Innovative Techniques and Applications of Entity Resolution

Hongzhi Wang
Harbin Institute of Technology, China

A volume in the Advances in Data Mining
and Database Management (ADMDM)
Book Series

Information Science
REFERENCE
An Imprint of IGI Global

Managing Director:	Lindsay Johnston
Production Manager:	Jennifer Yoder
Development Editor:	Austin DeMarco
Acquisitions Editor:	Kayla Wolfe
Typesetter:	Christina Barkanic
Cover Design:	Jason Mull

Published in the United States of America by
Information Science Reference (an imprint of IGI Global)
701 E. Chocolate Avenue
Hershey PA 17033
Tel: 717-533-8845
Fax: 717-533-8661
E-mail: cust@igi-global.com
Web site: http://www.igi-global.com

Library of Congress Cataloging-in-Publication Data

Wang, Hongzhi, 1978-Innovative techniques and applications of entity resolution / by Hongzhi Wang.
    pages cm
  Includes bibliographical references and index.
    ISBN 978-1-4666-5198-2 (hardcover) -- ISBN 978-1-4666-5199-9 (ebook) -- ISBN 978-1-4666-5201-9 (print & perpetual access) 1. Database management. 2. Data mining. I. Title.
  QA76.9.D3W355 2014
  006.3'12--dc23
                                    2013044978

This book is published in the IGI Global book series Advances in Data Mining and Database Management (ADMDM) Book Series (ISSN: 2327-1981; eISSN: 2327-199X)

British Cataloguing in Publication Data
A Cataloguing in Publication record for this book is available from the British Library.

All work contributed to this book is new, previously-unpublished material. The views expressed in this book are those of the authors, but not necessarily of the publisher.

For electronic access to this publication, please contact: eresources@igi-global.com.

Advances in Data Mining and Database Management (ADMDM) Book Series

David Taniar
Monash University, Australia

ISSN: 2327-1981
EISSN: 2327-199X

MISSION

With the large amounts of information available to businesses in today's digital world, there is a need for methods and research on managing and analyzing the information that is collected and stored. IT professionals, software engineers, and business administrators, along with many other researchers and academics, have made the fields of data mining and database management into ones of increasing importance as the digital world expands. The **Advances in Data Mining & Database Management (ADMDM) Book Series** aims to bring together research in both fields in order to become a resource for those involved in either field.

COVERAGE

- Cluster Analysis
- Customer Analytics
- Data Mining
- Data Quality
- Data Warehousing
- Database Security
- Database Testing
- Decision Support Systems
- Enterprise Systems
- Text Mining

IGI Global is currently accepting manuscripts for publication within this series. To submit a proposal for a volume in this series, please contact our Acquisition Editors at Acquisitions@igi-global.com or visit: http://www.igi-global.com/publish/.

Titles in this Series

For a list of additional titles in this series, please visit: www.igi-global.com

Innovative Techniques and Applications of Entity Resolution
Hongzhi Wang (Harbin Institute of Technology, China)
Information Science Reference • copyright 2014 • 354pp • H/C (ISBN: 9781466651982) • US $205.00 (our price)

Innovative Document Summarization Techniques Revolutionizing Knowledge Understanding
Alessandro Fiori (IRCC, Institute for Cancer Research and Treatment, Italy)
Information Science Reference • copyright 2014 • 363pp • H/C (ISBN: 9781466650190) • US $175.00 (our price)

Emerging Methods in Predictive Analytics Risk Management and Decision-Making
William H. Hsu (Kansas State University, USA)
Information Science Reference • copyright 2014 • 367pp • H/C (ISBN: 9781466650633) • US $175.00 (our price)

Data Science and Simulation in Transportation Research
Davy Janssens (Hasselt University, Belgium) Ansar-Ul-Haque Yasar (Hasselt University, Belgium) and Luk Knapen (Hasselt University, Belgium)
Information Science Reference • copyright 2014 • 350pp • H/C (ISBN: 9781466649200) • US $175.00 (our price)

Big Data Management, Technologies, and Applications
Wen-Chen Hu (University of North Dakota, USA) and Naima Kaabouch (University of North Dakota, USA)
Information Science Reference • copyright 2014 • 342pp • H/C (ISBN: 9781466646995) • US $175.00 (our price)

Innovative Approaches of Data Visualization and Visual Analytics
Mao Lin Huang (University of Technology, Sydney, Australia) and Weidong Huang (CSIRO, Australia)
Information Science Reference • copyright 2014 • 464pp • H/C (ISBN: 9781466643093) • US $200.00 (our price)

Data Mining in Dynamic Social Networks and Fuzzy Systems
Vishal Bhatnagar (Ambedkar Institute of Advanced Communication Technologies and Research, India)
Information Science Reference • copyright 2013 • 412pp • H/C (ISBN: 9781466642133) • US $195.00 (our price)

Ethical Data Mining Applications for Socio-Economic Development
Hakikur Rahman (University of Minho, Portugal) and Isabel Ramos (University of Minho, Portugal)
Information Science Reference • copyright 2013 • 359pp • H/C (ISBN: 9781466640788) • US $195.00 (our price)

Design, Performance, and Analysis of Innovative Information Retrieval
Zhongyu (Joan) Lu (University of Huddersfield, UK)
Information Science Reference • copyright 2013 • 508pp • H/C (ISBN: 9781466619753) • US $195.00 (our price)

www.igi-global.com

701 E. Chocolate Ave., Hershey, PA 17033
Order online at www.igi-global.com or call 717-533-8845 x100
To place a standing order for titles released in this series, contact: cust@igi-global.com
Mon-Fri 8:00 am - 5:00 pm (est) or fax 24 hours a day 717-533-8661

Table of Contents

Section 1
Principles of Entity Resolution

Section 2
Entity Resolution on Various Types Of Data

Section 3
Database Techniques and Entity Resolution

Section 4
Applications for Entity Resolution

Foreword

Entity resolution has attracted significant attention from many researchers in computer science during the last three decades. Entity resolution can play an important role in data cleaning and integration in many real-world applications (e.g., e-commerce, healthcare information managing, Web information management, and CRM). Therefore, many techniques for entity resolution have been proposed from the database and machine-learning communities, such as similarity join, blocking, and graph approximate matching.

This book covers many aspects of entity resolution including all of basic concepts, algorithms, and applications. It presents the latest research and application results in entity resolution.

This book is the first one that covers a wide spectrum of entity resolution issues. As I am also working on entity resolution from the database perspective, I found this book contains a lot of useful information including entity resolution algorithms for several data models, a complete reference list for new results in entity resolution, and applications of entity resolution. In current textbooks of database management, entity resolution has not received much attention. This book provides supplementary material for database courses.

In a nutshell, it will appeal to various kinds of readers, including researchers, students, and developers, and have a global view of entity resolution.

Guoliang Li
Tsinghua University, China

Guoliang Li *is an Associate Professor of Department of Computer Science, Tsinghua University, Beijing, China. He received his PhD degree in Computer Science from Tsinghua University in 2009, and his Bachelor degree in Computer Science from Harbin Institute of Technology in 2004. His research interests include data cleaning and integration and crowdsourcing. He has published more than 60 papers in premier conferences and journals, such as SIGMOD, VLDB, ICDE, TODS, VLDB Journal, and TKDE. He is a PC co-chair of the 14th International Conference on Web-Age Information Management (WAIM 2014) and 17th International Workshop on the Web and Databases (WebDB 2014, in conjunction with SIGMOD). He has served on the program committees of many premier conferences, such as SIGMOD, VLDB, KDD, ICDE, and IJCAI. His papers have been cited more than 1400 times. He received New Century Excellent Talents in University Award, Beijing Excellent Doctoral Dissertation Award, Nomination Award of National Excellent Doctoral Dissertation, and SCOPUS National Youth Science Star Award.*

Preface

The task of entity resolution is to identify difference representations referring to the same real-world entity. In many applications, users may input data with multiple representations to the same real-world object and the same representation. For example, for the same author named "Wei Wang," in the publications, the name can be "Wei Wang," "Wang Wei," or "W. Wang." Multiple authors share name "Wei Wang." During the processing of such data, it is necessary to identify the representations referring to the same real-world entity.

According to the form of results, entity resolution can be classified to pair-wise entity resolution and group-wise entity resolution. The former one is to obtain pairs of data objects with each pair referring to the same real-world entity. The later is to cluster the data set, such that the data objects in each cluster refer to the same real-world entity.

Entity resolution has wide applications such as information integration, e-commerce, and bibliography management. In Web, the same entity has different representation in different data sources. With entity resolution techniques, some representations can be detected, and the information from different data sources can be used more sufficiently. For example, in Web 2.0, on e-commerce Websites, such as eBay, the same product may have multiple names. For the convenience of users to browse and compare the same products from different buyers, entity resolution is in demand.

For its importance, entity resolution has become one the hottest research topics in the research field of database, machine learning, and natural language processing. Many techniques and applications have been proposed. This book attempts to give an introduction to these techniques and applications.

This book has three objectives. Firstly, this book will summarize the state-of-art techniques of entity resolutions. It provides researchers a reference of entity resolution for their research works. The possible areas where researchers will be interested include database, data quality, information system, and information integration. Since entity resolution is an important content of the course of data quality, database or information system, the second objective of this book is to provide a textbook or reference book for students with majors in computer science, information systems, and management. Entity resolution has wide applications in many systems, such as e-commerce, management information systems, and Web information systems. Therefore, the third objective of this book is to provide a reference book for developers for such systems. In summary, the potential audiences would be educators, information system designers, and graduate students.

In particular, the book is divided into four section.

The first section introduces basic principles of entity resolution and gives an overview of the whole area. The second section proposes entity resolution on various types of data including entity resolution on names, context, XML data, graph databases, and complex networks. Since data management has a natural relationship with entity resolution, the third section discusses the database techniques and entity resolution including basic operators for entity resolution, data cleaning based on entity resolution, and query processing based on entity resolution. The fourth section focuses on four applications of entity resolution including information integration, bibliography management, e-commerce, and healthcare.

The contents of chapters in this book are introduced as follows.

Entity resolution is one of many importation operations for data quality management, information retrieval, and data management. It has wide applications in Web search, ecommerce search, data cleaning, and information integration. Due to its importance, entity resolution has been studied by researchers in multiple fields including database, machine learning, information retrieval, as well as high performance computation. This book contains a number of chapters, which are carefully chosen in order to discuss the broad research issues in entity resolution. In addition, a number of important applications of entity resolution are also covered in the book. The purpose of chapter 1 is to provide an overview of the concepts, applications, and research topics of entity resolution, as well as the coverage of these topics in this book.

Chapter 2 discusses the measures of entity resolution. This is the base of entity resolution. The goal is to evaluate entity resolution techniques. Traditional measures include precision and recall, and F-measure as the combination of precision and recall. Sometimes, such simple measures are not sufficient. In some cases, the entity resolution results sharing same precision and recall may have significant difference in quality. To distinguish the entity resolution techniques, many new measures are proposed, especially for large data. In this chapter, some traditional measures are discussed with some state-of-the-art entity resolution results evaluation measures.

Chapter 3 surveys entity resolution techniques on names. The original goal of entity resolution is to identify the real-world entities according to the names in the flat text. Thus, this is the basic version of entity resolution. The difficulty of this problem is led by synonym, ambiguity, and typos in the text. This problem is related to natural language processing. Additionally, entity resolution on complex data types such as records and XML data requires entity resolution on names. This problem is related to natural language processing, data management, and even programming language. This problem has been studied for more than 50 years, and many solutions have been proposed. This chapter gives a survey of related techniques. Three kinds of methods are introduced. The first is the similarity measure between strings as fundamental techniques. The second is the transformation methods to handle the difference other than the textual differences. The third is the learning algorithm for string transformation rules for more complex cases.

Chapter 4 proposes context-based entity resolution framework. Names are not sufficient for entity resolution when the names have ambiguity or the data structure is complex. With the consideration that in real applications names are related to each other, the context information in data could be extracted to compare for the entity resolution. Additionally, context-based entity resolution provides an effective approach for entity resolution on mixed data in various types, since context information could be extracted according to the structure of various types of data. Thus, in chapter 4, we present Context-Based Entity Description (CED) to make context information help entity resolution. In our framework, each entity is described by a set of CEDs. During entity resolution, objects are only compared with CEDs to determine the corresponding entity. Additionally, we propose efficient algorithms for CED discovery, maintenance, and CED-based entity resolution. From the experimental results on real datasets, the context-based method outperforms existing methods.

Chapter 5 is a survey for entity resolution on a single relation. Many data are in relational databases due to the success of relational databases in the market. The relational model is also used in many information integration systems such as federal databases and mediate-wrapper-based systems. Hence, entity resolution on relational databases is in demand. The challenges of entity resolution on relational database include not only the synonym, ambiguity, and typos in attributes but also the determination of importance of them. Many techniques have been proposed. Chapter 5 surveys related work. The basic operation is attribute similarity computation. Based on the attribute similarity computation methods, many techniques for different areas are proposed to fulfill the process of entity resolution. Among the techniques, we focus on record similarity computation, rule-based approach, similarity threshold computation, and blocking. The former three are the framework of entity resolution on relations, and the latter one is the acceleration strategy for entity resolution on a single relation.

Chapter 6 discusses the methods of entity resolution on multiple relations to use join to get more information from multiple relations to support more accurate entity resolution. The complex structure for prime-foreign keys in multiple relations brings difficulty to this problem. Chapter 6 defines the problem of entity resolution on multiple relations. Then the similarity measures and reasonable algorithm are proposed to solve the problem. The efficiency and effectiveness of the proposed algorithm are verified with extensive experiments.

Chapter 7 summarizes state-of-art techniques for entity resolution on XML data. Currently, XML is the standard of the Web, e-commerce, and e-government due of its flexibility. Additionally, since XML data is in semi-structured data model, it has been widely used for data organization in databases and information integration systems. Entity resolution on XML data is helpful to improve database quality in both XML databases and information integration based on XML. The challenge of entity resolution brought by XML is its hierarchy structural information. In chapter 7, we survey entity resolution on XML data, the concrete applications of which include XML document management in highly dynamic applications such as the Web and peer-to-peer systems, detection of duplicate elements in nested XML data, and finding similar identities among objects from multiple Web sources. We survey techniques of pair-wise and group-wise entity resolution for XML data, respectively. We summarize the representations for XML structure and content including as a tree, Bayesian network, and set. We also introduce some well-known entity resolution algorithms for XML data based on these various structures.

Chapter 8 surveys the algorithms for entity resolution for graphs. Many data could be naturally represented as graph, such as organic molecular in chemistry and protein interaction network. Data quality management for graph-structured data requires entity resolution for graphs. The difficulties of entity resolution on graph data set include the measure of similarity between graphs and the computational difficulty in similarity comparison problems for popular measures such as graph edit distance and the largest common subgraphs. In chapter 8, we introduce the distance measures between graphs as well as their applications, which require approximation algorithms for some difficult problems. The approximate graph matching algorithms may be index-based like the NH-Index method, or kernel function-based like G-hash method. Other methods concentrate on providing new definitions of similar graphs that are easier to compute than traditional methods, like the Web-collection method and the Grafil method. To increase the resolution ability of traditional methods, researchers provide some methods to recognize similar graphs, such as graph bounded simulation and p-homomorphism.

Chapter 9 summaries and compares entity resolution algorithms on complex networks. In complex networks, the basic unit for entity resolution is vertex. Entity resolution on a complex network should consider two kinds of information, tags on vertices and the structure of the network. The applications of entity resolution on complex network include the detection of mirror Websites, name recognition in social network, and information searching on the Internet. The difficulties are from the definition of similarity vertex according to both of structural and content information and make the clustering algorithm suitable for large networks. This chapter will mainly introduce some applications including the detection of mirror Websites and name recognition in social network in detail, as well as node similarity description and clustering method including SimRank, PSimRank, and other related methods.

Chapter 10 presents an entity resolution algorithm on cloud for big data. With the increasing of data, entity resolution is required to be executed on large data sets in many applications. For two reasons, entity resolution is quite suitable to be performed in the cloud. One is that entity resolution is expensive in computation for large data sets. The other is entity resolution could be processed offline for most of the applications. Entity resolution on cloud is not straightforward since it often requires computing the similarities among data objects while cloud computation requires the partition of the data objects. Chapter 10 shows that it is necessary to use wave of strings to compute records similarity in cloud computing and provides a method based on wave of strings of entity resolution. Theoretical analysis and experimental results show that the method proposed in this chapter is efficient and effective.

Chapter 11 introduces basic data operators for entity resolution with implementation algorithms. From the aspect of data management, entity resolution can be considered as a series of basic data operators. Data operators for entity resolution are different from traditional relational data operators in two aspects. One aspect is that those for entity resolution are similar entity resolution due to possible errors in data while relational operators are accurate operators. The other is that the conversion and knowledge should be embedded in the operators for entity resolution since entity resolution requires conversion and knowledge due to ambiguity. The major concern of the basic data operators for entity resolution is efficiency. For efficient implementation of the operators, some database ideas are adopted to them such as index. In chapter 11, we first introduce the solution of similarity search, covering gram-based algorithms and sketch-based algorithms. Then we turn to the solution of similarity join, covering both exact and approximate algorithms. At last, we deal with the problem of clustering similar strings in a set that can be applied to duplicate detection in databases.

Chapter 12 proposes truth discovery methods for data cleaning based on entity resolution. During data cleaning, entity resolution could be applied at first. Then, if the values in the same attribute in different data objects referring to the same real-world entity are different, conflicts occur. To clean the data, it is necessary to resolve the conflicts, which requires truth discovery, which is to find true facts from a large amount of conflicting information provided. The challenge brought by truth discovery is to find sufficient information to determine the truth. In chapter 12, we review state-of-the-art approaches to processing truth discovery including trivial method, fixpoint method, approaches based on copying detection, and semi-supervised learning approaches.

In chapter 13, we propose query-processing strategies based on entity resolution including query semantics, basic data operator, and query optimization algorithms. Organizing the tuples in a database according to the referred real-world entity has three benefits: (1) duplicated tuples are merged together and the storage space and disk IO during query processing are saved; (2) the data quality of original data is identified according to the entity-based organization and the dirty-data tolerant operations could be applied on such data is convenient; (3) the query results on such data are organized based on referred entity and such interface could increase the efficiency for users to use the query results. As a result, it is a good choice to organize data based on referred real-world entity. The semantic of query on entity resolution is different from those in traditional data model. The basic data operators are also different from traditional relational data operators and so are query optimization strategies. Chapter 13 presents EntityManager, a dirty data management system with entity as the basic unit, and keep conflicts in data as uncertain attributes. Even though the query language is also SQL, the query in the system has different semantics on entity-based organized data. To process queries efficiently, this chapter introduces index structure, data operator implementation, and query optimization algorithms for entity-based data management.

Chapter 14 discusses the application of entity resolution in information integration systems. Information integration brings many data quality problems due to the schema mismatch and ambiguous description in autonomous data sources. Thus, quality assurance mechanism is required in information integration system. During quality assurance in information integration, entity resolution is a basic operation. Entity resolution technique could be applied to different components such as schema mapping and integrated data cleaning. For schema mapping, entity resolution is embedded into the schema matching rules as a function. Entity resolution in integrated data cleaning step should handle the conflict in not only attribute value but also the schema. In chapter 14, we focus on these two steps. To represent the similarity between two records from different data sources with different schemas, the optimal bipartite graph matching is adopted on the attributes of them, and the similarity is measured as the weight of such matching. Based on similarity estimation, the basic idea in this chapter is to estimate the range of the records similarity and to determine whether they are duplicate records according to the estimation. When data integration is performed on XML data, there are many problems because of the flexibility of XML. One of the current implementations is to use entity resolution to carry out the above operations. This chapter proposes the concept of quality assurance mechanisms besides the data integrity and reliability.

In chapter 15, the techniques for entity resolution in bibliography management are proposed. Bibliography information may be collected from various data sources. As a result, bibliography management system may contain different representations for the same reference as well as synonym in the author name. This is a classic problem of entity resolution. Many entity resolution techniques focus on this problem. Chapter 15 introduces EIF as a framework suitable for bibliography information management system. Such framework considers both kinds of confusion, ambiguous and synonym. In this framework, effective clustering techniques, approximate string matching algorithms, and a flexible mechanism of knowledge integration are involved. Extensive experimental results are presented to verify the effectiveness and efficiency of the proposed framework.

Chapter 16 discusses the systems for entity resolution on products in e-commerce. There are huge amounts of commodity data on the e-commerce Websites on the Internet. Such Websites often provide search interface to retrieve suitable products with given keywords. Since the information of products is from autonomous data sources, even various individual users, the same product may have many different descriptions. In some Web 2.0 e-commerce Websites, such as eBay or Taobao, such descriptions may have even larger diversity. To make users browse and use such retrieved products information effectively, if the products are classified according to referred real-world entity, the efficiency of purchasing could be improved. Due to frequently missing or wrong values, and subjective difference in description, traditional method of entity resolution may not have a good result on e-commerce data. Therefore, in this chapter a set of algorithms are proposed in data cleaning, attribute and value tagging, and entity resolution, which are specialized for e-commerce data. Additionally, user's actions are collected to improve the classification result. We evaluate the effectiveness of the proposed algorithms with real-life datasets from e-commerce sites. The experimental results demonstrate that the proposed method is effective and suitable for improve the experiences for users.

Chapter 17 discusses the entity resolution techniques for healthcare information management systems. In healthcare information management systems, some medical documents may contain data quality problems. A significant example is that the names for the same patients may be different in various documents, especially for the documents from different data sources. For effective management of medical documents in healthcare information management systems, entity resolution should be applied. In this section, some techniques for entity resolution on medical documents, especial for Word Sense Disambiguation are described. We compare the effectiveness of a variety of knowledge sources of WSD in the biomedical domain. These include features that have been commonly used for WSD of general text as well as information derived from domain-specific resources. One of these features is MeSH terms, which we find to be particularly effective when combined with generic features.

In a nutshell, the book provides a comprehensive summary from both the algorithmic and the applied perspectives. It will provide the reader with a better understanding of how entity resolution on data can be efficiently and effectively performed for different applications.

Hongzhi Wang
Harbin Institute of Technology, China

Acknowledgment

The author would like to acknowledge the help of all involved in the collation and review process of the book, without whose support the project could not have been satisfactorily completed.

Thanks go to NGFR 973 grant (No. 2012CB316200), NSFC grant (61003046, 61111130189), and NGFR 863 grant 2012AA011004, Doctoral Fund of Ministry of Education of China (No.20102302120054), Key Laboratory of Data Engineering and Knowledge Engineering (Renmin University of China), Ministry of Education (No.KF2011003), the Fundamental Research Funds for the Central Universities (No. HIT. NSRIF. 2013064). With the support, I can perform the research on entity resolution.

Thanks go to Prof. Jianzhong Li and Prof. Hong Gao of Harbin Institute of Technology for the suggestions of this project. Thanks go to Qiang Ren, Ming Yan, Rong Zhu, Anzhen Zhang, Zhenhua Zhu, Lingli Li, Qingyu Zhou, Chunxian He, Xueli Liu, Xiaodong Zhang, Huabin Feng, Yongnan Liu, Jian Yang, and Xiong Zhou from Harbin Institute of Technology for collecting materials for this book. The support of the Massive Data Computing Research Lab (MDC) in the Department of Science and Technology at Harbin Institute of Technology is acknowledged for providing office, equipment, and materials to this project.

Special thanks also go to the publishing team at IGI Global, whose contributions throughout the whole process from inception of the initial idea to final publication have been invaluable. In particular, thanks go to Christine E. Smith, who assisted in keeping this project on schedule, to Jan Travers, who signed the contract with me, and to Kayla Wolfe, who approved the decision of the proposal of this book.

Last but not least, thanks go to my wife, Lingli, for her unfailing support and encouragement during the months it took to give birth to this book.

Hongzhi Wang
Harbin Institute of Technology, China

Section 1
Principles of Entity Resolution

Chapter 1
Overview of Entity Resolution

ABSTRACT

Entity resolution is one of many importation operations for data quality management, information retrieval, and data management. It has wide applications in Web search, ecommerce search, data cleaning, and information integration. Due to its importance, entity resolution has been studied by researchers in multiple fields including database, machine learning, information retrieval, as well as high performance computation. This book contains a number of chapters, which are carefully chosen in order to discuss the broad research issues in entity resolution. In addition, a number of important applications of entity resolution are also covered in the book. The purpose of this chapter is to provide an overview of the concepts, applications, and research topics of entity resolution, as well as the coverage of these topics in this book.

BASIC CONCEPTS OF ENTITY RESOLUTION

Entity resolution is to distinguish the representations referring to the same real-world entity in one or more databases and recognize all different real-world entities in the databases.

Entity resolution plays an important role in data management. It is one of the major research problems in data quality management.

From the result form of entity resolution, it could be classified into two types. One is pairwise entity resolution. The results are pairs of data objects which refer to the same real-world entity. The other is group-wire entity resolution, whose result is a family of clusters with each one containing the data objects referring to the same real-world entity.

Entity resolution has wide applications in many steps in data management and data quality management. We use two examples to explain entity resolution and its applications.

Example 1: In a management information system for an enterprise, different departments of marketing, sales and server may maintain autonomous databases. These databases may have different types such as relational database, XML documents and OO database. The data in the databases may have different schemas. The name of attribute of the same entity may have different description method. As an example, a custom with name "Wei Wang" may be represented as "Wang Wei", "W Wang" even pairs (Wei, Wang) or XML data fragment <Customer><FamilyName>Wang</FamilyName><GivenName>Wei</GivenName

DOI: 10.4018/978-1-4666-5198-2.ch001

></customer> in different databases. The acquiring and reorganizing of enterprises will result in more such instances, since the databases of enterprises involving the acquiring may have many different representations referring to the same real-world entity. Information integrated from such databases may mislead the decision. For example, during the statistics of the number of customers, if the same customer from various databases is treated as different customers, the result is larger than the real result. In order to support the decisions with management information system, it is necessary to detect the data object referring to the same real-world entity in different databases correctly. Additionally, the data quantity in enterprise gets very large. According to the panel in VLDB 2002 (42), in 2002, the data amount of manufacturing enterprises reaches 100TB and increases 20% each year. Therefore, entity resolution techniques for massive and frequent-updating data in various structures are in demand for enterprise data management.

Example 2: Web sites in the Internet are autonomous. Information in Web 2.0 sites is inputted by various non-expert users. Therefore, one real-world entity may have different descriptions in different web sites even in different part of the same website. Thus, the search results from the Internet may contain various descriptions of the same real-world entity. On one hand, such duplicated results make users browse many similar information and their time is wasted. On the other hand, inconsistent information and wrong statistics results from retrieval results may lead to wrong decisions. If entity resolution is applied on the retrieval results to cluster them according to the referred entities and make the data objects in each cluster referring to the same real-world entity, retrieval results in higher quality are provided to users. Such

that the effectiveness of information use is increased. However, entity resolution on Internet brings challenges. The first challenge is that the data quantity of information in the Internet is very large. The number of pages indexed by Google exceeds 1T. Due to the involving of many users, the information in Internet updates frequently and is in various types including XML, relational database, RDF in graph structure and HTML. Internet information collection and retrieval system with quality assurance requires entity resolution on dynamic massive data in various types.

Other examples of entity resolution include finding special structure in network and IP alias discovery (Getoor & Machanavajjhala, 2012).

From these examples, entity resolution is important for data quality management and data management. Formally, these two kinds of entity resolution are defined as follows.

Definition 1 (Pair-wise Entity Resolution) Given S, a set of objects, the output is a set of pairs $\{(o_i, o_j)| o_i, o_j \in S, o_i$ and o_j refer to the same real-world entity$\}$.

Definition 2 (Group-wise Entity Resolution) Given S, a set of objects, the output is a family of sets $\{S_i |$ all objects in S_i refer to the same real-world entity$\}$ where for $i \neq j$, $S_i \cap S_j = \emptyset$.

As an example, for entity resolution on name set $\{o_1$="Wei Wang", o_2="W Wei", o_3="Wang Wei", o_4="Jian Pei"$\}$, the result of pair-wise entity resolution is $\{(o_1, o_2), (o_1, o_3), (o_2, o_3)\}$, while the result of group-wise entity resolution is $\{\{o_1, o_2, o_3\}, \{o_4\}\}$.

Entity resolution could be applied on data in different models or environments. Environments for entity resolution include single machine and cloud in clusters. Classifications of entity resolution according to data model are shown as follows.

- **Unstructured Data:** The data objects for entity resolution have no structural information. The entity resolution is performed only on the name of the data object and the context.
- **Structured Data:** The data objects for entity resolution have a regular structure. Structured data often refer to relational database. For structured data, the entity resolution can be applied on a single relation or multiple relations.
- **Semi-Structured Data:** Such kind of data has abundant but not necessarily regular structural information and the entity resolution on such data should take the structural information into consideration. Typical semi-structured data include XML data that are often modeled as trees, graph database with many graphs and complex network with massive vertices. The difference of entity resolution on graph database and complex network is that the data objects of entity resolution on graph database are graphs while those on complex network are vertices.

Ironically, entity resolution itself has many duplicate names including reference resolution, record linkage, duplicate detection, reference reconciliation, fuzzy match, objection identification, object consolidation, deduplication, object identification, approximate match, entity clustering identity uncertainty, merge/purge, household matching, hardening sort databases, house holding, reference matching and doubles (Getoor & Machanavajjhala 2012).

Even though all these terms refer to an entity resolution, they have subtle differences. Record linkage, fuzzy match and approximate match often refer to pair-wise entity resolution on relational database. Duplication detection and hardening sort databases often refer to group-wise entity resolution on relational database. Reference matching often refers to the entity resolution on names.

Object identification often refers to entity resolution on complex data set such as graphs and XML. Household matching and house holding refer to a special kind of group-wise entity resolutions that each entity is described with multiple attributes and the entity that a data object refers to is determined by the comparison of the data object and descriptions of entities. Deduplication and merge/purge often refer to the group-wise entity resolution on relational databases with an extra operation of merging the tuples referring to the same entity.

From the aspect of data mining, group-wise entity resolution is a special kind of clustering with a large number of clusters and small size clusters. Entity resolution is different from classification since it is unsupervised learning while classification is supervised learning.

CENTRAL ISSUES OF ENTITY RESOLUTION

Because of its importance, many research works on entity resolution are performed from various aspects. In this section, we propose the different aspects of the study of entity resolution.

Well-Define Entity Resolution Results

As discussed above, entity resolution is roughly classified into two types, pair-wise and group-wise entity resolution. They have different semantics and applications. The former one is used to find inconsistent data objects in the data set for data cleaning. The latter one outputs groups for entity-based search or data management. Unfortunately, these two types of entity resolution are not always consistent.

Generally speaking, if we consider "referring to the same real-world entity" as a binary relation defined on the data object. This should be an equivalent relation.

However, most current pair-wise entity resolution depends on similarity functions of data objects. If two data objects o1 and o2 satisfy the constraint $sim(o_1, o_2) > \varepsilon$ or distance $distance(o_1, o_2) < \varepsilon$, they are considered as referring to the same entity. In practice, the similarity function sim and distance often do not satisfy the transitivity. As examples, edit distance (Bille 2005) and Jaccard similarity (Strehl, Ghosh & Mooney 2000) are popular measures for pair-wise entity resolution. None of them satisfy the transitivity.

Thus to make the entity results correct, it is necessary to define proper criterions for entities. That is, which kind of data objects is considered as referring to the same real-world entity?

Research Challenges of Entity Resolution

Even though entity resolution has been studied for a long time, this problem is not solved satisfactorily. Currently, entity resolution research has following challenges:

1. Many applications have big data. Big data bring challenges to entity resolution. Most traditional entity resolution algorithms are in super-linear time complexity while big data require linear or sub-linear algorithms. How to perform entity resolution on big data efficiently and effectively is the first challenge.
2. In many applications such as accessed web page streams on Internet and financial data, data update frequently. Current entity resolution techniques scan data multiple times. Hence they do not support entity resolution on frequently updated data. The second challenge is to how to perform effective and efficient entity resolution on dynamic data that update frequently.
3. Data in modern information systems are often complex, including non-structured (such as flat text), semi-structured (such as graph data

and complex network) and structured data (such as relational database). How to use structural information and content effectively for entity resolution is the third challenge.
4. The evaluation of entity resolution results efficiently and accurately is the fourth challenge.

APPLICATIONS FOR ENTITY RESOLUTION

This section will provide a chapter-by-chapter overview of different applications of entity resolution. The aim is to cover the applications in data database management, e-commerce, web management and healthcare. Besides these applications, other applications with entity resolution include linking census records, comparison shopping, counter-terrorism, spam detection and machine reading (Getoor & Machanavajjhala 2012).

Data Quality Management

The results of entity resolution are different descriptions of the same entity in databases. The results of entity resolution have widely applications in data quality management such as deduplication, error data detection, outdated data discovery. For deduplication, entity resolution is applied for finding duplication tuples. For error data detection, the comparisons between the same attributes of tuples tell the possible errors as the conflict values. Outdated data could be detected with entity resolution results with rules (Fan, Geerts & Wijsen 2012).

Entity-Based Data Management

Since the conflict in data is a major source of dirty data, dirty data management requires to detect the data objects referring to the same real-world entity. Although such data objects could be detected, the true values for conflicting values could hardly be determined due to the lack of knowledge. In order not to lose information, the data could be managed without revising and removing data. The data is organized according to the entities for easy management of dirty data such that the query results are in the form of referred entities (Wang, Li, Wang & Gao 2011). In such data management system, entity resolution is a basic technique.

Entity-Based e-Commerce Information Search

Currently, many e-commerce web sites provide interfaces for retrieving products information. It is commonly that the same product has multiple descriptions. It is necessary to obtain various descriptions of the same product for the convenience of price comparison and product review. In order to support such application efficiently, entity resolution for products is in demand (Köpcke, Thor, Thomas & Rahm 2012).

Entity-Based Web information Search

For the information retrieval on web, entity-based search (Bagga & Baldwin 1998) is to obtain the data objects on web instead of documents. Accurate entity-based information retrieval on the Internet requires the distinguishing of documents or data objects referring to the same real-world entity, since the same entity may have different description over Internet. For such application, entity resolution should be performed on either the names of entities or the context of the entities. For example, for a costumer with name "Wei Wang", the name can be described as "W. Wang", "Wang Wei". Additionally, another costumer may share the name "Wei Wang". In such cases, context information is required to distinguish the entities.

Entity in Healthcare

In medical information integration system, it is common that a person has different name and a name shared by different persons. Healthcare system requires integrating information from various data sources as the reference for treatment. This application requires the entity resolution on the names in medical documents. Entity resolution techniques for healthcare are different from traditional entity resolution in that the medical documents have special attributes.

OVERVIEW FOR ENTITY RESOLUTION

Due to its importance, entity resolution has been studied for many years and many techniques have been proposed especial entity resolution for relational data and names (references) to the entities.

Currently, the entity resolution is one of the hottest research problems in database and related area. The state-of-art techniques of entity resolution include entity resolution for big data, entity resolution for complex data such as XML and graphs and combining new machine learning and knowledge management techniques in entity resolution.

In this book, we discuss techniques and applications for entity resolutions including both traditional and the state-of-art techniques. The broad areas covered in this book are as follows:

- **Entity Resolution on Various Types of Data:** With the existing of many data types, such as strings (flat text), relation databases, XML data, graph and complex network, in various data sources especially on the web, it is necessary to perform entity resolution for data in various data types. The methods of entity resolution on different data type are different due to the differences in the structure of data. The entity resolution uses no structure information but only context of strings. As a comparison, more structural information could be helpful for entity resolution on structural or semi-structure data such as relations or XML data. As an extreme, for entity resolution on graphs or complex networks, structural information is even more important than context on the labels. For each type of data, special algorithms are designed to make sufficient usage of available information. Furthermore, algorithms for entity resolution on mixed data with various types are in demand.

- **Database Techniques and Entity Resolution:** Processing objects of entity resolution are data objects in databases or other data sources. Thus, entity resolution is naturally related to the database. During entity resolution, data operations are the bases. Database techniques are helpful to entity resolution especially for that on big data. On such case, efficiency becomes a crucial issue. On another aspect, entity resolution organizes the data objects according to the referred real-world entity. Such organization increases the usability of data in two aspects. One is to support the cleaning of data by resolving the inconsistency discovered by entity resolution. The other is to provide the results clustered according to the referred entities to improve the efficiency and experience of the usage of the search or query results. As a result, database techniques for entity resolution and the application of entity resolution in database areas are needed to be designed.
- **Applications for Entity Resolution:** Entity resolution has widely applications in many areas. Even though general entity resolutions can be applied in applications, the background knowledge of applications is helpful to improve the accuracy of entity resolution. Some researchers also develop special entity resolution algorithms for applications according to the features of applications. Thus, we chose four applications that require entity resolution techniques, information integration, e-commerce, healthcare and bibliography

information management to show the entity resolution techniques requirements for special applications as well as entity resolution algorithms and systems for these applications.

Then this section will provide a chapter-by-chapter overview of the different topics which are discussed in this book. The aim is to cover the basic concept, entity resolution for various data types, database techniques and entity resolution as well as applications for entity resolution topics fairly comprehensively. The key algorithms and methods in the field are described fairly comprehensively in the different chapters and the relevant pointers are provided. The key topics discussed in the book are as follows:

- **Measures of Entity Resolution:** At the base of entity resolution, it requires to know what entity resolution techniques are good. Even though precision and recall are often used in current entity resolution research, they are too rough for many applications. In some cases, two entity resolutions sharing the same precision and recall may be different in result quality. Hence proper measures of entity resolution are to be designed. Another issue of entity resolution measurement is its practicability since for big data. Some measures are difficult to compute, such as recall. Some state-of-arts measures of entity resolution are described in Chapter 2.
- **Entity Resolution on Names:** Originally, entity resolution is proposed to identify the real-world entity referring by a name in the text. This is a basic problem of natural language understanding and machine translation. It is also a basic operation of entity resolution on complex data as the name of an object is one of its most important attributes. Entity resolution on names is interdisciplinary among natural language

processing, artificial intelligence and data management. Even though this problem has been studied for more than 50 years, it is not solved satisfactorily due to synonym, ambiguity and typos in the text. In Chapter 3, techniques for entity resolution on names are discussed.

- **Context-based Entity Resolution:** Names are not sufficient for entity resolution in many cases, especially when the names have ambiguity. With the consideration that names are not isolated in data, the context information in data could be referred for the entity resolution. Additionally, context-based entity resolution provides an effective approach for entity resolution on mixed data in various types, since context information could be extracted according to the structure of various types of data. The difficulties in entity resolution based context include the extraction of context information and the judgment of whether two data objects refer to the same entity. Chapter 4 proposes the solutions of these two difficulties.

- **Entity Resolution on Relations:** Many data are in relational databases due to the success of relational databases in the market. Relational model is also used in many information integration systems such as federal databases and mediate-wrapper based system. Hence entity resolution on relational databases is in demand. The challenges of entity resolution on relational database include not only the synonym, ambiguity and typos in attributes but also the determination of importance of them. Many researches have been done on this topic. Thus, Chapter 5 and Chapter 6 discuss the techniques on this topic. Chapter 5 focuses on the techniques of entity resolution on single relation to identify the tuples referring to the same entity. Chapter 6 discusses the methods of entity resolution on

multiple relations to use join to get more information from multiple relations to support more accurate entity resolution.

- **Entity Resolution on XML Data:** XML becomes the standard of the web because of its flexibility and ability of self-description. It is widely used for data representation in databases and information integration systems. Therefore, entity resolution on XML data is helpful to improve database quality. The challenge of entity resolution brought by XML is its rich in hierarchy structural information. On one hand, structural information provides more information for entity resolution. On the other hand, structural information brings difficulties in the definition of data objects in XML data, measure the similarity of

- **Entity Resolution on Graph Data Set:** Many data could be naturally represented as graph, such as organic molecular in chemistry and protein interaction network. The cleansing and integrating such kind of data needs entity resolution on graph data set to identify graphs representing to the same real-world entity. The difficulty of entity resolution on graph data set is the measure of similarity between graphs. The computations of similarities in most measures on graph such as graph edit distance and largest common subgraphs are NP-hard problems. As a result, both pair-wise and group-wise entity resolutions are difficult for large graph set. Techniques handling these difficult problems are proposed in Chapter 8.

- **Entity Resolution on Complex Network:** In complex network, the basic unit for entity resolution is vertex. The basis of entity resolution on complex network includes the tags on vertices and the structure of the network. The applications of entity resolution on complex network include author identification on bibliography network and account identification on social network. The central problem of entity resolution on complex network is the criterions of vertices referring to the same real-world entity that combines the structural information and tags on vertices. Another research issue for this topic is efficient since a complex network is often in size of billions of nodes. In Chapter 9, the algorithms for entity resolution on complex network are introduced.

- **Entity Resolution on Cloud:** With the increasing of data, entity resolution is required to be executed on large data set in many applications. For two reasons, entity resolution is quite suitable to be performed in cloud. One is that entity resolution is expensive in computation for large data set. The other is entity resolution could be processed offline for most of the applications. Entity resolution on cloud is not straightforward since it often requires computing the similarities among data objects while cloud computation requires the partition of the data objects. For efficient entity resolution on big data set, we propose entity resolution on the cloud in Chapter 10.

- **Basic Data Operators for Entity Resolution:** From the aspect of data management, entity resolution is split in a series of basic data operators. Data operators for entity resolution are different from traditional relational data operators in two aspects. One aspect is that those for entity resolution are similar entity resolution due to possible errors in data while relational operators are accurate operators. The other is that the conversion and knowledge should be embedded in the operators for entity resolution since entity resolution requires those conversion and knowledge due to ambiguity. The major concern of the basic data operators for entity resolution is efficiency. For efficient implementation of

the operators, some database ideas are adopted to them such as index. The definition and implementation algorithms for basic data operators are discussed in Chapter 11.

- **Data Cleaning Based on Entity Resolution:** Entity resolution is a basic operation for data cleaning since a basic step of data cleaning is to know the data objects referring to the same real-world entity such that the incompleteness, inconsistency and incurrences could be discovered according to the comparisons between the data objects referring to the same real-world entity. In order to clean data according to the results of entity resolution, inconsistency in the same attribute of the data objects referring to the same entity is to resolve. Thus, the major technique for data cleaning based on the results entity resolution is to find the true value from the inconsistencies for the same attribute in data objects referring to the same entity. Chapter 12 proposes truth discovery methods for data cleaning based on entity resolution.

- **Query Processing Based on Entity Resolution:** Organizing the tuples in a database according to the referred real-world entity has three benefits. (1) Duplicated tuples are merged together and the storage space and disk IO during query processing are saved. (2) The data quality of original data is identified according to the entity-based organization and the dirty-data tolerant operations could be applied on such data is convenient. (3) The query results on such data are organized based on referred entity and such interface could increase the efficiency for users to use the query results. Thus it is a good choice to organize data based on referred real-world entity. The semantic of query on entity resolution is different from those in traditional data model. The basic data operators are also different from traditional relational data operators and so are query optimization strategies. In Chapter 13, we propose query processing strategies for entity resolution including query semantics, basic data operator and query optimization algorithms.

- **Entity Resolution in Information Integration System:** Information integration brings many data quality problems. Thus it requires entity resolution since entity resolution is an effective way to improve data quality. To assure the quality of integrated data, entity resolution can be applied on different phrases of information integration including schema mapping and integrated data cleaning. These two steps provide different requirements for entity resolution techniques. For schema mapping, entity resolution should be able to be embedded into the schema matching rules as a function. Entity resolution in integrated data cleaning step should handle the conflict in not only attribute value but also the schema. Chapter 14 discusses the application of entity resolution in information integration systems.

- **Entity Resolution in Bibliography Management:** Bibliography information often from different data sources maintained with different managers. Hence bibliography management system may contain various representations for the same reference. A more serious problem is the ambiguity and synonym in the author name. A classic problem for entity resolution is the entity resolution for name "Wei Wang", which is shared by the same authors in similar research area. It has also many representations. Thus many techniques are proposed for author resolution for bibliography. In Chapter 15, the techniques for entity resolution in bibliography management are proposed.

- **Entity Resolution in E-Commerce:** E-commerce sites contain a large amount of product information. They often provide search interfaces for convenient find required products. The descriptions of products in e-commerce web site have large diversity since they are input by different users. Such case is more critical in web 2.0 e-commerce web sites such as ebay. The confusion in product description brings troubles for users. Users have to browse and compare prices among a large amount of search results. To increase the experience and browsing efficiency of users, it is an effective approach to cluster the search results according to refereed real-world entities. The entity resolution for product information in e-commerce systems requires entity resolution on various types of product information including product names and description even the pictures. Another challenge is that the product distinguishing is objective in some time. To meet these challenges, Chapter 16 discusses the systems for entity resolution in E-commerce.

- **Entity Resolution in Healthcare:** Medical documentations contain much information, which possibly has data quality problems. As an example, the names in various documentations have ambiguities. For effective management and usage of medical documents in healthcare management, entity resolution should be applied on the healthcare information. Chapter 17 proposes the entity resolution techniques for healthcare information management systems.

Practical Entity Resolution

Since entity resolution plays an important role in many applications. In many systems, the component of entity resolution is to be developed. As entity resolution is not a trivial job, the development of entity resolution may require much time and cost. Fortunately, some entity resolution tools or packages have been released. Thus, for developers, it is unnecessary to develop the whole component for entity resolution. Existing components could be used. Some representative entity resolution tools or packages are summarized as follows.

D-Dupe is an interactive tool for entity resolution with data mining. This system models the relationship between data objects as a graph. In this graph model, users resolve ambiguities either by merging nodes or by marking them distinct. This system also provides interactive tools for more accurate entity resolution. The system is published in http://www.cs.umd.edu/projects/linqs/ddupe/licensing.shtml.

SERF is a generic infrastructure for entity resolution developed by Stanford. In this system, the pair-wise entity resolution (as is called match) and merging are viewed as black-boxes. With this mechanism, SERF provides a generic and extensible ER solution. The input of this system includes a data set of records and a class "MatcherMerger" which implement the matching and merging of records. The output is a dataset of resolved records. The system can be downloaded in http://infolab.stanford.edu/serf/serf.zip.

DataMatch is a commercial tool for pair-wise entity resolution. DataMatch is a desktop software including multiple record matching algorithms. This system can handle up to 100 million records. It can be used to find and link customer data, consolidate data across multiple sources, and remove deceased and unwanted records - quickly and easily improving your marketing and mailing performance. With the DataMatch Enterprise suite, you can automate daily maintenance functions. The webpage of this software is http://dataladder.com/Products_DataMatch_Enterprise.html.

OYESTER is an open-source entity resolution system that supports probabilistic direct matching, transitive linking, and asserted linking. The system builds and maintains an in-memory index of attribute values to identities. OYSTER attaches and maintains unique IDs for entities. This system provides the ability to fix false-positive and false-negative resolutions. The homepage of OYSTER is shown in http://sourceforge.net/projects/oysterer/.

Another practical issue for entity resolution is to select the proper method and parameters for entity resolution. Some tips for method and parameters selections are shown as follows.

- Both effectiveness and efficiency are to be considered. Some entity resolution algorithms have high efficiency but low effectiveness while some are in the opposite. Whether to choose a more efficient or effective algorithms depends on the application. Therefore, the application of entity resolution algorithms requires considering not only the data type and running environment but also the priority of efficiency and effectiveness.

- Preprocess are required to improve the effectiveness of entity resolution. In many real applications, the input data are in chaos. In such case, the effectiveness of entity resolution is reduced. Thus for effective entity resolution, the input data should be cleaned as possible. The input data cleaning strategy includes imputation of missing attributes, revision of inconsistent data and format formalization.

- Choose proper parameters. Entity resolution has two core parameters, function and the threshold. The former is to compute the similarity between two data objects and the latter is used to judge whether two data objects refer to the same real-world entity. Thus these two parameters should be chosen carefully. The criterions of parameter selection include data type and the features of data. For data type, the developer should choose similarity function according to proper similarity functions for special data. For data features, both the distribution and source of data are considered. A practical way is to sample some data and determine the parameters manually.

- Some preliminary experiments are required to test the effectiveness of entity resolution and tune the parameters. Manual parameter selection method has the problem that the data objects referring to the same real-world entity are hardly obtained when the data size is large. Hence before the algorithms are to apply, some data could be sampled and preliminary experiments are performed on the sample to check whether the parameters are suitable.

- Multiple entity resolution methods could be used to cross check the effectiveness of the method. Some entity resolution method is suitable for some specific data set. However, for a given application, it is difficult to know which one is the most suitable. Thus, a feasible way is to adopt multiple entity resolution methods and cross check the results to find the most suitable method.

FUTURE RESEARCH DIRECTIONS

Even though entity resolution has widely studied and many techniques and applications are proposed, many problems are left unsolved. Additionally, effectiveness and efficiency of existing entity resolution techniques are still unsatisfactory. All of these are future research directions in this area. We summarize the possible research topic in entity resolution as followings.

- The measure of entity resolution results. The evaluation of entity resolution remains a difficult problem. Precision and recall are commonly used for evaluating the quality. The drawback is that the correct results are difficult to know for large data set. Without the baseline, it is impossible to evaluate them. For the convenient comparison of entity resolution algorithms, the

benchmarks for entity resolution are also in demand.

- Entity resolution for big data. Big data require linear or sub-linear algorithm. However, current algorithms do not satisfy this requirement. Entity resolution on big data motivates researchers to develop more efficient algorithms.

- Information collection for entity resolution. Insufficient information may lead to wrong entity resolution results. While in many cases, explicit information is insufficient for effective information integration. Thus a research topic for entity resolution is to find proper information for entity resolution.

- Knowledge-driven entity resolution. In entity resolution, one of the problems emergences to be solved is to recognize the synonyms and descriptions in the same area. In many cases, these problems could hardly be solved with data themselves. For these cases, external knowledge is in demand. Such knowledge could be from expert systems and Web (Wu, Li, Wang & Zhu 2012). A research issue is how to enhance entity resolution with the knowledge base. Another research issue in this problem is that how to embed the huge knowledge base into the process of entity resolution efficiently.

- Entity resolution on dirty data. Dirty data will disturb the entity resolution. For example, when one person graduated from *A* university joins *B* university, his email and address will change. Thus the entity resolution based on the similarity of email and address becomes invalid due to the outdated. Another example is that incomplete data do not provide sufficient data for entity resolution. As a result, for incomplete data, the relations of referring to the same real-world entity for many object pairs remain undetermined.

- New trends in entity resolution theory. Even though many theories have been proposed for entity resolution theory, it is not sufficient. There are also space for the study of basic theory for entity resolution includes the trade-off relationship between efficiency and effectiveness of entity resolution, the bound of time and space complexity for entity resolution on various data types with different measures and hierarchy entity resolution theory.
- Privacy issues for entity resolution. In many applications, entity resolution has to be performed on the data that have been anonymized. Entity resolution for such data requires two aspects of considerations. On one hand, the effectiveness of entity resolution on anonymized data may be affected due to the revision of data. On the other hand, entity resolution should keep the property of anonymized data. Thus privacy issues and the applications of entity resolution for privacy protection are new research directions for entity resolution.

This book studies a number of important problems in the entity resolution in the aspect of data management. We also introduce some of the recent trends for entity resolution applications.

CONCLUSION

This book provides an introduction to the problem of entity resolution. We will present the key techniques for entity resolution. We will show that these techniques can be very useful in a wide variety of applications such as information retrieval, E-commerce and healthcare. The book also presents some of the latest trends for entity resolution and their applicability across different domains. This book studies a number of important problems in the entity resolution in the aspect of data management. We also introduce some of the recent trends for entity resolution applications.

REFERENCES

Bagga, A., & Baldwin, B. (1998). Entity-based cross-document coreferencing using the vector space model. In *Proceedings of the 17th International Conference on Computational Linguistics* (vol. 1, pp. 79-85). Association for Computational Linguistics.

Bille, P. (2005). A survey on tree edit distance and related problems. *Theoretical Computer Science*, *337*(1), 217–239. doi:10.1016/j.tcs.2004.12.030

Fan, W., Geerts, F., & Wijsen, J. (2012). Determining the currency of data. *ACM Transactions on Database Systems*, *37*(4), 25. doi:10.1145/2389241.2389244

Getoor, L., & Machanavajjhala, A. (2012). Entity resolution: theory, practice & open challenges. *Proceedings of the VLDB Endowment*, *5*(12), 2018–2019.

Köpcke, H., Thor, A., Thomas, S., & Rahm, E. (2012). Tailoring entity resolution for matching product offers. In *Proceedings of the 15th International Conference on Extending Database Technology* (pp. 545-550). ACM.

Strehl, A., Ghosh, J., & Mooney, R. (2000, July). Impact of similarity measures on web-page clustering. In *Proceedings of Workshop on Artificial Intelligence for Web Search* (AAAI 2000) (pp. 58-64). AAAI.

Wang, H., Li, J., Wang, J., & Gao, H. (2011). Dirty data management in cloud database. In *Grid and cloud database management* (pp. 133–150). Berlin: Springer. doi:10.1007/978-3-642-20045-8_7

Wu, W., Li, H., Wang, H., & Zhu, K. Q. (2012). Probase: A probabilistic taxonomy for text understanding. In *Proceedings of the 2012 International Conference on Management of Data* (pp. 481-492). ACM.

ADDITIONAL READING

Bhattacharya, I., & Getoor, L. (2006). Entity resolution in graphs. *Mining graph data*, 311.

Brizan, D. G., & Tansel, A. U. (2006). A survey of entity resolution and record linkage methodologies. *Communications of the IIMA, 6*(3), 41–50.

Calado, P., Herschel, M., & Leitão, L. (2010). An overview of XML duplicate detection algorithms. In *Soft Computing in XML Data Management* (pp. 193–224). Springer Berlin Heidelberg. doi:10.1007/978-3-642-14010-5_8

Christen, P. (2012). A survey of indexing techniques for scalable record linkage and deduplication. *Knowledge and Data Engineering. IEEE Transactions on, 24*(9), 1537–1555.

Christen, P., & Goiser, K. (2007). Quality and complexity measures for data linkage and deduplication. In *Quality Measures in Data Mining* (pp. 127–151). Springer Berlin Heidelberg. doi:10.1007/978-3-540-44918-8_6

Cochinwala, M., Dalal, S., Elmagarmid, A. K., & Verykios, V. S. (2001). Record matching: Past, present and future.

Cohen, W. W., Ravikumar, P., & Fienberg, S. E. (2003). A comparison of string distance metrics for name-matching tasks. In *Proceedings of the IJCAI-2003 Workshop on Information Integration on the Web (IIWeb-03)* (Vol. 47).

Dai, H. J., Wu, C. Y., Tsai, R. T. H., & Hsu, W. L. (2012). From Entity Recognition to Entity Linking: A Survey of Advanced Entity Linking Techniques. In *The 26th Annual Conference of the Japanese Society for Artificial Intelligence*.

Dorneles, C. F., Gonçalves, R., & dos Santos Mello, R. (2011). Approximate data instance matching: a survey. *Knowledge and Information Systems, 27*(1), 1–21. doi:10.1007/s10115-010-0285-0

Elmagarmid, A. K., Ipeirotis, P. G., & Verykios, V. S. (2007). Duplicate record detection: A Survey. *Knowledge and Data Engineering. IEEE Transactions on, 19*(1), 1–16.

Galhardas, H., Florescu, D., Shasha, D., & Simon, E. (2000). AJAX: an extensible data cleaning tool. *SIGMOD Record, 29*(2), 590. doi:10.1145/335191.336568

Gollapalli, M., & Li, X. (2011). *Survey on Data Linkage and Ontology Matching Techniques*. Submitted for VLDB.

Gu, L., Baxter, R., Vickers, D., & Rainsford, C. (2003). Record linkage: Current practice and future directions. *CSIRO Mathematical and Information Sciences Technical Report, 3*, 83.

He, Q., Li, Z., & Zhang, X. (2010). Data deduplication techniques. In *Future Information Technology and Management Engineering (FITME), 2010 International Conference on* (Vol. 1, pp. 430-433). IEEE.

Karthigha, M., & Anand, S. K. (2013). A Survey on Removal of Duplicate Records in Database. *Indian Journal of Science and Technology, 6*(4), 4306–4311.

Köpcke, H., & Rahm, E. (2010). Frameworks for entity matching: A comparison. *Data & Knowledge Engineering, 69*(2), 197–210. doi:10.1016/j.datak.2009.10.003

Köpcke, H., Thor, A., & Rahm, E. (2010). Evaluation of entity resolution approaches on real-world match problems. *Proceedings of the VLDB Endowment, 3*(1-2), 484–493.

Luebbers, D., Grimmer, U., & Jarke, M. (2003). Systematic development of data mining-based data quality tools. In *Proceedings of the 29th international conference on Very large data bases-Volume 29* (pp. 548-559). VLDB Endowment.

Missier, P., Embury, S., Greenwood, M., Preece, A., & Jin, B. (2006). Quality views: capturing and exploiting the user perspective on data quality. In *Proceedings of the 32nd international conference on Very large data bases* (pp. 977-988). VLDB Endowment.

Navigli, R. (2009). Word sense disambiguation: A survey. [CSUR]. *ACM Computing Surveys*, *41*(2), 10. doi:10.1145/1459352.1459355

Subramaniyaswamy, V., & Chenthur Pandian, S. (2012). A complete survey of duplicate record detection using data mining techniques. *Inform Technol J*, *11*, 941–945. doi:10.3923/itj.2012.941.945

Thor, A., & Rahm, E. (2009). MOMA-a mapping-based object matching system. CIDR, 2007.

Weis, M., & Naumann, F. (2005). DogmatiX tracks down duplicates in XML. In *Proceedings of the 2005 ACM SIGMOD international conference on Management of data* (pp. 431-442). ACM.

Winkler, W. E. (1999). *The state of record linkage and current research problems*. Statistical Research Division, US Census Bureau.

Zhao, J. (2009). A Survey on Named Entity Recognition, Disambiguation and Cross 2 Lingual Conference Resolution. *Journal of Chinese Information Processing*, *23*(2), 3–17.

KEY TERMS AND DEFINITIONS

Big Data: A collection of data sets so large and complex that it becomes difficult to process using on-hand database management tools or traditional data processing applications.

Entity Resolution: Identify the data objects referring to the same real-world entity in a data object set.

Group-Wise Entity Resolution: Given S, a set of objects, the output is a family of sets $\{S_i \mid$ all objects in S_i refer to the same real-world entity$\}$ where for $i \neq j$, $S_i \cap S_j = \varnothing$.

Pair-Wise Entity Resolution: Given S, a set of objects, the output is a set of pairs $\{(o_i, o_j) \mid o_i, o_j \in S, o_i$ and o_j refer to the same real-world entity$\}$.

Precision: The fraction of matched data objects that refer to the same real-world entity.

Recall: The fraction of the data objects referring to the same real-world entity that are matched.

Record Matching: Find the record pairs that refer to the same real-world entity.

Chapter 2
Measures of Entity Resolution Result

ABSTRACT

In this chapter, the authors introduce how to measure Entity Resolution (ER) result. As the authors have already made the entity resolution process, they need to know how much better this result is. This is often done by comparing the ER result with the ground truth. First, two important parameters, precision and recall, that are commonly used in measuring the ER result today are shown. Then, there is a discussion of three categories of measure methods: pairwise, distance, and cluster. The authors stress talking about the distance-based measuring method in section two. In section three, there is a comparison made between these methods, and the authors discuss how to choose them in specific applications or circumstance.

INTRODUCTION

Entity Resolution (ER) is a fundamental and important problem in data cleaning. In real world applications, we may want to merge records from one or more data resources. In this process, a fatal task is to identify data records that actually represent the same entity in different ways in the whole dataset. Entity, here, may refers to a person, an item or any other things that described by data. This identifying and merging process is called entity resolution or ER in short. For example, in natural language processing, before analyzing sentence structures, our first task is to find items that represent the same thing in reality, e.g. "the United States of American" and "USA" all refers to the same country. Another example in real applications is data merging. Supposed that we need to merge financial data records from different banks together, we need to identify each person

which may be represented in different names in several datasets. We use ER algorithms to identify each person and put all his accounts from different banks together. Since the condition that the same entity represented in different forms commonly occurred, the ER problem is widely used in many domains such as natural language processing (NLP), machine learning, database and so on.

Since its importance and practice, this problem has been deeply researched in long terms. Many algorithms focus on how to identify the same entity. However, with more and more algorithms appear, there new problems emerge. Obviously, different methods will solve the ER problem in different way produce different results. Then the new problem is which results are the "best" among all these candidates. To answer this question, we should proceed in the most common ways to select candidates. That is to define measures to examine each candidate and choose the one with highest

DOI: 10.4018/978-1-4666-5198-2.ch002

score. However, this time the measures are on ER results. Each ER result should be evaluated to produce scores and at last we choose which one is the best.

Measures on ER results are very important since they directly tell us which ER results produced by different algorithms is the best. To summarize, it evaluates the existing algorithms. And in future, it gives directions in later works on how to improve the quality of ER results. Nowadays, many methods on evaluating ER results have been proposed. In this chapter we will have an overview on them and make a discussion in details on some respective ones. Also, we will make a contrast on differences between these measure methods and guide users how to choose the proper one in specific circumstance.

There is an old English saying which goes "Nothing is good or bad but by comparison", so the evaluation on the ER results is all based on comparison. Generally when we compare different ER algorithms, we run them on a given data source and compare the results with the pre-defined ground truth (Menestrina 2005). The ground truth result is commonly generated by confidential human experts or by exhaustive algorithm in large data scale, well like the standard key answers in examinations. Then measure methods are used to compute how close the ER results to the ground truth. Commonly, result of this measure algorithm will give out in a quantification way, may be a score value between 0 and 1 to represent the closeness. Finally, the closest ER results is claimed to be the best one. However, different measures have different computation ways, based on how they compute the closeness score; they were separated into three categories: pairwise based method, cluster based method and distance based method (Maidasani 2012). The pairwise based way generally count the same pairs occurred both in the results and in the ground truth and then to compute the ratio in all pairs. However, the cluster way may be more concentrate on same or similar cluster emerged both in ER results and the ground truth. In sec-

tion 3, we will discuss several kinds of pairwise based measure methods and cluster based ways. Then we will make a comparison between them. The distance-based way evaluate the closeness between ER results and the ground truth by an indicator called distance. In section 2, we will talk about the Basic Merge Distance method and the Generalized Distance Method based on the edit distance concept and another distance based measure method called Variation of Information (VI) based on measuring the amount of information lost and gain by transferring ER result into the ground truth. Moreover, we note that different measures may cause different best answers, which means there may exist conflicts between different evaluation results. So we will analyze why these conflicts occur and how they explain ER results in different views in the following content. This analysis guides us to choose the proper measures in our specially applications. Overall, all of these measures are based on two important parameters named precision and recall. Precision is used to measure how accurate our ER result is while recall tell how integrity our ER result is. They reflect the quality of our ER result from different views. Sometimes, we may need to make a compromise between them by a so-called F function. We will give the definitions and the common computation way of them in section 1. In different measure methods, precision and recall may compute in different ways. We will give out how to compute them after outlining the details of each ER measure algorithm. Also, the concept of precision and recall will be commonly used in the later chapters.

Before reading this chapter, readers aren't requested to know well about ER algorithms, we just concentrate on evaluations on the ER results but not concern about how they generated. We regard them from an auditing view but not a producing side. After learning the later chapters and have a deeply understanding on various ER algorithms, we recommend reading this chapter again to understand the how to measure ER results in depth.

BACKGROUND

Researchers have already developed many different ER measure methods. In our content, we will introduce pairwise measure method, distance-based measure method (BMD, GMD and VI) and cluster measure method (the Cluster F_1 (cF_1), the Closest Cluster F_1 (ccF_1), the MUC F_1 score method and the B^3F_1 score method). Also, we will discuss on how to choose the ER measure methods based on a survey made by researchers before.

PRECISION AND RECALL

In this section we will introduce two important metric that are commonly used in measures. While the general definition of these terms is consistent, the computation ways varies in different measures. And an important term, F_1 score, which is determined by the harmonic mean of precision and recall, is usually to measure the closeness between ER results and the ground truth. Firstly we will formulize the ER problem and introduce the general definition of precision and recall. Then we will take an example on how precision and recall computed in the pairwise measure method. After all, we present the meaning of the F_1 score and make some extensions on the F_1 score computation formula.

The ER problem is the process that identifies the same real world entity represented differently in different datasets. For an ambiguous record set $R = \{r_i\}$ which includes unknown set of entities. The ER algorithm may decide whether two records r_i and r_j where $i \neq j$ refers to the same real world entity. The ER results could be represented as set of clusters, where each cluster refers to the same entity. We could denote the ER result as $R = \{R_1, R_2 \cdots R_N\}$, where R_j represent a cluster and $R_j = \{r_1, r_2 \cdots r_m\}$ represent the records that belongs to the same "entity" called

R_j. We will use the formula $R = \{R_1, R_2 \cdots R_N\}$ or $R = \{\langle r_1, r_2 \rangle, \langle r_3, r_4, r_5 \rangle \cdots\}$ interchangeably to represent the ER result. And we will use R^1, R^2 to represent the different ER results.

In ER results, there exists several conditions, we take two records r_i and r_j for example. Firstly, if the records r_i and r_j refer to the same real world entity in the ground truth, they may be identified as the same or different entities in the result. We called the former one true positive condition and the later false negative condition. If the records r_i and r_j don't refer to the same real world entity in the ground truth, we may predict them as the same entity in the result, this condition is called false positive. So we could summarize, the true positive condition identifies the truly real world entity in the result, the false negative identifies the records as not the same entity in the result but in fact refer to the same entity in the ground truth, while the false positive predicts the records to be the same entity in the results but in fact refer to different entity in the ground truth. The precision and recall are defined based on these three conditions and describe the result from different aspects.

Precision is the fraction of the correct predicted records in all predicted records. In other world, it is the ratio of the result accuracy. We could define it as:

$$precision = \frac{T_p}{T_p + F_p}$$

Where T_p is the number of the true positives and F_p is the number of the false positives. So the precision tells us how many records in the ER results that we predict to be the same entity, we could use precision to measure the accuracy of the ER results.

Recall is the fractions of all records refer to the same entity that we found in our ER result. In other world, it is the ratio of the result integrity. We could define it as:

$$recall = \frac{T_p}{T_p + F_n}$$

where T_p is the number of the true positives and F_n is the number of the false negatives. The recall tells us how many records in ER results we succeed to predict in all records that belong to the same real world entity in the ground truth. We could use recall to test the integrity of our ER results.

Now we have introduced the general definition of precision and recall. However, the problem on how the number of T_p, F_p and F_n be computed isn't mentioned above. Generally, different ER measures methods often define different computation method on counting the number of T_p and etc. In pairwise measure method, it regards ER result as pairs of records and result pairs are compared to the truth pairs. In cluster measure method, it counts the number of cluster and compares the number of same or similar cluster. Here we take the pairwise method as an example and introduce how to compute precision and recall in this method.

In pairwise method, pairs represent the combinations between records. In the following Table 1, we list two possible ER result R^1 and R^2 and the ground truth result. As an example, in ER result R^2, the cluster $\langle r_5, r_6, r_7 \rangle$ represent an entity and could count the pair (r_5, r_6), (r_6, r_7) and (r_5, r_7). Naturally, T_p means all the true positives and could be defined as all the pairs both in ground truth and in result. However, F_p means all the false positives and could be defined as all the pairs in results but not in the ground truth. So on, F_n represents all the pairs in ground truth but not in the result. Extended from the general definition of precision and recall above, we could have the definition of precision and recall in the pairwise measure method.

$$PR_{pair} = \frac{\left| Pair_T \cup Pair_R \right|}{\left| Pair_R \right|}$$

$$RE_{pair} = \frac{\left| Pair_T \cap Pair_R \right|}{\left| Pair_T \right|}$$

In the definition, $Pair_T$ and $Pair_R$ means the set of the ground truth pairs and the ER result pairs. $|X|$ denotes the size of the set X. So $T_p + F_p$ ($|Pair_R|$) means all the positive pairs and $T_p + F_n$ ($|Pair_T|$) means all the true pairs. We could compute the precision and recall of R^1 and R^2 here. In ground truth we have 12 different pairs, and $\left| Pair_{R^1} \right| = 6$, we could count the same pairs in R^1 and T to compute precision and recall. We list the results of R^1 and R^2 in the following Table 2.

From the result in Table 2 we could see that a natural conflict exists between precision and recall. The ER result R^1 has a higher precision but a lower recall. This is due to precision and recall measures the result from different aspect. Precision concentrates on accuracy, so we are more careful to merge records in case of causing errors. Recall concentrates on integrity, so we dare to merge records in case of leaving out possible pairs. We need to make a trade-off between precision and recall so as to evaluate the ER as a whole; we could make some average on precision recall, which leads to the definition of an important term, F_1 score.

The F_1 score is the harmonic mean of precision and recall and is computed as following:

Table 1. Ground Truth and two ER result

Ground Truth	$\langle r_1, r_2 \rangle, \langle r_3, r_4 \rangle, \langle r_5, r_6, r_7, r_8, r_9 \rangle$
R¹	$\langle r_1, r_2 \rangle, \langle r_3, r_4 \rangle, \langle r_5, r_6, r_7 \rangle, \langle r_8, r_9 \rangle$
R²	$\langle r_1, r_2, r_3, r_4 \rangle, \langle r_5, r_6, r_7, r_8, r_9 \rangle$

$$F_1 = \frac{2}{\dfrac{1}{precision} + \dfrac{1}{recall}} = 2 \bullet \frac{precision \bullet recall}{precision + recall}$$

The F_1 score balance the features of precision and recall and give a single value to measure the result. So F_1 score is widely used to measure closeness between ER results and the ground truth. The higher F_1 score is, the much closer to the ground truth the ER result is. In our example above, the F_1 score of R^1 and R^2 is 0.667 and 0.857. So we could say R^2 are better than R^1 under pairwise F_1 score measure method.

However, in some condition we may not want to simply make a harmonic mean between precision and recall, we may more concern about one of them. This could be done from an extension of the F_1 score by give a weight on precision or recall. We called this extension computation method F_X.

$$F_X = \frac{2}{\dfrac{1+w}{precision} + \dfrac{1-w}{recall}} =$$
$$2 \bullet \frac{precision \bullet recall}{\left(1-w\right) \bullet precision + \left(1+w\right) \bullet recall}$$

Here w represents the weight, and we have $-1 < w < 1$. If $w \geq 0$, we more concern about recall, while if $w \leq 0$, we are more concern about

precision. When $w = 0$, F_X is the same with F_1. If we take $w = 0.8$ and compute the F_X score of the above example. The F_X score of R^1 and R^2 is 0.909 and 0.769. In this condition, we could say R^1 is better than R^2. This is conflict to result of the F_1 score measure method due to we measure ER results from different aspect. We could adapt proper method in specific applications. We will see more conflicts in section 3 and discuss why this occurs in depth. Readers could refer to the mathematic book for more properties on harmonic mean.

DISTANCE-BASED MEASURES

In this section we will introduce a category of widely used measure methods: distance-based measure method. One kind of this method computes the edit distance of the ER results and the ground truth to evaluate ER results. We will firstly present the concept of distance and the edit distance. Then we will give a discussion on two ER edit-distance based metrics: the Basic Merge Distance (BMD) method and the Generalized Distance Method (GMD) which is proposed in recent years. Another closest work to edit distance is called Variation of Information (VI), which measures the information lost and gained in converting ER result to the ground truth. We will introduce how to weight information and the VI method in the later of this section. The comparison between

Table 2. precision and recall of ER results

Result	Precision	Recall	$\mathrm{Pair_T} \cap \mathrm{Pair_R}$
R^1	1.000	0.500	$(r_1,r_2),(r_3,r_4),(r_5,r_6),(r_6,r_7),(r_5,r_7),(r_8,r_9)$
R^2	0.750	1.000	$(r_1,r_2),(r_3,r_4),(r_5,r_6),(r_5,r_7),(r_5,r_8),(r_5,r_9),$ $(r_6,r_7),(r_6,r_8),(r_6,r_9),(r_7,r_8),(r_7,r_9),(r_8,r_9)$

all these methods will be made in the next section of this chapter.

Distance is the property created by the space between two objects. The space can be physical space or defined in other ways. For example, there is two men A and B in London and New York, we could say the distance between A and B is 3467 miles. This distance is the common physical space distance. In other scene, different kinds of distance are defined. For example, to test the distance between two n-dimension vector **X** and **Y**, we could define the distance as

$$Distance\left(\boldsymbol{X},\boldsymbol{Y}\right)=\frac{1}{n}\bullet\sum_{i=1}^{n}\left(x_i-y_i\right)^2$$

This kind of distance is abstract and mathematic. All definition of distance must obey the following three properties of distance.

1. **Nonnegative:**

$$D\left(X,Y\right)^3 0, and D\left(X,Y\right)=0 \text{ iff } X=Y$$

2. **Symmetrical:** $D(X,Y) = D(Y,X)$
3. **Triangle Inequality:**

$$D\left(X,Y\right)\le D\left(X,Z\right)+D\left(Z,Y\right)$$

Reasons for distance definition obeying these properties and how to prove a definition of distance subject to these properties are beyond scope of this book. Readers could refer to relevant mathematic books for more information. Now we will introduce a more specific distance definition called edit distance metric that evaluate difference between strings.

Edit distance was proposed by Russian scientist Vladimir Levenshtein in 1965 and is widely used to measure the distance between strings. It is called "edit", so it only allows three basic "edit" operations on strings: delete a character, insert a character and replace a character. Edit distance is defined as the minimum operations needed to transfer one string A to another string B by aforementioned three basic edit operations:

1. Delete a character in every possible position in string A.
2. Insert a character in every possible position in string A.
3. Replace a character to other character in every possible position in string A.

For example, the string S="eeba" could transfer to string T="abac" by three operations. Firstly we replace the first 'e' in S to 'a', we get S_1 ="aeba"; secondly we delete the second 'e' and we get S_2 ="aba"; Last, we insert a 'c' in the last position of S_2 and we could get T="abac". So the edit distance of S and T is 3. Here we present a dynamic programming algorithm to solve the edit distance problem. Readers could refer to algorithm books for more information about this algorithm; we just give out the conclusion here.

Suppose we want to compute the edit distance between string M and N. We suppose the length of string M is m and the length of string N is n, and we use i and j to point to the position in M and N, then we could get:

1. ED (0,0)= 0, if i=0 and j=0
2. ED (0,j)= ED (0,j-1)+ 1 if i=0 and j>0
3. ED (i,0) = ED (i-1,0) +1, if i>0 and j=0

4. $ED(i,j) = min\begin{cases} ED(i,j-1), ED(i-1,j), \\ ED(i-1,j-1) \end{cases} +$

   $f(i,j), if \ i>0 \ and \ j>0$

Inside the formula, $f(i,j)$ means the cost from M_i to N_j. If $M_i \ne N_j$, which means we need to replace M_i to N_j, so $f(i,j)=1$, else when $M_i = N_j$, $f(i,j)=0$.

By the above formula and the cost function $f(i,j)$, it is simple to compute edit distance between string M and N. Firstly $ED(0,0) = 0$, then $\forall 0 \le i \le m$ and $\forall 0 \le j \le n$, we could calculate $ED(i,j)$ by recursion, the value $ED(m,n)$ is the edit distance between M and N. The time complexity of this algorithm is $O(mn)$.

Now readers may have a primary understanding on the concept "edit" and know well on how to compute the edit distance between strings. The edit distance based evaluation method is similar to the edit operations on the strings, but only with different operated objects and different operations. Now the operated objects are the ER results with set of clusters and the operations should be put on these clusters. We will first introduce the Basic Merge Distance (BMD) method and then the Basic Merge Distance (BMD) method.

The Basic Merge Distance (BMD) method was first proposed by Al-Kamha et al. in 2004. The BMD method defines two basic operations on the clusters in the ER result: split and merge. And it requires that all splits precede any merges. It counts the minimum number of operations needed to transfer the ER result to the ground truth and define this number as the distance between them.

For a split operation, we take in a cluster t and return two clusters that don't overlap with each other.

$$split(t) = \{(t_1, t_2) \mid t_1 \cap t_2 = \emptyset, \ t_1 \cup t_2 = t, \ t_1 \ne \emptyset, t_2 \ne \emptyset\}$$

So applying a split to a cluster set P will cause $\{P - (t_1, t_2)\} \cup \{t\}$, where $t_1, t_2 \in P$.

For a merge operation, we take in two cluster and output union set cluster as the result.

$$merge(t_1, t_2) = \{t \mid t = t_1 \cup t_2\}$$

Thus applying a merge to a cluster set P will cause $\{P - (t)\} \cup \{t_1, t_2\}$, where $t \in P$.

BMD restricts that splits must be done before merges and involves a path from ER result to the ground truth with splits and merges. For our example in Table 1, we just need one split to convert R^2 to the ground truth (split the $\langle r_1, r_2, r_3, r_4 \rangle$ to $\langle r_1, r_2 \rangle, \langle r_3, r_4 \rangle$) and one merge to convert R^1 to the ground truth (merge the $\langle r_5, r_6, r_7 \rangle, \langle r_8, r_9 \rangle$ to $\langle r_5, r_6, r_7, r_8, r_9 \rangle$). So the BMD distance between R^1 and the ground truth is 1 (so as to the result R^2). We now take a more complex example to present the process of the BMD method.

Suppose the ER result

$$R^3 = \{\langle r_1 \rangle, \langle r_2, r_3 \rangle, \langle r_4 \rangle, \langle r_5, r_6, r_7 \rangle, \langle r_8, r_9 \rangle\}$$

and the ground truth is the same in the Table 1. To convert R^3 to the ground truth, we need first do the splits and then the merges. Firstly we split $\langle r_2, r_3 \rangle$ and get two cluster $\langle r_2 \rangle$ and $\langle r_3 \rangle$. Compared with the ground truth, we need do the merges. We merge $\langle r_1 \rangle$ with $\langle r_2 \rangle$, returns $\langle r_1, r_2 \rangle$, $\langle r_3 \rangle$ with $\langle r_4 \rangle$, returns $\langle r_3, r_4 \rangle$, $\langle r_5, r_6, r_7 \rangle$ with $\langle r_8, r_9 \rangle$ returns $\langle r_5, r_6, r_7, r_8, r_9 \rangle$. To convert R^3 to the ground truth, we need one split and three merges, so the BMD distance between R^3 and the ground truth is 4.

To perform the process of split and merge, we describe the transformation path using a graph. In this graph, each node represents an operation (split or merge) and each edge represents a cluster. A split node inputs a cluster edge and outputs two cluster edges and vice versa. The path in this graph indicates the BMD process and we illustrate the process of converting R^3 to the ground truth in Figure 1. We will frequently use this graph to show the process in the later of this section.

Now we already have an understanding about BMD method. It is simple and easy to operate, just count the numbers of splits and merges. However, simple may represent useless, we could see there are two kinds of problems on the BMD

Figure 1. Transformation graph

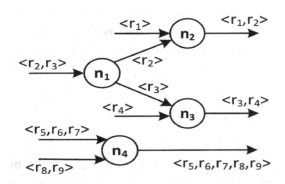

method. The first problem is in some cases we may want to penalize splits more than mergers (or vice versa) instead of simply counting the number of splits and merges. In some condition, the split (merge) operation may have more weight than merge (split), which isn't reflected in the BMD method. The second problem is BMD just concern about the operation numbers but not the operation size. In many cases, split (or merge) on a cluster with bigger size should power more than on small size. To reflect the different effect of split and merge and the effect of different size, we should make an improvement on BMD method. Here we present a new method called Generalized Distance Method (GMD) which is proposed in recent years.

The Generalized Distance Method was proposed by Menestrina et al. (2010). It is also based on the elementary operations of splitting and merging. However, GMD method is more advanced than BMD on the term generalized. The generalized term expresses two points. Firstly, the GMD method allows us to configure the cost of the cluster operation and the splitting operation. Thus, we could use different functions in different applications, which create lots of measure methods by configuring different cost functions. Second the GMD method relaxes the restriction in the BMD method that all splits must precede the merges, in corresponding, it defines a new concept called

legal-path. In the later of this section, we will first introduce the basic concepts and proving method in the GMD method and then make a discussion on the cost function to conduct users on how to select cost functions in specially applications.

Operations in GMD are the same as that in BMD method: merges and splits. We have already defined them in the BMD section and readers could review them. In BMD method we restrict that all splits must proceed merges, however in GMD method we relax this constriction to that the merge and split operations must be a legal path. To introduce this concept, we first analyze the reason that BMD make this constriction.

Here we just take a simple example, we want to convert the ER result $R = \{\langle r_1, r_2 \rangle, \langle r_3, r_4 \rangle\}$ to the ground truth $T = \{\langle r_1, r_3 \rangle, \langle r_2, r_4 \rangle\}$. According to the restriction, we must first split the ER result R into four independent clusters $R' = \{\langle r_1 \rangle, \langle r_2 \rangle, \langle r_3 \rangle, \langle r_4 \rangle\}$ and then merge them to be the ground truth (merge $\langle r_1 \rangle, \langle r_3 \rangle$ to be $\langle r_1, r_3 \rangle$ and merge $\langle r_2 \rangle, \langle r_4 \rangle$ to be $\langle r_2, r_4 \rangle$). This process includes two splits and two merges. So the edit distance between R and T is 4. However, we may find a small edit path regardless of this constriction. We could firstly merge $\langle r_1, r_2 \rangle$ and $\langle r_3, r_4 \rangle$ to be $\langle r_1, r_3, r_2, r_4 \rangle$ and then split this cluster into $\langle r_1, r_3 \rangle, \langle r_2, r_4 \rangle$. This process only needs two operations. However we consider this kind of operation invalid. In this process, we produce a new cluster $\langle r_1, r_3, r_2, r_4 \rangle$ which is not occurred in the ground truth. As in the process of editing clusters, we could only use the given cluster information based on R and T. Creating new cluster that never occurs produce new information that never be confirmed, do this is forbidden in this process. We could only do based on what we know but not by predicting or assuming. So intuitively, we should first remove the cluster information in R and then add the cluster information in T. In BMD method, the corresponding operations are splits and merges, which will never produce new cluster, so this restriction is guaranteed. In GMD method, the same restriction that new cluster never occur is also required, here we use the concept legal path to guarantee it.

We denote every operation, split or cluster as o (o_s for split and o_m for merge). In the transformation from R to T, we could denote the process as $T = R : o_1, o_2 \ldots o_N$. To every merge operation o_i, where $o_i(t_1, t_2) = t$, there exists a cluster c in the ground truth T and $t \subseteq c$. We say that this path is legal path. In this definition, we restrict every merge operation to never produce new cluster. Compared to the BMD method, we no longer require all splits proceed merges but use a much more relax concept legal path. In the example above, the path merges $\langle r_1, r_2 \rangle$ and $\langle r_3, r_4 \rangle$ to be $\langle r_1, r_3, r_2, r_4 \rangle$ is illegal. We will show a method to find the optimal legal path from ER result to the ground truth.

In the BMD method, we simply configure the cost of operation a constant number one, we have already mentioned this method is naive. In GMD method, however, we could configure the cost function. Functions are more accurate and powerful than constant numbers. We formalize the cost function in the GMD method.

In the GMD method, there exist a split operation cost function f_s and a merge operation cost function f_m. The cost functions f_s and f_m map two input cluster size to cost weight where the split function f_s is concerned with split operations, to a split operation $split(t) = (t_1, t_2)$, the cost is $c = f_s(|t_1|, |t_2|)$; the merge function f_m is concerned with merge operations, to a merge operation $merge(t_1, t_2) = t$, the cost is $c = f_m(|t_1|, |t_2|)$;

Also, the cost function f_s and f_m should subject to some properties.

1. **Non negative:** The cost function must always be non-negative, that is $f_s(x, y) \geq 0$ and $f_m(x, y) \geq 0$ where $x, y > 0$

2. **Symmetric:** The cost function must be symmetric to the input, that is $f_s(x, y) = f_s(y, x)$ and $f_m(x, y) = f_m(y, x)$

3. **Monotonicity:** The cost function must be monotone non-decreasing, that is $\forall i \geq 0, j \geq 0$ we have

$$f_s(x + i, y + j) \geq f_s(x, y)$$

and

$$f_m(x + i, y + j) \geq f_m(x, y)$$

The cost function could be configured according to these three properties. Specially, in BMD method, we just set $f_m(x, y) = 1$, $f_s(x, y) = 1.1$. And the GMD cost from ER result to the ground truth is the minimum total cost in all legal paths. David Menestrina etc. proved that there exists a minimum cost legal path in which all split precede merges from ER result to the ground truth. Here we just show the key ideas.

To illustrate the process that produces the minimum cost legal path, we should use the transformation graph mentioned above. Here we use a different example which was proposed by David Menestrina etc. in the paper and we have made a little change; we may want to convert the ER result $R = \{\langle r_1, r_2, r_3 \rangle, \langle r_4, r_5 \rangle, \langle r_6 \rangle, \langle r_7 \rangle\}$ to the ground truth $T = \{\langle r_1, r_2, r_3, r_4, r_5, r_6, r_7 \rangle\}$. In this example, the simple method is to merge all clusters in the result. However, here we show another operation sequences to illustrate the method used to construct the minimum cost legal path.

In Figure 2 we show the operation sequence that convert ER result to the ground truth. The dashed arrows represent the input and output of the transformation process and the operations o_i represents a merge operation or split operation. This operation process is legal according to our definition on legal path. Now we start to convert this graph to the path that cost is minimum, the path is legal and all splits precede merges.

Firstly we give out the method to move all split operation front. We see that in Figure 2 some operations are commutable for their inputs and outputs nerve overlap. For example, we could execute o_1, o_2 and o_3 in arbitrary order. However, o_1 must do precede o_2 because o_2 uses the output of o_1. So find the operation path from our ER result to the ground truth is same as to find the topological ordering in the directed graph. Readers could refer to data structure book for the simple algorithm to generate the topological ordering.

To construct the path with all splits preceding merges, we could simply use commutatively to move all splits in front of merges like do o_1, o_2 before o_3. However, to the condition that a merge must do before a split like o_1 and o_2, we may need a complex method called "merge-split" swap to move split in front of merge. Here we illustrate this method in the following graph.

In the merge-split swap process, we suppose a merge operation a points to a split operation b. Since the split b uses the output of the merge operation a, a must do before b. And we construct another two operations a' and b' where a' is a split operation precede the merge operation b'. In details, we could formalize this swap process as followed.

In the origin operation sequences, we have $o_a(c_1, c_2) = c_{1,2}$ and $o_b(c_{1,2}) = d_1, d_2$. And we let $|c_1| \geq |c_2|$, $|d_1| \geq |d_2|$. Then we construct two new operations $o_{a'}(c_1) = c_{1'}, d_{2'}$ and $o_{b'}(c_{1'}, c_2) = d_{1'}$. Here we choose $d_{2'}$ which subject to

1. $d_{2'} \subseteq c_1$
2. $|d_{2'}| = |d_2|$

And we could easily have that $c_{1'} = c_1 - d_{2'}$ and $d_{1'} = c_{1'} + c_2$. The remaining changes in the path is to replace inputs using $d_{1'}, d_{2'}$ instead of d_1, d_2. The merge-split swap ends when we process all these conditions. We take the example o_1, o_2 mentioned above to show this process more clearly.

Here in operation o_1 and operation o_2 we have $c_1 = \langle r_1, r_2, r_3 \rangle$ and $c_2 = \langle r_4, r_5 \rangle$, $d_1 = \langle r_2, r_3, r_4 \rangle$ and $d_2 = \langle r_1, r_5 \rangle$. Subject to the constrictions on $d_{2'}$, we could have three choices $(\langle r_1, r_2 \rangle, \langle r_2, r_3 \rangle, \langle r_1, r_3 \rangle)$. Here we choose

Figure 2. Transformation graph

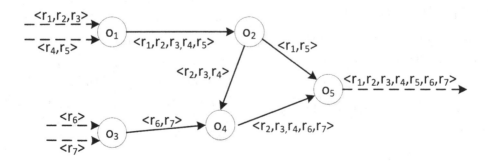

Figure 3. Merge-split swap

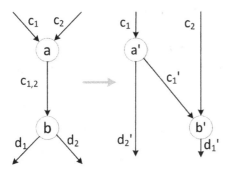

$d_{2'} = \langle r_1, r_2 \rangle$. Then we could have $c_{1'} = \langle r_3 \rangle$ and $d_{1'} = \langle r_3, r_4, r_5 \rangle$. We could redraw the transformation graph in Figure 4.

We could find a path from the ER result to the ground truth, that is $o_1', o_2', o_3, o_4, o_5$. We use the commutable property to swap o_1, o_2 before o_3 and use the merge-split swap method to build two new operations o_1', o_2'. In this path, we have all splits before merges. This guarantees that the path must to be legal. For the reason that suppose we merge two clusters and the resulted cluster is never occurred in the ground truth, the subsequent will not be splits, so we may never get the ground truth. So this split-first method guarantees the legality of the path, also, the authors proved after this merge-split swap the cost of the path p' will not bigger the cost of the origin path p. Readers could refer to the origin paper for proof in much more details. So we have this following theorem that there exists a legal path with minimum cost

in which all splits precede merges. The method is to use the commutable property and merge-split swap repeatedly on a legal path until we get the desired result.

After the discussion on the path processing, we now should concentrate on the core of the GMD method, which is the cost functions. We first discuss an important property on the cost function called operation order independence which is useful to compute the cost and then make an analysis on configuring the cost functions.

We called a function f is operation order independence if and only if it subjects to:

$$\forall x, y, z \quad f(x, y) + f(x + y, z) = f(x, z) + f(x + z, y)$$

For example, the two-dimensional linear function $f(x, y) = k_1 xy + k_2$, we could verify it by plugging it into the equation. The left of the equation is:

$$left = k_1 xy + k_2 + k_1(x + y)z + k_2 = k_1(xy + yz + xz) + 2k_2$$

The right of the equation is:

$$right = k_1 xz + k_2 + k_1(x + z)y + k_2 = k_1(xy + yz + xz) + 2k_2$$

Figure 4. Swapped transformation graph

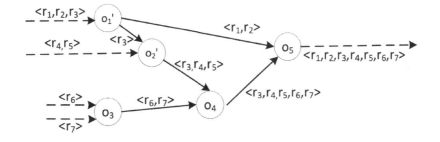

So we have verified our claim.

This operation order independence greatly helps our computation on the cost. Suppose we want to merger cluster c_x, c_y, c_z into a single cluster and the merger cost function f_m is operation order independent. We could have:

$$f_m\left(\left|c_x\right|,\left|c_y\right|\right) + f_m\left(\left|c_x + c_y\right|,\left|c_z\right|\right) = f_m\left(\left|c_x\right|,\left|c_z\right|\right) + f_m\left(\left|c_x + c_z\right|,\left|c_y\right|\right)$$

to the split operation cost function f_s the equation is about the same, which means we could compute the cost of this path in arbitrary order.

Combined with our discussions about the path above, we could easily construct a legal path with the minimum cost. Suppose the cost function f_s and f_m are operation order independent, we could easily compute the cost of the total path. We call this path the bare necessities path. When there exists more than one bare necessities path, we could prove the coat of them are equal and minimum. Menestrina et al. (2009) had given a slice algorithm to compute the cost by using the bare necessities path for its simple structure. (See Algorithm 1.)

Algorithm 1 Slice Algorithm

Input: R, T: our ER result and the ground truth
R_i, T_i represents the i-th cluster in R, T
f_m, f_s: the merge and split cost functions
Output: edit distance from R to T (the total cost)
Cost(R, T)

1. // build a map from record to cluster number and store size of each cluster in R
2. **for each** R_i **in** R
3. **for each** r **in** R_i
4. $M[r] \leftarrow i$
5. **end for**
6. $RSize[i] \leftarrow R_i$
7. **end for**
8. // compute the cost
9. $cost \leftarrow 0$
10. **for each** T_i **in** T
11. // determine which cluster in R contains the record in T_i
12. $pMap \leftarrow \{\}$
13. **for each** r **in** T
14. // if we haven't seen this R then add it into the map
15. **if** $M[r] \notin keys(pMap)$
16. $pMap[M[r]] \leftarrow 0$
17. **end if**
18. // increase the count for this partition
19. $pMap[M[r]]++$
20. **end for**
21. //compute the cost
22. $SiCost \leftarrow 0$
23. $totalRecs \leftarrow 0$
24. **for each** $(i, count)$ **in** pMap
25. // add the cost to split R_i
26. **if** $RSize[i] > count$
27. $SiCost \leftarrow SiCost + f_s(count, RSize[i]-count)$
28. **end if**
29. $RSize[i] \leftarrow RSize[i] - count$
30. **if** $totalRecs \neq 0$
31. // add the cost to merge
32. $SiCost \leftarrow SiCost + f_m(count, RSize[i]-count)$
33. **end if**
34. $totalRecs \leftarrow totalRecs + count$
35. **end for**
36. $cost \leftarrow cost + Sicost$
37. **end for**
38. **return** cost

We now explain the algorithm in details with an example that we want to convert

$$R = \{\langle r_1, r_3, r_5\rangle, \langle r_2, r_4, r_6\rangle\}$$

to

$$T = \left\{ \langle r_1, r_2, r_3 \rangle, \langle r_4, r_5, r_6 \rangle \right\}.$$

In line 2 to 7 we make a loop to set a map M mapping all records in R to the cluster number it owns to and set an array RSize to store the size of each cluster in R. So we have $M[r_1] = 1$ and $RSize[1] = 3$.

The algorithm continues to compute the cost to generate T. The first step Line 11 to 20 is to determine which cluster in R contains records in T_j. In the structure pMap we store the number of the records in R_i and in T_j. In our example, to T_1, we have $pMap[1] = 2$ and $pMap[2] = 1$. To generate T_j, we must first split all the relevant records in all in cluster in R and split them out. Then we must merge those split clusters into a single cluster, that is T_j. In line 24 to 37 we compute for this process. We use pMap to determine how many records we should split for each cluster R_i. And we compute the cost of the split as $f_s \left(count, RSize[i] - count \right)$. Then we compute the cost to merge them as $f_m \left(count, RSize[i] - count \right)$. In this process we update the RSize each time for the remaining records in cluster R_i. Finally we could return the resulted cost.

Now we could take about on how to choose the cost functions. We have always use the term configuring to mean that the cost function should set the metric based on the specific applications. By detailed analysis on the ER applications, we should carefully know the influence of the operations and the effect of the different size. We define three kinds of possible conditions.

First the effect of the operation is constant which means the influence of the operations have no relations with its size. We may set $f(x, y) = k$.

Second the effect of the operation is additively on the size inputs. We may set $f(x, y) = k(x + y)$.

Third the effect of the operation is multiplicative on the size input. We may set $f(x, y) = kxy$.

There are also many other possible conditions (logarithmic or exponential). We could do experiments to module the applications and choose the best measured cost functions. And there may be obvious difference between function f_m and f_s. So we recommend configuring split function and merging function independently. Sometimes, we could simply combine these basic functions and get the desired results. For example, we may set $f_m = log(xy) + k$, which means there is a basic effect value k of each merge operation and an additional influence value based on the size of x and y. The $log(xy)$ function grows more slowly larger, which shows that we want to penalize large size but not more.

After former discussion on the BMD and GMD method, we are convinced readers have already have detailed understanding on the core of the distance-based measure method. The BMD and GMD are all based on the edit distance and define the basic edit operations: split and merge. In fact, we could also define other distance-based measures as long as this definition observes the constrictions on definition of distance we proposed before. Here we show another distance-based measure method called Variation of Information (VI), which measures the information lost and gained in between ER result and the ground truth. We will first introduce what is information and how to measure information, and then we give out the method to compute in VI method.

We all talk about information every day and the current times is called "Times of Information". However, to define the words of information seems to be very difficult for its abstract and intangible. Some people takes information as the signals transferred in circuits or physical space. In fact, information is different to signals. Signals hold information but not represent information itself. Supposing that we want to research information, we must describable it clearly. Suppose that we want to describable it clearly, we must define information in mathematic ways. A good saying in science is to make an object into mathematic modules makes reliable and consecutive research on it, so as to information. Shannon & Weaver (1948) firstly proposed his probability information in his A Mathematical Theory of Communication, which was regarded as the beginning of the Information Theory.

Shannon regarded information as "the object to eliminate uncertainty". Once the information comes then the uncertainty disappears. For example we may not know whether it is sunny or snowy tomorrow. However, on the next day it snows then this uncertainty disappears. We could say we get information from this process. The more uncertainty the information eliminates, the more information we get. We just take a daily condition to explain this claim. Before a football match between a very weak team A and a very strong team B, the strong team B would have great chance to win this match, in mathematic saying, the probity that team B win the chance is very big or the uncertainty that team B win the team is small. After the team, if team B wins the match as expected, the uncertainty be eliminated is small and we get little information. However, if the team A wins this match in a surprise, the information we get is much more. So we could same the amount of the information we get is proportional to the uncertainty, or in mathematic saying the amount of information is inversely proportional to the probability (Cover & Thomas, 2012). As we could compute the probability the event occurs then we could measure the amount of the information.

As the probity p obeys $0 \le p \le 1$, and the amount of the information obeys $I \ge 0$. Thus we need a function maps p to I. Shannon defined this function as the reciprocal of the logarithmic function. To an event x, the information of x defined as:

$$I(x) = log_2 \frac{1}{p(x)} = log_2 \left(-p(x)\right)$$

the unit of the information is bit. In normal cases, we could omit the base number 2 of the logarithmic function. And this function has several good properties.

1. **Monotonicity:**

$$\forall 0 \le p(x_i) \le p(x_j) \le 1, \ I(x_i) \ge I(x_j)$$

2. **Limitation:**

$$p(x) = 0, \ I(x) = +\infty \quad p(x) = 1, \ I(x) = 0$$

3. **Additively:** $\forall$ independent event x_i and x_j obeys $p(x_i x_j) = p(x_i) p(x_j)$, we have

$$I(x_i x_j) = log_2 \frac{1}{p(x_i x_j)} = log_2 \frac{1}{p(x_i) \bullet p(x_j)}$$
$$= I(x_i) + I(x_j)$$

These three properties are totally in coincidence with the natural conditions, which shows this function is suit to describe the information. Shannon called this definition of information the probabilistic information.

We have just defined the information amount of a single event x. However, to an information source, it may occurs many possible event in random. We use the module probability space to represent each possible event and the corresponding probability.

$$probability \ space = \{\langle x_i, p(x_i)\rangle \mid 1 \le i \le n\}$$

where

$$\sum_{i=0}^{n} p(x_i) = 1$$

To measure the total average information provided by this information source, we could compute the mathematical expectation on the I, which we defines:

$$H(X) = E(I(x_i)) = \sum_i p(x_i) \log \frac{1}{p(x_i)} = -\sum_i p(x_i) \log p(x_i)$$

We call $H(X)$ the entropy of this information source, which tells us how many amount of information provides from an event occurred from this source on average. We take an simple example here. Suppose we throw a coin and guess which side face up. We have $p(0) = p(1) = 0.5$, so $H(X)$, the entropy of source, is just 1 bit.

The $H(X)$ function also has lots of properties and readers could refer to the relevant information theory books. Based on these priority knowledge, we have already hold a basic understanding on the concept of information and how to compute the information. Now we analysis the specially condition that between our ER result and the ground truth.

Suppose our ER result R contains N clusters $c_1, c_2 \ldots c_N$, and we denote $n_k = |c_k|$ to stand by the size of the cluster. We just imagine this game: to pick one record from the result set R randomly. We could easily know that the probability that the record comes from cluster c_k is:

$$p(k) = \frac{n_k}{n}$$

we could use the discrete random variable k to represent the cluster the record comes from. So we could know the entropy of the cluster in our game is:

$$H(C) = -\sum_k p(k) \log p(k) = -\sum_k \frac{n_k}{n} \log \frac{n_k}{n}$$

the value $H(C)$ tells us on average how much information we could get from the ER result clusters. This values just concerns with the ER result itself and express the amount of information performed by this classification. So we could defines the entropy both on ER result R and the ground truth T. We denote them as $H(R)$ and $H(T)$ and compute them by the above formula.

As the entropy represents the information on the classification itself, we must find the method to express the connectivity between two classifications. Suppose we have two classifications C and C', and we use two random variable k and k' to represent the cluster number associated with C and C'. The joint probability $p(k, k')$ means the probability that a record comes from c_k in C and c_k' in C'. We could compute:

$$p(k, k') = \frac{|c_k \cap c_k'|}{n}$$

to imitate the definition of the entropy, we could define the mutual information between C and C' as followed:

$$I(C, C') = \sum_k \sum_{k'} p(k, k') \log \frac{p(k, k')}{p(k) p(k')}$$

The mutual information $I(C, C')$ tells us as if we know the information in one classification C and want to know the information in the other classification C'. The $I(C, C')$ tells us how much uncertainty has be eliminated in this condition. The information in one may help us the know the other but not all of the other. From this formula, we could have:

$$I\left(C,C'\right)=I\left(C',C\right)\geq 0$$

And

$$I\left(C,C'\right)\leq H\left(C\right)\quad I\left(C,C'\right)\leq H\left(C'\right)$$

the equality found if and only if $C=C'$.

So we defines VI as the independent information holds in this two clusters as:

$$VI\left(C,C'\right)=H\left(C\right)+H\left(C'\right)-2I\left(C,C'\right)$$

or in a more pretty formula as:

$$VI\left(C,C'\right)=\left[H\left(C\right)-I\left(C,C'\right)\right]+\left[H\left(C'\right)-I\left(C',C\right)\right]$$

We could use the Venn graph to illustrate their relationship. See Figure 5.

The $VI\left(C,C'\right)$ express the amount of information C still contains when it has already got the information of C' and the amount of information C' still contains when it has already got the information of C. In our condition between $VI\left(R,T\right)$, we have known the distribution of our ER result R and the ground truth T and information represents uncertainly. So $VI\left(R,T\right)$ tells us how many uncertainly still exists between R and

Figure 5. Venn graph

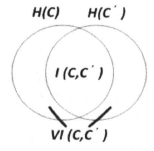

T and measures the distance between them. We could prove the VI satisfies the properties of the distance definition.

1. **Nonnegative:** Since $I\left(C,C'\right)=H\left(C\right)$ and $I\left(C,C'\right)=H\left(C'\right)$ if and only if $C=C'$. So we have $VI\left(C,C'\right)=0$ if and only if $C=C'$. This means the distance between R and T equal zero if and only if $R=T$.

We could also prove that $VI\left(C,C'\right)$ has a upper bound. Since we could prove that $H\left(C\right)\leq logk$ if and only if $\left|c_1\right|=\left|c_2\right|=...=\left|c_N\right|$ by Jenson non-equality. So we could have $VI\left(C,C'\right)\leq logk+logk'$. Since k has the max value n (each record is a cluster), so we could have

$$0\leq VI\left(C,C'\right)\leq 2\bullet logn$$

2. **Symmetrical:** Since $I\left(C,C'\right)=I\left(C,C'\right)$, it is easy to prove that:

$$VI\left(C,C'\right)=VI\left(C',C\right)$$

3. **Triangle inequality:** For three classification C_1, C_2 and C_3, we have:

$$VI\left(C_1,C_3\right)\leq VI\left(C_1,C_2\right)+VI\left(C_2,C_3\right)$$

We have:

$$VI\left(C_1,C_2\right)+VI\left(C_2,C_3\right)=H\left(C_1\right)+2H\left(C_2\right)+H\left(C_3\right)-2I\left(C_1,C_2\right)-2I\left(C_2,C_3\right)$$

And

$$VI\left(C_1,C_3\right)=H\left(C_1\right)+H\left(C_3\right)-2I\left(C_1,C_3\right)$$

minus these two equations we have:

$$minus = 2H\left(C_2\right) + 2I\left(C_1, C_3\right) - 2I\left(C_1, C_2\right) - 2I\left(C_2, C_3\right)$$

We could extend this *minus* and prove *minus* ≥ 0, we reserve this proof to be an exercise for readers.

We now use the example mentioned above to show the process to compute VI. We have

$$R = \left\{\langle r_1, r_3, r_5\rangle, \langle r_2, r_4, r_6\rangle\right\}$$

and

$$T = \left\{\langle r_1, r_2, r_3\rangle, \langle r_4, r_5, r_6\rangle\right\}.$$

We could have

$$p\left(i\right) = \begin{bmatrix} 1/2 & 1/2 \end{bmatrix}, \ p\left(j\right) = \begin{bmatrix} 1/2 & 1/2 \end{bmatrix}$$

and so we have

$$H\left(R\right) = H\left(T\right) = 1bit, \ I\left(R,T\right) = 0.08bit.$$

So $VI\left(R,T\right) = 1.84bit$. We recommend user to list the $p\left(i,j\right)$ as a matrix, which will make the computation of $I\left(R,T\right)$ much more clearly and easier.

From the above discussion, we think readers must have a deep understanding on the distance metric measures concepts and methods. We have talked about edit distance and two measures BMD and GMD based on this. Another distance based measure method is the VI. It measures the distance between ER result and the ground truth by the information lost and gained. Distance-based measures are widely used and developed in measuring ER result, we will make a comparison between themselves and with others in the next section to display advantages and disadvantages.

THE COMPARISONS OF MEASURES

Before this chapter, we have already introduced several kinds of metrics on ER result. In section 1, to explain the concept precision and recall, we introduced the pairwise method, which measures the ER result by counting the pairs in ER result and the ground truth. And in section 2, we learned a cluster of measure methods (BMD, GMD and VI) based on distance. We measure the ER result by computing the distance between the ER result and the ground truth. The method of computing distance differs in different algorithms. In BMD we count the number of basic operations (splits or merges) and in GMD method we could configure the cost of each operation. However, in VI method we evaluate the distance by the amount of information changed. We have already separated the measures into three categories: pairwise, cluster and distance. In the view of different measure method, different methods may have different answers. An ER result which was thought to be good in method may be evaluated as bad in method M_2. This conflict may occur and we should analysis why this condition occurs and direct users to choose the best measure method in specific applications. Thus, we need a comparison on different method from advantages and disadvantages. In this section, we will do these works. Firstly we replenish to introduce the cluster based measure method and then make the comparison on different measure methods.

The cluster measures compare the cluster in ER result and the ground truth. Clusters are the basic result units in ER result and the ground truth and one cluster contains one or more records. Based on different measures on cluster, we have several cluster based measures. We will introduce the Cluster F_1 (cF_1), the Closest Cluster F_1 (ccF_1), the MUC F_1 score method and the B^3F_1 score method.

The Cluster F_1 method is the simplest cluster based measures. It is only compare at the cluster level and counts the number of clusters that exactly match. Between the ER result R and the ground truth T, we define the precision to be the fraction of the number of all exactly matched cluster to the total number of clusters in ER result.

$$precision = \frac{|R \cap T|}{|R|}$$

and the recall is defined as the fraction of the number of all exactly matched cluster to the total number of clusters in the ground truth.

$$recall = \frac{|R \cap T|}{|T|}$$

cF_1 is the harmonic mean of precision and recall.

$$cF_1 = 2 \bullet \frac{precision \bullet recall}{precision + recall}$$

For example, the ER result

$$R = \left\{ \left\langle r_1, r_2, r_3 \right\rangle, \left\langle r_4, r_5 \right\rangle, \left\langle r_6 \right\rangle, \left\langle r_7 \right\rangle \right\}$$

and the ground truth

$$T = \left\{ \left\langle r_1, r_2, r_3 \right\rangle, \left\langle r_4, r_5 \right\rangle, \left\langle r_6, r_7 \right\rangle \right\}.$$

So the precision is 0.500 and the recall is 0.667, we could get the cF_1 is 0.572.

The Closest Cluster F_1 method was proposed by Benjelloun et al. (2009). It doesn't checks for the completely match but use the Jaccard function to measure the similarity of clusters. The Jaccard function is firstly to measure the similarity of strings, and we define the Jaccard of two cluster R_i and T_j here as:

$$Jaccard = \frac{|R_i \cap T_j|}{|R_i \cup T_j|}$$

To compute the similarity of each cluster r in ER result, we could compute the Jaccard value with each cluster t in the ground truth and choose the maximum one. And we define the precision that sums all the similarity of all cluster in ER result R.

$$precision = \frac{\sum_{R_i \in R} max_{T_j \in T} \left(Jaccard \left(R_i, T_j \right) \right)}{|R|}$$

As the same, we could also compute the similarity of each cluster t in the ground truth and define the recall as:

$$recall = \frac{\sum_{T_j \in T} max_{R_i \in R} \left(Jaccard \left(T_j, R_i \right) \right)}{|T|}$$

Thus, the ccF_1 is the harmonic mean of precision and recall.

$$ccF_1 = 2 \bullet \frac{precision \bullet recall}{precision + recall}$$

For the same example in the cF_1 method, we could compute each cluster in ER result and in the ground truth in the following Table 3.

So the precision is 0.750 and the recall is 0.833, the ccF_1 is 0.789.

Vilain et al. (1995) proposed MUC F_1 score in 1995 during the Message Understanding Conference. In MUC method, it regards each cluster as links of records and restrict that all links generate the minimum spanning tree of the record node. For example, we illustrate the links as the graph view, the above cluster R_1 could be regards as (a) or (b) in Figure 6.

Table 3. Similarity of each cluster

ER Result R		Ground Truth T	
Cluster	**Similarity**	**Cluster**	**Similarity**
R_1	1.000	T_1	1.000
R_2	1.000	T_2	1.000
R_3	0.500	T_3	0.500
R_4	0.500		

In MUC method, we count the number of link modifications that between the ER result and the ground truth. In the paper, authors defined a function Intersect (c, S) that takes in a cluster c and a set of clusters S and returns the set of clusters in S which intersect with c.

$$Intersect\left(c, S\right) = \left\{s \mid s \in S \, and \, s \cap c \neq \varnothing\right\}$$

For each cluster R_i and the function $Intersect\left(R_i, T\right)$ returns the number of the clusters in the ground truth which intersect with R_i. This number means the missing links in R_i. For the links in R_i generate the minimum spanning tree, the number of links is $|R_i| - 1$, so the precision is defined as the sum of all fraction of the correct links in the total links.

Figure 6. Links between records

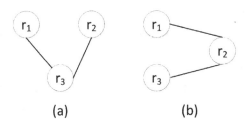

(a)   (b)

$$precision = \sum_{R_i \in R} \frac{\left|R_i\right| - \left|Intersect\left(R_i, T\right)\right|}{\left|R_i\right| - 1}$$

On the same, we could define the recall as

$$recall = \sum_{T_j \in T} \frac{\left|T_j\right| - \left|Intersect\left(T_j, R\right)\right|}{\left|T_j\right| - 1}$$

So the MUC F_1 score is the harmonic mean of precision and recall.

$$\mathrm{MUC}F_1 = 2 \bullet \frac{precision \bullet recall}{precision + recall}$$

Bagga & Baldwin (1998) proposed B^3 F_1 score that improved from the MUC F_1 score method.

Here in B^3 F_1 method, we defines a function $remap\left(r\right)$ which takes a record r as input and outputs the set of clusters which contain r.

And we define the precision and recall as.

$$precision = \frac{1}{|T|} \sum_{T_j \in T} \sum_{t \in T_j} \sum_{R_i \in remap(t)} \frac{\left|R_i \cap T_j\right|}{\left|R_i\right|}$$

$$recall = \frac{1}{|T|} \sum_{T_j \in T} \sum_{t \in T_j} \sum_{R_i \in remap(t)} \frac{\left|R_i \cap T_j\right|}{\left|T_j\right|}$$

The B^3F_1 is the the harmonic mean of precision and recall.

$$B^3F_1 = 2 \bullet \frac{precision \bullet recall}{precision + recall}$$

Above all, we have already introduced three categories of measures: pairwise, cluster and distance and showed the typical measure method in this category. In pairwise we showed pairwise F_1, in cluster category we showed cF_1, ccF_1, MUC F_1 and B^3 F_1 score method, in distance category we showed BMD, GMD and VI method. Since we have already have a deep understanding on these ER result measure methods, we could make an comparison between them. The comparison could be made on two sides: advantages and disadvantages of each method. And since we know the strong and weak points of each method, we could make the decision that which method is suitable for which applications. In a specific condition, we could choose the best ER result measure method according to these decisions. We recommend readers could review the former chapters when we discuss the corresponding measure methods in the following passages.

Firstly we discuss the pairwise F_1 method, this method is a good way to represent clusters. The pairs are thought to be the natural way to represent relations between records and require that transitivity should hold for records of pairs in this application. So pairwise method is widely used in such condition such as active learning that use pairs. In some applications where transitivity may not hold we may not use this pairwise method. However, this pairwise method is simple and easy to compute. Another disadvantage of this method is that it could not take into account the singleton entity, which is the cluster that only contains one record. So we may not choose this method in an application where singleton entity occurs frequently.

In cluster based measure methods, we will discuss the strong and weak points of cF_1, ccF_1, MUC F_1 and B^3 F_1 score method.

The cF_1 method measures the accuracy of ER result on the completely correct clusters but not the partially matched clusters. This is an advantage for it restricts exact and strict matching, which improves accuracy. Also this is a disadvantage for it lose the information of partially matched clusters, which effect the resulted precision and recall on evaluating the ER result. In applications which need exact and completely matching and evaluating, we could choose this cF_1 method.

The ccF_1 method overcomes the disadvantages of cF_1 method. It reflects the entire completely and partially matched cluster in precision and recall values. Also this method is easy to compute and for understanding. Although this is a new method, I think it will be widely used and improved in the coming future.

The MUC F_1 score have several shortcomings. The MUC method could process singleton entity but never penalize separation of a singleton entity from a cluster. Also, this method may cause unintuitive errors for it regards all errors to be equal. It considers all the missing links as the same. Unlike MUC F_1 score, B^3 F_1 score overcomes these shortcomings. The errors are not considered equal in B^3 F_1 score method. However, B^3 F_1 score method could process the twinless mentions. Twinless mentions are the conditions where records in ER result never occur in the ground truth. This may occur in some applications in the Natural Language Processing (NLP) area. Stoyanov et al. (2010) proposed B_3all and B_3^0, which could deal with twinless mentions.

In section 2 we discuss the distance based measure method. We talked about BMD, GMD and VI method. BMD is simple but couldn't configure by users. So we could only use this method in some rough applications (like estimation). VI could be thought to measure the distance from another view side. However, GMD method could be thought as a better and standard way to evaluate ER result. It could configured based on operations and clusters size. Also, authors proposed in paper that both VI method and pairwise method could be computed use the Slice Algorithm in the GMD method.

In GMD method, we could set the cost functions f_s and f_m as:

$$f_m\left(x+y\right) = f_s\left(x+y\right) = h\left(x+y\right) - h\left(x\right) - h\left(y\right)$$

Where:

$$h\left(x\right) = \frac{x}{N} \log \frac{x}{N}$$

Readers could prove this as an excises.

Also, we could prove that, in pairwise method, we could compute the precision and recall as:

$$precision = 1 - \frac{GMD\left(R,S\right)}{GMD\left(R,\perp\right)} \quad when$$

$$f_m\left(x,y\right) = 0 \ and \ f_s\left(x,y\right) = xy$$

$$recall = 1 - \frac{GMD\left(R,S\right)}{GMD\left(\perp,S\right)} \quad when$$

$$f_m\left(x,y\right) = xy \ and \ f_s\left(x,y\right) = 0$$

Readers could refer to the proof in the paper. Since GMD method is powerful and easy to compute, we recommend regarding it as the standard measure method. The key points in GMD method is to choose the suitable cost functions which we have already discussed in section 2.

Above all, we have talked about the weak and strong points and the relations of different measure methods. We could now decide to choose the suitable measure method in specific domains. In a survey made by Maidasani et al. (2012), he chose 21 ER papers and record the measure methods used in the paper. Here we give it out.

We could see that pairwise method is widely used in almost every domain. MUC and method

is only widely used in NLP area. and are used in databases domain but not widely as pairwise for they are new methods. BMD/GMD method is used very little for this method is very new. We could summarize these methods as three kinds.

1. Traditional and widely used methods: like pairwise method.
2. Professional methods for specific domain: like MUC F_1 and B^3F_1 method for NLP.
3. New mentioned method: like cF_1, ccF_1 and BMD/GMD.

We could recommend that firstly users should familiar with the application domain and use the classic method in this domain. Then user could use some universal method to evaluate the ER result like the pairwise method. The end but not the least, we suggest to use some new method such as GMD. Users could construct the cost function for GMD method and measure the ER result. By this triple-multi evaluation way and compare them with each other, I think we could have a deep understanding on our ER result all round. Also, users should focus on the developments in ER domain for new mentioned methods to measure ER results.

FUTURE RESEARCH DIRECTIONS

We think there are two main issues that are needed to be addressed in future research. First is the new model to measure ER result. In different applications and specific usages, we need different ER metrics. The second is a deeper research on GMD method. As we have talked, GMD is a generalized metric except the problem of how to choose measure functions and threshold depend on users. We propose to deal with this problem automatically by a machine learning methods in the future.

Table 4. Measure methods in papers

Source	Domain	Pairwise			MUC		BMD/GMD
(Laender et al., 2008)	Databases	√	√	---	---	---	---
(Whang et al., 2009)		√	---	---	---	---	---
(Menestrina et al., 2010)		√	√	√	---	---	√
(Kopcke et al., 2010)		√	---	---	---	---	---
(Rastogi et al., 2011)		√	---	---	---	---	---
(Junker et al., 1999)	Vision	√	---	---	---	---	---
(Bertini et al., 2006)		√	---	---	---	---	---
(Hamdoun et al., 2008)		√	---	---	---	---	---
(Zhang et al., 2011)		√	---	---	---	---	---
(Lin et al., 2010)	Natural Language Processing	---	---	---	---	√	---
(Recasens & Hovy, 2010)		√	---	---	---	√	---
(Stoyanov et al., 2010)		---	---	---	√	√	---
(Raghunathan et al., 2010)		√	---	---	√	√	---
(Cai & Strube, 2010)		---	---	---	√	√	---
(Singh et al., 2010)		√	---	---	---	√	---
(McCallum et al., 2000)	Machine Learning	√	---	---	---	---	---
(Bilenko & Mooney,2003)		√	---	---	---	---	---
(Bhattacharya & Getoor, 2007)		√	---	---	---	---	---
(Arasu et al., 2009)		√	---	---	---	---	---
(Kopcke et al., 2010)		√	---	---	---	---	---
(Kolb et al., 2011)		√	---	---	---	---	---

Notes: √ : used measures in this paper

--- : not used measures in this paper

CONCLUSION

In this chapter, we showed why and how to measure ER result. We could summarize this chapter as follows.

- Introduce the concept of precision and recall and how to compute them.
- Make a discussion on three categories measure methods: pairwise, distance and cluster. And we stress on the distance-based method.
- Make a comparison between these methods and talked on how to choose the suitable method in applications.

REFERENCES

Al-Kamha, R., & Embley, D. W. (2004). Grouping search-engine returned citations for person-name queries. In Proceedings of the 6th Annual ACM International Workshop on Web Information and Data Management (pp. 96-103). ACM.

Arasu, A., Ré, C., & Suciu, D. (2009). Large-scale deduplication with constraints using dedupalog. In *Proceedings of Data Engineering* (pp. 952–963). IEEE.

Bagga, A., & Baldwin, B. (1998). Algorithms for scoring coreference chains. In Proceedings of the First International Conference on Language Resources and Evaluation Workshop on Linguistics Conference (Vol. 1, pp. 563-6). Academic Press.

Benjelloun, O., Garcia-Molina, H., Menestrina, D., Su, Q., Whang, S. E., & Widom, J. (2009). Swoosh: A generic approach to entity resolution. The VLDB Journal—The International Journal on Very Large Data Bases, 18(1), 255-276.

Bertini, M., Del Bimbo, A., & Nunziati, W. (2006). Video clip matching using mpeg-7 descriptors and edit distance. In Image and video retrieval (pp. 133-142). Berlin: Springer.

Bhattacharya, I., & Getoor, L. (2007). Collective entity resolution in relational data. *ACM Transactions on Knowledge Discovery from Data*, *1*(1), 5. doi:10.1145/1217299.1217304

Bilenko, M., & Mooney, R. J. (2003). Adaptive duplicate detection using learnable string similarity measures. In Proceedings of the Ninth ACM SIGKDD International Conference on Knowledge Discovery and Data Mining (pp. 39-48). ACM.

Cai, J., & Strube, M. (2010). Evaluation metrics for end-to-end coreference resolution systems. In Proceedings of the 11th Annual Meeting of the Special Interest Group on Discourse and Dialogue (pp. 28-36). Association for Computational Linguistics.

Cover, T. M., & Thomas, J. A. (2012). *Elements of information theory*. New York: Wiley-Interscience.

Hamdoun, O., Moutarde, F., Stanciulescu, B., & Steux, B. (2008). Person re-identification in multi-camera system by signature based on interest point descriptors collected on short video sequences. In *Proceedings of Distributed Smart Cameras* (pp. 1–6). IEEE.

Junker, M., Hoch, R., & Dengel, A. (1999). On the evaluation of document analysis components by recall, precision, and accuracy. In *Proceedings of Document Analysis and Recognition* (pp. 713–716). IEEE.

Kolb, L., Kopcke, H., Thor, A., & Rahm, E. (2011). Learning-based entity resolution with MapReduce. In Proceedings of the Third International Workshop on Cloud Data Management (pp. 1-6). ACM.

Kopcke, H., Thor, A., & Rahm, E. (2010). Evaluation of entity resolution approaches on real-world match problems. *Proceedings of the VLDB Endowment*, *3*(1-2), 484–493.

Kopcke, H., Thor, A., & Rahm, E. (2010). Learning-based approaches for matching web data entities. *IEEE Internet Computing*, *14*(4), 23–31. doi:10.1109/MIC.2010.58

Laender, H., Gongalves, M. A., Cota, R. G., Ferreira, A. A., Santos, R. L., & Silva, A. J. (2008). Keeping a digital library clean: new solutions to old problems. In Proceedings of the Eighth ACM Symposium on Document Engineering (pp. 257-262). ACM.

Lin, B., Shah, R., Frederking, R., & Gershman, A. (2010). Cone: Metrics for automatic evaluation of named entity co-reference resolution. In Proceedings of the 2010 Named Entities Workshop (pp. 136-144). Association for Computational Linguistics.

Maidasani, H., Namata, G., Huang, B., & Getoor, L. (2012). Entity resolution evaluation measures.

McCallum, A., Nigam, K., & Ungar, L. H. (2000). Efficient clustering of high-dimensional data sets with application to reference matching. In Proceedings of the Sixth ACM SIGKDD International Conference on Knowledge Discovery and Data Mining (pp. 169-178). ACM.

Meila, M. (2007). Comparing clusterings—An information based distance. *Journal of Multivariate Analysis*, *98*(5), 873–895. doi:10.1016/j.jmva.2006.11.013

Menestrina, D., Whang, S. E., & Garcia-Molina, H. (2009). Evaluating entity resolution results (extended version).

Menestrina, D., Whang, S. E., & Garcia-Molina, H. (2010). Evaluating entity resolution results. *Proceedings of the VLDB Endowment, 3*(1-2), 208–219.

Raghunathan, K., Lee, H., Rangarajan, S., Chambers, N., Surdeanu, M., Jurafsky, D., & Manning, C. (2010). A multi-pass sieve for coreference resolution. In Proceedings of the 2010 Conference on Empirical Methods in Natural Language Processing (pp. 492-501). Association for Computational Linguistics.

Rastogi, V., Dalvi, N., & Garofalakis, M. (2011). Large-scale collective entity matching. *Proceedings of the VLDB Endowment, 4*(4), 208–218.

Recasens, M., & Hovy, E. (2010). Coreference resolution across corpora: Languages, coding schemes, and preprocessing information. In Proceedings of the 48th Annual Meeting of the Association for Computational Linguistics (pp. 1423-1432). Association for Computational Linguistics.

Shannon, E., & Weaver, W. (1948). A mathematical theory of communication.

Singh, S., Subramanya, A., Pereira, F., & McCallum, A. (2011). Large-scale cross-document coreference using distributed inference and hierarchical models. In Proceedings of the 49th Annual Meeting of the Association for Computational Linguistics: Human Language Technologies (vol. 1, pp. 793-803). Association for Computational Linguistics.

Stoyanov, V., Cardie, C., Gilbert, N., Riloff, E., Buttler, D., & Hysom, D. (2010). Reconcile: A coreference resolution research platform.

Vilain, M., Burger, J., Aberdeen, J., Connolly, D., & Hirschman, L. (1995). A model-theoretic coreference scoring scheme. In Proceedings of the 6th Conference on Message Understanding (pp. 45-52). Association for Computational Linguistics.

Whang, E., Benjelloun, O., & Garcia-Molina, H. (2009). Generic entity resolution with negative rules. The VLDB Journal—The International Journal on Very Large Data Bases, 18(6), 1261-1277.

Zhang, L., Vaisenberg, R., Mehrotra, S., & Kalashnikov, D. V. (2011). Video entity resolution: Applying ER techniques for smart video surveillance. In Proceedings of Pervasive Computing and Communications Workshops (PERCOM Workshops), (pp. 26-31). IEEE.

ADDITIONAL READING

Al-Kamha, R., & Embley, D. W. (2004). Grouping search-engine returned citations for person-name queries. In Proceedings of the 6th annual ACM international workshop on Web information and data management (pp. 96-103). ACM.

Bagga, A., & Baldwin, B. (1998). Algorithms for scoring coreference chains. In The first international conference on language resources and evaluation workshop on linguistics coreference (Vol. 1, pp. 563-6).

Maidasani, H., Namata, G., Huang, B., & Getoor, L. (2012). Entity Resolution Evaluation Measures.

Meila, M. (2007). Comparing clusterings—an information based distance. *Journal of Multivariate Analysis, 98*(5), 873–895. doi:10.1016/j.jmva.2006.11.013

Menestrina, D., Whang, S. E., & Garcia-Molina, H. (2010). Evaluating entity resolution results. *Proceedings of the VLDB Endowment, 3*(1-2), 208–219.

KEY TERMS AND DEFINITIONS

Basic Merge Distance (BMD): Evaluate the ER result based on the basic operations (splits and merges).

Cluster: Evaluate the ER result by comparing the clusters in ER result and the ground truth.

Entity Resolution (ER): Entity resolution, the process that identify and merge similar or the same record represent the same entity in the real world from multi data source.

Generalized Merge Distance (GMD): Evaluate the ER result based on the configured cost functions defined on the operations (splits and merges).

Pairwise: Evaluate the ER results based on counting how many pairs are found in both ER result and the ground truth.

Precision: The parameters shows how many records in the ER result is accurate.

Recall: The parameters shows how many records are found in the ER results.

Variation of Information (VI): Evaluate the ER result based on the information lost and gained between the ER result and the ground truth.

Section 2
Entity Resolution on Various Types of Data

Chapter 3
Entity Resolution on Names

ABSTRACT

Errors with names occur frequently. "California" and "CA" refer to the same state of the USA; however, they may both appear as records in a database at the same time. Several techniques need to be proposed to solve these problems. In this chapter, the authors introduce the methods of entity resolution on names. They propose three methods. Similarity measure between names is a kind of fundamental techniques; it makes a significant contribution to the textual similarity. The method of string transformations can handle some situations beyond textual similarity. Recently, learning algorithms on string transformations have been proposed to make matching robust to such variations. Examples illustrate the benefits of each approach.

INTRODUCTION

In the real world, we may be confronted with many errors about names. Record matching is a well-known problem of matching records that can handle this situation. Most approaches to record matching just rely on textual similarity of each pair record. The applications include entity resolution in E-Commerce (Chapter 16), bibliography (Chapter 15) and medical health information system (Chapter 17).

In section 1, we will introduce several metrics computed using a similarity function. Levenshtein (1966) has proposed a metric to calculate the distance between two sequences called *Edit-Distance*. The edit distance metrics work well for catching typographical errors, but they are typically ineffective for other types of mismatches. In Elmagarmid, Ipeirotis, and Verykios (2007),

Smith and Waterman describe an extension of edit distance and affine gap distance in which mismatches at the beginning and the end of strings have lower costs than mismatches in the middle. This approach is a well-known algorithm for performing local sequence alignment, that is, for determining similar regions between two nucleotide or protein sequences. Instead of looking at the total sequence, the Smith-Waterman algorithm compares segments of all possible lengths and optimizes the similarity measure in Smith & Waterman (1981). Jaro-Winkler Distance in Jaro (1989) and Winkler (1990) introduces a string comparison algorithm that is used in the area of record linkage (duplicate detection). The higher the two strings' Jaro-Winkler distance, the more similar the strings are. The Jaro-Winkler distance metric is designed and best suited for short strings such as person names. The above three algorithms

DOI: 10.4018/978-1-4666-5198-2.ch003

are character-based similarity metrics that are designed to handle typographical errors. Token-based similarity metrics are widely used in the domain of information retrieval. Scientists have proposed TF-IDF that is a numerical statistic which reflects how important a word is to a document in a data collection in Manning, Raghavan, and Schütze (2008). Cosine similarity in Tan (2007) is often coming along with TF-IDF. Cohen described a system named WHIRL in Cohen (1998, June) that adapts from information retrieval the cosine similarity combined with the TF-IDF weighting scheme to compute the similarity of two fields in Elmagarmid, Ipeirotis, & Verykios (2007). Character-based and token-based similarity metrics focus on the string-based representation of the database records. However, strings may be phonetically similar even if they are not similar in a character or token level. Soundex is a phonetic algorithm for indexing name by sound, as pronounced in English. The goal is for homophones to be encoded to the same representation so that they can be matched despite minor differences in spellings in R.C. Russell Index and R.C. Russell Index.

Record matching infrastructure does not allow a flexible way to account for synonyms that refer to the same name with different manifestations, and forms of string transformation such as abbreviations. In section 2, we will introduce a transformation-based framework for record matching. At first, we introduce preliminary knowledge about Context-Free grammar which is also referred as CFG in Hopcroft (2008). The context-free grammar is widely used in compiler theory. The parse tree that based on CFG, is one of the most efficient method to parse grammar. It can be constructed easily and it is effective to process semantic actions. Two frameworks have been proposed as transformation-based entity representation that has been shown in Arasu, Chaudhuri & Kaushik (2008) and Arasu & Kaushik (2009). In this section, we mainly introduce the grammar-based entity representation framework.

At first, the framework generates productions based the real world to construct a context free grammar. Then it utilizes the parse tree technique to analysis how a record is generated by the extension grammar of the CFG, and adds semantic actions to the parse tree in order to determine whether two records are the same. For example, "Dr Andrew J. Smith" will be analyzed as first name is Andrew, and last name is Smith. Then, "Smith, Andy J." will also be analyzed as first name is Andrew, and last name is Smith. Therefore, this framework can solve this problem.

Recently, both machine learning and data mining algorithms are widely used in computer science. Learning algorithm is important and effective to solve the problem of entity resolution on names. S. Tejada has proposed a system on learning algorithm to handle this situation in his Ph. D thesis (in Tejada, Knoblock & Minton 2001). There are two stages in the system architecture. The stage of computing similarity scores takes advantage of the methods about textual similarity that we introduce in section 1. The next stage is mapping learner. The first part of the mapping learner is mapping rule learner that uses decision to classify whether the rules are mapped or not. The transformation weight learner computes the weight of each transformation in order to get higher accuracy by recalculating similarity scores. The experimental results show high accuracy outcome of the processing.

At last, we will list some books and papers for further work as the expansion of knowledge.

BACKGROUND

Reduce error or duplicate records is one of the difficult problems in data cleaning. As the number of entities increasing fast, errors or duplicate records occur in databases more frequently. Traditional methods mainly rely on textual similarity. Recently, scientists have proposed some approaches that deal with these situation with higher accuracy.

There are more and more scientists researching Transformation-based data cleaning algorithms. Then learning algorithm will be gradually proposed with the development of machine learning and data mining.

SIMILARITY MEASURE BETWEEN NAMES

Entities have two or more representations in databases. Duplicate records of sequences data in databases is one of the most common sources of mismatches. Therefore, detection of duplicate records relies on sequence comparison, and we will introduce three techniques to deal with it. First of all, we will introduce the Character-Based Similarity Metric, then the Token-Based Similarity Metric will be presented. In the end of this section, we will introduce the Phonetic Similarity Metric.

Character-Based Similarity Metric

The Character-Based Similarity Metrics focus on typographical errors, such as words spelling errors (e.g. "Johnson" and "Jansen") (in Elmagarmid, Ipeirotis & Verykios 2007). In this part, we will introduce three algorithms to resolve these errors.

Edit Distance

Edit Distance, also referred as the Levenshtein Distance in Levenshtein (1966), is a string metric for measuring difference between two sequences. Edit Distance between two strings is equal to the minimum number of single character edit operations, which are required to transform one string into the other one, with three kinds of edit operations:

1. *insert* a character into the string(e.g. fightin →fighting, insertion of 'g' at the end)
2. *delete* a character from the string(e.g. above →abov, deletion of 'e' at the end)
3. *substitute* one character with a different character(e.g. hello →tello, substitution of 't' for 'h')

A basic dynamic programming algorithm, presented in the following, can be used for computing edit distance between two strings.

Edit-Distance(S, T):

1. $n \leftarrow$ length(S), m $\leftarrow$ length(T)
2. **For** $i \leftarrow 0$ to n:
3. $D[i,0] \leftarrow i$
4. **For** $j \leftarrow 0$ to m:
5. $D[0,j] \leftarrow j$
6. **For** $i \leftarrow 0$ to n:
7. **For** $j \leftarrow 0$ to m:
8. **If** $S[i] = T[j]$:
9. $COST \leftarrow 0$
10. **Else**:
11. $COST \leftarrow 1$
12. $D[i,j] \leftarrow$ Minimum of(
13. $D[i-1,j]+1$,
14. $D[i,j-1]+1$,
15. $D[i-1,j-1]+COST$)
16. **Return** $D[n,m]$

In the first line, we get the length of the string S and the string T. And it's going to initialize the first row to 0…n and the first column to 0…m of the matrix D from the line 2 to 5. We will compute the Edit Distance with the dynamic programming algorithm when the initialization has been done. It's respectively corresponding to the three edit operations (delete, insert and substitute) from the line 13 to 15. After filling up the entire D table, the value of D[n,m] is the Edit Distance we are looking for. Here is an example that shows how the algorithm works:

There are two strings "luckys" and "lucky", we want to transform the "luckys" into the "lucky",

Therefore, the Edit Distance between "luckys" and "lucky" is D[6,5], i.e., 2.

Smith-Waterman Distance

Smith-Waterman Distance in Smith, & Waterman (1981), based on dynamic programming, is a well-known algorithm for sequences alignment. Different from the Edit Distance, the Smith-Waterman Distance compares all possible tokens, and computes the similarity.

We assume there are two strings $A=\{a_1 a_2 \ldots a_n\}$ with the length of n, and $B=\{b_1 b_2 \ldots b_m\}$ with the length of m. The similarity between string A

Figure 1. An example on edit distance

Step 1: Initialization

		l	u	c	k	y
	0	1	2	3	4	5
l	1					
u	2					
c	3					
k	4					
y	5					
s	6					

Step 2: Compute the Edit Distance iteratively

		l	u	c	k	y
	0	1	2	3	4	5
l	1	0	1	2	3	4
u	2					
c	3					
k	4					
y	5					
s	6					

Step 3: Get the result

		l	u	c	k	y
	0	1	2	3	4	5
l	1	0	1	2	3	4
u	2	1	1	2	3	4
c	3	2	2	1	2	3
k	4	3	3	2	1	2
y	5	4	4	3	2	1
s	6	5	5	4	3	2

and string B is denoted as *sim*(A,B). Deletions of length k are given weight W_k. We will define a matrix *H* to discover possible pairs of tokens with higher similarity. First of all,

$$\begin{cases} H_{k0} = 0 \, for \, 0 \leq k \leq n \\ H_{0l} = 0 \, for \, 0 \leq k \leq m \end{cases} \quad (1)$$

Then, the value of H_{ij}, representing the maximum similarity of the two strings that end with a_i and b_j respectively, is obtained from the formula as:

$$H_{ij} = \begin{cases} H_{i-1,j-1} + sim\left(a_i, b_j\right) \\ max\left\{H_{i-k,j} - W_k\right\} for \, k \geq 1 \\ max\left\{H_{i,j-1} - W_l\right\} for \, l \geq 1 \\ 0 \end{cases} \quad (2)$$

$1 \leq i \leq n$ and $1 \leq j \leq m$

If are associated, the value of H_{ij} will be

$$H_{i-1,j-1} + sim\left(a_i, b_j\right),$$

And then with the consideration of a_i is at the end of a deletion of length k, the similarity will be:

$$max\left\{H_{i-k,j} - W_k\right\} for \, k \geq 1,$$

So does the situation that b_j is at the end of a deletion of length l, thus the similarity will be

$$max\left\{H_{i,j-1} - W_l\right\} for \, l \geq 1,$$

Finally, if there is no similarity between a_i and b_j, the value of H_{ij} will be zero.

The pair of tokens with the maximum similarity will be found in the matrix H by locating the maximum element of H. It is determined with a trace back procedure ending with an element of

H that equals to zero by the other elements of matrix H that lead to the maximum value in Smith & Waterman (1981).

We will show how the algorithm works with the example:

- Stringσ$_1$ = ACACACTA
- Stringσ$_2$ = ACACACTA
- W(gap)= -1
- W(match)= +2
- W(mismatch)= -1= W(a,-) = W(-b)

And then, the matrix H is as follows:

$$
H = \begin{pmatrix}
 & - & A & C & A & C & A & C & T & A \\
- & 0 & 0 & 0 & 0 & 0 & 0 & 0 & 0 & 0 \\
A & 0 & 2 & 1 & 2 & 1 & 2 & 1 & 0 & 2 \\
G & 0 & 1 & 1 & 1 & 1 & 1 & 1 & 0 & 1 \\
C & 0 & 0 & 3 & 2 & 3 & 2 & 3 & 2 & 1 \\
A & 0 & 2 & 2 & 5 & 4 & 5 & 4 & 3 & 4 \\
C & 0 & 1 & 4 & 4 & 7 & 6 & 7 & 6 & 5 \\
A & 0 & 2 & 3 & 6 & 6 & 9 & 8 & 7 & 8 \\
C & 0 & 1 & 4 & 5 & 8 & 8 & 11 & 10 & 9 \\
A & 0 & 2 & 3 & 6 & 7 & 10 & 10 & 10 & 12 \\
\end{pmatrix}
$$

Then we mark the trace in the matrix with black, and we get the result:

- Stringσ$_1$ = A - CACACTA
- Stringσ$_2$ = AGACAC - A

Jaro-Winkler Distance

Jaro-Winkler Distance is a measure of similarity between two strings (mainly used for comparison of last and first names). The Jaro Distance in Jaro (1989) of two strings and is defined as:

$$
d_j = \begin{cases}
0 & if\ m = 0 \\
\frac{1}{3}\left(\frac{m}{|S_1|} + \frac{m}{|S_2|} + \frac{m-t}{m}\right) & otherwise
\end{cases} \quad (3)
$$

- m is the number of matching characters
- t is the number of swap characters

We consider two characters from S$_1$ and S$_2$ respectively match only when the distance of the two characters is no larger than

$$
\left\lfloor \frac{MAX(|S_1, S_2|)}{2} \right\rfloor - 1
$$

and these characters determine t which is the number of swap characters. Simply, t is half the number of transpositions. For example, "MARTHA" and "MARHTA" has the same characters, but we need swap the character "T" with "H" if "MARTHA" transforms into "MARHTA". Thus, the character "T" and "H" are the match characters with different order, and t=2/2=1.

Therefore, the Jaro Distance of the two strings will be:

$$
d_j = \frac{1}{3}\left(\frac{6}{6} + \frac{6}{6} + \frac{6-1}{6}\right) = 0.944
$$

The Jaro-Winkler Distance in Winkler (1990) values the prefix more scores, it defines a prefix p which gives more favorable ratings to strings that match from the beginning for a set of prefix length l. The Jaro-Winkler Distance is:

$$
d_w = d_j + \left(lp\left(1 - d_j\right)\right) \quad (4)
$$

The meaning of d$_j$ is the Jaro Distance, and l means the number of common characters of the prefix and is up to a maximum of 4. p is a constant for adjusting score, and should not exceed 0.25. The standard value for the constant in Winkler's work is 0.1. Therefore, the Jaro-Winkler Distance of the last example is:

$$
d_w = 0.944 + \left(3 \times 0.1 \times \left(1 - 0.944\right)\right) = 0.961
$$

Token-Based Similarity Metrics

Character-based similarity metrics cannot deal with situations that involve rearrangement of words (e.g. "John Smith" versus "Smith, John"). The following two algorithms are proposed to solve this problem.

Atomic Strings

Atomic Strings in Monge & Elkan (1996), which is a sequence of alphanumeric characters delimited by punctuation characters, is one of the basic algorithms for matching text fields. Only if the two strings are equal or one is the prefix of the other, we will describe that the two strings match.

Therefore, the similarity of two fields based on the Atomic Strings algorithm is the number of matching atomic strings divided by their average number of atomic strings.

TF-IDF and Cosine Similarity

TF-IDF in Manning, Raghavan & Schütze (2008), abbreviation of the *Term Frequency-Inverse Document Frequency*, based on statistic, is a measure for analyzing how important a word or a string is to a data collection.

TF means frequency of a term occurs in document d which could be computed as:

$$tf_{i,j} = \frac{n_{i,j}}{\sum_k n_{k,j}} \tag{5}$$

The meaning of $n_{i,j}$ is the number of times this term appears in document d_j, and the denominator is the number of times that all terms appear in document d_j.

IDF is a measure of whether a term is common across all documents. It could be got by dividing the number of all documents by the number of documents that contain some particular term, and computing the logarithm of the result. The IDF could be described as follow:

$$idf\left(t, D\right) = \log \frac{|D|}{\left|\left\{d \in D : t \in d\right\}\right|} \tag{6}$$

The |D| represents the number of all documents in the data collection.

The denominator means the number of documents that contain the term . However, if does not occur in all the documents, the denominator will be zero and it will result to dividing zero. Therefore, it is a better way to solve this problem by adjusting the denominator to $1 + \left|\left\{d \in D : t \in d\right\}\right|$.

Cosine Similarity in Tan (2007) is a method to measure the similarity between two vectors by computing the cosine of the angle between them.

The cosine of two vectors could be described easily by the Euclidean Distance:

$$\vec{x} \bullet \vec{y} = \| x \| \| y \| \cos è \tag{7}$$

Therefore, the similarity can be defined as follow with two vector $\vec{A} = \left\{a_1, a_2, \bullet \bullet \bullet, a_n\right\}$ and $\vec{B} = \left\{b_1, b_2, \bullet \bullet \bullet, b_n\right\}$:

$$sim\left(\vec{A}, \vec{B}\right) = \frac{\sum_{i=1}^{n} a_i \times b_i}{\sqrt{\sum_{i=1}^{n} \left(a_i\right)^2} \times \sqrt{\sum_{i=1}^{n} \left(b_i\right)^2}} \tag{8}$$

The value of the similarity is ranging from -1 to 1.

A system named WHIRL in Cohen (1998), developed by Cohen, combines the cosine similarity with the TF-IDF weighting scheme to obtain the similarity of two text fields. It separates string into tokens, and then each tokens will be assigned a weight with consideration of the TF-IDF:

$$v_\delta\left(\hat{o}\right) = \log\left(tf_\delta + 1\right) \bullet \log\left(idf_\delta\right) \tag{9}$$

Then the cosine similarity of two strings is described as:

$$sim\left(\acute{o}_1, \acute{o}_2\right) = \frac{\sum_{i=1}^{|D|} v_{\acute{o}_1}\left(i\right) \bullet v_{\acute{o}_2}\left(i\right)}{v_{\acute{o}_1} \bullet v_{\acute{o}_2}} \qquad (10)$$

D represents a database that contains kinds of tokens, and $|D|$ means the number of records in the database D.

In summary, this method we introduced has a better performance in the large data collection, and can handle the situation that several different strings has the same words in different order. For example, both string "Kobe Bryant" and string "Bryant, Kobe" refer the same person, and it can be distinguished easily with this method. Also, "King James, LeBron" and "LeBron James" would have similarity close to one because both "LeBron" and "James" will have a great weight with the TF-IDF in the area of NBA Sports. Unfortunately, this similarity metric cannot deal with words spelling errors well.

Phonetic Similarity Metrics

Character-Based and Token-Based Similarity Metrics focus on the sequence-based records. However, when two strings are in phonetic but not in characters or tokens, the sequence-based similarity will fail to handle this situation. Therefore, we propose the Soundex Algorithm to solve this problem.

Soundex

Soundex is one of the most common phonetic algorithm for indexing names by sound, as pronounced in English. Our purpose is for homophones to be translated to the same representation so that it could be matched despite differences in spelling. This method is based on the assignment of identical code digits to phonetically similar groups of consonants, and a vowel will never be encoded unless it is the first letter.

As is shown in Knuth (1973), the rules of the Soundex coding are as follows:

1. Retain the first letter of the name as the prefix letter and drop all other occurrences of A, E, I, O, U, Y, H and W
2. Replace the remaining consonants after the first letter with the following value:
    a. B, F, P, V →1,
    b. C, G, J, K, Q, S, X, Z →2,
    c. D, T →3,
    d. L →4,
    e. M, N →5 and
    f. R →6.
3. Two adjacent letters with the same number will be coded as a single number, and two letters divided by 'H' or 'W' with the same number will also be coded as a single number.
4. Retain the prefix and three other numbers. Fill in zeros until there are three numbers if there are fewer than three codes.

We will show how the algorithm works with the examples "Knuth" and "Kant".

Keep the first letter, and ignore "A, E, I, O, U, H, W, Y". So the string "Knuth" will be coded as follow:

Knuth→K53

Then we will fill in zeros, because there are fewer than three codes:

Knuth→K53→K530

"Kant" will also be coded:

Kant→K53→K530

Therefore, the two strings will return the same code value.

STRING TRANSFORMATION FOR ENTITY RESOLUTION

In this section we introduce a transformation-based method to solve the entity resolution problem. We propose a framework based on *Context-Free* Grammar and show how it works. There are two subsections: the first is to introduce preliminary knowledge, the second is to introduce the framework based on transformation to handle this situation.

Preliminary Knowledge: Context-Free Grammar and Language

Context-Free Grammar is widely used in Computer Science. It is easy to construct efficient parsing algorithms for a given sequence to decide whether it will be generated and how it can be generated by the productions of the grammar. Especially, Context-Free Grammar is important to generate *LL* and *LR* parsers in the field of compiler theory. We will show what the Context-Free Grammar is and how to parse with the grammar.

Definition of Context-Free Grammar

When grammar's production rules can be applied regardless of the context of a non-terminal, then the grammar will be considered as *Context-Free Grammar*. We will give the definition of Context-Free Grammars as follows (Hopcroft 2008),

There are four essential components in a description of a grammar or a language:

1. There is a finite set of symbols that form the sequences of the language being defined, and we define this alphabet the *terminals*, or the *terminal symbols*.
2. There is a finite set of *variables* called *non-terminals*, or *syntactic categories*. Each non-terminal represents a set of sequences.
3. The non-terminal, one of the variables, representing the language being defined, is called the *start symbol*. The other variables represent auxiliary classes of strings that used to help define the language of the start symbol.
4. There is a finite set of *rules* also referred as *productions* represent the recursive definition of a language, and each production consists of:
   a. A variable which is often called the head of the production must be defined by the production.
   b. The symbol of the production '→'.
   c. A string of zero or more terminals and variables, called the body of the production, represents one way to form strings in the language of the variable of the head, and then we keep the terminals unchanged and replace for each variable of the body any sequence that is in the language of the variable.

These four components we proposed above construct a Context-Free grammar. We should present a CFG *G* by its four components like G={V,T,P,S} where V represents the set of variables, T represents the set of terminals, P represents the set of productions, and S is the start symbol. There is a simple example of the Context-Free Grammar:

1. E→I
2. E→E+E
3. E→E*E
4. E→(E)
5. I→a
6. I→b
7. I→Ia
8. I→Ib
9. I→I0
10. I→I1

The grammar of this example can be represented as:

$$G = \left\{ \begin{matrix} \{E, I\}, \{a, b, 0, 1, (,), +, *\}, \\ \{1, 2, 3, 4, 5, 6, 7, 8, 9, 10\}, E \end{matrix} \right\}$$

Derivations Using a Grammar

We can infer that certain strings are in the language of a certain non-terminal by the productions of a CFG. It is more often to take advantage of the rules from the body to the head. Then we take strings which are in the language of each of the non-terminals of the body, concatenate them in a proper order with any terminals appearing in the body, and infer that the resulting string is in the language of the non-terminal in the head (Hopcroft 2008).

We have another method to defining the language of a grammar, in which we use the productions from head to body. We expand the start symbol or the resulting string by substituting one of the non-terminals using one of productions of a grammar iteratively until we derive a string only consisting of terminals. There are two examples we prepare to explain the two approaches:

Inferring the string "a*(a+b00)" using the grammar we introduced above.

In Table 1, Line (5) and (6) exploit production 1 to infer that. Line (7) uses production 2 to infer that the sum of these identifiers is an expression. Line (8) uses production 4 to infer that the same string with parentheses around it is also an expression, and line (9) uses production 3 to multiply the identifier *a* by the expression we had discovered in line (8).

Then we will explain another method:

The string "a*(a+b00)" can be derived in the language. Here is the derivation:

$$E \overset{3}{\Rightarrow} E * E \overset{1}{\Rightarrow} I * E \overset{5}{\Rightarrow} a * E \overset{4}{\Rightarrow} a * \left(E\right) \overset{2}{\Rightarrow}$$
$$a * \left(E + E\right) \overset{1}{\Rightarrow} a * \left(I + E\right) \overset{5}{\Rightarrow}$$
$$a * \left(a + E\right) \overset{1}{\Rightarrow} a * \left(a + I\right) \overset{9}{\Rightarrow} a * \left(a + I0\right) \overset{9}{\Rightarrow}$$
$$a * \left(a + I00\right) \overset{6}{\Rightarrow} a * \left(a + b00\right)$$

First of all, E is replaced by $E*E$ with the production 3, and then E is replaced by I with the production 1, and so on until there are no non-terminals in the strings.

Parse Tree

Parse Tree is a representation for the derivations of strings. This tree can show us very clearly how

Table 1. derivation of string "a(a+b00)"*

	String Inferred	For Language of	Production Used	String(s) Used
(1)	*a*	*I*	5	
(2)	*b*	*I*	6	
(3)	*b0*	*I*	9	*(2)*
(4)	*b00*	*I*	9	*(3)*
(5)	*a*	*E*	1	*(1)*
(6)	*b00*	*E*	1	*(4)*
(7)	*a+b00*	*E*	2	*(5),(6)*
(8)	*(a+b00)*	*E*	4	*(7)*
(9)	*a*(a+b00)*	*E*	3	*(5),(8)*

the symbols of a terminal string are generated into substrings. A parse tree is widely used in the Compiler Theory which is known as "*Syntax Spanning Tree*". We will introduce the parse tree and show how a parse tree generates the derivations of strings (in Hopcroft (2008)).

When we focus on the leavers of a parse tree and concatenate them from the left to the right, we will get a string, called the yield of the tree, which is always a string that is derived from the root of the parse tree. There are two fundamental rules.

First, all the leaves of a parse tree are terminals or , and then the root must be labeled by the start symbol.

For example, we will show how to construct a parse tree also with the string "a*(a+b00)" in Figure 2.

Starting at the top with the start symbol, a variable will be expanded, until there is no more non-terminals remaining.

Transformation-Based for Entity Resolution

We all know that the primary source of data in the real world entities may not have high quality (in Arasu, Chaudhuri & Kaushik 2008). For example, we will sometimes find that the US state of California could be represented in different names, such as "*California*" and "*CA*" when we read newspaper or watch a basketball game. Sometimes, a string with spelling errors will also be recorded. Then, the representation of

Figure 2. A parse tree of "a(a+b00)" (Hopcroft 2008)*

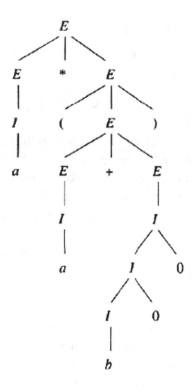

an entity could be a string just like the examples above, however, it is more generally stored as a structured record in the database. The following records derived from a database (Table 2) with the columns of "*Id*", "*Author*" and "*Affiliation*" that has been shown in Arasu & Kaushik (2009).

The main point of data cleaning is to transform "dirty" input records to one or more "clean" output records. We want to normalize records to

Table 2. Sample author records

Id	Author	Affiliation
1	Jerfrey D. Ullman	Department of Computer Science, Stanford University, Stanford, CA,USA
2	Jeff Ullman	Stanford University, Stanford CA 94305
3	J D Ullman	Stanford Univ., Stanford, Calif.
4	M. Stonebraker	M.I.T.
5	Michael Stonebraker	Department of EECS and Laboratory of Computer Science, M.I.T., MA 02139, Cambridge, USA

Table 3. Transformed output records for input records of Table 2

Id	First-Name	Last-Name	University
1	Jeffrey	Ullman	Stanford University
2	Jeffrey	Ullman	Stanford University
3	J	Ullman	Stanford University
4	M	Stonebraker	Massachusetts Institute of Technology
5	Michael	Stonebraker	Massachusetts Institute of Technology

the standard rules that we formulate. Table 3 shows the result we want from the Table 2.

The first name Jeff has been normalized to Jeffrey in the record *Id* 2, and all the information in the *Affiliation* column of Table 3 that does not describe the University, has been cleaned up. Then the names of Universities have been normalized by the standard rules. Arasu and Kaushik have proposed a *grammar-based entity representation framework* to solve this problem. The framework is *programmatic* that using a program method to transform an input record to output records. It is based on *Context-Free Grammar* that we introduced above, and there are three parts of the framework that can be defined as *<R,P,A>*. *R* is a grammar rule, *P* is a predicate, and *A* is an action.

A grammar rule is just the CFG rule we have introduced. It has a head and a body, and consists of non-terminals and terminals. A grammar is used to analysis an input record, and we assume that each attributes of an input record could be generated by a unique non-terminal, or it will be an error.

A predicate is the body of a data log rule. Every variable in the rule *<R, P, A>* is constrained to occur at least once in an extensional database predicate of *P*. The last constraint is analogous to be the limited variable constraint to make data log rules safe. An action is a function that uses input records and produces a record as the output record. Then, we will show how the framework works.

There is a given program *G*, and input record *r*. We utilize the rules of the program *G* to parse the input record r, and then construct a *parse tree*

Table 4. A program in the framework for processing names

Id	Rule	Predicate	Action
1	$<name> \rightarrow <prefix>_1 <fname>_2 <mname>_3 <lname>_4$.		fname= 2.value lname= 4.value
2	$<name> \rightarrow <lname>_1 ',' <fname>_2 <mname>_3$		fname= 2.value lname= 1.value
3	$<fname> \rightarrow <letter>_1 .''$		value=1.value
4	$<fname> \rightarrow F$	FNames (I,F,G)	value= F
5	$<fname> \rightarrow N$	NickNames (I,N,F,G)	value= F
6	$<mname> \rightarrow M$	LNames (I,M)	
7	$<mname> \rightarrow <letter>_1 '.'$		
8	$<lname> \rightarrow L$	LNames (I,L)	value= L
9	$<prefix> \rightarrow S$	Prefix(I,S)	

Table 5. Example tables used in sample program

1	Andrew	M	1	Alex	Alexander	M	1	Smith	1	Mr
2	John	M	2	Andy	Anderson	M	2	Johnson	2	Ms
3	Mary	F	3	Andy	Andrew	M	3	Williams	3	Dr
4	...	...	4	Becky	Rebecca	F	4	...	4	...
	FNames			NickNames				LNames		Prefix

just like we introduced above. The *action* function executes the semantic actions. It analyses nodes of the parse tree by the grammar, and generates output record. We will give a grammar and rules as an example. Table 4 will show us a grammar in our framework for processing names, and Table 5 will show us the *extensional database* used in the program (in Arasu & Kaushik 2009).

In Table 4, Rule 1 show us that a person's name can be generated by concatenating a prefix, first name, middle name and last name. Certainly, a name can also be generated by concatenating last name, notation ',', first name and middle name. We will define an expanded program *G'* for the given program *G* to present the semantics of the framework. We include as part of G' the rule <R',true,A'> obtained by substituting variables in <R,P,A> with the corresponding constant values. Table 6 shows part of the *expanded* program G'.

The column of the *Source Id* contains the *Id* of the rules in Table 4 from which the rule was generated. We use the *expanded* program *G'* to parse the input record, and we construct a parse tree to parse the input record. Then we will show how to parse the given strings, such as "Dr Andrew J. Smith", with the program we introduced. The parse tree will be shown as follow, and the rectangular represents non-terminal and terminals are represented by ellipses.

Each non-leaf node is associated with the rule <R,true,A> of G', and use the Action A to evaluate nodes N. All the output records for the parse tree are generated by evaluating the action corresponding to the root node of the parse tree. Therefore, the input record "Dr Andrew J. Smith" will be parsed and generates the output record <fname: Andrew, lname:Smith> from the root of the parse tree. The derivation of fname uses the rule 1 <fname>→Andrew, and uses the action

Table 6. Expanded program for program in Table 4

Id	Source Id	Rule	Action
1	4	<fname>→Andrew	value= Andrew
2	4	<fname>→John	value= John
3	5	<fname>→Andy	value= Anderson
4	5	<fname>→Andy	value= Andrew
5	8	<lname>→Smith	value= Smith
6	9	<prefix>→Dr	
		...	...

value=Andrew. Then it produces the record <value:Andrew>. Therefore the root node will produce the record <fname:Andrew,lname: Smith> with the fname node and the lname node. There is another example "Smith, Andy J." will be presented as follow:

The parse tree for "Smith, Andrew J." is shown in Figure 4. We note that the program produces the same out output record <fname: Andrew, lname=Smith> for both "Dr Andrew J. Smith" and "Smith, Andrew J.".

In particular, the framework can be used to preprocess records to simplify subsequent record matching logic.

LEARNING ALGORITHMS FOR ENTITY RESOLUTIONS ON NAMES

Preliminary Knowledge: Decision Tree

Decision Tree is a simple but widely-used technique for classification. There are three kinds of nodes:

- **Root Node:** It has no in-edges but has zero or some out-edges.
- **Internal Node:** It has only one in-edge and two or more out-edges.
- **Leaf Node:** It is also called *terminal node*. It has only one in-edge but has no out-edges.

In a decision tree, each leaf node has a class number. Non-terminal node (including root node and internal node) has attribute test condition in order to classify records with different characteristics. Once a decision tree has been constructed, it is easy to test records and to classify records. Starting at the root node, a test condition will be used to determine which branch is approximate for the records. Go along this branch or meet another internal node, and then use a new test condition or reach a leaf node. Once reach a leaf node, the

test record will be assigned by the value of the class of the leaf node.

In principle, the number of decision trees that we can construct for the given attribute set is exponential. Even though there are some decision trees have higher accuracy than the other, it is impossible to find out the optimal decision tree. However, scientists have proposed some efficient algorithm to construct a suboptimal decision tree with a reasonable time complexity. These algorithm often use the greedy algorithm. When choose to partition attributes of data set, they will use series of local optimum strategies to construct a decision tree. Hunt algorithm is one of these algorithms. It is the basis of many methods. In the Hunt algorithm, it constructs decision tree recursively by partitioning the training set into pure subsets. We assume that D_t is a training set that associated with node t, and $y=\{y_1,y_2,...,y_c\}$ is the labels of classes. Hunt algorithm will be described here:

1. If all the records of D_t are belonged to a same class y_t, then t will be a leaf node that labeled by y_t.
2. If the records of D_t are belonged to different classes, it will choose an attribute test condition, and then partition the records into smaller sets. For each output of the test condition, it will create a child node and records of D_t will be distributed to child nodes according to the result of testing condition.
3. For each child node, this algorithm will be called recursively until all the records are belonged to the same class.

Hunt algorithm will be effective if each combination of attributes appears in the training set and has a unique label of class. However, it is so difficult to meet this situation in the real world that we need some additional condition to solve the problems.

Then we will give a framework called Tree Growth for constructing decision tree. The input

Figure 3. Parse tree for "Dr Andrew J. Smith" (Arasu & Kaushik 2009)

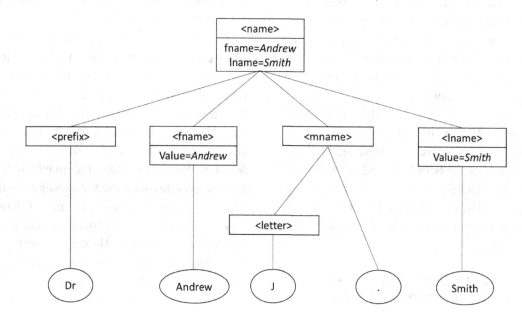

Figure 4. Parse tree for "Smith, Andrew J." (Arasu & Kaushik 2009)

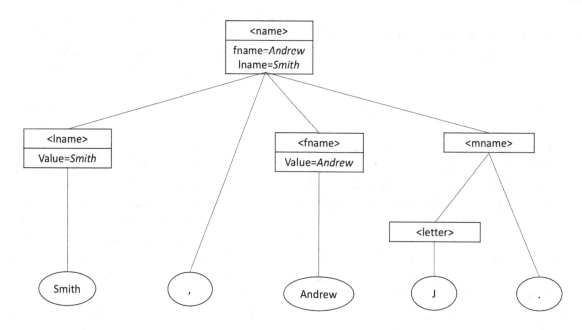

of this algorithm is the training set of records E, and attribute set F. It chooses the optimal attribute to partition data, and expands nodes of the tree until meet the stopping condition. See the following algorithm:

TreeGrowth (E,F):
1. **IF** stopping_cond (E,F) = true **then**
2. leaf = createNode()
3. leaf. label= Classify (E)
4. **return** leaf
5. **ELSE**
6. Root = createNode()
7. root.test_cond = find_best_split(E,F)
8. We assume that V= {v|v is one of the possible output of root.test_cond}
9. **For** each v ∈ V **do**
10. E_v= {e|root.test_cond(e) = v and e∈ E}
11. child= TreeGrowth (Ev,F) child
12. add the child to the tree as the derivation of the root, and label the edge root→child as v.
13. **Return** root

The details of this algorithm is:

1. Function createNode() create new node for the decision tree. A node or an attribute test condition of the decision tree will be labeled as , or a label of a class, as .
2. Function find_best_split() determine which attribute should be used as test condition to partition training set. For example, the selection of test condition will be determined by some measure for purity, such as *Entropy*, *Gini* and so on, and we will introduce this later in detail.
3. Function Classify() will determine the labels of classes of leaves nodes. For each leaf node t, p(i|t) represents the proportion of the training records of class *i* in this node. In most cases, we stipulate:

$$leaf.label = \operatorname*{argmax}_{i} p(i \mid t) \qquad (11)$$

The operation return the parameter of the maximum . not only provides the definite the information of the class label of leaf node, but also estimates the probability of the records distributed to the leaf node *t*.

4. Function stopping_cond() determined whether the tree are stopped growing or not by checking whether all the records are belonged to a same class, or they all have the same attribute value. There is another method to stop growing by checking the number of records, and judge if it less than some threshold.

Once the decision tree has been constructed, we can utilized the tree-pruning method to reduce the scale of decision tree. Then we will introduce how to determine the attribute test condition.

There are many metrics can be used to determine the partition records by optimal methods. We assume p(i|t) represents the proportion of the training records of class *i* in a given node. To choose the optimal partition is often according to the impurity of the child node. The lower the impurity is, the more inclination of the class is distributed. There is an example that calculates the impurity.

$$\text{Entropy} = -\sum_{i=0}^{c-1} p(i|t) \log_2 p(i \mid t) \qquad (12)$$

$$\text{Gini} = 1 - \sum_{i=0}^{c-1} \left[p(i|t) \right]^2 \qquad (13)$$

$$\text{Classification} - \text{Error}(t) = 1 - \max_{i}[p(i \mid t)] \quad (14)$$

Table 7.

Node	Count	$\text{Gini} = 1 - \left(0/6\right)^2 - \left(6/6\right)^2 = 0$
Class 0	0	$\text{Entropy} = -\left(0/6\right)\log_2\left(0/6\right) - \left(6/6\right)\log_2\left(6/6\right) = 0$
Class 1	6	$\text{Error} = 1 - \max\left[0/6, 6/6\right] = 0$
Node	Count	$\text{Gini} = 1 - \left(1/6\right)^2 - \left(5/6\right)^2 = 0.278$
Class 0	1	$\text{Entropy} = -\left(0/6\right)\log_2\left(0/6\right) - \left(6/6\right)\log_2\left(6/6\right) = 0.650$
Class 1	5	$\text{Error} = 1 - \max\left[1/6, 5/6\right] = 0.167$
Node	Count	$\text{Gini} = 1 - \left(3/6\right)^2 - \left(3/6\right)^2 = 0.5$
Class 0	3	$\text{Entropy} = -\left(3/6\right)\log_2\left(3/6\right) - \left(3/6\right)\log_2\left(3/6\right) = 1$
Class 1	3	$\text{Error} = 1 - \max\left[3/6, 3/6\right] = 0.5$

c is the number of classes, and we stipulate when calculating entropy. Then we will give an example.

We can find that different metrics on the impurity have the same trend. According to the calculation, Node N_1 has the lowest impurity, the second is N_2 and the last is N_3. In order to determine the effect of the test condition, we need to compare the impurity of the parent node (before partition) with the child node (after partition). The greater the result of the subtraction, the better the test condition is. The Gain Δ is a criterion that can be used to determine the effect of the partition:

$$\Delta = I\left(\text{parent}\right) - \sum_{j=1}^{k} \frac{N\left(v_j\right)}{N} I\left(v_j\right) \qquad (15)$$

The I(.) is the given impurity, N is the number of the records in parent node, k is the number of attributes, $N(v_j)$ is the number of the nodes that have association with child node v_j. Decision tree often chooses the greatest *Gain* as the condition test, because I(parent) is constant for every test condition, and then the maximum *Gain* equals to the minimum of the weighted average of the impurity of child node. At last, when choosing as the formula to measure the impurity, the subtraction of entropy is the so-called information gain.

In summary, decision tree is an efficient technique to classify data set. We just introduced the outline of decision tree. Refer to Tan (2007) for more discussions.

Learning String Transformation

"Robert" and "Bob" refer to the same name. However, they have long distance in textual similarity. Traditional methods on string similarity metric cannot identify such synonyms, abbreviations and aliases. An object identification system called Active Atlas is developed, and Tejada, Knoblock & Minton (2002) give extensions to the Active Atlas system. In this section, we mainly talk about learning string transformation based on the Active Atlas system that has been shown in Tejada, Knoblock & Minton (2002) and Tejada, Knoblock & Minton (2001).

In the real world, entities will arise in many different text format. Examples of the entities identification problem are shown in Table 8.

In the first example, the restaurant is shown as "Art's Deli" on the Zagat's website, and it also appears as "Art's Delicatessen" on the Department of Health's website. When the two entities are decided as the same entity, a mapping will be created between them. There are two types entities information that will be determined whether to create a mapping. The first type is a set of the domain independent string transformation for judging textual similarity, such as *prefix*, *acronym* and *abbreviation* and so on. These transformations will be used to identify the possible relationships of mappings. The second type is the importance of some key attribute or combination of several attributes. They will determine whether to create a mapping. In the Table 8 the first and the last examples will be determined as the same by the above rules, and the mapping will be created between them respectively.

For the Active Atlas System this process has two stages. In the first stage, the candidate generator generates the set of all possible mappings between the two sets of entities. At first, we do not know which transformations are correct or proper. Therefore all the transformations are regarded as the same when computing similarity. The second stage is mapping learner, which learns to tailor both types of entity identification information as mapping rules and transformations. The mapping learner will filter which transformation is correct. The goal of learning the mapping rules is to achieve the highest possible accuracy. This approach is for the mapping rules learner to choose the most informative candidate mappings for the user to classify as mapped or not mapped. Then the general system architecture shown in Tejada, Knoblock & Minton (2001) will be described in Figure 5.

At first, we will introduce how to *compute similarity scores* by applying transformations. There are two basic types of the transformations. The unary transformations need only one token as input in order to computer its transformation, and N-ary transformations compare multiple tokens from two entities.

Unary transformations:

- **Equality:** Detects if a token has the same character at the same position.
- **Stemming:** Converts a token into its stem or root.
- **Soundex:** Encodes a token by Soundex that we just introduced in section 1.
- **Abbreviation:** Substitutes a token with corresponding abbreviation (e.g., 1st or first).

N-ary transformations:

- **Initial:** Detects if one token is equal to the first character of the other.
- **Prefix:** Detects if one token is the prefix of the other.
- **Suffix:** Detects if one token is the suffix of the other.

Table 8. Matching restaurant objects

Name	Street	Phone		Name	Street	Phone
Art's Deli	12224 Ventura Boulevard	818-756-4124		Art's Delicatessen	12224 Ventura Blvd	818/755-4100
Teresa's	80 Montague St.	718-520-2910		Teresa's	103 1ˢᵗ Ave. between 6ᵗʰ and 7ᵗʰ St.	212/228-0604
Steakhouse The	128 Fremont St.	702-382-1600		Binion's Coffee Shop	128 Fremont St.	702/382-1600
Les Celebrites	155 W. 58ᵗʰ St.	212-484-5113		Les Celebrites	160 Central Park S	212/484-5113
Zagat's Restaurants				Department of Health		

- **Substring:** Detects if one token is the substring of the other but not the prefix or the suffix.
- **Computed Abbreviation:** Detects if one token is a subset of the other (e.g., Blvd, Boulevard).
- **Acronym:** Detects if one token is composed of the first letters of the words in a phrase (e.g., CPK, California Pizza Kitchen).
- **Drop:** Determine if one token does not match any other token.

If there is a transformation between tokens, a mapping will be generated between them. For example, a candidate mapping will be generated for the entities "Art's Deli" and "Art's Delicatessen". Therefore the mappings will be (Equality – "Art", "Art"), (Equality – "s", "s"), and (Prefix – "Deli", "Delicatessen") between them.

Then we will show how to compute attribute similarity scores. In this part, the system utilizes the TF-IDF and cosine similarity that we introduced in section 1 to compute the similarity scores with the following formula:

$$\text{sim}(A, B) = \frac{\sum_{i=1}^{t}\left(w_{ia} \bullet w_{ib}\right)}{\sqrt{\sum_{i=1}^{t} w_{ia}^2 \bullet \sum_{i=1}^{t} w_{ib}^2}} \quad (16)$$

- w_{ia}: $(0.5+0.5\text{freq}_{ia})$ x IDF
- w_{ib}: freq_{ib} x IDF_i
- freq_{ia}: Is the frequency that token I of attribute value a.
- IDF_i: Is IDF of the token i in the date collection.
- freq_{ib}: Is the frequency that token i of attribute value b.

Once the first stage is finished, it outputs all the possible mappings it has generated. The set of candidate mappings can be reduced further by simply setting a limit on the maximum number of mappings per entity. This reduced set of mapping information is then given as input to the mapping learner.

Then we will introduce the *mapping learner*.

Mapping rules are created to classify the candidate mappings as mapped or not mapped based on the attribute similarity scores. They determine which attributes are the key attributes, or which combination of attributes are needed to classify the candidate mappings. Accurate transformation weights for the specific domain must be used to compute the next attribute similarity scores. When the candidate mappings have been classified as mapped or not mapped, the transformation weights could be determined by the user-labeled mappings and those labeled by the mapping-rule learner. Certainly, it is a circular problem that the

Figure 5. General system architecture (Tejada, Knoblock & Minton 2001)

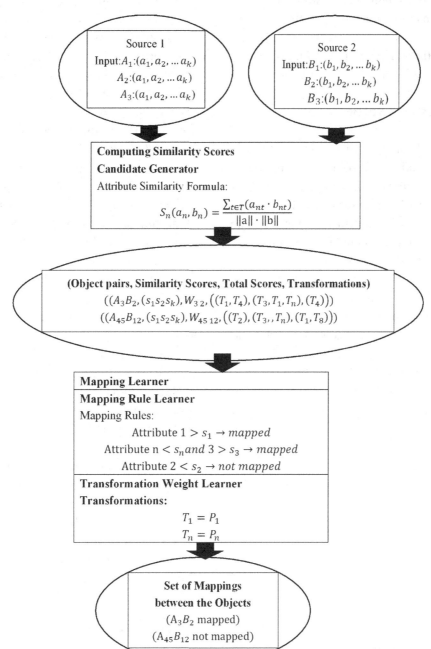

accuracy of the mapping rules relies on the accuracy of the transformations, and then the accuracy of the transformations is also determined by the accuracy of the mappings rules. The Mapping Learner module will be shown in Figure 5.

Mapping–Rule Learner

Mapping-Rule Learner will determine which attributes or combinations of attributes are important. Learning the mapping rules in order to obtain the highest possible accuracy, and the system will choose the most informative mappings as the training set so that it could judge whether the objects are mapped or not, based on the attributes similarity scores. The mapping-rule learner will be generated by a decision tree that we introduced above. The decision tree will classify an example from the root node to the leaf node, and each node of the tree will contain an attribute-based test so that each sub-tree will be labeled by a possible outcome of result. Here, we will give an example as the mapping rules:

- **Rule 1:** Name > 0.859 and Street > 0.912 → mapped
- **Rule 2:** Name > 0.859 and Phone > 0.95 →mapped

Figure 6. Mapping learner (Tejada, Knoblock & Minton 2001)

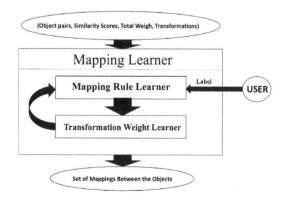

In the first rule, if the similarity score of the name is greater than 0.859 and the similarity score of the street is greater than 0.912, the mapping rule learner will label this situation as mapped. If either similarity score does not meet the conditions, it will be labeled as not mapped, and it is also applied to the rule 2. Once we get the rules, the decision tree that based on the rules will be constructed. mapped

In Figure 7 we can clearly find how the mappings are determined. According to the above example, N. A. and H. M. proposed a learning algorithm called query by bagging in order to learn mapping rules effectively. This technique will generate a committee of decision trees, and they vote on the most informative example to classify next. A single decision tree can learn the mapping rules by its own, however, it may need a lot of user-labeled examples. With a committee decision trees, the classification of an example or candidate mapping by one decision tree is considered its vote on the example. There is an example about committee votes that shown in Table 9.

When an example has been chosen, the user is asked to label the example. After that, the learner will reconstruct the decision tree and apply the new mapping rules, and then classify the examples again. This learner will process iteratively until all the learners in the committee converge to the same decision tree.

Then we will introduce the next part: Transformation Weight Learner.

The similarity scores of correct mappings should have much higher scores than incorrect mappings' scores. Therefore the Transformation Weight Learner must learn how to increase the scores of the correct mappings with the given values from the mapping-rule learner, and decrease the scores of the incorrect mappings with the given values from the mapping-rule learner. These will help the mapping-rule learner to construct higher accuracy decision trees with few labeled examples.

Transformation weight learner will first calculate transformation weight of each transformation,

Figure 7. Decision tree of the Rule 1 and Rule 2

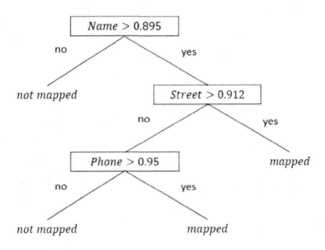

Table 9. Committee votes

Examples	L1	L2	L3	L4	L5	L6	L7	L8	L9	L10
Art's Deli, Art's Delicatessen	Yes	Yes	Yes	Yes	Yes	Yes	Yes	Yes	Yes	Yes
CPK, California Pizza Kitchen	Yes	No	Yes	No	Yes	Yes	Yes	No	No	No
Ca'Brea, La Brea Bakery	No	No	No	No	No	No	No	No	No	No

and then utilize the new probability scores to recalculate the similarity score of each example. After that, they will be ordered by the total object similarity scores. The total object similarity score will be calculated with the following formula:

$$TotalObjectSimilarity\left(S,W\right) = \sum_{i=1}^{n} s_i w_{ia} w_{ib} \quad (17)$$

- **S:** The set of attribute similarity scores, with the size n.
- **n:** The number of entities attributes.
- **W:** The set of uniqueness weight pairs.

The method for calculating transformation weights utilizes the classifications of both user-labeled and unlabeled examples. At first, we do not know which transformation is approximate for the domain we need, and the attribute similarity scores are determined by the generator. Therefore, the scores could not present the real similarity between the two entities. Even there exists a set of misclassification of the unlabeled data and some errors in the mapping rules; they still help to increase the accuracy of transformation weights. Using an efficient algorithm reduces the number of user-labeled data, so there are sparse number of labeled examples to learn the correct transformation weights from. The population of each of the labeled examples will be increased by adding duplicates of each of the labeled examples to the training set so that the labeled examples will be more informative than the unlabeled ones. If two objects are classified as mapped m and the transformation tf is applied between them, the likelihood can be described as follow:

Table 10. Recalculating attribute similarity scores

Transformation	p(m|t)	-p(m|t)
(EQUAL: "Art", "Art")	0.9	0.1
(EQUAL: "s", "s")	0.9	0.1
(PREFIX: "Deli", "Delicatessen")	0.3	0.7

$$p\left(m|tf_i\right) = \frac{positive\,classifications\,with\,transformation_i}{total\,number\,of\,transformation_i} \quad (18)$$

The p(m|tf$_i$) will be calculated for each of general transformation, just like "Equality", "Acronym" and so on. When all the transformation weights have been calculated, the attribute similarity scores will be computed. The product of the probabilities of the applied transformation weights will be computed to determine the attribute similarity scores for each candidate mapping, and then the outcome of result will be normalize.

$$AttributeSimilarityScore\left(A, B\right) = \prod_{i=1}^{t} tf_i \quad (19)$$

There is an example show the mapping "Art's Deli" and "Art's Delicatessen":

According to the example in Table 10, the total mapped score m=0.9 *0.9* 0.9=0.243, and the total not mapped score n= 0.1* 0.1* 0.7= 0.007. Then the output of result will be normalized as:

$$NormalizedAttributeSimilarityScore =$$
$$\frac{m}{\left(m + n\right)} = \frac{0.243}{\left(0.243 + 0.007\right)} \quad (20)$$

Once the attribute similarity scores have been calculated, the total object similarity scores will be computed again for each candidate mapping, and then ordered by the new total similarity scores. The new scores and the attribute similarity scores

will be sent to the mapping-rule learner to create some more accuracy mapping rules.

In summary, learning-based approach will have a higher accuracy of discovering similar entities. The experimental results of this learning-based approach are presented in the Ph. D. thesis of Sheila Tejada with the title "*Learning Object Identification Rules for Information Integration*", and if you care about details of the implement of the system, you can refer to this thesis.

Solutions and Recommendations

There are many kinds of errors on names in the real world. Some records referring to the same entity appear in a database at the same time. They can be summarized into several situations. Typographical errors, such as spelling errors, can be handled with the character-based similarity metrics. Token-level are widely used for similarity metrics in many domains. When we want to determine whether two records are similar, transformation-based methods and their learning algorithms will be useful.

FUTURE RESEARCH DIRECTIONS

Similarity functions, such as *edit-distance*, *Smith-Waterman distance* and *TF-IDF*, have been proposed for many years. They can calculate similarity between strings. However, textual similarity can be imperfect indicator of whether or not two records are matches; in particular, two matching records can be textually dissimilar. Then transformation-based methods and their learning algorithms are more useful in the real world. There are several issues for future work that we are pursuing, such as providing a method to minimize noise or error in the framework of the transformation-based methods. We would also like to increase the accuracy of these algorithms, such as reduce errors of the classification module in the learning algorithm.

CONCLUSION

In this chapter, we introduce three methods for entity resolution on names. Character-based metrics, token-based metrics and phonetic metrics focus on word-level metrics. Character-based metrics and token-based metrics can determine whether two strings are similar in a character or token level, and phonetic metrics can judge if the two words are phonetically similar. Transformation-based methods focus on record-level. It can determine whether two records refer to the same. As size of data sets increasing in TB-level or PB-level, learning algorithm is an effective algorithm to solve this problem. In addition, this chapter shows us some important approaches to entity resolution on names.

REFERENCES

Arasu, A., Chaudhuri, S., & Kaushik, R. (2008). Transformation-based framework for record matching. In *Proceedings of Data Engineering* (pp. 40–49). IEEE.

Arasu, A., & Kaushik, R. (2009). A grammar-based entity representation framework for data cleaning. In *Proceedings of the 2009 ACM SIGMOD International Conference on Management of Data* (pp. 233-244). ACM.

Cohen, W. W. (1998). Integration of heterogeneous databases without common domains using queries based on textual similarity. *SIGMOD Record*, *27*(2), 201–212. doi:10.1145/276305.276323

Elmagarmid, A. K., Ipeirotis, P. G., & Verykios, V. S. (2007). Duplicate record detection: A survey. *IEEE Transactions on Knowledge and Data Engineering*, *19*(1), 1–16. doi:10.1109/TKDE.2007.250581

Hopcroft, J. E. (2008). *Introduction to automata theory, languages, and computation* (3rd ed.). New Delhi: Pearson Education India.

Jaro, M. A. (1989). Advances in record-linkage methodology as applied to matching the 1985 census of Tampa, Florida. *Journal of the American Statistical Association*, *84*(406), 414–420. doi:10.1080/01621459.1989.10478785

Knuth, D. E. (1973). Sorting and searching. *The Art of Computer Programming, 3*.

Levenshtein, V. I. (1966). Binary codes capable of correcting deletions, insertions and reversals. *Soviet Physics, Doklady, 10*, 707.

Manning, C. D., Raghavan, P., & Schütze, H. (2008). *Introduction to information retrieval* (Vol. 1). Cambridge, UK: Cambridge University Press. doi:10.1017/CBO9780511809071

Monge, A. E., & Elkan, C. (1996). The field matching problem: Algorithms and applications. In *Proceedings of the Second International Conference on Knowledge Discovery and Data Mining* (pp. 267-270). Academic Press.

Russell Index, R. C. (1992). *U.S. patent 1,435,663*. Retrieved from http://patft.uspto.gov/netahtml/srchnum.htm

Russell Index, R. C. (1998). *U.S. patent 1,261,167*. Retrieved from http://patft.uspto.gov/netahtml/srchnum.htm

Smith, T. F., & Waterman, M. S. (1981). Identification of common molecular subsequences. *Journal of Molecular Biology, 147*(1), 195–197. doi:10.1016/0022-2836(81)90087-5 PMID:7265238

Tan, P. N. (2007). *Introduction to data mining*. New Delhi: Pearson Education India.

Tejada, S., Knoblock, C. A., & Minton, S. (2001). Learning object identification rules for information integration. *Information Systems, 26*(8), 607–633. doi:10.1016/S0306-4379(01)00042-4

Tejada, S., Knoblock, C. A., & Minton, S. (2002). Learning domain-independent string transformation weights for high accuracy object identification. In *Proceedings of the Eighth ACM SIGKDD International Conference on Knowledge Discovery and Data Mining* (pp. 350-359). ACM.

Winkler, W. E. (1990). String comparator metrics and enhanced decision rules in the Fellegi-Sunter model of record linkage.

ADDITIONAL READING

Arasu, A., Chaudhuri, S., & Kaushik, R. (2008, April). Transformation-based framework for record matching. In *Data Engineering, 2008. ICDE 2008. IEEE 24th International Conference on* (pp. 40-49). IEEE.

Arens, Y., Chee, C. Y., Hsu, C. N., & Knoblock, C. A. (1993). Retrieving and integrating data from multiple information sources. *International Journal of Intelligent and Cooperative Information Systems, 2*(02), 127–158.

Bhattacharya, I., & Getoor, L. (2004, August). Deduplication and group detection using links. In KDD workshop on link analysis and group detection.

Bilenko, M., & Mooney, R. J. (2003, August). Adaptive duplicate detection using learnable string similarity measures. In *Proceedings of the ninth ACM SIGKDD international conference on Knowledge discovery and data mining* (pp. 39-48). ACM.

Bitton, D., & DeWitt, D. J. (1983). Duplicate record elimination in large data files. [TODS]. *ACM Transactions on Database Systems, 8*(2), 255–265. doi:10.1145/319983.319987

Brill, E., & Moore, R. C. (2000, October). An improved error model for noisy channel spelling correction. *In Proceedings of the 38th Annual Meeting on Association for Computational Linguistics* (pp. 286-293). Association for Computational Linguistics.

Chaudhuri, S., Chen, B. C., Ganti, V., & Kaushik, R. (2007, September). Example-driven design of efficient record matching queries. *In Proceedings of the 33rd international conference on Very large data bases* (pp. 327-338). VLDB Endowment.

Chaudhuri, S., Ganti, V., & Kaushik, R. (2006, April). A primitive operator for similarity joins in data cleaning. In *Data Engineering, 2006. ICDE'06. Proceedings of the 22nd International Conference on* (pp. 5-5). IEEE.

Christen, P., & Churches, T. (2005, April). A probabilistic deduplication, record linkage and geocoding system. *In Proceedings of the Australian Research Council Health Data Mining Workshop, Canberra, Australia.*

Cohen, W. W. (2000). Data integration using similarity joins and a word-based information representation language. [TOIS]. *ACM Transactions on Information Systems*, *18*(3), 288–321. doi:10.1145/352595.352598

Cohen, W. W., & Richman, J. (2002, July). Learning to match and cluster large high-dimensional data sets for data integration. In *Proceedings of the eighth ACM SIGKDD international conference on Knowledge discovery and data mining* (pp. 475-480). ACM.

Cohen, W. W., & Sarawagi, S. (2004, August). Exploiting dictionaries in named entity extraction: combining semi-markov extraction processes and data integration methods. In *Proceedings of the tenth ACM SIGKDD international conference on Knowledge discovery and data mining* (pp. 89-98). ACM.

Cormen, T. H., Leiserson, C. E., Rivest, R. L., & Stein, C. (2001). *Introduction to algorithms*. MIT press.

Frakes, W. B. (1992). *Information retrieval: Data structures & algorithms*. Pearson Education India.

Grünwald, P. D. (2007). *The minimum description length principle*. The MIT Press.

Hopcroft, J. E. (2008). *Introduction to Automata Theory, Languages, and Computation, 3/E*. Pearson Education India.

Jaro, M. A. (1978). *Unimatch: A record linkage system: Users manual*. Bureau of the Census.

Koudas, N., Sarawagi, S., & Srivastava, D. (2006, June). Record linkage: similarity measures and algorithms. In *Proceedings of the 2006 ACM SIGMOD international conference on Management of data* (pp. 802-803). ACM.

Mamitsuka, N. A. H. (1998). Query Learning Strategies using Boosting and Bagging. In *Machine Learning: Proceedings of the Fifteenth International Conference* (ICML'98) (pp. 1). Morgan Kaufmann Pub.

Miller, D. R., Leek, T., & Schwartz, R. M. (1999, August). A hidden Markov model information retrieval system. In *Proceedings of the 22nd annual international ACM SIGIR conference on Research and development in information retrieval* (pp. 214-221). ACM.

Minton, S. N., Nanjo, C., Knoblock, C. A., Michalowski, M., & Michelson, M. (2005, November). A heterogeneous field matching method for record linkage. In *Data Mining, Fifth IEEE International Conference on* (pp. 8-pp). IEEE.

Ristad, E. S., & Yianilos, P. N. (1998). Learning string-edit distance. *Pattern Analysis and Machine Intelligence. IEEE Transactions on*, *20*(5), 522–532.

Roth, D., & Yih, W. (2007). Global inference for entity and relation identification via a linear programming formulation. In L. Getoor, & B. Taskar (Eds.), *Introduction to Statistical Relational Learning*. MIT Press.

Salton, G., & Buckley, C. (1988). Term-weighting approaches in automatic text retrieval. *Information Processing & Management*, *24*(5), 513–523. doi:10.1016/0306-4573(88)90021-0

Sarawagi, S., & Bhamidipaty, A. (2002, July). Interactive deduplication using active learning. In *Proceedings of the eighth ACM SIGKDD international conference on Knowledge discovery and data mining* (pp. 269-278). ACM.

Smith, T. F., & Waterman, M. S. (1981). Identification of Common Molecular Subsequences. *Journal of Molecular Biology, 147,* 195–197. doi:10.1016/0022-2836(81)90087-5 PMID:7265238

Ullmann, J. R. (1977). A binary n-gram technique for automatic correction of substitution, deletion, insertion and reversal errors in words. *The Computer Journal, 20*(2), 141–147. doi:10.1093/comjnl/20.2.141

Waterman, M. S., Smith, T. F., & Beyer, W. A. (1976). Some biological sequence metrics. *Advances in Mathematics, 20*(3), 367–387. doi:10.1016/0001-8708(76)90202-4

KEY TERMS AND DEFINITIONS

Active Atlas System: A system based on the Ph. D. thesis of S. Tejada.

Character-Based Similarity Metrics: Compute similarity between strings in character level.

Context-Free Grammar: A grammar that widely used in compiler theory etc.

Decision Tree: A kind of classification method.

Learning Algorithm: A method based on machine learning and data mining.

Token-Based Similarity Metrics: Compute similarity between strings in token level.

Transformation-Based: A method based on transformation can solve the problems of record matching.

Chapter 4
Context–Based Entity Resolution

ABSTRACT

Prior work of entity resolution involves expensive similarity comparison and clustering approaches. Additionally, the quality of entity resolution may be low due to insufficient information. To address these problems, by adopting context information of data objects, the authors present a novel framework of entity resolution, Context-Based Entity Description (CED), to make context information help entity resolution. In this framework, each entity is described by a set of CEDs. During entity resolution, objects are only compared with CEDs to determine its corresponding entity. Additionally, the authors propose efficient algorithms for CED discovery, maintenance, and CED-based entity resolution. The authors experimentally evaluated the CED-based ER algorithm on the real DBLP datasets, and the experimental results show that this algorithm can achieve both high precision and recall as well as outperform existing methods.

INTRODUCTION

Entity resolution (ER) is the process of identifying objects that refer to the same real-world entity. ER is one of the most important problems in data cleaning and arises in many applications. For example, in publications, two identical author names may represent different persons and an author may have different name spellings; same address might have multiple entries due to different spelling; a person can have quite different descriptions on web.

Because of its importance, ER has attracted general attention in the literatures. Most algorithms and frameworks of ER involve two steps. One is similarity comparison between objects (Koudas, Sarawagi & Srivastava 2006), the other

is clustering objects(Fan, Wang, Pu, Zhou & Lv 2011, Bansal, Blum & Chawla 2002, Chaudhuri, Ganjam, Ganti & Motwani 2003), in which objects in the same cluster represent the same entity. Even though existing methods can perform ER effectively in many cases, these ER approaches have following five limitations.

1. **Lack of Consideration of Updating:** In many systems, the number of objects increases rapidly. If we search one of the hottest products iPhone 4 on eBay, there are more than 2.5 million results; more than 1.5 million publications have been added in DBLP since 2010. Unfortunately, current ER approaches seldom consider the update problem. Both comparing new objects with old ones and re-clustering are quite expensive.

DOI: 10.4018/978-1-4666-5198-2.ch004

2. **Expensive Time Complexity:** Computing the similarity between pairs of objects is too expensive when the data size becomes large. Moreover, since the similarity relationship between objects is not transitive, after the pair-wise matching between objects, the clustering step has to be involved next, which is also an expensive operation.

3. **Order Dependent:** Since the similarity relationships are not transitive, the results of ER can be order dependent, which means if different matching orders are selected; the clustering results might be different as well. As the result, inconsistency exists in ER results.

4. **Sensitive to Training Data:** For learning-based strategies of ER (Chaudhuri, Chen, Ganti & Kaushik, R. 2007, Arasu, A., Chaudhuri, S. and Kaushik, R. 2009, Singla, P., Domingos, P. 2005, Verykios, V. S., Moustakides, G. V., Elfeky, M. G. 2003), they usually assume the training data is similar to the test data. In real world, since data can be obtained from various sources continuously, for an entity e, more and more objects referring to e with new attributes and quite different values from the old objects may come, thus this assumption cannot always be guaranteed.

5. **Monotonicity Assumption of Similarity Functions:** The similarity functions can be divided into two kinds. One is feature-based

similarity, the other is relational similarity. Most approaches of ER are based on feature similarity comparison between object pairs. They are all based on the intuition of the monotonicity of similarity, which means that the matching pairs in real world are more similar in features than the non-matching pairs. We will soon use Example 1 to show that this intuition is incorrect sometimes. Differently with feature similarity, (Fan, X., Wang, J., Pu, X., Zhou, L., Lv, B. 2011, Bansal, N., Blum, A., Chawla, S. 2002, Chaudhuri,S., Ganjam, K., Ganti, V., Motwani, R. 2003) focus on the relationships among objects. They solve the ER problem on a relationship graph, which requires a quite large space and as far as we know, they are not as efficient as feature-based similarity approaches.

We use Example 1 to illustrate the limitations of prior work.

Example 1: Consider 8 authors o_{11}-o_{32} with name ''wei wang'' in Table 1 corresponding to persons e_1-e_3 in real world. We suppose each data object o_{ij} refers to the entity e_i. The task of entity resolution is to identify the person each author referring to with the information in Table 1. Since all these objects have identical name but different coauthor set in different papers, the similarity between any two objects o_i and o_j, denoted by $Sim(o_i,o_j)$,

Table 1. Objects for Example 1

eid	id	name	coauthors	title
e_1	o_{11}	wei wang	zhang	inferring...
	o_{12}	wei wang	duncan, kum, pei	social...
	o_{13}	wei wang	chang, kum	sequential...
e_2	o_{21}	wei wang	lin, pei	threshold...
	o_{22}	wei wang	lin, hua, pei	ranking...
e_3	o_{31}	wei wang	shi, zhang	picturebook...
	o_{32}	wei wang	pei, shi, xu	utility...

is determined by the similarity of coauthors. To measure the similarity between sets, Jaccard similarity(Cohen, W. W. 1998) is often used, thus the similarity between any two objects o_i, o_j is defined as:

$$Sim(o_i, o_j) = \frac{|\ coauthors(o_i) \cap coauthors(o_j)\ |}{|\ coauthors(o_i) \cup coauthors(o_j)\ |}.$$

Then we have the similarities between objects as follows:

1. $Sim(o_{11}, o_{12}) < Sim(o_{11}, o_{31})$, since $Sim(o_{11}, o_{12})$ $= 0, Sim(o_{11}, o_{31}) = 1/2$;
2. $Sim(o_{12}, o_{13}) < Sim(o_{12}, o_{21})$, since $Sim(o_{12}, o_{13})$ $= 1/4, Sim(o_{12}, o_{21}) = 1/3$.

In this example we observe that, parts of the matching pairs have lower similarities than non-matching pairs. Additionally, pair-wise ER requires comparison between each object pair. Even though similarity join algorithms(Xiao, C., Wang, W., Lin, X., Yu, J., X. 2008, Xiao, C., Wang, W., Lin, X., Shang, H. 2009) can accelerate the processing in database, for new-coming object, such comparisons are still required. In contrast, if we have the rule-based entity descriptions for e_1-e_3 shown in Table 2.

we compute the similarity between object o and entity e denoted as Sim(o, e) by counting the

Table 2. Entity descriptions for Example 1

ent	descriptions
e_1	r_1 = <name>''wei wang'' $\wedge$ <coauthors>''zhang ''$\wedge \neg$<coauthors>''shi''
	r_2 = <name>''wei wang'' $\wedge$ <coauthors>''kum''
e_2	r_3 = <name>''wei wang'' $\wedge$ <coauthors>''lin''
e_3	r_4 = <name>''wei wang'' $\wedge$ <coauthors>''shi''

number of rules of e been matched by o, i.e., for object o_1, <coauthors>''zhang''$\in o_1$ while <coauthors>''shi''$\notin o_1$, thus o_1 matches the rule r_1, so $Sim(o_1, e_1) = 1$. The worst cost of comparison between rule and object is much smaller than the cost of object comparison. And all the objects are identified correctly in this case.

Therefore, based on the feature descriptions of entities, the ER problem can be reduced to a pair-wise matching problem between object and entity descriptions. Since entity descriptions are highly extracted information from the objects representing the same entity, thus comparing objects with entity descriptions has a lower cost than object comparison; the result accuracy will also be better, since entity descriptions include more comprehensive information than object. Thus the pair-wise matching between object and entity will be more efficient, scalable and effective than pair-wise matching between objects. Moreover, the pair-wise matching between object and entity has advantages of both pair-wise matching and clustering, such as easy to implement; amenable to incremental and distributed processing; and accurate of result.

Based on these properties, in this chapter, we propose a framework of general entity description rules for various forms of data and rule-based ER algorithms. We also present the discovery and maintenance of entity description rules to make the ER algorithm more robust on accuracy. The content of this chapter are summarized as following points. The major content is from Li, L., Li, J., Wang, H. & Gao, H.(2011). The applications of the techniques could be applied in E-commerce (Chapter 16) and medical information system (Chapter 17) for identifying entities based on the context of data objects. In E-commerce, the context includes the descriptions of products. In medical information systems, the context includes the related information of persons other than the attributes.

1. We propose a novel tool, Context-based Entity Description (CED), to describe entity features based on contexts of objects representing identical entity and we formalize the ER problem based on CEDs . Properties of entity description rules are also been discussed.

2. Based on the definition of entity description rules, we present an efficient ER algorithm by comparing objects with entity description rules.

3. In order to describe entity effectively, conditions of entity description rules are discovered. Based on these conditions, we develop an entity description rule discovery algorithm.

4. When updating is involved, more useful features of entities can be discovered from new objects. Thus we optimize the ER algorithm by utilizing entity description rules discovered from new objects.

5. Extensive experiments verified the effectiveness and efficiency of our algorithms on real data sets.

BACKGROUND

Definitions

An instance of an entity is called an object. For structured data, an object is a record; for unstructured data, an object is a phrase; while for semi-structured data such as XML, an object is an element.

The information related to an object is called the context of the object. For structured data, the context of an object is the values of other attributes in the same record. For unstructured data, the context of an object is the text near the phrase. For XML data, the context of an object o can be defined as the set of elements satisfying:

$$C(a) = \{e| \; dis(LCA(a, e), e) < K\},$$

where $dis(a, b)$ is the distance between elements a and b, $LCA(a, b)$ is the least common ancestors of a and b and K is a predefined threshold.

Example 2: o_1 and o_2 are two objects referring to Wei Wang in UNC, the contexts of o_1 and o_2 are shown as the following,

- the context of o_1 in XML

```
<inproceedings>
<author>wei wang< /author>
<author>ning jin</author>
<author>calvin young< /author>
<title>graph classification based on
...co-ocurrence</title>
<conference>cikm</conference>
</inproceedings>
```

- The context of o_2 in web as unstructured data,

Session 4-Wednesday, Nov 4, 10:10-12:00
Graph Classification Based on Pattern Co-occurrence
nin jin, calvin young, wei wang

By the extraction of values and their position information from context, an object o can be represented as follows,

$$o = \{<a_1>b_1, <a_2>b_2,...,<a_n>b_n\},$$

i.e. for o_1 in Example 2, it can be written as

$o_1 = \{<author>''wei \; wang'', <author>''ning \; jin'', ...,<conference>''cikm''\}$.

In the description of an object o, each $<a_i>b_i$ in o is defined as a feature element, where a_i is a place constraint and b_i is a value; and a describes where the value b should appear in the context of an object. i.e. t = <author>"*zhang*" means value "*zhang*" should appear in value of the attribute author. The form of place constraint can be defined by users according to various requirements under different data types.

Similarly, by discovering common feature elements of the objects referring to an entity e, e can be described as a set of feature elements. With the consideration of distinguishing from other entities, the conjunctions and negations will enhance the express power of the description. Based on the discussion, we define the Context-based Entity Description (CED).

Definition 1(CED): A CED r is defined recursively,

1. a feature element t is a CED
2. if r is a CED, then ¬r is a CED
3. if r_1 is a CED and r_2 is a CED, then $r_1 \wedge r_2$ is a CED
4. if r_1 and r_2 are CEDs, then $r_1 \vee r_2$ is a CED

Examples of CEDs on various data types are shown as follows.

Example 3: We denote the entity of Wei Wang in Fudan as e_1, the entity of Wei Wang in UNC as e_2. The CEDs for e_1 and e_2 as follows:
1. r1 = <author>"Baile Shi",
2. r_2= <author>"zhang" ∧ ¬(<author>"Baile Shi"),
3. r_3 = <dis=100bytes>"Baile Shi",

where r_1 and r_2 are instances of CEDs on semi-structured or structured data and r_3 is an instance of CED on unstructured data. For a CED r, the length of r, denoted as |r|, is the number of feature elements in r, i.e. in Example 3, $|r_1|=|r_3|=1$, $|r_2|=2$.

Based on the CED and feature-based description of objects, the judgment of whether an object o matches a CED r is represented as a Boolean function match rule M(o, r). M(o, r) returns true when o matches r, otherwise M(o, r) returns false. And the matching condition between o and r is defined recursively as following where t is an atom feature description.

1. if r=t, o matches r if and only if t ∈ o
2. if r =¬ r_1, o matches r if and only if o does not match r_1
3. if r = $r_1 \wedge r_2$, o matches r if o matches r_1 and o matches r_2
4. if r = $r_1 \vee r_2$, o matches r if o matches r_1 or o matches r_2

Considering the difference of importance of attributes, different CEDs may have different weights. We further describe an entity e with a set R of CEDs and a cost function W, denoted by e=(R, W), where W(r) represents the weight of r which describes the confidence of object o referring to e if o satisfies r. The larger the value of W(r) is, the more possible the object satisfying r represents e.

For simplicity, in the following of the chapter, we use entity instead of entity description. The possibility of an object referring to an entity is computed with similarity function described as following.

Definition 2(similarity function): For a given entity e=(R, W and an object o, the similarity function between o, e is defined as:

$$Sim(o, e)=\Sigma\, M(o, r)*W(r),\ r \in R.$$

Given two objects o_1, o_2, if they have identical or similar representations, they are an ambiguous object pair.

Given a set O of objects, if $\forall o_i \in O$, $\exists o_j$ satisfying o_i and o_j are an ambiguous object pair, We call O is an ambiguous object set. The most famous example is person name ambiguity that many objects share identical or similar name.

Correctness Verification

In this section, we study the properties of CEDs required by ER. As defined in Definition 1, each atom element in a CED is a bool variable and each CED is represented as a Boolean expression. Thus the problem of determining whether $\exists$ object o, satisfying o matches a CED p is reduced to a satisfiable problem of the Boolean expression by truth assignment as the judgment of the atom feature element, i.e. for CED $p = t \wedge \neg t$, p cannot be satisfied by any object; in contrast to p, $q = t$ is a satisfiable CED.

For two CEDs p and q, we say p dominates q (denoted as $p \leq q$) if $\forall$ object o, if o matches p then o matches q. If $p \neq q$ and $p \leq q$, then we say p strongly dominates q, denoted as $p < q$. From the aspect of Boolean expressions, following two propositions are obvious.

Proposition 1: For two satisfiable CEDs p and q, if p dominates q, they must satisfy the constraint that $\exists$ CED p' satisfying that $p = q \wedge p'$.

For two satisfiable CEDs p and q, we say p conflicts with q if $p \wedge q$ is unsatisfiable.

Proposition 2: For two satisfiable CEDs p and q, if p conflicts with q, then $\exists$ CED p' satisfying that $p = \neg q \wedge p'$.

Based on the notations of conflict and domination, we define an entity $e = (R, W)$ as a logical valid entity if there is no conflict and no domination in R, which means e should satisfy:

1. There is no feature element t satisfying that $\exists r_i, r_j \in R, r_i \neq r_j, r_i \leq t$ and $r_j \leq \neg t$
2. There is no two CEDs $r_i, r_j \in R, r_i \neq r_j$, satisfying $r_i \leq r_j$.

Given a set E of entities, E is a logical valid entity set if each entity is a logical valid entity and there is no domination between CEDs, which means E should satisfy:

1. $\forall e_i \in E$, e_i is a logical valid entity,

2. $\forall e_i, e_j \in E$, $e_i = (R_i, W_i)$, $e_j = (R_j, W_j) \in E$, $e_i \neq e_j$, e_i and e_j satisfy that there is no two CEDs p, q, $p \in R_i$, $q \in R_j$, satisfying that $p \leq q$.

In order to guarantee a good performance of ER problem, CED-ER enforces the following two conditions:

1. **Each entity should be a logical valid entity:** Since in the ER problem, when we compute the similarity between entity e and object o, we sum up the weights of all the matching CEDs with o of e. Therefore, the CEDs of e should be independent. We call this independency property.

2. **An entity set should be a logical valid entity set:** For e_i, e_j, if $\exists p \in R_i$, $q \in R_j$, satisfying that $p \leq q$, and $W(p) < W(q)$, then for an object o representing e_i, o will always be deemed to represent e_j if o matches p; unless o also matches some other CEDs in e_i to increase the similarity between o and e_i. Therefore p cannot be used independently to distinguish objects representing e_i and e_j. This also violate the independency property of CEDs of each entity.

Proposition 3: Given an entity $e = (R, W)$, $\forall r \in R$, there is a DNF r' which is equivalent with r.

Proposition 4: $\forall$ entity $e = (R, W)$ can be converted to an equivalent (R', W') with R' as a DNF set.

Proof: According to Proposition 3, $\forall r \in R, \exists$ an equivalent DNF of r, denoted as r' such that, $r' = r_1 \wedge r_2 \wedge \ldots \wedge r_k$, then e can be written as $e = (R', W')$, where $R' = (R/\{r\}) \cup \{r_1, r_2, \ldots, r_k\}$, $W'(r_i) = W(r_i)$, if $r_i \neq r$, $W'(r_1) = W'(r_2) = \ldots = W'(r_k) = W(r)$.$\square$

According to Proposition 4, for an entity $e = (R, W)$, we can modify e into (R', W'), where each CED $p \in R'$ do not contain logical OR($\vee$), thus p can be written as $p = t_1 \wedge \ldots \wedge t_i \wedge \neg t_{i+1} \wedge \ldots \wedge \neg t_k$. Therefore in the following chapter, the CEDs we discussed all do not contain logical OR.

Proposition 5: The time complexity of checking whether there is a dominate relationship between two CEDs p, q is $O(|p|+|q|)$.

Proof: For two CEDs p and q, obviously, the problem of checking whether there is a dominate relationship between p and q is equivalent to the problem of checking whether there is a dominate relationship between two sets S_1 and S_2, where $|S_1|=|p|$ and $|S_2|=|q|$.

Similar as the proof of Proposition 5, the following properties can be proven. For the interest of space, the proofs are eliminated.

Proposition 6: The time complexity of checking whether there is a conflict relationship between two CEDs p, q is $O(\max\{|p|,|q|\})$.

Proposition 7: The time complexity of logical valid judgment for an entity e = (R, W) is $O(|R|^2 * \max\{|r|\}, r \in R)$.

In most occasions, the lengths of CEDs are small, i.e., in our experiments on DBLP, the lengths of most CEDs are no more than 2, so $\max\{|r|\}$ can be considered as a constant. Since entities seldom do have many features. Thus $|R|$ can also be viewed as a constant value. Moreover, efficient index structure such as Hash can be applied to improve the efficiency.

Proposition 7: For a set E of entities, the worst time complexity of identifying whether E is valid is $O(|E|^2)$.

As mentioned earlier, we focus on the ER problem for each ambiguous object set in O. Thus the value of $|E|$ is always small, e.g., the number of authors sharing identical name is small.

MAIN FOCUS OF THE CHAPTER

Since from the representation, objects referring to different entities can be distinguished directly, we focus on the ER problem for each ambiguous object set in O. For simplicity, in the following, the object set we discussed all refer to the ambiguous object sets.

Definition 3 (CED-ER model): Given a set O of objects, a set E of entities and a similarity threshold θ, a valid classification result C= CED-ER(R) satisfies that, for $\forall$object $o_i \in O$,

1. If maximal$\{Sim(o, e_j)\} < \theta$ then $C(o_i) = \phi$,
2. Otherwise, $Sim(o, C(o)) = \text{maximal}\{Sim(o, e_j)\}$,

where C(o) represent the entity of object o represents.

Our main idea is for each object o, to find the entity e which matches o most and if Sim(o,e) is larger than θ, o is deemed to present e, otherwise, o is not similar enough to e to be deemed to represent e.

LEVERAGING CED FOR ENTITY RESOLUTION

In this section, we show how to apply CEDs on ER problem. In subsection 3.1, we present a U-CED algorithm which uses CEDs directly. In subsection 3.2, we present our second algorithm, GenCED, a CED discovery strategy based on training data. In subsection 3.3, we adopt a more optimized algorithm than U-CED, P-CED which can discover new CEDs on object set by leveraging GenCED.

U-CED Algorithm for ER

In this subsection, we present U-CED algorithm of using CEDs to perform ER. The pseudo code of U-CED is shown in Algorithm 1. U-CED is a pair-wise matching strategy between object and entity based on CEDs. The algorithm has two phrases. First, for each object o_i, we compute the similarity between o_i and each entity (lines 2-6). Then the entity e_j with the biggest value of similarity with o_i is selected as the entity o_i referring to (lines 7-10).

Algorithm 1 U-CED

Input: A set O of objects, a set E of entities, and a similarity threshold θ.

Output: A classification C of O.

1.   for i←1 to |O| do
2. $Sim(o_i, e_j)=0$;
3.   for j ←1 to |E| do
4.   For each CED $r \in R_j$ do
5.   if o_i matches r then
6. $Sim(o_i, e_j) += W(r)$;
7.   if $Sim(o_i, FindMatch(o_i)) > \theta$ then
8. $C(o_i) = FindMatch(o_i)$;
9.   else
10. $C(o_i) = \phi$;
11.   Return C;

The function FindMatch(o) is to find entity e satisfying, $Sim(o, e) = maximal\{Sim(o, e_j)\}$ $1 \leq j \leq |E|$. This algorithm is illustrated in Example 4.

Example 4: There are a set O of objects and a set of E of entities with their CEDs shown in Table 3 and Table 4, supposing θ=1. For the interests of space, we omit place constraint coauthor of feature element in CED in Table 4.

Table 3. An ambiguous object set

obj	name	coauthor	coauthor	entity
o_1	wei wang	zhang	shi	e_1
o_2	wei wang	wang	shi	e_1
o_3	wei wang	zhang	lin	e_2
o_4	wei wang	jin		e_2

Table 4. An entity set

entity	CED	description	W
e_1	r_1	shi	2
	r_2	wang	1
e_2	r_3	lin	1
	r_4	jin	1
	r_5	zhang ∧ ¬shi	1

We run U-CED on the data sets in the first phrase and find all the matching CEDs of each object as shown in Table 5. Then, the similarities between objects and entities are computed by summing up the weights of matching CEDs as Table 6 shows.

At last, for each object, its corresponding entity is selected according to the similarity. The result C is shown as following:

$$C(o_1) = C(o_2) = e_1, \quad C(o_3) = C(o_4) = e_2.$$

Complexity: We suppose the maximal length of a CED is l_{max}, the maximal number of CEDs in an entity is R_{max}. We can get that the complexity of line 5 is $O(l_{max})$, thus the complexity of lines 3-6 is $O(l_{max}*R_{max}*|E|)$. The complexity of lines 7-10 is $O(|E|)$. Therefore the time complexity of Algorithm 1 is $O(|O|*|E|*l_{max}*R_{max})$.

CED Discovery

In this subsection, we present a discovery strategy of CED set. The training data for CED discovery can be obtained by manually labeling on objects or by extracting from reliable data sources such as Wikipedia, personal homepages, databases and so on, by utilizing IR techniques. Before the introduction of CED discovery problem, we introduce some notations used in this subsection.

Table 5. Matching CEDs for Example 4

entity	o_1	o_2	o_3	o_4
e_1	r_1	r_1, r_2		
e_2			r_3, r_5	r_4

Table 6. Similarities for Example 4

entity	o_1	o_2	o_3	o_4
e_1	2	3	0	0
e_2	0	0	2	1

The goal of CED discovery is to find valid CED sets. Therefore, we discuss what are valid CED sets.

For a CED r of entity e, we say r is a valid CED of e on object set O, if r satisfies that $\forall o \in O$, if o matches r then o represents e. In another word, r can only be matched by the objects representing e. We define this property of valid CED as uniqueness property.

Proposition 8: For a logical valid entity set E, $\forall e = (R, W) \in E$ satisfies that $\forall CED$ $r \in R$ is a valid CED.

Proof: Since for a CED r, r dominates itself. Thus if r does not satisfy the uniqueness property, there is a dominate relationship between CEDs in different entities. Thus it conflicts to the definition of logical valid entity set.

For a CED r, the number of objects in object set O which matches CED r is the frequency of r on O, denoted as frq(r). A CED r is a pCED if r is in the form of $t \wedge t'$ or t, where t and t' are feature elements. For a pCED r, |r| is no more than 2, besides, there is no $\neg$ in pCED. A CED r is an nCED if r is in the form of $t \wedge \neg t_1 \wedge \neg t_2 \ldots \wedge \neg t_k$ with t and t_1-t_k as feature elements.

Based on above concepts, the valid entity set is defined as follows.

Definition 4 (valid entity set): Given a set O of objects, a classification C of O and an entity set E, E is a valid entity set if E satisfies the following conditions:

1. E is a logical valid entity set.
2. $\forall e = (R, W) \in E$ satisfies that $\forall r \in R$ is a valid CED of e on O.
3. $\forall e = (R, W) \in E$ satisfies that $\forall r \in R$, r is a pCED or r is a nCED.
4. $\forall e = (R, W) \in E$ satisfies that $\forall r \in R$, if r is a nCED, $r = t \wedge \neg t_1 \wedge \neg t_2 \ldots \wedge \neg t_k$ then $\exists$ pCED $r' \in R$, satisfying $r' = t \wedge t'$.

The first two conditions are intuitive. The reasons of condition 3 and condition 4 are explained as follows.

In most conditions, we prefer using pCED to describe entity feature, it is intuitive and easy. However, when we cannot discover enough feature elements to distinguish an entity from others, nCEDs have to be used. For example, considering for Wei Wang in Fudan as e_1 and Wei Wang in UNC as e_2, they both have a coauthor named "Qi Zhang". Additionally, we know Baile Shi is a supervisor of e_1. The nCED r=<coauthor>Qi Zhang$\wedge$ $\neg$<coauthor>Baile Shi can be used to distinguish e_2 from e_1 when we have no other features element of e_2 which usually co-occurs with <coauthor>Qi Zhang in the contexts.

The reason of limiting the maximal length of pCED as two is to guarantee that the feature elements we picked is representative enough. Actually, the longer the rule is, the less representative the rule is. This is also the reason that only one feature element without $\neg$ is allowed in nCED. If there are more than two feature elements without $\neg$ in the nCED, and we still have to add $\neg t_1 \wedge \ldots \wedge \neg t_i$ in the rule in order to satisfy the uniqueness property, it means the feature elements without $\neg$ are not representative enough for this entity. Condition 4 guarantees the correctness of the CEDs generated by Algorithm 3. Otherwise, identical nCEDs might appear in different entities, thus the uniqueness property of valid CED is violated.

Now we present the model of CED-discovery in Definition 5.

Definition 5 (CED-discovery model): Given an object set O, a classification C of O and a threshold θ, the valid result of CED-discovery is an entity set E, which satisfies the following conditions:

1. E is a valid entity set.
2. $\forall$ $e = (R, W) \in E$ satisfies $\forall$pCED $r \in R$, frq(r) $\geq \theta$.

We can see that, pCED is the core rules which describes entity features, however nCED is just a complementary of pCED. In order to generate pCEDs, finding the feature elements in pCEDs are the key problem of CED discovery.

In order to discover useful feature elements for pCED, we define two metrics of relevance between feature element t and entity e.

Given an entity e and a feature element t, we observe that in order to describe features of e effectively, t should have two properties in two levels:

1. t should be matched by a great part of the objects representing e.
2. t should seldom be matched by objects not representing e.

Based on the properties and inspired by TF/IDF model in IR, we use two parameters GF and ITF defined as follows to measure the relevance between feature element and entity.

Given an object set O and an entity set E, for an entity $e \in E$ and a feature element t, we have:

$GF(t, O(e)) = \Sigma w(t, o_i)$, $o_i \in O(e)$, O(e) is the object set representing e,

where $w(t, o_i) = 1$ if and only o_i matches t, otherwise, $w(t, o_i) = 0$.

$TF(t) = \Sigma u(t, e_i)$, $e_i \in E$,

where $u(t, e_i) = 1$ if and only if $\exists o_j$, $o_j \in O(e_i)$ and o_j matches t, otherwise, $u(t, e_i) = 0$.

$ITF(t) = 1/TF(t)$

According to the definitions, GF(t, O(e)) is the frequency of t on O(e). ITF(t) is the inverse frequency of t on entity set. Thus for a feature element t and an entity e, the larger the values of GF(t, O(e)) and ITF(t) are, the more relevant t is to e. Then we formalize the problem of generating Candidate Feature Element(CFE)s of pCED as follows.

Definition 6 (CFE discovery model): Given a set O of objects, a classification C of O, a threshold θ of GF, and a threshold of ITF, θ_{ITF}, the valid result is a set T of CFEs satisfying following conditions:

1. $\forall$ feature element $t \in T$, $ITF(t) \geq \theta_{ITF}$
2. $\forall$ feature element $t \in T$, $\forall$ entity e, if $t \in T(e)$, then $GF(t, O(e)) \geq \theta$, where T(e) is the CFE set of e.

Based on this model, we present the GenCFE algorithm of discovering CFEs for pCEDs in Algorithm 2. In lines 1-3, we initialize T and Cla, where T stores the feature element set of each entity at first, and Cla is a family with each set $C_E \in Cla$ containing all the objects referring to entity e. In lines 4-5, we compute the values of TF and GF and stores them in TF and GF.

Algorithm 2 GenCFE

Input: A set O of objects, a classification C of O, thresholds θ and θ_{ITF}.
Output: R=(GF, ITF, T, I)

1. for each $o \in O$ do
2. T[C(o)]= T[C(o)]∪Split(o);
3. Cla[C(o)].insert(o)
4. TF=ComputeTF(T,Cla);
5. GF=ComputeGF(T,Cla);
6. for i←1 to |Cla| do
7. for each feature element $t \in T[i]$ do
8. if $1/TF(t) \geq \theta_{ITF}$ && $GF(t, i) \geq \theta$ then
9. I(t).insert(i);
10. else
11. T[i].delete(t);
12. Return (T, GF, TF, I);

In Algorithm 2, the function Split(o) is to transform object o into a feature element set.

Complexity Analysis: Since |Cla| is equal to the number of entities, we use |E| to represent |Cla|. We suppose the maximal number of feature elements in an object o is o_{max}. Thus, the complexity of computing TF and GF is $O(|O|*o_{max})$. Since for each entity e_i, there are at most $|O|*o_{max}$ feature elemnts in T[i], the complexity of lines 6-11 is $O(|E|*|O|*o_{max})$. Thus the worst time complexity of Algorithm 2 is $O(|E|*|O|*o_{max})$. If |E| is considered as a constant, thus the time complexity of Algorithm 2 is linear to the size of data.

Then we present GenCED, the CED generation algorithm with CFEs generated by GenCFE. The pseudo code is shown in Algorithm 3.

In this algorithm for generating pCEDs, we consider how to combine CFEs in order to satisfy the uniqueness property of CED. If a CFE t already satisfies uniqueness property, t becomes a pCED directly; otherwise, we should identify whether t can combine with other feature element t'. If $t \wedge t'$ satisfies both the uniqueness property and $frq(t \wedge t') \geq \theta$, it becomes a pCED. All the valid combinations should be found in this way.

As a complementary of pCEDs, once a pCED in the form of $t \wedge t'$ of entity e is generated, for other entity e' which also has t as a CFE, corresponding nCED in form of $t \wedge t'$ is generated for e'. We use Example 5 to illustrate the relationship between nCEDs and pCEDs.

Example 5: There are three entities e_1, e_2 and e_3. Suppose they share a CFE t.

The pCEDs of e_1-e_3 are as follows:

1. pCEDs of e_1: $t \wedge t_1$, $t \wedge t_2$
2. pCEDs of e_2: $t \wedge t_3$
3. pCEDs of e_3: $t \wedge t_4$

Then the corresponding nCEDs of e_1-e_3 are as follows:

4. nCEDs of e_1: $t \wedge \neg t_3 \wedge \neg t_4$
5. nCEDs of e2: $t \wedge \neg t1 \wedge \neg t2 \wedge \neg t4$
6. nCEDs of e3: $t \wedge \neg t1 \wedge \neg t2 \wedge \neg t3$

The importance of condition 4 in the definition of valid entity set can also be illustrated using Example 5. If condition 4 is not satisfied, we assume that for e_2-e_3, there is no pCED containing t. Therefore, the corresponding nCED for e_2 and e_3 are identical, that is $t \wedge \neg t_1 \wedge \neg t_2$. Thus the uniqueness property is violated.

The flow of GenCED is as follows: In line1 we run GenCFE to obtain CFEs; then in lines 4-8, for each CFE t in each entity, all the possible pCEDs and corresponding nCEDs containing t are generated by function Add; before pCEDs are stored in R, line 10 checks whether there is a dominate relationship, the dominated rules are excluded from the results; in lines 12-17, nCEDs are stored in R.

Algorithm 3 GenCED

Input: A set O of objects, a classification C of O, Thresholds θ_{ITF}.

Output: A set E of entities

1. (T, GF, ITF, I)=Gen_CFE();
2. for k←1 to |E| do
3. for each $t_i \in T[k]$ do
4. if $I(t_i)$.size=1 then
5. $W(t_i)=GF(t_i,k)$;
6. R.insert(t_i);
7. else
8. $(P(t_i), N(t_i))=Add(t_i,k)$;
9. for each $t_j \in P(t_i)$ do
10. if $t_j \notin R$ then
11. R.insert($t_i \wedge t_j$);
12. CED r= t_i;
13. for each $t_j \in N(t)$ do
14. $r=r \wedge \neg t_j$;
15. for each $j \in I(t_i)$ do
16. $W(r)+=ComputeGF(r,k)$;
17. $R[j]$.insert(r);
18. $e_i=(R, \{W(r)|r \in R\})$;
19. E.insert(e_i);
20. Return E;
21. Add(t_i,k)
22. for each $t_j(j>i)$ in T[k] do
23. $W(t_i \wedge t_j)+=ComputeGF(t_i \wedge t_j,k)$;
24. If ComputeITF($t_i \wedge t_j$)=1 && $W(t_i \wedge t_j) \geq \theta$ then
25. P.insert(t_j);
26. N.insert(t_j);
27. Retun (P,N);

We use Example 4 to illustrate Algorithm 3. Suppose $\theta_{ITF} = 0.5$, $\theta = 1$, we run GenCED on the data set in Example 4. At first, all the CFEs of entity are generated by CFE. The result is shown in Table 7. For the interests of space, we omit place constraint of feature element. Secondly, for each CFE t in each entity, we compute all the possible pCEDs and nCEDs containing t. The result is shown in Table 8. Then, we delete all the pCEDs been dominated. Since $t_2 \wedge t_3$ is dominated by t_3, $t_2 \wedge t_5$ is dominated by t_7, thus $t_2 \wedge t_3$ and $t_2 \wedge t_5$ are deleted.

Complexity Analysis: We suppose the maximal length of nCEDs is l_n, the maximal number of CFEs in an entity is l_e, the maximal value of GF of CFEs is gf_{max}, and the maixmal value of TF of CFEs is tf_{max}. Thus, we can get the complexity of ComputeGF(r, k) is $O(|r|*gf_{max})$; the complexity of ComputeITF(r, k) is $O(|r|*tf_{max})$. Since the length of pCEDs is no longer than 2, the complexity of line 23 is $O(gf_{max})$; the complexity of line 16 is $O(l_n*gf_{max})$. So the complexity of Add is $O(l_e*\max\{gf_{max}, tf_{max}\})$. Since the maximal size of $P(t_i)$ and $N(t_i)$ is l_e, the complexity of lines 9-11

and lines 13-14 are both $O(l_e)$ and the complexity of lines 16 is $tf_{max}*l_e$. If tf_{max} and l_n are viewed as constants, thus the time complexity of Algorithm 3 is $O(|E|* l_e^2* gf_{max})$ in the worst case.

P-CED Algorithm for ER

As mentioned before, there are two ways of obtaining CEDs. No matter the CEDs are obtained manually or by learning from training data, CEDs can never capture the full feature information of entities due to continuously new-coming objects. Taking author identification as an example, people may change their research areas or teams. Due to lack of new feature descriptions, running U-CED directly on the new-coming object set can hardly achieve good performance. However, the classification result of U-CED can provide us new feature information of entities. Based on this classification, we can discover new entity description rules using GenCED, which leads to a better accuracy. Before presenting the algorithm, another property of CED set is shown.

Table 7. CFEs for Example 4

e₁				e₂			
ID	CFE	GF	ITF	ID	CFE	GF	ITF
t_1	wei wang	2	0.5	t_1	wei wang	2	0.5
t_2	zhang	1	0.5	t_2	zhang	1	0.5
t_3	shi	2	1	t_5	lin	1	1
t_4	wang	1	1	t_6	jin	1	1

Table 8. CEDs for Example 4

e₁			e₂		
ID	pCED	nCED	ID	pCED	nCED
t_1			t_1		
t_2	$t_2 \wedge t_3$	$t_2 \wedge \neg t_5$	t_2	$t_2 \wedge t_5$	$t_2 \wedge \neg t_3$
t_3	t_3		t_5	t_5	
t_4	t_4		t_6	t_6	

Proposition 9: Given a set E of entities and a set O of objects. If E is a valid entity set on S, $\forall E' \subseteq E$ is also a valid entity set on S.

Based on Proposition 9, when rules are deleted from the original valid entity set, the new entity set is still valid.

The update of entity set including two parts: deleting invalid old rules and generating new CEDs. In order to guarantee the old CED set is still valid on the new object set, we should delete rules which no longer satisfy the uniqueness property. Proposition 9 guarantees the safety of deletion. Besides, we should discover new CEDs using GenCED according to the classification result generated by U-CED on original CEDs.

Algorithm 4 P-CED

Input: A set O of objects, a set E of entities, thresholds θ_{ITF}, θ.

Output: A classification C of O.

1. For $k \leftarrow 1$ to |E| do
2. For each $r_i \in R_k$ do
3. If ComputeITF(r_i)<1 then
4. $R_k = R_k / \{r_i\}$;
5. C=U-CED(O,E, θ);
6. E=GenCED(O,C, θ_{ITF}, θ);
7. C=U-CED(O,E, θ);
8. Return C;

Complexity Analysis: We suppose the number of CEDs is N_c, the other variations are the same as we mentioned before. The time complexity of lines 1-3 is $O(N_c * l_n * tf_{max})$, the time complexity of lines 5-7 is $O(2|O|*|E|*l_{max} * R_{max} + |E|*|O|*o_{max} + |E|* l_e^2 * gf_{max})\} = max\{O(|O|*|E|*l_{max} *R_{max})$, $O(|E|*|O|*o_{max})$, $O(|E|* l_e^2 * gf_{max}))\}$. If we assume tf_{max} and l_n as constants, and $N_c << |O|$ then the time complexity of P-CED is $max\{O(|O|*|E|*l_{max} *R_{max})$, $O(|E|*|O|*o_{max})$, $O(|E|* l_e^2 * gf_{max}))\}$. Since the values of |E|, l_{max}, R_{max}, o_{max}, l_e^2, gf_{max} are usually quite small in real world applications. Thus, the time complexity of Algorithm 4 is linear to the size of objects.

EXPERIMENTAL EVALUATION

In this section, we present our empirical evaluation of P-CED on real datasets and show how P-CED outperforms both in accuracy and runtime.

Experimental Setting

Experimental Environment: Our experiments were run on a 2.67 GHz Intel(R) Core 2 processor with 4GB of RAM. The operation system is Microsoft Windows 7.

Datasets: Since author identification is one of the most difficult ER problems, and current ER approaches we discussed in section 1 result in the low accuracy and efficiency in author identification problem. Thus we evaluate our algorithm on DBLP(http://dblp.uni-trier.de). The DBLP dataset is a famous computer science bibliography database, which provides bibliographic information on major computer science journals and proceedings.

For simplicity, for a given name s, we use pub(s) to denote the set of publications which includes as an author name, aut(s) to denote the set of authors with name s. In order to evaluate the effectiveness of our algorithms, we select 10 representative author names shown in Table 9. They have the following properties:

1. A large number of authors sharing this name.
2. A large number of publications written by the authors sharing this name.
3. In DBLP, the authors sharing the same name are distinguished by a suffix, i.e. for "wei wang 0001" and "wei wang 0002."

In our experiments, we ignore the authors the numbers of whose publications are no more than one and the publications of which the above names are not been distinguished by DBLP. In order to obtain the training data, we randomly chose a subset of the test data. Figure 1 shows the number of publications of each author. It can be seen that almost 80% authors have less than 20 publications.

Table 9. Names corresponding to multiple authors

Name	#pub	#aut	Name	#pub	#aut
jing wang	115	11	ping zhang	164	4
yan liu	118	10	hui wang	171	11
jian zhang	147	8	xin zhang	173	13
lei chen	149	4	jun yang	202	9
jun sun	152	7	wei wang	421	25

Due to the small numbers of publications for most authors, for each author a_i, we randomly choose n_i = maximal {1, 20%*#pub} publications as the training data.

Measures: Similar to (Fan, X., Wang, J., Pu, X., Zhou, L., Lv, B. 2011, Yin, X., Han, J., Yu, P. S. 2007), we measure the accuracy of P-CED by precision, recall and f-score. According to the definitions in (Yin, X., Han, J., Yu, P. S. 2007), we define the real cluster is C, and the experimental results of P-CED is C*. Let TP (true positive) be the number of pairs of objects that are in the same cluster in both C and C*. Let FP (false positive) be the number of pairs of objects in the same cluster in C* but not in C, and FN (false negative) be the number of pairs of references in the same cluster in C but not in C*. Therefore the precision, recall and f-score are defined as follows:

precision = TP / (TP + FP),

recall = TP / (TP + FN),

f-score = (2 * precision * recall) / (precision + recall).

Comparison with GHOST

As far as we know, GHOST(Fan, X., Wang, J., Pu, X., Zhou, L., Lv, B. 2011) is the best author identification algorithm both in accuracy and efficiency. Therefore, we compare P-CED with GHOST both in accuracy and efficiency, and

the comparison results are shown in Table 10. We can make the following observations from these results.

1. **Precision:** We can see that GHOST shows a slight boast in precision for all names except "xin zhang" and "wei wang". This is because GHOST works based on the hypothesis that different persons with the same name should have quite different author communities. However, this hypothesis does not hold for the cases of "wei wang" and "xin zhang". For example, more than two authors named "wei wang" ever cooperated with the author Pei Jian. For P-CED, some of the feature elements in the rules learned by training data might not be representative, which might also appear in publications of other authors. This will cause the decrease of precision. However, the result shows P-CED is more robust than GHOST. The lowest precision of P-CED on this dataset is 0.89, while it is

Figure 1. Number of objects per entity (Li, L., Li, J., Wang, H. & Gao, H. 2011)

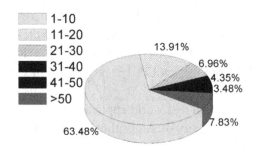

0.49 for GHOST. Besides, P-CED achieves a better performance of precision in average.

2. **Recall:** We observe that P-CED offers considerably better recall than GHOST. As mentioned in (Fan, X., Wang, J., Pu, X., Zhou, L., Lv, B. 2011), inadequate relationship may result in low similarity of two tuples, which may cause them to be separated into two clusters by GHOST. However, we can see this situation can hardly affect the recall result of P-CED. This shows how robust P-CED is again.

3. **Runtime:** We can see that P-CED can be executed significantly more efficiently than GHOST. The time complexity of GHOST is $O(|O|*\log|O|)$, while our algorithm is approximate linear to $|O|$, therefore our algorithm can outperforms GHOST in efficiency.

Impact Factors of Quality

1. **Effect of Updating Rules:** In this subsection, we evaluate the impact of updating CEDs on quality by comparing the two algorithms U-CED, and P-CED, shown in Table 11. The CEDs are learned from two train data sets. One (the other) is generated by randomly choosing 20%(30%) of the whole data. In Table 10, "U-20" represents the result of U-CED, and the CEDs are discovered from the training data whose size is 20% of the whole data, while "P-30" represents the result of P-CED, and the CEDs are discovered from the train data whose size is 30% of the whole data.

As we mentioned in section 3, differently with U-CED, P-CED updates the input CEDs by discovering new CEDs from object set. We also know that by enlarging the training data size, more CEDs will also be discovered, which can improve the accuracy of result.

From Table 10, we have the following observations:

a. P-CED outperforms U-CED overall under the same CEDs.

   i. **Precision:** For the same size of training data, the result of U-CED shows a slight boast in precision than the result of P-CED. This is because during the process of discovering new CEDs, due to some publications which are partitioned into the wrong author cluster, false information of this author will be learned and will cause the new CEDs containing improper CFEs. For the publications of other authors satisfying these CEDs containing improper CFEs, they might be classified into this class. This will cause the decrease of precision. However, the precision of P-CED is still quite comparable with U-CED.

   ii. **Recall:** P-20(P-30) shows a much better performance in recall than U-20(U-30). The lowest recall of U-20 is 0.63 while the lowest of P-20 is 0.88; the lowest recall of U-30 is 0.77 while the lowest of P-30 is 0.90.

b. ER algorithm with updating rules incrementally outperforms ER algorithm with large training data.

From the experimental results, it is observed that even P-20 provides a better accuracy improvement than U-30. It means that by rule updating algorithm, more new effective rules can be discovered than using training the whole training data set at the beginning.

2. Varying the training size.

In order to test the impact of training data size on accuracy, we pick two names, "jian zhang" and "ping zhang". One has the worst accuracy

Table 10. Effect of updating rules

Accuracy Comparison	Precision				Recall				F-Score			
	U-20	P-20	U-30	P-30	U-20	P-20	U-30	P-30	U-20	P-20	U-30	P-30
hui wang	1.00	1.00	1.00	1.00	0.65	0.93	0.76	0.93	0.79	0.96	0.88	0.96
jian zhang	1.00	1.00	0.99	1.00	0.46	**0.79**	0.72	0.90	**0.63**	**0.88**	**0.77**	0.94
jing wang	0.98	0.98	1.00	1.00	0.87	0.95	0.94	0.96	0.92	0.96	0.96	0.98
jun sun	1.00	0.97	1.00	0.97	0.96	0.97	0.96	0.97	0.98	0.97	0.99	0.97
jun yang	1.00	1.00	1.00	0.98	0.82	0.95	0.96	0.97	0.90	0.97	0.94	0.98
lei chen	0.96	0.96	1.00	0.98	0.84	0.98	0.89	0.99	0.90	0.97	0.94	0.99
yan liu	0.91	0.89	0.99	0.90	0.64	0.87	0.52	0.90	0.75	0.88	0.85	**0.90**
ping zhang	1.00	1.00	1.00	1.00	0.86	0.99	0.91	0.99	0.92	0.99	0.96	0.99
xin zhang	0.99	0.99	1.00	1.00	0.98	0.98	0.99	1.00	0.99	0.98	0.99	1.00
wei wang	0.97	0.92	0.97	0.96	0.83	0.85	0.79	0.97	0.89	0.88	0.93	0.97
average	0.98	**0.97**	**0.99**	0.98	0.79	**0.93**	**0.84**	0.96	0.88	**0.95**	**0.93**	0.97

Table 11. Performance comparison(P-CED vs GHOST)

	Precison		Recall		F-Score		Run Time(ms)	
	GHOST	P-CED	GHOST	P-CED	GHOST	P-CED	GHOST	P-CED
hui wang	1.00	1.00	0.19	0.93	0.32	0.96	1196	55
jian zhang	1.00	1.00	0.16	**0.79**	**0.28**	**0.88**	962	45
jing wang	1.00	0.98	0.91	0.95	0.95	0.96	854	50
jun sun	1.00	0.97	0.90	0.97	0.95	0.97	1072	47
jun yang	1.00	1.00	0.60	0.95	0.75	0.97	1580	67
lei chen	1.00	0.96	**0.13**	0.98	0.23	0.97	937	48
yan liu	1.00	**0.89**	0.26	0.87	0.42	0.88	836	43
ping zhang	1.00	1.00	0.16	0.99	0.28	**0.99**	1026	54
xin zhang	0.90	0.99	0.96	0.98	0.93	0.98	1354	60
wei wang	**0.49**	0.92	0.39	0.85	0.43	0.88	6806	144
average	0.94	0.97	0.47	0.93	0.55	0.95	1662	61

result with P-20 and the other gets the best result. From Figure 2 we observe that, for both names, the accuracy result can reach a high value even when the size of training data is small. With the growth of the training data size, the recall increases gradually, while precisions are insensitive to the training data size.

Efficiency and Scalability

In Figure 3, we test the impact of number of tuples on efficiency. In order to vary the values of numbers of publications of each name, we pick 14 names with publication numbers varying from 11 to 421. From Figure 3, it can be observed that the run time is approximately linear to the number of objects. This result is in accordance with our time complexity analysis in section 2.

From the experimental result, we can draw following conclusions,

1. P-CED is flexible than GHOST. P-CED neither care about whether the authors having the same name unlikely have similar research area, share a research community nor assume authors seldom change their research teams or labs. Without domain knowledge, P-CED still shows a robust high performance on test data.
2. Insensitive to the size of the training data. Due to the contribution of new CEDs been discovered, P-CED only requires a small size of training data. Even when the training data size is small, P-CED can get a high accuracy.

3. Good scalability and high efficiency. The experiments show P-CED has a good scalability, with the increase of size of data, the runtime increase approximately linearly.

FUTURE RESEARCH DIRECTIONS

We plan to design cloud-based entity resolution method to handle very large data set. The extraction and matching of attributes and values from various data format is another further research issue.

Figure 2. Training data size impact on accuracy (a)jian zhang (b)ping zhang

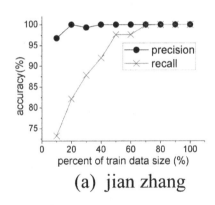
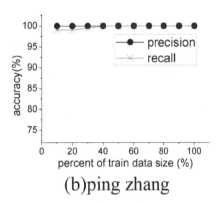

(a) jian zhang　　　　(b)ping zhang

Figure 3. Runtime decomposition (Li, L., Li, J., Wang, H. & Gao, H. 2011)

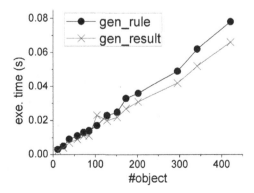

CONCLUSION

Current ER approaches mostly based on object comparison and similarity functions. This chapter addressed the limitations of comparison between objects on ER, and developed a strategy based on comparison between object and entity. We present a context-based entity description rule (CED) to describe the features of entity. Thus the ER problem is reduced to that for each object, to identify the entity which is most similar with the object. We develop an algorithm P-CED for ER problem and present a CED discovery strategy. We experimentally evaluated our algorithm on real data set, and the experimental results show that our algorithm can achieve a good performance in accuracy and outperforms existing algorithm both in efficiency and accuracy.

REFERENCES

Arasu, A., Chaudhuri, S., & Kaushik, R. (2009). *Learning string transformations from examples.* VLDB.

Bansal, N., Blum, A., & Chawla, S. (2002). Correlation clustering. In *Proceedings of FOCS*. FOCS.

Chaudhuri, S., Ganjam, K., Ganti, V., & Motwani, R. (2003). Robust and efficient fuzzy match for online data cleaning. In *Proceedings of SIGMOD*. ACM.

Chaudhuri, S., Sarma, A. D., Ganti, V., & Kaushik, R. (2007). Leveraging aggregate constraints for deduplication. In *Proceedings of SIGMOD*. ACM.

Fan, X., Wang, J., Pu, X., Zhou, L., & Lv, B. (2011). On graph-based name disambiguation. *J. Data and Information Quality*, 2(2), 10.

Koudas, N., Sarawagi, S., & Srivastava, D. (2006). Record linkage: Similarity measures and algorithms. In *Proceedings of SIGMOD*. ACM.

Li, L., Li, J., Wang, H., & Gao, H. (2011). Context-based entity description rule for entity resolution. [CIKM.]. *Proceedings of CIKM, 2011*, 1725–1730.

Singla, P., & Domingos, P. (2005). Object identification with attribute-mediated dependences. In *Proceedings of PKDD*. PKDD.

Verykios, V. S., Moustakides, G. V., & Elfeky, M. G. (2003). A Bayesian decision model for cost optimal record matching. *The VLDB Journal*, 12(1), 28–40. doi:10.1007/s00778-002-0072-y

Xiao, C., Wang, W., Lin, X., & Shang, H. (2009). Top-k set similarity joins. In *Proceedings of ICDE*, (pp. 916-927). ICDE.

Xiao, C., Wang, W., Lin, X., & Yu, J. X. (2008). Efficient similarity joins for near duplicate detection. In *Proceedings of WWW*, (pp. 131-140). IEEE.

Yin, X., Han, J., & Yu, P. S. (2007). Object distinction: Distinguishing objects with identical names by link analysis. In *Proceedings of ICDE*. ICDE.

ADDITIONAL READING

Arasu, A., Chaudhuri, S., & Kaushik, R. (2009). *Learning string transformations from examples.* VLDB.

Bansal, N., Blum, A., & Chawla, S. (2002). Correlation clustering. In FOCS, pp. 238.

Bekkerman, R., & McCallum, A. (2005). *Disambiguating web appearances of people in a social network.* WWW. doi:10.1145/1060745.1060813

Bilenko, M., Kamath, B., & Mooney, R. (2006). *Adaptive blocking: learning to scale up record linkage.* ICDM. doi:10.1109/ICDM.2006.13

Bilenko, M., & Mooney, R. J. (2003). *Adaptive duplicate detection using learnable string similarity measures.* KDD. doi:10.1145/956755.956759

Chaudhuri, S., Chen, B.-C., Ganti, V., & Kaushik, R. (2007). *Example-driven design of efficient record matching queries*. VLDB.

Chaudhuri, S., Ganjam, K., Ganti, V., & Motwani, R. (2003). *Robust and efficient fuzzy match for online data cleaning*. SIGMOD. doi:10.1145/872794.872796

Chaudhuri, S., Sarma, A. D., Ganti, V., & Kaushik, R. (2007). *Leveraging aggregate constraints for deduplication*. SIGMOD.

Cohen, W. W. (1998). *Integration of heterogeneous databases without common domains using queries based on textual similarity*. SIGMOD. doi:10.1145/276304.276323

Dong, X., Halevy, A. Y., & Madhavan, J. (2005). *Reference reconciliation in complex information spaces*. SIGMOD.

Fan, X., Wang, J., Pu, X., Zhou, L., & Lv, B. (2011). On Graph-Based Name Disambiguation. J. *Data and Information Quality*, 2(2), 10.

Gravano, L., Ipeirotis, P. G., Koudas, N., & Srivastava, D. (2003). *Text joins in an rdbms for web data integration*. WWW. doi:10.1145/775165.775166

Hernandez, M. A., & Stolfo, S. J. (1995). *The merge/purge problem for large databases*. SIGMOD. doi:10.1145/223784.223807

Jaro, M. A. (1984). *Advances in record linkage methodology as applied to matching the 1985 census of tampa*. American Statistical Association.

Koudas, N., Sarawagi, S., & Srivastava, D. (2006). *Record linkage: similarity measures and algorithms*. SIGMOD.

Newcombe, H. B., Kennedy, J. M., Axford, S. J., & James, A. P. (1959). Automatic linkage of vital records. *Science*, *130*(3381), 954–959. doi:10.1126/science.130.3381.954 PMID:14426783

Sarawagi, S., & Bhamidipaty, A. (2002). *Interactive deduplication using active learning*. SIGKDD.

Singla, P., & Domingos, P. (2005). *Object identification with attribute-mediated Dependences*. PKDD.

Tejada, S., Knoblock, C. A., & Minton, S. (2001). Learning object identification rules for information integration. *Information Systems Journal*, *26*(8), 635–656.

Verykios, V. S., Moustakides, G. V., & Elfeky, M. G. (2003). A Bayesian decision model for cost optimal record matching. *The VLDB Journal*, *12*(1), 2840. doi:10.1007/s00778-002-0072-y

Whang, S. E., Benjelloun, O., & Molina, H. G. (2009). Generic entity resolution with negative rules. *The VLDB Journal*, *18*, 1261–1277. doi:10.1007/s00778-009-0136-3

Whang, S. E., Menestrina, D., Koutrika, G., Theobald, M., & Molina, H. G. (2009). *Entity Resolution with Iterative Blocking*. SIGMOD.

Xiao, C., Wang, W., Lin, X., Shang, H. (2009). Top-k Set Similarity Joins. ICDE, 916-927.

Xiao, C., Wang, W., Lin, X., & Yu, J. X. (2008). Efficient similarity joins for near duplicate detection. In WWW, 131-140.

Yin, X., Han, J., & Yu, P. S. (2007). *Object Distinction: Distinguishing Objects with Identical Names by Link Analysis*. ICDE. doi:10.1109/ICDE.2007.368983

KEY TERMS AND DEFINITIONS

Context: The information related to an object is called the context of the object. For structured data, the context of an object is the values of other attributes in the same record. For unstructured data, the context of an object is the text near the phrase. For XML data, the context of an object o can be defined as the set of elements satisfying,

$$C(a) = \left\{ e \mid dis\left(LCA\left(a,e\right),e\right) < K \right\}, \quad \text{where}$$

dis(a, b) is the distance between elements a and b, LCA(a, b) is the least common ancestors of a and b and K is a predefined threshold.

Entity Resolution: Given an data object set U, entity resolution is to partition U into groups $R_U=\{R_1,...,R_k\}$ such that objects which are determined to refer to the same real-world entity are in the same group while objects which are determined to refer to different entities are in different groups and R_U also satisfies that, i) $R_1\cup...\cup R_k=U$; ii) $\forall R_i$, $R_j\in R_U$, $R_i\cap R_j = \emptyset$.

Matching Pair: Given a data object pair (o_i, o_j), (o_i, o_j) is a matching pair if they represent the same real-world entity.

Monotonicity of Similarity Function: Given a matching object pair (o_i, o_j) and a non-matching pair (o_i', o_j'), the property monotonicity of similarity function requires that the value of $sim(o_i,o_j)$ should be larger than $sim(o_i', o_j')$.

Non-Matching Pair: Given a data object pair (o_i, o_j), (o_i, o_j) is a non-matching pair if they does not represent the same real-world entity.

Object: An instance of an entity is called an object. For structured data, an object is a record; for unstructured data, an object is a phrase; while for semi-structured data such as XML, an object is an element.

Similarity Function: Taken a data object pair (o_i, o_j) as input, similarity function $sim(o_i, o_j)$ returns a non-negative number such that the more similar o_i and o_j are, the larger the value of $sim(o_i, o_j)$ is.

Chapter 5
Entity Resolution on Single Relation

ABSTRACT

A basic work of entity resolution is to detect duplicate records in single relation. To address this problem, many different approaches for different areas are proposed. The basic process of entity resolution is attribute similarity computation. Based on the attribute similarity computation methods, many techniques for different areas are proposed to fulfill the process of entity resolution. Rule-based approach is one of the main techniques for entity resolution. To speed up the process of duplicate record detecting, the authors use techniques such as canopy and blocking. In this chapter, the authors focus on the record similarity computation, rule-based approach, similarity threshold computation, and blocking.

INTRODUCTION

This chapter introduces some basic entity resolution methodologies and technics on single relation.

The target of entity resolution is to recognize all the same entities in one or more databases. The result of entity resolution is the sets and representations of different entities. The result can be used in other step of quality management, such as redundant data deduplication, checking errors on data, inconsistent data discovery, conflict Resolution, etc. Entity resolution techniques for single relations could be applied on information integration (Chapter 14) and healthcare information management system (Chapter 17).

Section 1 introduces some basic record similarity computation approaches, including similarity computation methods on attributes and approaches on records, along with some improvement techniques. Section 2 introduces the basic terms and approaches used in rule-based entity resolution. It first introduces matching dependencies and keys, and then gives algorithms for deducing the dependencies and keys. Section 3 introduces how to compute thresholds for the rule-based entity resolution approaches. Section 4 introduces a traditional but efficient technique to speed up the process of duplicate record detection, blocking. It first establishes models for blocking and iterative blocking, and then gives two blocking algorithms.

DOI: 10.4018/978-1-4666-5198-2.ch005

RECORD SIMILARITY COMPUTATION

In this section, we focus on the problem of lexical heterogeneity and explore various techniques for addressing this problem. We introduce basic record matching criteria in section 1.1, and approaches for detecting duplicate record in section 1.2, and two basic and traditional techniques to improve the efficacy of detection are presented in section 1.3.

Establishing Record Matching Criteria

Before we start to detect duplicate record, we should establish record matching criteria. Approaches for computing similarity of two records include character-based, token-based, phonetic and numeric computation.

Character-Based Similarity Computation

Exact Match

The basic way in record matching is the exact matching. For example, if a relation schema contains student ID and student name, we can perform exact matching on the student ID attribute. The data set should be clean enough to perform exact matching, i.e., two tuples are free from data entry errors (e.g., Google versus Googel).

Distance Match

One of the methodologies to compute similarity between character strings is the distance match method. There are different similarity metrics of distance match method; here we cover the following computation methods

Edit Distance

Edit distance, specifically refer to Levenshtein distance, is defined as the smallest number of insertions, deletions, and substitutions required to change one string or tree into another. For example, the Levenshtein distance between "kitten" and "sitting" is 3, since the following three edits change one into the other, and there is no way to do it with fewer than three edits:

Kitten → **s**itten (substitution of "s" for "k")

sitten → sitt**i**n (substitution of "i" for "e")

sittin → sittin**g** (insertion of "g" at the end)

The basic algorithm to compute edit distance between two strings s_1 and s_2 takes $O\left(\left|s_1\right| \cdot \left|s_2\right|\right)$ time complexity. Landau et al. presented an algorithm in $O\left(max\left(\left|s_1\right|, \left|s_2\right|\right) \cdot k\right)$ which can determine whether the edit distance between two strings is less than k.

Keyboard Distance

Keyboard distance is a measure of the physical distance between two keys on a keyboard. For example, 'g' has a distance of 1 from the keys 'r', 't', 'y', 'f', 'h', 'v', 'b', and 'n'. Immediate diagonals (like ''r', 'y', 'v', and 'n') are considered to have a distance of 1 instead of 1.414 to help to prevent horizontal/vertical bias. Knowing each character's cost, we can get the keyboard distance by summing the costs of inserts, deletes and substitutions required to change one string to another.

Affine Gap Distance

The edit distance described above does not work well when it comes to some abbreviated or truncated strings. To address this problem, the affine gap distance introduces two extra edit operations:

open gap and *extend gap*. To make the gap mismatches cost fewer penalties under the edit distance metric; the cost of extending a gap is usually smaller than the cost opening a gap. The algorithm to compute the affine gap distance takes $O\left(a \cdot |s_1| \cdot |s_2|\right)$ time, in which a gap $a \ll min\left(|s_1|, |s_2|\right)$. Bilenko et al. proposed a method of training an edit distance model with affine gaps.

Smith-Waterman Distance

Another extension of edit distance method and affine gap distance method is Smith-Waterman distance metric. It is well known for performing local sequence alignment (i.e., substring matching). The algorithm allows the mismatches at the beginning and the end have fewer costs than the mismatches in the middle of strings. For example, the two strings "Prof. J. R. Smith, University of Calgary" and "J. R. Smith, Prof" can have a short distance between them because the prefixes and the suffixes are ignored. The basic algorithm to compute Smith-Waterman distance is a dynamic programming algorithm, based on the Needleman and Wunsch algorithm. The algorithm requires $O\left(|s_1| \cdot |s_2|\right)$ time and space to compute the distance between the two strings of length $|s_1|$ and $|s_2|$, respectively. There are many improved algorithms in the context of computational biology because the Smith-Waterman distance was proposed for determining similar regions between two nucleotide or protein sequences. A similarity metric proposed by Pinheiro and Sun is to find the best character alignment to make the number of mismatches minimized.

Jaro Distance

Jaro introduced a measure of similarity between two strings, and the distance metric is designed and best suited for short strings such as person names. The higher the Jaro distance for two strings is, the more similar the strings are. The Jaro distance of two strings s_1 and s_2 are defined as follows.

$$Jaro\left(s_1, s_2\right) = \frac{1}{3}\left(\frac{c}{|s_1|} + \frac{c}{|s_2|} + \frac{c - t}{c}\right),$$

where c is the number of matching characters; common are all the characters $s_1[j]$ and $s_2[j]$ for which $s_1[j] = s_2[j]$ and $|i - j| \leq \frac{1}{2}min\left\{|s_1|, |s_2|\right\}$. t is half the number of transpositions; the number is computed as follows: each nonmatching character is a transpositions after comparing the common ith charater in s_1 with ith common character in s_2.

From the definition above we can see that the algorithm takes $O\left(|s_1| \cdot |s_2|\right)$ time because the computation of c, the matching characters in the two strings.

Q-Grams

The *q-grams* are short character substring of length q of the database string. We use the q-grams because when two string s_1 and s_2 are similar, they share a large number of q-grams in common. One natural extension of q-grams is the positional q-grams which also record the position of the q-gram in the string. Given a string s, we can compute the q-gram by sliding a window of length q over the string s.

Token-Based Similarity Computation

To address the problem of computing similarity of strings whose words are rearranged, some token-based metrics are proposed.

Atomic Strings

An atomic string is a sequence of alphanumeric characters delimited by punctuation characters. We say two strings match if they are equal or one of them is the prefix of the other. So the similarity of two strings is number of their matching atomic strings divided by the number of the two strings average number of atomic strings.

Cosine Similarity Matches

This metrics match criteria independent from word ordering in two strings. Respectively, the similarity is defined as the sum of matching words between the two strings. Gravano et. al. (2003) suggested that this method is not limited to compute the similarity of strings consisting of component words, it can also compare any strings by its substrings.

Phonetic Similarity Computation

The character-based and token-based metrics both focus on the string-based representation of the database records. Some strings are not very similar in a character or token level, However, they may be similar phonetically similar. To address this problem, some phonetic similarity computation methods were proposed.

Soundex

Invented by Russel, soundex, is the most common phonetic coding scheme. The goal is for homophones to be encoded to the same representation so that they can be matched despite minor differences in spelling. The algorithm mainly encodes consonant and is mainly used to match surnames.

The rules of Soundex coding are as follows:

1. Retain the first letter of the name and drop all other occurrences of a, e, i, o, u, y, h, w.

2. Replace consonants with digits as follows (after the first letter):

b, f, p, v → 1

c, g, j, k, q, s, x, z → 2

d, t → 3

l → 4

m, n → 5

r → 6

3. Consolidate the sequences of similar codes by keeping only the first character of the code.
4. Keep the first letter and the three first numbers; if there are fewer than three codes, concatenate zeros to the back of the code.

For example, using this algorithm, both "Robert" and "Rupert" return the same string "R163" while "Rubin" yields "R150".

The code of Soundex is designed for Caucasian surnames, but it works well for names of different origins. However, when it comes to the East Asian names, the result of the code is not satisfying, because the vowel sounds occurs so frequently that the algorithm ignores them.

Numeric Similarity Computation

Compared to methodologies described above, methods for numeric similarity computation are rather primitive. Traditionally, we treat the numbers as strings to perform the methods above or simple range queries. As a future research direction, suggested by Koudas et al., technics such as cosine similarity for numeric data can be extended to work well for entity resolution.

Detecting Duplicate Record

In the previous section, we introduced some methods to compute the similarity between individual fields of a record. In the real world, the tuples always consists of multiple fields, which makes the entity resolution problem more complicated and difficult. In this section, we introduce some technics based on the previous methods to address this problem.

SYMBOLS NOTATION

In this section, we define the following symbols to describe the problems and the methods.

We use R_1 and R_2 etc. to denote the schema of the relations, in which R_1 and R_2 have n comparable fields. We use the lowercase letters such as t to denote the tuples of a specified schema. The M and N refer to the set of tuple pairs that *matches* and *not matches*. For example, if the tuple pair t_1, t_2 matches under some particular method, t_1, t_2 will be assigned to the set M; otherwise, t_1, t_2 will be assigned to the set N.

We use the vector $\underline{v} = \left(v_1, v_2, \cdots, v_n \right)$ to represent the n comparable fields of the two tuples t_1 and t_2. The value of each v_k can be both real value and binary value, which represent the similarity of the specific filed v_k between the two tuples. Many approaches tend to use binary values.

Probabilistic Record Matching Methods

Newcombe et al. recognize the record duplicate detection problem as a Bayesian inference problem first, which means we can address this problem with probabilistic methods. After Newcombe, Fellegi and Sunter proved the intuition and propose the notation we defined before.

The vector $\underline{v} = \left(v_1, v_2, \cdots, v_n \right)$ is the input to an decision algorithm that assigns t_1, t_2 to M or N. The assumption is that $\vec{v}$ is a random vector whose probability density function is different for M and N. If the probability density function is already known, the record matching problem then becomes a Bayesian inference problem. In the following section, we will introduce some methods to address the problem.

The Bayes Decision Rule for Minimum Error

The goal of duplicate detection is to assign the tuple pair to a specific set, M or N. We describe the simplest rules to accomplish this job as follows:

$$t_1, t_2 \in \begin{cases} M, \; p\left(M \mid \underline{v} \right) \geq p\left(N \mid \underline{v} \right) \\ N, \; otherwise \end{cases}$$

The rule indicates that if the probability of the match set M is larger than the probability of the not match set N, then the tuple pair is assigned to M, and vice versa. Using the Bayes' theorem, we can change the rule to the following form:

$$t_1, t_2 \in \begin{cases} M, \; if \, l\left(\underline{v} \right) = \dfrac{p\left(\underline{v} \mid M \right)}{p\left(\underline{v} \mid N \right)} \geq \dfrac{p\left(N \right)}{p\left(M \right)} \\ N, \; otherwise \end{cases}$$

$$(1)$$

The ratio $l\left(\underline{v} \right) = \dfrac{p\left(\underline{v} \mid M \right)}{p\left(\underline{v} \mid N \right)}$ is called the *likelihood ratio*. The ratio $\dfrac{p\left(N \right)}{p\left(M \right)}$ is a threshold denotes that if $l\left(\underline{v} \right)$ is larger than it, the tuple pair t_1, t_2 is assigned to M, and vice versa. We call the decision function (1) as the *Bayes' test for minimum error*. It is easy to prove that the Bayes' test results in the smallest probability of errors, which means the decision rule is an optimal classifier. However, the prerequisite is that the distribution of $p(\underline{v} \mid M)$, $p(\underline{v} \mid N)$, $p(N)$ and $p(M)$ are already known, which, unfortunately is nearly impossible.

One of the methods to address this problem is called Naive Bayes Classifier. The method make a condition independence assumption that the probabilities of $p(v_i \mid M)$ and $p(v_j \mid M)$ are independent where $i \neq j$, similar to $p(v_i \mid N)$ and $p(v_j \mid N)$. From the assumption, we can get:

$$p(\underline{v} \mid M) = \prod_{i=1}^{n} p(v_i \mid M)$$

$$p(\underline{v} \mid N) = \prod_{i=1}^{n} p(v_i \mid N)$$

We can use some pre-labeled records to helping training compute the value of $p(v_i \mid M)$ and $p(v_i \mid N)$. However, the probabilistic model can work well without training data set. Jaro suggested using *expectation maximization* (EM) algorithm to compute probability $p(v_i = 1 \mid M)$ and taking random tuple pairs to estimate the probability $p(v_i = 1 \mid N)$, and the v_i is binary value.

Winkler proposed an algorithm called *general expectation maximization* algorithm to estimate $p(\underline{v} \mid M)$ and $p(\underline{v} \mid N)$ when the assumption, conditional independent, is not reasonable.

Decision with a Reject Region

We can get optimal results using the Bayes' Decision rule when we know the parameters. In fact, the likelihood ratio $l(\underline{v}) = \dfrac{p(\underline{v} \mid M)}{p(\underline{v} \mid N)}$ is close to

the threshold, the error of any decision is very high. To address this problem, Fellegi and Sunter suggested adding an extra class, "reject" in addition to *M* and *N*. The reject class means that if one tuple pair t_1, t_2 assigned to this class, the decision rule cannot make a definite decision. The tuple pairs in the *reject region* are usually examined by experts to decide whether they belong to *M* or *N*. We can define the *reject region* and *reject probability* by setting thresholds for the conditional error on *M* and *N* to express the probability of need to be review by the experts.

Since we define the reject region and reject probability, we can extend this method to a larger number of decision areas which can make the decision rules more accurate. But the problem of the generalization is that how to set the thresholds to make sure no region disappears.

Rule-Based Record Matching Methods

Rule-based record matching methods can be seen as a kind of distance-based techniques, where the distance between two tuples is either 0 or 1. Wang and Madnick propose to use the rules developed by experts to derive a set of fields as "key", which can be used to detect the duplicate records. For example, the rules developed by experts may be as follows:

If*age < 17*

Then*status = minor*

Else*status = adult*

If the experts can develop rules like above, we can use the derived key to cluster the multiple records which represent the same entity in the real world. The rules should not be heuristically developed but should reflect the absolute truths and server as *functional dependencies*.

Hernandez and Stolfo developed the above idea and proposed an equational theory which dictates the logic of domain equivalence. The theory specifies the method about the similarity of records. For example, if two students have similar name and the same student ID, we can infer that they are the same student. The following example shows one of the axioms of the equational theory derived for a student database:

For all tuple pairs t_1, t_2 in STUDENT

If $t_1.name$ is similar to $t_2.name$

AND

$t_1.ID = t_2.ID$

Then

t_1 matches t_2

In the above example, the "similar to" is defined by one or some of the techniques introduced in the previous section; the "matches" means that the tuple pair t_1, t_2 belongs to the "Matches" set M, and the two students t_1 and t_2 refer to the same real-world entity.

The rule-bases approaches need human experts to develop matching rules, so the results in these systems usually have high accuracy. However, these rule-based approaches require extremely high human efforts and make it hard to promote. Fortunately, we can develop a system that can generate rules from a trained data set and manually adjust the automatically generated rules later.

We will discuss rule-based entity matching approaches in depth in Section 2.

IMPROVEMENT OF THE DETECTING TECHNICS ON EFFICACY AND THE APPLICATIONS

In section 1 and section 2, we have discussed the record matching criteria and methods, the criteria and method mainly focus on the accuracy and the quality of entity resolution problems other than the efficiency of the duplicate records detection. In this section, we turn to focus on the efficiency of entity resolution approaches and introduce some techniques to improve the speed of duplicate record matching.

To compare each pair of tuples, we need to execute a "nested-loop" on database A and B, which means we compare each record of A with each record B. Obviously, the "nested-loop" needs $|A| \cdot |B|$ comparisons. The cost in not acceptable because even the size of both table are moderate, we still need expensive time to finish the comparison.

The cost required for a single comparison is another factor that increase the total cost. Suppose we have two strings s_1 and s_2, and use edit distance to compute the similarity, we will need $O\left(|s_1| \cdot |s_2|\right)$ time.

To reduce time complexity, we present some useful techniques to reduce the number of comparisons and the cost of record comparison.

Reducing the Number of Comparisons

The basic force method needs the greatest running time because each tuple in a relation is compared to every other tuple. We have some more efficient methods to address the problem:

- Canopy / Sliding Window
- Blocking
- Hierarchical
- Bucketing

Canopy / Sliding Window

If t_1 is similar to t_2, and t_2 is similar to t_3, then t_1 is similar to t_3, which means the relation "similar to" is *transitive*. Monge and Elkan proposed an approach to improve the performance of force method by assuming that duplicate record detection is *transitive*.

Based on the above assumption, we can treat entity resolution problem in a database as detecting connected components in an undirected graph. We use the term "transitive closure" to describe the set of record matches tuples. To improve the efficiency, we can use the data structure Disjoint-set to implement the union step. In the union step, we merge the duplicate records into a cluster and select or synthesize a representative record of the cluster.

The main technique we use here to reduce the number of comparisons is that, if a tuple t is not similar to one of the tuples in a cluster, and then t will not match any tuple in the cluster according to the transitive property.

McCallum et al. proposed to use canopies to speed up the process of duplicate record detection. The idea is to use some metric to group the records into *overlapping* canopies. The strategy is different from blocking, we will discuss it later. After grouping the records, we use the basic force method to compare each pair in each canopy.

Blocking

Blocking is one of the traditional techniques to speed up the comparison process. Before we introduce blocking, we will introduce a term, *bucket*. The basic idea is to apply a *hash function* to each tuple in the table, and the hash value will determine the "bucket" that the tuple will be assigned in. If two tuples are assigned to the same bucket, we say the two tuples are similar. Therefore, we only need to compare the tuples which are assigned to the same bucket. The problem is that there is no guarantee that the hash value of two tuples will be the same. However, blocking is some kind of bucketing to address this problem.

Utilizing the hash function to speed up the entity resolution process, blocking refers to the process of subdividing the table into a set of mutually exclusive subsets, under the assumption that tuples from different blocks do not match. We can use the approaches such as Soundex to form the blocks.

One of the shortcomings of blocking is that the false mismatches rate and missed matches rate. One of the approaches to address this problem is to run the duplication detection algorithm multiple runs using different fields for blocking. We will discuss blocking in depth in Section 4.

Reducing the Cost of Record Comparisons

Another kind of approaches that can speed up the process of entity resolution is to reduce the cost of single record comparison.

First, we can terminate the process of a single comparison. For example, when comparing some fields of two tuples, it may be obvious that the pair of tuples does not match. Then we can terminate the comparison process to save time, and vice versa. The assumption is that when we terminate the process, we are sure enough the remaining fields cannot reverse the current situation that the pair matches or not matches.

Second, we can develop some algorithms to reduce the dimension of the input tables, such as a subset selection algorithm to reduce the number of fields to be compared.

Last but not the least, we can use some techniques to prune the decision trees that are used to decide two tuples matches or not.

Rule-Based Entity Resolution on Relation

In the previous section, we introduced some basic record resolution methods. In this section, we will discuss a special technique, rule-based entity resolution approach (Fan, Jia, Li & Ma 2009).

No matter what method to use, we often need to select some fields to compare and consider how to compare these fields. Real life data is usually dirty, and may not have a uniform representation in different database for the same entity. To address this problem, we can use domain knowledge to select the attributes or deduce attributes by analyzing the semantic of data. For example, we have two tables as following:

Customer (ID, FN, LN, addr, tel, email, gender, type)

Due to errors in the database, two different tuples may refer to the same customer. To detect to duplication, we can develop a rule as following. Give two tuples t_1 and t_2, if $t_1[ID] = t_2[ID]$, we say $t_1[Y]$ and $t_2[Y]$ refer to the same customer, where Y is the attribute list: $Y = [FN, LN, addr, tel, email, gender]$. Due to errors of the data source, $t_1[Y]$ and $t_2[Y]$ may not match even if $t_1[ID] = t_2[ID]$. However, domain knowledge suggest that we can only compare FN, LN, addr when comparing $t_1[Y]$ and $t_2[Y]$, which means if two tuples have the similar first name, same last name and address, we treat them as the same entity in the real world. In this process, we use the three attributes, FN, LN, addr as a "key".

In this section, we first introduce the matching dependencies and keys as basics, and then give the algorithms for deducing matching dependencies and compute the "keys" called relative candidate key.

MATCHING DEPENDENCIES AND KEYS

Matching Dependencies

Before we define matching dependencies, we define similarity operators and comparable list first.

We use the similarity operators to describe the similarity relation between two tuples. One of the operators is $\approx$, the operator describe the similarity between two tuple using some specific similarity metric, such as edit distance. So $x \approx y$ is true if x and y are similar enough *w.r.t* a predefined threshold. The $\approx$ operator has two basic properties, reflexive and symmetric. Except the equality relation, $\approx$ is not transitive in general. The $=$ is reflexive, symmetric and transitive.

We denote the length of X by $|X|$, and the i-th element of X by $X[i]$, where X is a list of attributes in a schema R. If two attribute lists have the same length and their elements are pairwise comparable, we say they are comparable.

A *matching dependency* (MD) φ for two schemas R_1 and R_2 is defined as follows:

$$\bigwedge_{j=1}^{|X_1|} \left(R_1[X_1[j]] \approx_j R_2[X_2[j]] \right)$$
$$\rightarrow R_1[Z_1] \rightleftharpoons R_2[Z_2]$$

In the definition the lists X_1 and X_2 are comparable, so the length of them is equal; the similarity operators $\approx_j$ can be $\approx$. or $=$. And we define the left part $\bigwedge_{j=1}^{|X_1|} \left(R_1[X_1[j]] \approx_j R_2[X_2[j]] \right)$. as LHS and the right part $R_1[Z_1] \rightleftharpoons R_2[Z_2]$ as RHS of MD φ. φ states that if $R_1[X_1]$ and $R_2[X_2]$ are similar, then compare $R_1[Z_1]$ and $R_2[Z_2]$. For example, in the schema Customer, we can express the duplicate detection pross into an MD, as follows:

$$\varphi_1 : \text{customer}\big[ID\big] = \text{customer}\big[ID\big]$$
$$\rightarrow \text{customer}\big[Y\big] \rightleftharpoons \text{customer}\big[Y\big] \, .$$

The MD states that for any two tuples in customer, if they have the same ID, then identify the attribute list Y.

Dynamic Semantics

First we recall the functional dependencies. A functional dependency (FD) $A \rightarrow B$ indicates that for any tuples t_1 and t_2, if $t_1\big[A\big] = t_2\big[A\big]$, then $t_1\big[B\big] = t_2\big[B\big]$. However, the real world data contains errors, even if if $t_1\big[A\big] = t_2\big[A\big]$, it is possible that $t_1\big[B\big] \neq t_2\big[B\big]$. To accommodate the unreliable data, we use the semantic of MDs.

Then we extend an instance of a schema by some kind of copy. For schema instance I and I', we write $I \sqsubseteq I'$ if for each tuple in I, there exists an corresponding tuple in I'. For instances pairs $D = \big(I_1, I_2\big)$ and $D' = \big(I_1', I_2'\big)$, we can write $D \sqsubseteq D'$ if $I_1 \sqsubseteq I_1'$ and $I_2 \sqsubseteq I_2'$. Now we give the semantic. A pair $\big(D, D'\big)$ is an instance pair of schema $\big(R, R'\big)$ and $D \sqsubseteq D'$. We denote $\big(D, D'\big) \vDash \varphi$ if for any tuples $\big(t_1, t_2\big) \in D$ match the LHS of φ, then in the other instance D', $\big(t_1', t_2'\big) \in D'$ also match the LHS of φ and $t_1'\big[Z_1\big] = t_2'\big[Z_2\big]$.

We can conclude that matching dependencies are different from traditional dependencies:

1. MDs have the ability to accommodate the errors and different representations by using the dynamic semantics.
2. MDs are defined by similarity operators based on similarity metrics, while FDs are defined only by equality.

Example 2.1:

Consider a FD defined on the schema $R(A,B)$:

$$f : A \rightarrow B$$

and a MD defined on R:

$$\varphi : R\big[A\big] = R\big[A\big] \rightarrow R\big[B\big] \rightleftharpoons R\big[B\big]$$

and the instance I of R is as shown in Table 1.

When we use the FD, we can find that the two tuples violate the FD because the values of attribute A are same, but the values of attribute B are different.

In contrast, we consider the MD on R. The MD states that for any instance $\big(I, I'\big)$ of $\big(R, R\big)$ and any tuple pair $\big(t_1, t_2\big)$ in the instance, if $t_1\big[A\big] = t_2\big[A\big]$, then identify $t_1\big[B\big]$ and $t_2\big[B\big]$. For the instance, $\big(t_1, t_2\big)$ does not violate the MD because we update the data by extending the instance to I_1 shown in Table 2.

In I_1, $t_1\big[B\big]$ and $t_2\big[B\big]$ are updated to b. That is how MDs accommodate the errors.

Table 1.

A	B
a	b1
a	b2

Table 2.

A	B
a	b
a	b

A pair (D, D') of instances satisfy a set Σ of MDs, if (D, D') satisfies each MD of Σ, denoted by $(D, D') \vDash \Sigma$.

Relative Candidate Keys

We define a special case MDs as keys to determine whether two tuples refer to the same entity or not. A key E relative to attribute lists (Z_1, Z_2) of schemas (R_1, R_2) is an MD

$$
\bigwedge_{j=1}^{|X_1|} \left(R_1 \left[X_1 [j] \right] \approx_j R_2 \left[X_2 [j] \right] \right) \\
\rightarrow R_1 \left[Z_1 \right] \rightleftharpoons R_2 \left[Z_2 \right]
$$

that the RHS is fixed to be (Z_1, Z_2). We write the key E as $(Z_1, Z_2 \| C)$, where C is the similarity operators $[\approx_1, \cdots, \approx_k]$.

The key assures that to identify $t_1 [Z_1]$ and $t_2 [Z_2]$, we can just identify $t_1 [X_1]$ and $t_2 [X_2]$. The key E is a relative candidate key (RCK) when (1) there is no other key É' that the length of attribute list in the LHS of É' is shorter than E , and (2) each element of LSH of É' is included in the LHS of E .

There are three differences between RCKs and traditional keys. First, we use domain-specific similarity operators to define the RCKs. Second, although we can use RCKs in single relation, in general, RCKs can be used across different relations; in contrast, traditional keys are only used in single relation. Third, RCKs can accommodate data errors by using dynamic semantics.

Deducing Matching Dependencies

A Generic Deducing Mechanism

An instance D of (R_1, R_2) is said to be stable for a set Σ of MDs if $(D, D') \vDash \Sigma$. For example, the instance I_1 in Example 2.1 is stable for the set $\{\varphi\}$, because it is an ultimate outcome of the MD set.

For a set Σ of MDs and a MD φ on (R_1, R_2) not in Σ, we say φ is deduced from Σ, denoted by $\Sigma \vDash_m \varphi$, if for any instance D of (R_1, R_2), and for each stable instance D' for Σ, if $(D, D') \vDash \varphi$. In other words, φ is a logical consequence of MDs in set Σ.

Inference of Matching Dependencies

Armstrong's Axiom is useful in implication analysis of FDs. Along the same line; we give an inference system for MDs which is sound and complete. The system consists of 11 axioms; we present the first four axioms in Table 3.

Algorithm for Deduction Analysis

We give an algorithm that accepts a set Σ of MDs and another MD φ as input and determines whether $\Sigma \vDash_m \varphi$ or not in $O(n^3 + h^3)$ time, where n is the size of Σ and φ, h is the total number of distinct attributes appearing in Σ or φ.

Algorithm *MDClosure* (Table 4) computes the closure Σ and $LHS(\varphi)$ using M, and concludes that $\Sigma \vDash_m \varphi$ if and only if $M\left(R_1 [C_1], R_2 [C_2], = \right)$ is 1. By Lemma 2.2, we can set $M\left(R_1 [C_1], R_2 [C_2], = \right) = 1$ if and only if $R_1 [C_1] \rightleftharpoons R_2 [C_2]$ is deduced from Σ and $LHS(\varphi)$.

Procedure AssignVal (Table 5) takes a similar pair $R[A] \approx R'[B]$ as input and checks whether ornot $M\left(R[A], R'[B], \approx\right)$ or $M\left(R[A], R'[B], =\right)$ is already set to 1. If not, set $M\left(R[A], R'[B], \approx\right)$ and $M\left(R'[B], R[A], \approx\right)$ to 1.

Table 3. First four axioms

Lemma 2.1: For any MD φ, any comparable attribute (A, B) over (R_1, R_2), and similarity operator $\approx$, the following MDs can be deuced from MD φ:

$$\left(LHS(\varphi) \wedge R_1[A] \approx R_2[B]\right) \rightarrow RHS(\varphi) \text{ and}$$

$$\left(LHS(\varphi) \wedge R_1[A] = R_2[B]\right) \rightarrow \left(RHS(\varphi) \wedge R_1[A] \rightleftharpoons R_2[B]\right)$$

To present to transitivity of MDs, we first show:

Lemma 2.2: Let $L = \wedge_{i \in [1,k]} \left(R_1\left[X_1[i]\right] \approx_i R_2\left[X_2[i]\right]\right)$

1. *For any MD* $\varphi = L \rightarrow R_1[Z_1] \rightleftharpoons R_2[Z_2]$, any instances $(D.D') \vDash \varphi$, and any $(t, t') \in (D, D')$, if (t, t') match $LHS(\varphi)$ in D, then $t[Z_1] = t'[Z_2]$ in D'.

2. *For any similarity operator* $\approx$, *from MD* $\left(L \wedge R_1[A] \approx R_2[B]\right) \rightarrow R_1[Z_1] \rightleftharpoons R_2[Z_2]$, the following MD can be deduced: $\left(L \wedge R_1[A] = R_2[B]\right) \rightarrow R_1[Z_1] \rightleftharpoons R_2[Z_2]$.

Lemma 2.3: For MDs φ_1, φ_2 and φ_3 given as follows:

$$\varphi_1 = \wedge_{i \in [1,k]} \left(R_1\left[X_1[i]\right] \approx_i R_2\left[X_2[i]\right]\right) \rightarrow R_1[W_1] \rightleftharpoons R_2[W_2],$$

$$\varphi_2 = \wedge_{i \in [1,k]} \left(R_1\left[W_1[j]\right] \approx_j R_2\left[W_2[j]\right]\right) \rightarrow R_1[Z_1] \rightleftharpoons R_2[Z_2],$$

$$\varphi_3 = \wedge_{i \in [1,k]} \left(R_1\left[X_1[i]\right] \approx_i R_2\left[X_2[i]\right]\right) \rightarrow R_1[Z_1] \rightleftharpoons R_2[Z_2],$$

$\Sigma \vDash_m \varphi_3$, where $\pounds$ consists of φ_1, φ_2, and $l = |W_1| = |W_2|$.

Lemma 2.4: Let L be $\wedge_{i \in [1,k]} \left(R_1\left[X_1[i]\right] \approx_i R_2\left[X_2[i]\right]\right), (D, D')$ be any instances of (R_1, R_2), and $(t, t') \in (D, D')$. Then:

1. *if* $\varphi = L \rightarrow R_1[A_1, A_2] \rightleftharpoons R_2[B, B], (D, D') \vDash \varphi$, and if (t, t') match $LHS(\varphi)$, then $t[A_1] = t[A_2]$ in D'; if in addition, $(D, D') \in \varphi'$, where $\varphi' = L \rightarrow R_1[A_1] \rightleftharpoons R_2[C]$, then $t[A_2] = t'[C]$ in D';

2. *if* $\varphi = \left(L \wedge R_1[A_1] \approx R_2[B]\right) \rightarrow R_1[A_2] \rightleftharpoons R_2[B], (D, D') \vDash \varphi$, and if (t, t') match $LHS(\varphi)$ in D, then $t[A_2] \approx t[A_1]$ in D'.

Procedure *Propagate* (Table 6) takes a newly deduced similar pair $R[A] \approx R'[B]$ as input and updates M. Procedure *Infer* (Table 7) takes queue Q, array M, a new similar pair $R[A] \approx R'[B]$ and relation R'' as input. The procedure infers other similar pairs and push them into Q, and then invokes AssignVal to update M.

Table 4. Algorithm MDClosure

Input: a set Σ of MDs and another MD φ, where $LHS\left(\varphi\right) = \wedge_{i=1}^{|X_1|}\left(R_1\left[X_1\left[i\right]\right] \approx_i R_2\left[X_2\left[i\right]\right]\right)$	
Output: The closure of Σ and $\mathrm{LHS}\left(\varphi\right)$, stored in array M.	
1.	initialize array M with 0
2.	**for** each $i \in \left[1, |X_1|\right]$ **do**
3.	**if** AssignVal $\left(M, R_1\left[X_1\left[i\right]\right], R_2\left[X_2\left[i\right]\right], \approx_i\right)$
4.	**then** Propagate $\left(M, R_1\left[X_1\left[i\right]\right], R_2\left[X_2\left[i\right]\right], \approx_i\right)$
5.	**repeat** until no further changes
6.	**for each** MD ϕ in Σ **do**
7.	**if** there is $d \in \left[1, \mathrm{m}\right]$ such that $M(R_1\left[U_1\left[d\right]\right], R_2\left[U_2\left[d\right]\right], =) = 0$ and $M(R_1\left[U_1\left[d\right]\right], R_2\left[U_2\left[d\right]\right], \approx_d) = 0$ $\left(1 \le d \le m\right)$
8.	**then continue;**
9.	**else** $\Sigma := \Sigma \setminus \left\{\phi\right\}$;
10.	**if** AssignVal $\left(M, R_1\left[A\right], R_2\left[B\right], =\right)$
11.	**then** Propagate $\left(M, R_1\left[A\right], R_2\left[B\right], =\right)$;
12.	**return** M;

Computing Relative Candidate Keys

We have mentioned that to raise the accuracy rate, we can compare different fields for several times. To achieve this goal, we need to select the fields to compare using different keys. To address this problem, we need to compute RCKs: given a set £ of MDs, a natural number m and a pair of comparable attribute lists $\left(Y_1, Y_2\right)$, to deduce a set of m MDs relative to $\left(Y_1, Y_2\right)$. To deduce the set, we need to decide what metrics to use, and how to find m MDs using the metrics. We first propose a model to assess the quality of the RCKs, and then propose the algorithm to deduce the RCKs.

Quality Model

We define the quality of RCK based on the following two properties:

1. The diversity of RCKs in Γ. Since we want Γ to include diverse attributes so that if

Table 5. Procedure AssignVal $\left(M, R[A], R'[B], \approx\right)$

Input: Array M with new similar pair $R[A] \approx R'[B]$	
Output: Updated M, return true if M is updated and false otherwise	
1.	**if** $M\left(R[A], R'[B], =\right) = 0$ **and** $M\left(R[A], R'[B], \approx\right) = 0$
2.	**then** $M\left(R[A], R'[B], \approx\right) := 1$; $M\left(R'[B], R[A], \approx\right) := 1$
3.	**return** true;
4.	**else return** false;

some attributes contain errors we can still find match pairs by comparing other attributes, we do not want the RCKs to be defined by those pairs that appear frequently in RCKs already in Γ. To achieve this goal, we can maintain a counter $ct\left(R_1[A], R_2[B]\right)$ for each pair. When we add an RCK with pair $\left(R_1[A], R_2[B]\right)$ to Γ, then we increase the counter of the pair.

2. Statistics. Suppose the accuracy of each attribute pair is given as $ac\left(R_1[A], R_2[B]\right)$, and average lengths $lt\left(R_1[A], R_2[B]\right)$. The longer the lt, the more likely errors occur in the attribute; the higher the ac, the more reliable the attribute pair is.

The cost of including attributes $\left(R_1[A], R_2[B]\right)$ in an RCK is defines as:

$$
\begin{aligned}
&cost\left(R_1[A], R_2[B]\right) \\
&= w_1 \cdot ct\left(R_1[A], R_2[B]\right) \\
&+ w_2 \cdot lt\left(R_1[A], R_2[B]\right) \\
&+ w_3 / ac\left(R_1[A], R_2[B]\right)
\end{aligned},
$$

where w_1, w_2 and w_3 are weights assigned to the factors. We say a RCK has high quality if it has low cost.

Algorithm for Finding RCKs

The algorithm takes number m, a set Σ of MDs, and pairwise comparable lists $\left(Y_1, Y_2\right)$ as input, and returns a set Γ of at most m RCKs. The algorithm selects RCKs with high quality in $O\left(m(l+n)^3\right)$ time, where l is the length $|Y_1|$ $\left(|Y_2|\right)$, and n is the size of Σ. Usually, the m is a predefined constant and the algorithm is in cubic-time.

The procedure minimize is described in Table 9. Procedure incrementCt takes a set S of attribute pairs and an RCK γ as input, and increases $ct\left(R_1[A], R_2[B]\right)$ by 1. Procedure sortMD sorts MDs in a list L_Σ in ascending order based on the sum of the costs the *LHS* attributes. The Algorithm findRCKs is described in Table 8.

Table 6. Procedure Propagate $\left(M, R_1\left[A\right], R_2\left[B\right], \approx\right)$

Input: Array M with updated similar pair $R_1\left[A\right] \approx R_2\left[B\right]$	
Output: Updated M to include similarity change propagation	
1.	$Q.\text{push}(M, R_1\left[A\right], R_2\left[B\right], \approx)$;
2.	**while**(Q is not empty) do
3.	$\left(R\left[C\right], R^{\prime\left[C^{\prime}\right]}, \approx_d\right) := Q.pop()$;
4.	**case** $\left(R, R^{\prime}\right)$ of
5.	**(1)** $R = R_1$ and $R^{\prime} = R_2$
6.	Infer $\left(Q, M, R_2\left[C^{\prime}\right], R_1\left[C\right], R_1, \approx_d\right)$;
7.	Infer $\left(Q, M, R_1\left[C\right], R_2\left[C^{\prime}\right], R_2, \approx_d\right)$;
8.	**(2)** $R = R^{\prime} = R_1$
9.	Infer $\left(Q, M, R_1\left[C\right], R_1\left[C^{\prime}\right], R_2, \approx_d\right)$;
10.	Infer $\left(Q, M, R_1\left[C^{\prime}\right], R_1\left[C\right], R_2, \approx_d\right)$;
11.	**(3)** $R = R^{\prime} = R_2$
12.	Infer $\left(Q, M, R_2\left[C\right], R_2\left[C^{\prime}\right], R_1, \approx_d\right)$;
13.	Infer $\left(Q, M, R_2\left[C^{\prime}\right], R_2\left[C\right], R_1, \approx_d\right)$;

SIMILARITY THRESHOLD COMPUTATION

In the previous section, we have discussed the rule-based entity resolution approaches. We defined similarity operators $(\approx)$, however, we did not define the specific similarity metrics and thresholds. In this section, we will introduce a method to address the following problem: given a dataset, a set of record matching rules and similarity functions, we want to identify the best thresholds for detecting the duplicate tuples in the table effectively.

In this section, (1) we first formulize the problem we meet. (2) We introduce the method to generate finite thresholds from infinite thresh-

Table 7. Procedure Infer $\left(Q, M, R[A], R'[B], R'', \approx\right)$

Input: Queue *Q*, array *M*, newly updated similar pair $R[A] \approx R'[B]$, and relation name R''.	
Output: New similar pairs stored in *Q* and updated *M*.	
1.	**for each** attribute C of R'' **do**
2.	**if** $M\left(R[A], R''[C], \rightleftharpoons\right) = 1$
3.	**then if** AssignVal $\left(M, R'[B], R''[C], \approx\right)$
4.	**then** Q.push $\left(R'[B], R''[C], \approx\right)$;
5.	**if** $\approx$ *is* $=$
6.	**then for each** similarity operator $\approx_d \left(1 \le d \le p\right)$ **do**
7.	**if** $M\left(R[A], R''[C], \approx_d\right) = 1$ **and** AssignVal $\left(M, R'[B], R''[C], \approx_d\right)$
8.	**then** Q.push $\left(R'[B], R''[C], \approx_d\right)$;

olds. (3) We introduce the method to eliminate the thresholds redundancy. The techniques of this section mainly are from Wang, Li, Yu & Feng (2011).

Problem Formulation

Given a database schema $R[a_1, a_2, \cdots, a_n]$, t is a tuple in R and $t[a_i]$ is the value of the attribute a_i in tuple t. Given a similarity function f, two tuples t and t', the function computes a similarity score $f\left(t[a_i], t'[a_i]\right)$ in $[0,1]$. In this section, the larger score indicates that $t[a_i]$ and $t'[a_i]$ is more similar. For example, see Table 10.

We consider the edit-distance similarity. The edit-distance similarity is defined as $1 - \dfrac{ed\left(s_1, s_2\right)}{\max\left(|s_1|, |s_2|\right)}$, where $ed\left(s_1, s_2\right)$ is the edit-

distance between string s_1 and s_2 as we described in section 1. For example, given $s_1 = $ "Jermey Lee", $s_2 = $ "Jeremy Lee", the edit-distance is 2, the similarity $f_{edit}\left(s_1, s_2\right) = 1 - \dfrac{2}{10} = 0.8$. Intuitively, the two strings are very similar. And q-gram (q=2) similarity $f_g\left(s_1, s_2\right) = \dfrac{6}{11} = 0.55$. In order to decide whether two records refer to the same real-world entity or not, we will give a new definition based on rule-based matching approaches.

Definition: An *explicit attribute-matching rule* (eAR) is such a triple $\lambda^e\left(e, f, \theta\right)$, that a is an attribute name, f is a similarity function and θ is a threshold. If $f\left(t[a], t'[a]\right) \ge \theta$, $t[a]$ and $t'[a]$ are considered to be the same. $t[a]$ and $t'[a]$ satisfying λ^e is denoted by $\left(t[a], t'[a]\right) \vDash \lambda^e$, and

Table 8. Algorithm findRCKs

Input: Number m, a set Σ of MDs, and pairwise comparable lists $\left(Y_1, Y_2\right)$.	
Output: A set Γ of at most m RCKs.	
1.	c:= 0; S:= pairing $\left(\Sigma, Y_1, Y_2\right)$
2.	**let** ct $\left(R_1\left[A\right], R_2\left[B\right]\right)$:=0 for each $\left(R_1\left[A\right], R_2\left[B\right]\right) \in S$
3.	$\gamma := \left(Y_1, Y_2 \;\|\; C\right)$, where $\left|C\right| = \left|Y_1\right|$ and C consists of = only;
4.	$\gamma' := minimize\left(^3, \pounds\right)$; $\Gamma := \left\{\gamma'\right\}$; incrementCt $\left(S, ^{3\prime}\right)$
5.	**for** each RCK $\gamma \in \Gamma$ **do**
6.	$L_\Sigma := sortMD\left(\Sigma\right)$;
7.	**for** each ϕ in L_Σ in the ascending order **do**
8.	$L_\Sigma := L_\Sigma \setminus \left\{\phi\right\}$;
9.	$\gamma' := apply\left(\gamma, \phi\right)$; flag:= true;
10.	**for** each $\gamma_1 \in \Gamma$ **do**
11.	flag:= flag **and** $\left(\gamma_1 \not\preceq \gamma'\right)$
12.	**if** flag **then**
13.	$\gamma' := minimize\left(\gamma', \Sigma\right)$; $\Gamma := \Gamma \bigcup \left\{\gamma'\right\}$;
14.	c:= c + 1; increment ct $\left(S, \gamma'\right)$; $L_\Sigma := sortMD\left(\Sigma\right)$;
15.	**if** c = m **then** return Γ ;
16.	**return** Γ ;

$t\left[a\right]$ and $t'\left[a\right]$ dissatisfying λ^e is denoted by $\left(t\left[a\right], t'\left[a\right]\right) \nvDash \lambda^e$.

From the definition we know that an eAR includes an explicit similarity function and a threshold which can be used to determine whether two tuples refer to the same entity or not. However, it is still hard to determine an appropriate threshold. We usually hope to use a threshold range in the

Table 9. Procedure minimize $\left(\left(X_1, X_2 \parallel C \right), \Sigma \right)$

Input: Relative key $\gamma = \left(X_1, X_2 \parallel C \right)$ and a set Σ of MDs.	
Output: An RCK.	
1.	$L := sort\left(X_1, X_2 \parallel C \right);$
2.	**for** each $V = \left(R_1\left[A\right], R_2\left[B\right] \parallel \approx \right)$ in L in the descending order **do**
3.	**if** $\Sigma \models m\ \gamma \setminus V \cdot / *$ using algorithm MDClosure $* /$
4.	**then** $\gamma := \gamma \setminus V$
5.	**return** γ;

Table 10. Example 3.1

Record	Name	Tel.	Email	Address	Gender
r_1	Jeremy Lee	1234	JerryL	04733	Male
r_2	Jerry Lee	1234-999999	JerryLee@mailbox.com	11111	Female
r_3	Jeremy YYi	1234-888888	JerryY@box.com	12345	Male
r_4	Lee Yi	1234	JerryY@box.com	12345	Male
r_5	Jermey Yi	1234	JerryL	11111	F.
r_6	Jermey Lee	1234	JerryL@mailbox.com	04733	M.
r_7	Jeremy Lee	1234	JerryL@mailbox.com	04733	M.

Positive example set $M : \left\{ RP_{1,6}, RP_{1,7}, RP_{2,5}, RP_{3,4}, RP_{6,7} \right\}$

Negative example set $N : \{ RP_{1,2}, RP_{1,3}, RP_{1,4}, RP_{1,5}, RP_{2,3}, RP_{2,4}, RP_{2,6},$
$RP_{2,7}, RP_{3,5}, RP_{3,6}, RP_{3,7}, RP_{4,5}, RP_{4,6}, RP_{4,7}, RP_{5,6}, RP_{5,7} \}$

record matching rules, and we call such rules as *implicit attribute-matching rules*:

Definition: An *implicit attribute-matching rules* (iAR) is such a triple $\lambda^i\left(e, \mathcal{F}, \Theta\right)$, that a is an attribute name, $\mathcal{F} = \left\{f_1, f_2, \cdots\right\}$ is a set of similarity functions and Θ is a threshold range. If there exists a similarity function f in F and $f\left(t[a], t'[a]\right) \geq \theta$, where θ is lower bound of Θ, then $t[a]$ and $\text{t'}[a]$ are considered to be the same.

From the definitions of eAR and iAR, we can see that eAR $\left(a, f, \theta\right)$ is an instance of the iAR $\left(a, \mathcal{F}, \Theta\right)$ if $f \in \mathcal{F}$ and $\theta \in \Theta$. The property lead us to generate eAR from iAR by enumerating the similarity functions in F and selecting a similarity threshold in Θ. For example, the attribute matching rules we use for example 3.1 are in Table 11.

Based on the definition of eAR and iAR, we give the definition of *record-matching rule* as follows:

Definition: A *record-matching rule* (RR) is a set of eARs or iARs, denoted by $\phi = \wedge_{i=1}^{k} \lambda_i$, where λ_i can be an eAR or iAR. A tuple pair $\left(t, t'\right)$ satisfies the record-matching rule, if $\left(t[a], t'[a]\right)$ satisfies *every* attribute-matching rule λ_i for $1 \leq i \leq k$, denoted by $\left(t, t'\right) \vDash \phi$. A tuple pair $\left(t, t'\right)$ dissatisfying the RR ϕ is denoted by $\left(t, t'\right) \nvDash \phi$.

According to the definitions of eAR and iAR, a record-matching rule (RR) $\phi = \wedge_{i=1}^{k} \lambda_i$ is called *explicit record-matching rule* (eRR) if *every* λ is eAR; otherwise, the RR ϕ is called *implicit record-matching rule* (iRR). For example, figure 3.1 shows 3 iRRs. $\phi_1 = \lambda_1^i \wedge \lambda_2^e$ indicates that if two records have the similar name and the same telephone number, the two records refer to the same person.

In this section, we will talk about eRRs, because eRR is the instance of iRR and can be deduced by some methods such as the schema-based methods. In applications, we suppose that experts can provide a set of examples denoted by E by domain knowledge to help us evaluate the quality of eRR, which includes positive examples denoted by M that records are known referring to the same real-world entity, and negative examples denoted by N that records are known to referring to different entities.

Given a eRR $\psi \in \Psi$, a record pair is generated by ψ if it satisfies ψ, denoted by $\left(t, t'\right) \vDash \psi$.

Table 11. Attribute-matching rules and record-matching rules

(a) ARs	(b) RRs	
$\lambda_1^i : \left(name, \left\{f_e, f_g\right\}, [0,1]\right)$	ϕ_1	$\lambda_1^i \wedge \lambda_2^e$
$\lambda_2^e : \left(tel, =, 1\right)$	ϕ_2	$\lambda_3^e \wedge \lambda_4^i$
$\lambda_3^e : \left(email, =, 1\right)$	ϕ_3	$\lambda_1^i \wedge \lambda_4^i \wedge \lambda_5^e$
$\lambda_4^i : \left(address, \left\{f_e, f_i\right\}, [0,1]\right)$		
$\lambda_5^e : \left(gender, =, 1\right)$		

All the pairs that can be generated by ψ is denoted by $\overline{M_\psi} = \{(t,t') \mid (t,t') \in E, (t,t') \vDash \psi\}$. The set of pairs generate by the eRRs in Ψ is denoted by $\overline{M_\Psi} = \bigcup_{\psi \in \Psi} \overline{M_\psi}$. We hope that $\overline{M_\psi}$ can be equal to M, however, there exists negative record pairs. To evaluate the quality of Ψ, we create a function $F(\Psi, M, D)$: the larger $\left|\overline{M_\psi} \cap M\right|$, the larger $F(\Psi, M, D)$; the smaller $\left|\overline{M_\psi} \cap D\right|$, the smaller $F(\Psi, M, D)$. Since our goal is to find the best similarity function and thresholds, now it turn to find a set of eRRs from Ψ to maximize a pre-defined objected function $F(\Psi, M, D)$.

From Infinite Thresholds to Finite Thresholds

A force method to find the eRR is enumerating all possible eRRs and select one to maximize the function $F(\Psi, M, D)$. However, the problem is that an iAR contains a thresholds range and it is impossible to enumerate the infinite numbers of thresholds. For example in figure 3.1, we can get many eRRs from $\phi_1 = \lambda_1^i \wedge \lambda_2^e$ because there are infinite values in the threshold range. Since we are only interested in the eRRs that can maximize the function, we want to generate finite eRRs that can also maximize the function.

Given iAR $\lambda^i(a, \mathcal{F}, \Theta)$ and its two eAR instances, $\lambda_1^e(a, f, \theta_1)$ and $\lambda_2^e(a, f, \theta_2)$. Suppose $\theta_1 < \theta_2$, it is obvious that the set of records that satisfy λ_2^e is a subset of the set of record that satisfy λ_1^e, denoted by $\overline{M_{\lambda_2^e}} \subseteq \overline{M_{\lambda_1^e}}$. The main idea for selecting finite thresholds from infinite thresholds is that, if there is no positive example in $\overline{M_{\lambda_1^e}} - \overline{M_{\lambda_2^e}}$ for any iRRs that contains λ^i, we will not use the eRRs with λ_1^e since they cannot get a better objective value than the eRRs with

λ_2^e. The idea can be described as the following theorem:

Theorem 3.1: Consider a set of RRs Φ, a set of positive examples M, a set of negative examples N, and an objective function $F(\Psi, M, N)$. Consider an iRR in Φ which contains an iAR $\lambda^i : (a, \mathcal{F}, \Theta)$, and two instances of λ^i, $\lambda_1^e : (a, f, \theta_1)$ and $\lambda_2^e : (a, f, \theta_2)$. Suppose Ψ_1 is an eRR set, Ψ_2 is another eRR set transformed from Ψ_1 by replacing λ_1^e in Ψ_1 with λ_2^e. If $\theta_1 < \theta_2$ and there is no positive examples in $\overline{M_{\lambda_1^e}} - \overline{M_{\lambda_2^e}}$, we have $F(\Psi_1, M, N) \leq F(\Psi_2, M, N)$.

Since we get the theorem, we can see that a lot of eRRs can be pruned since they cannot help improve the value of the objective function. For example in Table 12. The data in Table 12 shows $f_e(t[name], t'[name])$ and $f_g(t[name], t'[name])$ of each record pair (t, t') in E, and the positive examples are marked by grey background. Consider two eARs $\lambda_1^e : (name, f_e, 0.6)$ and $\lambda_2^e : (name, f_e, 0.7)$.

$$\overline{M_{\lambda_1^e}} = \begin{Bmatrix} RP_{1,2}, RP_{1,3}, RP_{1,5}, RP_{1,6}, \\ RP_{1,7}, RP_{2,6}, RP_{2,7}, RP_{3,5}, \\ RP_{3,6}, RP_{3,7}, RP_{5,7}, RP_{6,7} \end{Bmatrix},$$

$$\overline{M_{\lambda_2^e}} = \begin{Bmatrix} RP_{1,2}, RP_{1,3}, RP_{1,5}, RP_{1,6}, \\ RP_{1,7}, RP_{2,6}, RP_{2,7}, RP_{3,5}, \\ RP_{3,7}, RP_{5,7}, RP_{6,7} \end{Bmatrix}.$$

$$\overline{M_{\lambda_1^e}} - \overline{M_{\lambda_2^e}} = \{RP_{3,6}\}.$$

As there is no positive example in $\overline{M_{\lambda_1^e}} - \overline{M_{\lambda_2^e}}$, we can prune λ_1^e.

Based on this idea, we can generate a finite set of eARs and take them as candidate eAR set. We can construct the candidate eAR set from an iAR $\lambda^i : \left(a, \mathcal{F}, \Theta\right)$ as follows: first, add $\lambda^e : f\left(a, f, \theta_{max}\right)$ into $\mathcal{P}\left(\lambda^i\right)$ where θ_{max} is the upper bound of Θ (we choose the upper bound because it is the maximal value so cannot be pruned) for each $f \in \mathcal{F}$; second, if $\theta \in \Theta$ and tuple pair $\left(t, t'\right)$ is a positive example compute $\theta = f\left(t\left[a\right], t'\left[a\right]\right)$, then add $\lambda^e : f\left(a, f, \theta_{max}\right)$ into $\mathcal{P}\left(\lambda^i\right)$. For all other thresholds we can prune them as described in the proposition:

Proposition: Given an iAR $\lambda^i : \left(a, \mathcal{F}, \Theta\right)$ and a set of positive examples M, we can use the candidate eAR set $\mathcal{P}\left(\lambda^i\right)$ to generate the best eRR set.

Example 3.2: We show how the algorithm computes $\mathcal{P}\left(\lambda_1^i\right)$ for $\lambda_1^i : \left(name, \left\{f_e, f_g\right\}, \left[0, 1\right]\right)$.

First, for f_e and f_g we add two eRRs with threshold 1 because 1 is the upper bound. Then we enumerate each pair in the set of positive examples M. We compute similarity between r_1 and r_6, and then get 0.8 for f_e and 0.5 for f_g, then we add $\left(name, f_e, 0.8\right)$ and $\left(name, f_g, 0.5\right)$ to $\mathcal{P}\left(\lambda_1^i\right)$. We enumerate the elements in M and get the result shown in Table 13.

Eliminating Thresholds Redundancy

As we described in Section 3.2, we can generate a set of eARs, however, the size of the set may be quite large. In this part, we will show how to prune the redundant eARs. To address the problem, we first define redundant eARs and show them cannot lead to optimal objective-function value. So we can eliminate the redundancy to reduce the size of candidate eAR set.

Table 12 Similarity for iAR $\lambda_1^i : \left(name, \left\{f_e, f_g\right\}, \left[0, 1\right]\right)$

pairs	f_e	f_g	pairs	f_e	f_g	pairs	f_e	f_g
$RP_{1,2}$	0.8	0.55	$RP_{2,4}$	0.2	0.18	$RP_{3,7}$	0.7	0.5
$RP_{1,3}$	0.7	0.5	$RP_{2,5}$	*0.4*	*0.2*	$RP_{4,5}$	0.22	0.5
$RP_{1,4}$	0.3	0.17	$RP_{2,6}$	0.8	0.55	$RP_{4,6}$	0.5	0.3
$RP_{1,5}$	0.7	0.55	$RP_{2,7}$	0.8	0.55	$RP_{4,7}$	0.22	0.3
$RP_{1,6}$	*0.8*	*0.5*	$RP_{3,4}$	*0.5*	*0.17*	$RP_{5,6}$	0.5	0.21
$RP_{1,7}$	*1*	*1*	$RP_{3,5}$	0.9	0.89	$RP_{5,7}$	0.7	0.55
$RP_{2,3}$	0.44	0.21	$RP_{3,6}$	0.67	0.2	$RP_{6,7}$	*0.78*	*0.5*

Table 13. Candidate eAR set of $\lambda_1^i : \left(name, \left\{ f_e, f_g \right\}, [0,1] \right)$

λ_1^e	$\left(name, f_e, 1 \right)$	λ_6^e	$\left(name, f_g, 1 \right)$
λ_2^e	$\left(name, f_e, 0.8 \right)$	λ_7^e	$\left(name, f_g, 0.5 \right)$
λ_3^e	$\left(name, f_e, 0.78 \right)$	λ_8^e	$\left(name, f_g, 0.2 \right)$
λ_4^e	$\left(name, f_e, 0.5 \right)$	λ_9^e	$\left(name, f_g, 0.17 \right)$
λ_5^e	$\left(name, f_e, 0.4 \right)$		

First, we divide a candidate eAR set $\mathcal{P}\left(\lambda^i \right)$ into $|\mathcal{F}|$ groups, where $|\mathcal{F}|$ is the size of similarity function set. We use $\mathcal{G}_f$ to refer to the group of candidate eARs whose similarity function is f. In one group, we say $\lambda_1^e > \lambda_2^e$ if and only if λ_1^e has a larger threshold than λ_2^e. If λ^e has the maximal (minimal) threshold, it can be called the maximal (minimal) function in the group. For example in Table 12, λ_1^i has two similarity functions f_e and f_g. $\mathcal{P}\left(\lambda^i \right)$ is divided into two groups $\mathcal{G}_{f_e} = \left\{ \lambda_1^e, \lambda_2^e, \lambda_3^e, \lambda_4^e, \lambda_5^e \right\}$ and $\mathcal{G}_{f_g} = \left\{ \lambda_6^e, \lambda_7^e, \lambda_8^e, \lambda_9^e \right\}$. We say $\lambda_3^e > \lambda_4^e$ since the threshold of λ_3^e is larger than that of λ_4^e. However, we cannot say $\lambda_3^e > \lambda_7^e$ because they do not belong to the same group.

We can see that in each group there may exist threshold redundancy. Given an iAR $\lambda^i : \left(a, \mathcal{F}, \Theta \right)$, we define redundancy as follows:

Given two eARs $\lambda_1^e : \left(a, f, \theta_1 \right)$ and $\lambda_2^e : \left(a, f, \theta_2 \right)$ in $\mathcal{P}\left(\lambda^i \right)$, without loss of generality, we suppose $\theta_1 > \theta_2$, and then $\overline{M}_{\lambda_1^e} \subset \overline{M}_{\lambda_2^e}$ (if $\overline{M}_{\lambda_1^e} = \overline{M}_{\lambda_2^e}$, λ_2^e will be moved based on Theorem 3.1). λ_1^e and λ_2^e generate the same record pairs set $\overline{M}_{\lambda_1^e}$, and

λ_2^e can identify more record pairs $\overline{M}_{\lambda_2^e} - \overline{M}_{\lambda_1^e}$. $\overline{M}_{\lambda_2^e} - \overline{M}_{\lambda_1^e} \subseteq M$ means that these pairs are all positive pair examples in M, so λ_2^e is better than λ_1^e. We say λ_1^e is redundant w.r.t λ_2^e. The idea is described in Theorem 3.2.

Theorem 3.2: Given a candidate eΛR set $\mathcal{P}\left(\lambda^i \right)$ and a set M of positive examples, $\lambda_1^e : \left(a, f, \theta_1 \right) \in \mathcal{P}\left(\lambda^i \right)$ is redundant w.r.t $\lambda_2^e : \left(a, f, \theta_2 \right) \in \mathcal{P}\left(\lambda^i \right)$ if $\overline{M}_{\lambda_2^e} - \overline{M}_{\lambda_1^e} \subseteq M$ and $\theta_1 > \theta_2$.

A simple force algorithm for eliminating the redundancy is to enumerate $|\mathcal{F}| \cdot |\mathcal{G}_f|$ candidate eARs and takes $O\left(|\mathcal{G}_f| \cdot |E| \right)$ time to verify each candidate eAR. The algorithm requires $O\left(|\mathcal{F}| \cdot |\mathcal{G}_f|^2 \cdot |E| \right)$ time. We next present another algorithm which can reduce the time complexity to $O\left(|\mathcal{F}| \cdot |K| \cdot |E| \right)$, where $|K| = log\left(|\mathcal{F}| \cdot |\mathcal{G}_f| \right)$.

To reduce time complexity, we use a *compressed inverted index* (*CIX*) to detect threshold redundancy. We first introduce compressed inverted index briefly and then introduce how to detect the threshold redundancy.

An *inverted index* over $\mathcal{P}\left(\lambda^i\right)$ maps each $\lambda^e \in \mathcal{P}\left(\lambda^i\right)$ to a list of record pairs that satisfy λ^e. We can *compress* the inverted list since if $\lambda_1^e > \lambda_2^e$, then $\overline{M}_{\lambda_1^e} \subseteq \overline{M}_{\lambda_2^e}$. Suppose that λ_1^e is the maximal eAR and λ_2^e is the second maximal eAR in $\mathcal{P}\left(\lambda^i\right)$. The compressed inverted list CIX (λ_2^e) of λ_2^e stores the records pairs in $\overline{M}_{\lambda_2^e} - \overline{M}_{\lambda_1^e}$. We can construct the compress inverted index for all the eARs iteratively. This can be demonstrated by the following example in Table 14.

According the Theorem 3.2, we need to check $\overline{M}_{\lambda_2^e} - \overline{M}_{\lambda_1^e} \subseteq M$ for every $\lambda_2^e \in \mathcal{P}\left(\lambda^i\right)$ that is smaller than λ_1^e to verify that whether λ_1^e is redundant. However, we can only check the maximal eAR λ_2^e such that $\lambda_2^e < \lambda_1^e$, since if λ_1^e is not redundant w.r.t λ_2^e, then for any smaller eAR $\lambda_x^e < \lambda_2^e$, we have $\overline{M}_{\lambda_2^e} \subseteq \overline{M}_{\lambda_3^e}$, so $\overline{M}_{\lambda_3^e} - \overline{M}_{\lambda_1^e} \nsubseteq M$. To check whether $\overline{M}_{\lambda_2^e} - \overline{M}_{\lambda_1^e} \subseteq M$, we can use the CIX to verify the this condition. We can only check the condition $CIX\left(\lambda_2^e\right) \subseteq M$, since $CIX\left(\lambda_2^e\right) = \overline{M}_{\lambda_3^e} - \overline{M}_{\lambda_1^e}$.

BLOCKING

In Section 1 we have introduced blocking briefly. Blocking divides data into blocks and only compares tuples in the same block, this is under the assumption that the matching tuple pairs must be in the same block and the tuple pairs in different block are unlikely to match. For example, we can partition a dataset of customer by the address.

Table 14. A compressed inverted index for $\mathcal{P}\left(\lambda_1^i\right)$

Candidate eARs	Compressed Inverted List	
	M	N
λ_1^e	$RP_{1,7}$	-
λ_2^e	$RP_{1,6}$	$RP_{1,2}, RP_{2,6}, RP_{2,7}, RP_{3,5}$
λ_3^e	$RP_{6,7}$	-
λ_4^e	$RP_{3,4}$	$RP_{1,3}, RP_{1,5}, RP_{3,6}, RP_{3,7}, RP_{4,6}, RP_{5,6}, RP_{5,7}$
λ_5^e	$RP_{2,5}$	$RP_{2,3}$
λ_6^e	$RP_{1,7}$	-
λ_7^e	$RP_{1,6}, RP_{6,7}$	$RP_{1,2}, RP_{1,3}, RP_{1,5}, RP_{2,6}, RP_{2,7}, RP_{3,5}, RP_{3,7}, RP_{4,5}, RP_{5,7}$
λ_8^e	$RP_{2,5}$	$RP_{2,3}, RP_{3,6}, RP_{5,6}$
λ_9^e	$RP_{3,4}$	$RP_{1,4}$

While using a single field as the blocking criteria may cause miss matches, we can use different fields for partition to improve accuracy. In this section, we are going to introduce an improved blocking model, called iterative blocking model (I-BlockER) (Whang, MenestrinaW & Koutrika 2009).

Blocking Model and Iterative Blocking Model

Before presenting the models, we give a simple example first. The schema is Customer (Name, Add, Email), and an instance of the schema is depicted in Table 16. We can use different fields to partition this instance, as is demonstrated in Table 16.

After blocking the data set, we can run the duplication detection algorithms on each block. Consider this situation of SC_2: if the tuples r and s are similar enough to combine, then they are merged into a new tuple denoted by r,s. The combination of the address and the email lead us to find a new match with t. You must have noticed

that we compared the new combined tuple with others again. After the iterative blocking, the final blocking solution becomes $\{r, s, t, u, v\}$. The iterative method improves the accuracy of the blocking result obviously.

In reality, the dataset can be very large, so it is nearly impossible to compare all the tuple pairs in the dataset. However, the iterative method can improve the speed although it is not obvious in this example. In Section 4.1, we will introduce three models: ER model, Blocking Model and Iterative Blocking Model.

ER Model

Before introducing the blocking model and the iterative blocking model, we first define a general model for entity resolution.

In the previous example, we use $\{r, s, t, u, v\}$ to represent the blocking result. The r,s,t in the result means that r,s and t are similar and *merged* into a new composite tuple. We do not actually merge the tuples into a new tuple in the ER

Table 15. Customer records

Record	Name	Address	Email
r	Jerry Brin	04733	JBrin@hotmail.com
s	Jerry Brin	11111	
t	J. Grey	11111	JBrin@hotmail.com
u	James Lee	12345	JL@gmail.com
v	James Lee	12345	JL@gmail.com

Table 16. Multiple blocking

Criterion	Partition by			
SC_1	address (zip code)	r	s,t	u,v
SC_2	Last name	r,s	t	u,v

model, but only use the symbol to represent the blocking results. The input records, denoted by R, we treat it as the base records and say that both the input records and the output records are partitions of the these base records. For example, the input records (r, s, t, u, v), and we omit the brackets for singleton blocks, so we write the input as (r, s, t, u, v).

A partition P_o *dominates* another partition P_i if $\forall r \in P_i, \exists s \in P_o \, s.t \, r \subseteq s$, denoted as $P_i \leq P_o$. An ER algorithm is valid if given an input record partition P_i of schema R, the algorithm returns a result partition P_o that $P_i \leq P_o$. We say tuples refer to the same entity if they are in the same block in the result partition P_o.

Blocking Model

Given r in the input partition P_i, our ER algorithm must compare it with any other s in P_i in general. This quadratic process is expensive for large datasets. A single blocking criterion can prune number of records that must be compare with r by reducing the number of candidates that may join r in the output partition P_o.

We use $b_{j,k}$ to represent a block, where subscript j indentifies the single blocking criterion and k identifies the block under the criterion. A blocking function SC_j maps a record to one or more blocks denoted by $b_{j,k}$. $SC_j(r) \cap SC_j(s) \neq \Phi$ which means that tuple r and s can be compared. We use $IN(b_{j,k})$ to represent the content of block $b_{j,k}$.

A *multiple blocking criteria* (MBC) uses a set of single criteria $SC_1, SC_2, \cdots, SC_n$, so blocks that a record r is mapped is denoted by $MBC(r) = \bigcup_{j=1,2,\cdots,n} SC_j(r)$. Similarly, $MBC(r) \cap MBC(s) \neq \Phi$ means that r and s can be compared.

We say that a MBC has the coverage property if all of its single blocking criteria determines the blocks by simply seeing where each base record in the cluster would be placed. The formal definition is: A multiple blocking criteria (MBC) satisfies the coverage property if $\forall j = 1, 2, \cdots, n, SC_j(r) = \bigcup_{z \in r} SC_j(z)$.

Iterative Blocking Model

The main idea of iterative blocking model is *reflecting*. Iterative blocking model (I-BlockER Model) is defined as follows:

Given a set of records R, a core ER algorithm (CER), and a multiple blocking criteria function MBC, a valid I-Blocking result $J = I\text{-}BlockER(R)$ satisfies the following conditions:

$$\bigcup_{r \in J} r = R \tag{1}$$

$$\forall r, s \in J \, s.t. \, r \neq s, r \cap s = \Phi \tag{2}$$

$$\begin{aligned} &\forall block \, b, IN(b) = CER(IN(b)) \\ &where \, IN(b) = \{r \mid r \in J, b \in MBC(r)\} \end{aligned} \tag{3}$$

For example, recall example of figure 4.2, the I-Blocking solution $J = \{r, s, t, \langle u, v \rangle\}$ satisfies the definition of I-BlockER Model. However, the solution $J = \{r, s, t, \langle u, v \rangle\}$ does not saitisfy the condition (3) because $IN(b_{1,2}) \neq CER(IN(b_{1,2}))$ where $IN(b_{1,2}) = \{r, s, t\}$.

Iterative Blocking Algorithm

First, we give an algorithm for iterative blocking in Table 17.

The algorithm consists of three parts: processing blocks, distributing records and gathering

Table 17. Algorithm iterative blocking

Input: A partition P_i of R and a core entity resolution algorithm *CER*	
Output: A partion P_o of R such that $P_i \leq P_o$	
1.	**for each** block $b_{j,k}$ **do**
2.	$IN\left(b_{j,k}\right) \leftarrow \{r \mid r \in P_i, b_{j,k} \in SC_j\left(r\right)\}$
3.	**end for**
4.	**repeat**
5.	$NewRec \leftarrow false$
6.	**for each** block $b_{j,k}$ **do**
7.	$R_i \leftarrow Preprocess\,IN\left(b_{j,k}\right)$ into a partition of base records
8.	$R_o \leftarrow CER\left(R_i\right)$
9.	**if** $R_o - IN\left(b_{j,k}\right) \neq \Phi$ **then**
10.	$NewRec \leftarrow true$
11.	**for each** $r \in R_o - IN\left(b_{j,k}\right)$ **do**
12.	**for each** $b \in MC\left(r\right)$ **do**
13.	$IN\left(b\right) \leftarrow IN\left(b\right) \bigcup \{r\}$ /* Distribute r to b */
14.	**end for**
15.	**end for**
16.	**end if**
17.	$IN\left(b_{j,k}\right) \leftarrow R_o$
18.	**end for**
19.	**until** $NewRec = false$ /* No new records created */
20.	**return** Union of all blocks

results. This can be demonstrated in the following example.

We use records in figure 4.1. The first step is blocking, the result is as shown in Table 18. The *SC* denotes the blocking criterion and *b* denotes the block. For instance, $b_{1,2}$ include the tuples *s* and *t*.

The second step is processing all the blocks. We process the blocks in the order of ascending subscript order. The first block that has tuples matches is block $b_{1,3}$, we merge *u* and *v* into a composite tuple $\langle u, v \rangle$. Then the distributing process follows because we assume the coverage property, $\langle u, v \rangle$ is distributed to the blocks that contains *u* and *v*. In this example, we distribute $\langle u, v \rangle$ to $b_{2,3}$. Then we process the block $b_{2,1}$ and then distribute the result $\langle r, s \rangle$ to $b_{1,1}$ and $b_{1,2}$. After processing all the blocks, the final result of the first iteration is shown in Table 19.

Then we repeat the iteration process again. We can see that in block $b_{1,1}$ the tuple *r* is included in $\langle r, s \rangle$, so we merge them to $\langle r, s \rangle$. After the CER algorithm is applied, the tuples in block $b_{1,2}$ is merged into $\langle r, s, t \rangle$, and then $\langle r, s, t \rangle$ is distributed to $b_{1,1}$, $b_{2,1}$ and $b_{2,2}$. The result after the second round loop is shown in Table 20.

We still need to repeat another time. After this iteration, we reach a final state shown in Table 21. Then we union the result of SC_1 and SC_2 to get the final partition result $\{r, s, t, \langle u, v \rangle\}$. In total, we have process 18 blocks in the iterations to derive the final result.

From the simple example we can see the iterative blocking algorithm can terminate and return a partition of *R* under the coverage property and connected component strategy. In the iterations, we use a strategy called *connected*

Table 18 After the initial blocking

Criterion		$b_{-,1}$	$b_{-,2}$	$b_{-,3}$
SC_1		r	s, t	u, v
SC_2		r, s	t	u, v

Table 19. The result after the first iteration

Criterion		$b_{-,1}$	$b_{-,2}$	$b_{-,3}$
SC_1		$r, \langle r, s \rangle$	$s, t, \langle r, s \rangle$	$\langle u, v \rangle$
SC_2		$\langle r, s \rangle$	t	$\langle u, v \rangle$

Table 20. The result after the second iteration

Criterion	$b_{-,1}$	$b_{-,2}$	$b_{-,3}$
SC_1	$r, s, \langle r, s, t \rangle$	$\langle r, s, t \rangle$	$\langle u, v \rangle$
SC_2	$\langle r, s, t \rangle$	$\langle r, s, t \rangle$	$\langle u, v \rangle$

Table 21. The final blocking result

Criterion	$b_{-,1}$	$b_{-,2}$	$b_{-,3}$
SC_1	$\langle r, s, t \rangle$	$\langle r, s, t \rangle$	$\langle u, v \rangle$
SC_2	$\langle r, s, t \rangle$	$\langle r, s, t \rangle$	$\langle u, v \rangle$

component strategy to address resolving the conflicts in the line 7 of the algorithm. In general we have two strategies to address the problem. One is *unmerge conflict records*, it does things as its name. For example, if we get the temporary result $\left\{ r, s, s, t, \langle u, v \rangle \right\}$, we change it into $\left\{ r, s, t, \langle u, v \rangle \right\}$ because $\langle r, s \rangle$ and $\langle s, t \rangle$ conflict. The other one is the strategy we used in the example, connected component strategy, we merge the conflicting tuples into $\langle r, s, t \rangle$ and we get the result $\left\{ r, s, t, \langle u, v \rangle \right\}$

The result of the iterative algorithm is determined by the order that the blocks are processed when the CER algorithm is order dependent. While if the CER algorithm is not order dependent and it merges records never unmerge.

We assume that each of N blocking criteria generates exactly blocks, then the time to run the algorithm is:

$$O\left(N \times B \times \frac{|R|^2}{B^2} \times \left(|R| - 1 \right) \right) = O\left(\frac{N \times |R|^3}{B} \right).$$

The Lego Algorithm

We can see that the iterative blocking algorithm is not very efficient; we developed an improved algorithm called *Lego algorithm* (Table 22) in two ways.

First, we use the "maximal" records of base records to manage merged records efficiently. The "maximal" record of a base record r is denoted by $max(r)$ and defined as the "largest" record that contains r as the following definition.

The maximal record of a base record r $max(r)$ is a record such that:

$$max\left(r \right) \in \bigcup_{j,k} b_{j,k} \ and$$
$$\forall r' \in \bigcup_{j,k} b_{j,k} \ s.t. \ r \subseteq r',$$
$$then \ r' \subseteq max\left(r \right)$$

Second, the blocks are no longer processed sequentially, but are managed by a *block queue Q*.

Procedure $Update\left(b_{j,k} \right)$ can be seen in Table 23.

Table 22. Algorithm The Lego algorithm

Input: A partition P_i of R and a core entity resolution algorithm CER	
Output: A partition P_o of R such that $P_i \leq P_o$	
1.	$Q \leftarrow \Phi$
2.	**for each** $r \in P_i$ **do**
3.	**for each** $r_b \in \left\{ Base\,records\,of\,r \right\}$ **do**
4.	$max\left(r_b\right) = r$
5.	**end for**
6.	**end for**
7.	Create blocks
8.	Push all blocks onto Q
9.	**while** $Q \neq \Phi$ **do**
10.	$b_{j,k} \leftarrow Q.pop()$
11.	$R_i \leftarrow Update\left(b_{j,k}\right)$
12.	$R_o \leftarrow CER\left(R_i\right)$
13.	**for each** $r \in R_o - R_i$ **do**
14.	**for each** $r_b \in \left\{ Base\,records\,of\,r \right\}$ **do**
15.	$max\left(r_b\right) = r$
16.	**end for**
17.	**for each** $b \in MBC\left(r\right)$ **do**
18.	**if** $b \notin Q$ **then**
19.	$Q.push\left(b\right)$

continued on following page

Table 22. Continued

20.	**end if**
21.	**end for**
22.	**end for**
23.	**end while**
24.	**return** $\bigcup_k Update\left(b_{0,k}\right)$

The Lego algorithm processes less blocks than the iterative blocking algorithm. In the example, Lego algorithm processes only 11 blocks, while the iterative blocking algorithm processes 18 blocks.

Disk-Based Iterative Blocking

In real applications, the datasets are usually too large to load in memory. We introduce a disk-based algorithm in this section that efficiently manages blocks on the disk. The algorithm improves the Lego algorithm in two ways. First, the blocks are stored in fixed-sized extents called *segments* on the disk. Second, the algorithm uses a *merge log* for managing maximal records.

Segments

We use fixed-sized extents called *segments* on the disk to store the blocks. A segment acts like a unit that should be read into the memory so the size of it cannot exceed the memory size. We allocate a fixed number of segments on the disk consecutively for each blocking criterion, so each segment belongs to one blocking criterion and contains the blocks of the criterion. The blocks are stored randomly to segments to make even distribution. The segment strategy can save space since the blocks may contain overlapping records. Each block can later be extracted from the segment when the *MBC* are applied to each record. So a segment is a set of records and we denote the records in segment s as $IN\left(s\right)$.

Table 23. Procedure $Update\left(b_{j,k}\right)$

1.	$b \leftarrow \Phi$
2.	**for each** $r \in IN\left(b_{j,k}\right)$ **do**
3.	**for each** $r_b \in \left\{Base\,records\,of\,r\right\}$ **do**
4.	$b \leftarrow b\bigcup max\left(r_b\right)$
5.	**end for**
6.	**end for**
7.	**return** b

Table 23. Assigning blocks to segments for Table 16

Criterion	$s_{-,1}$	$s_{-,2}$
SC_1	$b_{1,1}, b_{1,3}$	$b_{1,2}$
SC_2	$b_{2,1}$	$b_{2,2}, b_{2,3}$

Because different blocks are distributed randomly to the segments, the different block sizes are even is the advantage of the using of segments. We can do the same amount of work for each segment processed approximately. However, the problem is that the segments may overflow during the iterative blocking process because of the fixed-size segments. For example, segment $s_{1,1}$ starts with the record $\{r, u, v\}$ and ends with $\{r, s, t, u, v\}$ where r, s, t can be larger than r while u, v has a similar size as u and v combined. To address the overflow problem, we can leave some extra space for each segment in case the sizes of the blocks grow (Table 24).

Merge Log

We use the merge log to update the records in a block to their maximal records. When we cannot manage the maximal records in memory for large datasets, we can use the merge log. We can also use a hash table so updating a block would involve many random IOs to find the maximal records. However, the merge log keeps track of record merges and can be read sequentially to update a block. For example, if two records r and s are merged into $\langle r, s \rangle$, then we add to the merge log the entries $r \rightarrow \langle r, s \rangle$ and $s \rightarrow \langle r, s \rangle$. After that, when we process a block containing r, we find

Table 24. Algorithm Updating a Block using the Merge Log

1.	$UpdateBlock\left(b, L\right)$
2.	Skip L entries with timestamps less than or equal to the timestamp of b
3.	**While** L has more entries **do**
4.	$r \leftarrow s \leftarrow L.nextEntry()$
5.	if $r \in IN\left(b\right)$ **then**
6.	$IN\left(b\right) \leftarrow IN\left(b\right) - \{r\} + \{s\}$
7.	**end if**
8.	**end while**
9.	**return** $IN\left(b\right)$

Table 25. Algorithm The Duplo algorithm

Input: A partition P_i of R and a core entity resolution algorithm CER	
Output: A partition P_o of R such that $P_i \leq P_o$	
1.	$L_1 \leftarrow \Phi$ /* Disk merge log for segments */
2.	$Q_1 \leftarrow \Phi$ /* Segment queue */
3.	Create segments
4.	Push all segments into Q_1
5.	**While** Q_1 is not empty **do**
6.	$s \leftarrow Q_1.pop()$
7.	$IN(s) \leftarrow UpdateSegment(s, L_1)$
8.	$L_2 \leftarrow \Phi$ /* In-memory merge log for blocks */
9.	Push all blocks in s into Q_2
10.	**while** Q_2 is not empty **do**
11.	$b \leftarrow Q_2.pop()$
12.	$R_i \leftarrow UpdateBlock(b, L_2)$
13.	$R_o \leftarrow CER(R_i)$
14.	Add to L_2 the new record merges in b
15.	Add to L_1 the new record merges in b
16.	**for each** record $r \in R_o - R_i$ **do**
17.	**for each** block $b' \in MBC(r)$ **do**
18.	$s' \leftarrow BlockToSegment(b')$ /* Return the segment where b' is */
19.	**if** $s = s'$ **then** /* Hit the same segment */

continued on following page

Table 25. Continued

20.	if $b \neq b'$ and $b' \notin Q_2$ then
21.	$Q_2.push\left(b'\right)$
22.	**end if**
23.	**else** /* Hit a different segment */
24.	if $s' \notin Q_1$ then
25.	$Q_1.push\left(s'\right)$
26.	**end if**
27.	**end if**
28.	**end for**
29.	**end for**
30.	**end while**
31.	write s back to disk
32.	**end while**
33.	$J \leftarrow \Phi$
34.	$J \leftarrow \left\{Records\,in\,R\,that\,were\,never\,merged\right\}$
35.	$J \leftarrow J \bigcup \left\{Records\,in\,L_1\,that\,are\,not\,contained\,by\,any\,other\,record\,in\,L_1\right\}$
36.	**return** J

the appropriate region of the log to find the entry $r \rightarrow \langle r, s \rangle$ and update r to $\langle r, s \rangle$.

The algorithm shows how to update a block by using the merge log (Table 24). The main advantage of the algorithm is that it only needs one single sequential scan to update block. Although the number of entries in the merge log could grow to $2|R| - 2$, the number of records merged is much smaller than $|R|$.

The Duplo Algorithm

The Duplo algorithm (Table 25) uses segments and merges log to scale iterative blocking. The main idea of the algorithm is processing N blocks at a time with assumption that a segment contains N blocks on average. So the iterative blocking is done in two levels: processing a segment and then processing the blocks within that segment.

In the algorithm we maintain two queues and two merge logs for managing the segments and the blocks within each segment. Segment queue Q_1 is used to determine which segment to process next, and merge log L_1 is used to keep track of all the record merges done until now. Block queue Q_2 is used to determine which blocks to process next, and merge log L_2 keeps track of the record merges done within the current segment. The function is called *UpdateSegment* that is identical to *UpdateBlock* except that a segment is updated instead of a block. The algorithm is as follows.

REFERENCES

Wang & Fan. (2011). Object identification on complex data: A survey. *Chinese Journal of Computers, 34*(10).

Elmagarmid, Ipeirotis, & Verykios. (2007). Duplicate record detection: A survey. *IEEE Transactions on Knowledge and Data Engineering, 19*(1).

Brizan & Tansel. (2006). A survey of entity resolution and record linkage methodologies. *Communications of the IIMA, 6*(3).

Fan, W., Jia, X., Li, J., & Ma, S. (2009). *Reasoning about record matching rules*. Paper presented at VLDB. Lyon, France.

Wang, J., Li, G., Yu, J. X., & Feng, J. (2011). Entity matching: How similar is similar. *Proceedings of the VLDB Endowment, 4*(10).

Whang, S. E., Menestrina, D., & Koutrika, G. (2009). *Entity resolution with iterative blocking*. Paper presented at SIGMOD. Providence, RI.

ADDITIONAL READING

Newcombe, H. B. (1967). Record Linking: The Design of Efficient Systems for Linking Records into Individual and Family Histories. *American Journal of Human Genetics, 19*(3), 335–359.

Fellegi, I. P., & Sunter, A. B. (1969). A Theory for Record Linkage. *Journal of the American Statistical Association, 64*(328), 1183–1210.

Sarawagi, S., & Bhamidipaty, A. (2002). *Interactive Deduplication Using Active Learning*. Paper presented at Eighth ACM SIGKDD Int'l Conf. Knowledge Discovery and Data Mining (KDD '02), pp. 269-278.

Bilenko, M., Mooney, R. J., Cohen, W. W., Ravikumar, P., & Fienberg, S. E. (2003). Adaptive Name Matching in Information Integration. *IEEE Intelligent Systems, 18*(5), 16–23.

Bhattacharya, I., & Getoor, L. (2006). *A Latent Dirichlet Allocation Model for Entity Resolution*. Paper presented at 6th SIAM Conference on Data Mining, Bethesda, MD.

Bilenko, M., & Raymond, J. Mooney, R. J. (2003). *Adaptive Duplicate Detection Using Learnable String Similarity Measures*. Paper presented at the Ninth ACM SIGKDD International Conference on Knowledge Discovery and Data Mining.

Christen, P., & Churches, T. (2006). *A Probabilistic Deduplication, Record Linkage and Geocoding System. Advances in Data Mining: Theory, Methodology, Techniques, and Applications. State-of-the-Art Lecture Notes in Artificial Intelligence* (Vol. 3755). Springer-Verlag.

Hipp, J., Guntzer, U., & Grimmer, U. (2001). *Data Quality Mining: Making a Virtue of Necessity*. Paper presented at the 6th ACM SIGMOD Workshop on Research Issues in Data Mining and Knowledge Discovery.

Raman, V., & Hellerstein, J. (2001). *Potter's Wheel: An Interactive Data Cleaning System*. Paper presented at the 27th VLDB Conference, 2001.

Fan, W., Gao, H., Jia, X., Li, J., & Ma, S. (2011). Dynamic constraints for record matching. *The VLDB Journal*. doi: doi:10.1007/s00778-010-0206-6

Monge, A.E. (2000). *Matching Algorithms within a Duplicate Detection System*. Bulletin of the Technical Committee.

Hellerstein, J. M. (February 2008). *Quantitative Data Cleaning for Large Databases*. White paper, United Nations Economic Commission for Europe.

Guo, Z., & Zhou, A. (2002). Research on Data Quality and Data Cleaning:a Survey. *Journal of Software*, *13*(11), 2076–2082.

Lup, L. W., Li, L. M., & Wang, L. T. (2001). Aknowledge-based approach for duplicate elimination in data cleaning. *Information Systems*, *26*(8), 585–606.

Baxter, R., Christen, P., & Churches, T. (2003). *A comparison of fast blocking methods for record linkage*. Paper presented at the 2003 ACM SIGKDD Workshop on Data Cleaning, Record Linkage, and Object Consolidation, pages 25–27.

Chaudhuri, S., Chen, B.-C., Ganti, V., & Kaushik, R. (2007). *Example-driven design of efficient record matching queries* (pp. 327–338). VLDB.

Cohen, W. W., Ravikumar, P., & Fienberg, S. E. (2003). A comparison of string distance metrics for name-matching tasks. In IIWEB, pages 73–78.

Hern'andez, M. A., & Stolfo, S. J. (1995). *The merge/purge problem for large databases* (pp. 127–138). SIGMOD.

Jaro, M. A. (1989). Advances in record-linkage methodology as applied to matching the 1985 census of tampa, florida. *Journal of the American Statistical Association*, *84*(406), 414–420.

Bhattacharya, I., & Getoor, L. (2004). *Iterative record linkage for cleaning and integration*. Paper presented at SIGMOD Workshop on Research Issues on Data Mining and Knowledge Discovery.

Chaudhuri, S., Ganti, V., & Motwani, R. (2005). *Robust identification of fuzzy duplicates*. Paper presented at ICDE, Tokyo, Japan.

Newcombe, H. B. (1988). *Handbook of record linkage: methods for health and statistical studies, administration, and business*. New York, NY, USA: Oxford University Press, Inc.

Abiteboul, S., Hull, R., & Vianu, V. (1995). *Foundations of Databases*. Addison-Wesley.

Ananthakrishna, R., Chaudhuri, S., & Ganti, V. (2002). *Eliminating fuzzy duplicates in data warehouses*. VLDB.

Anish Das Sarma, J. W. Jeffrey Ullman. (2009). *Schema design for uncertain databases*. Paper presented at the 3rd Alberto Mendelzon Workshop on Foundations of Data Management.

Batini, C., & Scannapieco, M. (2006). *Data Quality: Concepts, Methodologies and Techniques*. Springer.

Chaudhuri, S., Sarma, A. D., Ganti, V., & Kaushik, R. (2007). *Leveraging aggregate constraints for deduplication*. SIGMOD.

Gupta, R., & Sarawagi, S. (2009). Answering Table Augmentation Queries from Unstructured Lists on the Web. *PVLDB*, *2*(1), 289–300.

Benjelloun, O., Garcia-Molina, H., Menestrina, D., Su, Q., Whang, S. E., & Widom, J. (2009). Swoosh: a generic approach to entity resolution. *The VLDB Journal*, *18*(1), 255–276.

I. Bhattacharya & L. Getoor (2007). Collective entity resolution in relational data. TKDD 1(1).

KEY TERMS AND DEFINITIONS

Explicit Attribute-Matching Rule (eAR): An *explicit attribute-matching rule* (eAR) is such a triple $\lambda^e\left(e, f, \theta\right)$, that a is an attribute name, f is a similarity function and θ is a threshold. If $f\left(t[a], t'[a]\right) \geq \theta$, $t[a]$ and $t'[a]$ are considered to be the same. $t[a]$ and $t'[a]$ satisfying λ^e is denoted by $\left(t[a], t'[a]\right) \vDash \lambda^e$, and $t[a]$ and $t'[a]$ dissatisfying λ^e is denoted by $\left(t[a], t'[a]\right) \nvDash \lambda^e$.

Implicit Attribute-Matching Rules (iAR): An implicit attribute-matching rules (iAR) is such a triple $\lambda^i\left(e, \mathcal{F}, \Theta\right)$, that a is an attribute name, $\mathcal{F} = \left\{f_1, f_2, \cdots\right\}$ is a set of similarity functions and Θ is a threshold range. If there exists a similarity function f in F and $f\left(t[a], t'[a]\right) \geq \theta$, where θ is lower bound of Θ, then $t[a]$ and $t'[a]$ are considered to be the same.

Matching Dependency: A *matching dependency* (MD) Æ for two schemas R_1 and R_2 is defined as $\bigwedge_{j=1}^{|X_1|}\left(R_1\left[X_1[j]\right] \approx_j R_2\left[X_2[j]\right]\right) \rightarrow R_1[Z_1] \rightleftharpoons R_2[Z_2]$, where the lists X_1 and X_2 are comparable; the similarity operators $\approx_j$ can be $\approx$ or $=$.

Maximal Record: The maximal record of a base record r $max(r)$ is a record that $max\left(r\right) \in \bigcup_{j,k} b_{j,k}$ and $\forall r' \in \bigcup_{j,k} b_{j,k}$ s.t. $r \subseteq r'$, . then $r' \subseteq max\left(r\right)$

Record-Matching Rule (RR): A *record-matching rule* (RR) is a set of eARs or iARs, denoted by $\phi = \wedge_{i=1}^k \lambda_i$, where λ_i can be an eAR or iAR. A tuple pair $\left(t, t'\right)$ satisfies the record-matching rule, if $\left(t[a], t'[a]\right)$ satisfies *every* attribute-matching rule λ_i for $1 \leq i \leq k$, denoted by $\left(t, t'\right) \vDash \phi$. A tuple pair $\left(t, t'\right)$ dissatisfying the RR ϕ is denoted by $\left(t, t'\right) \nvDash \phi$.

Relative Candidate Key: A relative candidate key E relative to attribute lists $\left(Z_1, Z_2\right)$ of schemas $\left(R_1, R_2\right)$ is an MD $\bigwedge_{j=1}^{|X_1|}\left(R_1\left[X_1[j]\right] \approx_j R_2\left[X_2[j]\right]\right) \rightarrow R_1[Z_1] \rightleftharpoons R_2[Z_2]$, that the RHS is fixed to be $\left(Z_1, Z_2\right)$. We write the key E as $(Z_1, Z_2 \| C)$, where C is the similarity operators $\left[\approx_1, \cdots, \approx_k\right]$.

Similarity Operator: A similarity operator, such as $\approx$, is an operator which describes the similarity between two tuple using some specific similarity metric, such as edit distance.

Chapter 6
Entity Resolution on Multiple Relations

ABSTRACT

Entity resolution is a central issue in data quality management. It has been proven extremely useful in data fusion, inconsistency and inaccuracy detection, knowledge extraction, and data repairing. Nevertheless, in the real world, entities often have two or more representations in databases. The complex structures of data introduce new challenges and make entity resolution much harder than record matching on relational data. Entity resolution on complex data is to find data objects that refer to the same real-world entity and to cluster such objects together. This chapter introduces an overview of recent advances in the study of entity resolution on complex data. At first, the authors make a definition of this problem. Then the authors discuss similarity measures and reasonable algorithm to solve the problem. Finally, the authors validate the resolution by the various experiments on different kind of datasets.

INTRODUCTION

Databases play an important role in today's IT-based economy. As studied in (Elmagarmid, Ipeirotis & Verykios, 2007), many industries and systems depend on the accuracy of database to carry out operations in. However, it's impossible to have absolute accurate data in the real world. The information stored in databases contains a varied of different kinds of errors such as incorrectness, inconsistency, duplication, incompleteness or data being out of date. Data often lack a unique identifier which consists of linking – in relational terms, joining – two or more tables on their key fields. Thus, data quality is often compromised by many factors, including data entity errors (e.g. *"Wei Wan"* instead of *"Wei Wang"*), missing integrity constraints (e.g. *"age = 234"*), and multiple conventions for recording information (e.g. *"W. Wei"* equals to *"Wei Wang"*). Therefore, the quality of information stored in the database can have significant cost implications to a system that relies on information to function and conduct business. Entity resolution is a central issue in data quality management, which is one of the most popular research directions.

DOI: 10.4018/978-1-4666-5198-2.ch006

The data in applications is probably that with complex structure, such as XML information in enterprises, in websites and social networks, chemical and biological databases and graph data. This was further explored in (Wang & Fan, 2011). Often, there are a variety of ways of referring to the same underlying entity. To use complex data effectively in practice, necessary techniques must be in place to improve the quality of the data. Although, traditional approaches to entity resolution and deduplication use a variety of attribute similarity measures, which often based on approximate string-matching criteria. In fact, determining that two records refer to the same individual may in turn allow us to make additional inferences. The problem involves resolving multiple types of entities at the same time using the different relations that are observed among them. In this chapter, we will define the problem and propose similarity measures and some reasonable algorithms on this problem.

PROBLEM DEFINITION

In the relational entity resolution problem, we have some collection of references to entities and from this set of references we would like to identify the unique collection of individuals or entities to which they should be mapped. The entity resolution on multiple relations has varied classification methods. According to the result of resolution, entity identification on complex data can classify into *pairwise entity resolution* and *group-wise entity resolution*. While according to the target of the resolution, entity identification on multiple relations includes resolution on XML, resolution on graph data and resolution on complex networks. Entity resolution on multiple relations can be applied on information integration (Chapter 14) and healthcare information management (Chapter 17).

Pairwise Entity Resolution

- Pairwise entity identification is to recognize whether two data objects and refers to the same real-world entity. Before going through this problem, we list the meanings of some symbols we will use frequently here.
- Lower case characters e, t and r denote entities, types and references.
- Upper case character labels like e.A and r.E to denote variables, while e.a and r.e denote values of them (shot-hand for e.A = a).
- Character $\mathcal{R} = \{r_i\}$ denotes the set of references, where each reference r has its attributes r.A.
- Character $\mathcal{T} = \{t_i\}$ denotes the set of the references' possible types.
- Character $\varepsilon = \{e_i\}$ denotes the set of entities the references correspond to, so that each reference r has its entity r.E.
- Character $\mathcal{H} = \{h_i\}$ denotes the set of hyper-edges to describe co-occurrence of references, which was further explored in (Bhattacharya & Getoor, 2005; Bhattacharya & Getoor, 2007).

We should note that each r in $\mathcal{R}$ has an observable type and r.e.T = r.T, which means that a reference r and its corresponding entity r.E are necessarily of the same type. And it is true that the entities and their attributes are often not observable. What we observe are the attributes r.A of individual references, which can be imagined being generated by some distortion process from the attributes of the corresponding entity r.E. Our target is to recover the set of underlying entities ε and figure out the unobservable attributes and types by the observed attributes and types from given references.

However, entity resolution on complex data is not only to find out the set of entities ε. The references are often unobservable individually. Instead, they co-occur as members of hyper-edges in complex data. For a better understanding of the word 'hyper-edge', we represent the relationships as a graph where the vertices represent the references, and then the hyper-edges represent the co-occurrence relations that hold between them. We use label r.H to mark the hyper-edge that the reference r belongs to. If reference r is occurs in hyper-edge h, then r.H = h. Unlike the association of a reference r and its entity r.E is hidden, we know which hyper-edge a reference r belongs to. Note that the entities of references that occur in the same hyper-edge are related to each other. That means the references help us build associative patterns between entities and hyper-edges. So, our resolution decisions are not independent. Instead of finding the set of entities and the association between entities and references, our problem is to predict the entities of the references collectively, where the entity r.E of any reference r is directly influenced by the choice of entity r'.E for another reference r' if they are associated with the same hyper-edge h, i.e. r.E= r'.E=h. When making decisions in multiple-related entity resolution, we would like to regard a data object as a hyper-edge which contains a set of entities rather than an individual entity.

To make these more concrete, consider an illustrative example from the bibliographic domain. When we trying to construct a database of papers, authors and citations, from a collection of paper references, authors often cannot be correctly identified and citations cannot be resolved, due to the fact that the same paper may have multiple references. Just consider the following example in (Sarawagi & Bhamidipaty; 2002):

- R. Agrawal, R. Srikant. Fast algorithms for mining association rules in large databases. In VLDB-94, 1994
- Rakesh Agrawal and Ramakrishnan Srikant. Fast algorithms for mining association rules in large databases. In Proc. Of the 20th Intl. Conference on Very Large Databases, Santiago, Chile, September 1994.

In this example, we just assume the fact is that the two citations are referring to the same paper. We have more direct and clear relations described in Table 1.

In this example, it turns out there are four underlying entities. But the fact is unknown to us. Now what we want is to find out whether each pair of these references in the given two papers refers to the same entities or refers to two different entities.

Each citation has 4 different references constituting the set $\mathcal{R} = \left\{ r_1, \cdots, r_8 \right\}$. In the first citation, r_1 and r_2 are author references with attributes $r_1.A=$'R.Agrawal' and $r_2.A=$'R.Srikant' and types $r_1.T=r_2.T=$ 'author'. Reference r_3 is a paper with title, so that $r_3.A=$ "Fast algorithms for mining association rules in large databases' and $r_3.T=$ "paper". The last reference r_4 is about venue with $r_4.A=$ 'VLDB-94' and $r_4.T=$ 'venue'. Similarly,

Table 1. The references in different papers

Paper 1	Fast Algorithms for mining association rules in large databases.	R. Agrawal	R. Srikant	VLDB-94
Paper 2	Fast Algorithms for mining association rules in large databases.	Rakesh Agrawal	Ramakrishnan Srikant	In Proc. Of…

we can deal with the second citation by references r_5, r_6, r_7 and r_8.

We use a set $\mathcal{E} = \{e_1, \cdots, e_4\}$ to represent the underlying entities, where e_1 and e_2 are the author entities with names $e_1.A = $ 'Rakesh Agrawal' and $e_2.A = $ 'Ramakrishnan Srikant', e_3 is a paper with title $e_3.A = $ 'Fast algorithms for mining association rules in large databases' and e_4 is a conference venue with name $e_3.A = $ '20th International Conference on Very Large Databases'. Easy to find that r_1 and r_5 correspond to author entity e_1 so that $r_1.E = r_5.E = e_1$, while r_2 and r_6 correspond to e_2 so that $r_2.E = r_6.E = e_2$. Also, reference r_3 and r_6 correspond to paper entity e_3 so that $r_3.E = r_6.E = e_3$ and r_4 and r_8 correspond to venue entity e_4 so that $r_4.E = r_8.E = e_4$. The relationships can be clearly performed in Figure 1.

We have a set $\mathcal{H} = \{h_1, h_2\}$ in which the two hyper-edges h_1 and h_2 represent two citations above. Easy to find that in the first citation the references $r_1, \cdots, r_4$ are associated with hyper-edge h_1 and the relation is represented as $r_1.H = r_2.H = r_3.H = r_4.H = h_1$. And we have similar relation in the second citation. Then we combined the hyper-edge and entities together. We can easily decide

that $h_1 = h_2$. Figure 2 shows the reference and entity graph of the example.

Group Wise Entity Resolution

In group-wise entity identification, we divide the dataset S into k subsets S_1, S_2, $\cdots$, S_k while both $S_1 \cap S_2 \cap ... \cap S_k = \varnothing$ and $S_1 \cup S_2 \cup ... \cup S_k = S$ are satisfied, so that $\forall i \in [1,k], \forall \sigma_1, \sigma_2 \in S_i, \sigma_1$ and σ_2 refer to the same real-world entity. In other words, our goal is to cluster the references so that those that correspond to the same entity end up in the same cluster.

We define the set of entity clusters $\mathcal{C} = \{c_i\}$ reflects our belief about the underlying entities. Thus, each entity cluster corresponds to one reconstructed entity and all references in a cluster correspond to the same entity. Memberships of references in the constructed clusters are represented using a cluster label r.C for each reference r. Note that all references in the same cluster should be of the same type, which is also the type c.T for the cluster. The process of solving this problem could be described as follow: At the beginning, each reference belongs to a separate cluster. Then

Figure 1. Corresponding attributes of entities

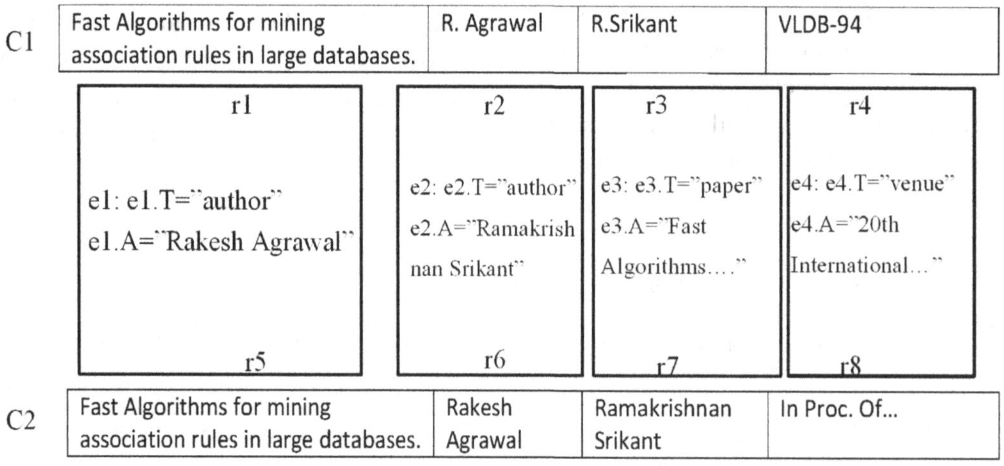

C1	Fast Algorithms for mining association rules in large databases.	R. Agrawal	R.Srikant	VLDB-94
	r1	r2	r3	r4
	e1: e1.T="author" e1.A="Rakesh Agrawal"	e2: e2.T="author" e2.A="Ramakrish nan Srikant"	e3: e3.T="paper" e3.A="Fast Algorithms...."	e4: e4.T="venue" e4.A="20th International..."
	r5	r6	r7	r8
C2	Fast Algorithms for mining association rules in large databases.	Rakesh Agrawal	Ramakrishnan Srikant	In Proc. Of...

Figure 2. Examples for reference graph and entity graph

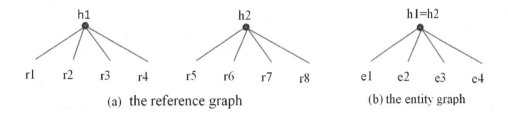

(a) the reference graph   (b) the entity graph

we run an iterative cluster algorithm, where at any stage the two clusters that are most possible to be the same entity are merged. The algorithm will stop when each two clusters are impossible to be the same entity. The key to the success of a clustering algorithm is the similarity measure which is to define the similarity between two clusters. In the following sections, we will describe the similarity measure and clustering algorithm.

SIMILARITY MEASURE

In collective entity resolution, the similarity measure takes into account the similarity in not only attributes of the references in the two clusters but also the relations that they participate in. The attribute similarity component of the similarity measure is focused on the similarity of the attributes r.A of the references in the two clusters. And the relational similarity component looks at the similarity of the relations that two entities or clusters participate in. Each cluster is associated with a set of edges to other references that we want to take into account. For the other references, we will focus on not their attributes values but the resolution decisions that have been taken on them, more exactly the labels r.C of these references.

(Bhattacharya & Getoor, 2005) formally define the similarity measure between two entity clusters as a weighted combination of the attribute similarity and relational similarity between then. For two entity clusters c_i and c_j, their similarity may be defined as:

$$\mathrm{sim}\left(c_i, c_j\right) = \left(1 - a\right) \times \mathrm{sim}_A\left(c_i, c_j\right) + a \times \mathrm{sim}_R\left(c_i, c_j\right), \quad \left(0 \leq a \leq 1\right)$$

where $\mathrm{sim}_A()$ is the similarity of the attributes and $\mathrm{sim}_R()$ is the relational similarity between the two entity clusters and they are linearly combined with weight α and $1\text{-}\alpha$. In the following subsections, we discuss the two similarity components in detail.

Attribute Similarity

The traditional approach (Fellegi & Sunter 1969; Cohen et al. 2003) is attribute-based entity resolution where the similarity $\mathrm{sim}_A(r_i, r_j)$ is computed for each pair of references r_i, r_j based on their attributes, and only those pairs that have similarity above some threshold are considered co-referent (Bhattacharya & Getoor, 2007). The similarity measure takes two references and returns a value between 0 and 1 that indicates the degree of similarity between them. A higher value indicates greater similarity between attributes. Several sophisticated similarity measure have been developed for names, such as the Jaro, Levenstein, Jaro-Winkler, among others, and popular TF-IDF schemes may be used for other textual attributes like keywords (Bhattacharya & Getoor, 2007). The measure that works best for each attribute can be used. Finally, a weighted combination of the similarity over the different attributes for each reference can be used to compute the attributes similarity between two references.

We have considered the attribute similarity measure in attribute-based entity resolution. Nevertheless, $\text{sim}_A()$ defines the similarity of attributes between two entity clusters instead of references, while each cluster is a collection of references with their own attributes. So we need to use the similarity measure between two attributes to define the similarity between two clusters of attributes.

This is similar to finding the aggregate distance between two clusters given a pairwise distance measure. Many sophisticated approaches have been proposed for aggregating over pair-wise distance between the two clusters (Berkhin, 2002). The duplicate relation is typically transitive: if reference r_i and r_j are duplicates, then all other duplicates of r_i will also be duplicates of r_j. So the single link measure that takes the minimum pair-wise distance (or the maximum pairwise similarity) between two clusters is the most relevant for our purposes. Computing single link similarity is quadratic in the average number of distinct attribute values in a cluster. A more efficient alternative to pairwise comparison might be to maintain a representative attribute for each entity cluster, which is the most likely attribute value for the underlying entity given the observed attributes of all references in that cluster. Then the attribute similarity for a cluster pair is the similarity of their representative attributes.

Relational Similarity

Then, we address the relational similarity measure between two entity clusters considering the clusters that they are related to via hyper-edges. There many possible ways to define this problem. We'll explore some possibilities here and focus on some issues that are of relevance.

Naïve Relational Similarity Measure

The simplest way to use relationships to resolve the similarity measure problem is to treat related references as additional attributes for matching. For instance, to determine if two author references in two different papers are co-referent, we can compare the names of their coauthors. In our running example, the naïve relational decision about the references 'R. Agrawal' and 'Rakesh Agrawal', would consider that both have co-authors with the name 'Ramakrishnan Srikant'.

A similar idea has been used in the context of matching in dimensional hierarchies. We generalize the idea for unordered relationships and define hyper-edge similarity $\text{sim}_H(h_i, h_j)$ between two hyper-edges h_i and h_j as the best pairwise attribute match between their references. Since the references in any hyper-edge are not ordered, each reference $r \in h_i$ can be matched to any reference $r' \in h_j$. So for each reference $r \in h_j$ we find the best match to $r \in h_j$:

$$\text{sim}_H\left(r, h_j\right) = \max_{r' \in h_j} \text{sim}_H\left(r, r'\right)$$

For symmetry, we also compute the best match to hyper-edge h_i for each reference in and then take the average over all of the reference in the two hyper-edges to get $\text{sim}_H\left(h_i, h_j\right)$. We then use this similarity measure between two hyper-edges to find the hyper-edge similarity $\text{sim}_H\left(r_i, r_j\right)$ between two references r_i and r_j by matching their hyper-edges.

When each references belongs to just one hyper-edge, $\text{sim}_H\left(r_i, r_j\right)$ can be computed simple as $\text{sim}_H\left(r_i.H, r_j.H\right)$. Otherwise, we need to make pairwise comparisons between their hyper-edges.

Finally, we take a simple linear combination of the attribute match $\text{sim}_A\left(r_i, r_j\right)$ and the hyper-edge match $\text{sim}_H\left(r_i, r_j\right)$ to get naïve relational similarity for two references r_i and r_j:

$$\text{sim}_R\left(r_i, r_j\right) = \left(1 - a\right) \times \text{sim}_A\left(r_i, r_j\right) + a \times \text{sim}_H\left(r_i, r_j\right), \quad \left(0 \leq a \leq 1\right)$$

Edge Detail Similarity

(Bhattacharya & Getoor, 2005) call this the edge detail similarity between two clusters since it explicitly considers every edge of all types associated with each cluster, instead of just treating the relations as additional attributes. Each entity cluster is associated with a set of edges that the references contained in it belong to. Recall that each reference r is associated with an observed hyper-edge r.H. Then the edge set c.H for an entity cluster c may be defined as:

$$c.H = U_{r \in \mathcal{R} \wedge r.C = c}\{ h \mid h \in \mathcal{H} \wedge r \in h.R\}$$

These hyper-edges connect c to other clusters. To ground this in terms of our example used above, after we have resolved the 'Agrawal' references so that cluster cluster c_1 contains references r_1 and r_5, then the edge set for cluster is $c_1.H = \{h_1, h_2\}$ having the edges corresponding to the two citations involving 'Agrawal'. We will now define a similarity measure for a pair of edges, so that given this pair-wise similarity measure, we can again use a linkage metric like single link to measure the relational similarity between two clusters.

Just like the naïve relational measure, we first need to define a pair-wise similarity measure

between two hyper-edges. Because we have already noted that what we want to consider for relational similarity are the cluster labels of the references in each edge, instead of their attributes. So for an edge, we consider the multi-set of cluster labels, one for each reference associated with it. However, the references and accordingly the cluster labels in a hyper-edge can be of multiple types. To look at the clusters of each type separately, we define a type projection for an edge as the set of cluster labels from it that are of a particular type. For example, the 'author projection' for edge h_1 in our example has the two author clusters c_1 and c_2. Formally, for a hyper-edge h and a type t, the projection $\Pi_t\left(h\right)$ is defined as:

$$\Pi_t\left(h\right) = U_{r \in h.R}\{ c \mid c = r.C \wedge c.T = t\}$$

To check two edges for similarity, we will consider their projections for each type separately. A common measure for set similarity is the Jaccard similarity. For two sets A and B, their Jaccard similarity is defined as $\text{Jaccard}\left(A, B\right) = \dfrac{\left|A \cap B\right|}{\left|A \cup B\right|}$. Then the similarity for the edges h_i and h_j for a particular type t is:

$$\text{sim}_t\left(h_i, h_j\right) = \text{Jaccard}\left(\Pi_t\left(h_i\right), \Pi_t\left(h_j\right)\right)$$

The overall similarity for edges may be obtained by using some appropriate aggregation operation Σ over all types:

$$\text{sim}\left(h_i, h_j\right) = \sum_{t \in \mathcal{T}} \text{sim}_t\left(h_i, h_j\right)$$

The aggregation operation could be a max or a weighted combination over the types. The same with naïve measures, we have relational similarity between two entity clusters as:

$$\text{sim}_R\left(c_i, c_j\right) = \max_{h_i \in c_i.H, \ h_j \in c_j.H} \text{sim}\left(h_i, \ h_j\right)$$

Neighborhood Similarity

Clearly, an issue with edge detail similarity is the computational complexity. Also, it is not trivial to incrementally update edge detail similarity when clusters merge. A second and probably more pertinent issue is whether it is necessary for the task at hand that we focus on the detailed pair-wise similarity computation for edges. While it may make sense for some other applications, it may not be necessary and efficiently to look at the structure of all the edges separately for the task of relational entity resolution. Using a more concrete example, for two author entities e_1 and e_1' to be considered similar, it is not necessary for both them to co-author a paper with entities e_2, e_3 and e_4 together. Instead, if e_1 participates in an edge $\{e_1, e_2, e_3, e_4\}$ and e_1' participates in three separate edges $\{e_1', e_2\}$, $\{e_1', e_3\}$ and $\{e_1', e_4\}$, then that also should count as significant relational evidence for their being the same author entity (if they have similar attributes as well). So whether or not two entity clusters with similar attributes have the same edge structures, if they have the same neighbor clusters to which they have edges, is sufficient relational evidence for collective entity resolution.

Now we will make formalized notion of neighborhood for a cluster. Recall that we have defined $\Pi_t\left(h\right)$ as the typed projection of cluster labels for an edge h. Also, for an entity cluster c, c.H is the set of edges associated with it. Then we can formally define the typed neighborhood $N_t(c)$ for c as follows:

$$N_t\left(c\right) = U_{h \in c.H}\Pi_t\left(h\right)$$

Again, we now go back to our example in the above. Just suppose that 'Agrawal' and 'Srikant' references have been resolved into author clusters c_1 and c_2 but the other references are still dispersed over paper clusters c_{3a} and c_{3b} and venue clusters c_{4a} and c_{4b}. Then the author neighborhoods for the paper clusters c_{3a} and c_{3b} are identical: $N_{\text{author}}(c_{3a}) = N_{\text{author}}(c_{3b}) = \{c_1, c_2\}$. But their venue neighborhoods are different: $N_{\text{venue}}(c_{3a}) = \{c_{4a}\}$ and $N_{\text{venue}}(c_{3b}) = \{c_{4b}\}$.

This defined the neighborhood as a set of related clusters, but the neighborhood can also be defined as a multiset in which the multiplicity of the different neighboring clusters is preserved. We will use $N_{\text{Mt}}\left(c\right)$ to denote the multiset of neighborhood clusters.

We have seen how the neighborhood of a cluster of references can be represented as a set of cluster labels and that we can compute relational similarity between two clusters by considering the similarity of their neighborhoods. Besides the Jaccard similarity we have just used in the edge detail similarity, there are many different metrics proposed and evaluated for measuring commonness between sets. Here we adapt and modify some of these measures and study their applicability for this problem (Bhattacharya & Getoor, 2007).

Common Neighbors: This is the simplest approach for measuring commonness between sets and the number of elements that occur in both. For two clusters and , their common typed neighbor score is defined as follows.

$$\text{CNS}_t\left(c_i, \ c_j\right) = \frac{1}{K} \times \left| N_t\left(c_i\right) \cap N_t\left(c_j\right)\right|$$

where K is a large enough constant such that the measure is less than 1 for all pairs of clusters. For two references which attributes similarity is not very informative, this score measures the overlap in their connected entity clusters. The greater the score of common entity clusters, the higher the possibility that the two references refer to the same entity as well. Then for the overall similarity between clusters we can aggregate over all types as before:

$$\text{sim}_R \left(c_i, \; c_j \right) = \sum_{t \in \mathcal{T}} \text{CNS}_t \left(c_i, \; c_j \right)$$

This definition ignores the frequency of connectivity to a neighbor. Then we also define a common neighbor score with frequencies that takes into account multiple occurrences of common clusters in the neighborhoods:

$$\text{CNS\_Fr}_t \left(c_i, \; c_j \right) = \frac{1}{K'} \times \left| N_{Mt} \left(c_i \right) \cap N_{Mt} \left(c_j \right) \right|$$

And we can have corresponding overall similarity for multi-set.

Jaccard Similarity: This has been mentioned in edge detail similarity. We can just do the same as before. So the overall similarity between clusters c_i and c_j:

$$\text{sim}_R \left(c_i, \; c_j \right) = \sum_{t \in \mathcal{T}} \text{Jaccard} \left(N_t \left(c_i \right), \; N_t \left(c_j \right) \right)$$

As before, we may consider neighbor counts to define the Jaccard coefficient with frequencies Jaccard_Fr$_t$(c_i,c_j), by using $N_{Mt}(c_i)$ and $N_{Mt}(c_j)$ in the definition.

Adamic/Adar Similarity: Both the common similarity and Jaccard similarity consider all cluster labels in the neighborhood as equally important and significant for determining co-reference. However, this is not always desirable. If a cluster is frequently linked with many different clusters, then its presence in a shared neighborhood is not as significant as a cluster which is less frequent. This similar to the idea behind inverse document

frequency in the commonly used TF-IDF scheme in information retrieval. (Adamic and Adar, 2003) use this idea for predicting friendship from web page features. They proposed a similarity measure between two web pages X and Y that individually considers the significance of each element that they share and assigns weights to them accordingly. This has come to be called the Adar/Adamic score:

$$\text{similarity} \left(X, \; Y \right) = \sum_{\text{shared feature } z} \frac{1}{\log \left(\text{frequency} \left(z \right) \right)}$$

(Liben-Nowell and Kleinberg, 2003) adapted this idea for the task of link prediction in social networks considering node neighborhoods where they used the size of a node's neighborhood for measuring frequency or commonness. We generalize this idea to propose a class of Adar/Adamic measures for our problem. If the uniqueness of a cluster label c is denoted as u(c), then we define the Adar similarity score of two typed clusters c_i and c_j:

$$\text{Adar}_t \left(c_i, \; c_j \right) = \frac{\sum_{c \in N_t(c_i) \cap N_t(c_j)} u \left(c \right)}{\sum_{c \in N_t(c_i) \cup N_t(c_j)} u \left(c \right)}$$

where the denominator normalized the score and the uniqueness u(c) are defined as:

$$u \left(c \right) = \frac{1}{\log \left(\left| N_t \left(c \right) \right| \right)}$$

Now the Jaccard similarity can be viewed as a special case of the Adar score when all nodes are equally unique. And the overall similarity can be defined as:

$$\text{sim}_R \left(c_i, \; c_j \right) = \sum_{t \in \mathcal{T}} \text{Adar}_t \left(c_i, \; c_j \right)$$

Ad before, we can define $Adar\_Fr_t(c_i, c_j)$ that takes into account the multiplicity of the neighbors.

Adar Similarity with Ambiguity Estimate: It may not always work well while we use the neighborhood size of a cluster to define its uniqueness, even though it has shown to be well performed in link prediction applications. When making entity resolution decisions, we often do not directly know the neighbors for each entity from the data. The true neighborhood size for any entity cluster is known only after the entity graph has been correctly reconstructed. So it is incorrect and of over-estimate on the actual neighborhood size when we use the neighborhood size as a measure of uniqueness at any intermediate stage of the resolution algorithm. We give a definition of uniqueness which incorporates a notion of the ambiguity of the attributes found in the shared neighborhood. We define the uniqueness of a cluster c as inversely proportional to the average ambiguity of its references:

$$u(c) = \frac{1}{Avg_{r \in c} \ Amb(r.A)}.$$

This measure is defined in terms of the ambiguity of a reference's attributes. For a reference attribute A, denoted $\mathcal{R}.A$ which means the attribute A of all the references, a naïve estimate for the ambiguity of a value of r.A for the attributes of reference r is:

$$Amb(r.A) = \frac{|\sigma_{R.A=r.A}(R)|}{|R|},$$

where

$$\sigma_{\mathcal{R}.A=r.A}(\mathcal{R}) = \{\ r' \mid r' \in \mathcal{R} \wedge r'.A = r.A\ \}$$

denotes the subset of references with value r.A for A. This estimate is clearly not good since the number of references with a certain attribute value

does not always match the number of different entity labels for that attribute. We can do much better if we add another attribute in. Given A', the ambiguity for value of A can be estimated as:

$$Amb(r.A \mid r.A') = \frac{|\ \delta(\pi_{\mathcal{R}.A'}(\sigma_{R.A=r.A}(\mathcal{R})))\ |}{|\mathcal{R}|},$$

Where

$$\delta(\pi_{R.A'}(\sigma_{R.A=r.A}(R))) =$$
$$\{\ r' \mid r' \in \sigma_{R.A=r.A}(R) \wedge r'.A' = r.A'\ \}$$

is the subset of distinct values observed for *A'* in references with *R.A = r.A*. For example, we can estimate the ambiguity of a last name by counting the number of different first names observed for it. This provides a better estimate of the ambiguity of any value of an attribute *A* when *A'* is not correlated with *A*.

Higher-Order Neighborhoods: Analysis of the commonness of neighborhoods can be viewed as an investigation of paths of length two between two clusters. We also investigate whether higher-order neighborhoods play a role in detecting co-reference. We evaluate measures which takes into account collaboration paths of length three when describe neighborhood similarity measures. As the clusters change, it becomes computationally infeasible to recompute all paths between all cluster pairs. Instead, we calculate the second-order typed neighborhood $N_t^2(c)$ for a cluster c by recursively taking the set union or multi-set union of the neighborhoods of all typed neighboring clusters: $N_t^2(c) = \cup_{c' \in N_t(c)} N_t(c')$. For paths of length three to be present between two clusters and , there must be intersections between the $N_t(c_i)$ and $N_t^2(c_i)$ or vice versa. Then, to find the similarity over paths of length three or less for and , we take the average of the similarities over length-2 paths and length-3 paths:

$$sim_t(c_i, c_j) = \frac{1}{3}[Jaccard(N_t(c_i), N_t(c_j)) +$$
$$Jaccard(N_t^2(c_i), N_t(c_j)) + Jaccard(N_t(c_i), N_t^2(c_j))].$$

And as before, we can measure the overall relational similarity and the similarity which takes into account the multiplicity of the neighbors.

Negative Constraints from Relationships

So far, we have considered relational structure as additional positive evidence for inferring that two author references refer to the same underlying author entity. However, there may be negative constraints as well. A 'soft' aspect of negative evidence is directly captured by the combined similarity measure. Just imagine two references with identical names. If we only consider attributes, their similarity would be very high. Yet, if they do not have any similarity in their hyper-edges, then we are less inclined to believe that they correspond to the same entity. This is reflected by the drop in their overall similarity when the relational similarity measure is factored in as well.

We may also imagine stronger relational constraints for clustering. In many relational domains, there is the constraint that no two references appearing in the same edge can be duplicates of each other. In our example, no matter how similar the names 'R. Srikant' and "R. Agrawal' are deemed to by the attribute similarity measure that is employed, they cannot be the same entity since they are co-authors. We have such constrains for every edge that has more than one reference. This can be taken into account by the relational similarity measure. The similarity between two cluster pairs is zero if merging them violates any relational constraint.

ENTITY RESOLUTION ALGORITHM ON MULTIPLE RELATIONS

Given the similarity measure for a pair of clusters, (Bhattacharya & Getoor, 2007) use a greedy agglomerative clustering algorithm that finds the closest cluster pair at each step and merges them. Here we discuss several implementation and performance issues regarding our relational clustering algorithm for entity resolution. The high-level pseudo code for the algorithm is provided as following:

1. Find similar references using blocking
2. Initialize clusters using bootstrapping
3. For clusters c_i, c_j such that similar (c_i, c_j)
4. Insert $< sim(c_i, c_j), c_i, c_j, >$ into priority queue
5. While priority queue not empty
6. Extract $< sim(c_i, c_j), c_i, c_j, >$ from queue
7. If $sim(c_i, c_j)$ less than threshold, then stop
8. Merge c_i and c_j to new cluster c_{ij}
9. Remove entries for c_i and c_j from queue
10. For each cluster c_k such that similar (c_{ij}, c_k)
11. Insert $< sim(c_{ij}, c_k), c_{ij}, c_k >$ into queue
12. For each cluster c_n neighbor of c_{ij} do
13. For c_k such that similar (c_n, c_k)
14. Update $sim(c_n, c_k)$ in queue

The algorithm inserts all candidate duplicate pairs – identified using a 'blocking' approach – into a priority queue considering their similarities. Then it iteratively picks the pair with the highest similarity and merges them. The algorithm terminates when the similarity for the closest pair falls below a threshold.

Blocking

It is impractical to consider all possible pairs as potential candidates for merging in most situations where the datasets are probably not small. Apart from the scaling issue, most pairs checked by an $O(n^2)$ approach will be rejected since usually only about 1% of all pairs are true matches. Blocking techniques (Hernandez & Stolfo, 1995; Monge & Elkan, 1997; McCallum et al. 2000) are usually employed to rule out pairs which are certain to be non-matches. The goal of blocking is to separate references into possibly overlapping buckets and only pairs of references within each bucket are considered as potential matches. In relational clustering algorithm, the blocking method is just as a black box and any method that can quickly identify potential matches minimizing false negatives can be used. We use a variant of an algorithm proposed by (McCallum et al. 2000).

The algorithm makes a single pass over the list of references and assigns them to buckets using an attribute similarity measure. Each bucket has representative reference that is the most similar to all references currently in the bucket. For assigning any reference, it is compared to the representative for each bucket. It is assigned to all buckets for which the similarity is above a threshold. If no similar bucket is found, a new bucket is created for this reference. A naïve implementation yields a $O(n(b+f))$ algorithm for n references and b buckets and when a reference is assigned to at most f buckets. This can be improved by maintaining an inverted index over buckets. For example, when dealing with names, for each character, we maintain the list of buckets storing last names starting with that character. Then buckets can be looked up in constant time for each reference leading to an $O(nf)$ algorithm.

Relational Bootstrapping

The relational clustering algorithm begins with each reference assigned to a separate entity cluster. So to start with, the clusters are disconnected and there is no relational evidence at all between clusters to depend upon for the initial iterations of the algorithm. In other words, the there are no shared neighbors for references that belong to different hyper-edges. As a result, the relational component of the similarity between clusters would be zero and merges would occur based solely on attribute similarity. Many of such initial merges can be inaccurate, particularly for the references with ambiguous attribute values. This is what we want to avoid. To deal with this, we would like to bootstrap the clusters so that some relational evidence may be leveraged. That is to make each reference to be not assigned to a distinct cluster. Specifically, if we are confident that some reference that some reference pair that has attributes v_1 and v_2 is co-referent, and then they should be assigned to the same initial cluster, where either v_1 is identical to v_2, or v_1 is an initialed form of v_2. It would also speed up the algorithm if initial clusters could be merged without similarity computations and updates. For example, we may merge 'Alfred Aho' references with other 'Alfred Aho' references or with 'A. Aho' references. However, for domains where last names repeat very frequently, like Chinese, Japanese or Indian names, this can affect precision quite adversely. For the case of such common last names, the same author label can be assigned to pairs only when they have document co-author with identical names as well. This should improve bootstrap precision significantly under the assumption that while it may be common for different authors to have the same name, it is extremely unlikely that they will collaborate with the same author, or with two other authors with identical names.

However, precision is crucial for the bootstrap process since out algorithm cannot undo any of these initial merge operations. Observe that this bootstrapping is not necessary for entity resolutions that are not on multiple relations. For such approaches, the decision for any reference pair is the same irrespective of the decisions for other pairs. So bootstrapping does not have any effect on subsequent decisions. We here describe our bootstrap-ping scheme for relational clustering that makes use of the hyper-edges for improved bootstrap performance. The basic idea is very similar to the naive relational approach described with the difference that we use exact matches instead of similarity for attributes. To determine if any two references should be assigned to the same initial cluster, we first check if their attributes match exactly. For references with ambiguous attributes, we also check if the attributes of their related references match. We now discuss this in greater detail.

The bootstrap scheme goes over each reference pair that is potentially co-referent (as determined by blocking) and determines if it is a bootstrap candidate. Consider the simple bootstrap scheme that looks only at the attributes of two references. It determines which attribute values are ambiguous and which are not using a data-based ambiguity estimate. References with ambiguous attribute values are assigned to distinct clusters. Any reference pair whose attribute values match and are not ambiguous is considered to be a bootstrap candidate. The problem with this simple approach is that it assigns all references with ambiguous attributes to distinct clusters leading to poor recall in datasets with high ambiguity. When hyper-edges are available, they can be used as evidence for bootstrapping of ambiguous references. A pair of ambiguous references forms a bootstrap candidate if their hyper-edges match. Two hyper-edges, h_1 and h_2, are said to have a k-exact-match if there are at least k pairs of references (r_i, r_j), $r_i \in h_1.R, r_j \in h_2.R$ with exact matching attributes, that is, $r_i.A = r_j.A$. Two references, r_1 and r_2, are

bootstrap candidates if any pair of their hyper-edges have a k. As a bibliographic example, two reference with the name 'W. Wang' will not be merged during bootstrapping on the basis of the name alone. However, if the first

'Wang' has co-author 'A. Ansari', then they have a 1-exact-match and, depending on a threshold for k, they would be merged. The value of k for the hyper-edges test depends on the ambiguity of the domain. A higher value of k should be used for domains with high ambiguity. Also, when matching hyper-edges, references with ambiguous attributes are not considered for matches in high ambiguity domains. For example, 'C. Chen' may not be considered for a co-author match since it is a common name. Other attribute of the reference, and also of the hyper-edges, when available, can be used to further constrain bootstrap candidates. Two references are considered only if these other attributes do not conflict.

Once bootstrap candidates have been identified, the initial clusters are created using the union-find approach so that any two references that are bootstrap candidates are assigned to the same initial cluster. In addition to improving accuracy of the relational clustering algorithm, bootstrapping reduces execution time by significantly lowering the initial number of clusters without having to find the most similar cluster-pairs or perform expensive similarity computations.

Merging and Updating

Once potential duplicate entity clusters have been identified and clusters have been bootstrapped, the algorithm iteratively merges the most similar cluster pair and updates similarities until the similarity drops below some specified threshold. Lines 5–14 of the pseudo code above have shown this process. The key steps are similarity update steps shown in lines 12–14 in the pseudo code that distinguish collective relational clustering from a traditional agglomerative clustering algorithm.

Here, we describe the data structure that we maintained for each cluster to perform update steps efficiently. We maintain three additional lists with each cluster, including the list of similar clusters for each cluster, the list to keep track of all neighboring clusters and the list to keep the track of all the queue entries that involve this cluster. For a cluster that has a single reference r, the similar clusters are those that contain references in the same bucket as r after blocking. Also, the neighbors for this cluster are the clusters containing references that share a hyper-edge with r. Then, as two clusters merge to form a new cluster, all of these lists can be constructed locally for the new cluster from those of its parents. All of the update operations can be performed efficiently using these lists. For example, updates for related clusters are done by first accessing the neighbor list and then traversing the similar list for each of them.

Complexity Analysis

Now that we have described each component of our relational clustering algorithm, let us analyze its time complexity.

We here discuss the time complexity of the similarity computations in lines 3-4 of the pseudo code. In the worst case scenario where the bootstrapping approach does not reduce any clusters at all, we need to compare every pair of references within each bucket. Suppose we have n references, i.e. $|\mathcal{R}| = n$, that are assigned to b buckets with each reference being assigned to at most f buckets. Then, using an optimistic estimate, we have references in each bucket, leading to $O((nf / b)^2)$ comparisons per bucket and a total of $O(n^2 f^2 / b)$ comparisons. If we assume that the number of buckets is proportional to the number of references, i.e. b is $O(n)$, and that f is a small constant independent of n, we have $O(n)$ computations. However, it should be noted that

this is not a worst case analysis for the bucketing. A bad bucketing algorithm that assigns $O(n)$ references to any bucket will lead to $O(n^2)$ comparisons.

Then, let us look at the time complexity of iteration in the algorithm. We first discuss the time taken by single iteration. We should analyze how many update or insert operations are required. Just assume that for each bucket that is affected by a merge operation, all the $O((nf / b)^2)$ computations need to be redone. Then we need to find out how many buckets may be affected by a merge operation. As we know two buckets are connected if any hyper-edge connects two references in the two buckets. So if any bucket is connected to k other buckets, each merge operation leads to $O(k(nf / b)^2)$ update or insert operations. This is still only $O(k)$ operations when f is a constant independent of n and b is $O(n)$. Using a binary-heap implementation for the priority queue, the extract-max and each insert and update operation take $O(\log q)$ time, where q is the number of entries in the queue. So the total cost of each iteration of the algorithm is $O(k \log q)$. Now, we count the total time of the whole iterations. In the worst case, the algorithm may have to exhaust the priority queue before the similarity falls below the threshold. So we need to consider the number of merge operations that are required to exhaust a queue that has q entries. If the merge tree is perfectly balanced, then the size of each cluster is doubled by each merge operation and as few as $O(\log q)$ merges are required. However, in the worst case, the merge tree may be q-deep requiring as many as $O(q)$ merges. With each merge operation requiring $O(k \log q)$ time, the total cost of the iterative process is $O(qk \log q)$.

Finally, in order to put a bound on the initial size q of the priority queue, we again consider the worst-case scenario where bootstrapping does not reduce the number of initial clusters. This results in $O(n^2f^2/b)$ entries in the queue as shown earlier. Since this is again O(n), the total cost of the algorithm can be bounded by O(nk log n). The one cost that we have not considered so far is that of bootstrapping. We can analyze the bootstrapping by considering it as a sequence of cluster merge operations that do not require any updates or inserts to the priority queue. Then the worst case analysis of the number of iterations accounts for the bootstrapping as well.

CONCLUSION

In this chapter, we address the problem of resolving references to multiple types of related entities. We have shown how entity resolution may be posed as a relational clustering problem where the entity labels of related references depend on each other. We propose two different similarity measures for references that consider relational similarity among them in addition to the attribute similarities. We show how these similarity measures may be used to resolve references into entities by clustering them. Then we described an algorithm for this problem. We investigated the effectiveness of these relational similarity measures on three real bibliographic datasets with different characteristic and levels of ambiguity. In all datasets, our similarity measures significantly outperformed the baseline algorithms, but the degree of improvement depended on the intrinsic ambiguity of the dataset—the greater the ambiguity, the greater the benefit obtained using collective resolution. To study the dependence of the algorithm's performance on different structural characteristics of the domain, we performed detailed experiments on synthetically generated data where we can vary the data characteristics in a controlled fashion. We present a relational bootstrapping scheme for clustering that significantly reduces execu-

tion time in addition to improve performance. We also illustrate the diverse issues that need to be addressed when resolving typed references in relational data.

There are still many interesting avenues for future work. While our algorithms are general and can handle multiple entity types, our experimental results have focused on a single entity and relation type. Also all our real-world datasets are bibliographic; it would be interesting to study our algorithms on different types of relational data including consumer data, social network data, and biological data. Our work starts from data in which the references have already been extracted; it would be interesting to integrate the collective resolution process with the extraction process.

REFERENCES

Adamic, L. A., & Adar, E. (2003). Friends and neighbors on the web. *Social Networks*, 25(3), 211–230. doi:10.1016/S0378-8733(03)00009-1

Berkhin, P. (2006). A survey of clustering data mining techniques. In *Grouping multidimensional data* (pp. 25–71). Berlin: Springer. doi:10.1007/3-540-28349-8_2

Bhattacharya, I., & Getoor, L. (2005). Relational clustering for multi-type entity resolution. In *Proceedings of the 4th International Workshop on Multi-Relational Mining* (pp. 3-12). ACM.

Bhattacharya, I., & Getoor, L. (2007). Collective entity resolution in relational data. *ACM Transactions on Knowledge Discovery from Data*, 1(1), 5. doi:10.1145/1217299.1217304

Cohen, W. W., Ravikumar, P., & Fienberg, S. E. (2003). A comparison of string distance metrics for name-matching tasks. In *Proceedings of the IJCAI-2003 Workshop on Information Integration on the Web (IIWeb-03)* (Vol. 47). IJCAI.

Elmagarmid, A. K., Ipeirotis, P. G., & Very-kios, V. S. (2007). Duplicate record detection: A survey. *IEEE Transactions on Knowledge and Data Engineering*, *19*(1), 1–16. doi:10.1109/TKDE.2007.250581

Fellegi, I. P., & Sunter, A. B. (1969). A theory for record linkage. *Journal of the American Statistical Association*, *64*(328), 1183–1210. doi:10.1080/0 1621459.1969.10501049

Hernández, M. A., & Stolfo, S. J. (1995). The merge/purge problem for large databases. *SIGMOD Record*, *24*(2), 127–138. doi:10.1145/568271.223807

Liben-Nowell, D., & Kleinberg, J. (2007). The link-prediction problem for social networks. *Journal of the American Society for Information Science and Technology*, *58*(7), 1019–1031. doi:10.1002/asi.20591

McCallum, A., Nigam, K., & Ungar, L. H. (2000). Efficient clustering of high-dimensional data sets with application to reference matching. In *Proceedings of the Sixth ACM SIGKDD International Conference on Knowledge Discovery and Data Mining* (pp. 169-178). ACM.

Monge, A., & Elkan, C. (1997). An efficient domain-independent algorithm for detecting approximately duplicate database records. In *Proceedings of the SIGMOD Workshop on Research Issues on Data Mining and Knowledge Discovery (DMKD)*. Tuscon, AZ: ACM.

Sarawagi, S., & Bhamidipaty, A. (2002). Interactive deduplication using active learning. In *Proceedings of the Eighth ACM SIGKDD International Conference on Knowledge Discovery and Data Mining* (pp. 269-278). ACM.

Wang, H. Z., & Fan, W. F. (2011). Object identification on complex data: A survey. *Jisuanji Xuebao*, *34*(10), 1843–1852.

ADDITIONAL READING

Ananthakrishna, R., Chaudhuri, S., & Ganti, V. (2002, August). Eliminating fuzzy duplicates in data warehouses. In Proceedings of *the 28th international conference on Very Large Data Bases* (pp. 586-597). VLDB Endowment.

Benjelloun, O., Garcia-Molina, H., Menestrina, D., Su, Q., Whang, S. E., & Widom, J. (2009). Swoosh: a generic approach to entity resolution. *The VLDB Journal—The International Journal on Very Large Data Bases*, 18(1), 255-276.

Bhattacharya, I., & Getoor, L. (2004, June). Iterative record linkage for cleaning and integration. In Proceedings of *the 9th ACM SIGMOD workshop on Research issues in data mining and knowledge discovery* (pp. 11-18). ACM.

Bhattacharya, I., & Getoor, L. (2005). A latent dirichlet model for unsupervised entity resolution. In *The SIAM Conference on Data Mining (SIAM-SDM)*. Bethesda, MD.

Bhattacharya, I., & Getoor, L. (2006). Entity resolution in graphs. *Mining graph data*, 311.

Bhattacharya, I., Getoor, L., & Licamele, L. (2006, August). Query-time entity resolution. In Proceedings of *the 12th ACM SIGKDD international conference on Knowledge discovery and data mining* (pp. 529-534). ACM.

Bontcheva, K., Dimitrov, M., Maynard, D., Tablan, V., & Cunningham, H. (2002, June). Shallow methods for named entity coreference resolution. In Chaînes de références et résolveurs d'anaphores, workshop TALN.

Chaudhuri, S., Ganjam, K., Ganti, V., & Motwani, R. (2003, June). Robust and efficient fuzzy match for online data cleaning. In *Proceedings of the 2003 ACM SIGMOD international conference on Management of data* (pp. 313–324). ACM. doi:10.1145/872757.872796

Cohen, W. W., & Richman, J. (2002, July). Learning to match and cluster large high-dimensional data sets for data integration. In Proceedings of *the eighth ACM SIGKDD international conference on Knowledge discovery and data mining* (pp. 475-480). ACM.

Culotta, A., & McCallum, A. (2005, October). Joint deduplication of multiple record types in relational data. In Proceedings of *the 14th ACM international conference on Information and knowledge management* (pp. 257-258). ACM.

Domingos, P. (2004). Multi-relational record linkage. In *In Proceedings of the KDD-2004 Workshop on Multi-Relational Data Mining*.

Dong, X., Halevy, A., & Madhavan, J. (2005, June). Reference reconciliation in complex information spaces. In *Proceedings of the 2005 ACM SIGMOD international conference on Management of data* (pp. 85-96). ACM.

Haghighi, A., & Klein, D. (2007, June). Unsupervised coreference resolution in a nonparametric bayesian model. In Annual meeting-Association for Computational Linguistics (Vol. 45, No. 1, p. 848).

Kalashnikov, D. V., Mehrotra, S., & Chen, Z. (2005, April). Exploiting relationships for domain-independent data cleaning. In SIAM data mining (SDM) conf.

McCallum, A., & Wellner, B. (2004). Conditional models of identity uncertainty with application to noun coreference. *Advances in Neural Information Processing Systems*, *17*, 905–912.

McCarthy, J. F., & Lehnert, W. G. (1995). Using decision trees for coreference resolution. *arXiv preprint cmp-lg/9505043*.

Pasula, H., Marthi, B., Milch, B., Russell, S., & Shpitser, I. (2002). Identity uncertainty and citation matching. Nips. In *The Annual Conference on Neural Information Processing Systems* (NIPS). Vancouver, Canada.

KEY TERMS AND DEFINITIONS

Attribute Similarity: The similarity of attributes between two entity clusters while each cluster is a collection of references with their own attributes.

Edge Detail Similarity: The similarity between two clusters considering every edge of all types associated with each cluster.

Entity Resolution on Multiple Relations: It's a kind of entity resolution in which entities for co-occurring references are determined jointly rather than independently as in the traditional approaches.

Group-Wise Entity Resolution: In Group-wise entity resolution, we cluster the references so that those that correspond to the same real-world entity end up in the same cluster.

Neighborhood Similarity: The similarity between two entity clusters considering the similarity of their neighborhoods.

Pairwise Entity Resolution: Pairwise entity resolution is to recognize whether two data objects and is referring to the same real-world entity.

Relational Clustering Algorithm: A greedy agglomerative clustering algorithm with given similarity measure for a pair of reference clusters.

Chapter 7
XML Object Identification

ABSTRACT

For the ability to represent data from a wide variety of sources, XML is rapidly emerging as the new standard for data representation and exchange on Web and e-government. To effectively use XML data in practice, entity resolution, which has been proven extremely useful in data fusion, inconsistency detection, and data repairing, must be in place to improve the quality of the XML data. In this chapter, the authors deal specifically with object identification on XML data, the application of which includes XML document management in highly dynamic applications like the Web and peer-to-peer systems, detection of duplicate elements in nested XML data, and finding similar identities among objects from multiple Web sources. The authors survey techniques of pairwise and groupwise entity resolution for XML data, which adopt structured information to describe the similarity or distance of XML data, like XML document and XML elements in document, and find the matching pairs which describe same object or classify them into separate groups, each group corresponding to the same object in real world. There are a lot of ways to describe the XML structure and content, such as a tree, Bayesian network, and set. The authors introduce some well-known algorithm base on these structures to solve matching XML data problems. Finally, the authors discuss directions for future research.

INTRODUCTION

The object identification problem is a central problem arising in data cleaning and data integration, where different objects must be compared to determine if they refer to the same real-world entity, even in the presence of errors such as misspellings. As the spread of the XML format as a data model increases, the need to develop effective strategies for XML object identification grows.

For the ability to represent data from a wide variety of sources, XML is rapidly emerging as the new standard for data representation and exchange on web and e-government etc. There are quantities of data represented in XML forms in information system nowadays, and XML document has becomes the standard of describing information of integrating different kind of data from sources in which XML data has different schema or there exists different forms of the same object. Query on data which has not been processed will lead to duplicate or inconsistent results. Statistics analysis on such data will count one object many times, which causes wrong decision making. If integrating XML data using object identification

DOI: 10.4018/978-1-4666-5198-2.ch007

method, making each class describing the same object, it will improve the quality of query and accuracy of statistics.

Although there exist a lot of object identification techniques, they mainly focus on duplicate record in literature or in a database. The research on object identification of complex data especially those in XML form is starting recently, the application of which mainly includes XML document management in Highly dynamic applications like the Web and peer-to-peer systems, detection of duplicate elements in nested XML data and finding similar identities among objects from multiple web sources.

Our focus in this chapter is on object identification on XML data, the rest of the paper is organized as follows. We begin with a brief overview of the definition of object identification on complex data and present our framework for pairwise and groupwise entity resolution on XML Next we introduce several algorithms to solve corresponding problems separately. We conclude with a discussion of the difficulties and challenges when solving XML object identification problem.

Since XML has been widely used in information integration due to its flexibility, entity resolution techniques could be applied to information integration based on XML (Chapter 14).

BACKGROUND

According to the different identification results, object identification on XML data can be classified into two categories, namely pairwise entity and groupwise entity resolution. The former is to determine whether two object o_1 and o_2 describe the same object in the real world; the latter is to classify the data set S into subset S_1, S_2, ..., S_k, which satisfy:

$$S_1 \cap S_2 \cap ... \cap S_k = \varphi \qquad (1)$$

and

$$S_1 \cup S_2 \cup ... \cup S_k = S \qquad (2)$$

making that $\forall i \in [1, k]$, $\forall o_1, o_2 \in S_i$, they describe the same object in real world.

MAIN FOCUS OF THE CHAPTER

In pairwise entity resolution, which is also named as XML document matching or element matching, the main work concentrates on the similarity or distance of XML data. Compared with structured or unstructured data, the outstanding feature of XML data is its abundant structure information, with this respect, the most used matching approach is to describe the similarity or distance of XML document with structure information. There are many ways to describe the similarity of XML document structure, such as similarity of tree when using tree to simulate XML document structure, XMLDup system using Bayesian network similarity(Leit et al. 2007), similarity of sets when extract XML documents into set.

In groupwise entity resolution, people often adopt object identification method based on similarity function, which means by definition of distance function distance or similarity function sim, given two objects o_1, o_2 and threshold ε, when $sim(o_1, o_2) \geq \varepsilon$ or $distance(o_1, o_2) \leq \varepsilon$, o_1 and o_2 will be regarded as the same object. According to objects, XML group-wise entity resolution can be classified into two categories, document level identification and element level identification. The former is to classify XML documents, making each category describes same object, which can be done with either neighbour ordering method(Puhlmann S et al. 2006)or identification based on tuple matching; the latter is to classify elements in same XML document, making each category describing same entity.

XML PAIRWISE ENTITY RESOLUTION

XML pairwise entity resolution is to find XML documents or element pair which describe the same object, which is also called XML document matching or element matching. The work mainly focuses on how to define the similarity or distance of XML data. Compared with structured or unstructured data, the most outstanding feature of XML data is the variety of its structure information, with this respect, using structured information to describe the similarity or distance is more frequently used.

Using Tree Structure to Describe the Similarity

Since the XML document can be described by tree structure, it is convenient to describe the similarity of the XML document with tree similarity. There are mainly two ways to calculate similarity of trees, one is based on tree edit distance (Tai et al. 1979), the other is based on overlap(Milano et al. 2006).

Tree Edit Distance

The tree-to-tree correction problem is to determine, for two labeled ordered trees T and T', the distance from T to T' as measured by the minimum cost sequence of edit operations needed to transform T into T'. The edit operations investigated allow changing one node of a tree into another node, deleting one node from a tree, or inserting a node into a tree. An algorithm is presented which solves this problem m time $O(V*\ V'*LZ*L'2)$, where V and V' are the numbers of nodes respectively of T and T', and L and L' are the maximum depths respectively of T and T'. Possible applications are to the problems of measuring the similarity between trees, automatic error recovery and correction of programming languages, and determining the largest common substructure of two trees.

In this paper all trees we discuss are rooted, ordered, and labeled. Let T be a tree. $|T|$ denotes the number of nodes of T. $T[i]$ denotes the node of T whose position in the preorder for nodes of T is i. The preorder traversal on T is to first visit the root of T and then traverse the subtrees of T from left to right, each subtree traversed in preorder. The following diagram illustrates how nodes of a tree T are denoted:

Let r be an arbitrary cost function which assigns to each edit operation b $\rightarrow$ c a nonnegative real number r(b $\rightarrow$ c). Extent r to a sequence of edit operations S = $s_1, s_2, ..., s_m$ by letting r(S) $= \sum_{l=1}^{m} r(s_l)$. Without loss of generality it may be assumed that r(b $\rightarrow$ b) = 0 and that r(b $\rightarrow$ a) + r(a $\rightarrow$ c) $\geq$ r(b $\rightarrow$ c).

The distance $d(T, T')$ from tree T to tree T' is defined to be the minimum cost of all sequences of edit operations which transform T into T', i.e., $d(T, T') = \min\{r(S)|S$ is a sequence of edit operations which transform T into $T'\}$.

- **Mapping:** Intuitively, a mapping is a description of how a sequence of edit operations transforms T into T', ignoring the order in which edit operations are applied. Consider the following diagram:

A dotted line from $T[i]$ to $T'[j]$ indicates that $T[i]$ should be changed to $T'[j]$ if $T[i]\ T'[j]$, or that $T[i]$ remains unchanged, but becomes $T'[j]$, if $T[i] = T'[j]$. Nodes of T not touched by dotted lines

Figure 1. Tree T (Tai K C et al. 1979)

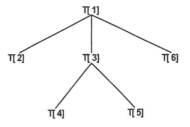

Figure 2. Transform T into T' (Tai K C et al. 1979)

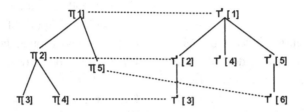

are to be deleted and nodes of *T'* not touched are to be inserted. Such a diagram is called a mapping, which shows a way of transforming *T* to *T'*. Let M he a mapping from *T* to *T'* and let *I* and *J* be the sets of untouched nodes of *T* and *T'* respectively. We define the cost of M:

Definition 1:

$$\text{cost}(M) \sum_{(i,j) \in M} r(T[i] \rightarrow T'[j]) + \sum_{i \in I} r(T[i] \rightarrow \wedge) + \sum_{j \in J} r(\wedge \rightarrow T'[j]).$$

Thus, the cost of M is just the cost of the sequence of edit operation which consists of a change operation $T[i] \rightarrow T'[j]$ for each line(i, j) of M, a delete operation $T[i] \rightarrow \wedge$ for each node T[i] not touched by a line of M, and an insert operation $\wedge \rightarrow T'[j]$ for each node T'[j] not touched by a line of M.

Theorem 1:

$d(T, T') = \min\{\text{cost}(M) \mid M$ is a mapping from *T* to *T'*$\}$.

MIN_M (i+1, j+1) min{cost(M)|M is a mapping from

T (1: i+1) to' (1: j+1) such that (i+1, j+1) $\in$ M}.

Theorem 2:

$$D(i+1, j+1) = \min\{D(i, j+1) + r(T[i+1]-> \wedge),$$
$$D(i+1, j) + r(\wedge -> T'[i+1]), \text{MIN\_M}(i+1, j+1)\}$$
for all i, j, $1 \leq i$ T, $1 \leq j$ T'

- **Computation of MIN_M(t + l, j + 1):** Assume that $s \leq u \leq t$, $t \leq v \leq j$, T[u] is on the path from T[s] to T[i], and T'[v] is on the path from T'[t] to T'[j]. Define E[s: u: I, t: v: j] to be min{ $\text{cost}(M)$ |M is a mapping from T(s:i) to $T'(t:j)$ such that(s, t) is in M and no descendant of T[s] (T'[t]) on the path from T[s] (T'[t]) to T[u] (T'[v]) is touched by a line of M}.

Theorem 3:

MIN_M (i+1, j+1)= T[i+1] $\rightarrow$ T'[j+1] +

$\min_{s,t}$ {MIN$_{M(s,t)}$+ E [s:f (i+1: i,t: f (j+1): j]-r(T[s] $\rightarrow$ T'[t]}

where T'[s] and T'[t] are ancestors of T[i+1] and T'[j+1], respectively.

- **Algorithm for the Tree-to-Tree Correction Problem:** An algorithm is presented which computes the distance from tree *T* to tree *T'* in polynomial time. This algorithm consists of the following three steps:

1. Compute $E[s:u:i,t:v:j]$ for all s, u, i, t, u, j, where $1 \leq i \leq T$, $1 \leq j \leq T'$, $T[u](T'[v])$ is on the path from $T[1](T'[1])$ to $T[i](T'[j])$, $T[s]$ $(T'[t])$ is on the path from $T[1](T'[1])$ to $T[u](T'[v])$;
2. Compute $MIN\_M(i, j)$ for all, i, j, where $1 \leq i \leq T$ and $1 \leq j \leq T'$;
3. Compute $D(i, j)$ for all i, j, where $1 \leq i \leq T$ and $1 \leq j \leq T'$;

Define $(x) = f((x))$ for $n \geq 1$ and $x > 1$, where $f(x)$ is the father of node x, and $f(x) = x$

Structure Aware XML Distance Based on Overlap (Milano D et al. 2006)

Tree distances are not fully able to capture the semantics of XML data, as they do not keep into account the semantics and structural relationships among XML elements. We propose a novel distance measure for XML data, the structure aware XML distance, which copes with the flexibility which is usual for XML documents, but takes into proper account the semantics implicit in structural information. The structure aware XML distance treats XML data as unordered. Nonetheless, differently from other distances for unordered trees, it can be computed in polynomial time. In this paper, we formally define the structure aware XML distance, we present an algorithm to measure the distance, prove its correctness and its computational cost, and we perform experiments to test the effectiveness and efficiency of our distance measure as a comparison function for XML object identification.

We consider XML trees as unordered. The above examples show that, when comparing XML trees, a good choice is to match subtrees that have similar structure and that are located under the same path from the root. These can be indeed interpreted as clues of the same semantics. If two trees have exactly the same structure, and only differ by the textual values present on the leaves, we can overlay the trees so that nodes with

the same path match. When multiple overlays are possible, then we choose one such that the distance among textual values on the leaves is minimal. If the structure of the two trees differs, due to additional information, we can still realize an overlay as above by deleting extra subtrees that do not match well.

The following definitions make the notion of overlay introduce above more formal. We assume a model of XML objects as labeled trees. All leaves are labeled with the same special label $\mathcal{T}$. Given a leaf l, its textual value (different from its label) is denoted by text(l).

Definition 2 (Overlay): An overlay O of T_1 and T_2 is a non-empty set of pairs of nodes from T_1 and T_2 with the following properties: $\forall v_i, v_i' \in T_i$, $\forall n_i \in T_i$ - leaves(T_i), i = 1,2,....n

If $<v_1, v_2>, <v_1', v_2'> \in O$, then $v_1 = v_1'$ iff $v_2 = v_2'$ 　　　　　(1)

If $<v_1, v_2> \in O$, then path(v_1) = path(v_2)　　(2)

$<n_1, n_2> \in O$ iff $\exists v_1, v_2$ s.t. $n_1 = parent^{(v_1)}$
$\wedge$　　　　　　　　　　　　　　　　(3)

Where path(v_i) denotes the sequence of node labels label($root_i$)....label(v_i) encountered when traversing T_i from the root to node v_i.

Definition 3 (Maximal Overlay): An overlay O of two trees is maximal if there is no other overlay O' such that $O \subset O'$

Definition 4 (Cost of a Match): Let sdist(s_1, s_2) be a string comparison function. The cost of match. For two nodes v, w is:

$$\mu(v, w) =$$
$$\begin{cases} sdist(text(v), text(w)) \text{ if } v, w \text{ are leaves} \\ \qquad\qquad 0 \text{ otherwise} \end{cases}$$

Definition 5(Cost of a Overlay): The cost of an overlay O is defined as $\Gamma_O = \Sigma_{\langle v,w \rangle} v(v,w)$.

Definition 6(Optimal Overlay): An overlay O of two trees is optimal if it is maximal an there is no other maximal overlay O' such that $\Gamma_{O'} < \Gamma_O$.

Definition 7(Structure Aware XML Distance): The structure aware XML distance of two comparable XML trees T_1 and T_2 is defined as the cost of an optimal overlay of T_1 and T_2.

We introduce an algorithm to measure the structure aware XML distance, and prove its correctness and its worst case complexity. Algorithm 1 analyzes two comparable trees recursively, starting from the roots. If the roots are leaf nodes, a distance measure for their associated text values is returned. Such function is denoted by the procedure sdist() in the algorithm. Otherwise, the algorithm considers their children, and computes a distance for each couple of subtrees rooted at children.

Algorithm 1 dist(T_1 , T_2):

If isLea*f*(r_1) and isLeaf(r_2) **then**
Return sdist(text(r_1),text(r_2))
else
xmldist:= ∞
for all l in labels(children(r_1) $\bigcup$ children(r_2)) **do**
for all v_i ϵ children(r_1) **do**
for all w_j ϵ children(r_2) **do**
D_l [i,j]:= dist($T_{(v_i)}$, $T_{(w_j)}$)
end for
assignment$_l$:= *f*indAssignment(D_l [])
for all <h,k> ϵ $assignment_l$ **do**
if xmldist = ∞ **then**
xmldist:= 0
end if
xmldist:= xmldist + D_l [h,k]
end for

end for
return xmldist
end if with the same label, recursively. After all distances have been calculated, the algorithm must assign each node to another node with the same label, minimizing the overall cost. This is an assignment problem and can be solved using a variation of the well-known Hungarian Algorithm. In the algorithm, this task is performed by a call to procedure findAssignment(). In particular, given a matrix of distances, the procedure returns a set of assignments containing couples of indices of assigned nodes. For ease of presentation, in the algorithm we denote the set of all children of node v having label l with childrenl(v). Results of distance calculations for a certain set of children having label l are stored in an array named D_l. The distance is initially set to 1, and reset to 0 only in the case that here is at least one assignment of root children.

Bayesian Network for Fuzzy Duplicate Detection(Leit et al. 2007)

Algorithms for fuzzy duplicate detection in more complex structures, e.g., hierarchies of a data warehouse, XML data, or graph data have only recently emerged. These algorithms use similarity measures that consider the duplicate status of their direct neighbors, e.g., children in hierarchical data, to improve duplicate detection effectiveness. In this paper, we propose a novel method for fuzzy duplicate detection in hierarchical and semi-structured XML data. Unlike previous approaches, it not only considers the duplicate status of children, but rather the probability of descendants being duplicates. Probabilities are computed efficiently using a Bayesian network. The duplicate detection method uses a Bayesian network model to compute the probability of any two XML objects, represented by XML elements, being duplicates. It considers the hierarchical structure of XML elements by considering probabilities for descendant XML elements as well.

The model is built automatically based on the structure of the objects being compared. Since the structure contains no cycles, the duplicate probability can be determined efficiently. Our approach not only provides a strong formal basis for the proposed solution, but it is also flexible enough to easily adapt to different databases from different Domains.

The goal of XML duplicate detection is to identify XML elements representing the same real-world object. In this work, we assume a schema mapping step has preceded duplicate detection, so that all XML documents comply to the same schema. As an example, consider the tree representation of two XML elements represented in Figure 3 (nodes are labeled by their XML tag name and an index for future reference). Both trees represent XML elements named mv. These elements have two attributes, namely year and title. They nest further XML elements representing directors (*dr*) and casts (*cst*). A cast consists of several actors (*ac*), represented as children XML elements of cst. Year, title, dr, and ac have a text node which stores the actual data. For instance, year has a text node containing 1983 as a string value.

For XML duplicate detection, we construct a Bayesian network as follows. Let us first consider the XML nodes tagged mv. The BN will have a node labeled mv_{11} representing the possibility of node mv_1 in the XML tree U being a duplicate of node mv_1 in the XML tree U˙. Node mv_{11} is assigned a binary random variable. This variable takes the value 1 (active) to represent the fact that the XML mv nodes in trees U and U˙ are duplicates. It takes the value 0 (inactive) to represent the fact that the nodes are not duplicates.

The probability of the two XML nodes being duplicates depends on (1) whether or not their values are duplicates, and (2) whether or not their children are duplicates. Thus, node mv_{11} in the BN has two parent nodes. Node V_{mv11} represents the possibility of the values in the mv nodes being duplicates. Node Cmv11 represents the possibility of the children of the mv nodes being duplicates.

As before, a binary random variable, that can be active or inactive, is assigned to these nodes, representing the fact that values and children nodes are duplicates or nonduplicates.

- **Bayesian Network Construction:** Formally, an XML tree is defined as a triple $U = (t, V, C)$, where
- t is a root tag label, e.g., for tree U in Figure 3, $t = mv_1$.
- V is a set of (attribute, value) pairs. If the node itself has a value, we can consider it as a special (attribute, value) pair. For tree U in Figure 3, we have

$$V = \{(year, '1983'), (title, 'Pros and Cons')\}.$$

- C is a set of XML trees, i.e., the sub-trees of U. For tree U in Figure 3, C contains subtrees rooted at dr and cst. These subtrees are again each described by a triple. We say that two XML trees are duplicates if their root nodes are duplicates.

Algorithm 2 BNGen(XTreeSet U, XTreeSet U′):

Input $U = \{(t_1, V_1, C_1), (t_2, V_2, C_2), \ldots\}$,

$$U' = \{(t_1', V_1', C_1'), (t_2', V_2', C_2'), \ldots\}$$

Output A directed graph G = (N,E)
/*--Initialization--*/
/* Root node tags of all XML trees in U and U' */

1. $S \leftarrow \{t_1, t_2, \ldots\}$;
2. $S' \leftarrow \{t_1', t_2', \ldots\}$;

/* Tags in S and S' representing real-world type r */

3. $S_r = \{ t_i \in S \mid T_{t_i} = r \};$

4. $S'_r = \{ t'_1 \in S' \mid T'_{t'_1} = r \};$

/*------------------------------------BN Construction------------------------------------*/

5.   **foreach** type $r \in S \cup S'$ do

/* Nodes with single occurrence */

6.   **if** $| S_r | \leq 1$ and $| S'_r | \leq 1$ **then**

7.   Insert into N a node t_{ii} ;

8.   **if** $V_i \cup V'_i \neq \varnothing$ **then**

9.   Insert into N a node $V_{t_{ii}}$;

10.   Insert into E an edge from this node to node t_{ii} ;

11.   **if** $C_i \cup C'_i \neq \varnothing$ **then**

12.   Insert into N a node $C_{t_{ii}}$;

13.   Insert into E an edge from this node to node t_{ii} ;

14.   **if** node $V_{t_{ii}}$ was created **then**

15.   **foreach** attribute $a \in V_i \cup V'_i$ **do**

16.   Create a node $t_{ii}[a]$;

17.   **Insert an edge from this node to node** $V_{t_{ii}}$;

18.   **if** node $C_{t_{ii}}$ was created **then**

19. $G' = (E', E') \leftarrow \text{BNGen}(C_i, C'_i);$

20.   **foreach** node $n \in N'$ **do**

21.   Insert n into N;

22.   **foreach** edge $e \in E'$ **do**

23.   Insert e into E;

24.   **foreach** node $n \in N'$ without outgoing edges **do**

25.   Insert an edge in E from n to node $C_{t_{ii}}$;

/* Nodes with multiple occurrences */

26.   **else if** S_r or S'_r contain more than one tag each **then**

27.   Insert into N a node t_{**} ;

28.   **foreach** tag $t_i \in S_r$ **do**

29.   Insert into N a node t_{i*} ;

Figure 3. Two XML trees, each representing a movie (mv) (Leit et al. 2007)

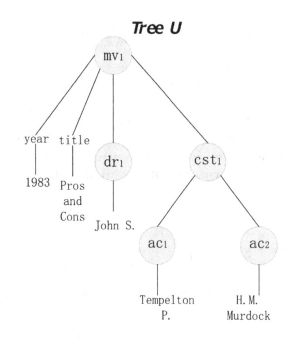

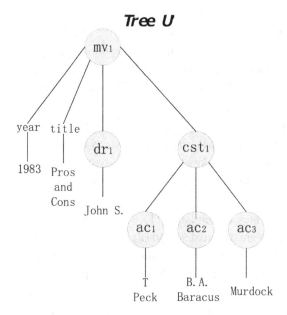

30. Insert into *E* an edge from this node to node t_{**} ;

31. foreach tag $t'_j \in S'_r$ do

32. Insert into N a node t_{ij} ;

33. Insert into E an edge from this node to node t_{i*} ;

34. foreach newly created node t_{ij} do

35. Similar to processing of node t_{ii} (line 8-25),

Second subscript I is replaced by j

- **Defining the Probabilities:** To complete the Bayesian network constructed as described previously, we need to define the prior probabilities associated with the networks leaf nodes and the conditional probabilities associated with the network's inner nodes. In both cases, our model takes an epistemological view of the problem, where probabilities are interpreted as the degree of belief that can be specified independently of experimentation.

In the following, for simplicity, we will use the notation $P(x)$ to mean $P(x = 1)$. We will assume that all probabilities $P(x = 0)$ are defined as $P(x = 0) = 1 - P(x = 1)$.

Prior Probabilities

$$P\left(t_{ij}[\boldsymbol{a}]\right) = \begin{cases} sim\left(V_i[a], V_j[a]\right) \\ k_a \end{cases} \tag{3}$$

if similarity was measured otherwise where Vi[a] is the value of attribute a of the i−th node with tag t in the XML tree, sim(.) is a similarity function normalized to fit between 0 and 1, and ka is a small constant, representing the probability of two values of attribute a being similar. We name constant ka the default probability

Conditional Probabilities

Conditional Probability CP1: CP1 denotes the probability of the values of the XML nodes being duplicates given that their attribute values are duplicates. Formally, this corresponds to $P(Vt_{ij}|t_{ij}[a1], t_{ij}[a2], \ldots)$ and is a function of the values of the Bayesian network nodes $t_{ij}[a1], t_{ij}[a2], \ldots$ This function can be arbitrarily defined, as long as it conforms to the axioms of probability. We therefore propose to define this probability as follows: (a) if all attribute values are duplicates, we consider the XML node values as duplicates; (b) if none of the attribute values are duplicates, we consider the XML node values as non-duplicates; (c) if some of the attribute values are duplicates, we determine that the probability of the XML nodes being duplicates equals a given value, w_a. This value represents the importance of the corresponding attribute in determining if the nodes are duplicates. This definition is represented in Equation (4).

$$P\left(Vt_{t_{ij}}|t_{ij}[a_1], t_{ij}[a_2], \ldots, t_{ij}[a_n]\right) \sum_{1 \leq k \leq n | t_{ij}[a_k]=1} w_{a_k} \tag{4}$$

Subject to $\displaystyle\sum_{1 \leq k \leq n} w_{a_k} = 1$

Conditional Probability CP2: The probability of considering children nodes as duplicates, given that each pair of comparable children nodes is a duplicate, is denoted *CP2* and formally defined as $P(Ct_{ij}|t_1 i_j, t_2 i_j, \ldots)$. Intuitively, it makes sense to say that two nodes are duplicates only if all of their child nodes are also duplicates. However, it may be the case that, for instance, the XML tree is incomplete or contains erroneous information. Thus, we relax this assumption and state that the more child nodes in both trees are duplicates, the higher the probability that the parent nodes are duplicates. This is represented by Equation (5).

$$P\left(Ct_{t_{ij}}\mid t_{ij}^1, t_{ij}^2, \ldots, t_{ij}^n\right) = \frac{1}{n} \times \sum_{k=1}^{n} t_{ij}^k \qquad (5)$$

According to Equation (5), the probability is directly proportional to the number of child nodes that are duplicates. Conditional Probability CP3. To define the probabilities of two nodes being duplicates given that their values and their children are duplicates, i.e., $P(t_{ij}\mid Vt_{ij}, Ct_{ij})$, we consider the nodes as duplicates if both their values and their children are duplicates. Thus, the probability is defined as in Equation (6).

$$P\left(t_{ij}\mid Vt_{t_{ij}}, Ct_{t_{ij}}\right) = \begin{cases} 1 & iff\ Vt_{t_{ij}} = Ct_{t_{ij}} = 1 \\ 0 & otherwise \end{cases} \qquad (6)$$

Conditional Probability CP4: Finally, we define the probabilities of a set of nodes of the same type being duplicates given that each pair of individual nodes in the set are duplicates, i.e., $P(t**\mid t1*, t2*, \ldots)$ and $P(ti**\mid ti1, ti2, \ldots)$. We start by defining the probability $P(t**\mid t1*, t2*, \ldots)$, of the set of nodes being duplicates given that each of its nodes is a duplicate. As before, we assume that the more nodes are duplicates, the higher the probability that the whole set of nodes is a duplicate. The probability can thus be defined as shown in Equation (7).

$$P\left(t_{**}\mid t_{1*}, t_{2*}, \ldots, t_{n*}\right) = \frac{1}{n} \sum_{k=1}^{n} t_{k*} \qquad (7)$$

We can now define the probability $P(ti*\mid ti1, ti2, \ldots)$, which reflects the fact that a node in a XML tree is a duplicate if it is a duplication of at least one node of the same type in the other XML tree. This is represented in Equation (8).

$$P\left(t_{i*}\mid t_{i1}, t_{i2*}, \ldots, t_{in}\right) = \begin{cases} 1 & iff\ \exists_j\mid t_{ij} = 1 \\ 0 & otherwise \end{cases} \qquad (8)$$

Final Probability

Once all prior and conditional probabilities are defined, the Bayesian network can be used to compute the probability of two XML trees being duplicates, i.e. $P(t_{11})$, where t is the tag for the root node of both trees. This can be achieved by any probability propagation algorithm. We can illustrate the probability computation for the network of Figure 4, where we wish to compute the probability of XML trees U and U being duplicates, i.e., $P(mv_{11})$. According to the network, and applying Equation (6), the probability is defined as:

$$\begin{aligned} P\left(mv_{11}\right) &= \sum_{V_{mv_{11}}, C_{mv_{11}}} P\left(mv11\mid V_{mv_{11}}, C_{mv_{11}}\right) P\left(V_{mv_{11}}\right) P\left(C_{mv_{11}}\right) \\ &= P\left(V_{mv_{11}}\right) P\left(C_{mv_{11}}\right) \end{aligned} \qquad (9)$$

Similarly, by applying Equation (4), probability $P(V_{mv11})$ is defined as:

$$P\left(V_{mv_{11}}\right) = w_{year} P\left(mv_{11}\left[year\right]\right) + w_{title} p\left(mv_{11} title\right) \qquad (10)$$

As for probability $P(C_{mv11})$, according to Equation (5), we have:

$$P\left(C_{mv_{11}}\right) = \frac{P\left(dr_{11}\right) + P\left(cst_{11}\right)}{2} \qquad (11)$$

We now proceed by computing probability $P(dr_{11})$, using Equations (6) and (4), as follows:

$$P\left(dr_{11}\right) = w_{value} P\left(dr_{11}\left[value\right]\right) = P\left(dr_{11}\left[value\right]\right) \qquad (12)$$

since w value $= 1$, according to Equation (4). Similarly, for $P(cst_{11})$, using Equations (5) and (7):

$$P\left(cst_{11}\right) = P\left(ac_{**}\right) = \frac{P\left(ac_{1*}\right) + P\left(ac_{2*}\right)}{2} \qquad (13)$$

Figure 4. Bayesian network to compute the similarity of the trees in Figure 3. (Leit et al. 2007)

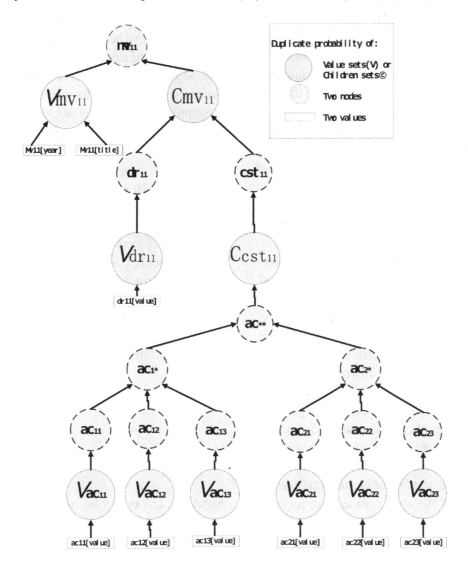

Using Equations (8) and (4) we can compute probability P(ac1∗)as:

$$P\left(ac_{1*}\right) = 1 - \prod_{i=1}^{3}\left(1 - P\left(ac_{1i}\left[value\right]\right)\right) \qquad (14)$$

A similar equation can be obtained for P(ac₂∗). Finally, joining Eqs. (9) through (14), we have:

$$P\left(mv_{11}\right) = (w_{year}P\left(mv_{11}\left[year\right]\right) + w_{title}p\left(mv_{11}title\right)) \times$$
$$(P\left(dr_{11}\left[value\right]\right) + 1 - \prod_{i=1}^{3}\left(1 - P\left(ac_{1i}\left[value\right]\right)\right)$$
$$+ 1 - \prod_{i=1}^{3}\left(1 - P\left(ac_{2i}\left[value\right]\right)\right))\frac{1}{2}\times) \times \frac{1}{2} \qquad (15)$$

Using Set Vector Model (Carvalho et al. 2003)

We propose a similarity-based approach to identify similar identities among objects from multiple Web sources. This approach works like the join operation in relational databases. In the traditional join operation, the equality condition identifies tuples that can be joined together. In our approach, a similarity function that is based on information retrieval techniques takes the place of the equality condition Our approach also uses the vector space model to determine the similarity among objects from multiple sources, but unlike the previously discussed ones it can be used to integrate objects with complex structure (e.g., XML documents) and not only objects with a flat structure as relations.

We present four different strategies to define the similarity function using the vector space model and describe experimental results that show, for Web sources of three different application domains, to characterize the object identification problem, let us consider without loss of generality the integration of two data sources Sp and Sq. Each source S_i contains a set of objects of type $t_i = (A_{i1}, A_{i2}, ..., A_{in})$, where A_{ij}, $1 \leq j \leq n$, is either an atomic attribute or a list of atomic attributes A defined as $l\{A\}$. We also consider that, for each data source Sp and Sq, There is a subset of their attributes, say $S_p^{'} \subseteq S_p$ and $S_q^{'} \subseteq S_q$, respectively, that are semantically equivalent.

Definition 8: Two attribute sets are semantically equivalent if they carry the same semantic meaning and if they share similar values.

Definition 9: Two objects $o_p \in S_p$ and $o_q \in S_q$ are semantically related if their similarity degree is greater than a parameter r, called the similarity factor, that depends on the application domain.

In this work we present four different strategies to determine the similarity degree between objects. All of them are based on the vector space model. For this, we assume that the objects $o_p \in S_p$ and $o_q \in S_q$ can be properly represented as vectors in a multidimensional space. We also assume that semantically equivalent attribute sets are previously determined, for example, by a schema matching approach. The basic difference among the four strategies is how we construct the vectors and that represent, respectively, and .

Strategy 1: To construct the vectors and , we consider a vector space , where is the term set that contains values of all attributes , 1jn, of all objects . The values of all attributes are used to construct the vector . The vector is constructed analogously. The similarity degree is calculated according to the vector space model.

For this strategy, the similarity degree is given by:

$$sim\left(o_1, o_2\right) = \frac{\overrightarrow{o_1} \cdot \overrightarrow{o_2}}{\left|\overrightarrow{o_1}\right| \times \left|\overrightarrow{o_2}\right|} \qquad (16)$$

Strategy 2: Let $S_p^{'}$ be an attribute subset of S_p and $S_q^{'}$ an attribute subset of S_q. We consider that $S_p^{'}$ and $S_q^{'}$ are semantically equivalent, according to Definition 1. To construct the vector $\overrightarrow{o_p}$ and $\overrightarrow{o_q}$ we consider a vector space $\mathfrak{R}^{\left|S_p^{'}\right|}$. The values of all attributes $A_{pj} \in S_p^{'}$ and $A_{qk} \in S_q^{'}$ are used, respectively, to form $\overrightarrow{o_p}$ and $\overrightarrow{o_q}$. The similarity degree is also calculated according to the vector space model.

Strategy 3. For each attribute $A_{pj} \in S_p^{'}$, a vector $\overrightarrow{o_{pj}}$ is constructed considering a space $\mathfrak{R}^{\left|T_{pj}\right|}$, where T_p is the set of all values of A_{pj}. The vector $\underset{O_{qk}}{\rightarrow}$ is constructed using the same

$\mathfrak{R}^{|T_{pj}|}$ space. The similarity degree is given by:

$$sim\left(o_p, o_q\right) = \sum_{j\in S_p', k\in S_q'} \grave{e}_p f_{sim}\left(\underset{O_{pj}}{\rightarrow}, \underset{O_{qk}}{\rightarrow}\right), \qquad (17)$$

Where $f_{sim}\left(\underset{O_{pj}}{\rightarrow}, \underset{O_{qk}}{\rightarrow}\right)$ is calculated according to vector.

Strategy 4. This strategy is similar to Strategy 3, but here $_{,p} \geq 0$ reflects the importance of the corresponding attributes in determining the identity of the objects.

$$sim\left(o_1, o_2\right) = \grave{e}_1 \frac{\underset{o_{11}}{\rightarrow} \cdot \underset{o_{21}}{\rightarrow}}{\left|\underset{o_{11}}{\rightarrow}\right| \times \left|\underset{o_{21}}{\rightarrow}\right|} + \grave{e}_2 \frac{\underset{o_{12}}{\rightarrow} \cdot \underset{o_{22}}{\rightarrow}}{\left|\underset{o_{12}}{\rightarrow}\right| \times \left|\underset{o_{22}}{\rightarrow}\right|} \qquad (18)$$

Combine Structure with Content

Using Average Similarity of Nodes(Kade et al. 2008)

However, performance limitation is not the only problem of tree edit distance when used to match XML documents, as it is pointed out in (Milano et al. 2006). The tree edit distance algorithms give more importance to the tree's topology than to the semantic information contained in the tree nodes' labels. The semantic information, however, is one of the XML's main strength. So, we would be throwing away a lot of information if we just ignore or disregard it, which is the case in tree edit distance techniques.

An alternative approach called structure aware XML distance is proposed in (Milano et al. 2006). It employs a strategy to identify common structures—called overlays—in two XML documents. This approach solves some deficiencies of the tree edit distance. It is not very flexible, however, in the sense that it requires the matching nodes' paths to be exactly the same. This is a strong restriction when we consider XML's flexible nature.

Two approaches are proposed in Apostolico et al. 1992): bag of paths and bag of XPaths. The distance between two documents is calculated by the identification of common paths (which are XPath expressions in the last case), using clustering techniques. They only consider the parent/child relationships between the elements when separating the documents into clusters. So, for their method to be effective it is necessary that the structure of the input documents be reasonably different. This can be a limitation if one needs to match data sources whose documents have a considerable degree of structural similarity.

The approaches described above use information from document's content and structure at various degrees, ranging from nodes' topology in the trees to parent/child relationships. None of them, however, consider both content and structure as first class features in the task of XML matching. We present a novel approach to match XML documents, which makes use of information from both content and structure for matching discovery.

XML integration is also a challenging task, due to the flexible nature of XML, which may lead to structure divergences and content conflicts between the documents. In this work, we present a novel approach to the matching problem, i.e., the problem of defining which parts of two documents contain the same information. Matching is usually the first step in an integration process. Our approach is novel in the sense it combines similarity information from the content of the elements with information from the structure of the documents. This feature, as our experiments confirm, makes our approach capable of dealing with content as well as structural divergences.

In this paper, we propose a novel approach for matching XML documents. In this context, we propose a similarity function to measure the similarity between two XML documents called XSim. This approach makes use of information from both structure and content of the elements of the documents, and comprises two main steps: node matching and document matching.

- **Node Matching:** Matching of nodes of two XML documents is assessed in two steps. In the first step, we decompose every XML document tree in subtrees. We consider, one at a time, every non-leaf node in the tree, starting from the root and traversing down to the leaves. In this process, each node of the tree is considered as the root of its own subtree. For each subtree we produce one string, which is made up of the contents of all the subtree's leaf nodes merged together. The result of this process is a set of tuples in the form (path, content), one for each node in the XML tree. We call this representation of a XML document list.

As described below, in the next step of the matching process, the tuples in the document list will be compared by applying similarity functions. Figure 6 highlights some subtrees produced by the application of this process to the tree (b) from the Figure 5. Three subtress are highlighted in the figure: the employee subtree (the continuous line); the address subtree (the dash-point line); and the city subtree (the dashed line). Note that the employee subtree in fact comprises all the elements of the document, for it is the root of the tree.

The decomposition process is detailed in Algorithm 1. It receives as input an XML document tree and generates as result a document list, as described above. The document list starts empty (line 1). Then, we use the DocIter() function to traverse the XML tree in document order and visit all its non-leaf nodes (line 2). For every node, we apply the GetAbsolutePath() function to get its path from the node up to the root (line 3). We test the node Type node's property to see if it is an element node or an attribute node (lines 4 and

7). Then, we use a suitable method to get the node's content. If it is an element node, we use the GetStringValue() function to get a string which comprises all the contents of the nodes on its subtree (line 5). If it is an attribute node, we simply get its textual content, by using the function GetNodeValue(). Next, we append the pair (path, content) to the document list (line 10). In the end, we return the full document list (line 12). In the second step we compare the tuples of the document lists, searching for matching nodes. To do this we employ three evidences of similarity for each node:

- The textual content of the subtree rooted at the node;
- The node's label (i.e., the tag of the XML element);
- The node's path up to the root of the document tree.

The first evidence comparison tells us how similar the contents of the nodes are, while the comparison of the two remaining evidences tells us about the structural similarity of the nodes. These two dimensions—content and structure—in an XML document complement each other, and we only get a partial document view if we consider only one of them. So, it is essential in a matching process not to disregard any one of these dimensions.

We combine the three individual similarity values obtained from the comparison of the similarity evidences (i.e., content, name, and path similarity) to evaluate the similarity between two nodes. To do this, we use thresholds for content similarity, name similarity, and path similarity. If the similarity value for a pair of nodes is higher than or equal to the thresholds values, we consider that the nodes match. We detail this process in Algorithm 2. The algorithm receives as input two document lists created by the application of the Algorithm 1, along with three threshold values.

Figure 5. Two different ways of representing personal data in XML.(Kade et al. 2008)

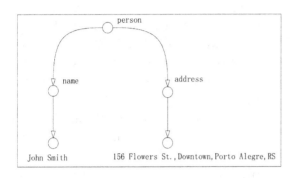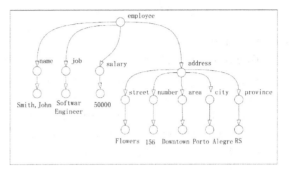

Figure 6. Sample subtrees highlighted in the tree from the Figure 5.(Kade et al. 2008)

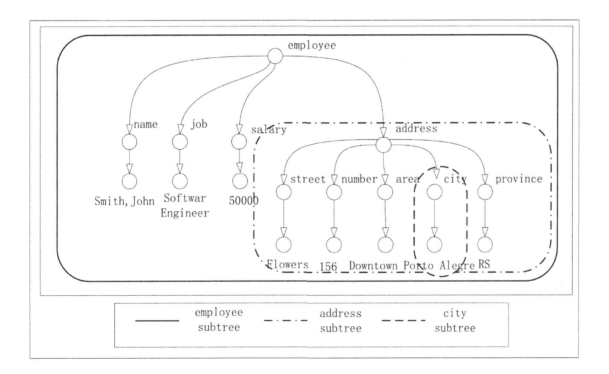

Algorithm 3:

   Input: An XML document tree

   Output: A document list with (path,content)
tuples

1.   docList ← [];
2.   **foreach** v ∈ DocIter(d) **do**
3.   path ← GetAbsolutePah(h)
4.   **if** v .nodeType = ELEMENT-NODE **then**
5.   content ← GetStringValue(n);
6.   endif
7.   **else if** i .nodeType = ATTRIBUTE-NODE
     then
8.   content ← GetNodeValue(n);
9.   endif

10. tuple = (path,content);
11. docList.append(tuple)
12. endfch
13. **return** docList
- **Document matching:** The node matching step results in a list containing all matching pairs of two given documents. This list is used to evaluate the similarity between two XML documents. In a way analogous to (Milano D et al. 2006), we consider that only the pairs of elements which effectively match are significant in the calculation of the similarity between two XML documents. So, we calculate the document similarity as the average between all the similarity values in the matching list. Consider that the number of elements in the matching list is given by its length, represented as, and the similarity value measured for each pair of elements is given by, where i is the position of the pair in the matching list. Then, the similarity of two XML documents, XSim, is given by:

$$XSim = \frac{\sum_{i=1}^{l} \sigma_i}{\ell} \qquad (19)$$

As an example of document similarity, consider the documents of Figure 7 The nodes job e salary in document (a) does no match with any other node in document (b). The individual nodes which form the address in (b) partially match with the address node in (a), but this matching is superseded by the matching of address in (b) with address in (a). So, we find the following matches:

- /person/name in (a) with /employee/name in (b);
- /person/address in (a) with /employee/address in (b).

$$XSim = \frac{\sum_{i=1}^{l} \sigma_i}{\ell} \qquad (20)$$

The similarity values of each evidence for these matching pairs are shown in Figure 7. The first column lists the evidences, the second shows the first matching pair, and the third shows the second matching pair. The similarity values were computed by the application of the following similarity functions: Jaro-Winkler, for the contents; PathSim, for the paths; and Edit Distance for node names. The last line of the table shows the global similarity of the nodes, calculated as the average between the evidences. Using similarity values from Figure 7, we calculate the XSim between documents (a) and (b) in Figure 5 as the average of 0.71 and 0.76, which gives 0.73.

Algorithm 4:

Data: two document lists D_1, D_2; CONTENT-THRESHOLD; NAME-THRESHOLD; NODE-THRESHOLD

Result: A list containing pairs of matching nodes

1. matchings $\leftarrow$ [];
2. **foreach** $d_1 \in D_1$ do
3. **foreach** $d_2 \in D_2$ do
4. contSim $\leftarrow$

GetContentSim(d_1.content, d_2.content);

1. **if** contSim $\geq$ CONTENT-THRESHOLD **then**
2. nameSim $\leftarrow$ GetNameSim(d_1.path, d_2.path);
3. **if**(nameSim < NAME-THRESHOLD)**then**
4. nameSim $\leftarrow$ 0.0;
5. endif
6. pathSim $\leftarrow$ GetPathSim(d_1.path, d_2.path);
7. nSim $\leftarrow$ (contSim + pathSim + nameSim)/3;
8. **if** (nSim > NODE-THRESHOLD) **then**
9. pair $\leftarrow$ (d_1, d_2, í Sim);
10. matchings.append(pair);

Figure 7. Object identification framework (Weis et al. 2005)

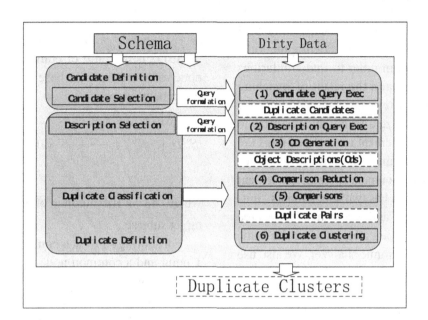

Table 1. Sample similarity values for the matching nodes

Evidence	/person /name X / employee / name	/person / address X /employee /address
Content Path Element Name	0.64 0.50 1.00	0.79 0.50 1.00
Node	0.71	0.76

11. endif
12. endfch
13. endfch
14. endfch
15. **return** matchings

Multiply of Content and Structure Similarity (Viyanon et al. 2009)

The traditional content similarity methods can be roughly separated into two groups: character-based techniques and vectorspace based techniques. Tree Edit Distance can be applied to measure context similarity as well for the character-based technique. This technique relies on character edit operations. The latter group transforms strings into vector representation on which similarity computations are performed.

In this paper, we describe a system based on our research incorporating additional improvements to XML Document Integration (XDoI) (Viyanon et al. 2008) which considers both the data structur and the content for approximately matching XML documents to integrate XML data sources together using keys. XDoI clusters an XML document into smaller subtrees, considered as individual objects using leaf-node parents which may generate a very large number of clustered subtrees due to overlapped subtrees. The large number of clustered subtrees would affect the computational time of comparison in order to find similarities among the subtrees and the result of matching subtrees. To eliminate unnecessary subtrees for comparison, we utilize a taxonomic analyzer to analyze how close element names' meanings are and transform them into the same category. For example, an XML document contains an element name "Pages" which has two subelements "initPage" and "endPage" as descendants. These three element names can be categorized in the same group using the taxonomic analyzer. We also use the instance statistics concept (Ananthakrishna, R et al. 2002] to determine the relationship of element names and keep subtrees that have a one-to-one relationship between XML elements. The system analyzes the information from the results of matching with keys by using improper matches to determine inappropriate leaf-node parents that are not relevant to the other document in order to be compared during the similarity comparison. The aftermath of the experiment shows that the system results in better improvement in the overall computation and still keeps the same result quality.

- **Content Similarity:** Subtree Similarity Degree based on the base document (SSD1) is the percentage of the number of leaf nodes having the same PCDATA value out of the total number of leaf nodes in t_{bi}. Let t_{bi}

and t_{tj} be two subtrees from the base document and target document respectively and assume nn is the number of leaf nodes having the same PCDATA value and n_{bi} represents the number of leaf nodes in t_{bi}. SSD1 can be calculated using the formula.

$$SSD_1\left(t_{bi}, t_{tj}\right) = \frac{n}{n_{bi}} \times 100\% \qquad (21)$$

SSD2 is the ratio of common matched leaf-node values between the base and target subtrees. It can be written as:

$$SSD_2\left(t_{bi}, t_{tj}\right) = \frac{2 \times n}{n_{bi} + n_{tj}} \times 100\% \qquad (22)$$

where n_{tj} is the number of leaf nodes in the target subtree.

For scoring rule each common node is worth 1 point and a common node defined as a key is worth 2 points. The scores SSD1 and SSD2 of all remaining subtree pairs are calculated and stored in the subtree_similarity_score relation. We select the matched pair by selecting subtree pairs having the highest similarity score.

However, the one-to-multiple matching may happen. To find out which subtree pair is the best match, we measure similarity on the signature of matched leaf-node values using Path Similarity Degree (PSD).

- **Structural Similarity:** Before performing path similarity measurements, we semantically transform XML element names of the both XML documents, using LCS discussed in order to get more precise similarity results. Path Similarity Degree (PSD) is the ratio of common labels N on paths from the base and target subtrees having the same PCDATA value to the number of path elements in the base subtree.

$$PSD\left(i\right) = \frac{N}{N_{bi}} \times 100\% \qquad (23)$$

- **Content and Structural Similarity:** Path Subtree Similarity Degree (PSSD) is an average of Path similarity degree for t_{bi} and t_{tj}. Let i be the total number of matched leaf node paths in the base subtree between 1 to k paths.

$$PSSD\left(t_{bi}, t_{tj}\right) = \frac{\sum_{i=1}^{k} PSD(i)}{k} \times SSD\left(t_{bi}, t_{tj}\right) \times 100\% \quad (24)$$

The matched subtree is defined as a pair of subtrees that has the maximum subtree similarity degree in terms of content and structural similarity which is greater than a given threshold.

- **System Design:** We discuss the system design, the requirements of the system and how the system has been implemented. Java 5.0 (JDK 5) and Oracle 10G are selected as a programming language and a relational database respectively. XRel exploits the functionalities of the validating XML parser and SAX (Simple API for XML) in order to convert XML documents into the relations mentioned using JDBC to connect to the database. For the interface, the XML documents are parsed by the Java API for XML Processing (JAXP) which enables applications to parse, transform, validate and query XML documents using an API independent of a particular XML processor implementation. The XML documents are then displayed in a tree data structure by JTree. 5.

Algorithm Our approach written in a pseudo-code is given below. This algorithm is processed after XML documents are parsed into a relational database. There are three main modules:

1. Subtree generator and validator
2. Key generator
3. Subtrees matching by similarity components.

The inputs of this algorithm are two XML documents stored in a relational database. First, the XML documents are fragmented into small subtrees using leaf-node parents. In Module 1, we find leafnode parents and validate them using the taxonomy analyzer and the instance statistics concepts before clustering the XML documents into subtrees. We then generate subtrees using the generated leaf-node parents. All possible key(s) are found in Module 2. They are used to identify their subtrees. At this point, the subtree relation is updated by marking the attribute "key" as 'Y' discussed. In Module 3, subtree matching, we separate this module into two sub-modules: Module 3.1 and Module 3.2.

First, the clustered subtrees from the both base and target documents are compared by the identified key(s) in the function "match_with_key()". The results of the matching with key(s) can possibly be the best matched subtrees or multiple matched subtrees. The best matched subtrees are stored as the outputs. Multiple-matched subtrees occur when the subtrees have more than one alternate key. These subtrees are not considered as the best matched subtrees. The results of multiple matched subtrees are analyzed by the "find_proper_leafnode_parent" in order to find and eliminate non-relevant subtrees by comparing with the median number of alternate keys per subtree. These onrelevant subtrees no longer count as subtrees so they are removed from the subtree relation. The remainder of non-matched subtrees and multiple-matched subtrees from this module are determined to find subtree similarity degrees in Module 3.2.

Algorithm 5: XDI-CSSK

Input: XML document tree T_b and T_t
Output: Set of matched subtree pairs $\{(t_{bi}, t_{tj})\}$
//Module 1:Generate and validate subtree
Find_leafnode_parent(); //Figure 5
Validate_leafnode_parent(); //Figure 6

Generate_subtree() //Figure 7

//Module 3: Subtree Matching

//Module 2: Identifying key(s)

Finding_key(); //Figure 8

//Module 3.1: Matching Subtrees

Match_with_key(); //Figure 9

Find_proper_lefanode_parent //Figure 10 and Figure 11

//Module 3.2: Subtree similarity degree

For (every t_{bi} in T_b { //non-matched subtrees from the base document tree

MaxSim[i] = 0;

for (t_{tj} in T_t){//Subtrees from the target document tree

CalSimilarity $S(t_{bi}, t_{tj})$ // Section 4.1.5.4

MaxSim[i] = Max(MaxSim[i],S(t_{bi}, t_{tj}));

}

StoreMSSD(t_{bi}, t_{tj},MaxSim[i]); //Store Max SSD in a temporary table

}

//Path Subtree Similarity degree computation

for (every t_{bi} in MSSD, such that Count(MaxSim()) > 1 and MaxSim > τ){

// Count the number of maximum similarity degrees

//Match subtree more than one pair

MaxPath[i] = 0

for(j=1 to k_t){

CalPathSimilarity PSSD(t_{bi}, t_{tj}) //Section 4.1.5.5

MaxPath[i] = Max(MaxPath[i],PSSD(t_{bi}, t_{tj}));

}

StoreMPSSD(t_{bi}, t_{tj},MaxPath[i]);

}

Return (t_{bi}, t_{tj})store in Max SSD and Max PSSD

XML Group-Wise Entity Resolution

According to the object to be identified, XML groupwise entity resolution can be classified into two categories, document level identification and element level identification.

DogmatiX Tracks Down Duplicates in XML *(Weis et al. 2005)*

we propose an XML duplicate detection method, DogmatiX, which compares XML elements based not only on their direct data values, but also on the similarity of their parents, children, structure, etc. We pro- pose heuristics to determine which of these to choose, as well as a similarity measure specially geared towards the XML data model. An evaluation of our algorithm using several heuristics validates our approach.

- **Framework:** We define a general framework for duplicate detection. To form an abstraction from any particular data model, we distinguish objects and elements. Objects are present in the real-world, while elements are present in a certain data model. Different elements and different kinds of elements can all represent the same real-world object. We perform duplicate detection among elements describing the same type of real-world object. Thus, we speak of the general problem of object identification. Our framework is flexible enough to cover a wide range of existing algorithms,

Figure 8. Sample XML schema (Weis et al. 2005)

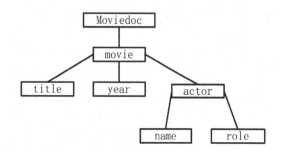

and new methods can easily be included. The framework is represented in Figure 8.

Briefly speaking, the framework consists of three main Components.

- **Candidate Definition:** The goal of candidate definition is to define which objects are relevant for object identification and thus need to be compared. It is based on three observations. (i) A data source may store information about various types of real- world objects, not all of which need to be considered for duplicate detection. (ii) Among the elements relevant to object identification, some may represent the same type of real-world object, just represented differently. These should be compared with each other. (iii) On the other hand, it makes no sense to compare objects of different real-world type, as they cannot be duplicates of each other. These observations yield the following definition, which formally describes duplicate candidates as a set of objects of the same real-world type and can be extracted from the entire data set by selection and projection operations. Let S be a schema containing schema elements $s_1,\ldots,s_n$. Further, let T be a real-world type describing real-world objects. In many scenarios a real world type is represented by many different schema elements. For instance, the real- world type motion-picture can be represented by schema elements movie and film. We assume a mapping M that associates element types to real-world types.

Definition 10 (Duplicate candidate): Let $S^T :=$ { $s_1,\ldots, s_L$ } be set be set of schema elements describing the same type T of real-world object according to M. Further, let $O_i^T = \{$ $o_{i1},\ldots, o_{in} \}$ be set of all instances of the schema elements s_i. Then we define the duplicate candidates of type T as $\Omega^T := \bigcup_{1\le i\le k} O_i^T$.

Definition 11(Duplicate): Towards the overall goal of identifying duplicate objects, it is essential to define what characterizes duplicates. We characterize them in the duplicate definition component by (i) their description, and (ii) a classifier for pairs of objects using a similarity measure.

Definition 12 (Descriptions): It is often the case that not all information of an object is useable or useful for object identification. For instance, a CD object might be effectively described using information about artist, track list, publisher, etc. However, the textual review of a CD is usually not a useful indicator. In principle, one could choose any data item as part of the description of an object.

Definition 13 (Description): For every candidate duplicate $o_i \in \Omega^T$ we define its description ID_i as a set of data instances from the data source. This set is specified by selections and projections in relation to o_i. In practice, an object's description comprises sibling, child, or parent data, such as attribute values of a tuple, or children of an XML element. We represent an object's description in a special data structure, called object description (OD).

Definition 14 (Object Description): An object description OD is a relation with schema OD(value; name). The attribute value describes an instance of some information and name identifies the type of information by a name. The 2-tuples within an OD are referred to as OD tuples. We believe that this OD schema can be used by a wide range of object identification algorithms. Nevertheless, the framework supports an easy replacement of the OD schema.

Example 2: Let us consider the an XML Schema de- scribing the tree structure of Figure 8. A

Figure 9. Sample XML elements (Weis et al. 2006)

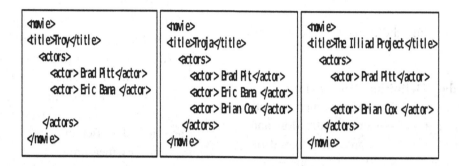

corresponding XML document contains 3 movies, their data being represented in Table 2. We assume that the description of a movie object is its title, the year, and their actors' name. The corresponding OD instances are shown in Table 3.

- **Duplicate Classification:** Using the ODs of objects, duplicate classification classifies every pair of candidates $(o_i, o_{\dot{i}})$, where both $o_i, o_{\dot{i}} \in \Omega_C^T$ into some class $C_i \in \Gamma = \{C_0, C_1, ..., C_n\}$, according to a classifier $\ddot{a}(o_i, o_{\dot{i}})$. In our framework, the class C_0 is the class dedicated to pairs of non-duplicates.

In practice, the duplicate detection problem uses two or three classes, i.e., C_1 being "o_i and o_j are duplicates", C_0 translating "o_i and o_j are no duplicates", and possibly C_2 that contains all pairs where "o_i and o_j may be duplicates". Typical examples for classification methods are thresholded similarity measures among objects, or rule based decisions. This framework provides a means to add new classifiers to the framework. For every classifier, classes and the corresponding classification methods can be added.

- **Duplicate Detection:** The duplicate detection component specifies the algorithm that actually performs object identification, using the information provided offline in the candidate definition and duplicate definition components. To prepare the XML data for duplicate detection, it undergoes three transformations, which can be expressed as queries: the first extracts the relevant candidates, the second selects for each candidate the relevant data, and the third flattens their structure to the OD representation. The remaining three steps perform the actual detection of duplicates, based on the OD representation. The different steps the algorithm performs are the subject of this section.

Step 1: Candidate Query Formulation and Execution: The first step of duplicate detection is to obtain duplicate candidates specified by S^T in the candidate definition component. To this end, query formulation generates a candidate query Q_C that selects all instances of a schema element $s_i \in S^T$. The result of candidate query execution is the set of duplicate candidates $\mathcal{T}$. The data structure for representing this instance can be any suited data structure.

Table 2. Sample XML data (Weis et al. 2005)

id	title	year	actor / name	actor /role
1	The Matrix	1999	Keanu Reeves	Neo
			L. Fishburne	Morpheus
2	Matrix	1999	Keanu Reeves	The One
3	Signs	2002	Mel Gibson	Graham Hess

Table 3. Examples for objects description (Weis et al. 2005)

id	OD
1	{(The Matrix , title), (1990 , year), (Keanu Reeves , actor /name), (L. Fishburne , actor /name) }
2	{(Matrix , title), (1999 , year), (Keanu Reeves , actor /name)}
3	{(Signs , title) , (2002 , year) , (Mel Gibson , actor / name)}

Step 2: Description Query Formulation and Execution: The description of an object $o_i \in \Omega^T$ can be expressed as a query Q_D in the query language appropriate to the data model at hand. In its current state, our framework automatically derives XQueries from a description specification the support of other query languages is under development. After execution, the schema of the query result is a subset (projection of schema elements selected by the description definition) of the original schema and still needs to be transformed to the OD-schema (value-attribute-pairs). This is the goal of OD generation.

Step 3: OD Generation: Since an OD is nothing other than a relation, it can be obtained by a mapping from the result of the description query formulation to the *OD* schema *OD*(value; name). The result of *OD* generation is a set $\{OD_1,....,OD_n\}$, where OD_i is the OD (the set of *OD* tuples) that describes object $o_i \in \dot{U}^T$. All above steps include the formulation and executions of queries. Indeed, we have three queries, namely the candidate query *QC*, the description query *QD*, and the query of the mapping used for *OD* Generation. Clearly, they are not independent of each other, and in practice the queries may be combined to increase efficiency.

Step 4: Comparison Reduction: Once the *OD* instance is generated, all necessary information about duplicate candidates is available, so we could start with comparisons of object pairs. However, for large data sets, the number of pairwise comparisons is computationally prohibitive, so an efficient algorithm should include a method to reduce the number of comparisons. Consequently, the comparison reduction provides a pruning method to efficiently prune pairs.

Definition 15 (pruning method): Let $\phi(o_i, o_j)$ be a pruning method on pairs of candidates o_i and o_j. $\phi(o_i, o_j)$ is a classifier with two classes that signify "pair (o_i, o_j) pruned" and "pair (o_i, o_j) not pruned", respectively.

Possible methods for reducing the number of pairwise comparisons are filtering and clustering. Alter reduces the set of candidate duplicates by pruning pairs of candidates that provably cannot be duplicates in Ω_C^T. In the case of clustering, candidates that are likely to be duplicates are grouped, and only candidates within a group are compared with each other. Hence, all pairs consisting of candidates in different clusters are pruned.

Step 5: Comparisons: During this step, the actual object identification is performed through pairwise comparisons. Pairs of *OD*s are compared and classified according to the duplicate classifier. In general, the result of the comparison step is a set of object pairs $\{(o_i, o_j) | (o_i \in OD_i) \wedge (o_j \in OD_j)\}$ for each class $C_k \in \Gamma$. In practice, pairs are instantiated only for those classes that are input to further processing. For example, for the three classes C_1 = "duplicates", C_2 ="possible duplicates", and C_0 ="non-duplicates", only C_1 and C_2 are instantiated. C_1 is required for data cleaning, whereas C_2 is subject to revision by a domain expert.

Step 6: Duplicate Clustering: The relationship "is- duplicate-of" is transitive. For instance, if o_1 is duplicate of o_2, and o_2 duplicate of o_3, then through transitivity o_1 is duplicate of o_3. So, if a class C_k represents pairs of duplicates, the pairs can be combined to duplicate clusters through transitivity. Once object identification has been performed according to the duplicate detection algorithm, duplicate representations of the same real-world entity are detected and object identification is complete. The resulting identified data may be input to many applications, such as data fusion methods or ETL tools. *W+e* now specialize this framework for detecting duplicates in XML data.

Element Level Identification (Weis et al. 2006)

Using Relationship Defined by Specialists

We proposed a similar approach for XML data in (Galhardas et al. 2001). However, as shown in (Chen et al. 2005), the top-down approach, as well as a bottom-up approach we envisioned, rely on the fact that parent and child elements are in a 1:n relationship, meaning that a parent can have several different children but a child is associated to a unique parent. Our classification technique relies on pairwise comparisons and classifications. Another publication on this topic is (Dong et al. 2005), where duplicate detection is performed for a personal information management (PIM) application. Dong et al.(Dong et al. 2005) proposes an algorithm that propagates similarities from one duplicate classification to another. Our basic idea of using references resembles the idea proposed in (Weis et al. 2006), but we consider different aspects of the problem. We are interested both in efficiency and effectiveness, whereas for low volume PIM data efficiency is not the crucial issue. Furthermore, we set an additional focus on a comparison order

- **Classification Strategies:** Before demonstrating our comparison strategy by example, we need to clarify terms. An XML element can play the role of being the XML element representing an object to which we detect duplicates, i.e., a duplicate candidate, or it can be an element describing a candidate, which we call an object description (*OD*). Consequently, duplicate detection of one candidate is not independent of the duplicate detection of another candidate, because candidates are compared based on similarities in their *OD*s. The comparison strategy we present is based on candidate and *OD* definitions provided by an expert. We say that a candidate c depends on another candidate *c'* if *c'* is part of the *OD* of c. As we will see, due to cyclic dependencies between candidates it is useful to classify pairs of objects more than once.

To demonstrate our comparison strategy, we consider the XML elements of Figure 9. The candidates and *OD* definitions, which are necessary input to the algorithm, are provided in Table 4. For instance, the candidate <movie> is described by its <title> and <actor> children. The <title> candidate depends on its text node and the <movie> element it is a child. We observe a cyclic dependency between <movie> and <title> candidates.

For ease of presentation, we identify XML element as follows. The three <movie> elements are duplicates, which we denote $m1$, $m1'$, and $m1''$. Their <title> elements are not duplicates, so we denoted them as $t1$, $t2$, and $t3$, respectively. Brad Pitt and its obvious duplicates are denoted $a1$, $a1'$, and $a1''$. Similarly, Eric Bana is $a2$ when nested under $m1$ and $a2$ when nested under m1. Brian Cox and its duplicate are denoted $a3$ and $a3'$.

For pairwise classification, we arbitrarily decide to consider pairs in the order $\{(m1,m1')$,

$(m1,m1'')$, $(m1',m1'')$, $(t1, t2)$, $(t1, t3)$, $(t2, t3)$, $((a1, a2), ...\}$. When comparing m1 and m1', they appear to have no related object in common because actor and titles have not yet been compared. We conclude for now that they are not duplicates. The same is true for all other comparisons between movies and between titles. Continuing along the list we start to compare actors and find duplicates $(a1, a1')$, $(a1, a1'')$, $(a1', a1'')$, $(a2, a2')$, and $(a3, a3')$. Knowing that movies depend on their actors, we compare movies again, with the additional knowledge of duplicates among actors.

We find that they are duplicates because they now share several actors. Titles being related to movies, we compare titles again, but do not find further duplicates. The point is that by reclassifying movies after duplicates in related objects have been detected, we were able to find duplicates where we could not before. Consequently, reclassifying pairs can increase effectiveness. However, classifications being an expensive operation, we should avoid to perform a classification too often. In the above example, it is easy to see that if we had started by comparing actors, we would have saved reclassifications in movies and titles a second time. Next, we introduce an order that reduces this number of reclassifications

- **Comparison Order:** For every candidate pair (v, v'), we compute a rank $r(v, v')$ whose ascending order is used as comparison order. Rank $r(v, v')$ estimates for every pair of candidates v and v' the number of reclassifications necessary if the similarity was calculated at the current processing state. A low rank implies few reclas-

Table 4. Sample OD definition (Weis et al. 2006)

Candidate	OD
movie	Title , actor
title	Movie , textnode
actor	textnode

sifications, so the pair with low rank is classified early. The estimation of r takes into account both an estimate of how often a pair (v, v') is reclassified, and an estimate of how many classifications of other pairs are triggered by pair (v, v') if v and v' are classified as duplicates. The value of r(v, v') depends on duplicates detected among elements composing v and v''s *OD*s. Consequently, r(v, v') needs to be recomputed whenever a duplicate is detected among their *OD*s. These computations can be saved using r−static(v, v'), a version of r that does not take into account duplicates in *OD*s.

Domain-Independent Algorithm

In this paper, we present a domain-independent algorithm that effectively identifies duplicates in an XML document. The solution adopts a top-down traversal of the XML tree structure to identify duplicate elements on each level. Pairs of duplicate elements are detected using a threshold similarity function, and are then clustered by computing the transitive closure. To minimize the number of pairwise element comparisons, an appropriate filter function is used. The similarity measure involves string similarity for pairs of strings, which is measured using their edit distance. To increase efficiency, we avoid the computation of edit distance for pairs of strings using three filtering methods subsequently. First experiments show that our approach detects XML duplicates accurately and efficiently.

Definition 16: Two XML elements *e* and *e'* are candidate duplicates if the following conditions are satisfied:
- The parent elements of *e* and *e'* are equal or similar
- *e* and *e'* have the same name (same XML tag)
- The data of *e* and *e'* is similar

- The children sets of *e* and *e'* have similar structure and contain similar data

- **Similarity Measure:** Our technique for detecting similar objects uses a thresholded similarity measure. That is, two objects are considered similar if the similarity measure yields a result above a given threshold. Our similarity measure is guided by the following intuition. Let O and O be two multisets of objects in a universe U. The larger the intersection between O and O, the more similar they are. On the other hand, the larger their multiset difference compared to their intersection, the We further adopt the notion that objects may have different relevance in distinguishing O and O, which is quantified by their inverse document frequency (IDF). The use of the IDF to quantify the notion of importance has been successfully used in information retrieval literature (Ciaccia et al. 1997). The IDF is defined as follows. Let $f_s(o)$ denote the frequency of an object $o \in O$. Then, $IDF_s(o) = \log(\frac{|U|}{f_s(o)})$. As in {3}, we further define the IDF of a set $S \subseteq O$, to be

$$IDF_s(S) := \sum_{o \in S} IDF(o) \qquad (25)$$

We introduce a similarity measure comparing two string sets, denoted S and S'.

$$sim(S, S') := \frac{IDF(S \cap S')}{IDF((S \cup S')(S \cap S'))} \qquad (26)$$

According to Definition 1, the calculation of two XML elements' similarity requires the determination of (i) the similarity between data contained in XML elements, called element data and (ii) the similarity of their children data in order to measure co-occurrence. Of course, two children elements can only co-occur if they have same name, that is, we have to consider their structure as well.

Both element and child data are considered as strings. Element data is further divided into a set of tokens. Two tokens or strings s and s are considered similar if their edit distance $d_{edit}(s, s')$ divided by the maximum length of s and s' is below a given threshold t_{edit}. The edit distance is a common measure for string similarity and is defined as the minimum number of insert, delete, and replace operations necessary to transform s into s. We divide $d_{edit}(s, s')$ by the maximum length of s and s' because more errors should be allowed in longer strings (intuitively, the longer a word, the more errors such as typographical errors may occur).Let E denote a set of elements that need to be compared. For an element $e \in E$, $TS(e)$ denotes the token set comprising the data in e, and $CS(e)$ denotes the set of strings composing e's children data. The similarity of two elements e and e' is then defined as:

$$s(e, e') = \text{sim}\left(TS(e) \cup CS(e),\ TS(e') \cup CS(e')\right) \quad (27)$$

We extend the classical definition of set intersection to include not only equal strings, but also tokens and children considered similar according to their edit distance. The efficient determination of this similarity employs the concepts described next.

- **Identifying Similar Data:** The similarity of two elements is based on the similarity of their data as well as their children data. In both cases, the data is considered as strings, so we need to determine pairwise string similarity, measured using edit distance. Computing the edit distance of two strings is an expensive operation. By applying the following general edit dis-

tance filters for pairs of tokens and pairs of children data, the number of edit distance computations can be substantially reduced. Edit distance filtering is applied once the graph is initialized.

- **Length Distance Filter:** When comparing two strings s and s of length $l(s)$ and $l(s')$, it is true that the following inequality holds:

$$\left| l(s) - l(s') \right| \leq d_{edit}(s, s'). \quad (28)$$

This property was already used in (Kade et al. 2008). In our approach, we first group strings by length, and we then prune out complete groups of string pairs that do not qualify to be similar: let L be the group of all strings of length l, and L' the group of all strings of length l'. As a reminder, two strings s and s' are duplicates if $d_{edit}(s, s') <$ tedit. Now, if $|l-l'| \geq t_{edit}$, there exists no string s $\in L$ that is a duplicate for a string s' $\in$ L', because Equation 3 holds for every sand s'. Therefore, we can prune out pairs of string groups, each time saving saving $|L| * |L'|$ edit distance operations by computing a single difference.

- **Filtering using Triangle Inequality:** A second method for saving expensive edit distance calculations makes use of the triangle property that holds for edit distance. Let x, y, and z be three strings. It can be shown that following inequality holds:

$$\left| d_{edit}(x, y) - d_{edit}(y, z) \right| \leq d_{edit}(x, z) \leq d_{edit}(x, y) + d_{edit}(y, z) \quad (29)$$

We can use this inequality to calculate a range [min, max] for $d_{edit}(x, z)$ by computing a simple substraction and addition. This is cheaper than calculating the edit distance. Then, there exist two filter methods:

1. $max < t_{edit} \Rightarrow x$ and z are similar
2. $min \geq t_{edit} \Rightarrow x$ and z are not similar

Bag Distance Filter: For the remaining strings, we use the bag distance between two strings, which was introduced in (Cobena et al. 2002) as a lower bound for the edit distance of those strings. Given a string x over an alphabet A, let $X = ms(x)$ denote the multiset of symbols in x. For instance, $ms("peer") = e, e, p, r$. Let the bag distance be defined as follows:

$$d_{bag}\left(x,\ y\right) = max(|\ X - Y\ |, |\ Y - X\ |) \quad (30)$$

where the difference has bag semantics (e.g., $\{\{a, a, a, b\}\} - \{\{a, a, b, c, c\}\} = \{\{a\}\}$), and $|.|$ counts the number of elements in a multiset (e.g., $|\{a, a\}| = 2$). In practice, $d_{bag}(x, y)$ first drops common elements, then takes the maximum considering the number of residual elements. It can be easily shown that $d_{bag}(x, y) \leq d_{edit}(x, y)$, so it is a potential filter function for edit distance. Its use is justified as its computation in $O(|X| + |Y|)$ is substantially cheaper than the calculation of the edit distance performed in $O(|X| * |Y|)$. Once similar tokens and children have been identified, we can apply the similarity measure (2) to identify pairs of duplicate XML objects.

- **Detecting Pairs of Duplicate Objects:** As mentioned earlier, we use a thresholded approach to detect pairs of duplicate objects. Formally, let t_{dup} be a threshold value, and isDup(e, e') be a function returning a boolean value such that:

$$isDup\left(e, e'\right) = \begin{cases} TRUE & if\ s\left(e, e'\right) > t_{dup} \\ FALSE & otherwise \end{cases} \quad (31)$$

If isDup(e, e') yields a positive result, e and e' are considered duplicate elements. Consider again the two elements of Figure 9. Set $t_{edit} = 0.15$

and $t_{dup} = 1.0$. The intersection of both elements is {"United", "States", "New", "York", "Los", "Angeles", "Lake Michigan"}. "Angeles" is part of the intersection because d_{edit}("Angeles", "Angels") $< t_{edit}$. The difference between the two elements consists of {"of", "America", "Chicago"}. Assuming all tokens and children data have equal IDF, we obtain a similarity s = 7/3 $> t_{dup}$, so both elements are considered duplicates. As $s(e, e')$ is applied to pairs of elements, the number of comparisons explodes for a large number of elements. Similar to our approach for reducing the number of edit distance computations, we developed a filter function for s, described next.

- **Object Filter:** We apply the following filter function to reduce the number of expensive pairwise object comparisons. The filter function represents an upper bound to our similarity measure s. With e being an XML element, $S(e) = TS(e) \cup CS(e)$ being the set of strings composing $e's$ data, and G being the set of data strings of all elements, the filter function f is defined as:

$$f\left(e\right) = \frac{IDF\left(S\left(e\right) \cap \left(G - \left\{S\left(e\right)\right\}\right)\right)}{IDF\left(S\left(e\right)\left(S\left(e\right) \cap \left(G - \left\{S\left(e\right)\right\}\right)\right)\right)} \quad (32)$$

Informally, $f(e)$ considers all data that e shares with any other element, relative to data unique to e. Thus, if e shares very few data with any other element in G, $f(e)$ yields a small result. As a consequence, it is likely that e is no duplicate of any other element, because it is too isolated. Formally, I can be easily shown that:

$$s\left(e,\ e'\right) \leq f\left(e\right) \quad (33)$$

for any $e' \in G$. As a reminder, two elements are considered duplicates if $s(e, e) > t_{dup}$. If $f(e) \leq t_{dup}$, it follows from (8) that $s(e, e) \leq f(e) \leq t_{dup}$

for any $e' \in G$, so we can conclude that e has no duplicates without calculating any similarity for e. The cost of computing $f(e)$ is comparable to the cost of calculating s. However, f only needs to be calculated once for every element, whereas s has to be computed for every pair of elements. Therefore, $f(e)$ is a suitable filter for reducing the number of pairwise element comparisons. So far, we have seen which measures are required in order to determine pairs of duplicate objects. We use these measures to reach our broader goal of efficiently identifying all duplicate elements at different levels in an XML document.

FUTURE RESEARCH DIRECTIONS AND CONCLUSION

With the widespread of the complex structure, it becomes more important to identify the similarities. In this chapter, we have introduced several methods to solve the identification problem in XML data, considering the content and structure information together.

There have several problems in XML object identification, for example, object identification on large complex data, complex data with multiply types, and the evaluation of results on XML object identification.

REFERENCES

Carvalho, J. C., & da Silva, A. S. (2003). Finding similar identities among objects from multiple web sources. In *Proceedings of the 5th ACM International Workshop on Web Information and Data Management* (pp. 90-93). ACM.

Dong, X., Halevy, A., & Madhavan, J. (2005). Reference reconciliation in complex information spaces. In *Proceedings of the 2005 ACM SIGMOD International Conference on Management of Data* (pp. 85-96). ACM.

Guha, S., Jagadish, H. V., Koudas, N., Srivastava, D., & Yu, T. (2002). Approximate XML joins. In *Proceedings of the 2002 ACM SIGMOD International Conference on Management of Data* (pp. 287-298). ACM.

Joshi, S., Agrawal, N., Krishnapuram, R., & Negi, S. (2003). A bag of paths model for measuring structural similarity in web documents. In *Proceedings of the ninth ACM SIGKDD International Conference on Knowledge Discovery and Data Mining* (pp. 577-582). ACM.

Leitão, L., Calado, P., & Weis, M. (2007). Structure-based inference of xml similarity for fuzzy duplicate detection. In *Proceedings of the Sixteenth ACM Conference on Conference on Information and Knowledge Management* (pp. 293-302). ACM.

Milano, D., Scannapieco, M., & Catarci, T. (2006). Structure aware xml object identification. In *Proceedings of VLDB Workshop on Clean Databases* (CleanDB). Seoul, Korea: VLDB.

Puhlmann, S., Weis, M., & Naumann, F. (2006). XML duplicate detection using sorted neighborhoods. [Berlin: Springer.]. *Proceedings of Advances in Database Technology-EDBT, 2006*, 773–791.

Tai, K. C. (1979). The tree-to-tree correction problem. *Journal of the ACM, 26*(3), 422–433. doi:10.1145/322139.322143

Viyanon, W., & Madria, S. K. (2009). A system for detecting xml similarity in content and structure using relational database. In *Proceedings of the 18th ACM Conference on Information and Knowledge Management* (pp. 1197-1206). ACM.

Viyanon, W., Madria, S. K., & Bhowmick, S. S. (2008). XML data integration based on content and structure similarity using keys. In *On the move to meaningful internet systems: OTM 2008* (pp. 484–493). Berlin: Springer. doi:10.1007/978-3-540-88871-0_35

Weis, M. (2005, August). Fuzzy duplicate detection on XML data. In *Proceedings of VLDB 2005 PhD Workshop*. VLDB. Kade, A. M., & Heuser, C. A. (2008). Matching XML documents in highly dynamic applications. In *Proceedings of the Eighth ACM Symposium on Document Engineering* (pp. 191-198). ACM.

Weis, M., & Naumann, F. (2004). Detecting duplicate objects in XML documents. In *Proceedings of the 2004 International Workshop on Information Quality in Information Systems* (pp. 10-19). ACM.

Weis, M., & Naumann, F. (2004). Detecting duplicate objects in XML documents. In *Proceedings of the 2004 International Workshop on Information Quality in Information Systems* (pp. 10-19). ACM.

Weis, M., & Naumann, F. (2005). DogmatiX tracks down duplicates in XML. In *Proceedings of the 2005 ACM SIGMOD International Conference on Management of Data* (pp. 431-442). ACM.

Weis, M., & Naumann, F. (2006). Detecting duplicates in complex xml data. In *Proceedings of Data Engineering* (pp. 109–109). IEEE.

ADDITIONAL READING

Chawathe, S. S., & Garcia-Molina, H. (1997, June). Meaningful change detection in structured data. [). ACM.]. *SIGMOD Record, 26*(2), 26–37. doi:10.1145/253262.253266

Chawathe, S. S., Rajaraman, A., Garcia-Molina, H., & Widom, J. (1996, June). Change detection in hierarchically structured information. [). ACM.]. *SIGMOD Record, 25*(2), 493–504. doi:10.1145/235968.233366

Cobena, G., Abiteboul, S., & Marian, A. (2002). Detecting changes in XML documents. In *Data Engineering, 2002. Proceedings. 18th International Conference on* (pp. 41-52). IEEE.

KEY TERMS AND DEFINITIONS

Cost of Match: The cost of M is just the cost of the sequence of edit operation which consists of a change operation.

Cost of Overlay: The cost of an overlay O is defined as $\Gamma_O = \Sigma_{\langle i,w \rangle}\mu(v,w)$.

Duplicate: Towards the overall goal of identifying duplicate objects, it is essential to define what characterizes duplicates. We characterize them in the duplicate definition component by (i) their description, and (ii) a classifier for pairs of objects using a similarity measure.

Duplicate Candidate: Let $S^T := \{ s_1,\ldots,s_k \}$ be set be set of schema elements describing the same type T of real-world object according to M. Further, let $O_i^T = \{ o_{i1},\ldots,o_{in} \}$ be set of all instances of the schema elements s_i. Then we define the duplicate candidates of type T as $\Omega^T := \bigcup_{1 \le i \le k} O_i^T$.

Maximal Overlay: An overlay O of two trees is maximal if there is no other overlay O' such that $O \subset O'$.

Optimal Overlay: An overlay O of two trees is optimal if it is maximal an there is no other maximal overlay O' such that $\Gamma_{O'} < \Gamma_O$.

Overlay: An overlay O of T_1 and T_2 is a non-empty set of pairs of nodes from T_1 and T_2 with the certain properties.

Pairwise Entity Resolution: Find XML documents or element pair which describe the same object, which is also called XML document matching or element matching.

Pruning Method: Let $\phi(o_i, o_j)$ be a pruning method on pairs of candidates o_i and o_j. $\phi(o_i, o_j)$ is a classifier with two classes that signify "pair(o_i, o_j) pruned" and "pair(o_i, o_j) not pruned", respectively.

Semantically Equivalent: Two attribute sets are semantically equivalent if they carry the same semantic meaning and if they share similar values.

Semantically Related: Two objects $o_p \in S_p$ and $o_q \in S_q$ are semantically related if their similarity degree is greater than a parameter r, called the similarity factor, that depends on the application domain.

Structure Aware XML Distance: The cost of an optimal overlay of T1 and T2.

Chapter 8
Entity Resolution on Graph Data Set

ABSTRACT

In this chapter, the authors study entity resolution on graph data set. In order to conduct entity resolution on graph data, the authors need to define the distance of graph. The authors compute these distances or approximately compute them for time efficiency. At last, the authors utilize the distances to get the final result of entity resolution. The approximate graph matching algorithms may be index-based like the NH-Index method or kernel function based like G-hash method. Other methods concentrate on providing new definitions of similar graph that are easier to compute than traditional methods, like the Web-collection method and the Grafil method. To increase the resolution ability of traditional methods, researchers provide some methods to recognize similar graphs, like graph-bounded simulation and p-homomorphism. Section 8.1 introduces existing methods on defining the distance of graph, which has a direct impact on the computation of graph similarity. Section 8.1 introduces pair-wise entity resolution on graph data set, including index techniques, graph-bounded simulation, and graph p-homomorphism.

INTRODUCTION

At earlier times, researchers concentrate on exact graph matching, for exact graph matching can get the same subgraph in the data graph. However, as the development of database theory, more none-relational database systems come into the world, and graph database system is one of the most suitable systems for the processing of big data. For many times, exact graph matching cannot express the query intention well. User queries include querying for whether there exists web store with similar production structure, querying for protein molecules with a given protein molecules, *etc*. As

the Chinese saying goes, "no clear water to fish", exact graph matching may lead to not enough number of matching results or even no matching result. So similar graph matching plays an important role in the database management world.

The approximate graph matching algorithms may be index-based like the NH-Index method, or kernel function based like G-hash method.

NH-Index(Tian, 2008), short for neighborhood index is an easy to implement index structure for similar graph matching. Traditional graph index methods only index subgraphs (paths, trees or general subgraphs), which can lead to index sizes that are exponential in the database size. The index

DOI: 10.4018/978-1-4666-5198-2.ch008

unit for NH-Index is the neighbor information of each node in database and the index size is linear in the database size. Also, the NH-Index is a disk-based index, which is suitable for big data that cannot be all put in main memory.

G-hash(Wang, 2009) is a kernel function based method to do pair-wise entity resolution on graphs. The basic idea of this method is mapping graph data into node vectors, and we can get graph similarity by computing similarity function on these node vectors. In order to get node vector, we first make use of wavelet functions, which transform the topology of graphs into node vectors. Kernel function refers to the operation of computing the inner product between two objects in feature space. Kernel function computes the similarity of node vectors, which reflect the similarity between graphs.

Other methods concentrate on providing new definitions of similar graph that are easier to compute than traditional methods, like the web-collection (Cho, 2000) method and the Grafil(Yan, 2005) method.

Web collection is a practical graph similarity measure method defined by the group who developed the Google search engine. Their aim is to find replicated web pages, and this is done by modeling web pages as a web graph. The basic processing unit is called collection in this method.

Grafil is a similarity measure for graph. This measure builds a connection between the structure-based measure and the feature-based measure so that we can use the feature-based measure to screen the database before performing the expensive pairwise structure-based similarity computation. When performing subgraph matching, too strict matching will induce a nearly empty result set. Grafil's basic idea is to extract features from query graph, and when the result set doesn't have enough elements, we gradually reduce the number of features to return more similar results. This process is called *query relaxation*. During the computation, feature filtering can then improve time efficiency.

To increase the resolution ability of traditional methods, researchers provide some methods to recognize similar graphs, like graph bounded simulation (Fan, 2010) and p-homomorphism (Fan, 2010).

Informally speaking, the graph isomorphism problem is to judge whether one graph G_1 can turn into G_2 only by relabelling node id. The subgrpah isomorphism problem is to determine whether G_1 is isomorphism to some subgraph of G_2. Subgraph isomorphism is a NP-complete problem and graph isomorphism problem is a NP-hard problem. The graph homomorphism problem is to find a mapping from V_1 to V_2 such that each node in V_1 is mapped to a node in V_2 with the same label, and each edge in E_1 is mapped to an edge in E_2, while the subgraph isomorphism problem is to find a 1-1 mapping.

We can modify the problems as follows. For node match, we introduce a similarity matrix *mat()* to measure the similarity of two nodes u and v between pattern graph and data graph. The matrix can be computed in terms of common shingles that u and v share. Then we can extend the mapping process. We can map edges in pattern graph to paths in data graph. The P-homomorphism and 1-1 P-homomorphism are extensions of graph homomorphism and subgraph isomorphism, respectively.

Bounded simulation is an extension of graph simulation. Its biggest change to graph simulation is mapping edges in pattern graphs to paths in data graphs, and the path's length is a user-controllable parameter k. We can see graph simulation as a special case of bound simulation when $k = 1$.

BACKGROUND

Defining the distance of graphs is an important problem for researchers. People have some successful definitions such like the graph edit distance and graph alignment distance. They are good to measure similarity but difficult to compute.

Then other easier computed index structures were introduced to measure graph similarity, like Closure-Tree, Treepi and Gstring in ICDE 2006 and ICDE 2007. Particularly, researchers in biology information produced a few high efficient methods inspired from pattern recognition and machine learning area, like SAGA and TALE.

DISTANCE DEFINITION OF GRAPH

Finding Similar Web Collections (Cho, Shivakumar & Garcia-Molina, 2000)

In this section, we will introduce a practical graph similarity measure method. This similarity measure method was defined by the group whose members developed the Google search engine. Their aim is to find replicated web pages, and this is done by modeling web pages as a web graph. The basic processing unit is called collection in this method.

Definition 1: Web Graph

Given a set of web pages, the we graph $G = (V, E)$ has a node v_i for each web page p_i, and a directed edge from v_i to v_j if there is a hyperlink from page p_i to p_j.

Definition 2: Collection

A collection is an induced subgraph of the web graph $G = (V, E)$. An induced subgraph $G' = (V', E')$ of a graph $G = (V, E)$ is the subgraph that only has edges between the vertices in the subgraph.

Definition 3: Identical Collections

Equi-sized collections C_1 and C_2 are identical ($C_1 \equiv C_2$) if there is a one-to-one mapping M that maps all C_1 pages to C_2 pages (and vise-versa) such that:

1. **Identical Pages:** For each page $p \in C_1$, $p \equiv M(p)$.
2. **Identical Link Structure:** For each link in C_1 from page a to b, we have a link from $M(a)$ to $M(b)$ in C_2.

As we know, there are many ways to define graph similarity. The basic idea is to identify the graph pairs that humans would call similar. But we need to convert this vague feeling into detailed rules. Besides, we need to control the complexity in a reasonable level.

Definition 4: Similar Collections

Equisized collections C_1 and C_2 are similar (i.e, $C_1 \cong C_2$) if there is a one-to-one mapping M (and vice-versa) that maps all C_1 pages to all C_2 pages such that:

1. **Similar Pages:** Each page $p \in C_1$ has a matching page $M(p) \in C_2$ such that $p \approx M(p)$.
2. **Similar Links:** For each page p in C_1, let $P_1(p)$ be the set of pages in C_1 that have a link to page p. Similarly define $P_2(M(p))$ for pages in C_2. Then we have pages $p_1 \in P_1(p)$ and $p_2 \in P_2(p)$ such that $p_1 \approx p_2$.

This kind of definition may miss some similar web graph pairs that humans tend to believe similar. For example, in order to improve compute efficiency, we only find *equal sized* clusters. This would miss graph pairs where one graph can be got by adding one node to another graph. The figure below shows this case of missing.

Look at another example. In this situation, the two graphs have an equal size. Moreover, there link structure is similar, i.e., a has links to b, and c has links to d. But we cannot identify the two graph as similar graphs, for we restrict the mapping to *1-1 mapping*. If we identify the two graphs as similar, three nodes labelled b in one graph are mapped to the same node in another graph, which

Figure 1. An example for the missing files

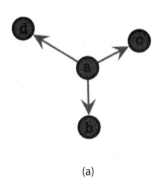

(a)

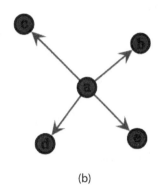

(b)

destroyed the Figure 2(a) mapping restriction. This restriction is also set out of the consideration of saving computation time.

To control complexity, we will again be more conservative and require that *all* pages be mapped to similar pages. That means if two graphs are similar for most node pairs(not all node pairs), we have to say sorry.

The cluster growing algorithm takes two tables as input, and they are TRIVIAL(rid, pid) and LINK(src, dest). TRIVIAL(rid, pid) contains tuple <R_i, p_j> to indicate that page p_j is in trivial cluster R_i. LINK(src, dest) indicate the links in the web graph. The output of growing algorithm is the set of similar clusters

First, we construct LinkSummary in a join-based method. LinkSummary table is computed like this. Join TRIVIAL as Ts, LINK, TRIVIAL as Td, and the join condition is Ts.PID = LINK. SRC and LINK.DEST= Td.PID. Group table by Ts.RID, Td.RID. And we get *s*, *d*, *a*, *b*, where s is count(distinct src), d is count(distinct dest), a is |Ts.RID|, and b is |Td.RID|. Two cluster can be joined if they satisfy the *merge condition*.

Suppose $s_{i,j}$ is the number of pages(i.e., nodes in graph) in cluster R_i links to cluster R_j, and $d_{i,j}$ is the number of pages(i.e., nodes in graph) in cluster R_j links from cluster R_i. The *merge condition* is defined as $|R_i| = s_{i,j} = d_{i,j} = |R_j|$.

After computing LinkSummary, we test each entry in LinkSummary.

Algorithm ClusterGrowing
Input: Tables *Trivial* and *Link*
Output: The set of similar clusters

Figure 2. An example for graph similarity

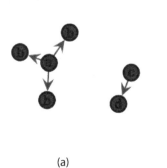

(a)

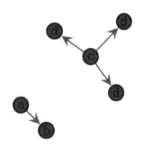

(b)

1. S <- {} //S: the set of similar clusters
2. Construct *LinkSummary* table with schema

<Ts.RID, Td.RID, a, b, s, d>

3. for each entry in LinkSummary
4. if $(a = s = d = b)$
5. S <- S ∪ { *<Ts.RID, Td.RID>*} //coalesce Ts.RID and Td.RID
6. return UNION-FIND(S) //find connected components

Graph Bounded Simulation (Fan, Li, Ma, Tang, Wu, & Wu, 2010)

In this section we will introduce a graph simulation based method called *bounded simulation* to define the similarity of graphs. We can design a cubic-time matching algorithm according to this graph similarity measurement. Moreover, the bounded simulation matching can be further accelerated by an incremental algorithm when provided a *result graph* and a list of updates.

Bounded Simulation (Fan, Li, Ma, Tang, Wu & Wu, 2010)

First we introduce some terms in bounded simulation.

*   Data graph $G = (V, E, f_A)$, where V is the node set and E is the edge set of $G. f_A(u)$ is a function such that for each node u in $V, f_A(u)$ is a tuple $(A_1 = a_1, A_2 = a_2, ..., A_n = a_n)$. In other words, $f_A(u)$ is the property list for node u.

Different from other query graph definitions, pattern graph is defined as follows.

*   Pattern graph $P = (V_p, E_p, f_v, f_e)$, where V_p is the node set and E_p is the edge set of $G. f_v$ is used for predication of u. That is, f_v

is a function defined on V_p such that for each node u, f_v is the *predicate* of u. Pridicate is defined as a conjunction of atomic folumas of the form: *A* op *a*; A is the property name, a is a constant property value, and op is a comparison operator in $<, \leq, =, \neq, >, \geq$.

1. Path A *path* $\rho = v_1, ..., v_n$ in graph G is a sequence of nodes $v_1, v_2, ..., v_n$ such that (v_i, v_{i+1}) is an edge in G.

Having these concepts above, we can define the problem.

2. Bounded simulation.

The graph *G* matches the pattern P via *bounded simulation*, denoted by $P \lhd G$, if there exists a binary relation $S \in V_p \times V$ such that for each $(u,v) \in S$: (1) the attributes $f_A(v)$ of v satisfies the predicate $f_v(u)$ of u; that is, for each atomic formula *A* op *a* in $f_v(u)$, $v.A = a'$ is defined in $f_A(v)$ and moreover, a' op *a*; and (2) for each edge (u, u') in E_p, there exists a nonempty *path* $\rho = v_1, ..., v_n$ in G such that (a) $(u', v') \in S$, and (b) $len(\rho) \leq k$ if $f_e(u, u')$ is a constant k.

Bounded simulation is an extension of graph simulation. Its biggest change is mapping edges in pattern graphs to paths in data graphs, and the path's length is a user-controllable parameter. We can see graph simulation as a special case of bound simulation when k = 1. Note that the result of bounded simulation is a relation rather than a function. So given input pattern graph P and data graph G, there can be multiple relations $S_1, S_2, ... S_n$ satisfying $P \lhd G$. The good news is that it is proven the existence of a single maximum matching. We call this maximum matching as *result graph*, and set the result graph as the output of bounded simulation.

Algorithm Match

Now we have defined the bounded simulation problem and the result graph. Then we design an algorithm for computing the result graph. The algorithm is shown below.

We use an auxilary distance matrix in this algorithm. At the beginning of Algorithm Match, we compute the distance between all pairs of nodes in G. After this, compute four sets for each node u in the pattern graph, including mat(u), premv(u), anc($f_e(u',u), f_v(u'), x$) and desc($f_e(u,u'), f_v(u'), x$). Set mat(u) records nodes in G that may match u. Set premv(u) records nodes that cannot match any parent of u. For each node $x \in V$ and edge $(u', u) \in E_p$, anc($f_e(u',u), f_v(u'), x$) records nodes x' in the graph G such that (i) the distance from x' to x is within the bound imposed by f_e, i.e., len(x', …, x) $\leq f_e(u',u)$, and (ii) $f_A(x')$ satisfies the predicate $f_v(u')$ defined on u'; similarity for desc($f_e(u,u'), f_v(u'), x$), for descendants of x.

For example, in Figure 3, graph P is the pattern graph and graph G is the data graph.

The distance matrix for graph G is

$$M = \begin{bmatrix} 0 & 1 & 2 & 1 & 2 & 3 \\ \infty & 0 & 1 & \infty & \infty & 2 \\ \infty & \infty & 0 & \infty & \infty & 1 \\ \infty & \infty & \infty & 0 & 1 & 2 \\ \infty & \infty & \infty & \infty & 0 & 1 \\ \infty & \infty & \infty & \infty & \infty & 0 \end{bmatrix}$$

Algorithm Match:

Input: Pattern $P = (V_p, E_p, f_v, f_e)$ and data graph $G = (V, E, f_A)$

Output: The maximum match S if $P \trianglelefteq G$, and $\varnothing$ otherwise.

1. compute the distance matrix M of G;

2. **for each** $(u', u) \in E_p$ and **each** $x \in V$ **do**

3. c o m p u t e $\quad anc(f_e(u', u), f_v(u'), x)$, $desc(f_e(u', u), f_v(u'), x)$;

4. **for each** $u \in V_p$ **do**

5. mat(u):= $\{x \mid x \in V, f_A(x)$ satisfies $f_v(u)$, and out-degree(x) $\neq 0$ if out-degree(a) $\neq 0\}$;

6. premv(u):= $\{x \mid x \in V$, out-degree(x) $\neq 0$, and $\nexists (u', u) \in E_p$ ($x' \in mat(u)$, $f_A(x)$ s a t i s f i e s $f_v(u')$, a n d $len(x, …, x') \leq f_e(u', u)$)$\}$

Figure 3. An example for graph pattern matching

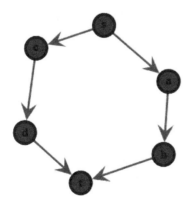

Graph G

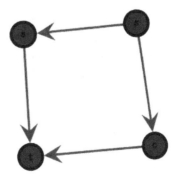

Graph P

7. **while** (there exists a node $u \in V_p$ with premv(u) $\neq \varnothing$) **do**

8.   **for** (each $(u', u) \in E_p$ and each $z \in premv(u) \cap mat(u')$) **do**

9. $mat(u') := mat(u') \setminus \{z\}$;

10.   **if** ($mat(u') = \varnothing$) **then return** $\varnothing$

11.   **for each** u'' with $(u'', u') \in E_p$ **do**

12.   **for(** $z' \in anc(f_e(u'', u'), f_v(u''), z) \wedge z' \notin premv(u'))$ **do**

13.   **if** $(desc(f_e(u'', u'), f_v(u'), z') \cap mat(u') = \varnothing)$

14.   **then** $premv(u') := premv(u') \cup \{z'\}$;

15. $premv(u) := \varnothing$

16. $S := \varnothing$ **for** ($u \in V_p$ and $x \in mat(u)$) **do** $S := S \cup \{(u, x)\}$;

17.   **return** S;

Incremental Graph Pattern Matching

Although better than intractable, the cubic-time complexity bound of Match is still too high to compute matches in large data graphs. In practice, the data graph's updating is very frequent, For example, adding a new friend is an operation frequently performed. If we call algorithm match each time updating the data graph, the operation is somewhat stupid. We can make use of existing resources to update the result graph. That leads us to design an *incremental graph pattern matching problem*. Given a graph pattern P, a data graph G, the maximum match S' in G for P, and a list δ of updates(edge insertions and deletions) to G, it is to compute the maximum match S' in G' for P if $P \lhd G'$.

Next, we analyze the problem structure and then provide an incremental graph pattern matching problem.

AFF_1 AFF_1 is the set of node pairs (v', v) in data graph G such that the distance between them is changed by δ, *i.e.*, the changes to M

AFF_2 AFF_2 is the difference between the new match S' and the old S, *i.e.*, the set of matches (u,v) added to or removed from S, along with nodes that are adjacent to u in P or to v in G.

Note that AFF is short for affected.

We give separate algorithm to handle a single single deletion and insertion. Algorithm for handling edge deletion is denoted by Match⁻.

Match⁻ first call procedure UpdateM to incrementally compute the distance matrix after updating. For each affected pair $(v', v) \in AFF_1$, Match⁻ identifies matches (u', v') directly affected by the distance change of (v', v). Then recursively finds all matches (u'', v'') affected by (u', v'), and updates S accordingly.

Algorithm Match⁻:

Input: Pattern $P = (V_p, E_p, f_v, f_e)$, data graph $G = (V, E, f_A)$ the old maximum match S, the distance matrix M of G, and an edge e to be deleted from G.

Output: The new maximum match S and the updated M.

1. $AFF_1 :=$ **UpdateM**(G, M, e); $wSet := \varnothing$

2. **for** all $(v', v) \in AFF_1$ **do**

3. **for** all $(u', u) \in E_p$ having $v' \in mat(u')$ and $v \in mat(u)$ **do**

4. **if** $desc(f_e(u', u), f_v(u), v') \cap mat(u) = \varnothing$ **then**

5. $wSet.push((u', v'))$;

6.   **while**($wSet \neq \varnothing$) **do**

7. $(u', v') := wSet.pop()$;

8. $mat(u') := mat(u') \setminus \{v'\}$; $S := S \setminus \{(u', v')\}$;

9.   **for** all $(u'', u') \in E_p$ **do**

10.   **for** all $v'' \in anc(f_e(u'', u'), f_v(u''), v') \cap mat(u'')$ **do**

11.   **if** $desc(f_e(u'', u'), f_v(u'), v'') \cap mat(u') = \varnothing$ **then**

12. $wSet.push((u'', v''))$;

13.   **if** there is a pattern node u having $mat(u) = \varnothing$ **then** $S := \varnothing$

14.   **return** S and M;

Match⁻ is in $O(|AFF_1| |AFF_2|^2)$ time.

The incremental algorithm Match⁺ handles insertion of an edge. The structure of this algorithm is similar to Match⁻. Moreover, for each pattern node $u \in V_p$, Match⁺ maintains a candidate match set can(u), consisting of nodes v in which $f_A(v)$ satisfies $f_v(u)$ and $v \notin$ mat(u), i.e., candidate matches of u.

Algorithm Match⁺:

Input: Pattern $P = (V_p, E_p, f_v, f_e)$, data graph $G = (V, E, f_A)$ the maximum match S, the distance matrix M of G, and an edge e to be inserted.

Output: The new maximum match S if $P \trianglelefteq G \cup \{e\}$ ($\varnothing$ otherwise) and the updated M.

1. AFF₁:= UpdateM(G, M, e);
2. *wSet*:= $\varnothing$;
3. **for all** $(v', v) \in AFF_1$ **do**
4. **for all** $(u', u) \in E_p$ having $v' \in$ can(u') and $v \in$ mat(u) **do**
5. **if for all** $(u', u_s) \in E_p$
    $desc(f_e(u', u_s), f_v(u_s), v') \cap mat(u_s) \neq \varnothing$ **then**
6. *wSet*.push((u', v'));
7. **while** (*wSet* $\neq \varnothing$) **do**
8. (u', v'):= *wSet*.pop();
9. mat(u'):= mat(u') $\cup \{v'\}$;
10. can(u'):= can(u') $\cup \{v'\}$;
11. S:= $S \cup \{(u', v')\}$;
12. **for all** $(u'', u') \in E_p$ **do**
13. **for all**
    $v'' \in anc(f_e(u'', u'), f_v(u''), v') \cap mat(u'')$ **do**
14. **if for all** $(u'', u_s') \in E_p$
    $desc(f_e(u'', u_s), f_v(u_s'), v'') \cap mat(u_s') \neq \varnothing$
15. *wSet*.push((u'', v''));
16. **return** S and M.

Match⁺ can solve the single edge insertion problem in $O(|AFF_1| |AFF_2|^2)$ time for DAG patterns.

We then try to handle multiple edge insertion and deletion together. We provide an algorithm for incremental graph pattern matching, referred to as IncMatch, which is a *batch update* algorithm.

IncMatch is also distance matrix based. For each pair $(v', v) \in AFF_1$ with increased distance, updates S along the same lines as Match⁻. For each pair in AFF_1 with decreased distance, updates S following Match⁺.

Algorithm IncMatch:

Input: Pattern $P = (V_p, E_p, f_v, f_e)$, data graph $G = (V, E, f_A)$ the maximum match S, the distance matrix M of G, a set of updates δ.

Output: The maximum match S if $P \trianglelefteq G \oplus \delta$ and $\varnothing$ otherwise

1. AFF₁:= UpdateM(G, M, e);
2. **for** each $(v', v) \in AFF_1$ **do**
3. **if** the distance from v' to v increases after applying δ **then**
4. invoke Match⁻ (lines 3-12) to update S;
5. **else**
6. invoke Match⁺ (lines 4-15) to update S;
7. **if** there is a pattern node u having mat(u) = $\varnothing$ **then**
8. S:= $\varnothing$;
9. **return** S.

IncMatch incrementally compute maximum matching graph in $O(|AFF_1| |AFF_2|^2)$ time for DAG patterns.

Graph P-Homomorphism (Fan, Li, Ma, Wang & Wu, 2010)

In traditional graph theroy, graph homomorphism and subgraph isomorphism are two important problems. Given two graphs $G_1 = (V_1, E_1)$ and $G_2 = (V_2, E_2)$, the graph homomorphism problem is to find a mapping from V_1 to V_2 such that each node in V_1 is mapped to a node in V_2 with the same label, and each edge in E_1 is mapped to an edge in E_2, while the subgraph isomorphism problem is to find a 1-1 mapping.

However, these two notions are often too restrictive for graph matching. In many cases, we cannot get enough amount of matches, while there exists many candidate matches need to be discovered.

We can modify the two problems as follows. For node match, we introduce a similarity matrix *mat()* to measure the similarity of two nodes u and v between pattern graph and data graph. The matrix can be computed in terms of common shingles() that u and v share. Then we can extend the mapping process. We can map edges in pattern graph to paths in data graph. The P-homomorphism and 1-1 P-homomorphism are extension of graph homomorphism and subgraph isomorphism, respectively.

Definition 1: P-Homomorphism

Graph G_1 is said to be *p*-homomorphism(*p*-hom) to G_2 w.r.t a similarity matrix *mat()* and a similarity thresholdξ, denoted by $G_1 \preceq_{(e,p)} G_2$, if there exists a mapping σ from V_1 to V_2 such that for each node v $\in V_1$,

1. If $\sigma(v) = u$, then mat(v, u) $\geq \xi$; and
2. For each edge (v, v') in E_1, there exists a nonempty path u/.../u' in G_2 such that $\sigma(v')$ = u', ie.e, each edge from v is mapped to a path emanating from u.

Definition 2 1-1: P-Homomorphism

A graph G_1 is 1-1 p-hom to G_2, denoted by $G_1 \preceq_{(e,p)}^{1-1} G_2$, if there exists a 1-1 (injective) p-hom mapping σ from G_1 to G_2, i.e., for any distinct nodes v_1, v_2 in G_1, $\sigma(v_1) \neq \sigma(v_2)$. We refer to σ as a 1-1 p-hom mapping from G_1 to G_2.

{\subsection Measure graph similarity via p-hom}

Now we have defined the p-hom matching and 1-1 p-hom matching. But if there are multiple matches, how can we know the similarity of each match? For there exists a kind of problem called *how similar is similar*. That means only when the

similarity of the match reach a threshold, we can return the match.

We define cardinality and overall similarity to measure graph similarity.

Definition 3: Cardinality

This metric evaluates the number of nodes in G_1 that σ maps to G_2. The cardinality of σ is defined as:

$$qualCard(\sigma) = \frac{|V_1'|}{|V_1|}$$

Now we can get the *maximum cardinality problem* for p-hom, denoted by CPH. Given graph G_1 and G_2, node similarity matrix *mat()* and similarity thresholdξ, find a p-hom mapping σ from G_1 to G_2 such that qualCard(σ) is maximum.

We can get the maximum cardinality problem for 1-1 p-hom in the same way, denoted by CPH$^{1-1}$.

Definition 4: Overall Similarity

Alternatively, we consider the overall similarity of mapping σ. Assume a weight w(v) associated with each node v, indicating relative importance of v, e.g., whether v is a hub, authority, or a node with a high degree. The metirc is defined to be

$$qualSim(\sigma) = \frac{\sum_{v \in V_1'} (w(v) * mat(v, \sigma(v)))}{\sum_{v \in V_1} w(v)}$$

This is simply a weighted sum of node similarity, and it can represent the overall similarity of mapping σ. The *overall similarity problem* for p-hom, denoted by SPH, can be defined as follows. Given graph G_1 and G_2, node similarity matrix *mat()* and similarity thresholdξ, find a p-hom mapping σ from G_1 to G_2 such that qualSim (σ) is maximum.

We can get the overall similarity problem for 1-1 p-hom in the same way, denoted by SPH$^{1-1}$.

179

It is hard to compute the maximum cardinality problem and the maximum overall similarity problem. They are NP-complete for p-hom and 1-1 p-hom. Even worse, they are also approximate hard problems. That is to say, there exists no polynomial time algorithm for finding (1-1) p-hom mappings such that the quality of each mapping found is guaranteed to be within $O(1/n^{1-\varepsilon})$ of its optimal solution. In fact these above problems can be reduced to the maximum weighted indepdent set problem (WIS)(). It is well known that WIS is NP-complete, and is approximate hard.

In the following section, we design an approximation algorithm for the maximum cardinality problem CPH. The approximation algorithms for CPH$^{1-1}$, SPH, SPH$^{1-1}$ are very similar to it. We leave these to readers.

Now let us look at the algorithm compMaxCard. It maintains four structures, a matching list H for nodes in G_1, an adjacency list H_1 for nodes in G_1, and an adjacency matrix H_2 for the transitive closure graph G_2^+, a set I of pairwise contradictory matching node pairs.

For each node v in H, H(v).good is a node set for nodes in G_2 that may match node v, and H(v).minus is a node set for nodes in G_2 that cannot match node v according to σ.

For each node v in H_1, $H_1(v)$.prev is a node set for v's parent nodes in G_2, and $H_1(v)$.post is a node set for v's children nodes in G_2.

Different from H and H_1, H_2 is not an adjacency list but an adjacency matrix. The transitive closure $G^+(V, E^+, L)$ of graph $G(V, E, L)$ is the graph such that for all nodes $v, v' \in V$, $(v, v') \in E^+$ iff there is a nonempty path from v_1 to v_2 in G. That means $H_2(u_1, u_2) = 1$ iff (u_1, u_2) is an edge in G_2^+.

The set of pairwise contradictory matching node pairs I, for any two pairs (v_1, u_1) and (v_2, u_2) in I, if v_1 is mapped to u_1, then v_2 cannot be mapped to u_2. This structure is used for finding the mapping σ with enough small size.

The algorithm compMaxCard works in this way. First, for each node in G_1, compute matching list H_1 and H. Then compute the transitive

closure of graph G_2 and compute H_2. Last, do the prune work until it find an enough small mapping σ. The prune step is done by calling procedure greedyMatch.

Algorithm compMaxCard:

Input: Two graphs $G_1(V_1, E_1, L_1)$ and $G_2(V_2, E_2, L_2)$, a similarity matrix mat(), and a similarity thresholdξ

Output: A p-hom mapping from subgraph of G_1 to G_2.

1. **for** each node $v \in V_1$ of graph G_1 **do**
2. $H_1(v)$.prev:= $\{v' \mid v' \in V_1, (v', v) \in E_1\}$;
3. $H_1(v)$.post:= $\{v' \mid v' \in V_1, (v, v') \in E_1\}$;
4. $H(v)$.good:= $\{u \mid u \in V_2, \text{mat}(v, u) \geq \xi\}$; $H(v)$.minus = $\varnothing$
5. compute the transitive closure $G_2^+(V_2, E_2^+, L_2)$
6. **for** each ordered node pair (u_1, u_2) in G_2 **do**
7. **if** $(u_1, u_2) \in E_2^+$ **then** $H_2(u_1)(u_2):= 1$; **else** $H_2(u_1)(u_2):= 0$;
8. $\sigma_m:= \varnothing$;
9. **while** sizeof(H) > sizeof(σ_m) **do**
10. $(\sigma, I):=$ greedyMatch(H_1, H_2, H); $H:= H \setminus I$;
11. **if** sizeof(σ) > sizeof(σ_m) **then** $\sigma_m:= \sigma$;
12. **return** σ_m.

The procedure greedyMatch computes p-hom matching for subgraph $G_1(H)$ to G_2. It works as follows. First call procedure trimMatching to .... Then for each node v' in H, partition H into two parts, namely H^+ and H^-. H^+ contains nodes in G_2 that can match v', i.e., nodes in $H(v')$.good. Respectively, H^- contains nodes in G_2 that cannot match v. We recursively call greedyMatch for the two partition and return the larger match. Also, updates I_2 by adding node pair (v, u) and return the larger contradictory matching pair set. (line 10-13)

Procedure Greedymatch:

Input: Graphs H_1, H_2, and matching list H for subgraph $G_1(H)$.

Output: A p-hom mapping σ for subgraph $G_1(H)$ to G_2 and a set I of pairwise contradictory matching pairs.

1. **if** H is empty **then return** $(\varnothing, \varnothing)$;
2. pick a node v of H and a node u from $H(v)$. good;
3. $H(v).minus := H(v).good \setminus \{u\}$; $H(v).good := \varnothing$;
4. $H := trimMatching(v, u, H_1, H_2, H)$;
5. **for** each node v' in H **do**
6. **if** $H(v').good$ is not empty
7. **then** $\{H^+(v').good := H(v').good; H^+(v').minus := \varnothing\}$
8. **if** $H(v').minus$ is not empty
9. **then** $\{H^-(v').good := H(v').minus; H^-(v').minus := \varnothing\}$
10. $(\sigma_1, I_1) := greedyMatch(H_1, H_2, H^+)$;
11. $(\sigma_2, I_2) := greedyMatch(H_1, H_2, H^-)$;
12. $\sigma := max(\sigma_1 \cup \{(v, u)\}, \sigma_2); I := max(I_1, I_2 \cup \{(v, u)\})$;
13. **return** (σ, I);

Below is the procedure trimMatching. This procedure assume the input (v, u) is a match and update the matching list H. Whether (v, u) is a chosen match or not is decided in procedure greedyMatch. The procedure trimMatching is only a worker, finishing the work assigned.

Procedure trimMatching:

Input: Node v with matching node u, H_1, H_2, and H

Output: Updated matching list H.

1. **for** each node v' in $H_1(v).prev \cap H$ **do** /* prune the matching nodes for v's parent nodes */
2. **for** any node u' in $H(v').good$ such that $H_2(u', u) = 0$ **do**
3. $H(v').good := H(v').good \setminus \{u'\}$
4. $H(v').minus := H(v').minus \cup \{u'\}$;
5. **for** each node v' in $H_1(v).post \cap H$ **do** /* prune the matching nodes for v's children nodes */
6. **for** any node u' in $H(v').good$ such that $H_2(u, u') = 0$ **do**
7. $H(v').good := H(v').good \setminus \{u'\}$;
8. $H(v').minus := H(v').minus \setminus \{u'\}$;

9. **return** H;

PAIR-WISE ENTITY RESOLUTION ON GRAPHS

Grafil (Yan, Yu & Han 2005)

In this section, we will introduce a new similarity measure for graph called Grafil. This measure builds a connection between the structure-based measure and the feature-based measure so that we can use the feature-based measure to screen the database before performing the expensive pairwise structure-based similarity computation. When performing subgraph matching, too strict matching will induce a nearly empty result set. Grafil's basic idea is to extract features from query graph, and when the result set doesn't have enough elements, we gradually reduce the number of features to return more similar results. This process is called *query relaxation*. During the computation, feature filtering can then improve time efficiency.

What is featured in graph data? Researchers have different definitions. The features could be path, discriminative frequent structures, or any structure in a graph. For example, construct feature for this query graph in Figure 4.

And we can get three different features in Figure 5.

These features are extracted following this rule: no matter which edge is relaxed, the query graph after relaxation will have at least three embeddings of these features. Or in other words, the query graph after relaxation can miss at most four embeddings of these features.

The Grafil method performs substructure search in the following four steps:

1. Build index
2. Evaluate feature misses upper bound
3. Query processing
4. Query relaxation

Figure 4. The query graph to construct feature

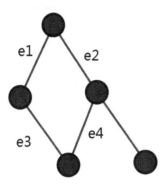

Where query relaxation is performed only when we don't have enough query results. After relaxation step, we continue to perform step 2, step 3 and step 4, until the result set reaches our demand.

Index

Grafil's index structure is a matrix called *Feature-Graph Matrix*. Each column of the matrix corresponds to a target graph in the graph database, while each row corresponds to a feature being indexed. We can build a feature-graph matrix for the graph p mentioned above.

We use another matrix called Edge-Feature Matrix to represent the relation between edges and features. If edge *e* has appeared *n* times in feature *f*, the corresponding matrix entry is *n*.

Otherwise, the corresponding matrix entry is 0. We can say an edge e_i hit a feature f_j if f_j covers e_i.

Feature Miss Upper Bound

Given a relaxation ratio θ, we can find the max number of features that can be missed.

The relaxation ratio is defined as follows.

Definition 1: Relaxation Ratio

Given two graphs G and Q, if P is the maximum common subgraph of G and Q, then the substructure similarity between G and Q is defined by $\frac{|E(P)|}{|E(Q)|}$, and $1 - \frac{|E(P)|}{|E(Q)|}$ is called relaxation ratio.

For example, we have graph a and graph b in Figure 6, compute their substructure similarity and relaxation ratio. $|E(a)| = 12$, $|E(b)| = 11$, the maximum common subgraph of a and b is b itself. Then $|E(p)| = 11$, so the substructure similarity between graph a and graph b is $\frac{11}{12} \approx 91.7\%$ and the relaxation ratio is $1 - \frac{11}{12} \approx 8.3\%$.

Now we get the feature miss estimation problem. Given a query graph Q and a set of features

Figure 5. Extracted features

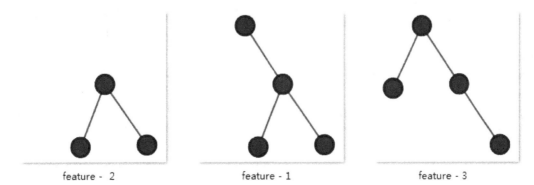

Table 1. Feature graph matrix

	G1	G2	G3	G4
f-a	0	1	0	0
f-b	0	0	1	0
f-c	2	3	4	4

Table 2. Edge-freature matrix for graph p

	f-a-1	f-a-2	f-a-3	f-a-4	f-a-5	f-b	f-c-1	f-c-2	f-c-3	f-c-4	f-c-5	f-c-6
e1	1	0	0	1	0	0	0	1	1	1	1	0
e2	1	1	0	0	0	1	1	0	1	1	1	0
e3	0	0	1	1	0	0	1	1	0	1	0	1
e4	0	1	1	0	1	1	1	1	1	0	0	1

contained in Q, if the relaxation ratio is θ, what is the maximal number of features that can be missed?

Suppose k is $\lfloor \theta \cdot \mid G \mid \rfloor$, the maximal number of features that can be missed equals the maximum number of columns that can be hit by k rows in the edge-feature matrix. This is a classic set k-coverage problem. The set k-coverage problem is given a universe U, and n sets constitute the universe, find the least number of sets which still consitute the universe. The set k-coverage problem is NP-complete, but the optimal solution can be approximated by a greedy algorithm. The greedy algorithm to approximate compute feature miss estimation problem is shown below. The algorithm chooses the row hit by the most number of columns, and then deletes all columns hit by his row. Repeat this process until only k rows are left. The columns deleted provide us the feature miss upper bound.

Algorithm 1 GreedyCover:

Input: Edge-feature Matrix M, Maximum edge relaxations k

Output: The number of feature misses W_{greedy}

1. let $W_{greedy} = 0$;
2. **for each** $l = 1 \dots k$ **do**
3. select row r_l that maximizes $|M(r_p \cdot)|$;
4. $W_{greedy} = W_{greedy} + |M(r_p \cdot)|$
5. **for each** column c s.t. $|M(r_p \ c)| = 1$ **do**
6. set $M(\cdot, c) = 0$;
7. **return** W_{greedy};

where $|M(r_p \cdot)|$ is the none zero elements in the lth row, $|M(r_p \ c)|$ is the entry in the lth row, cth column, and W_{greedy} is the maximum of feature misses.

The greedy algorithm has the best approximation performance in therory. However, in this problem we can further improve the performance in practice using a brance-and-bound approach.

NH-Index (Tian & Patel 2008)

In this section, we will introduce a highly efficient graph data index called NH-Index.

NH-Index, short for neighborhood index, first appears in Yuanyan Tian and Jignesh Patel's paper. Traditional graph index methods only index subgraphs (paths, trees or general subgraphs), which can lead to index sizes that are exponential in the

Figure 6. The Structures of Some Compounds (Yan, Yu & Han 2005)

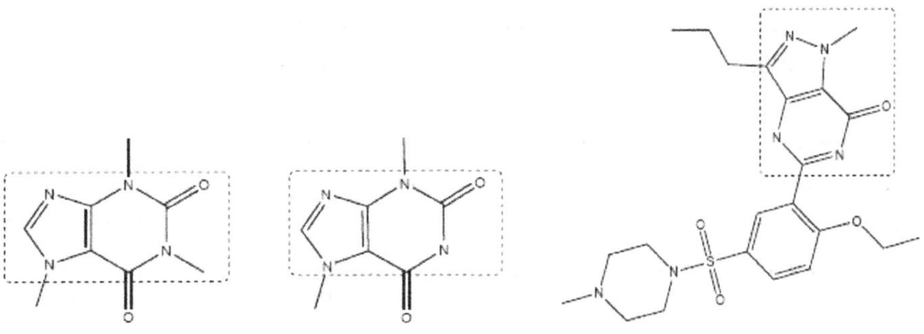

(a) caffeine   (b) thesal   (c) viagra

database size. The index unit for NH-Index is the neighbor information of each node in database and the index size is linear in the database size. Also, the NH-Index is a disk-based index, which is suitable for big data that cannot be all put in main memory.

The following describes the composition of the index, and the graph node query method using NH-index.

NH-Index Structure

NH-Index has a hybrid two-level index structure. The first level of the index structure is a B+-tree index on node (label, degree, neighbor connection). Label and degree are self-explained properties, and the neighbor connection is defined by the number of edges between neighbor nodes. For example, for the graph p in Figure 7, we build a first level for this graph.

In this graph, label = a, degree = 4, neighbor connection = 2, so the index entry is (a, 4, 2).

The second level of NH-Index is a bit array, and each bit in the array indicates whether a neighbor with a specific label exists (set to 1) or not(set to 0). When we have a big number of nodes in the graph data, the bit array is often very large. To handle this situation, we can employ a Bloom filter approach(). The Bloom filter is a simple space-

efficient randomized data structure for representing a set. Using Bloom filter we can fix the bit array's size to a user-controllable parameter S_{bit}.

In this way, we have built the hybird index, and the index unit of NH-Index contains (label, degree, nbConnection, nbArray).

Query Processing

Now we show the graph query method using NH-Index. First we consider a simple case: similar node query. Given a node u, how to find the nodes same or similar to it in a graph?

Figure 7. The Example Graph for NH-Index

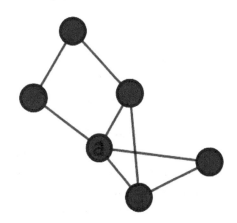

For exact node query, suppose the query node is N_q, data node is N_{db}, we have $N_q.label = N_{db}.label$, $N_q.degree \leq N_{db}.degree$, and $N_q.nbConnection \leq N_{db}.nbConnection$. Additionally, $N_q.nbArray = N_{db}.nbArray$.

For approximate node query, we can tolerate some missing in the matching. Given a neighbor missing fraction ρ, we can use $\rho \times N_q.degree$ to represent the max number of neighbors missing in data graph, denoted by nb_{miss}. Suppose the missing neighbor nodes have an edge between each pair of nodes, then the number of missing edges caused by missing nodes can be up to $nb_{miss} \times (nb_{miss} - 1) / 2$. But remember the edge missing caused by the neighbor nodes and the missing neighbor nodes, this number is $(N_q.degree - nb_{miss}) \times nb_{miss}$. In total, we can have up to $(nb_{miss} \times (nb_{miss} - 1) / 2) + (N_q.degree - nb_{miss}) \times nb_{miss}$ missing edges, denoted by nbc_{miss}. In summary, we can use the following four equations to judge the similarity between nodes.

$$N_{db}.label = N_q.label$$

$$N_{db}.degree = N_q.degree - nb_{miss}$$

$$\sum_{i=1}^{S_{bit}} Miss(N_{db}.nbArray[i], N_q.nbArray[i]) \leq nb_{miss}$$

$$N_{db}.nbConnection \geq N_q.nbConnection - nbc_{miss}$$

Because the first level index is implemented using existing relational system, condition 1 and 2 can also get in existing relational DBMS. The second level index can be implemented by a table with node and its nbArray. So we need to design an efficient algorithm to perform similar node querying. This is shown below in Algorithm 1.

Algorithm 1 contains two steps. The first step (line 1 to 17) counts the number of missing neighbors of the query node in the match. This is done by simulating counting in binary numbers. The second step (line 18 to 30) prunes all the database nodes with the number of missing neighbors higher than the user-defined threshold.

In step 1, variable *Count* is the counter representing the number of missing neighbors nb_{miss}, and *countSize* denotes its binary digit size. In other words, we keep a counter of *countSize* + 1 bits for each database node to recod the number of misses. In step 2, we use two bit vectors $Result_{eq}$ and $Result_{lt}$ to record the nodes with nb_{miss} misses. The final result is the bitwise OR of $Result_{eq}$ and $Result_{lt}$.

Algorithm 1 Bitmap Probe for Approximate Subgraph Matching (N_q, *Bitmap*, ρ):

Input: N_q is the query node, *Bitmap* is the bitmap index to be probed, assuming that there are n nodes in the bitmap index and the size of neighbor array is S_{bit}, ρ is the percentage of neighbors of a query node that can be missing in the match to a database node.

Output: $Result_{le}$ is the bit vector indicating which nodes satisfy the query

1. // (Step 1) count the number of missing neighbors
2. $nb_{miss} = \lfloor \rho \times N_q.degree \rfloor$ // the threshold for the number of missing neighbors
3. $countSize = \lfloor \log_2(nb_{miss}) \rfloor + 1$
4. **for** i from 0 to *countSize* **do**
5. $Count(i) = (0,0, ..., 0)$ // $Count(i)$ is a bit vector of size n
6. **end for**
7. **for** j from 0 to $S_{bit} - 1$ **do**
8. **if** $N_q.nbArray(j) = 1$ **then**
9. $Carries = $ NOT $Bitmap.B_j$
10. **for** k from 0 to *countSize* $- 1$ **do**
11. $Temp = Count(k)$ AND $Carries$
12. $Count(k) = Count(k)$ XOR $Carries$
13. $Carries = Temp$
14. **end for**
15. $Count(countSize) = Count(countSize)$ OR $Carries$

16. **end if**
17. **end for**
18. // (Step 2): only return nodes with no more than nb_{miss} missing neighbors
19. $Result_{lt} = (0,0,...,0)$ // $Result_{lt}$ is a bit vector of size n
20. $Result_{eq} = (1,1,...,1)$ // $Result_{eq}$ is a bit vector os size n
21. **for** k from *countSize* to 0 **do**
22. **if** bit k of nb_{miss}'s binary format is 1 **then**
23. $Result_{lt} = Result_{lt}$ OR ($Result_{eq}$ AND (NOT *Count*(k)))
24. $Result_{eq} = Result_{eq}$ AND *Count*(k)
25. **else**
26. $Result_{eq} = Result_{eq}$ AND (NOT *Count*(k))
27. **end if**
28. **end for**
29. $Result_{le} = Result_{lt}$ OR $Result_{eq}$
30. **return** $Result_{le}$

Now we have got an algorithm for node query processing using NH-Index. Let us continue to see how to perform subgraph matching.

Many existing subgraph matching methods have made use of this property that the importance of each node in a graph is very different. In graphs, deleting some nodes will break the graph structure, while deleting some other nodes will have almost no influence on the graph structure. This property is very like in a rail transport network, the breakdown of railway hub node is much more fatal than the edge nodes. There are various ways of measuring the importance of a node in a graph. For example, closeness, betweenness, and eigenvecter centralities. We consider to use the degree of a node to represent this importance for simplicity.

Following this observation, the subgraph matching method is shown in Algorithm 2. The procedure of subgraph matching contains two steps. The first step is to match important nodes and the second step is to extend the matching results in the first step.

In step 1, the algorithm selects a number of important nodes from the query and probes the NH-Index to match these important nodes. We introduce a parameter P_{imp}, defined as the fraction of important nodes in the query. Given P_{imp}, we sort the nodes in the query by their importance and select the top P_{imp} percent as the important nodes. After selecting important nodes, we match the nodes in Algorithm 1, and we get a list of matching database graphs. For the node mapping from query graph node to data graph node, we can use the traditional maximum weighted bipartie graph matching algorithm. For each node pair in the matching list, we define the *quality* of a node match w, as

$$w = \begin{cases} 2 - f_{nbc} & \widetilde{nb}_{miss} = 0 \\ 2 - (f_{nb} + \dfrac{f_{nbc}}{\widetilde{nb}_{miss}}) & otherwise \end{cases}$$

In step 2, for each candidate graph, utilizes the node matches produced by step 1 as anchor points to match the remaining nodes in the database and query graphs, and produce the final graph match. Algorithm 2 is a simple process, put important nodes into a queue, and pop the most important node from the queue each matching times until the queue is empty. Each time, the node is processed by Algorithm 3, which checks all nodes directly connect to the current node. And Algorithm 4 is the matching process in detail, including the operation of the auxilary queue.

Algorithm 3 and Algorithm 4 are shown next.

Algorithm 2: GrowMatch(G_q, G_{db}, M_{imp}):
Input: G_q is the query graph, G_{db} is the database graph, M_{imp} contains the matches for the important nodes in G_q

Output: M contains the node matches for the resulting graph match

1. put all node matches from M_{imp} to a priority queue Q sorted by their qualities

2. **while** Q is not empty **do**
3. pop up the best node match (N_q, N_{db}) from Q
4. put (N_q, N_{db}) into M
5. **ExamineNodesNearBy**(G_q, G_{db}, N_q, N_{db}, M, Q) //finding new matches for nodes nearby N_q
6. **end while**
7. **return** M

Algorithm 3: ExamineNodesNearBy (G_q, G_{db}, N_q, N_{db}, M_c, Q_c):

Input: G_q is the query graph, G_{db} is the database graph, N_q is a node in G_q, N_{db} is the node in G_{db} matched to N_q, M_c contains all the current node matches found so far, Q_c contains all the candidate node matches to be examined

1. $NB1_q$ = immediate neighbors of N_q that have no matches in M_c
2. $NB2_q$ = nodes two hops away from N_q that have no matches in M_c
3. $NB1_{db}$ = immediate neighbors of N_{db} that have no matches in either M_c or Q_c
4. $NB2_{db}$ = nodes two hops away from N_{db} that have no matches in either M_c or Q_c
5. **MatchNodes**(G_q, G_{db}, $NB1_q$, $NB1_{db}$, M_c, Q_c)
6. **MatchNodes**(G_q, G_{db}, $NB1_q$, $NB2_{db}$, M_c, Q_c)
7. **MatchNodes**(G_q, G_{db}, $NB2_q$, $NB1_{db}$, M_c, Q_c)

Algorithm 4: MatchNodes(G_q, G_{db}, S_q, S_{db}, M_c, Q_c):

Input: G_q is the query graph, G_{db} is the database graph, S_q is a set of nodes in G_q, S_{db} is a set of nodes in G_{db}, M_c contains all the current matches found so far, Q_c contains all the candidate matches to be examined

1. **for** every node N_q in S_q **do**
2. N_{db} = the best mapping of N_q in S_{db}
3. **if** N_{db} = null **then**
4. **continue**
5. **end if**

6. **if** N_q has no matches in Q_c **then**
7. put (N_q, N_{db}) into Q_c
8. remove N_{db} from S_{db}
9. **else if** (N_q, N_{db}) is a better node match **then**
10. remove the existing match of N_q from Q_c
11. put (N_q, N_{db}) into Q_c
12. remove N_{db} from S_{db}
13. **end if**
14. **end for**

G-Hash (Wang, Smalter, Huan & Lushington, 2009, Wang, Huan, Smalter, & Lushington, 2010)

In this section, we will look at a kernel function based method to do pair-wise entity resolution on graphs. Kernel methods and radial-basis function networks are widely used methods in machine learning area.

This G-hash method's basic idea is mapping graph data into node vectors, and we can get graph similarity by computing similarity function on these node vectors. In order to get node vector, we first make use of wavelet functions, which transform the topology of graphs into node vectors. Kernel function refers to the operation of computing the inner product between two objects in feature space. Kernel function computes the similarity of node vectors, which reflect the similarity between graphs.

Kernel Function

First we introduce some basic concepts.

Definition 1: Symmetric Function: A binary function is symmetric if K(x,y) = K(y,x) for all x,y $\in$ X.

Definition 2: Complex Conjugate: Complex conjugates are a pair of complex numbers, both having the same real part, but with imaginary parts of equal magnitude and opposite signs.

Definition 3: Positive Semi-Definite Function:
A binary function K: $X \times X \rightarrow \mathbb{R}$ is a positive semi-definite function if

$$\sum_{i,j=1}^{m} c_i c_j K(x_i, x_j) \geq 0$$

for any $m \in \mathbb{N}$, any selection of samples $x_i \in X$ (i = (1,n)), and any set of coefficients $c_i \in \mathbb{R}$ (i = (1,n)).

Definition 4: Hilbert Space: A Hilbert space H is a real or complex inner product space that is also a *complete metric space* with respect to the distance function induced by the inner product. To say that H is a complex inner product space means that H is a complex vector space on which there is an inner product *<x,y>* associating a complex number to each pair of elements *x, y* of H that satisfies the following properties: The inner product of a pair of elements is equal to the *complex conjugate* of the inner product of the swapped elements:

$$\overline{<y, x>} = <x, y>$$

The inner product is *linear* in its first argument. For all complex numbers *a* and *b*,

$$<ax_1 + bx_2, y> = a <x_1, y> + b <x_2, y>$$

The inner product of an element with itself is *positive definite*:

$$<x, x> \geq 0$$

where the case of equality holds precisely when x = 0.

Mercer's Theorem

A symmetric, positive semi-definite function ensures the existence of a Hilbert space H and a map $\Phi : X \rightarrow H$ such that

$$k(x, x') = <\Phi(x), \Phi(x')>$$

The result is known as the Mercer's theorem, and this function is known as a Mercer kernel function, or *kernel function*.

An alignment of graph G and G' is a 1-1 mapping $\pi : V(G) \rightarrow V(G')$. Given an alignment, we can define the similarity of G and G':

$$k_A(G, G') = \max_{\pi} (\sum_{v \in V[G]} k_n(v, \pi(v)) +$$
$$\sum_{u,v \in V[G]} k_e((u, v), (\pi(u), \pi(v))))$$

where k_n is the kernel function to measure the similarity of nodes, k_e is the function to measure the similarity of edges, and their sum constitute the similarity of graphs. Of course, its computational complexity is too high in this definition of graph similarity. It is at least no easier than subgraph isomorphism problem(), which is a NP-hard problem.

To increase the computational complexity, we can revise graph similarity in this way:

$$k_M(G, G') = \max_{\pi} \sum_{v \in V[G]} k_a(f(v), f(\pi(v)))$$

where π is an alignment from $V(G)$ to $V(G')$, $f(v)$ is the feature set of node v. We will explain how to compute feature set $f(v)$ in detail in the following paragraphs. The revised equation is to compute the *maximal weighted bipartite graph*. It has an efficient solution in $O(|V(G)^3|)$ time.

Wavelet Alignment Kernel

Kernel functions map a set of data to a high dimensional Hilbert space without explicitly computing the coordinates of the data, and this provide a uniformed analytical environment for many kinds of data including graph data. This a a widely used method in machine learning area.

As mentioned above, a symmetric, semidefinite function ensures the existence of Hilbert sapce, and we need this kind of functions. But how to define the functions?

Let us look at the two wavelet functions below.

Haar Function

$$\bar{f}_j(v) = \frac{1}{\left|N_j(v)\right|} \sum_{u \in N_j(v)} f_u$$

This is the earliest and simplest wavelet function. Its function image is shown in Figure 8.

Mexican Hat Function

$$\varphi(x) = \frac{2}{\sqrt{3}\sigma\pi^{\frac{1}{4}}}(1 - \frac{x^2}{\sigma^2})e^{\frac{-x^2}{2\sigma^2}}$$

Mexican hat function has another name *Ricker wavelet*. Its function image's curve in Figure 9from is very like Mexican hat, so American researchers tend to call it Mexican hat function. By the way, the Mexican hat function is frequently employed to model seismic data, and as a broad spectrum source term in computational electrodynamics.

To make a connection between graph object structures, we define *discrete wavelet function*. The h-hop neighborhood of one node v, denoted by $N_h(v)$, refers to a set of nodes which are h hops away from the node v according to the shortest path. The discrete wavelet function is defined as:

$$\psi_{j,k} = \frac{1}{h+1}\int_{j/(k+1)}^{(j+1)/(k+1)} \varphi(x)dx$$

Figure 8. Image for Wavelet Function (http://en.wikipedia.org/wiki/Haar_wavelet)

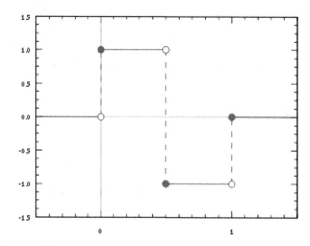

Figure 9. The Curve of Function Images (http://en.wikipedia.org/wiki/Mexican_hat_wavelet)

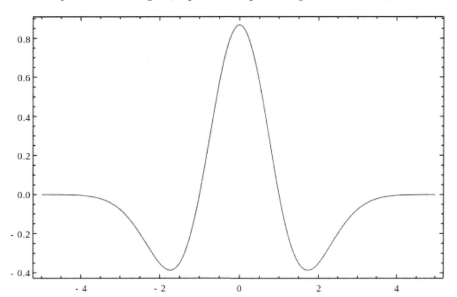

where $\varphi(x)$ is Haar function or Mexican hat function, and h is the *h*th partition after partition domain $(0,1)$ into $(h+1)$ intervals, and *j* is between 0 and *h*. Discrete wavelet denotes employing wavelet functions on discrete objects. We use discrete wavelet function to measure the local topology of node *v*, and the result is represent by feature vector, denoted by $\Gamma_h(v)$.

$$\Gamma_h(v) = C_{h,v} \times \sum_{j=0}^{k} \psi_{j,k} \times \overline{f}_j(v)$$

where $C_{h,v}$ is a normalization factor with:

$$C_{h,v} = (\sum_{j=0}^{h} \frac{\psi_{j,h}^2}{|N_h(v)|})^{-1/2}$$

where $|N_h(v)|$ is the number of nodes in *h* hops away from *v*, and $\psi_{j,h}$ is discrete wavelet function defined above.

And $\overline{f}_j(v)$ is the average feature vector value of atoms that are at most *j*-hop away from *v* with

$$\overline{f}_j(v) = \frac{1}{|N_j(v)|} \sum_{u \in N_j(v)} f_u$$

f_u denotes the feature vector value. There are four types of feature vector value: nominal, ordinal, and internal and ratio. For ratio and internal node feature vector value, we directly use wavelet analyses to get local feature vector. For nominal and ordinal node feature, we can first construct a histogram, and then perform wavelet analyzing. At last we get a list of feature vectors $\Gamma^h(v) = \{\Gamma_1(v), \Gamma_2(v), \dots, \Gamma_h(v)\}$, called *wavelet measurement vector*. This vector list constitutes a matrix, and we call it *wavelet measurement matrix*.

For feature vectors of node *u* and node *v*, kernel function is defined by this equation:

$$k_m(G, G') = \sum_{(u,v) \in V(G) \times V(G')} K(\Gamma^h(u), \Gamma^h(v))$$

$$K(X,Y) = e^{\frac{-\|X-Y\|_2^2}{2}}$$

Wavelet Graph Matching Kernel

Having the wavelet measurement matrix, we can construct the kernel function, and then compute the distance between graphs. The graph distance is defined as:

$$
\begin{aligned}
d(G,G') &= \sqrt{\left\|\phi(G)-\phi(G')\right\|_2^2} \\
&= \sqrt{\left\langle \phi(G)-\phi(G'),\phi(G)-\phi(G')\right\rangle} \\
&= \sqrt{\left\langle \phi(G),\phi(G)\right\rangle+\left\langle \phi(G'),\phi(G')\right\rangle-2\left\langle \phi(G),\phi(G')\right\rangle} \\
&= \sqrt{k_m(G,G)+k_m(G',G')-2k_m(G,G')}
\end{aligned}
$$

where $k_m(G,G)$ is the kernel function of graph G and itself, $k_m(G',G')$ is the kernel function of graph G' and itself, and $k_m(G,G')$ is the kernel function between graph G and G'.

Now we get local topology vector $\Gamma_h(v)$ of each node v, and they are the input parameter of kernel function. For node u and node v, the kernel function can be computed by this equation:

$$
k_m(G,G') = \sum_{(u,v)\in V(G)\times V(G')} K(\Gamma^h(u),\Gamma^h(v))
$$

$$
K(X,Y) = e^{\frac{-\|X-Y\|_2^2}{2}}
$$

Suppose the database' size is n and the average node number of all graphs is m, then the overall time complexity of the kernel matrix is $O(n^2\times m^2)$. When dealing with big data, this complexity is still inadequate.

Is there a way to avoid pair-wise computation, and still get the similarity relation among nodes? The answer is yes, for we can use the similar nodes to represent the graph. In this way, we develop a hash based k-NNs query method called G-hash. First discretize each feature in the node vector to an integer, and encode a node label directly as a n bit-string with all zeros except a single 1 which

indicate the label. After the node vector is changed to a list of integer, we then convert a node vector to a string. Such string is the hash key of the corresponding node. Let us see an example, the hash table for graph P in Figure 10 is also shown.

If we put two graph together to build hash index, we only need to count the nodes who have the same number as node v. And the kernel function value is the count.

If we choose RBF kernel, the $K(\Gamma^h(u),\Gamma^h(v))\approx 1$ for similar nodes u and v. For the unsimilar nodes u and v, $K(\Gamma^h(u),\Gamma^h(v))\approx 0$. In this way, the similarity of two graphs is determined only by similar node pairs instead of all node pairs. The kernel function is simplified as:

$$
k_m(G,G') \approx \sum_{v\in G',u\in simi(v)} 1 = \sum_{v\in G'}\left|simi(v)\right|
$$

where *simi(v)* is a node set which contains the nodes hash to the same cell as node v, and $\left|simi(v)\right|$ is the number of nodes in the set.

FUTURE RESEARCH DIRECTIONS

Discuss future and emerging trends. Provide insight about the future of the book's theme from the perspective of the chapter focus. Viability

Figure 10. Graph P

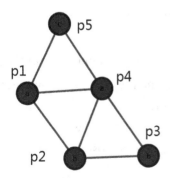

of a paradigm, model, implementation issues of proposed programs, etc., may be included in this section. If appropriate, suggest future research opportunities within the domain of the topic.

CONCLUSION

In this chapter, we discussed the pairwise similarity measurement of graphs, and mainly focus on the representative ones. These measurements all have their own employment area and perform quite differently in other areas. After reading this chapter, readers can have a general idea on using these graph similarity measurements in the right suitable case.

REFERENCES

Cho, J., Shivakumar, N., & Garcia-Molina, H. (2000). Finding replicated web collections. *SIGMOD Record*, *29*(2), 355–366. doi:10.1145/335191.335429

Fan, W., Li, J., Ma, S., Tang, N., Wu, Y., & Wu, Y. (2010). Graph pattern matching: from intractable to polynomial time. *Proceedings of the VLDB Endowment*, *3*(1-2), 264–275.

Fan, W., Li, J., Ma, S., Wang, H., & Wu, Y. (2010). Graph homomorphism revisited for graph matching. *Proceedings of the VLDB Endowment*, *3*(1-2), 1161–1172.

Tian, Y., & Patel, J. M. (2008). Tale: A tool for approximate large graph matching. In Proceedings of Data Engineering, (pp. 963-972). IEEE.

Wang, X., Huan, J., Smalter, A., & Lushington, G. H. (2010). Application of kernel functions for accurate similarity search in large chemical databases. *BMC Bioinformatics*, *11*(Suppl 3), S8. doi:10.1186/1471-2105-11-S3-S8 PMID:20438655

Wang, X., Smalter, A., Huan, J., & Lushington, G. H. (2009). G-hash: Towards fast kernel-based similarity search in large graph databases. In *Proceedings of the 12th International Conference on Extending Database Technology: Advances in Database Technology* (pp. 472-480). ACM.

Yan, X., Yu, P. S., & Han, J. (2005). Substructure similarity search in graph databases. In *Proceedings of the 2005 ACM SIGMOD International Conference on Management of Data* (pp. 766-777). ACM.

ADDITIONAL READING

Blondel, V. D., Gajardo, A., Heymans, M., Senellart, P., & Van Dooren, P. (2004). A measure of similarity between graph vertices: Applications to synonym extraction and web searching. *SIAM Review*, *46*(4), 647–666. doi:10.1137/S0036144502415960

Bloom, B. H. (1970). Space/time trade-offs in hash coding with allowable errors. *Communications of the ACM*, *13*(7), 422–426. doi:10.1145/362686.362692

Bunke, H. (1997). On a relation between graph edit distance and maximum common subgraph. *Pattern Recognition Letters*, *18*(8), 689–694. doi:10.1016/S0167-8655(97)00060-3

Chen, L., Gupta, A., & Kurul, M. E. (2005, August). Stack-based algorithms for pattern matching on dags. In *Proceedings of the 31st international conference on Very large data bases* (pp. 493-504). VLDB Endowment.

Cheng, J., Yu, J. X., Ding, B., Yu, P. S., & Wang, H. (2008, April). Fast graph pattern matching. In *Data Engineering, 2008. ICDE 2008. IEEE 24th International Conference on* (pp. 913-922). IEEE.

Gärtner, T., Flach, P., & Wrobel, S. (2003). On graph kernels: Hardness results and efficient alternatives. In *Learning Theory and Kernel Machines* (pp. 129–143). Springer Berlin Heidelberg. doi:10.1007/978-3-540-45167-9_11

He, H., & Singh, A. K. (2006, April). Closure-tree: An index structure for graph queries. In *Data Engineering, 2006. ICDE'06. Proceedings of the 22nd International Conference on* (pp. 38-38). IEEE.

Henzinger, M. R., Henzinger, T. A., & Kopke, P. W. (1995, October). Computing simulations on finite and infinite graphs. In *Foundations of Computer Science, 1995. Proceedings., 36th Annual Symposium on* (pp. 453-462). IEEE.

JIS, M. T. C. S. (1979). Computers and intractability A Guide to the Theory of NP-Completeness.

Kann, V. (1992). On the approximability of the maximum common subgraph problem. In STACS 92 (pp. 375-388). Springer Berlin Heidelberg.

Melnick, S., Molina-Garcia, H., & Rahm, E. (2002). Similarity flooding: a versatile graph matching algorithm. In *proc. of the International Conference on Data Engineering–ICDE, San José* (pp. 117-128).

Ramalingam, G., & Reps, T. (1993, March). A categorized bibliography on incremental computation. In *Proceedings of the 20th ACM SIGPLAN-SIGACT symposium on Principles of programming languages* (pp. 502-510). ACM.

Ramalingam, G., & Reps, T. (1996). An incremental algorithm for a generalization of the shortest-path problem. *Journal of Algorithms*, *21*(2), 267–305. doi:10.1006/jagm.1996.0046

Ramalingam, G., & Reps, T. (1996). On the computational complexity of dynamic graph problems. *Theoretical Computer Science*, *158*(1), 233–277. doi:10.1016/0304-3975(95)00079-8

Saha, D. (2007). An incremental bisimulation algorithm. In FSTTCS 2007: Foundations of Software Technology and Theoretical Computer Science (pp. 204-215). Springer Berlin Heidelberg.

Shasha, D., Wang, J. T., & Giugno, R. (2002, June). Algorithmics and applications of tree and graph searching. In *Proceedings of the twenty-first ACM SIGMOD-SIGACT-SIGART symposium on Principles of database systems* (pp. 39-52). ACM.

Smalter, A., Huan, J., & Lushington, G. (2009). Graph wavelet alignment kernels for drug virtual screening. *Journal of Bioinformatics and Computational Biology*, *7*(03), 473–497. doi:10.1142/S0219720009004187 PMID:19507286

Tian, Y., Mceachin, R. C., Santos, C., & Patel, J. M. (2007). SAGA: a subgraph matching tool for biological graphs. *Bioinformatics (Oxford, England)*, *23*(2), 232–239. doi:10.1093/bioinformatics/btl571 PMID:17110368

Ukkonen, E. (1992). Approximate string-matching with *q*-grams and maximal matches. *Theoretical Computer Science*, *92*(1), 191–211. doi:10.1016/0304-3975(92)90143-4

Ullmann, J. R. (1977). A binary n-gram technique for automatic correction of substitution, deletion, insertion and reversal errors in words. *The Computer Journal*, *20*(2), 141–147. doi:10.1093/comjnl/20.2.141

Vazirani, V. V. (2004). *Approximation algorithms*. springer.

Williams, D. W., Huan, J., & Wang, W. (2007, April). Graph database indexing using structured graph decomposition. In *Data Engineering, 2007. ICDE 2007. IEEE 23rd International Conference on* (pp. 976-985). IEEE.

Yan, X., Yu, P. S., & Han, J. (2004, June). Graph indexing: a frequent structure-based approach. In *Proceedings of the 2004 ACM SIGMOD international conference on Management of data* (pp. 335-346). ACM.

Zhang, S., Hu, M., & Yang, J. (2007, April). Treepi: A novel graph indexing method. In *Data Engineering, 2007. ICDE 2007. IEEE 23rd International Conference on* (pp. 966-975). IEEE.

Zhao, P., Yu, J. X., & Yu, P. S. (2007, September). Graph indexing: tree+ delta<= graph. In *Proceedings of the 33rd international conference on Very large data bases* (pp. 938-949). VLDB Endowment.

Zou, L., Chen, L., & Özsu, M. T. (2009). Distance-join: Pattern match query in a large graph database. *Proceedings of the VLDB Endowment*, 2(1), 886–897.

KEY TERMS AND DEFINITIONS

1-1 P-Homomorphism: An extension of subgraph isomorphism that support edge-to-path mappings and node similarity, and this is also an NP-hard problem.

Bounded Simulation: An extension of graph simulation that allows mapping edges in pattern graph to paths in data graph.

Incremental Graph Matching: A graph matching method with much faster speed, but requires graph pattern matching result and update area as input.

Kernel Function: A node vector based graph similarity measure that computes the inner product between node sets of graphs.

Neighborhood Index: A bit-array based index structure built on relational database system.

P-Homomorphism: An extension of graph homomorphism that allows edge-to-path mappings, and this is an NP-hard problem.

Relaxation Ratio: A none-symmetric graph similarity measure defined through their maximum common subgraph.

Similar Collection: Equal sized subgraphs that ensure a 1-1 mapping with similar pages and similar links.

Web Graph: A graph model of Web that regards web pages as nodes, links between pages as directed edges.

Chapter 9
Entity Resolution on Complex Network

ABSTRACT

Complex networks can be used to describe the Internet, social network, or more broadly describe a binary relation of a set of objects. Structure information of complex network helps the identification of the entity corresponding to nodes in the network. There is much research in this area, and the authors introduce these studies and their results in this chapter. The authors mainly present two practical applications as an example. Through these examples, the authors explore the research ideas in entity resolution on complex network. The applications of entity resolution on complex network include the detection of mirror Websites, name recognition in social network, and information searching on the Internet. This chapter introduces some applications, including the detection of mirror Websites and name recognition, in social network in detail.

INTRODUCTION

What is complex network? a network which has parts or all of the nature of self-organization, self-similar, attractor, small-world and scale-free is called a complex network, which can be used to describe the Internet, social network, or more broadly describe a set which has a binary relation. The structural information of complex network will be helpful to the identification of the entity where each node corresponds to a data objet.

This chapter mainly describes entity resolution on a complex network. The applications of entity resolution on a complex network include the detection of mirror websites, name recognition in social network. The following will introduce these applications in this area and in the end, we

will briefly introduce some description methods of node similarity and formula corresponding to them.

BACKGROUND

The study of complex networks is a young and active area of scientific research inspired largely by the empirical study of real-world network such as computer network and social network. In recent years, the academic study of complex network is in the ascendant. In particular, two international pioneering works set off a boom of complex network's study. Watts & Strogatz (1998) introduces a small-world network model to describe a conversion from completely regular network to a

DOI: 10.4018/978-1-4666-5198-2.ch009

completely random network. Small-world network not only has clustering characteristics similar to the regular network, but also has a smaller average path length similar to the random network. Barabási & Albert (1999) pointed out that many practical connectivities on complex network spread in a power-law form. .

With no obvious characteristic length, such networks are called scale-free network. Then, scientists have studied the various characteristics of a variety of complex network.

Domestic scholars have noticed this trend, and began to expand research. The scholars who join the study of complex network are mainly from the field of graph theory, statistical physics, computer network research, ecology, sociology and economics. The network involved in the research included all kinds of network in the field of life sciences (such as cellular networks, protein - protein interaction networks, protein folding networks, neural networks, ecological networks), Internet / WWW network, social networks, network of epidemic spread of the disease, scientists cooperation network, the network of human sexual relations, linguistics network, and so on. The primary methods include graph theory, statistical physics and social network analysis.

THE DETECTION OF MIRROR WEBSITES (BARABÁSI & ALBERT 1999)

What is mirroring? There is no crisp definition but it is obvious that no one can say that two sites are mirrored only if their content is byte-wise identical. In practice this definition is too restrictive, even on successive accesses to the same URL the fetched content may differ slightly because of dynamic components, time stamps, transaction-ids, etc. What's more, this definition does not address the issue of structure. When two sites have different structures, the proof offered by content similarity is not compelling. Krishna Bharat and Andrei Broder have good insights in

this field. They were able to detect both partial and total mirroring, and handle cases where the content is not byte-wise identical. Furthermore, their technique is computationally very efficient and does not assume that the initial set of URLs gathered from each host is comprehensive. They defined two hosts to be mirrors if: (1) A high percentage of *paths* (that is, the portions of the URL after the host name) are valid on both Web sites, and (2) these common paths link the documents that have similar content. Therefore, hosts that replicate content but rename paths are not considered mirrors under their definitions. The technique that they devised to detect mirrored hosts from large data sets depends mostly on the syntactic analysis of URL strings and requires fetching and content analysis only for a small number of pages. They use probabilistic tests for establishing the degree of mirroring. This makes their technique computationally very efficient. They are able to detect both partial and total mirroring, and handle cases where the content is not exactly identical. Furthermore, their strategy does not assume that the initial set of URLs from each host is comprehensive. Hence, their technique has practical uses beyond our study, and can be applied to other settings.

The following are the specific studies:

1. **Classification of Mirroring**

Level 1: Structural and Content Identity: Every page on host A with relative path P, (i.e., a URL of the form http://A/P) is represented by a byte-wise identical page on host B, at location http://B/P, and vice versa.

Level 2: Structural identity. Content equivalence: Every page on host A with relative path P, is represented by an equivalent content page on host B, at location http://B/P, and vice versa.

Level 3: Structural identity. Content similarity: Every page on host A with relative path P, is represented by a highly similar page on host B, at location http://B/P, and vice versa.

Level 4: Partial structural match. Content similarity: Some pages on host A with relative path P, are represented by a page on host B, at location http://B/P, and vice versa, and these pairs of pages are highly similar.

Level 5: Structural identity. Related content: Every page on host A with relative path P, is represented by a page on host B, at location http://B/P, and vice versa. The pages are pairwise related (e.g., every page is a translation of its counterpart) but in general are not syntactically similar.

Mismatch: None of the above: The consideration of similarity is as follows.

Structure: Is defined by the set of valid paths relative to the host under consideration.

Structurally Identical: If two hosts have exactly the same set of paths, we say that they are structurally identical

Content Identical: With regard to content, we say that two pages are *content identical* if they are byte-wise equal.

Content Equivalent: We say that two pages are *content equivalent* if pages change at the byte level (e.g., by the addition of blank lines, by HTML reformatting, etc.) without any change of content.

Highly Similar: If pages change in content (e.g., due to a banner ad or other forms of dynamic content) but remain highly similar at the syntactic level, we call them *highly similar*.

Related: If pages change substantially at the syntactic level but are semantically similar (e.g. translated content), we call them *related*.

After defining mirror segments, the solution strategies are given.

Stage I: Candidate Pair Detection

In this stage, we consider the URLs available from each of the hosts in our database, sample a subset of these URLs and compute syntactic similarity between these subsets. As explained below, we use coordinated sampling to increase the likelihood of selecting the same paths from

hosts that happen to be mirrors. The output from this stage is a list of host pairs that are potential mirrors, ordered by likelihood.

First, from the practical considerations of using full paths as features is not practical. Instead, they use fragments of the path and the host name as features. In the feature selection, they use pairs of consecutive directories' names along the path (called word bigrams) as features. For large data sets (179 million URLs in our case) reducing the number of features to be considered is a priority. One step to do this is to ignore hosts which contribute a small number of URLs to the collection. For every host we first sort the list of URLs, and then only consider those paths whose strings upon hashing yielded a value which is 0 mod m. The aim of this step is to increase the correlation between the selected paths.

Of course, this is not enough. Let us talk about the feature generation that is how to do with. The hostname and the set of paths derived from a given host as described above, contribute a set of features associated with host. Each string is converted to a list of following terms.

Converting to Lowercase: Paths may or may not be case sensitive, but hostnames are not. We ignore case for both.

Treating Sequences of Non-Alphabetical Characters as Word-Breaks: This gives a list of words. Thus, www7.infoseek.com and www6.infoseek.com will yield the same list:(www,infoseek,com). We generate *word bigrams* by treating every contiguous pair of terms as a feature. For example, the hostname www.infoseek.com generates: (www,infoseek) and (infoseek,com). In fragmenting the path, we also associate depth information. This gives us *positional word bigrams*.

For example: /Education/Alice-Lee-Institute-of-Advanced-Nursing/Pages/Overview. aspx gives(Education,Alice-Lee-Institute-of-Advanced-Nursing,0)(Alice-Lee-Institute-of Advanced-Nursing,Pages,1)(Pages,Overview,2) (Overview,aspx,3)as features.

Position is useful because we are trying to find mirror sites that share the same path structure.

Finally, to reduce the set of features to be considered and reduce noise in the matching process we do following three things:

1. Eliminate stop terms such as: htm, html, txt, main, index, home, bin, cgi.
2. Avoid URLs that have terms like nph, dynaweb, and zyview, which are characteristic of websites created automatically by tools. Such sites lead to spurious matches because they use a standard naming scheme.
3. Eliminate path features that do not occur at least twice on the host.

After feature generation has been solved, we need to solve the last problem, *Feature matching*.

For each valid feature we write the tuple <*feature, host*> to a file, and the file of tuples is sorted by the first element of the tuple in order to compute the similarity between pairs of hosts that share common features. Like the usual IDF (inverse document frequency) weighting used in information retrieval, they prescribed that features are weighted in inverse proportion to the number of hosts which they occur in in the feature matching scheme. This means that features that occur in many hosts are considered too common to be significant, and correspondingly their IDF weight is low. To further optimize, they skip all features that occur within more than 20 hosts and, for the rest, they consider each pair of hosts that share it and increment the Similarity_Score(*Host1, Host2*) by the weight of the feature, FW(*f*) (*f* means feature) as follows.

$$FW(f) = S(f)/N(f) \qquad (1)$$

where S(*f*) is a measure of the significance of f independent of its distribution, and N(*f*) is the number of hosts in which f occurs. They set S(*f*) to 4 for host features and to 1 for path features, since a host feature match offers evidence that the two sites are part of the same organization.

The Normalized Similarity Score of each pair (*Host1, Host2*) is computed thus:

$$
\begin{aligned}
&Normalized\_Score(Host_1, Host_2) \\
&= \frac{Similarity\_Score(Host_1, Host_2)}{1 + 0.1 * (Log(N_1) + Log(N_2))}
\end{aligned} \qquad (2)
$$

N1 and *N2* represent the number of URLs in the input from *Host1* and *Host2* respectively, and are assumed to be proportional to their sizes. The denominator helps normalize the score by host size, to compensate for the fact that large hosts will have more feature matches than small hosts. Our parameters appear to perform satisfactorily but may afford some tuning.

After the normalized similarity score of every pair of hosts computed, a list of <*score, host-pair*> tuples is written to a file. To reduce mismatches, they filter out host pairs that have only one feature in common. Besides, the remaining host pairs are sorted in the descending order of normalized similarity score. And this optional step reduces false positives at the risk of skipping some mirrored pairs.

Stage II: Host Pair Classification

In this stage we process the list of candidate host pairs from Stage I, and test in each case if the hosts are indeed mirrors and estimate the extent of their overlap.

In Stage I, they have got a descending order of normalized similarity score, a list of <*score, host-pair*>. In Stage II, they will classify each host pair into one of many categories based on the classification of mirroring hosts discussed in classification of mirroring.

To classify a host pair we estimate the fraction of the paths from one host that are valid on the other host, and the extent to which the pages referenced by the common paths are similar. Thus, there are two steps: (i) selecting paths to test, and

(ii) checking for validity of paths and computing similarity between pages corresponding to the valid paths. Since any given host may occur in many host pairs, the same paths are reused. The first step is done only once per host. In the second step the selected paths are used to fetch documents from both hosts, namely the source host where the path is known to be valid, and the target host, where the validity of the path is to be tested. How to estimate the validity of the path? After the GET is successful, the checking is done if the content is the same. This can be done at various levels of tolerance to change. For instance, this can be done by fingerprinting both documents. Of course, this is not entirely feasible, since the content is often non fingerprint-identical. And this can happen even on successive GETs to the same server, since variable server-side includes or dynamically generated Web-pages, to say nothing of mirrored content to be even greater likelihood of a discrepancy, due to version inconsistencies and local server-side includes. To compensate for this, they de-tag the content and ignore whitespace and check for syntactic similarity, that is, closeness of textual content, instead of fingerprint equality. They use the mathematical concept of 'resemblance' to capture the informal notion of syntactic similarity.

The resemblance, r(A, B), of two documents A and B is defined as follows: first each document is transformed into a set of word k-grams, S(A) and S(B), also called 'shingles'. And then compute:

$$r(A, B) = \frac{|\,S(A) \cap S(B)\,|}{|\,S(A) \cup S(B)\,|} \qquad (3)$$

where |S| is the size of the set S.

The resemblance can be estimated using a fixed size 'sketch' for each document, and the size of this sketch is of the order of a few hundred bytes per document. Namely, the resemblance value, r(A,B), is a number between 0 and 1, which we can use to express the similarity between A and B as a percentage.

After the work is done, the host pairs will be classified into one of many levels. Between any pair of hosts, there are 19 Web page comparisons in all: a pair of root pages and 9 source pages sampled from each host.

In each case one of the following outcomes is possible:

- **Source Failure (SF):** GET failed at source host.
- **Target Failure (TF):** GET failed at target host.
- **Fingerprint Match (FM):** Content is byte-wise identical.
- **Full Similarity (FS):** The documents are 100% equivalent after de-tagging.
- **High Similarity (HS):** Common content is above the threshold for high similarity.
- **Trace Similarity (TS):** A small (non-zero) portion of the document is common.
- **NS:** Path is valid, but no syntactic similarity.

Based on what is observed in the 19 tests, each host pair is assigned a classification level. The assignment criterion for various classification levels is summarized in Table 1.

In the previous part, we have already mentioned the description of the five levels. Now the test for Level 5 similarity is stricter than the previous definition, which does not require trace similarity testing. This criterion was added to compensate for the case when all paths seem valid on the target host because it returns its own error page for mismatches instead of a 404 HTTP result.

About Cross Domain Mirroring

This table shows the distribution of cross-domain mirrors. These are pairs of mirrored hosts in which the domains of the two hosts differ. Cross-domain mirroring is interesting because it often reveals mirroring across organizational boundaries. In other cases it reveals mirroring for geographical

Table 1. Classification of host pairs

Classification	Criterion	Implication
Level 1	All tests show SF or FM and Not all are SF	Same structure: identical content
Level 2	All tests show SF or FM or FS, and not all are SF	Same structure: equivalent content
Level 3	All tests show SF or FM or FS or HS, and not all are SF	Same structure: similar content
Level 4	Some tests show HS or FM	Structure is partially replicated: for replicate paths, content is similar
Level 5	No test yields TF and at least one with TS	Same structure (since all paths are valid):some of the contest appears related.
Mismatch	All tests result in TF or NS	Not similar
DNS failure	DNS lookup failed for one of the hosts	No information: presently inaccessible
Server failure	One of the two servers was inaccessible	No information presently inaccessible

reasons, within the same organization. The table shows the 10 most common domain combinations we encountered for various mirroring classifications.

When one considers hosts that are fully replicated (Levels 1–3), the most common case is when a 'com' site is mirrored as an 'org' site. Almost as frequent is the 'com-net' combination. We then see several instances of a 'com' site being mirrored under a country's domain.

The 'com-edu' combination seems to occur more with partial replication (Level 4). This suggests the sharing of databases rather than a replication of the site's main functionality.

A cluster of research sites found to have Level 4 similarity because they all had copies of date resource. And with structural cross-domain replication (Level 5) we tend to find Web sites by the same organization mirrored in other languages or catering to local content, e.g., (www.yahoo.ca, www.yahoo.co.jp) or (infoart.stanet.ru, infoart.baku.az).

The examples below were chosen to illustrate the various levels in our hierarchy. They behave as described at the time of writing. Since the Web is constantly changing, it is impossible to guarantee that they will continue to do so in the future.

Level 1 Examples (Cross Domain)

- www.boutiques-de-gestion.asso.fr (20 samples)
- www.boutiques-de-gestion.com (19 samples)
- www.ruskin-sch.milohedge.com (20 samples)
- www.ruskin-sch.ox.ac.uk (20 samples)
- www.upa.net (20 samples)
- www.upaccess.com (20 samples)

Level 2 Examples

These sites do virtual hosting from the same server, and have content that differs in minor ways:

- sys1.tpusa.com (20 samples)
- www.i-trade.com (20 samples)
- www.palladium.net (20 samples)
- www.parroty.com (20 samples)

Table 2. Distribution of cross-domain mirrors

Rank Based on Frequency of Occurrence	Full Replication Levels 1–3	Partial Replication Level 4	Structural Replication Level 5
1	com-org (12.1%)	com-net (14.3%)	com-net (19.23%)
2	com-net (10.06%)	com-edu (3.08%)	ca-edu (19.23%)
3	com-de (5.17%)	com-org (3.08%)	edu-us (11.53%)
4	com-uk (4.89%)	de-edu (2.94%)	ca-com (11.53%)
5	com-fr (4.48%)	ca-com (2.32%)	az-ru (11.53%)
6	edu-org (3.8%)	com-de (2.19%)	com-sg (7.69%)
7	com-jp (3.53%)	au-com (2.12%)	cl-org (3.84%)
8	net-org (2.44%)	edu-uk (1.77%)	kz-ru (3.84%)
9	at-com (2.44%)	edu-jp (1.5%)	mx-org (3.84%)
10	com-kr (2.17%)	com-fr (1.5%)	ca-jp (3.84%)
Cross-domain mirrors	735	1461	26

Level 3 Examples

These are hosted by the same server but appear to be different because of dynamic content (a visitor counter):

- www.dancecorner.com (20 samples)
- www.swingdance.com (20 samples)

Level 4 Examples

These are mirror sites in French and English. They have the same path hierarchy but with translated content. This is characteristic of Canadian organizations with bilingual content. Some pages are common, so this does not appear to be Level 5:

- www.cbsc.org (56 samples)
- www.rcsec.org (63 samples)

These mirrors have identical content, but with French accented characters replaced with their HTML entity equivalents in one case. Consequently the pages that were compared appeared to have high or trace similarity rather than full similarity or fingerprint equivalence:

- bleue.ac-aix-marseille.fr (20 samples)
- www.ac-aix-marseille.fr (20 samples)

These are 2 different school sites, built with the same tool (Microsoft Communication Tool for Schools). Hence, they have a similar hierarchy, and layout, but differ in content:

- wchs02.washington.high.washington.k12.
- ga.us (20 samples)
- www.sd70.bc.ca (20 samples)

Although these have different IP addresses and their root pages are different, paths from one source seem to produce identical pages on the other. This led us to the discovery that DesertNet implements the newspaper, Tucson Weekly:

- www.desert.net (111 samples)
- www.tucsonweekly.com (66 samples)

Level 5 Examples

These two differ only in their encoding of Cyrillic. The content is the same:

- www-ibm866.consultant.ru (20 samples)
- www-windows-1251.consultant.ru (20 samples)

Two libraries that use the same query engine. Consequently queries on one are valid on the other:

- leagle.wcl.american.edu (127 samples)
- library.cwu.edu (102 samples)

Same content, mirrored in Spanish and English:

- tribute.lronhubbard.cl (20 samples)
- tribute.lronhubbard.org (18 samples)

All in all,mirroring information is useful in the implementation of smart caching proxies and efficient crawlers. A proxy that maintains such a list of mirrors can serve as a cached page from any of the mirrors of a given host, provided that the path is the same. A smart proxy can also try and compensate for broken links or server failure by transparently checking if the page is available on a mirror site. A crawler that tries to cover as much as the Web as possible in the shortest possible time can use mirroring information to avoid redundant crawling over mirrored parts of the Web. Also, in the interests of load balancing or in the interests of speed it can selectively download a path from an equivalent host.

NAME RECOGNITION IN SOCIAL NETWORK (FAN, WANG, PU, ZHOU & LV 2011)

Why name ambiguity exists in social networks? It is corresponding to the fact that many people or objects share identical names in the real world. And name disambiguation contains the actual value because such name ambiguity decreases the performance of document retrieval, Web search, information integration, and may cause confusion in other applications. Since they share same name

and we lack sufficient information, it is a nontrivial task to distinguish them accurately. What's more, different names may correspond to the identical entity, and this is difficult too. There are some researches on these two aspects but most research focuses on only one aspect and cannot solve the problem completely. Therefore, we choose two remarkable researches as reference. One of them is on graph-based name disambiguation (FAN, WANG, PU, ZHOU & LV 2011). Their research focus on the former, namely different entities share a common name. In their study, they used digital libraries as background to distinguish publications written by authors with identical names, and the specific contents will be described in the following. And the other gives a framework from Li, Wang, Gao & Li (2010). In the research, both kinds of confusions are considered, and with effective clustering techniques, approximate string matching algorithms and a flexible mechanism of knowledge integration, EIF can be widely used to solve many different kinds of entity identification problems. Similarly, this study makes author identification as topic to verify the feasibility of the EIF, and the specific contents will also be described in the following.

On Graph-Based Name Disambiguation (FAN, WANG, PU, ZHOU & LV 2011)

For some reasons like personalized styles and contextual requirements, name variation, identical names for different persons, and name misspellings are not uncommon in various information sources. They often appear in the web documents, bibliographies, and so on. Because we can't assign a unique identifier to every name, there may be a lot of confusions in many cases if people use names to identify specified persons. Generally, the problems caused by name ambiguity can be classified into two categories. The first popular case is called reference disambiguation or duplicate detection, and we will not focus on it in this section. The second case called name disambiguation is the focus of this part. Such techniques could be applied in Bibliography information management as shown in Chapter 15. Think about the problems raised in their research.

Problem I: We are looking for all publications authored by "Lei Wang" in a digital library. Without loss of generality, we take DBLP and CiteSeer as examples. When the query is submitted, about 151 publications are retrieved in DBLP and 123 in CiteSeer. As far as we know, there are no fewer than 39 different persons with this identical name, and it is difficult to differentiate the publications written by a person one really cares about from the remaining ones belonging to other persons who happen to share the same author name. As an example, Table 3 shows four names and for each name we list four distinct authors, their present affiliations, and the corresponding number of publications.

Problem II: Name ambiguity also brings confusion when we try to merge multiple tables from different data sources into a single table and it may decrease the performance of information retrieval and Web search as well.

As can be seen from the above problem, the objective of name disambiguation is to group objects (e.g., publications) into clusters so that the elements in each cluster belong to the same entity (e.g., author), while all the objects of the same entity are grouped in the same cluster. The following is the steps:

The first step is problem formulation. The problem definition is formalized in the setting of an academic publication record database. Let D be a database which contains a set of academic publications. Each publication has a set of attributes, such as a list of authors, a title, and a venue (e.g., a conference or a journal). We suppose r is an author name whose publications are to be distinguished, and denote the subset of D which contains the publications coauthored by any person whose name is r by R. Let the number of publications in R be |R|, the number of distinct

Table 3. Different authors with identical names

Name	Present Affiliation	# Publications
Wei Wang	University of North Carolina at Chapel Hill	57
	Fudan University, China	31
	The University of New South Wales, Australia	19
	The State University of New York at Buffalo	5
Jim Smith	University of the West of England	13
	University of Newcastle upon Tyne	15
	The University of Melbourne, Australia	2
	University of Wisconsin	1
Lei Wang	Nanyang Technological University, Singapore	14
	Zhejiang University, China	8
	University of Texas at Dallas	7
	Harvard University	2
Jing Zhang	Tsinghua University, China	5
	Tsinghua University, China	1
	Tsinghua University, China	2
	Carnegie Mellon University	5

authors with name r be k, the ith publication in R be Pir ($1 \leq i \leq$ |R|), the author whose name is r in publication Pir be ri ($1 \leq i \leq$ |R|). The notations used in this article are summarized in Table 4.

After introducing some basic notations, the formal definition of the problem studied in this article is given as follows. Given a database D consisting of |D| publications and an author name r, our task is to automatically group the publications authored by any person with a name of r (i.e., publications in R) into k disjoint clusters (where k is the number of distinct authors with a name r) C = {c1, . . ., ck} such that each publication within a cluster is authored by the same person and the publications of the same person are not split across clusters.

In the second step, an effective framework named GHOST (abbreviation for GrapHical framewOrk for name diSambiguaTion) is intro-

Table 4. Notations (FAN, WANG, PU, ZHOU & LV 2011)

Name	Description
D	a database of academic publications
|D|	the number of publications in D
R	the author name which needs to resolve
R	the set of publications with the author name r
|R|	the number of publications in R
P_r^i	the ith publication in R (coauthored by ri, $1 \leq i \leq$ |R|)
Ri	the author whose name is r in P_r^i
K	the number of distinct authors with name r ($k \leq$ |R|)
c j	set of publications written by the jth distinct author ($1 \leq j \leq k$)

duced. GHOST consist of five subtasks, that is, graphical view of the database, valid path selection, similarity computation, name clustering, and user feedback(in this book, this section will be ignored).

Graphical View of the Database

In general, it is a natural idea to represent the database D as a graph G = {V, E}, where each node $v \in$ V represents a distinct author name (or an instance of the queried author name r in a certain publication), and an undirected edge represents a coauthorship. According to the preceding definition, even multiple different names correspond to the same person, we do not merge them in the graph. For example, if "Philip S. Yu" and "Philip Yu" correspond to the same author, they will be represented as two different nodes in the graph. Each edge between node vi and node vj has a label S(i, j), which denotes the complete set of publications coauthored by both vi and vj. This means that we collect all publications coau-

thored by vi and vj in order to denote a unique edge. For convenience, only the nonempty sets are taken into account. Here we give an example to illustrate the graphical model more clearly. Assume that a tiny database containing several papers is available as shown in Example 1, and the name to resolve is "Wei Wang". Note that in Example 1, Pj as opposed to P_r^i represents a publication that does not mention the author name of "Wei Wang". Since our method does not utilize the paper titles, they are omitted in this example.

P_r^1: Jiong Yang, Wei Wang, Philip S. Yu, Jiawei Han. SIGMOD'02.

$P1$: Jiawei Han, Jian Pei, Guozhu Dong, Ke Wang. SIGMOD'01.

P_r^2: Jinze Liu, Wei Wang, Jiong Yang. SIGKDD'04.

$P2$: Charu C. Aggarwal, Jiawei Han, Jianyong Wang, Philip S. Yu. VLDB'03.

P_r^3: Jinze Liu, Wei Wang. ICDM'03.

P_r^4: Jian Pei, Jiawei Han, Wei Wang. CIKM'02.

P_r^5: Peng Wang, Haixun Wang, Xiaochen Wu, Wei Wang, Baile Shi. ICDM'05.

P_r^6: Chen Wang, Wei Wang, Jian Pei, Yongtai Zhu, Baile Shi. SIGKDD'04.

The graph generated from Example 1 is shown in Figure 1. For simplicity, other authors (e.g., Jianyong Wang and Charu Aggarwal) who never coauthored with r (i.e., "Wei Wang") or only coauthored one publication (e.g., Peng Wang, Haixun Wang, and Xiaochen Wu in P_r^5, Chen Wang and Yongtai Zhu in P_r^6) are omitted. There are six nodes labeled with "Wei Wang" in Figure 1, each of which represents an instance of "Wei Wang" in one of the publications coauthored by "Wei Wang". Two authors are linked by an edge if they have coauthored a paper, and we ignore other types of attributes and their corresponding links. For example, in Figure 1, there is an edge between the nodes of "Jiawei Han" and "Philip

S. Yu", and the edge label of $\{P_r^1, P2\}$ means Jiawei Han and Philip S. Yu are coauthors of publications P_r^1 and P2.

Valid Path Selection

The design philosophy of GHOST is based on the observation that the research interests of a researcher usually do not change too frequently during a short period of time, and in particular, he/she would stay in the same institution for a relatively long time. We can infer that a researcher usually has a relatively stable set of coauthors (i.e., author community) during a certain period of time. Also, we expect that different persons with the same name seldom work in the same institution and thus they should have quite different author communities. In addition, it is a natural idea that the coauthors usually focus on some close research topics and share some common research interests. If the same name which needs to be disambiguated (e.g., "Wei Wang") appears in both author lists of two publications and corresponds to the same person. These two publications are expected to share some coauthors either directly or by some other intermediate publications. On the other

hand, if they are not written by the same person, their coauthor sets likely do not overlap or there are few paths which link them. GHOST tries to unearth some valuable hidden information based on both short and long coauthorship linkages in order to compute the similarity of two authors with identical name. Thus, the first task of GHOST is to retrieve paths linking two nodes in the graph view.

A naive way to compute the similarity between two nodes in the coauthorship graph is based on the length of their shortest path. However, it may neglect valuable information which can be derived from other paths linking the two nodes in the graph. For example, if five paths of length 3 link two nodes of vi and vj which need to be disambiguated, they should be regarded to be more similar to each other than another two nodes of vi and vk which are linked by just one path of length 3 or even shorter. Therefore, more precise similarity computing strategy is required, and it is imperative for GHOST to exploit all simple paths, where a path is said to be simple if it does not contain any duplicate nodes. Because we assign equal weight to edges, breadth-first search appears to be a natural strategy to find out all loopless paths. As we know, however, the runtime

Figure 1. Graphical view of the example database with respect to the name of "Wei Wang." (FAN, WANG, PU, ZHOU & LV 2011)

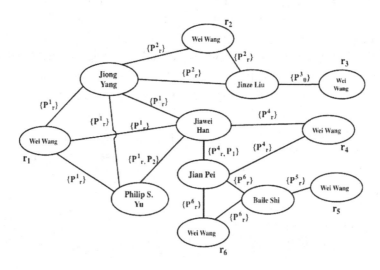

complexity of breadth-first search is O(|V| + |E|), thus we need to propose a faster search strategy to reduce the time complexity. But before we go further, let us first investigate a substructure of the coauthorship graph shown in Figure 1, which will lead to the definition of valid path.

Valid Path

Suppose we want to find paths linking nodes of r1 and r6 in Figure 1, the shortest path is obviously "Wei Wang—Jiawei Han—Jian Pei—Wei Wang". The two intermediate nodes representing "Jiawei Han" and "Jian Pei" connect the starting node and ending node. In addition, we can easily figure out another 19 paths which link nodes of r1 and r6 from the graph structure. This is because there are a total of 5 simple subpaths linking "Wei Wang(i.e., r1)" and "Jiawei Han", 2 simple subpaths linking "Jiawei Han" and "Jian Pei", and 2 simple subpaths linking "Jian Pei" and "Wei Wang (i.e., r6)". Take the 5 simple subpaths connecting "Wei Wang(i.e., r1)" and "Jiawei Han" as an example. They form a substructure which is shown in Figure 2. We can derive the other four simple subpaths shown as follows besides the shortest subpath introduced before (i.e., "Wei Wang — Jiawei Han").

1. "Wei Wang — Jiong Yang — Jiawei Han"
2. "Wei Wang — Philip S. Yu — Jiawei Han"
3. "Wei Wang — Jiong Yang — Philip S. Yu — Jiawei Han"
4. "Wei Wang — Philip S. Yu — Jiong Yang — Jiawei Han"

An intuitive observation from the previous example is that there is some redundancy among all the five simple subpaths (e.g., the two paths of "Wei Wang — JiongYang — Philip S. Yu — Jiawei Han" and "Wei Wang — Philip S. Yu — Jiong Yang — Jiawei Han"). Therefore, GHOST should discriminate different paths based on the graph structure and eliminate those redundant

subpaths that make no sense in similarity computation. Besides, the coauthorship graph could be so huge, resulting in high time complexity to find all simple paths. For this purpose, GHOST calls for a criterion to judge whether a path deserves to be searched for. Before we present a generalized definition of a valid path, it is necessary to present the following lemma first.

Lemma: Consider two nodes of v1 and v2 both of which connect to another node v0 via sets of publications of S01 and S02, respectively. If S01 and S02 share a common publication, which is denoted by Pc, we come to the conclusion that v1 and v2 also connect via a publication set containing at least one publication of Pc.

Proof: Because S01 and S02 share a common element Pc, we know that v0 and v1 have coauthored the publication Pc, so have v0 and v2. This implies that v0, v1, and v2 are all in the author list of Pc. So the lemma holds.

In the following, we will develop the valid path selection criterion. For each of the intermediate vertices V in a specific path, the vertex itself and its two adjacent vertices will form a triangle-like structure if there exists an edge between the two adjacent vertices, taking Vk for example as illustrated in Figure 3. If no publication is shared by the publication sets $S(k-1)k$, $Sk(k+1)$ and $S(k-1)(k+1)$, Vk is a valid vertex in the specific path. If any two publication sets of the three edges contain

Figure 2. A substructure of the coauthorship graph. (FAN, WANG, PU, ZHOU & LV, 2011)

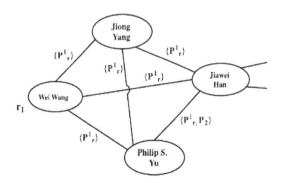

a same publication, denoted by Pc, we can infer from the Lemma mentioned above that the third set must also contain Pc. In this case, if there are at least two sets with cardinality no smaller than two, Vk is also considered to be valid as the three authors are coauthored frequently. However, when two of the three sets both consist of only Pc, we consider Vk as an invalid vertex.

Exactly, the following two paths are equivalent to similarity between Vs and Ve.

$$V_s \xrightarrow{S_{s1}} V_1 \xrightarrow{S_{12}} V_2 ... V_{k-1} \xrightarrow{S_{(k-1)k}} V_k$$
$$\xrightarrow{S_{k(k+1)}} V_{k+1} ... V_{n-1} \xrightarrow{S_{(n-1)n}} V_n \xrightarrow{S_{ne}} V_e$$

$$V_s \xrightarrow{S_{s1}} V_1 \xrightarrow{S_{12}} V_2 ... V_{k-1} \xrightarrow{S_{(k-1)(k+1)}}$$
$$V_{k+1} ... V_{n-1} \xrightarrow{S_{(n-1)n}} V_n \xrightarrow{S_{ne}} V_e \quad .$$

Therefore, Vk is called an invalid vertex in path P if Vk ∈ {V1, V2, · · ·, Vn−1, Vn} such that at least one of the following three conditions holds.

1. $S(k-1)k = Sk(k+1)$ and $|S(k-1)k||= 1$
2. $S(k-1)k = S(k-1)(k+1)$ and $|S(k-1)k| = 1$
3. $Sk(k+1) = S(k-1)(k+1)$ and $|Sk(k+1)| = 1$

Definition 1 (Invalid Path): A path P is an invalid path if and only if P contains at least one invalid vertex.

Definition 2 (Valid Path): A path P is said to be valid if it contains no invalid vertex.

While searching in the graph, GHOST will eliminate all the invalid paths. What GHOST needs to do is to check the intermediate vertices in turn for each path and eliminate the path once the first invalid vertex is found in it.

The Search Strategy

Now we consider how to shorten the runtime. The runtime complexity of the breadth-first search strategy is O(|V| + |E|). Suppose the set of names to resolve is R, it would result in a total time of |R|(|R|-1)/2×O(|V|+|E|), that is, O(|R|^2×(|V|+|E|)) . Therefore, we need to put forward a search strategy to reduce the time complexity. Obviously, the longer a path is, the less contribution it makes to the total similarity, which will be validated in next subsection. Therefore, in the practical application of the path search process should be terminated when it reaches the limit of a predefined length of the path (indicated by L). In other words, only when the intermediate node of a path is not more than (L - 1), the path can be saved.

Dynamic Programming Algorithm

Dynamic programming algorithm solves the problem by combining the solutions to independent subproblems. In general, dynamic programming solves every subproblem just once and then saves its answer, avoiding the overhead of computing the answer to the subproblems once again. In practice L = 4 is enough for most ambiguous names, and we start from each node $v \in R$ and take L2 = 2 steps forward, saving subpaths into memory. For any pair of nodes $vi, v j \in R$, we check whether

Figure 3. A triangle-like structure (FAN, WANG, PU, ZHOU & LV, 2011)

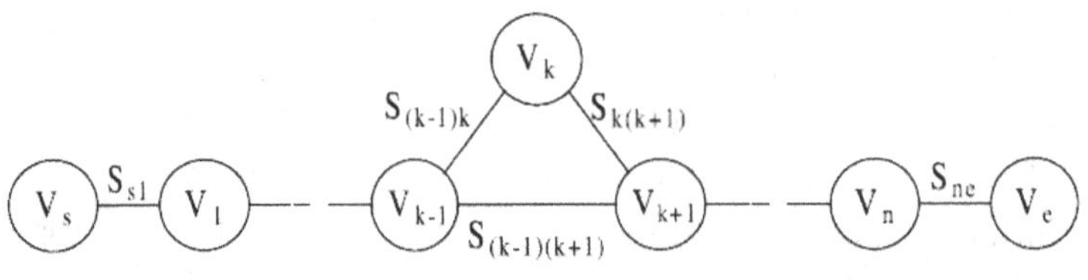

there exists any intermediate node shared by any two subpaths starting from v_i and v_j, respectively, and if the answer is yes, two subpaths would be merged to form a valid path linking v_i and v_j. The algorithm is as follows:

```
Q ← θ;
forall r ∈ R do
    ENQUEUE(Q, r);
    while Q ≠ θ do
        u ← DEQUEUE(Q);
        forall v ∈ Adj[u] do
            forall s ∈ step(r,v) do
                if s.length = 1 then
                    if v ∉ i then
                        insert v into I;
                    if r ∉ source(v) then
                        insert r into source(v);
                    path = "r-v"
                    insert path into sub path(r);
                    ENQUEUE(Q,v);
                else if s.length = 2 then
                    path = "r-s.intermediate-v";
                    if path is simple and valid then
                        if v ∉ I then
                            insert v into I;
                        if r ∉ source(v) then
                            insert r into source(v);
                        insert path into sub path(r);
```

This part searches for all the simple and valid paths whose length is less than or equal to two for each of the nodes to be resolved.

```
forall v ∈ I do
    forall pair (rᵢ,rⱼ), such that rᵢ,rⱼ ∈ source(v) do
        forall pathᵢ ∈ sub path(rᵢ) such that pathᵢ ends with v do
            forall pathⱼ ∈ sub path(rⱼ) such that pathⱼ ends with v do
                path ← merge pathᵢ and pathⱼ;
                if path is valid then
                    insert path into path(rᵢ,rⱼ);
```

This part merges the subpaths obtained from the first part. For each intermediate node v belonging to I, each pair of subpaths that end with v will be merged to a full path. The full path is inserted into $path(r_i, r_j)$ if it is valid.

```
forall pair (rᵢ,rⱼ), such that rᵢ,rⱼ ∈ R do
    Output path(rᵢ,rⱼ);
```

This part outputs path(ri, rj)and the whole algorithm runs in time $O(|R| \times \log(|R|))$.

Notes for the algorithm:

1. Sub path(r) denotes the set of subpaths starting from any node r ∈ R. For example, the value of sub path(r6) in Figure 1 is {Wei Wang—Jian Pei, Wei Wang—Jian Pei —Jiawei Han, Wei Wang — Baile Shi, Wei Wang — Baile Shi — Jian Pei}.

2. Path(ri, rj) denotes the set of paths connecting nodes ri and rj, where ri, rj ∈ R. It is the output of Algorithm 1.

3. I denotes the set of nodes in V-R which are reachable from at least one node in R. For example, the value of I in Figure 1 is the set of all the nodes in Figure 1 except the six "Wei Wang"s.

4. Source(v) denotes a set of nodes in R which are reachable from v within two steps where v is a node in I. For example, the value of source(Philip S. Yu) in Figure 1 is {r1, r2, r4}.

5. Step(r, v) denotes a set of paths with length 1 or 2 that begin with r ∈ R and end with v ∈ V. For each path p ∈ step(r, v), p.length denotes the length of the path and p.intermediate denotes the intermediate node if the length of the path is 2. For example, the value of step(r1, Jiawei Han) in Figure 1 is {{length=1, intermediate=NULL}, {length=2, intermediate=Jiong Yang}, {length=2, intermediate= Philip S. Yu}}.

Similarity Computation

Now, we have found all valid paths and then we will compute the similarity of the two nodes based on the following heuristics.

- The shortest path is the most indicative one among all valid paths in similarity computation, and the shorter it is, the more similar two nodes may be.
- The more paths there exist between two nodes, the more "similar" the two nodes may be.

Formally, suppose we get sum(i, j) valid paths connecting authors r_i and r_j, then the similarity function can be described in the following mathematical formula.

$$Sim(r_i, r_j) = -1 / \{ \sum_{h=1}^{sum(i,j)} \frac{1}{l_h} \} \qquad (4)$$

where lh denotes the number of intermediate nodes along the hth path. l_h can be zero if r_i and r_j represent two different authors who ever coauthored the same paper. In the framework we will merge the two nodes of ri and rj into one node when this happens. The value of $Sim(r_i, r_j)$ ranges from $-\infty$ to 0 and is obviously a symmetric measure, that is, $Sim(r_i, r_j) = Sim(r_j, r_i)$. The similarity is equal to 0 only when there exist an infinite number of valid paths connecting two specified nodes, which is the ideal condition. On the other hand, for the sake of simplicity, we set the similarity between two isolated nodes not to $-\infty$ but to a fixed negative value (e.g., -10), leading to no change of final results.

However, because every individual is on an average six "steps" away from one another, even in the case when two individuals are randomly selected, every pair of authors could be highly likely connected to each other when we constrain the problem in the social network. Therefore, we modify formula (4) to the following form.

$$Sim(r_i, r_j) = -1 / \{ \sum_{h=1}^{sum(i,j)} \frac{1}{f(l_h)} \} \qquad (5)$$

where f(lh) is a monotonic increasing function, and satisfies the constraint: $f(lh) \geq l_h$. Polynomial

in one indeterminate and exponential functions are good choices. Nevertheless we require that the corresponding value of the similarity function decrease slowly when the independent variable is relatively small, and sharply when it is large. This constraint determines that an exponential function is an ideal model. In our experiments, we set f(lh) = (α)($lh-1$), where $\alpha = 2.1$.

Name Clustering

In previous sections, we developed methods for valid path selection and similarity computation between any two nodes in a coauthorship graph, which can be used to compute the similarity matrix for a set of publications that need to be disambiguated. Given a similarity matrix, GHOST tries to group "different" authors into clusters so that each cluster corresponds to a distinct author. Similarly to traditional clustering algorithms, the objective is to produce high-quality clusters with high intraclass similarity and low interclass similarity.

Our clustering problem has several features. First, the similarity measure defined in Equation (2) means that the corresponding distance (which is defined as the negative similarity here) metric does not satisfy the triangle inequality (namely, $-Sim(ri, rk) < -Sim(ri, rj) - Sim(rj, rk)$ does not hold). One such situation is that when author rj is a coauthor with author ri and author rk separately, but author ri has never been a coauthor with author rk. Second, the number of clusters is completely unknown. Third, the ideal clustering results are unique and unchangeable, and therefore it is easy to evaluate the quality of clustering results.

According features above, we adopt a powerful new clustering algorithm called Affinity Propagation (AP for short) for GHOST. Frey & Dueck (2007) introduced it first based on the message-passing techniques from the perspective of max-sum algorithm in a factor graph. AP does not need the user to specify a fixed number of potential cluster centers in advance, but instead chooses to simultaneously consider all data points as potential cluster centers (also known as exemplars). From this perspective, the AP algorithm is quite suitable for clustering in the name disambiguation problem setting. Following we introduce its main ideas.

First, besides a similarity matrix with n×n elements, AP also takes as input a self similarity Sim(k, k) for each data point k, which is named "preference." The larger is the preference of point k, the more likely it is chosen as an exemplar. Thus the final number of clusters is influenced by the values of input exemplars (and the message passing procedure). Without any prior knowledge about the underlying clusters, AP recommends that preferences be set to a global (shared) value, the median of all the input similarities in order to produce a moderate number of clusters.

Next, every pair of data points exchanges two kinds of messages. The responsibility r(i, k) sent from point i to candidate point k indicates how well-suited point k is as the exemplar for point i in contrast to other potential exemplars, while the availability a(i, k) sent from candidate point k to point i indicates how much support point k has received from other points for being an exemplar. The responsibility and availability are set to new values through the following formulae (6) and (7) at the beginning of each iteration until exemplars emerge.

$$r(i,k) = s(i,k) - \max_{k' s.t. k' \neq k} \{a(i,k') + s(i,k')\} \quad (6)$$

$$a(i,k) = \min\{0, r(k,k) + \sum_{i' s.t. i' \notin \{i,k\}} \max\{0, r(i',k)\}\} \quad (7)$$

In formula (6), the term s(i, k) is the similarity value between point i and point k. At any point during the procedure of affinity propagation, extra computation is utilized to check whether changes in the messages fall below a threshold or the local decision stays constant for some number of

iterations. Finally, for point i, the value of k that maximizes a(i, k) + r(i, k) identifies the exemplar for point i. GHOST tries to draw on AP to group authors with identical names into disjoint clusters by taking as input the values of similarities generated in the way described in preceding subsections.

The last step is how to analysis and test results. We measure the performance of GHOST by precision, recall, and f-score in the context of pairwise comparison based on traditional information retrieval measures. Suppose the set of real clusters is Cstd and the set of clusters generated by GHOST is Cghost. Let TP (true positive) be the number of pairs of publications that are in the same cluster in both Cstd and Cghost, FP (false positive) be the number of pairs of publications in the same cluster in Cghost but not in Cstd, and FN (false negative) be the number of pairs of publications in the same cluster in Cstd but not in Cghost. The two measures, precision and recall, are defined as:

$$precison = \frac{TP}{TP \perp FP}, recall = \frac{TP}{TP \perp FN} \quad (8)$$

f-score is the harmonic mean of precision and recall, and is defined as follows:

$$precison = \frac{TP}{TP \perp FP}, recall = \frac{TP}{TP \perp FN} \quad (9)$$

In this article, we have explored the problem of name disambiguation. We develop an effective five-step framework, GHOST, which employs only one type of relationship, namely, coauthorship. In GHOST, we propose a novel similarity metric and adopt the affinity propagation algorithm to group intermediate results into clusters. User feedback can also be used as an option to improve the performance if the publications belong to dense authors.

DESCRIPTION METHODS OF NODE SIMILARITY

SimRank (Jeh & Widom 2002)

Basic SimRank Equation: The similarity between objects a and b by $s(a, b) \in [0, 1]$. This is Equation for $s(a, b)$. If $a = b$ then $s(a, b)$ is defined to be 1.

$$s(a,b) = \frac{C}{|I(a)||I(b)|} \sum_{i=1}^{|I(a)|} \sum_{j=1}^{|I(b)|} s(I_i(a), I_j(b)) \quad (10)$$

where C is a constant between 0 and 1. A slight technicality here is that either a or b may not have any in-neighbors. Since we have no way to infer any similarity between a and b in this case, we should set $s(a, b) = 0$, so we define the summation in Equation (10) to be 0 when $I(a) = \emptyset$ or $I(b) = \emptyset$.

Bipartite SimRank

Next we extend the basic SimRank Equation (10) to bipartite domains consisting of two types of objects. Suppose persons A and B purchased item sets {eggs, frosting, sugar} and {eggs, frosting, flour} respectively. Clearly, the two buyers are similar, both are baking a cake, say, and so a good recommendation to person A might be flour. One reason we can conclude that A and B are similar is that they both purchased eggs and frosting. But moreover, A purchased sugar while B purchased flour, and these are similar items, in the sense that they are purchased by similar people, cake-bakers like A and B. Here, the similarity of items and similarity of people are mutually-reinforcing notions:

- People are similar if they purchase similar items.
- Items are similar if they are purchased by similar people.

The mutually-recursive Equations that formalize these notions are analogous to Equation (10). Let s(A, B) denote the similarity between persons A and B, and let s(c, d) denote the similarity between items c and d. Since, as discussed above, directed edges go from people to items, for A and B we write the Equation:

$$s(A,B) = \frac{C_1}{|O(A)||O(B)|} \sum_{i=1}^{|O(A)|} \sum_{j=1}^{|O(B)|} s(O_i(A), O_j(B)) \quad (11)$$

and for $c \neq d$ we have following Equation:

$$s(c,d) = \frac{C_2}{|I(c)||I(d)|} \sum_{i=1}^{|I(c)|} \sum_{j=1}^{|I(d)|} s(I_i(c), I_j(d)) \quad (12)$$

If $A = B$, $s(A, B) = 1$, and analogously for $s(c, d)$. Neglecting C1 and C2, Equation (11) says that the similarity between persons A and B is the average similarity between the items they purchased, and Equation (12) says that the similarity between items c and d is the average similarity between the people who purchased them. The constants C1, C2 have the same semantics as C in Equation (10).

Bipartite SimRank in Homogeneous Domains

It turns out that the bipartite SimRank Equations (11) and (12) can also be applied to homogeneous domains, such as Web pages and scientific papers. Although a bipartite distinction is not explicit in these domains, it may be the case that elements take on different roles, or those in-references and out-references give different information. For example, two scientific papers might be similar as survey papers if they cite similar result papers, while two papers might be similar as result papers if they are cited by similar survey papers. In analogy with the HITS algorithm, we can associate a "points-to" similarity score $sl(a, b)$ to each pair of nodes a and b, as well as a "pointed-to" similarity score s2(a, b), and write the same Equations (11) and (12) as if the domain were bipartite:

$$s_1(a,b) = \frac{C_1}{|O(a)||O(b)|} \sum_{i=1}^{|O(a)|} \sum_{j=1}^{|O(b)|} s_2(O_i(a), O_j(b))$$

$$s_2(a,b) = \frac{C_2}{|I(a)||I(b)|} \sum_{i=1}^{|I(a)|} \sum_{j=1}^{|I(b)|} s_1(I_i(a), I_j(b))$$

$$(13)$$

Depending on the domain and application, either score or a combination may be used.

Computing SimRank

A solution to the SimRank Equations (or bipartite variations) for a graph G can be reached by iteration to a fixed-point. Let n be the number of nodes in G. For each iteration k, we can keep n^2 entries Rk(*,*) of length n^2, where Rk(a,b) gives the score between a and b on iteration k. We successively compute Rk+l(*, *) based on Rk (*, *). We start with Ro(*, *) where each Ro(a, b) is a lower bound on the actual SimRank score s(a, b):

$$R_0(a,b) = \begin{cases} 0 & (if \quad a \neq b) \\ 1 & (if \quad a = b) \end{cases}$$

$$(14)$$

To compute Rk+l(a, b) from Rk(*, *), we use Equation (10) to get:

$$R_{k+1}(a,b) = \frac{C}{|I(a)||I(b)|} \sum_{i=1}^{|I(a)|} \sum_{j=1}^{|I(b)|} R_k(I_i(a), I_j(b))$$

$$(15)$$

for $a \neq b$, and Rk+l(a,b) = 1 for $a = b$. That is, on each iteration k + 1, we update the similarity of (a, b) using the similarity scores of the neighbors of (a, b) from the previous iteration k according to Equation (10). The values Rk(*, *) are nondecreasing as k increases. The SimRank scores s(*, *), i.e., for all a, b $\in$ V, $\lim_{k \to \infty} R_k(a,b) = s(a,b)$. In all of our experiments we have seen rapid convergence, with relative rankings stabilizing within 5 iterations, so we may choose to fix a number K$\approx$5 of iterations to perform.

Let us analyze the time and space requirements for this method of computing SimRank. The space required is simply O(n^2) to store the results Rk. Let d2 be the average of |I(a)||I(b)| over all node-pairs (a, b). The time required is O(K n^2 d2), since on each iteration, the score of every node-pair (n^2 of these) is updated with values from its in-neighbor pairs (d2 of these on average). As it corresponds roughly to the square of the average in-degree, d2 is likely to be a constant with respect to n for many domains. The resource requirements for bipartite versions are similar.

SimRank+ + (Antonellis, GarciaMolina & Chang, 2008)

Revising Simrank

Consider a bipartite graph G=($V1$, $V2$,E) and two nodes a,b $\in$ $V1$. We will denote as evidence(a, b) the evidence existing in G that the nodes a, b are similar. The definition of evidence(a, b) that we used is shown on Equation 16.

$$evidence(a,b) = \sum_{i=1}^{|E(a) \cap E(b)|} \frac{1}{2^i}$$

$$(16)$$

The intuition behind choosing such a function is as follows. We want the evidence score evidence(a,b) to be an increasing function of the common neighbors between a and b. In addition we want the evidence scores to get closer to one as the common neighbors increase. We can now incorporate the evidence metric into the Simrank Equations.

For $q \neq q'$, we write the Equation:

$$S evidence(q,q') = evidence(q,q') \cdot s(q,q') \quad (17)$$

where s(q,q') is the Simrank similarity between q and q'

Notice that we could use k only iterations to compute the Simrank similarity scores and then multiply them by the evidence scores to come up with evidence-based similarities after k iterations. We will be loosely referring to these scores as evidence-based similarity scores after k iterations and we will be denoting them by $S_{evidence}^{(k)}(q, q')$.

Theorem 1: Consider the two complete bipartite graphs $G = Km,2$ and $G' = Kn,2$ with m<n and nodes sets $V1$, $V2 = \{A,B\}$ and $v'1, v'2 = \{C,D\}$ correspondingly. Let $sim^{(k)}(A, B)$ and $sim^{(k)}(C, D)$ denote the similarity scores that bipartite evidence-based Simrank computes for the node pairs $(A;B)$ and $(C;D)$ after k iterations and let $C1,C2 > 1/2$, where $C1,C2$ are the decay factors of the bipartite Simrank Equations. Then,

$$sim^{(k)}(A, B) < sim^{(k)}(C, D), \forall\ k > 1, \text{ and}$$
$$\lim_{k\to\infty} sim^{(k)}(A, B) < \lim_{k\to\infty} sim^{(k)}(C, D).$$

This Theorem indicates that the evidence-based Simrank scores in complete bipartite graphs will be consistent with the intuition of query similarity even if we effectively limit the number of iterations we perform.

Weighted Simrank

We explore ways to derive query-query similarity scores that (i) are consistent with the graph's weights and (ii) utilize the edge weights in the computation of similarity scores.

In general, we dene the notion of consistency as follows:

Definition 3: (Consistent similarity scores) Consider a weighted bipartite graph $G = (V1,V2,E)$. Consider also four nodes $i1, j1, i2, j2 \in V1$ and two nodes $v1,v2 \in V2$. We now define the sets $W(v1) = \{w(i1,v1),w(j1,v1)\}$ and $W(v2) = \{w(i2,v2),w(j2,v2)\}$ and let variance($v1$)

(variance($v2$)) denote a measure of W($v1$)'s (W($v2$)'s) variance respectively. We will be saying that a set of similarity scores sim(i,j) $\forall i, j \in V1$ is consistent with the graph's weights if and only if $\forall i1, j1, i2, j2 \in V1$ and $\forall v1, v2 \in V2$ such that $\exists (i1,v1),(j1,v1),(i2,v2),(j2,v2) \in E$ both of the following are true:

1. If variance($v1$) < variance($v2$) and w($i1,v1$) > w($i2, v2$)) then sim($i1,j1$) > sim($i2,j2$)
2. If variance($v1$) = variance($v2$) and w($i1,v1$) > w($i2, v2$)) then sim($i1,j1$) > sim($i2, j2$)

This definition utilizes the notion of the set variance which can be computed by averaging the squared distance of all the values belonging to the set from their mean value.

Revising Simrank

Now, we modify the underlying random walk model of Simrank. Remember that Simrank's random surfers model implies that a Simrank score sim(a, b) for two nodes a, b measures how soon two random surfers are expected to meet at the same node if they started at nodes a, b and randomly walked the graph. In order to impose the consistency rules in the similarity scores we perform a new random walk where its transition probabilities p(a, i), $\forall \partial \in E(\partial)$ are defined as follows:

$$p(\alpha, i) = spread(i) \cdot normalized\_weight(\alpha, i), \forall i \in E(\alpha), and$$
$$p(\alpha, \alpha) = 1 - \sum_{i \in E(\alpha)} p(\alpha, i)$$

where,

$$spread(i) = e^{-\,variance(i)}, and$$
$$normalized\_weight(\alpha, i) = \frac{\omega(\alpha, i)}{\sum_{j \in E(\alpha)} \omega(\alpha, j)}$$

The value variance(i) corresponds to the variance of the weights of all edges that are connected with the node i.

Theorem 2: Consider a weighted bipartite graph $G = (V1, V2, E)$ and let w(e) denote the weight associated with an edge $e \in E$. Let also $sim(i,j)$ denote the similarity score that weighted Simrank computes for two nodes $i, j \in V1$. Then, $\forall i, j \in V_1$, $sim(i, j)$ is consistent with the graph's weights.

The actual similarity scores that weighted Simrank gives after applying the modified random walk are:

$$S_{weighted}(q, q') = evidence(q, q') \cdot C_1 \cdot \sum_{i \in E(q)} \sum_{j \in E(q')} W(q, i)W(q', j)s_{weighted}(i, j) \quad (18)$$

$$S_{weighted}(\alpha, \alpha') = evidence(\alpha, \alpha') \cdot C_2 \cdot \sum_{i \in E(\alpha)} \sum_{j \in E(\alpha')} W(\alpha, i)W(\alpha', j)s_{weighted}(i, j) \quad (19)$$

where the factors $W(q; i)$ and $W(a; i)$ are defined as follows:

$W(q, i) = spread(i) \cdot normalized\ weight(q, i)$

$W(a; i) = spread(i) \cdot normalized\ weight(a, i)$

We can finally get the Equation as follow:

$$\frac{C}{|I(u)||I(v)|} \sum_{l=1}^{|I(u) \cap I(v)|} \frac{1}{2^l} \sum_{i=1}^{|I(u)|} \sum_{j=1}^{|I(v)|} sim_k(I_i(u), I_j(v)), C \in (0,1) \quad (20)$$

PSimRank (Fogaras & Rácz 2005)

In this section we give a new SimRank named PSimRank. In PSimRank, the new similarity function will be expressed as an expected f-meeting distance by modifying the distribution of the set of random walks and by keeping f(t) = c^t. We define PSimRank as the expected f-meeting distance of a set of random walks, which are not independent, as in case of SimRank, but are coupled so that a pair of them can find each other more easily.

We allow the random walks to meet with higher probability when they are close to each other: a pair of random walks at vertices u', v' will advance to the same vertex with probability of the Jaccard coefficient $\frac{|I(u') \cap I(v')|}{|I(u') \cup I(v')|}$ of their in neighborhoods I(u') and I(v').

Definition 4: PSimRank is the expected f-meeting distance with f(t) = c^t (for some $0 < c < 1$) of the following set of random walks. For each vertex u, the random walk Xu makes ` uniform independent steps on the transposed web graph starting from point u. For each pair of vertices u, v and time t, assume that the random walks are at position $Xu(t) = u'$ and $Xv(t) = v'$. Then

- With probability $\frac{|I(u') \cap I(v')|}{|I(u') \cup I(v')|}$ they both step to the same uniformly chosen vertex of $I(u') \cap I(v')$;

- With probability $\frac{|I(u') \cap I(v')|}{|I(u') \cup I(v')|}$ the walk Xu steps to a uni- form vertex in $I(u') \setminus I(v')$ and the walk Xv steps to an independently chosen uniform vertex in I(v');

- With probability $\frac{|I(u') \cap I(v')|}{|I(u') \cup I(v')|}$ the walk Xv steps to a uniform vertex in $I(v') \setminus I(u')$ and the walk Xu steps to an independently chosen uniform vertex in I(u').

We give a set of random walks satisfying the coupling of the definition. For each time t 0 we choose an independent random permutation t on the vertices of the web graph. At time t if the random walk from vertex u is at $X_u(t) = u'$, it will step to the in-neighbor with smallest index given by the permutation σ_t, i.e.,

$$X_u(t+1) = \arg\min_{u'' \in I(u')} \sigma_t(u'') \qquad (21)$$

It is easy to see that the random walk Xu takes uniform independent steps, since we have a new permutation for each step. The above coupling is also satisfied, since for any pair u', v' the vertex $\arg\min w \in I(u') \cup I(v')\sigma_t(w)$ falls into the sets $I(u') \cap I(v')$, $I(u') \setminus I(v')$, $I(v') \setminus I(u')$ with respective probabilities:

$$\frac{|I(u') \cap I(v')|}{|I(u') \cup I(v')|}, \frac{|I(u') \setminus I(v')|}{|I(u') \cup I(v')|} \; and \; \frac{|I(v') \setminus I(u')|}{|I(u') \cup I(v')|} \quad (22)$$

Let u,v denote the first meeting time of the walks of Xu,Xv starting from vertices u, v; and $\tau_{u,v} = \infty$ if the walks never meet. Then PSimRank scores for path length ℓ can be expressed by definition as $psim_\ell(u,v) = E(c^{\tau_{u,v}})$. It is trivial that psim0$(u, v) = 1$, if $u = v$; and otherwise psim0$(u, v) = 0$. By applying the law of total expectation on the first step of the walks Xu and Xv, and time shift we get the following PSimRank iterations:

$$
\begin{aligned}
&psim_{\ell+1}(u,v) = 1, if \quad u = v; \\
&psim_{\ell+1}(u,v) = 0, if \quad I(u) = \theta \, or I(v) = \theta; \\
&psim_{\ell+1}(u,v) = c \cdot
\end{aligned}
$$

$$
\left[
\begin{aligned}
&\frac{|I(u) \cap I(v)|}{|I(u) \cup I(v)|} \cdot 1 + \frac{|I(u) \setminus I(v)|}{|I(u) \cup I(v)|} \cdot \frac{1}{|I(u) \setminus I(v)||I(v)|} \\
&\qquad psim_\ell(u',v') + \frac{|I(v) \setminus I(u)|}{|I(u) \cup I(v)|} \cdot \\
&\sum_{\substack{u' \in I(u) \setminus I(v) \\ v' \in I(v)}} \frac{1}{|I(v) \setminus I(u)||I(u)|} \sum_{\substack{v' \in I(v) \setminus I(u) \\ u' \in I(u)}} psim_\ell(u',v')
\end{aligned}
\right] \quad (23)
$$

Other Description Methods of Node Similarity

MatchSim (Lin, Lyu & King, 2009)

We model the Web graph as a directed graph G $= (V,E)$ with vertices V representing web pages vi(i = 1, 2,…, n) and directed edges E representing hyperlinks among web pages. Given two pages a and b in a web graph of size n, we obtain a weighted bipartite graph Ga,b = (I(a) + I(b),E,w), where E = $\{(u,v)|u \in I(a), v \in I(b)\}$ and w(u,v) = sim(u,v). Based on the recursive intuition of "similar pages have similar neighbors", MatchSim measures the similarity between pages by "the average similarity of the maximum matching between their neighbors". Formally, the MatchSim score between two different pages a and b is defined by:

$$sim(a,b) = \frac{\hat{W}(a,b)}{\max(I(a),I(b))} \qquad (24)$$

In the cases that $|I(a)| = 0$ or $|I(b)| = 0$, since there is no way to infer any similarity, we simply define sim(a,b) = 0. If $a = b$, we have sim(a,b)=1, which is obviously.

In Eq. (24), $\hat{W}(a,b)$ denotes the weight of maximum matching between I(a) and I(b), i.e.,

$$\widehat{W}(a,b) \overset{\Delta}{=} W(m_{ab}^*) = \sum_{(u,v) \in m_{ab}^*} sim(u,v) \qquad (25)$$

where m_{ab}^* is a maximum matching between I(a) and I(b).

$\hat{W}$ (a,b) can be calculated using algorithms for the assignment problem. This chapter adopts the Kuhn-Munkres (K-M) algorithm. Since the K-M algorithm always convert I(a) and I(b) to be "equally-sized" before computing $m_{ab}{}^*$, we define

$$l_{ab} \overset{\triangle}{=} \mid m_{ab}^* \mid = \max(I(a), I(b)).$$ Obviously, any matching between I(a) and I(b) is of size lab.

Therefore, in Eq. (24), the factor $\dfrac{\hat{W}(a,b)}{\max(I(a), I(b))}$ max(I(a);I(b)) is exactly the average similarity of a maximum matching between the neighbors of a and b.

Other Related Research

A concept of similarity between vertices of directed graphs is introduced. Let GA and GB be two directed graphs with respectively n_A and n_B vertices. We define a $n_A \times n_B$ similarity matrix S whose real entry Sij expresses how similar vertex j (in GA) is to vertex i (in GB): we say that Sij is their similarity score. The similarity matrix can be obtained as the limit of the normalized even iterates of $S_{k+1} = BS_k A^T + B^T S_k A$ where A and B are adjacency matrices of the graphs and S(0) is a matrix whose entries are all equal to one.

FUTURE RESEARCH DIRECTIONS

Based on this chapter, we believe that entity resolution on complex network has many issues to be examined. Foremost, we need to address the efficiency issues. In particular, we need to address how to conduct entity resolution efficiently in massive complex data. As the second issue, we need to discuss how to solve the rapid data update in real world. As the third issue, the integration of different types of data will be solved as the issue of multi-source. At last, we hope to have an effective mechanism for evaluation whether the results meets the needs. That is the issue of scalability.

CONCLUSION

In this chapter, we mainly summarize previous research in this regard. There is a brief introduction about what entity resolution on complex network, specific genre on it and common methods used. We discuss about it via two concrete examples. Specifically, when we identify mirror websites, we first define mirroring classification level. After that, we use two different strategies of "Candidate Pair Detection" and "Host Pair Classification" to make the level as a numeric value in a way. Finally, we divide them into corresponding levels by comparing the value. In the name recognition, we study in the same lines. Slightly different from the former issue, we analysis of this issue from the perspective of FIG. In the end, we have listed some node similarity solution algorithms in recent years. In this section, we pick particular kernels to these methods for reference.

REFERENCES

Barabási, A., & Albert, R. (1999). Emergence of scaling in random networks. *Science*, *286*(5439), 509–512. doi:10.1126/science.286.5439.509

Barabási, A., & Albert, R. (1999). Mirror, mirror on the web: A study of host pairs with replicated content. *Computer Networks*, *31*, 1579–1590. doi:10.1016/S1389-1286(99)00021-3

Fan, X., Wang, J., Pu, X., Zhou, L., & Lv, B. (2011). On graph-based name disambiguation. *Journal of Data Quality*.

Fogaras, D., & Rácz, B. (2005). Scaling link-based similarity search. In *Proceedings of the 14th International Conference on World Wide Web*. IEEE.

Frey, B. J., & Dueck, D. (2007). Clustering by passing messages between data points. *Science*, *315*, 972. doi:10.1126/science.1136800

Jeh, G., & Widom, J. (2002). SimRank: A measure of structural-context similarity. In *Proceedings of KDD*. KDD. Antonellis, I., GarciaMolina, H., & Chang, C. (2008). Simrank++: Query rewriting through link analysis of the click graph. In *Proceedings of PVLDB 2008*. PVLDB.

Li, L., Wang, H., Gao, H., & Li, J. (2010). EIF: A framework of effective entity identification. In *Proceedings of WAIM 2010*. WAIM.

Lin, Z., Lyu, M. R., & King, I. (2009). MatchSim: A novel neighbor-based similarity measure with maximum neighborhood matching. In *Proceedings of the 18th ACM Conference on Information and Knowledge Management*. ACM.

Watts, D. J., & Strogatz, S. H. (1998). Collective dynamics of 'small-world' networks. *Nature, 393*(6684), 440–442. doi:10.1038/30918

ADDITIONAL READING

Arasu, A., Chaudhuri, S., & Kaushik, R. (2008). Transformation-based framework for record matching. In ICDE 2008

Arasu, A., Chaudhuri, S., & Kaushik, R. (2009). Learning string transformations from examples. In VLDB 2009

Arasu, A., & Kaushik, R. (2009). A grammar-based entity representation framework for data cleaning. In SIGMOD, pp. 233–244

Arasu, A., Re, C., & Suciu, D. (2009). Large-scale deduplication with constraints using Dedupalog. In ICDE 2009

Barabási, A.-L. et al. (2003). Scale-Free Networks. *Scientific American, 288*, 50–59. doi:10.1038/scientificamerican0503-60

Bekkerman. R., & Mccallum, A. (2005). Disambiguating web appearances of people in a social network. In Proceedings of the International World Wide Web Conference (WWW'05). 463–470.

Bharat, K., & Henzinger, M. (1998). Improved algorithms for topic distillation in hyperlinked environments, In Proc. ACM SIGIR '98, pp. 111–104

Bhattacharya, I., & Getoor, L. (2007). Collective entity resolution in relational data. ACM Trans. Knowl. Discov. Data 1, 1, 1–36.

Bilenko. M., & Mooney, R. J. (2003). Adaptive duplicate detection using learnable string similarity measures. In Proceedings of the International SIGKDD Conference on Knowledge Discovery and Data Mining (KDD'03). 39–48.

Bilenko, M.,Mooney, R., Cohen, W., Ravikumar, P., & Fienberg, S. (2003). Adaptive name matching in information integration. IEEE Intell. Syst 18, 5, 16–23. Brusco, M. J., & K''OHN, H.-F. 2008. Comment on clustering by passing messages between data points. *Sci., 319*, 726c.

Bilenko. M., & Mooney, R. J. (2004). A probabilistic framework for semi-supervised clustering. In Proceedings of the International SIGKDD Conference on Knowledge Discovery and Data Mining (KDD'04). 59–68.

Brin, S., & Page, L. (1998). The anatomy of a large-scale hypertextual Web search engine, In Proc. 7th Int. World Wide Web Conference, Brisbane, Australia.

A. Broder, S. Glassman, M. Manasse & G. Zweig (1997). Syntactic clustering of the Web, In Proc. 6th Int. World Wide Web Conference.

Chakrabarti, S., Dom, B., Raghavan, P., Rajagopalan, S., Gibson, D., & Kleinberg, J. (1998). Automatic resource compilation by analyzing hyperlink structure and associated text, In Proc. 7th Int. World Wide Web Conference, Brisbane, Australia.

M.L. Creech (1996). Author-oriented link management, In Proc. 5th Int. World Wide Web Conference, Paris, France.

R.K. Jones & J. Pitkow (1996). Supporting the Web: a distributed hyperklink database, In Proc. 5th Int. World Wide Web Conference, Paris, France.

Chaudhuri. S., Ganjam, K., Ganti, V., & Motwani, R. (2003). Robust and efficient fuzzy match for online data cleaning. In Proceedings of the ACM SIGMOD International Conference on Management of Data. 313–324.

Chaudhuri, S., Chen, B. C., Ganti, V., & Kaushik, R. (2005). Example-driven design of efficient record matching queries. In VLDB 2007 (2007)

Chen. Z., Kalashnikov, D. V., & Mehrotra, S. (2007). Adaptive graphical approach to entity resolution. In Proceedings of the ACM/IEEE-CS Joint Conference on Digital Libraries (JCDL'07). 204–213. DBLP. 2010.

Chen, Z., Kalashnikov, D. V., & Mehrotra, S. (2009). Exploiting context analysis for combining multiple entity resolution systems. In SIGMOD, pp. 207–218

Culotta, A., & McCallum, A. (2005). Joint deduplication of multiple record types in relational data. In Proc. CIKM 2005, pp. 257–258.

Dong. X., Halevy, A., & !, J. (2005). Reference reconciliation in complex information spaces. In Proceedings of the ACM SIGMOD International Conference on Management of Data. 85–96.

Dong, X., Halevy, A., & Madhavan, J. (2005). Reference reconciliation in complex information spaces. In Proc. SIGMOD 2005, pp. 85–96

Dueck. D., & Frey, B. J. (2007). Non-metric affinity propagation for unsupervised image categorization. In Proceedings of the IEEE International Conference on Computer Vision (ICCV'07). 1–8.

Dueck. D., & Frey, B. J. (2008). Constructing treatment portfolios using affinity propagation. In Proceedings of the Annual Conference on Research in Computational Molecular Biology (RECOMB'08). 360–371.

Fan. X., Wang, J., LV, B., Zhou, L., & Hu, W. (2008). Ghost: An effective graph-based framework for name distinction. In Proceedings of the ACM International Conference on Information and Knowledge Management (CIKM'08). 1449–1450.

Fellegi, I. P., & Sunter, A. B. (1969). A theory for record linkage. *Journal of the American Statistical Association*, *64*(328), 1183–1210. doi:10.1080/0 1621459.1969.10501049

Frey, B. J., & Dueck, D. (2007). Clustering by passing messages between data points. *Sci.*, *315*, 972–976. doi:10.1126/science.1136800

Frey, B. J., & Dueck, D. (2008). Response to comment on clustering by passing messages between data points. *Sci.*, *319*, 726d. doi:10.1126/ science.1151268

Han. H., Giles, L., Zha, H., LI, C., & TSIOUT-SIOULIKLIS, K. (2004). Two supervised learning approaches for name disambiguation in author citations. In Proceedings of the ACM/IEEE-CS Joint Conference on Digital Libraries (JCDL'04). 296–305.

Han. H., Zha, H., & GILES, C. L. (2005). Name disambiguation in author citations using a k-way spectral clustering method. In Proceedings of the ACM/IEEE-CS Joint Conference on Digital Libraries (JCDL'05). 334–343.

Hern´Andez. M. A., & Stolfo, S. J. (1995). The merge/purge problem for large databases. In Proceedings of the ACM SIGMOD International Conference on Management of Data. 127–138.

Jiang. L.,Wang, J., AN, N.,Wang, S., Zhan, J., & LI, L. (2009). GRAPE: A graph-based framework for disambiguating people appearances in web search. In Proceedings of the IEEE International Conference on Data Mining (ICDM'09). 199–208.

Kalashnikov, D. V., & Mehrotra, S. (2006). Domain-independent data cleaning via analysis of entityrelationship graph. ACM Trans. Datab. Syst. 31, 2, 716–767.

Kleinberg, J. (1998). Authoritative sources in a hyperlinked environment, In Proc. ACM SIAM Symp. on Discrete Algorithms, pp. 668-677.

Koudas, N., Saha, A., & Srivastava, D., et al. (2009). Metric functional dependencies In ICDE

Koudas, N., Sarawagi, S., & Srivastava, D. (2006). Record linkage: similarity measures and algorithms. In SIGMOD Conference, pp. 802–803

Krishnan, P., & Sugla, B. (1998). Utility of co-operating Web proxy caches, In Proc. 7th Int. World Wide Web Conference, Brisbane, Australia.

Lawrence. S., Giles, C. L., & Bollacker, K. D. (1999). Autonomous citation matching. In Proceedings of the AGENTS'99 Conference. 392–393.

Lee. D., On, B.-W., Kang, J., & Park, S. (2005). Effective and scalable solutions for mixed and split citation problems in digital libraries. In Proceedings of the International Workshop on Information Quality in Information Systems (IQIS'05). 69–76.

Leone, M., Sumedha, & Weigt, M. (2007). Clustering by soft-constraint affinity propagation: Applications to gene-expression data. *Bioinf.*, *23*(20), 2708–2715. doi:10.1093/bioinformatics/btm414

Malpani, R., Lorch, J., & Berger, D. (1995). Making World Wide Web caching servers cooperate, In Proc. 4th Int. World Wide Web Conference, Boston, MA.

Mccallum. A., Nigam, K., & Ungar, L. H. (2000). Efficient clustering of high-dimensional data sets with application to reference matching. In Proceedings of the SIGKDD International Conference on Knowledge Discovery and Data Mining (KDD'00). 169–178.

Milch, B., Marthi, B., Sontag, D., Russell, S., & Ong, D. L. (2005). BLOG: Probabilistic models with unknown objects. In Proc. IJCAI 2005, pp. 1352–1359

Minkov. E., Cohen, W. W., & Ng, A. Y. (2006). Contextual search and name disambiguation in email using graphs. In Proceedings of the Annual ACM SIGIR Conference on Research and Development in Information Retrieval. 27–34.

N. Shivakumar & H. Garcia-Molina (1998). Finding near-replicas of documents on the Web In Proc. Workshop on Web Databases (WebDB'98)

Newcombe, H., Kennedy, J., & Axford, S. (1959). Automatic Linkage of Vital Records. *Science*, *130*, 954–959. doi:10.1126/science.130.3381.954

O'Neill, E. T., McClain, P. D., & Lavoie, B. F. (1997). A methodology for sampling the World Wide Web. In *OCLC Annual Review of Research*. Online Computer Library Center Inc.

On. B.-W., Elmacioglu, E., Lee, D., Kang, J., & Pei, J. (2006). Improving grouped-entity resolution using quasi-cliques. In Proceedings of the IEEE International Conference on Data Mining (ICDM'06). 1008–1015.

On. B.-W., & Lee, D. (2007). Scalable name disambiguation using multi-level graph partition. In Proceedings of the SIAM International Conference on Data Mining (SDM'07). 575–580.

Pasula. H.,Marthi, B.,Milch, B., Russell, S., & Shpitser, I. (2002). Identity uncertainty and citation matching. In Proceedings of the Conference on Advances in Neural Information Processing Systems (NIPS'02).

Pei. J., Jiang, D., & Zhang, A. (2005). On mining cross-graph quasi-cliques. In Proceedings of the International SIGKDD Conference on Knowledge Discovery and Data Mining (KDD'05). 228–238. PUBMED. 2010. bibliography.

Research Division, U.S. Bureau of the Census.

Sarawagi. S., & Bhamidipaty, A. (2002). Interactive deduplication using active learning. In Proceedings of the International SIGKDD Conference on Knowledge Discovery and Data Mining (KDD'02). 269–278.

Selingo, J. (1998). Information technology: in attempting to archive the entire Internet, a scientist develops a new way to search it, In The Chronicle of Higher Education, Washington D.C.

Shakes, J., Langheinrich, M., & Etzioni, O. (1997). Dynamic reference sifting — case study in the homepage domain, In Proc. 6th Int. World Wide Web Conference. .

Singla, P., & Domingos, P. (2005). Object identification with attribute-mediated dependences. In A. M. Jorge, L. Torgo, P. B. Brazdil, R. Camacho, & J. Gama (Eds.), *PKDD 2005. LNCS (LNAI)* (Vol. 3721, pp. 297–308). Heidelberg: Springer.

Sparck-Jones, K., & Willett, P. (1997). *Readings in Information Retrieval, Morgan Kaufman. D. Wessels (1997). Configuring hierarchical squid caches*. Online Tutorial.

Travers, J., & Milgram, S. (1969). An experimental study of the small world problem. *Sociometry, 32*(4), 425–443. doi:10.2307/2786545

Whang, S. E., Menestrina, D., Koutrika, G., Theobald, M., & Garcia-Molina, H. (2009). Entity resolution with iterative blocking. In SIGMOD, pp. 219–232

Winkler. (1999). *The state of record linkage and current research problems. Tech. rep.* W.: Statistical.

Yin. X., Han, J., & YU, P. S. (2007). Object distinction: Distinguishing objects with identical names. In Proceedings of the IEEE International Conference on Data Engineering (ICDE'07). 1242–1246.

Yin, X., Han, J., & Yu, P. S. (2007). Object Distinction: Distinguishing Objects with Identical Names. In ICDE 2007

Yu, P. S., & MacNair, E. A. (1998). Performance study of a collaborative method for hierarchical caching in proxy servers, In Proc. 7th Int. World Wide Web Conference, Brisbane, Australia

Zhang. D., Tang, J., LI, J., & Wang, K. (2007). A constraint-based probabilistic framework for name disambiguation. In Proceedings of the ACM International Conference on Information and Knowledge Management (CIKM'07). 1019–1022.

KEY TERMS AND DEFINITIONS

Content Equivalent: We say that two pages are content equivalent if pages change at the byte level (e.g., by the addition of blank lines, by HTML reformatting, etc.) without any change of content.

Content Identical: With regard to content, we say that two pages are content identical if they are byte-wise equal.

Fingerprint Match (FM): Content is byte-wise identical.

Full Similarity (FS): The documents are 100% equivalent after de-tagging.

Highly Similar: If pages change in content (e.g., due to a banner ad or other forms of dynamic content) but remain highly similar at the syntactic level, we call them highly similar.

High Similarity (HS): Common content is above the threshold for high similarity.

NS: Path is valid, but no syntactic similarity.

Related: If pages change substantially at the syntactic level but are semantically similar (e.g. translated content), we call them related.

Source Failure (SF): GET failed at source host.

Structurally Identical: If two hosts have exactly the same set of paths, we say that they are structurally identical.

Structure: Structure is defined by the set of valid paths relative to the host under consideration.

Target Failure (TF): GET failed at target host.

Trace Similarity (TS): A small (non-zero) portion of the document is common.

Chapter 10
Entity Resolution on Cloud

ABSTRACT

Large quantities of records need to be read and analyzed in cloud computing; many records referring to the same entity bring challenges for data processing and analysis. Entity resolution has become one of the hot issues in database research. Clustering based on records similarity is one of most commonly used methods, but the existing methods of computing records similarity often cost much time and are not suitable for cloud computing. This chapter shows that it is necessary to use wave of strings to compute records similarity in cloud computing and provides a method based on wave of strings of entity resolution. Theoretical analysis and experimental results show that the method proposed in this chapter is correct and effective.

INTRODUCTION

In the collections of data, some records referring to the same entity have different presentations, and the process of finds them is called entity resolution. Without good results of entity resolution to take as a unit records referring to the same entity, confusion between information arises to afftect the use of information. Hence in the processes where data plays an important role, such as information integration, data cleansing, information ex-change etc., entity resolution is an important step.

With the development of information techniques, people are faced with large quantities of data to query, handle and analyze. Different data sources and data quality amplifies the probability of different presentations of the same entity in data collections, so direct analysis of the collections leads to an incomplete view, which impacts the

final decision and wastes lots of time and internet bandwidth as well. It is necessary to perform entity resolution in large quantities of data.

To address entity resolution in large quantities problems in cloud computing, we adopt widely used Mapreduce paradigm(Dean & Ghemawat 2008) to design algorithms, and to make use of it, our algorithm based on wave similarity of strings based on Jaccard similarity function, which uses wave of strings to describe features of strings and calculates similarity to cluster records with high similarity. Wave of strings generated by our algorithms, can re-arrange characters by features, which can be filtered easily and need not access files, and decreases transported information. Meanwhile, wave of strings can be used on Chinese word attributes without performing Chinese word segmentation, which avoids errors made by bad Chinese word segmentation.

DOI: 10.4018/978-1-4666-5198-2.ch010

Our contributions are as follows:

1. We study entity resolution in large quantities problem in cloud computing.
2. We propose a method based on wave of strings generated by Mapreduce paradigm to address the problem.
3. We show the feasibility and correctness of our algorithm by experiments.

Since cloud computing is one of the feasible solutions for big data processing, entity resolution techniques based on cloud could be applied in e-commerce (Chapter 16) and healthcare information systems (Chapter 17).

BACKGROUND

Entity resolution in large quantities of data is faced with many challenges, such as:

Firstly, large quantities of data lead to so many accesses and computation that expensive computers with high performance cannot handle it well.

Secondly, different representations exist in different sources. Such as:

1. Different orders of description,
2. Spelling mistakes in an attribute,
3. Different choices of attributes. For example, consider two records R1(006,Jones Smith, America, 8678901 8276571) and R2(019,Jonse R . Smith,8276571 8678901). R1 has attributes of name, nationality, phone number, while R2 only has attributes of only name and nationality. Besides, there are spelling mistakes in name and different orders in phone number.

Thirdly, there are also large quantities of intermediate data, and frequently accessing of data brings large cost.

Current methods cannot solve these problems well. Some methods do not have good scalability, such as (Hassanzadeh, & Miller, 2009), which need the similarity values between every two strings in the candidate set to get a high precision and leads to high computation cost, so they cannot handle large quantities of data. Some parallel methods (Xiao, Wang, Lin, Yu & Wang, (2011), Vernica, Carey & Li. 2010), based on the analysis of tokens extracted from strings, need Chinese word segmentation to prepare the data, whose results are determined by the results of Chinese word segmentation.

Cloud computing(Brian, Brunschwiler, Dill, Christ, Falsafi, Fischer & Zollinger, 2008) reduces the pressure of computation by parallel computing. So it is a good way to solve entity resolution problem by making good use of cloud computing. But there are few methods suitable for the cloud computing. Most of current methods are based on string similarity (Elmagarmid, Ipeirotis, & Verykios, 2007), which need inverted-gram files for computing. If these functions are used directly in cloud computing, nodes need to access inverted files frequently, which increases the dependency of name node and information transported.

Preliminaries

Definitions about Wave of Strings

Definition 1: (ε-single directional neighborhood) Single directional neighborhood of character c is characters beginning at position p, with length of ε to the right of c.

Due to the comparison between long strings, ignoring separators between attributes, we need single directional neighborhood to prevent impacts between attributes. Besides, frequencies of characters nearby are strengthened obviously by the single directional neighborhood. We shall describe it in Section 2.2.

Definition 2: (Total frequencies f(c) with ε-single directional neighborhood) Suppose the position of c is p, f(c) is total number of c appearing from position p with length of p+ε-1.

Definition 3: (Wavepart P(ε,W) of string S in ε-single directional neighborhood) It's a 2-tuple <Integer N, sorted sequence C> where $\forall c \in C,\ f(c) = N$

Definition 4: (wave W(S) of string S) It is a triple:
$$< M, L, \{< f(c_1), C_1 >, ... < f(c_n), C_n >\} >,$$
where L is the total length of string, and
$$M = \sum_{i=1}^{n} f(c_i),\ f(c_1) < f(c_2) < ... < f(c_n).$$

Example 1: Suppose there only two records R="labbcldbl",S="lacdl"(l is the separator between attributes).

Suppose ε=3. The second 'b' is in the directional neighborhood of the first 'b', which adds the frequency to be 2, and the third 'b' is not in the directional neighborhood of the second 'b' and the first 'b', which makes the frequency of 'b' is only 1. So wavepart of R is {<1,b>,<2,abbd>}, and the wave of R is <3,5, {<1,b>,<2,abbd>}>.

Mapreduce Paradigm

Mapreduce is a Data-intensive parallel com-putation paradigm, whose data is stored in distributed file system (DFS), represented as (key, value) pair and its computation can be divided into two parts of map and reduce:

Map (k1,v1)→list(k2,v2)

Reduce (k2,list(v2))→list(k3,v3)

The data flow of Mapreduce is shown in Figure 1, data is partitioned in master node, and transported to slave nodes to run map tasks, and the output of map tasks is shuffled by the hash values of keys, which makes the keys sharing the same hash value in the same reduce task, and the output of reduce task is written into DFS.

Formalization of Entity Resolution Problem

Given a collection of records from relation R, and similarity function between record r, s: Sim(r,s), and the result of clustering is a set of C={c_1, . . ., c_k},

$$where\ \forall r, s \in c_i, \mathrm{Sim}(r, s) \geq threshold.$$

In this chapter, we use Jaccard similarity based on n-gram sets of strings as the similarity function.

AN ENTITY RESOLUTION METHOD BASED ON MAPREDUCE

In this section, we shall introduce an entity resolution based on MapReduce. In Section 2.1, we will show the framework of our algorithm, and in Section 2.2-2.4, we will show the three parts of the algorithm.

Framework of the Clustering Algorithm

Input: A set of records R, similarity threshold *Th*, length of single-direction neighborhood ε, max total frequencies of difference of frequencies *TF*.

Output: A Set S, where different clusters represent different entities.

1. Access set R, and generate total frequencies f(c) with ε-single directional neighborhood.
2. Access set R, and generate wave W(S) of string S according to the frequencies got in the first step.
3. According to the W(S) of string S, calculate similarity values between two strings, and cluster records with similarity values no less than threshold *Th* between each pairs.

Figure 1. Data flow in MapReduce

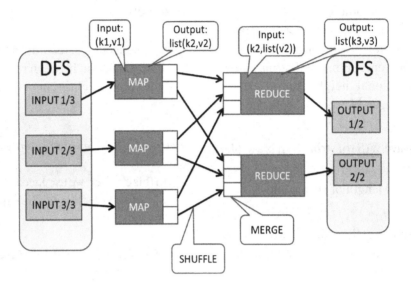

The algorithm takes as input the data set, with parameters of similarity threshold *Th*, length of single-direction neighborhood *ε*, max total frequencies of difference of frequencies *TF*. Firstly, it generates total frequencies f(c) with ε-single directional neighborhood using Mapreduce, which will be shown in Section 2.2, and secondly generates wave W(S) of string S according to the frequencies got in the first step, which will be shown in section 2.3, and thirdly calculates the similarity values between records with wave of strings, where only map-process is used, which will be shown in section 2.4. Similar records are rearranged in the master node, and are output by clusters. The key-value pair is shown as <key,value> in the algorithm.

Example 2: Given a data set R={{1,Abc....} {2,Ebks....},{3,Ajlm...}.....}, where the first record is shown as {1,Abc...}, whose content is "Abc...", and data is partitioned in the master node (a.k.a namenode in Hadoop) and total frequencies f(c) with ε-single directional neighborhood are generated shown in Figure 2, and waves W(S) of

string S according to the frequencies got in the first step are generated shown in Figure 3, and similarity values can be calculated according to waves of strings.

Generate Total Frequencies F(C) with E-Single Directional Neighborhood

The step of generating total frequencies f(c) with ε-single directional neighborhood is as follows:

Input: Set of data records *R*, Length of ε-single directional neighborhood *ε*

Output: Set F of total frequencies f(c) with ε-single directional neighborhood.

Map-Process

- **Input:** Offset of data records *offset_S*, content of data *index*.
- **Output:** key-value pair flow, whose form is <character, (position of the character, offset *offset_S*, 1)>
- **Parameter:** Length of ε-single directional neighborhood *ε*

- **Process:** Scan the index of data records, and analyze them, and output the result flow as designed.
- **Reduce-Process**
- **Input:** Data flow of Map-process.
- **Output:** Key-value flow, whose form is <offset of a record in data set *offset_S*, (character, frequency of a character)>
- **Process:**
  - $T \leftarrow \varnothing$ /*Initialize a balanced tree T, whose node is {position *pos*, frequency *f*}*/
  - Foreach value do

p=T. FindPostion (value.pos+1-ε)

Fre = -1;/*frequency of a character */

/*Function FindPostion (x) returns the first existing node whose value is no less than x, otherwise NULL*/

If p = NULL do

T.addnode(value.pos,1) /*Add this node*/

Else do

While(T[p].pos <=value.pos) do

T[p].f = T[p].f +1;

Fre = T[p].f;

If(T.FindPostion(value.pos)=NULL)

If(fre = -1) do

T.addnode(value.pos,1)

/*Add this node*/

Else

T.addnode(value.pos,Fre)

/*Add this node, whose frequency is frequency of previous character in the single-direction neighborhood*/

- Output the key-value pairs when traversing the tree T.

The algorithm first does simple computation to get characters and their positions to prepare computations for single-direction neighborhood in map-process, and in reduce-process, the algorithm try to increase frequencies of characters in a single-direction neighborhood by 1, to make local features of strings obvious.

Figure 2 shows the data flow of the algorithm. After the algorithm, frequency of a character is less influenced by farther characters in other attributes, which can distinguish appearances of the same character in different attributes. Besides, the increments of characters in a single-direction neighborhood strengthen impact between characters nearby, and make features of strings more obvious.

Suppose the average length of records is l, and the number of records is N. The time complexity is $O(N \cdot l)$, which can be viewed as $O(N)$, due to smallness of l.

Generate Wave of Strings

The step of generating wave of strings is as follows:

- **Input:** Key-value pairs file, generated from reduce-process in Section 2.2.
- **Output:** Key-value pair flow, whose form is as <offset set *offset_S* of every record in the data set R, wave set *W* of records>
- **Map-Process**
- **Input:** Key-value pair flow, whose form is as <Offset of data records *offset_S*, content of data *index*>.

Figure 2. Data flow in computing frequencies in a single direction scope

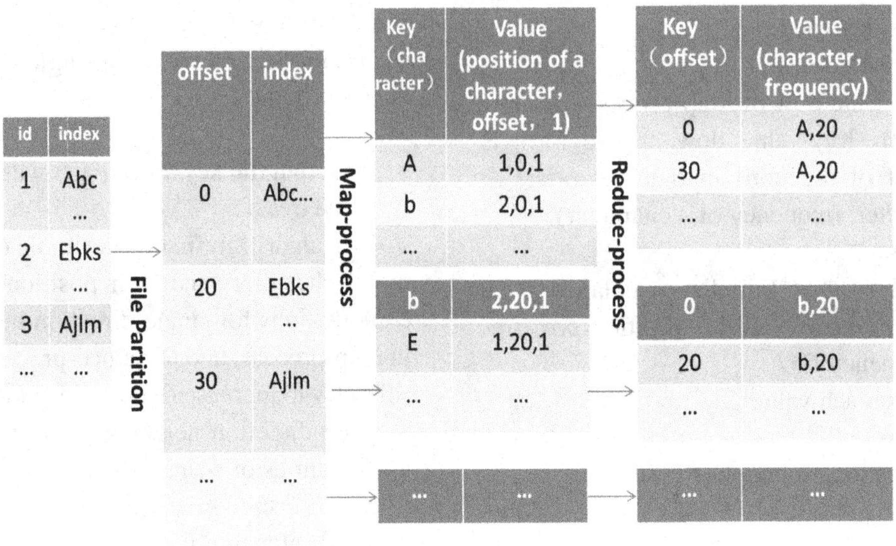

- **Output:** Key-value pair flow, whose form is as <offset *offset_S* of records which contain the character, in the data set, (character *c*, frequency *f* of the character) >
- **Process:** Read the content of each record, analyze the structure of it, and output the pairs as designed.

/*Map-process only reads the file generated by the reduce-process in Section 2.2, and prepares input for the next reduce-process.*/

- **Reduce-Process**
- **Input:** Key-value pair flow, whose form is <offset *offset_S* of records which contain the character, in the data set, (character *c*, frequency *f* of the character)>
- **Output:** Key-value pair flow, whose form is as < offset *offset_S* of records in the data set, wave set *W* of records>
- **Process:**
  - ○ $T \leftarrow \varnothing$ /*Initialize a balanced tree, whose comparison key is the frequency of a character, and the node is as {frequency *f*, sorted string *S*}*/
  - ○ foreach value do

p =T. FindPostion (value.f)

/*Function FindPostion(f) returns the position of the existing character in the tree whose frequency is *f*, otherwise returns NULL*/

If(p = NULL) do

T.addnode(f,"value.c") /*Add this node */

Else

T[p].S.addchar(value.c) /*Add this character into sorted string *S*, whose frequency is *f**/

  - ○ Traverse the tree T to output key-value pairs in ascending order of frequency.

Figure 3 shows the data flow of reduce-process. First, the algorithm reads the file generated by the reduce-process in Section 2.2, performs the Map-process, and output key-value pairs as they are written. Due to MapReduce paradigm, key-value pairs with the same key are sent to the same node to perform Reduce-process, which generates wave of a record. Suppose the number of records is N, the time complexity is $O(N)$. Re-arranging the records in ascending order of frequency, and partitioning the records by their wave, features of records are shown obviously, which can filter dissimilar records as early as possible (Vernica et al. 2010).

Computing Similarity Values

Waveparts, generated from methods above, can partition records into different clusters, when a filtering method based on properties below can be used:

Lemma 1:(Arasu, Ganti & Kaushik, 2006) If strings are r and s, with length |r| and |s|, then the Jaccard similarity value between them satisfies:

$$If \ J_s\left(r,s\right) \geq \gamma, then \ \gamma \leq \frac{|r|}{|s|} \leq \frac{1}{\gamma}$$

Property 1: Suppose there are two strings R and S, whose real Jaccard similarity value is Js, and parts compared are R_p and S_p, where $R_p \cap S_p = A_1, m_1 = R_p - A_1, n1 = S_p - A_1$, parts to be compared are $R_t = R - R_p, S_t = S - S_p, R_t \cap S_t = A_2, m2 = Rt - A_2, n_2 = S_t - A_2$. Jaccard similarity estimated is Js', and we have Js'≥Js, where Js' is as below, and it is no more than 1.

$$J_s' = \frac{|A_1| + |A_2| + |m_2|}{|A_1| + |A_2| + |n_2|}$$

According to Property 1, we can estimate the max Jaccard similarity between remaining parts of the strings to quit the comparison as soon as possible.

Algorithms to computing similarity values between records are as below:

- **Input:** A wave file *Frw*, consists of set of 2-tuples <offsets *offset_S* of records set R, set *W* of wave of each record>, similarity threshold *Th*, max of the difference value between frequencies of two records *TF*.
- **Output:** Stream of 2-tuple <*offset_S_r*, which is offset of a record r in the records set, offsets of records, whose similarity to the record r is no less than *Th*. (which is similar to the set *offset_S_s*)>
- **Map-Process**

Figure 3. Data flow in generating wave of strings in reduce phase

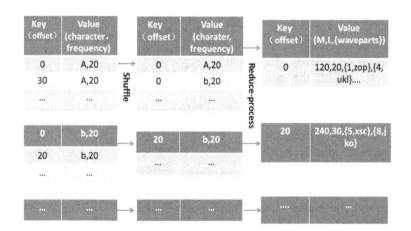

- **Input:** *Offset_S_r*, which is the offset of a record *r*, and *W*, which is the wave of the record.
- **Output:** 2-tuple<offset of the record *r*, offset of set of records, whose similarity value to the record *r* is no less than *Th*>
- **Parameters:** SIMILARITY threshold Th, max of the difference value between frequencies of two records TF.
- **Process:**
  - $C \leftarrow \varnothing$ /*C stores records similar to the record *r* */
  - for each Wave of s in *Frw* do
  - if(abs(r.M -s.M)> *TF*) /*too large differences of frequencies of two records, not similar*/
  - Continue; /*quit this comparison, and continue next*/
  - Else do
  - *Min* = min(s.L,r.L);
  - *Max* = max(s.L,r.L);
  - If(*Min*/*Max* < *Th*) /*comparison between float numbers*/
  - Continue; /*not similar according to the lemma*/
  - *CurSim* = *Min*/*Max*;
  - While r and have other waveparts do
  - Compare waveparts of s and r till one character is different and update the com
  - /*compare the records by character frequency and sequence, and the record number of common characters *comm*/
  - *Min* = min(rem(s).L,rem(r).L); /*find the shorter one of the remaining parts*/
  - *Max* = max(rem(s).L,rem(r).L)); /*find the longer one*/
  - *CurSim* = (com+*Min*)/(com+*Max*);
  - /*estimate the similarity value*/
  - If(*CurSim*<*Th*) continue; /*if it is too small, quit and continue*/
  - End while from line 11

  - Calculate real Jaccard similarity *JS*;
  - If (*JS* >= *Th*)
  - C.add(s); /*add s*/
  - End else from line 5
  - End foreach from line 2
  - output C in the format designed

Due to frequency of a wavepart when comparing, the time complexity is O(min(r.L,s.L)) for each iteration.

Due to the comparison between each two records, the time complexity is O(N^2), which does not happen often according to experimental results.

Example 3: Suppose we want to compute similarity values between each two of three strings: *R,S* and *H*, and *TF*=3,*Th*=0.8, and we have waveparts as below:

R = <11,10,{1,"acz"},{4,"mn"},{6,"bnxyz"}>;
S = <4,5,{1,"xyz"},{3,"ab"}>; H = <11, 9, {2,"acx"},{3,"bcn"},{6,"cmq"}>;

When in comparison, since the total frequency of *S* is 4, which makes the difference to *R* larger than 3, besides max similarity between *S* and *R* is (5/10=0.5<0.8), so *S* is not similar to *R* and filtered.

While *H* will be compared to *R* by every wavepart, due to the frequency of first wavepart of *R* is 1, smaller than that of *H*, 2. The second wavepart of *R* will be obtained to prepare for the next comparison. Due to the length of R is 7, and H, 9, max similarity value estimated is (7/9=0.78<0.8), showing *H* is not similar to *R*, which ends the comparison.

Theoretical Analysis

We evaluate the clustering results by *Recall* and *Precision* calculated by Hassanzadeh & Miller, (2009).

Supposed we have ground truth data consisting of k clusters, G = {$g_1,g_2,...,g_k$}, which is extracted from a relation R. And we have a set of clusters, by our algorithm, C = {$c_1, ..., c_k$}. And *f* is a mapping from G to C, where g_i is mapped to C_j, i.e. $C_j = f(g_i)$, and satisfying that the common ones between C_j and g_i is the largest proportion of g_i. We can define *Precision* and *Recall* of every cluster as Pr_i and Re_i, for $1 \leq i \leq k$, as follows:

$$\Pr{}_i = \frac{\left| f(g_i) \cap g_i \right|}{\left| f(g_i) \right|} \text{ and } \mathrm{Re}_i = \frac{\left| f(g_i) \cap g_i \right|}{\left| g_i \right|}$$

And we can evaluate the total *Precision* and *Recall* as:

$$\Pr = \sum_{i=1}^{k} \frac{\left| g_i \right|}{\left| R \right|} \Pr{}_i \text{ and } \mathrm{Re} = \sum_{i=1}^{k} \frac{\left| g_i \right|}{\left| R \right|} \mathrm{Re}_i$$

Due to different data sources, most records may have different schemas, leading to a low probability of same length between records. Hence we can assume that different records are in different length.

We can define *Comparison Ratio* as follows.

$$R_{com} = \frac{Number\ of\ kinds\ of\ length\ of\ records\ to\ compare}{Number\ of\ kinds\ of\ length\ of standard\ records}$$

Comparison Ratio approximately shows how many kinds of records to compare, which can also shows how many records to compare.

Conclusion 1: Suppose the total number of standard records is Ni, the length of each standard record in the ground truth of α_i, and the similarity value SJ, average length α_{avg}, and we have follows.

$$R_{com}^{i} = \alpha_{avg} \left(\frac{1}{S_J} - S_J \right) + 1$$

The expectation value is shown as follows.

$$E\left(R_{com}^i \right) \leq \frac{\sum_{i=1}^{N_i} E\left(n_{i1} \right)_{max} + \sum_{i=1}^{N_i} E\left(n_{i2} \right)_{max}}{N_i}, where$$

$$E\left(n_{i1} \right)_{max} = \frac{m_{i1}^4 + 8m_{i1}^3 + 23m_{i1}^2 + 28m_{i1} + 12}{12m_{i1}}, m_{i1} = \alpha_i \left(\frac{1}{S_J} - 1 \right)$$

$$E\left(n_{i2} \right)_{max} = \frac{m_{i2}^3 + 4m_{i2}^2 + 5m_{i2} + 2}{12}, m_{i2} = \alpha_i \left(1 - S_J \right)$$

Conclusion 2: When computing similarity according to Property 1, false negative does not happen.

Conclusion 3: Given m nodes, the time complexity of Clustering Algorithm in Section 2.1 is $O(N^2/m)$, and speed-up is $O(m)=O(1)$, and efficiency is $O(m)/m=O(1)/m=O(1)$.

EXPERIMENTAL RESULTS

Experimental Setup

Hadoop implements MapReduce paradigm, which has similar performance as MapReduce. Our experiments are based on Hadoop 0.20.2, and the codes are in Java, and data set crawled from yellow pages, whose average length is 340 Byte. And the clusters consists of 1 name node, and 10 data nodes, whose CPU Frequency is 2.63GHz, with 8 cores, and RAM 2GB. The operating system is 64-bit Red Hat Enterprise Linux AS release 4. Size of file block is 1M, and the max number of map tasks is 4, and the number of reduce tasks is 4.

The ground truth set of the data set is classified by human, and we chose some records in different clusters of the ground truth set, and modified them in random attributes and positions, and added them into the set in random offsets of the file, and we perform our algorithm on this file.

We set the length of single-direction neighborhood as 4 and the max of the difference value between frequencies of two records as 300, and similarity threshold as 0.8.

Experimental Results

From Figure 4 to Figure 7, the number in x-axis is the experimental number divided by 3830, i.e. 2 is actually 2*3830 in experiments.

In Figure 4, we can see that the growth of time of calculating frequencies in single-direction neighborhood (GetFre) and Generating wave of strings (GenWave) is nearly linear with the growth of file size. More calculating and accesses of file bring more time cost.

In Figure 5, we can see the growth of similarity computing (GetSim) seldom reach the worst growth case (N*N growth, where, based on the time of first case, 3 times of it is increased from the second case, and the values in y-axis is shown in log (actual time / 100), while the values is (actual time / 100).) Due to small file size and the worse performance of Hadoop of dealing with small size of file, more time cost is brought in. Due to fewer records, the wave generated is not useful enough, which leads to worse filtering result. As the records grows, more records are filtered, which leads to less growth in time.

In Figure 6, due to conclusion 3, real similarity value can always be computed, so the *Precision(Pr)* and *Recall(Re)* are relative high.

Figure 5. Time cost of computation of similarity with the increment of tuples

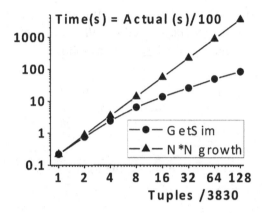

As the number of records grows, more records are filtered, which contributes to higher precision. Due to modification in random positions and addition in random characters, some records, consisting of low frequency words seldom showing up in life, are filtered, which leads to fewer records in a cluster and low recall. Sometimes these happen with more records. But these will not happen so much in life, the Recall may be higher in practice.

In Figure 7, the total time of the serial algorithm (SerTotal) is 3 to 4 times as long as that of the

Figure 4. Time cost of computing frequencies in a single direction and generating waves with the increment of tuples

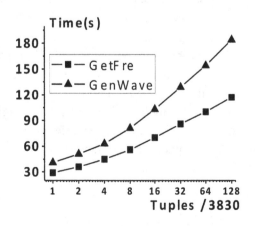

Figure 6. Precision and recall with the increment of tuples

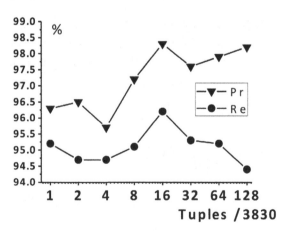

Figure 7. The total time cost of serial and parallel computing with the increment of tuples

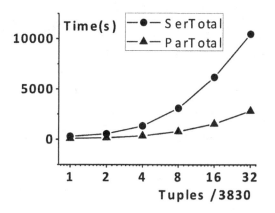

Figure 9. Time cost of generating wave of strings with the increment of nodes

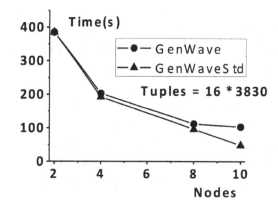

parallel algorithm, so the speed-up is 3 to 4, and the efficiency is 0.3 to 0.4.

In Figure 8, there is a distance between the time of calculating frequency in single-direction neighborhood (GetFre) and that of ideal time (GetFreStd) got by continuous halving the value in y-axis of the previous case, due to more data transmission via network, with the growth of nodes, and more merges and reduces.

In Figure 9, with the growth of nodes, there is small distance between the time of generating wave (GenWave) and that of ideal time (GenWaveStd) got by continuous halving the value in y-

axis of the previous case, due to good use of MapReduce paradigm to generate wave quickly.

In Figure 10, there is a distance between the time of computing similarity values (GetSim) and that of ideal time (GetSimStd) obtained by continuous halving the value in y-axis of the previous case, due to more clustering results transmission via network, with the growth of nodes, and more time cost brought by that.

Based on results and analysis above, the generation of string similarity measure proposed can be performed quickly in MapReduce paradigm and the clustering method based on it can also be performed efficiently.

Figure 8. Time cost of computing frequencies in a single direction with the increment of nodes

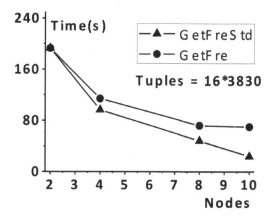

Figure 10. Time cost of computing similarity with the increment of nodes

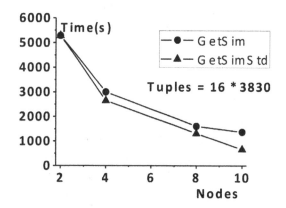

STRATEGIES TO IMPROVE PERFORMANCE

Due to the only filtering strategy, size filter (Arasu, Ganti, & Kaushik, 2006), in the algorithm, the effect can be impacted by skew data (Vernica, Carey & Li, 2010). Due to the adoption of string wave to describe features, the records have been rearranged and partitioned, so the algorithm in Section 2 can adopt filtering strategies based on token(Xiao, Wang, Lin, Yu & Wang, 2011, Vernica, Carey & Li 2010), to improve performance.

FUTURE RESEARCH DIRECTIONS

Due to the only consideration of stationary length of single-direction neighborhood, the performance of dealing with records, with different length of attributes varying frequently, is not high. How to improve performance at this situation is future work.

CONCLUSION

In this chapter, we study the entity resolution in large quantities of data problem, and propose a method of entity resolution based on wave of strings, and propose a fast method of generating string wave and computing similarity values based on string wave using Mapreduce paradigm to accelerate the clustering algorithm. We show the effectiveness of our algorithm by theoretical analysis and experimental results.

REFERENCES

Arasu, A., Ganti, V., & Kaushik, R. (2006). Efficient exact set-similarity joins. In *Proceedings of the 32nd International Conference on Very Large Data Bases* (pp. 918-929). VLDB Endowment.

Brian, H. A. Y. E. S., Brunschwiler, T., Dill, H., Christ, H., Falsafi, B., Fischer, M., & Zollinger, M. (2008). Cloud computing. *Communications of the ACM, 51*(7), 9–11. doi:10.1145/1364782.1364786

Dean, J., & Ghemawat, S. (2008). MapReduce: Simplified data processing on large clusters. *Communications of the ACM, 51*(1), 107–113. doi:10.1145/1327452.1327492

Elmagarmid, A. K., Ipeirotis, P. G., & Verykios, V. S. (2007). Duplicate record detection: A survey. *IEEE Transactions on Knowledge and Data Engineering, 19*(1), 1–16. doi:10.1109/TKDE.2007.250581

Hassanzadeh, O., & Miller, R. J. (2009). Creating probabilistic databases from duplicated data. *The VLDB Journal—The International Journal on Very Large Data Bases, 18*(5), 1141-1166.

Vernica, R., Carey, M. J., & Li, C. (2010). Efficient parallel set-similarity joins using MapReduce. In *Proceedings of the 2010 International Conference on Management of Data* (pp. 495-506). ACM.

Xiao, C., Wang, W., Lin, X., Yu, J. X., & Wang, G. (2011). Efficient similarity joins for near-duplicate detection. *ACM Transactions on Database Systems, 36*(3), 15. doi:10.1145/2000824.2000825

ADDITIONAL READING

Benjelloun, O., Garcia-Molina, H., Kawai, H., Larson, T. E., Menestrina, D., Su, Q., & Widom, J. (2006). Generic entity resolution in the serf project. [*Issue.*]. *A Quarterly Bulletin of the Computer Society of the IEEE Technical Committee on Data Engineering*, (June): 2006.

Benjelloun, O., Garcia-Molina, H., Menestrina, D., Su, Q., Whang, S. E., & Widom, J. (2009). Swoosh: a generic approach to entity resolution. *The VLDB Journal—The International Journal on Very Large Data Bases, 18*(1), 255-276.

Bhattacharya, I., & Getoor, L. (2004). Iterative record linkage for cleaning and integration. In *Proceedings of the 9th ACM SIGMOD workshop on Research issues in data mining and knowledge discovery* (pp. 11-18). ACM.

Bhattacharya, I., & Getoor, L. (2007). Online collective entity resolution. In Proceedings of the National Conference on Artificial Intelligence (Vol. 22, No. 2, p. 1606). Menlo Park, CA, Cambridge, MA, London, AAAI Press, MIT Press, 1999.

Garcia-Molina, H. (2005). Handling data quality in entity resolution. In *Information Quality in Informational Systems: Proceedings of the 2nd international workshop on Information quality in information systems* (Vol. 17, No. 17, pp. 1-1).

Kawai, H., Garcia-Molina, H., Benjelloun, O., Menestrina, D., Whang, E., & Gong, H. (2006). P-swoosh: Parallel algorithm for generic entity resolution.

Kenig, B., & Gal, A. (2012). MFIblocks: an effective blocking algorithm for entity resolution. *Information Systems*.

Kirsten, T., Kolb, L., Hartung, M., Groß, A., Köpcke, H., & Rahm, E. (2010). Data partitioning for parallel entity matching. *arXiv preprint arXiv:1006.5309*.

Kolb, L., Köpcke, H., Thor, A., & Rahm, E. (2011). Learning-based entity resolution with MapReduce. In *Proceedings of the third international workshop on Cloud data management* (pp. 1-6). ACM.

Kolb, L., Thor, A., & Rahm, E. (2011). Block-based load balancing for entity resolution with MapReduce. In *Proceedings of the 20th ACM international conference on Information and knowledge management* (pp. 2397-2400). ACM.

Kolb, L., Thor, A., & Rahm, E. (2012). Load balancing for mapreduce-based entity resolution. In *Data Engineering (ICDE), 2012 IEEE 28th International Conference on* (pp. 618-629). IEEE.

Kolb, L., Thor, A., & Rahm, E. (2012). *Don't match twice: redundancy-free similarity computation with MapReduce*. Tech. rep. http://dbs. uni-leipzig. de/de/publication/redfree

Köpcke, H., & Rahm, E. (2010). Frameworks for entity matching: A comparison. *Data & Knowledge Engineering, 69*(2), 197–210. doi:10.1016/j.datak.2009.10.003

Menestrina, D., Benjelloun, O., & Garcia-Molina, H. (2005). Generic entity resolution with data confidences.

Menestrina, D., Whang, S. E., & Garcia-Molina, H. (2010). Evaluating entity resolution results. *Proceedings of the VLDB Endowment, 3*(1-2), 208–219.

Omar, B., Hector, G. M., Hideki, K., Tait, L., David, M., & Sutthipong, T. (2006). *D-swoosh: A family of algorithms for generic, distributed entity resolution*. Technical Report, Stanford InfoLab.

Papadakis, G., Ioannou, E., Niederée, C., Palpanas, T., & Nejdl, W. (2012). Beyond 100 million entities: large-scale blocking-based resolution for heterogeneous data. In *Proceedings of the fifth ACM international conference on Web search and data mining* (pp. 53-62). ACM.

Papadakis, G., & Nejdl, W. (2011). Efficient entity resolution methods for heterogeneous information spaces. In *Data Engineering Workshops (ICDEW), 2011 IEEE 27th International Conference on* (pp. 304-307). IEEE.

Shu, L., Chen, A., Xiong, M., & Meng, W. (2011). Efficient spectral neighborhood blocking for entity resolution. In *Data Engineering (ICDE), 2011 IEEE 27th International Conference on* (pp. 1067-1078). IEEE.

Shu, L., Long, B., & Meng, W. (2009). A latent topic model for complete entity resolution. In *Data Engineering, 2009. ICDE'09. IEEE 25th International Conference on* (pp. 880-891). IEEE.

Wang, J., Kraska, T., Franklin, M. J., & Feng, J. (2012). Crowder: Crowdsourcing entity resolution. *Proceedings of the VLDB Endowment, 5*(11), 1483–1494.

Whang, S., Marmaros, D., & Garcia-Molina, H. (2012). Pay-as-you-go entity resolution.

Whang, S. E., & Garcia-Molina, H. (2010). Entity resolution with evolving rules. *Proceedings of the VLDB Endowment, 3*(1-2), 1326–1337.

Whang, S. E., & Garcia-Molina, H. (2012, April). Joint entity resolution. In *Data Engineering (ICDE), 2012 IEEE 28th International Conference on* (pp. 294-305). IEEE.

Whang, S. E., Lofgren, P., & Garcia-Molina, H. (2013). Question selection for crowd entity resolution.

Whang, S. E., Menestrina, D., Koutrika, G., Theobald, M., & Garcia-Molina, H. (2009). Entity resolution with iterative blocking. In *Proceedings of the 35th SIGMOD international conference on Management of data* (pp. 219-232). ACM.

KEY TERMS AND DEFINITIONS

Cloud Computing: Cloud computing is the use of computing resources (hardware and software) that are delivered as a service over a network (typically the Internet).

Entity Resolution: Entity resolution refers to the task of finding records in a data set that refer to the same entity across different data sources.

MapReduce: MapReduce is a programming model for processing large data sets, typically used to do distributed computing on clusters of computers.

Wave of Strings: A wave of strings consists of different substrings of a record, showing both frequency and content information.

Section 3
Database Techniques and Entity Resolution

Chapter 11
Basic Data Operators for Entity Resolution

ABSTRACT

This chapter focuses on the basic data operators for entity resolution, which include similarity search, similarity join, and clustering on sets or strings. These three problems are of increasing complexity, and the solution of simpler problems is the building blocks for the harder problem. The authors first introduce the solution of similarity search, covering gram-based algorithms and sketch-based algorithms. Then the chapter turns to the solution of similarity join, covering both exact and approximate algorithms. At last, the authors deal with the problem of clustering similar strings in a set, which can be applied to duplicate detection in databases.

INTRODUCTION

As discussed in previous chapters, entity resolution has many models. Most of entity resolution methods focus on the effectiveness of entity resolution on various data types. With the increasing of data size, efficiency is another issue that is noticed by the literature. To perform entity resolution on big data, many algorithms have been developed. However, most of these algorithms are memory-based algorithms without efficiency assurance. To solve the efficiency problem, some methods have been proposed in database literature.

To solve the problem in the aspect of database, some operators for entity resolution are extracted and efficient algorithms are designed for these operators. With efficient implemented operators, entity resolution could be performed efficiently.

Since entity resolution is to identify different representations for the same real-world entity. With the consideration of errors in data, to identify different representations, one basic operator is to find descriptions that are similar to a given description and the other operator is to find pairs of similar descriptions. The first one is defined as similarity search and the second is defined as similarity join. This chapter focuses these two basic operators. We use an example to illustrate these two operators. Consider a query "stick" on a set $S=\{$stuck, schick, trick, chunk$\}$ with threshold=1, the result is "stuck" since the edit distance between "stick" and "stuck" is 1 while larger than 1 with other strings. For similarity self-join with threshold 2 on the set S is {(stuck, trick)} since the threshold of these two strings is equal or smaller than 2.

DOI: 10.4018/978-1-4666-5198-2.ch011

As the base of the similarity search and similarity join, similarity function should be defined at first for different data type. For numerical data types, the similarity search and similarity join can be performed directly with SQL language on database. For example, consider a relation R with numerical attribute A. For the similarity search on A with query value v and the threshold r, the query is "select A from R where $A<=v+r$ AND $A>=v-r$"

For complex data types such as string and set, things are more complex since the similarity comparison process could not be described as SQL expression and thus hardly performed with database engine. As a result, researchers show more interests in the similarity operator for complex data types. Many methods are proposed. Thus, in this chapter, we propose the algorithms for these three operators for common-used data types of string and set.

Additionally, with the result of similarity search and similarity join, the final results of group-wise entity resolution require clustering with the result. Thus clustering is another important operator for entity resolution.

SIMILARITY SEARCH

The goal of similarity search is to find similar strings for a given query string. As the readers might have noticed, this problem exists ubiquitously entity resolution, and solution of this problem serves as a powerful weapon for tackling more complicated problems, such as similarity join and clustering.

Problem Formulation and Related Definitions

Find strings similar to a given string: dist (Q, D) $<= \delta$

Example: Find strings similar to "hadjeleftheriou"

Similarity Measures and Distances (Xiao, Wang, Lin, Yu & Wang, 2011)

- Jaccard Similarity is defined as
$$J(x,y) = \frac{|x \cap y|}{|x \cup y|}$$
- Cosine similarity is defined as
$$C(x,y) = \frac{\vec{x} \cdot \vec{y}}{\|\vec{x}\| \cdot \|\vec{y}\|}$$
- Overlap similarity is defined as
$$O(x,y) = |x \cap y|$$
- Hamming distance between x and y is defined as the size of their symmetric difference: $H(x,y) = |(x-y) \cap (y-x)|$
- Edit distance, also known as Levenshtein distance, measures the minimum number of edit operations needed to make two strings identical.

$$H(x,y) = |(x-y) \cap (y-x)|$$

Q-Gram

Let Σ be an alphabet. For a string s of the characters in Σ, we use "|s|" to denote the length of s, "s[i]" to denote the i-th character of s (starting from 1), and "s[i, j]" to denote the substring from its i-th character to its j-th character.

We define q continues characters as q-gram. Formally, given a string s and a positive integer q, a positional q-gram of s is a pair (i, g), where g is the q-gram of s starting at the i-th character, i.e., g = s[i, i + q - 1]. The set of positional q-grams of s, denoted by G(s, q), is obtained by sliding a window of length q over the characters of string s. There are |s| - q + 1 positional q-grams in G(s, q). For instance, suppose q = 3, and s = university, then G(s, q) = {(1, uni), (2, niv), (3, ive), (4, ver), (5, ers), (6, rsi), (7, sit), (8, ity)}. This example is illustrated in Figure 1.

Since for q-gram, k operations could affect $k * q$ grams, if ed(s_1, s_2) <= k, then their number of common grams >= $(|s_1| - q + 1) - k * q$. With this

Figure 1. An example for q-gram

property, we could process similarity search on string set efficiently.

To process similarity search, we organize the q-grams with corresponding string id with an inverted list. For example, let the target collection *D* be {"rich", "stick", "stich", "stuck", "static"} and query string *Q* be "shtick". First we should construct inverted index from the target collection *D* as shown in Figure 2.

To illustrate the processing, we use a query of "shtick" and require ed(shtick, ?)$\leq$1. If ed(shtick, s) <= 1, then their number of common grams >= (6 − 2 + 1) − 1 * 2=3. So, their number of common grams should be equal to or more than 3. At first, the grams of "shtick" are generated as "sh", "ht", "ti", "ic" and "ck".

We can see that "sh" and "ht" are not in the inverted index. Gram "ch" is in string 1 and 3. "ic" is in string 0, 1, 2 and 4. "ti" is in string 1, 2 and 4. Only string 1 contains three grams which are also in the query string. So, the edit distance between string 1, i.e. "stick", and query string "shtick" is smaller than 1.

The standard q-gram algorithm is quite straight forward. At the same time, it also leaves much opportunity for optimization. There are generally three directions of optimization. One is tackling the process of finding the id of strings which appear more times than the threshold number, which results in several list-merging algorithms. Another direction is optimizing the length of grams, like VGRAM [?]. The third direction is optimizing the storing structure of target collection D, and at the same time one can take advantage of the structure for special purposes, like the trie-based algorithm for incremental-search.

From the example, a basic operation is to choose the number of ids that exists in more than T ordered lists. Then, we propose the algorithms to implement this operation efficiently.

List-Merging (Sarawagi & Kirpal, 2004)

The topic of this section is the T-occurrence of problem. That's given n sorted lists with ascending order, find elements whose occurrence in the lists is larger than T times. This problem is shown in Figure 3

Let n_w denote the number of records containing word w and t denote the average number of words per record. In the remaining part of this section, we discuss various solution of this problem.

Figure 2. An example for organizing q-gram with inverted index

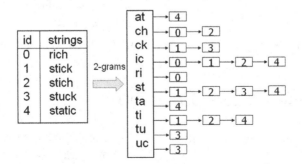

Figure 3. Find elements whose occurrences ≥ T

Merge

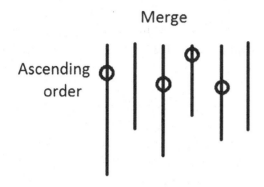

Ascending order

Heap-Merger (Probe-Count) (Sarawagi & Kirpal, 2004)

The established method of doing the merge is to insert the frontier of the sorted lists in a heap. Then repeatedly find the minimum and accumulate its weight if successive minimum values are the same.

When solving the T-occurrence problem, one naïve solution is that for each possible RID, traverse the n lists to find the number of occurrences, this solution requires $O(t * \text{sum over w } n_w)$ comparisons. One common improvement is that we can sort by ascending order the RIDs in each list. Then we can use a min heap to maintain the frontiers of each list. The detailed operations are as follows:

1. Sort each list by ascending order (note that the key used by comparison is RID);
2. Construct a min heap with the frontiers of each list, resulting in a heap of n elements (as the algorithm goes on, the heap might be smaller, because some lists might go out of elements)
3. Pop the min RID of the heap. Accumulate its weight if successive pop RIDs are the same.
4. Push the frontier of the list associated with the popped RID into the heap.
5. Repeat until there is nothing in the lists and pop remaining elements in the heap.

The trick is in step 3. It is true that all occurrences of an element are popped in a row, so we only need to count the occurrence of the current element. Since we have sorted the lists, it is impossible that a RID smaller than the heap top is anywhere in the heap or the lists, it must have been popped. And yet we can assure, by the property of heap, that the RIDs which are the same would be popped in a row, all other RIDs are larger than them, so they would remain in the heap until the smallest RIDs are all popped. It is also impossible that there is any RID smaller than the heap top is stuck in the lists, because there is at most one element of each list in the heap, and the one in the list is the smallest in that list.

MergeOPT (Sarawagi & Kirpal, 2004)

Beyond the basic scheme of heap-merger, (Sarawagi & Kirpal, 2004) proposed mergeOPT algorithm that exploits the threshold T. The idea originates from the stop words (words with very high frequency) trick of IR community. The stop words are associated with a few large lists, which take a lot of time when merging. We can exploit by marking the top T-1 highest frequency words as stop words and reducing the threshold for a record T by the number of stop words that it contains.

The mergeOPT algorithm adopts a more gradual method of exploiting the threshold parameter T. Given a set of lists to be merged, first sort the lists in an increasing order of size. Scanning from the large end, then select the largest set L of lists with total weight less than T. Let the remaining lists be S. A record that satisfies the threshold condition must appear in at least one of the lists in S. We therefore use the heap data structure to merge only the lists in S instead of all the lists. The advantage is that we do not waste time processing records that appear only in the lists in L. For each record returned during the merge, we perform a doubling binary search over each list in L in increasing order of size to accumulate the true match count. During this search within L, after each failed search, we check if the remaining lists are sufficient to meet the threshold condition for the current minimum record even if the record were to appear in all of them. If not, we terminate the search early and repeat for the next minimum record from the heap.

The sketch of the algorithm is shown below.

Algorithm 1 MergeOpt (r, T, I):

1. Let $A = l_1, l_2, \ldots l_t$ be the record lists of index I in decreasing order of length corresponding to t words $w_1 \ldots w_t$ of r
2. Computing cumulative $Wt\left(l_i\right) = \Sigma_{j=1}^{i}$ weight(w_j)
3. $L = l_1, l_2, \ldots, l_k$ such that k is the largest index for which cumulativeWt(l_k) < T
4. Insert frontiers of lists $S = A - L$ in a heap H.
5. **While** H not empty **do**
6. pop from H current minimum record m along with total weight m.w of all lists in H where m appears
7. push in H next records from lists in S that popped.
8. **For** $i = k$ down to 1 **do**
9. if (m.w + cumulativeWt(l_i) using a doubling binary search method, and if found,
10. increment m.w with weight(word(l_i)).

Scan Count Merge-Skip Divide-Skip

Scan Count (Li, Lu, & Lu 2008)

This algorithm is shown in Algorithim 2. It adapts the naïve idea of directly counting the occurrences of RIDs (record id) to real world. The main feature of this algorithm is that it uses an array of |S| counters to record the occurrences of each RID, so one pass counting is enough. Though this algorithm is simple, it can still achieve high performance when combined with some optimization, see (Li, Lu & Lu, 2008) for details.

Algorithm 2 Scan-Count:

Input: Set of RID lists and a threshold T:

Output: Record ids that appear at least T times on the lists.

1. Initialize the array C of |S| counters to 0's;
2. Initialize a result set R to be empty;
3. **FOR** (each record id r on each given list) {
4. Increment the value of C[r] by 1;
5. **IF** (C[r] == T)
6. Add r to R;
7. }
8. **RETURN** R;

Merge-Skip (Barbay & Kenyon, 2002, Li, Lu & Lu, 2008)

Formal description of this algorithm is shown in Algorithm 3. This algorithm is based on the heap-merger algorithm. It also exploits the parameter T, but different from MergeOpt, by aggressively discarding the RIDs whose times of appearance must be smaller than the threshold T.

Algorithm 3 Merge-Skip:

Input: A set of RID lists and a threshold T;

Output: Record ids that appear at least T times on the list.

1. Insert the frontier records of the lists to a heap H;
2. Initialize a result set R to be empty;
3. While (H is not empty) {
4. Let t be the top record on the heap;
5. Pop from H those records equal to t;
6. Let n be the number of popped records;
7. If (n ≥ T) {
8. Add t to R;
9. Push next record (if any) on each popped list to H;
10. }
11. Else {

12. Pop T-1-n smallest records from H;
13. Let t' be the current top record on H;
14. For (each of the T-1 popped lists) {
15. Locate its smallest record r ≥ t' (if any);
16. Push this record to H;
17. }
18. }
19. }
20. Return R;

Divid-Skip

The main idea of DivideSkip (Li, Lu & Lu 2008) is to combine MergeSkip and MergeOpt. It can be seen that both of the two algorithms try to skip irrelevant records on the lists, but using different strategies. DivideSkip uses the strategy of MergeOpt to divide the lists into long lists and short lists, and uses the strategy of MergeSkip to improve the merging process of short lists, rather than simply using heap merger algorithm. One important feature of DivideSkip is that L, the number of long lists, is a tunable parameter. While for MergeOpt, L is fixed to be T-1 assuming the weight of each list is set to 1. The tunable feature of DivideSkip creates chance for optimization, similar scenario can be found when discussing VGRAM algorithm.

Algorithm 4 Divid-Skip:

Input: Set of RID lists and a threshold T;
Output: Record ids that appear at least T times on the lists.

1. Initialize a result set R to be empty;
2. Let L_{long} be the set of L longest lists among the lists;
3. Let L_{long} be the remaining short lists;
4. Use MergeSkip on L_{short} to find ids that appear at least T-L times;
5. For (each record r found) {
6. For (each list in L_{long})
7. Check if r appears on this list;

8. If (r appears ≥ T times among all lists)
9. Add r to R;
10. }
11. Return R;

VGRAM

The methods discussed before suppose the length of q-gram is fixed. To improve the performance of gram-based algorithm, VGRAM is proposes with grams in variable length.

Before actually introducing VGRAM (Li, Wang & Yang, 2007), we have a glance at the Dilemma of Choosing Gram Length, which is the direct driving force for the advent of VGRAM. This dilemma means that when we use small gram length, the size of lists in the inverted-list based algorithms will increase and it would take more time to merge the lists. The advantage of smaller gram length is that the number of common grams required by the filtering process would be larger, which leads to more effective filtering. When using bigger gram length, the inverted lists would be shorter which reduces merging time. At the same time, the filtering would be less efficient, which allows more false positives to pass the count filtering, causing more time to compute their real edit distances (a costly computation) in order to verify if they are in the answer to the query.

Now we turn our attention to VGRAM, it is a novel technique for improving the performance of approximate string matching algorithms. Its main idea is to judiciously choose high-quality grams of variable lengths from a collection of strings to support queries on the collection. The basic steps are selecting high-quality grams from the collection, generating variable-length grams for a string based on the preselected grams and deciding which strings are in the range of desired edit distance. One primary advantage of the VGRAM is that it can be adopted by a plethora of algorithms without the need to modify them substantially. It has also been shown by experiments that, by applying VGRAM, the improvements on existing algorithm are significant.

To implement the idea VGAM, there are several challenges which can also be served as the steps of the implementation. We will deal with them one by one.

Challenge 1: Generating Variable-Length Grams

The algorithm for generating variable-length gram is formally described in Algorithm 5. In this algorithm the gram dictionary D is given as an input variable, the construction of such a dictionary will be discussed in the next step. In step (5), (p,t) is subsumed by (p',t') means that t is a substring of t'.

Algorithm 5: VGEN

Input: Gram dictionary D, string s, bounds q_{min}, q_{max}

Output: The variable length graph VG

1.   Position p=1; VG=empty set;
2.   While (p $\leq$|s|-q_{min} + 1) {
3.   Find a longest gram in D using the trie to match a substring t of s starting at position p;
4.   If (t is not found) t=s[p, p+q_{min}-1];
5.   If (positional gram (p,t) is not subsumed by any positional gram in VG;
6.   Insert(p, t) to VG;
7.   p=p+1;
8.   }
9.   Return VG;

Let's illustrate this algorithm by an example. Consider a string s=universal and a gram dictionary D = {ni, ivr, sal, uni, vers}. Let q_{min} be 2 and q_{max} be 4. By setting p = 1 and G = {}, the algorithm starts at the first character u. The longest substring starting at u that appears in D is uni. Thus the algorithm produces a positional gram

(1, uni) and inserts it to VG. Then the algorithm moves to the next character n, starting from this character, the longest substring that appears in D is ni. However, since this candidate positional gram (2, ni) is subsumed by the previous one, the algorithm does not insert it into VG. The algorithm moves to the next character i. There is no substring starting at this character that matches a gram in D, so the algorithm produces a positional gram (3, iv) of length q_{min} = 2. Since it is not subsumed by any positional gram in VG, the algorithm inserts it to VG. The algorithm repeats until the position is at the (|s| - q_{min} + 2)-nd character, which is the character l. The generated positional gram set is VG = {(1, uni), (3, iv), (4, vers), (7, sal)}.

Challenge 2: Constructing Gram Dictionaries

In this section, we show how to construct a high-quality gram dictionary. We assume q_{min} and q_{max} are given. We introduce a two-step algorithm to achieve the goal. The first step is to collect the gram frequencies; the second step is to select grams with a small frequency.

Step 1: Collecting Gram Frequencies

To find all q-gram frequencies within qmin and qmax, one naïve way to generating all grams within range for each string s. Then count separately for each gram. However, this algorithm is not efficient. We can improve time and space efficiency by using a trie to collect gram frequencies. Each path from the root node to a leaf node represents a gram. Observe that whenever a gram of length q_{max} is generated, this path also contains all grams which are prefix of the q_{max}-gram. So before the end of a string s, we only need to generate the q_{max}-gram from position p, and we treat the grams near the end of a string separately.

We collect gram frequencies as follows with the algorithm shown in Algorithm 6.

We store the frequencies of each gram is a frequency trie, each node n in the frequency trie has a frequency value n:freq.

Algorithm 6: Frequency Generation

1. Initialize the frequency trie to be empty.
2. **For** each string s
3. **For** p from 1 to length(s) – qmin + 1
4. Generate the positional gram (p, s[p: min(p + qmax – 1, length(s))])
5. **If** the gram does not exist
6. Insert it to the trie
7. Initialize the leaf node to be 0
8. **For** each node n on the path from the root to the leaf node for this gram
9. n.freq++
10. **If** qmin <= length(root, n) && length(root,n) < qmax
11. **If** there is no leaf node of n with the special endmarker symbol #
12. Create a leaf node by appending an edge with the special enmarker symbol #

Step 2: Selecting High-Quality Grams

The intuition of the pruning process is as follows. (1) Keep short grams if possible: If a gram g has a low frequency, we eliminate all the extended grams of g from the trie. (2) If a gram is very frequent, keep some of its extended grams. As a simple example, consider a gram ab. If its frequency is low, then we will keep it in the gram dictionary. If its frequency is very high, we will consider keeping this gram and its extended grams, such as aba, abb, abc, etc. The goal is that, by keeping these extended grams in the dictionary, the number of strings that generate an ab gram by the VGEN algorithm could become smaller, since they may generate the extended grams instead of ab.

Algorithm 7: Function Prune (Node n, Threshold T)

1. **If** each child of n is not a leaf node
2. // the root →n path is shorter than q_{min}
3. **for** (each child c of n
4. CALL Prune(c, T)
5. Return; // a gram corresponds to the leaf-node child of n
6. L = the (only) leaf-node child of n;
7. **If** n.freq ≤ T
8. Keep L, and remove other children of n;
9. L.frep = n.freq;
10. Else
11. Select a maximal subset of children of n (excluding L), so that the summation of their freq values and L.freq is still not greater that T;
12. Add the freq values of these children to that of L, and remove these children from n;
13. For (each remaining child c of n excludeing L)
14. CALL Prune(c, T);

Challenge 3: Edit Operation's Effect on Grams

The third challenge is to make clear the relationship between the similarity of two strings and the similarity of their gram sets generated using the same gram dictionary. We have shown the relationship for fixed length gram in earlier sections. Now we will deal with the case of variable length gram. Suppose we have a given gram dictionary D, two gram length parameter q_{min} and q_{max}. For two strings s1 and s2, we have the positional gram sets VG (s1) and VG (s2) based on the given parameters.

We then separate the grams into two categories. One is the preserved positional gram. For each character s1[i] ins s1 that is aligned with a character s2[j] in s2, if there is positional gram (i, g) in VG(s1), and there is a positional gram (j, g) in VG(s2), such that |i-j| <= ed(s, s'), we call (i, g) a preserved positional gram. The other category of positional grams is called affected positional gram. To achieve the goal of this section, the key is to find the number of preserved positional grams.

First, we analyze the effect of a deletion on i-th character of s. Consider the following window [a, b] including the character s[i], where a = max $\{1, i - q_{max} + 1\}$, and b = min $\{|s|, i + q_{max} - 1\}$. The effect of the deletion on each positional gram (p,g) can be summarized into 4 categories, based on the relative position between the window and the gram.

Category 1: If the positional gram is not contained in the window, i.e., $p < i - q_{max} + 1$ or $p + |g| - 1 > i + qmax - 1$, this deletion does not affect the positional gram.

Category 2: If the positional gram overlaps with the character, it could be affected by the deletion.

Category 3: Consider a positional gram (p, g) on the left of the i-th character, and contained in the window [a, i-1]. These positional grams could be potentially affected due to the deletion. To find out which positional grams could be affected, we use the algorithm described in Algorithm 8.

Algorithm 8: Find_Positional_Gram

1. For j from a to i-qmin+1
2. If s[j, i-1] is a prefix of a gram g' in the dictionary D
3. mark all the positional grams contained in the interval [j, i-1] to be potentially affected
4. Break
5. End If
6. End For

Category 4: This category is symmetric to Category 3. We consider the positional grams in window [i+1, b]. To find which grams are affected. We use the algorithm described in Algorithm 9.

Algorithm 9: Find_affected_Gram

1. For j from b to i+qmin-1
2. If s[i+1, j] is a suffix of a gram g' in the dictionary D
3. mark all the positional grams contained in the interval [i+1, j] to be potentially affected
4. Break
5. End If
6. End For

Note the operation of finding if s[i+1, j] is a suffix of a gram g'. This test could be done efficiently with the support of a reversed-gram trie, which is part of the VGRAM index.

NAG Vectors

In this section, we introduce the key concept *vector of affected grams* ("NAG vector" for short). For a give string s and *VG*(s), this vector is precomputed and stores an upper bound of affected number of grams for each possible k value. The NAG vector for a string s is denoted by *NAG(s, k)*. The *k*-th number in the vector is denoted by NAG(s, k). Given integer k and string s, for each of |s| characters and |s|+1 gaps in *s*, we calculate the set of positional grams that could be affected due to an edit operation at that position. For these $2|s|+1$ numbers, we take the k largest numbers, and use their summation as *NAG(s, k)*.

Then we arrive at our destination, we use the follow lemma to compute the similarity of the variable-gram sets of two similar strings.

LEMMA 1: For a string s_i, let VG (s_i) and NAG (s_i) be the corresponding set of variable-length positional grams and NAG vector of s_i, respectively. Suppose two string s_1 and s_2 have $ed(s_1, s_2) <= k$.

The following is a lower bound on the number of common grams (ignoring positional information) between $VG(s_1)$ and $VG(s_2)$ (using the same gram dictionary).

$$\max (|VG(s_1)|\text{-}NAG(s_1,k), |VG(s_2)|\text{-}NAG(s_2,k))$$

The following is an upper bound on the hamming distance between the bit vectors (ignoring positional information) corresponding to $VG(s_1)$ and $VG(s_2)$ (using the same gram dictionary):

$$NAG(s_1,k)+ NAG(s_2,k)$$

Implementation Issues

The idea of VGRAM is quite intuitive, but it is not easy to implement. The basic steps are constructing a high-quality dictionary, generating variable length gram of string s using the dictionary, compute the NAG vectors for the strings to be compared and use NAG vectors to compute string similarity. By using VGRAM technique, the performance of existing algorithms can be improved significantly and the reader can refer to (Li, Wang & Yang, 2007) for detailed benchmarking.

Besides VGram, several other strategies are proposed to accelerate similarity join. Then we discuss these strategies.

Gram Signature Algorithms

When executing selection queries, it is inefficient to compare the query string to every string in the data set. We can use an approximate representation of the string, a sketch, to filter out those strings which are surely not in the answer. A sketch should have a size much smaller than the string, and it must be able to be used as an upper bound similarity (or lower bound the distance). To perform filtering, we first compute the sketch of query string s, denoted as sig(s). Then for each candidate t, if the similarity between sig(s) and sig(t) is lower than θ, we can prune t safely. It should be noticed that the similarity between sketches are much easier to compute than the similarity between actual strings. Different algorithms use different sketches and we will cover prefix filter and minhash.

Prefix Filtering

Let string s be a set of q-grams, sketch for prefix filtering is constructed by first sorting the grams by some order and taking its prefix. For example, if we have $s = \{q_4, q_1, q_2, q_7\}$, we first sort it by lexicographical order. We get $s = \{q_1, q_2, q_4, q_7\}$ and the prefix sketch is $sig(s) = \{q_1, q_2\}$. So how is the length, i.e. $|sig(s)|$, determined? Basically, the rule we use to do filtering is that if $|s \cap t| \geq \theta$ then $\forall (t' \subset t$ and $|t'| \geq |s|\text{-}\theta+1)$ $t' \cap s \neq \varnothing$, where t' is the sketch. If we want there are at least 3 common grams for query string s and candidate string t, we need $|t'| \geq |s|\text{-}\theta+1=4\text{-}3+1=2$. That's why sig(s) should be the first two grams.

Next we show a more concrete example. Suppose we have string s and t.

$$s = \{q_1, q_2, q_4, q_6, q_8, q_9, q_{10}, q_{12}\}.$$

$$t = \{q_1, q_2, q_5, q_6, q_8, q_{10}, q_{12}, q_{14}\}$$

If we want $|s \cap t| \geq \theta = 6$ then it must be true that $\forall (t' \subset t$ and $|t'| \geq 3)$ $t' \cap s \neq \varnothing$. It is easy to observe this fact from the diagram. In worse case, we can choose q_5, q_{14} from t and we cannot find the third gram which is in t but not in s. We can avoid taking a subset of t by sorting and taking prefixes from both s and t: $pf(s)=\{q_1, q_2, q_4\}$, $pf(t)= \{q_1, q_2, q_5\}$ then if $|s \cap t| \geq 6$ then $pf(s) \cap pf(t) \neq \varnothing$. Why prefix filtering works? Because when $pf(s) \cap pf(t) = \varnothing$, we are left with at most 5 grams in common between s and t, but we need at least 6 grams.

Prefix sketch provides a loose bound, which results in a large number of candidates. But it is easy to construct and compare, it is worth a try when strings are long.

Minhash

In prefix filtering, we use sorting to help pruning. We can also use hashing as in minhash. Minhash is a scheme used to estimate the similarity of two sets. Basically, we use minhash to estimate the Jaccard similarity between two strings. Give a string $s = \{q_1, ..., q_m\}$. Use k functions $h_1, ..., h_k$ from independent family of hash functions, which are defined as, $h_i: q \rightarrow [0, 1]$. Hash s by each of the k hash functions, and keep the k q-grams which have the smallest hash-value for a specific hash function. The set of the minimum values is sig(s). Given two sketches sig(s) and sig(t), the percentage of matched values is an estimation of Jaccard(s, t).

SIMILARITY JOIN

In this section, we discuss similarity join.

Problem Definition and Classification

Given two sets of objects R and S, a similarity function sim(r, s) and a threshold t, we need to find all pairs of objects $r \in R$, $s \in S$, such that $sim(r, s) \geq t$. Alternatively, we can find the pairs within certain distance ε. There are many existing ideas and techniques for solving this this problem. Both exact and approximate approaches are used.

Exact Similarity Join in Euclidean Space: ORE/MSJ/GESS

The representative algorithms picked for this section are Orenstein's algorithm (Orenstein 1991), Multidimensional Spatial Join (MSJ) (Koudas & Sevcik, 1998), Generic External Space Sweep

(GESS) (Dittrich & Seeger, 2001). These are exact algorithms for solving similarity join in Euclidean Space.

Orenstein's algorithm, latter referred as ORE, can be treated as this origin of the serials of algorithms. ORE is relatively simple and at the same time provides a clear view of the framework. But ORE is actually dealing with a problem which is a little different from ours. ORE solves the problem of computing the overlay of two arbitrary shapes in k-dimensional space. In similarity join, we represent the objects in R and S as hypercube, which has a side length of ε and with the object point at its center.

Basically, the steps of these algorithms are shown in Algorithm 10.

Algorithm 10: Framework of Orenstein Algorithm

1. Assign a code to each of the objects in R and S;
2. Sort the objects according to code order, typically lexicographical order;
3. Merge objects using Orenstein's Merge Algorithm, at the same time generate candidates;
4. Refine the results obtained by step 3.

Figure 4. Hilbert curve

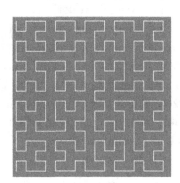

Encoding

Different approaches in step 1 can result in different algorithms. Space filling curve or space splitting can be utilized to encode the objects. For example, Hilbert curve is a space filling curve as shown in Figure 4. As the order of Hilbert curve increase, it can split the space into finer grains. We can calculate for an object the so-called Hilbert value, which is the number of line segments from the origin to a corner on the curve. The value can be calculated for different orders of Hilbert value and the sequence of those values can be used as the code of the objects.

Space splitting is another technique for encoding. This approach is quite intuitive as demonstrated in Figure 5. In this example, a space is recursively split into four sub-spaces, numbered from 0 to 3. The code of an object is derived by concatenating the space number it lies in.

As intuitive as it is, there are two details people are not agreed upon. One is how many pieces a space should be split into for one time. ORE adopts a binary splitting strategy, which results in binary string for encoding object, e.g. 10101. Latter researchers adopt a 2^d splitting strategy, where d is the dimension of the object. Then the code for an object should also change accordingly.

Another issue is how to deal with replication encountered during splitting. That is when an

object hypercube is standing on the boundary of subspaces, how should we encode this object? One approach is to allow replication. We give several codes for the same objects and eliminate duplicate results in the refining steps. Another approach is forbidding replication. When an object is standing on the boundary, its code will not grow longer and thus has limited resolution.

Now, we can see that the example above adopts a 2^2 splitting strategy for a two-dimensional space and forbids replication. Sorting the codes is straight forward. If the codes are strings, we can use lexicographical order, e.g. 10<101. Sorting is applied to R and S respectively.

Orenstein's Merge Algorithm

Orenstein's Merge Algorithm is an important innovation of ORE. The algorithm is a heuristic. The original version is described below and the version adapted for similarity join is in Algorithm 10.

Algorithm 11: Original Orenstein's Merge Algorithm

1. g = input stream of ordered codes
2. stack = empty // stack of codes
3. while g.has_next()
4. if stack is not empty and top code doesn't contain g.code()
5. generate_candidates();
6. stack.pop() until stack.isempty() or statck.top() contains g.code();
7. push g.code() onto stack.;
8. generate_candidates();

The original version does that push codes onto a stack, pop codes as a group when the nested property does not hold and meanwhile generate them as candidates. In ORE, candidates are a group of shapes. However, in similarity join, a candidate is a pair of objects. The nested property is used to filter out the pairs of objects which are impossible to be in the result set. The key for

Figure 5. An example for space splitting

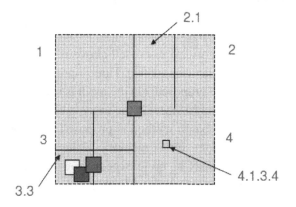

Figure 6. An ORE's example

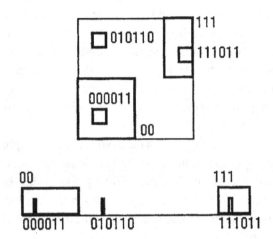

maintaining nested property is the *contain* test. When the codes are strings, if code s is a prefix of code t, we say that s *contains* t. It is most appropriated to illustrate the idea by ORE's example, see Figure 6. Every code derived by ORE's binary splitting strategy can be seen as a rectangle. Take 00 and 000011 for example, the space encoded by 000011 is contained by the space encoded by 00 and 00 is a prefix of 000011. The code is a 1D representation of the 2D space.

Algorithm 12: Orenstein's Merge Algorithm

1. While(both sorted streams are not empty) {
2. Choose minial hypercude H(x) from the streams;
3. Ensure prefix-property for Stack_R and Stack_S;
4. If(H(x) is hypercude of R) {
5. Stack_S.query(H(x));
6. Stack_R.insert(H(x));
7. }
8. Else { //H(x) is hypercude of S
9. Stack_R.query(H(x));
10. Stack_S.insert(H(x));
11. }
12. }

We can easily adapt the merge algorithm for similarity join. The two streams are sorted respectively. For each time, we choose the minimal hypercube from either of the streams, which can ensure that the picked hypercube must be no smaller than previously chosen ones. In step 3, ensure prfix-property for Stack_R and Stack_S means the poping step for the original algorithm. We use the chosen hypercube to test angainst Stack_R and Stack_S. After that, if the chosen hypercube is from R, then use this hypercude to query all elements in Stack_S. It means we generate a candidate for each element in Stack_S with the hypercube from R. Last we push the hypercube onto Stack_R. If the hypercube is from S, it is performed vise versa.

The refinement step can be implemented by brute force. However, various technique can also be applied to improve performace. We can use hashing to cache candidates. Sarawagi, S., & Kirpal, A. (2004) also proposed an on-line algorithm called Reference Point Method(RPM) to refine the results.

Similarity Join on Sets and Strings

Similarity join on between the attribute with type sets or strings depends on the similarity functions. Since the edit distance between strings could be bounded with the Jaccard similarity on the set of corresponding q-gram sets. Therefore, we discuss set similarity join algorithm.

The basic algorithm is Probe-Count-Opt algorithm (Sarawagi & Kirpal, 2004). This algorithm build index on candidates and perform nested-loop join the candidates. For each tuple, list merge with threshold algorithm discussed above is invoked to find similar candidates. Three optimization strategies are proposed: (1) the input is sorted by increasing record size; (2) the input is clustered; (3) partition-based method is proposed to adapt the method for external memory. In this method, verification may be quite expensive with many generated unnecessary candidates.

Prefix filtering strategy is to establish an upper bound of the overlap between two set based on a part of them with a global order defined on elements in all sets. For example, for two sorted sets $S_1=\{1,3,5,7,9\}$ and $S_2=\{2,4,6,8,10\}$, the prefixes of these two sets with length $=2$ share no elements. As a result, just from the prefix, it can be judged that the overlapping of these two set must be smaller than 3. Formally, we denote the $|U|-(t-1)$ prefix of a set U is $prefix_t(U)$. $Prefix_t(U) \cap Prefix_t(V)=\varnothing \Rightarrow overlap(U, V)<t$. It means that (U, V) can be safely pruned.

With this idea, the similarity join could be performed on a RDBMS. The algorithm has three phrases. The first phrase computes the prefix for each set; the second phrase generates the candidate pairs and the third phrase verifies the candidates. Only in the third phrase, original records are accessed for verification. This framework is firstly proposed as SSJoin (Chaudhuri, Ganti & Kaushik, 2006).

An algorithm improving SSJoin in this framework is All-Pairs (Bayardo, Ma, Y., & Srikant, R. 2007). This algorithm use prefix-filtering in an asymmetric way. The pseudo code is shown in Algorithm 12, where the function Verity(x, S) is to output the pair (x, s_i) with $s_i \in S$ and overlap $(x, s_i) \geq t$.

Algorithm 13: All-Pairs

for each $S_j \in S$ in increasing size
Candidates = $\varnothing$
prefix-len = calc_probing_prefix_len()
for i=1 to prefix-len
w = $S_j[i]$
for each $S_k \in$ Inverted-list(w) & len-filter
Candidates = Candidates$\cup S_k$
If i < calc_indexing_prefix_len() do
Inverted-list(w) = Inverted-list(w) $\cup S_j$
Verify(S_j, Candidates)

PPJoin (Xiao, C., Wang, W., Lin, X., Yu, J. X., & Wang, G. 2011) improves All-Pairs to optimize the algorithm for Jaccard/cosine similarity constraints. The algorithm has following two strategies by recording the positions of the tokens in the prefix:

1. Derive an upper bound of the overlap based on position information in the prefixes;
2. Apply multiple probes in a divide-and-conquer manner to accelerate the stopping.

With the strategy, PPJoin generates less candidates and the cost of verification is less. The pseudo code of PPJoin is shown in Algorithm 14.

Algorithm 14: PPJoin(R,t)

Input: R is a multiset of records sorted by the increasing order of their sizes;

Each record has been canonicalized by a global ordering O;

A Jaccard similarity threshold t

Output: All pairs of records <x,y>, such that $sim(x,y) \geq t$

1. $S \leftarrow \varnothing$;
2. $I_i \leftarrow \varnothing$ $(1 \leq i \leq |U|)$;
3. **for** each $x \in R$ **do**
4. $A \leftarrow$ empty map from record id to int;
   $p \leftarrow |x| - \lceil t \cdot |x| \rceil + 1$;
5. **for** i = 1 to p **do**
6. $w \leftarrow x[i]$;
   for each $(y,j) \in I_w$ such that $|y| \geq t \cdot |x|$ **do**
7. $\alpha \leftarrow \left\lceil \dfrac{t}{1+t}(|x|+|y|) \right\rceil$;
8. ubound $\leftarrow$ 1 + min(|x|-i, |y|-j);
9. **if** A[y]+ubound$\geq\alpha$**then**
10. A[y] $\leftarrow$ A[y] + 1;
11. **else**
12. A[y] $\leftarrow$ 0 ;
13. $I_w \leftarrow I_w \cup \{(x,i)\}$;
14. Verify(x,A,α);
15. **return** S

CLUSTERING

The definition of clustering algorithm is shown as below.

Given a set S of data objects, parititon S into a set of clusters C_1, C_2, ..., C_n, such that the data objects in each cluster are similar.

Since clustering is a research area of data mining, many techniques are proposed in this problem (Xu & Wunsch, 2005). However, most of them are not suitable for entity resolution since they require Eular distance between objects (Han & Kamber, 2000), they are not suitable of the feature of entity resolution with many small clusters (Hassanzadeh, Chiang, Miller & Lee, 2009) or the efficiency is not satisfatory for clustering on large data set. In this section, we focus on the clustering algorithm for entity resolution.

Partitioning

An intuitive solution is to model the similarity join results L as a graph with each node as a data object and each edge as a pair in L. The clustering is to find the connected component in the graph. In this algorithm, L is scanned. When a vertex is met for the first time in L, a cluster is created. If a (u, v) is scanned with u and v belonging to different clusters, these two clusters are merged.

Algorithm 15: Partition

Input: A list L of pairs (u, v)
Output: clusters C_1, C_2, ..., C_n

H=∅
C=∅
for each (u, v) in L do
if u∈H then
if v ∈H then
merge C_u and C_v
else
add v to C_u
else

create a cluster C_u
add v to C_u
add C_u to C
return C

This algorithm may lead to large clusters with data objects that are not similar.

CENTER

The CENTER algorithm (Haveliwala, Gionis & Indyk, 2000) is some kind of greedy algorithm. A list of similar pairs as the result of similarity join is sorted by decreasing order of the similarity. The algorithm performs clustering by scanning the sorted list only once. When a node v is accessed for the first time, it is set as a center of a cluster. The following nodes that exist in any pair of v are set to be in the same cluster with v as the center. The pseudo algorithm is shown in Algorithm 16.

Algorithm 16: Center

Input: A list L of pairs (u, v)
Output: clusters C_1, C_2, ..., C_n

H=∅
C=∅

for each (u, v) in L doif u∈H thenadd v to $C_u$elsecreate a cluster $C_u$add u to Hadd C_u to Creturn C

This algorithm could generate more cluster than Partitioning but only the data objects connected to the center are included in the same cluster.

MERGECENTER

To overcome the shortcomings of CENTER, the MERGE-CENTER algorithm (Hassanzadeh & Miller, 2009) is proposed. The framework of MERGE-CENTER is the same as CENTER but merge the two clusters C_1 and C_2 with some record similar to the centers of both C_1 and C_2. The process is the similar as CENTER but the records that are clustered as recorded. The first time a node u is visited. A cluster C_u is created and u is assigned as the center. If the nodes v in pair (u, v) is not in any cluster, it is in C_u. If v has been in some cluster C_v, C_v and C_u are merged. If u and v has been assigned to cluster C_u and C_v for a scanned pair (u, v), C_u and C_v are merged. The algorithm is shown in Algorithm 17.

Algorithm 17: MERGE-CENTER

1. **Input:** A list L of pairs (u, v)
2. **Output:** clusters C_1, C_2, ..., C_n
3. H=∅
4. T=∅
5. C=∅
6. **for** each (u, v) in L **do**
7. **if** u∈H **then**
8. **if** v∈H **then**
9. merge C_v and C_u
10. else
11. add v to C_u
12. add v to H
13. else
14. **if** v∈H **then**
15. add v to C_u
16. else
17. create a cluster C_u
18. add v to C_u
19. add u to H
20. add C_u to C
21. add u to H
22. return C

From the algorithm, MERGE-CENTER creates fewer clusters than the CENTER algorithm, but more than the Partitioning algorithm.

Star Clustering Algorithm (Aslam, Pelekhov & Rus, 2004)

This algorithm models the result of similarity join in PARTITIONING. The framework is similar as CENTER but the generated cluster could be overlapping. The algorithm is shown in algorithm 18. This algorithm requires another scan of the list to compute the degree of each vertex and sort them according to the degrees. The algorithm sorts the vertices according to the degrees. When an unmarked vertex u is met, a cluster is created and u is marked. Then all nodes with edge connected to u are assigned to the cluster. The algorithm stops when all vertices are marked.

Algorithm 18: Star-Clustering

1. **Input:** A list L of pairs (u, v)
2. **Output:** Clusters C_1, C_2, ..., C_n
3. G=(V, L) is constructed with L as the edge set
4. **for** each v in G **do**
5. v is set to be unmarked
6. the degree of v is calculated as d_v
7. sort V according to the degree of vertices in it
8. H=∅
9. C=∅
10. **for** each u in V **do**
11. **if** u is unmarked
12. create a cluster C_u
13. **for** each edge (u, v)∈L **do**
14. add v to C_u
15. v is marked
16. u is marked
17. add C_u to C
18. return C

Markov Clustering Algorithm (Dongen, 2000)

Natural clusters in a graph are characterized by the presence of many edges between the members of that cluster, and one expects that the number of higher-length (longer) paths between two arbitrary nodes in the cluster is high. In particular, this number should be high, relative to node pairs lying in different natural clusters. A different angle on this is that random walks on the graph will infrequently go from one natural cluster to another.

The MCL algorithm finds cluster structure in graphs by a mathematical bootstrapping procedure. The process deterministically computes (the probabilities of) random walks through the graph, and uses two operators transforming one set of probabilities into another. It does so using the language of stochastic matrices (also called Markov matrices) which capture the mathematical concept of random walks on a graph.

The MCL algorithm simulates random walks within a graph by alternation of two operators called expansion and inflation. Expansion coincides with taking the power of a stochastic matrix using the normal matrix product (i.e. matrix squaring). Inflation corresponds with taking the Hadamard power of a matrix (taking powers entrywise), followed by a scaling step, such that the resulting matrix is stochastic again, i.e. the matrix elements (on each column) correspond to probability values.

A column stochastic matrix is a non-negative matrix with the property that each of its columns sums to 1. Given such a matrix M and a real number $r > 1$, the column stochastic matrix resulting from inflating each of the columns of M with power coefficient r is written $\Gamma_r(M)$, and Γ_r is called the inflation operator with power coefficient r. denote $\Sigma_{r,j}(M)$ as the summation of all the entries in column j of M raised to the power r (sum after taking powers). Then $\Gamma_r(M)$ is defined in an entry-wise manner by setting

$$\Gamma_r(M_{ij}) = M_{ij}^{\ r} / \Sigma_{r,j}(M)$$

Each column j of a stochastic matrix M corresponds with node j of the stochastic graph associated with M. Row entry i in column j (i.e. the matrix entry M_{ij}) corresponds with the probability of going from node j to node i. It is observed that for values of $r > 1$, inflation changes the probabilities associated with the collection of random walks departing from one particular node (corresponding with a matrix column) by favoring more probable walks over less probable walks.

Expansion corresponds to computing random walks of higher length, which means random walks with many steps. It associates new probabilities with all pairs of nodes, where one node is the point of departure and the other is the destination. Since higher length paths are more common within clusters than between different clusters, the probabilities associated with node pairs lying in the same cluster will, in general, be relatively large as there are many ways of going from one to the other. Inflation will then have the effect of boosting the probabilities of intra-cluster walks and will demote inter-cluster walks. This is achieved without any a priori knowledge of cluster structure. It is simply the result of cluster structure being present.

Eventually, iterating expansion and inflation results in the separation of the graph into different segments. There are no longer any paths between these segments and the collection of resulting segments is simply interpreted as a clustering. The inflation operator can be altered using the parameter r. Increasing this parameter has the effect of making the inflation operator stronger, and this increases the granularity or tightness of clusters.

With this, the MCL algorithm can be written as Algorithm 19.

Algorithm 19: MCL Algorithm

1. **G** is a graph
2. add loops to **G** # see below
3. set Γ to some value # affects granularity

4. set **M_1** to be the matrix of random walks on **G**
5. **while** change
6. **M_2 = M_1 * M_1** # expansion
7. **M_1 = Γ(M_2)** # inflation
8. change = difference(**M_1, M_2**)
9. set CLUSTERING as the components of **M_1** # see below

It is possible to compute change in a simpler way, directly from **M_2** and using the characteristics of the limits of the MCL process. This is beyond the scope of this introduction however.

Informally, cast in the language of stochastic flow, we can state that expansion causes flow to dissipate within clusters whereas inflation eliminates flow between different clusters. Expansion and inflation represent different tidal forces which are alternated until an equilibrium state is reached. An equilibrium state takes the form of a so-called doubly idempotent matrix, i.e. a matrix that does not change with further expansion or inflation steps. The graph associated with such a matrix consists of different connected directed components. Each component is interpreted as a cluster, and has a star-like form, with one attractor in the center and arcs going from all nodes of that component to the attractor. In theory, attractor systems with more than one attractor may occur (these do not change the cluster interpretation). Also, nodes may exist that are connected to different stars, which are canonically interpreted as cluster overlap, or in other words nodes may belong to multiple clusters.

With respect to convergence, it can be proven that the process simulated by the algorithm converges quadratically around the equilibrium states. In practice, the algorithm starts to converge noticeably after 3-10 iterations. Global convergence is very hard to prove; it is conjectured that the process always converges if the input graph is symmetric. This conjecture is supported by results concerning the matrix iterands. For symmetric input graphs, it is true that all iterands have real spectrum (the set of eigenvalues), and that all iterands resulting from expansion have non-negative spectrum and are diagonally symmetric to a positive semi-definite matrix. It can be shown that these matrices have a structural property which associates a directed acyclic graph (DAG) with each of them. It turns out that inflation strengthens (in a quantitative sense) this structural property and will never change the associated DAG, whereas expansion is in fact able to change the associated DAG. This is a more mathematical view on the tidal forces analogy mentioned earlier. DAGs generalize the star graphs associated with MCL limits, and the spectral properties of MCL iterands and MCL limits can be related via the inflation operator. These results imply that the equilibrium states can be viewed as a set of extreme points of the set of matrices that are diagonally similar to a positive semi-definite matrix. This establishes a close relationship between the MCL iterands, MCL limits, and cluster (and DAG) structure in graphs.

The MCL algorithm also associates return probabilities (or loops) with each node in the initial input graph. The flow paradigm underlying MCL naturally requires this, and it can be motivated in terms of the spectral and structural properties mentioned earlier. As for the loop weights that are chosen, experience shows that a neutral value works well. It is possible to choose larger weights, and this will increase cluster granularity. The effect is secondary however to that of varying the inflation parameter, and the algorithm is not very sensitive to changes in the loop weights.

A very important asset of the algorithm is its bootstrapping nature, retrieving cluster structure via the imprint made by this structure on the flow process. Further key benefits of the algorithm are:

1. It is not misled by edges linking different clusters.
2. It is very fast and very scalable.
3. It has a natural parameter for influencing cluster granularity.

4. The mathematics associated with the algorithm shows that there is an intrinsic relationship between the process it simulates and cluster structure in the input graph.

5. Its formulation is simple and elegant. From the definition of the MCL algorithm it is seen that it is based on a very different paradigm than any linkage-based algorithm. One possible view of this is that MCL, although based on similarities between pairs, recombines these similarities (via expansion) and is thus affected by similarities on the level of sets (as generalizing pairs). Alternating expansion with inflation turns out to be an appropriate way of exploiting this recombination property.

Other Graph Theory Algorithms

From the aspect of graph theory, some algorithms for clustering are proposed. We will propose a brief introduction of these models and algorithms.

Correlation Clustering: Another clustering strategy on graph model is to label each edge with either + or -. If two objects are similar, + is added two the edge. – represents that two objects are not similar. Thus the clustering problem is converted to a problem of partition G with the goal to minimize the number of – edges inside clusters and the number of + edges between clusters. It is proven that the problem is an NP-hard problem (Bansal, Blum & Chawla, 2004). Several approximate algorithms have been proposed. (Bansal, Blum & Chawla, 2004, Charikar, Guruswami & Wirth, 2005, Demaine, Emanuel, Fiat & Immorlica, 2006, Swamy, 2004)

Cut Clustering: In the graph model of clustering, a weight could be attached to each edge as the similarity between two objects. With treating the weights on edges as the capacities, the clustering problem could be modeled as the minimum cutting problem to find clusters with small inter-cluster cuts. This model treats a pseudo sink into the graph and computes the minimum cut from each node to the sink. For the convenience of the computation of clustering, a minimum cut tree could be generated and the each connected component in the cut tree after the sink is removed is a cluster. The cut algorithm in (Flake, Tarjan & Tsioutsiouliklis, 2004) could be applied to solve this problem.

Articulation Point Clustering: Another definition of cluster is biconnected component in the graph. To find biconnected components, all articulation points, the removal of which will make the graph disconnected, are found. A graph is biconnected if it contains no articulation points. A biconnected component of a graph is a maximal biconnected graph. Finding biconnected components of a graph is a well-studied problem that can be performed in linear time (Cormen, Leiserson & Rivest, 1990).

FUTURE RESEARCH DIRECTIONS

For these three basic operators, even though many methods have been proposed, with the increasing of data size, current methods are not sufficient. In literature, the algorithms for these three operators are still hot research topics. The future research directions include:

- **Similarity Operators on Big Data:** Currently, most algorithms are designed for single computer. They could not scale to large data set. Therefore, efficient parallel algorithms for these operators are in demand. Even though some researchers notice this topic, this problem is not solved satisfactorily.

- **Complex Similarity Function:** Current methods focus on edit distance and jaccard similarity which are easy to perform. However, in practice, the similarity function may be more complex. As an example, for the similarity join on word set, the consideration of synonym will increase the effectiveness. However, this topic is not considered currently.

- **Similarity Function with Different Weights:** The similarity function considers the errors in data for effective entity resolution. However, different error has different probability. For example, the possibility that 'b' is misspelled to 'd' is higher than 'x' for human input. However, no solution considers this status. The consideration of the different weight will lead to more accurate results.

- **Similarity Function Selection:** For similarity operators, some different similarity functions have been proposed. They have different scope of application and efficiency. For a given data set, which similarity to choose is a research issue for the balance of efficiency and effectiveness?

CONCLUSION

From the aspect of database, entity resolution is treated as a series of basic operators. Fast entity resolution requires efficient implementations of the basic operators. In this chapter, we discuss three basic operators for entity resolution, similarity search, similarity join and clustering. Additionally, these operators have widely applications besides entity resolution and they become hot research topics in database literature. Thus, we focus on the implementation algorithms for these three operators that are suitable for entity resolution. We present a survey of these algorithms in this chapter and propose further research directions.

REFERENCES

Aslam, J. A., Pelekhov, E., & Rus, D. (2004). The star clustering algorithm for static and dynamic information organization. *J. Graph Algorithms Appl.*, 8, 95–129. doi:10.7155/jgaa.00084

Bansal, N., Blum, A., & Chawla, S. (2004). Corrlation clustering. *Machine Learning*, 56(1-3), 89–113. doi:10.1023/B:MACH.0000033116.57574.95

Barbay, J., & Kenyon, C. (2002). *Adaptive intersection and t-threshold problems*.

Bayardo, R. J., Ma, Y., & Srikant, R. (2007). Scaling up all pairs similarity search. In *Proceedings of WWW*, (pp. 131-140). IEEE.

Charikar, M., Guruswami, V., & Wirth, V. (2005). Clustering with qualitative information. *Journal of Computer and System Sciences*, 71(3), 360–383. doi:10.1016/j.jcss.2004.10.012

Chaudhuri, S., Ganti, V., & Kaushik, R. (2006). A primitive operator for similarity joins in data cleaning. *ICDE, 5*.

Cormen, T. H., Leiserson, C. E., & Rivest, R. L. (1990). *Introduction to algorithms*. Cambridge, MA: McGraw Hill and MIT Press.

Demaine, E. D., Emanuel, C., Fiat, A., & Immorlica, A. (2006). Correlation clustering in general weighted graphs. *Theoretical Computer Science*, 361(2), 172–187. doi:10.1016/j.tcs.2006.05.008

Dittrich, J.-P., & Seeger, B. (2001). *GESS: A scalable similarity-join algorithm for mining large data sets in high dimensional spaces*.

Dongen, S. V. (2000). *Graph clustering by flow simulation*. (PhD thesis). University of Utrecht, Utrecht, The Netherlands.

Flake, G. W., Tarjan, R. E., & Tsioutsiouliklis, K. (2004). Graph clustering and minimum cut trees. *Internet Mathematics, 1*(4), 385–408. doi:10.1080/15427951.2004.10129093

Han, J., & Kamber, M. (2000). *Data mining: Concepts and techniques*. San Francisco: Morgan Kaufmann.

Hassanzadeh, O., Chiang, F., Lee, H. C., & Miller, R. J. (2009). Framework for evaluating clustering algorithms in duplicate detection. *Proceedings of the VLDB Endowment, 2*(1), 1282–1293.

Hassanzadeh, O., Chiang, F., Miller, R., & Lee, H. C. (2009). Framework for evaluating clustering algorithms in duplicate detection. *PVLDB, 2*(1), 1282–1293.

Hassanzadeh, O., & Miller, R. J. (2009). Creating probabilistic databases from duplicated data. *The VLDB Journal, 18*(5), 1141–1166. doi:10.1007/s00778-009-0161-2

Haveliwala, T.H., Gionis, A., & Indyk, P. (2000). Scalable techniques for clustering the web. *WebDB*, 129-134

Koudas, N., & Sevcik, K. (1998). High dimensional similarity joins: Algorithms and performance evaluation. In *Proceedings of Data Engineering*. IEEE.

Li, C. Bin Wang, & Yang, X. (2007). VGRAM: Improving performance of approximate queries on string collections using variable-length grams. In *Proceedings of the 33rd International Conference on Very Large Data Bases*. VLDB Endowment.

Li, C., Lu, J., & Lu, Y. (2008). *Efficient merging and filtering algorithms for approximate string searches*.

Orenstein, J. (1991). An algorithm for computing the overlay of k-dimensional spaces. In O. Günther, Oliver, & H.-J. Schek (Eds.), Lecture Notes in Computer Science: Advances in Spatial Databases (Vol. 525, pp. 381–400). Berlin: Springer. http://dx.doi.org/ doi:10.1007/3-540-54414-3_48

Sarawagi, S., & Kirpal, A. (2004). *Efficient set joins on similarity predicates*.

Swamy, C. (2004). Correlation clustering: Maximizing agreements via semidefinite programming. In *Proceedings of the Annual ACM-SIAM Symposium on Discrete Algorithms* (SODA), (pp. 526–527). New Orleans, LA: ACM.

Xiao, C., Wang, W., Lin, X., Yu, J. X., & Wang, G. (2011). Efficient similarity joins for near-duplicate detection. *ACM Transactions on Database Systems, 36*(3), 15. doi:10.1145/2000824.2000825

Xu, R., & Wunsch, D. (2005). Survey of clustering algorithms. *IEEE Transactions on Neural Networks, 16*(3), 645–678. doi:10.1109/TNN.2005.845141 PMID:15940994

ADDITIONAL READING

Alsubaiee, S., Behm, A., & Li, C. (2010). *Supporting Location-Based Approximate-Keyword Queries*. ACM GIS.

Andritsos, P. (2004). *Scalable Clustering of Categorical Data And Applications*. PhD thesis, University of Toronto, Toronto

Aslam, J. A., Pelekhov, E., & Rus, D. (2004). The Star Clustering Algorithm For Static And Dynamic Information Organization. *Journal of Graph Algorithms and Applications, 8*(1), 95–129. doi:10.7155/jgaa.00084

Bansal, N., Blum, A., & Chawla, S. (2004). Correlation Clustering. *Machine Learning*, *56*(1-3), 89–113. doi:10.1023/B:MACH.0000033116.57574.95

Bansal, N., Chiang, F., Koudas, N., & Tompa, F. W. (2007). *Seeking Stable Clusters in the Blogosphere*. VLDB.

Behm, A., Ji, S., Li, C., & Lu, J. (2009). *Space-Constrained Gram-Based Indexing for Efficient Approximate String Search*. ICDE. doi:10.1109/ICDE.2009.32

Behm, A., Li, C., & Carey, M. (2011). *Answering Approximate String Queries on Large Data Sets Using External Memory*. ICDE. doi:10.1109/ICDE.2011.5767856

Bhattacharya, I., & Getoor, L. (2006). *A Latent Dirichlet Model for Unsupervised Entity Resolution*. SDM. doi:10.1137/1.9781611972764.5

Brandes, U., Gaertler, M., & Wagner, D. (2003). Experiments on Graph Clustering Algorithms. In *The 11th Europ. Symp. Algorithms*, pages 568–579. Springer-Verlag CanadaSeptember.

Charikar, M., Guruswami, V., & Wirth, A. (2005). Clustering with Qualitative Information. *Journal of Computer and System Sciences*, *71*(3), 360–383. doi:10.1016/j.jcss.2004.10.012

Cheng, D., Kannan, R., Vempala, S., & Wang, G. (2003). On a Recursive Spectral Algorithm for Clustering from Pairwise Similarities. Technical Report MIT-LCS-TR-906, MIT LCS.

Chierichetti, F., Panconesi, A., Raghavan, P., Sozio, M., Tiberi, A., & Upfal, E. (2007). *Finding Near Neighbors Through Cluster Pruning* (pp. 103–112). Beijing, China: PODS.

Day, W. H., & Edelsbrunner, H. (1984). Efficient Algorithms for Agglomerative Hierarchical Clustering Methods. *Journal of Classification*, *1*(1), 7–24. doi:10.1007/BF01890115

Demaine, E. D., Emanuel, D., Fiat, A., & Immorlica, N. (2006). Correlation Clustering In General Weighted Graphs. *Theoretical Computer Science*, *361*(2), 172–187. doi:10.1016/j.tcs.2006.05.008

Deng, D., Li, G., & Feng, G. (2013). *Top-k String Similarity Search with Edit-Distance Constraints*. ICDE. doi:10.1109/ICDE.2013.6544886

Deng, D., Li, G., & Feng, J. (2012). An Efficient Trie-based Method for Approximate Entity Extraction with Edit-Distance Constraints. ICDE, 762-773.

Fan, J., Li, G., Zhou, L., Chen, S., & Hu, J. (2012), SEAL Spatio-textual Similarity Search. VLDB:824-835.

Feng, J., Li, G., & Wang, J. (2011). Finding Top-k Answers in Keyword Search over Relational Databases Using Tuple Units. [TKDE]. *IEEE Transactions on Knowledge and Data Engineering*, *23*(12), 1781–1794. doi:10.1109/TKDE.2011.61

Feng, J., Wang, J., & Li, G. (2012). Trie-join: a trie-based method for efficient string similarity joins. *The VLDB Journal*, *21*(4), 437–461. doi:10.1007/s00778-011-0252-8

Filippone, M., Camastra, F., Masulli, F., & Rovetta, S. (2008). A Survey of Kernel and Spectral Methods for Clustering. *Pattern Recognition*, *41*(1), 176–190. doi:10.1016/j.patcog.2007.05.018

Flake, G. W., Tarjan, R. E., & Tsioutsiouliklis, K. (2004). Graph Clustering and Minimum Cut Trees. *Internet Mathematics*, *1*(4), 385–408. doi:10.1080/15427951.2004.10129093

Halkidi, M., Batistakis, Y., & Vazirgiannis, M. (2001). On clustering validation techniques. *Journal of Intelligent Information Systems*, *17*(2-3), 107–145. doi:10.1023/A:1012801612483

Hassanzadeh, O., Sadoghi, M., & Miller, R. J. (2007). Accuracy of Approximate String Joins Using Grams. In *Proc. of the International Workshop on Quality in Databases (QDB)*, pages 11–18, Vienna, Austria.

Haveliwala, T. H., Gionis, A., & Indyk, P. (2000). Scalable Techniques for Clustering the Web. In *Proc. of the Int'l Workshop on the Web and Databases (WebDB)*, pages 129–134, Dallas, Texas, USA.

Huang, W., Li, G., Tan, K., & Feng, J. (2012). Efficient Safe-Region Construction for Moving Top-K Spatial Keyword Queries. CIKM:932-941.

Jain, A., & Dubes, R. (1988). *Algorithms for Clustering Data*. Prentice Hall.

Jain, A. K., Murty, M. N., & Flynn, P. J. (1999). Data Clustering: A Review. *ACM Computing Surveys*, *31*(3), 264–323. doi:10.1145/331499.331504

Kannan, R., Vempala, S., & Vetta, A. (2004). On clusterings: Good, bad and spectral. *Journal of the ACM*, *51*(3), 497–515. doi:10.1145/990308.990313

King, A. D. (2004). Graph Clustering with Restricted Neighbourhood Search. Master's thesis, University of Toronto, 2004.

Kogan, J. (2007). Introduction to Clustering Large and High-Dimensional Data. Cambridge Univ. Press, 2007.

Li, C., Lu, J., & Lu, Y. (2008). *Efficient Merging and Filtering Algorithms for Approximate String Searches*. ICDE. doi:10.1109/ICDE.2008.4497434

Li, G., Deng, D., & Feng, J. (2013). *Pass-Join+: A Partition-based Method for String Similarity Joins with Edit-Distance Constraints. ACM Transactions on Database Systems*. TODS.

Li, G., Deng, D., Wang, J., & Feng, J. (2012). Pass-Join: A Partition-based Method for Similarity Joins. VLDB: 253-264.

Li, G., Feng, J., & Li, C. (2013). Supporting Search-As-You-Type Using SQL in Databases. [TKDE]. *IEEE Transactions on Knowledge and Data Engineering*, *25*(2), 461–475. doi:10.1109/TKDE.2011.148

Li, G., Feng, J., Zhou, X., & Wang, J. (2011). Providing Built-in Keyword Search Capabilities in RDBMS. *The VLDB Journal*, *20*(1), 1–19. doi:10.1007/s00778-010-0188-4

Li, G., Ji, S., Li, C., & Feng, J. (2011). Efficient Fuzzy Full-Text Type-Ahead Search. *The VLDB Journal*, *20*(4), 617–640. doi:10.1007/s00778-011-0218-x

Li, G., Li, C., Feng, J., & Zhou, L. (2009). SAIL: Structure-Aware Indexing for Effective and Progressive Top-k Keyword Search over XML Documents. *Information Sciences*, *179*(21), 3745–3762. doi:10.1016/j.ins.2009.06.025

Liu, S., Li, G., & Feng, J. (2013). *A Prefix-Filter based Method for Spatio-Textual Similarity Join. IEEE Transactions on Knowledge and Data Engineering*. TKDE.

Lu, J., Senellart, P., Lin, C., Du, X., Wang, S., & Chen, X. (2012). Optimal top-k generation of attribute combinations based on ranked lists. SIGMOD Conference: 409-420

Pelleg, A. M. D. (2000). X-Means: Extending K-Means with Efficient Estimation of the Number of Clusters. In *Proc. Of the Int'l Conf. on Machine Learning*, pages 727–734, San Francisco, CA, USA, 2000.

Sarawagi, S., & Kirpal, A. (2004). Efficient Set Joins On Similarity Predicates. In *ACM SIGMOD Int'l Conf. on the Mgmt. of Data*, pages 743–754, Paris, France.

van Dongen, S. (2000). *Graph Clustering By Flow Simulation*. PhD thesis, University of Utrecht, 2000.

Vernica, R., Carey, M., & Li, C. (2010). *Efficient Parallel Set-Similarity Joins Using MapReduce.* SIGMOD.

Wang, J., Cetindil, I., Ji, S., Li, C., Xie, X., Li, G., & Feng, J. (2010). Interactive and fuzzy search: a dynamic way to explore MEDLINE. *Bioinformatics (Oxford, England)*, *26*(18), 2313–2320. doi:10.1093/bioinformatics/btq414 PMID:20660296

Wang, J., Li, G., & Feng, J. (2010). Trie-Join: Efficient Trie-based String Similarity Joins with Edit-Distance Constraints. *VLDB*, *2010*, 1219–1230.

Wang, J., Li, G., & Feng, J. (2011). Fast-Join: An Efficient Method for Fuzzy Token Matching based String Similarity Join. *ICDE*, *2011*, 458–469.

Wang, J., Li, G., & Feng, J. (2012). Can we Beat the Prefix Filtering? An Adaptive Framework for Similarity Join and Search. SIGMOD:85-96.

Wang, J., Li, G., Yu, J.X., & Feng, J. (2011) Entity Matching: How Similar Is Similar. VLDB:622-633.

Whitney, J. A. (2006). Graph Clustering With Overlap. Master's thesis, University of Toronto.

Wijaya, D. T., & Bressan, S. (2009). Ricochet: A Family of Unconstrained Algorithms for Graph Clustering. In *Proc. Of the Int'l Conf. on Database Systems for Advanced Applications (DASFAA)*, pages 153–167, Brisbane, Australia.

Xu, R., & Wunsch, I. (2005). Survey of clustering algorithms. *IEEE Transactions on Neural Networks*, *16*(3), 645–678. doi:10.1109/TNN.2005.845141 PMID:15940994

Yang, X., Wang, B., & Li, C. (2008). *Cost-Based Variable-Length-Gram Selection for String Collections to Support Approximate Queries Efficiently.* ACM SIGMOD. doi:10.1145/1376616.1376655

Zupan, J. (1982). *Clustering of Large Data Sets.* Research Studies Press.

KEY TERMS AND DEFINITIONS

Clustering: Given a set S of data objects, parititon S into a set of clusters $C_1, C_2, ..., C_n$, such that the data objects in each cluster are similar.

Edit Distance: For two string r and s, the edit between them is the minimal number of operators that are required to convert r to s. The operators includes insertion, deletion or change of a character.

Jaccard Similarity: Given two sets x and y, the Jaccard similarity is defined as $J(x,y) = \frac{|x \cap y|}{|x \cup y|}$.

N-Gram: n continues characters in a string.

Similarity Join: Given two sets of objects R and S, a similarity function sim(r, s) and a constraint for similarity, we need to find all pairs of objects $r \in R$, $s \in S$, such that r and s are similar.

Similarity Search: Find strings similar to a given query Q in a set D such that the each result r is similar to Q.

Thershold Similarity Query: Retrieve the results with similarities larger than a given threshold.

Top-K Similarity Query: Retrieve the results with top K similarities.

Chapter 12
Data Cleaning Based on Entity Resolution

ABSTRACT

Data quality is one of the most prevalent problems in data management. A traditional data management application typically concerns the creation, maintenance, and use of a large amount of data, focusing only on clean datasets. However, real-life data are often dirty: inconsistent, duplicated, inaccurate, incomplete, or out of date. Derived from these issues, the problem of conformity of facts from a large amount of conflicting information provided by various Web sets or different data sources to be integrated receives increasing attention. False data can generate misleading or biased analytical results and decisions and lead to loss of revenue, credibility, and customers. Based on the results of entity resolution, truth discovery shares an important role in modern data management applications. In this chapter, the authors review approaches to processing truth discovery related to central aspects of data quality (i.e., data consistency, data reduplication, data accuracy, data currency, and information completeness).

INTRODUCTION

Many data management applications require integrating data from multiple sources (or views), each of which provides a set of values as "facts". We do not distinguish between the terms of "data sources" and "views" in the following. However, different data sources can often provide conflicting values, some being true while some being false. Considering an example illustrated in Table 1(a), there are five data sources providing information on affiliations of five researchers and only s_1 provides all correct data. All these five data

sources provide a set of "facts" about the affiliation information, but "facts" often does not mean the truth, so these sources may give true values as well as false values. When integrating data from these data sources, we have to find out the truth (trustworthy affiliations) of these five researchers. The world-wide web has become the most important information source for most people. Unfortunately, there is no guarantee for the correctness of information on the web. Moreover, different web sites often provide conflicting information on a subject, such as different release date for a new coming product. Table 1(b) depicts authors of the book "Rapid Contextual Design"

DOI: 10.4018/978-1-4666-5198-2.ch012

Table 1(a). The motivating example: information on the affiliations of researchers.

	S1	S2	S3	S4	S5
Stonebraker	MIT	Berkeley	MIT	MIT	MS
Dewitt	MSR	MSR	UWisc	UWisc	UWisc
Bernstein	MSR	MSR	MSR	MSR	MSR
Carey	UCI	AT&T	BEA	BEA	BEA
Halevy	Google	Google	UW	UW	UW

(ISBN: 0123540518) searched from different online bookstores. From the image of the book cover we found that A1 Books provides the most accurate information. In comparison, the information from Powell's books is incomplete, and that from Lakeside books is incorrect. Likewise, we have to extract truth from the many conflicting "facts" provided by different websites.

The above task, which has been studied as the truth discovery problem is defined as follows. Given a set of data sources (e.g., different web sites or databases) and a set of facts, and that each fact is provided by one or more data sources. How do we predict the confidence of each fact (i.e., likelihood of being true) and the trustworthiness of each data source? In our usage the word "fact" is used to represent something claimed as true, whether or not it is right. Typically, we can expect a true value to be provided by more sources rather than any particular false one, so we can apply voting and take the value provided by the majority of the sources as the truth. Unfortunately, copying between data sources is common

in practice, especially on the web (Dong et al. 2010); a value provided by one data source, no matter true or false, can be copied by many other sources. Besides, large amounts of out-of-data facts may exist in many data sources. Finally, there may exist negative facts in the data sources. Thus, the problem of truth discovery is challenging.

Yin, Han & Yu (2007) firstly propose the truth discovery problem, they provide a probabilistic approach based on the assumption that different data sources are independent and thus false values appearing in different data sources should be different from each other. They assign confidence scores to facts based on the principle that a fact provided by more (and more trustworthy) data sources is more likely to be correct. A data source is more trustworthy if more of the facts it provides are of high confidence. A data source providing mostly high-confidence facts is more trustworthy. This assumption holds when different data sources are independent. But this is generally not true as data copying is prevalent on the web. Under the same assumption, Galland, Abiteboul, Marian &

Table 1(b). The motivating example: information about a book's authors from webs.

Web Site	Authors
A1 Books	Karen Holtzblatt, Jessamyn Burns Wendell, Shelley Wood
Powell's books	Holtzblatt, Karen
Cornwall books	Holtzblatt-Karen, Wendell-Jessamyn Burns, Wood
Mellon's books	Wendell, Jessamyn
Lakeside books	WENDELL, JESSAMYNHOLTZXBLATT, KARENWOOD, SHELLEY
Blackwell online	Wendell, Jessamyn, Holtzblatt, Karen, Wood, Shelley

Senellart (2010) apply a different model to estimating the confidence of facts. The model takes into consideration negative views from data sources and proposes fixpoint algorithm to discover true real-world and the trustworthiness of data sources.

Dong, Berti-Equille & Srivastava (2009a) propose a method that considers the dependencies among data sources, such dependencies need to be inferred from the confidence associated with each fact. Their proposed algorithm detects copying relationships during the iterative process of truth discovery with incorporating of trustworthiness of data sources.

By using a small set of ground truth data to help distinguish true facts from false ones as well as identifying trustworthy data sources, Yin & Tan (2011) proposed to use semi-supervised graph learning method to cope with truth discovery problem, in 2011.

In this survey, we review these various approaches proposed under different assumptions to process truth discovery with the result of entity resolution. All approaches reviewed in this survey can be easily implemented by iterative algorithms. We also discuss the future research direction for this area.

BACKGROUND

Formally, the truth discovery problem is defined as follows. We consider a set of data sources $\mathcal{V}$ and a set of objects $\mathcal{O}$. An object represents a particular aspect of a real-world entity, such as the director of a movie; in a relational database, an object corresponds to a cell in a table while in a website, an object may refer to a piece of extracted useful information for a kind of knowledge. For each object $O \in \mathcal{O}$, a data source $V \in \mathcal{V}$ can (but not necessarily) provide a value. These values provided are called "facts". Among different facts provided for an object, one correctly describes the real world so it is true, and the rest are false. Given a set of data sources data sources $\mathcal{V}$, it is

to decide the true fact for each object $O \in \mathcal{O}$. Note that a value provided by a data source can either be atomic, or a set or list of atomic values (e.g., author list of a paper). In the latter case, we consider the value as true if the atomic values are correct and the set or list is complete (and order preserved for a list). Figure 1 shows an example set of data sources. Each data source can provide various numbers of facts for different objects, but can only provide at most one fact for an object.

Based on the input data sources of the truth discovery problem, we formally give the definition of the properties of input datasets and the interdependence of data sources and facts.

Definition 1. (Confidence of Facts): The confidence of a fact f (denoted by $c(f)$) is the probability of f being correct, according to the best of our knowledge.

Definition 2. (Trustworthiness of Data Sources): The trustworthiness of a data source V (denoted by $t(V)$) is the expected confidence of the facts provided by V.

Different facts about the same objects may be conflicting as well as supportive to each other. For example, one data source claims that the average height of an adult is "175cm" and another one claims "176cm". If one of them is true, the other is also likely to be true. So, we have the following definition of Implication between facts.

Definition 3 (Implication Between Facts): The implication from facts f1(f2) to f2(f1), imp(f1→f2) (imp(f2→f1)), is f1's(f2's) influence on f2's(f1's)

Definition 3 (Implication Between Facts): The implication from facts f1(f2) to f2(f1), imp(f1→f2) (imp(f2→f1)), is f1's(f2's) influence on f2's(f1's) confidence, i.e., how much f2's(f1's) confidence should be increased (or decreased) according to f1's(f2's) confidence.

Figure 1. The input of truth discovery problem

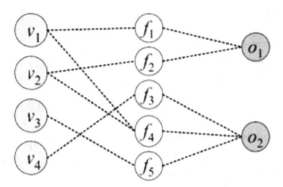

Note that, imp(f1→f2) should be a value between -1 and 1. A positive value indicates if f1 is correct, f2 is likely to be correct while a negative value means that if f1 is correct, f2 is likely to be wrong. Also the definition of imp(f1→f2) is often domain specific and usually needs to be provide with the help of domain knowledge. Often, the implication function is symmetric, i.e., imp(f1→f2) = imp(f2→f1), and imp(f→f) = 1 for any fact f.

Likewise, there exists inter-dependence between data sources as data copying between sources is ubiquitous (Dong et al., 2010).

Definition 4 (Dependence Between Data Sources): We say that there exists a dependence between two data sources V_1 and V_2 if they derive the same part of their data directly or transitively from a common source (can be one of V_1 and V_2). Accordingly, there are two types of data sources: independent sources and copiers.

An independent source provides values independently. It may provide erroneous values. Good independent sources are more likely to provide the true value for each object rather than any particular false value, compared to bad independent sources. A copier copies a part (or all) of data from other sources (independent sources or copiers). It can copy from multiple sources by union, intersection, etc. In addition, a copier may revise some of the copied values or add additional values; though, such revised and added values are considered as independent contributions by the copier.

When we only consider the direct copying between data sources in truth discovery, we say a source V_1 depends on V_2 if V_1 copies directly from V_2.

DIFFERENT TRUTH DISCOVERY APPROACHES

A Trivial Approach

As stated before, we can expect a true value to be provided by more sources rather than any particular false one, so we can apply a trivial approach called "VOTING" and take the value provided by the majority of the sources as the truth. Formally, Let O be an object and V be a set of independent data sources (views) providing facts for O. Among the different values on O provided by V, the one provided by the maximum number of data sources has the highest probability to be true and should be regarded as the true value. This method can be treated as the baseline of other more complex approaches.

A Basic Iterative Approach Considering Accuracy

Yin, Han & Yu (2007) provide a probabilistic approach based on the assumption that the data source set $\mathcal{V}$ only contains independent data sources (they focused on web sites as data sources), i.e., they only consider the confidence of facts and trustworthiness of data sources and the implication between facts. They propose TRUTH-FINDER based on the following four basic heuristics that serve as the bases of the computational model.

- **Heuristic 1:** Usually there is only one true fact for an object.
- **Heuristic 2:** This true fact appears to be the same or similar in different data sources.
- **Heuristic 3:** The false facts from different data sources are less likely to be the same or similar.
- **Heuristic 4:** In a certain domain, a data source that provides mostly true facts for many objects will likely provide true facts for other objects.

Based on the above heuristics, we know that if a fact is provided by many trustworthy data sources, it is likely to be true; if a fact conflicts with the facts provided by many trustworthy data sources, it is unlikely to be true. On the other hand, a data source is trustworthy if it provides facts with high confidence. So the data source trustworthiness and fact confidence are determined by each other, and an iterative method can be used to compute both of them. Next is the model of inference between data source trustworthiness and fact confidence.

As defined in Definition 2, the trustworthiness of a data source is just the expected confidence of facts it provides. For data source V its trustworthiness $t(V)$ is computed by calculating the average confidence of facts provided by V.

$$t(V) = \frac{\sum_{f \in F(V)} c(f)}{|F(V)|} \qquad (1)$$

Where $F(V)$ is the set of facts provided by V.

Assuming that there is no related fact, and f is the only fact about object O. All the data sources providing f are independent. Thus we can compute f's confidence as

$$c(f) = 1 - \prod_{V \in W(f)} \left(1 - t(V)\right) \qquad (2)$$

Where $W(f)$ is the set of data sources providing f.

In order to facilitate computation and veracity exploration, Yin et al., define the trustworthiness score of a data sources as

$$\tau(V) = -\ln\left(1 - t(V)\right) \qquad (3)$$

Similarly, the confidence score of a fact is defined as

$$\sigma(f) = -\ln\left(1 - c(f)\right) \qquad (4)$$

A very useful property is that, the confidence score of a fact f is just the sum of the trustworthiness scores of data sources providing f. This is shown in the following equation (Yin et al., 2007).

$$\sigma(f) = \sum_{V \in W(f)} \tau(V) \qquad (5)$$

However, there are usually many different facts about an object (such as f_1 and f_2 in Figure 2, w_i denotes data sources), and these facts influence each other. So when computing the confi-

Figure 2. Computing confidence of a fact

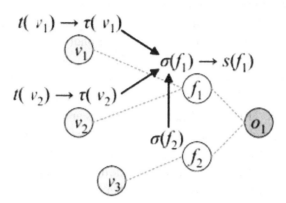

dence score of f, we should adjust its confidence score by summing the confidence scores of f' that provide the fact for the same object as f. So the adjusted confidence score of a fact f is

$$\sigma^*(f) = \sigma(f) + \rho \sum_{o(f'=o(f))} \sigma(f') \cdot imp(f' \to f) \quad (6)$$

ρ is a parameter between 0 and 1, which controls the influence of related facts. It is obvious to see that $\sigma^*(f)$ is the sum of confidence score of f and a portion of the confidence score of each related fact f' multiplies the implication from f' to f. When f' is conflicting with f, $imp(f' \to f) < 0$.

Similar to Equation (4), the adjusted confidence of a fact f can be computed from its adjusted confidence score.

$$c^*(f) = 1 - e^{-\sigma^*(f)} \quad (7)$$

As is stated in Yin et al., (2007), there are still two main problems with the above model. Under the actually incorrect assumption that all data sources are independent with each other, the computational confidence of a fact f provided by several data sources with quite low trustworthiness, i.e., 0.6, can be very high, i.e., 0.99. But actually some of the data sources may copy contents from others. By adding a dampening factor γ into Equation (7) to compensate for the problem of overly high confidence, the redefined fact confidence is $c^*(f) = 1 - e^{-\gamma \cdot \sigma^*(f)}$, where $0 < \gamma < 1$.

Another problem with the above model is that the confidence of a fact f can easily be negative if it is conflicting with some facts provided by trustworthy data sources, which makes $\sigma^*(f) < 0$ and $c^*(f) < 0$. This is obviously unreasonable because even with negative evidence, there is still a chance that f is correct, so its confidence should still be positive. By adopt the Logistic function, the final definition for fact confidence is

$$c(f) = \frac{1}{1 + e^{-\gamma \cdot \sigma^*(f)}} \quad (8)$$

When $\gamma \cdot \sigma^*(f)$ is significantly greater than zero, $c(f)$ is very close to $c^*(f)$ because $\frac{1}{1 + e^{-\gamma \cdot \sigma^*(f)}} \approx 1 - e^{-\gamma \cdot \sigma^*(f)}$. When $\gamma \cdot \sigma^*(f)$ is significantly less than zero, $c(f)$ is close to zero but remains positive, which is consistent with the real situation.

As described by the above models, we can infer the data source trustworthiness if we know the fact confidence, and vice versa. The proposed TRUTHFINDER in Yin et al., (2007) adopts an iterative method to compute the trustworthiness of data sources and confidence of facts. Initially, it has very little information about the data sources and the facts. At each iteration, TRUTHFINDER tries to improve its knowledge about their trustworthiness and confidence, and it stops when the computation reaches a stable state. Begin with the initial state in which all data sources have a uniform trustworthiness (set to the estimated average trustworthiness, such as .9). In each iteration, TRUTHFINDER first uses the data source trustworthiness to compute the fact confidence, and then re-computes the data source trustworthiness from the fact confidence. It stops iterating when it reaches a stable state. The stableness is measured by the change of the trustworthiness of all data sources. If the trustworthiness only changes a little after an iteration (measured by cosine similarity between old and new trustworthiness vector) then TRUTHFINDER will stop.

Yin et al. evaluated the effectiveness of TRUTHFINDER on a real dataset with a baseline approach called VOTING that chooses the fact that is provided by most data sources. TRUTHFINDER is also compared with Google by comparing the top data sources (web sites) found by each of them. As is reported in Yin et al. (2007), TRUTHFINDER is significantly more accurate than VOTING and its accuracy can increase to about 95% at the stable state on an real data set. Also as stated in Yin et al., (2007), TRUTHFINDER converges in a steady speed. Experiment also shows that TRUTHFINDER can do better than Google for finding accurate information on the web.

Fixpoint Approaches

Galland, Abiteboul, Marian & Senellart (2010) proposed different probabilistic model taking into account trust in the data sources under the assumption of independence between data sources and independence between facts. The model can cope with negative facts in the data sources through functional dependencies. They introduced three fixpoint algorithms corresponding to different levels of complexity of the underlying probabilistic model. The algorithms estimate both truth values of facts and trust in the data sources.

In the presence of negative statement of views, Galland, Abiteboul, Marian and Senellart view the truth discovery problem as a mapping problem that decides whether any views in the set should be true or false. Let $\mathcal{F}$ be a set $\{f_1 \ldots f_n\}$ of facts. A view V can be described as a (partial) mapping from $\mathcal{F}$ to the set $\{T, F\}$ (T stands for true, and F for false). Given a set of views $\mathcal{V} = \{V_1 \ldots V_m\}$, they try to estimate the real world W, a total mapping form $\mathcal{F}$ to the set $\{T, F\}$. The underlying probabilistic model they assumed is as follows:

$$
\begin{cases}
\mathbb{P}\left(V_i\left(f_j\right) \text{ is undefined}\right) = \varphi\left(V_i\right)\varphi\left(f_j\right) \\
\mathbb{P}\left(V_i\left(f_j\right) = \neg W\left(f_j\right)\right) = \\
\left(1 - \varphi\left(V_i\right)\varphi\left(f_j\right)\right)\varepsilon\left(V_i\right)\varepsilon\left(f_j\right) \\
\mathbb{P}\left(V_i\left(f_j\right) = W\left(f_j\right)\right) = \\
\left(1 - \varphi\left(V_i\right)\varphi\left(f_j\right)\right)\left(1 - \varepsilon\left(V_i\right)\varepsilon\left(f_j\right)\right)
\end{cases}
$$

In the above mode, views ignore some facts and make errors. First, with some probability $\varphi\left(V_i\right)\varphi\left(f_j\right)$, view V_i ignores fact f_j, i.e., $V_i\left(f_j\right)$ is undefined. While when $V_i\left(f_j\right)$ is defined V_i makes an error on f_j (w.r.t W) with probability $\varepsilon\left(V_i\right)\varepsilon\left(f_j\right)$. The functions φ, ε define the ignorance and error factors respectively. Besides estimating W, these factors are also estimated.

The work presents three algorithms to estimate the real world W and error factors $\varepsilon\left(V_i\right), \varepsilon\left(f_j\right)$. The ignorance factors $\varphi\left(V_i\right)$ and $\varphi\left(f_j\right)$ are independent of these parameters and their estimation is relatively straightforward given the structure of the views,

$$S = \left(\left(V_i, f_j\right) \in V \times F \mid V_i\left(f_j\right)\right)$$

is defined. In the following, $\Theta(\bullet)$ denotes the estimates (given by each algorithm) of the different parameters (notably, error factors and truth values).

The first algorithm COSINE is a heuristic approach for estimating the truth values of facts and the trustworthiness of views. It is based on the classical cosine similarity measure. The algorithm use an alternative representation where these variables have values -1 (false facts), 0 (undetermined facts) or 1 (true facts). The idea is then to compute, for each view V_i, given a set of truth values for views, the similarity between the statements of V_i, viewed as a set of ± 1 statements on views, and the predicted real world. The technique is precisely described in Algorithm 1. Note that to improve the stability of the method, the algorithm set the new value of the estimation to be a linear combination of the old value and the predicted cosine similarity. As for the estimate of the truth value of facts given the trustworthiness of views, it uses a simple averaging, except that it gives more weight to predictable views, which are views with high $\Theta\left(\varepsilon\left(V_i\right)\right)^2$ (consistently often correct, or consistently often wrong). In the initialization phase, estimates are set as if all facts were true. Trustworthiness of views are estimated as $\Theta\left(\varepsilon\left(V_i\right)\right)+1 \Big/ 2$ and facts are predicted as true when $\Theta\left(W\left(V_i\right)\right) > 0$.

Algorithm 1: The COSINE Algorithm (Galland, Abiteboul, Marian and Senellart 2010)

Input: $\mathcal{F}$, $\mathcal{V}$, $\mathcal{S}$

Output: An estimate of $\varepsilon\left(V_i\right)$ for each view, an estimate of $W\left(f_i\right)$ for each fact

1 for each $V_i \in \mathcal{V}$ do

2 $\Theta\left(\varepsilon\left(V_i\right)\right) \leftarrow \dfrac{|\{f_j \mid V_i\left(f_j\right) = T\}| - |\{f_j \mid V_i\left(f_j\right) = F\}|}{|\{f_j \mid V_i\left(f_j\right) \in \mathcal{S}\}|}$

//initialization of error factor

3 end for

4 for each $f_j \in \mathcal{F}$ do

5 $\Theta\left(W\left(f_j\right)\right) \leftarrow 1$

6 end for

7 while not convergence

8 for each $V_i \in \mathcal{V}$ do //{ç is a constant, i.e., 0.2}

9 $posFacts \leftarrow \displaystyle\sum_{f_j \in \mathcal{F} \&\& V_i\left(f_j\right) = T} \Theta\left(W\left(f_i\right)\right)$

10 $negFacts \leftarrow \displaystyle\sum_{f_j \in \mathcal{F} \&\& V_i\left(f_j\right) = F} \Theta\left(W\left(f_i\right)\right)$

11 $norm \leftarrow \sqrt{\left|f_j \in \mathcal{F} \mid V_i\left(f_j\right) \in \mathcal{S}\right| \times \displaystyle\sum_{f_j \in \mathcal{F} \&\& V_i\left(f_j\right) \in \mathcal{S}} \Theta\left(W\left(f_i\right)\right)^2}$

$\Theta\left(\varepsilon\left(V_i\right)\right) \leftarrow \left(1 - ç\right) \times \Theta\left(\varepsilon\left(V_i\right)\right) +$

12 $ç \times \dfrac{posFacts - negFacts}{norm}$

13 end for

14 for each $f_j \in \mathcal{F}$ do

15 $posViews \leftarrow \displaystyle\sum_{V_i \in \mathcal{V} \&\& V_i\left(f_j\right) = T} \Theta\left(\varepsilon\left(V_i\right)\right)^3$

16 $negViews \leftarrow \displaystyle\sum_{V_i \in \mathcal{V} \&\& V_i\left(f_j\right) = F} \Theta\left(\varepsilon\left(V_i\right)\right)^3$

17 $norm \leftarrow \displaystyle\sum_{V_i \in \mathcal{V} \&\& V_i\left(f_j\right) \in \mathcal{S}} \Theta\left(\varepsilon\left(V_i\right)\right)^3$

18 $\Theta\left(W\left(f_j\right)\right) \leftarrow \dfrac{posViews - negViews}{norm}$

19 end for

20 end while

21 return Θ

The second algorithm, 2-ESTIMATES depicted in Algorithm 2, is more closely related to the probabilistic model. The idea is to iteratively find a good estimate of the $\varepsilon(V_i)$ given $\mathbb{P}(W(f_j)=T)$, and conversely, using a fixpoint computation. The algorithm first initializes the parameters as if all the views were true about W, then successively estimates one set of parameters given the other one and the views, until convergence. It is possible to prove that the estimates which are used in 2-ESTIMATES are valid when $\mathcal{S}$ is given, in the sense that the expectation of $\Theta(W(f_j))$ given the correct set of $\varepsilon(V_i)$'s and the views, is indeed the expectation of $\mathbb{P}(W(f_j)=T)$; similarly for $\Theta(\varepsilon(V_i))$ given the correct set of $W(f_j)$'s and the views.

Algorithm 2: The 2-ESTIMATES Algorithm (Galland, Abiteboul, Marian and Senellart 2010)

Input: $\mathcal{F}$, $\mathcal{V}$, $\mathcal{S}$
Output: An estimate of $\varepsilon(V_i)$ for each view, an estimate of $W(f_i)$ for each fact

1 for each $V_i \in \mathcal{V}$ do
2 $\Theta(\varepsilon(V_i)) \leftarrow 0$ //initialization to zero
3 end for
4 while not convergence
5 for each $f_j \in \mathcal{F}$ do
6 $posViews \leftarrow \sum_{V_i \in \mathcal{V} \&\& V_i(f_j)=T} (1-\Theta(\varepsilon(V_i)))$
7 $negViews \leftarrow \sum_{V_i \in \mathcal{V} \&\& V_i(f_j)=F} \Theta(\varepsilon(V_i))$
8 $nbViews \leftarrow |\{V_i \in \mathcal{V} \,|\, (V_i,f_j) \in \mathcal{S}\}|$
9 $\Theta(W(f_j)) \leftarrow \dfrac{posViews + negViews}{nbViews}$
10 end for
11 for each $V_i \in \mathcal{V}$ do
12 $posFacts \leftarrow \sum_{f_j \in \mathcal{F} \&\& V_i(f_j)=T} (1-\Theta(W(f_i)))$
13 $negFacts \leftarrow \sum_{f_j \in \mathcal{F} \&\& V_i(f_j)=F} \Theta(W(f_i))$
14 $nbFacts \leftarrow |\{f_j \in \mathcal{F} \,|\, (V_i,f_j) \in \mathcal{S}\}|$
15 $\Theta(\varepsilon(V_i)) \leftarrow \dfrac{posFacts + negFacts}{nbFacts}$
16 end for
17 end while
18 return Θ

The 2-ESTIMATES algorithm may converge on local optima. To avoid this, they first normalize $\Theta(W(f_j))$ to the closest value in $\{0,1\}$, which constrains W to map each fact to either T or F, and $\Theta(\varepsilon(V_i))$ to the whole range $[0,1]$. This is still not satisfactory because the estimation becomes quite unstable then. They then fixed the problem using a linear combination between the non-normalized value and the normalized value, as described in algorithm 3 for the truth values of facts. Algorithm 3 uses a weight ë progressively (and linearly) decreasing from 1 to 0. Lastly, a remaining issue of 2-ESTIMATES is that for one set of views, a given distribution of estimates is always as likely its dual one, where W is replaced by its negation and each error factor $\varepsilon(V_i)$ is replaced by $1-\varepsilon(V_i)$.

Algorithm 3: Normalize WFacts (Galland, Abiteboul, Marian and Senellart 2010)

Input: $\mathcal{F}, \Theta, \lambda$
Output: A normalized value of Θ

1 $maxW \leftarrow max_{f_j \in \mathcal{F}} \Theta(W(f_j))$
2 $minW \leftarrow min_{f_j \in \mathcal{F}} \Theta(W(f_j))$
3 for each $f_j \in \mathcal{F}$ do

$$4 \ value_1 \leftarrow \frac{\Theta\big(W\big(f_j\big)\big) - minW}{maxW - minW}$$

$$5. \ value_2 \leftarrow round(\Theta\big(W\big(f_j\big)\big)$$

$$6 \ \Theta\big(W\big(f_j\big)\big) \leftarrow \lambda \times value_1 + \big(1 - \lambda\big) \times value_2$$

7 end for

8 return Θ

Another algorithm proposed by Galland et al. (2010), 3-ESTIMATES as shown in Algorithm 4, is aimed at overcoming the limitations of 2-ESTIMATES. It concerns about an additional series of parameters, namely, the error factor of facts. The algorithm is founded on the full underlying probabilistic model. It estimates $W\big(f_j\big)\,(f_j \in \mathcal{F})$, $\varepsilon\big(f_j\big)$ $(f_j \in \mathcal{F})$ and $\varepsilon\big(V_i\big)$ $(V_i \in \mathcal{V})$. The algorithm assumes that the errors of the views are null and that all the facts are easy to guess as an initialization. The algorithm then successively estimates one parameter given the other two (and the views) and iterates until convergence with a fixpoint computation very similar to 2-ESTIMATES. Here again, $\Theta\big(W\big(f_j\big)\big)$ is more precise given a numerical value that is an estimation of $\mathbb{P}\big(W\big(f_j\big) = T\big)$. Also, as for 2-ESTIMATES, they proved that the three estimators used in 3-ESTIMATES are valid given the other correct sets of parameters.

Algorithm 4: The 3-ESTIMATES algorithm (Galland, Abiteboul, Marian and Senellart 2010)

Input: $\mathcal{F}$, $\mathcal{V}$, $\mathcal{S}$

Output: An estimate of ε for each view and fact, an estimate of $W\big(f_i\big)$ for each fact

1 for each $V_i \in \mathcal{V}$ do

2 $\Theta\big(\varepsilon\big(V_i\big)\big) \leftarrow 0$ //initialization of error factor

3 end for

4 for each $f_j \in \mathcal{F}$ do

5 $\Theta\big(\varepsilon\big(f_j\big)\big) \leftarrow 0.1$

6 end for

4 while not convergence

5 for each $f_j \in \mathcal{F}$ do

$$6 \ posViews \leftarrow \sum_{V_i \in \mathcal{V}\&\&V_i\big(f_j\big)=T} \big(1 - \Theta\big(\varepsilon\big(V_i\big)\big)\Theta\big(\varepsilon\big(f_j\big)\big)\big)$$

$$7 \ negViews \leftarrow \sum_{V_i \in \mathcal{V}\&\&V_i\big(f_j\big)=F} \Theta\big(\varepsilon\big(V_i\big)\big)\Theta\big(\varepsilon\big(f_j\big)\big)$$

$$8 \ nbViews \leftarrow |\{V_i \in \mathcal{V} \,|\, \big(V_i, f_j\big) \in \mathcal{S}\}|$$

$$9 \ \Theta\big(W\big(f_j\big)\big) \leftarrow \frac{posViews + negViews}{nbViews}$$

10 end for

5 for each $f_j \in \mathcal{F}$ do

$$6 \ posViews \leftarrow \sum_{V_i \in \mathcal{V}, V_i\big(f_j\big)=T, \Theta\big(\varepsilon\big(V_i\big)\big)\neq 0} \frac{1 - \Theta\big(W\big(f_j\big)\big)}{\Theta\big(\varepsilon\big(V_i\big)\big)}$$

$$7 \ negViews \leftarrow \sum_{V_i \in \mathcal{V}, V_i\big(f_j\big)=F, \Theta\big(\varepsilon\big(V_i\big)\big)\neq 0} \frac{\Theta\big(W\big(f_j\big)\big)}{\Theta\big(\varepsilon\big(V_i\big)\big)}$$

$$8 \ nbViews \leftarrow |\{V_i \in \mathcal{V} \,|\, \big(V_i, f_j\big) \in \mathcal{S}, \Theta\big(\varepsilon\big(V_i\big)\big) \neq 0\}|$$

$$9 \ \Theta\big(W\big(f_j\big)\big) \leftarrow \frac{posViews + negViews}{nbViews}$$

10 end for

11 for each $V_i \in \mathcal{V}$ do

$$12 \ posFacts \leftarrow \sum_{f_j \in \mathcal{F}, V_i\big(f_j\big)=T, \Theta\big(\varepsilon\big(f_j\big)\big)\neq 0} \frac{1 - \Theta\big(W\big(f_j\big)\big)}{\Theta\big(\varepsilon\big(f_j\big)\big)}$$

$$13 \ negFacts \leftarrow \sum_{f_j \in \mathcal{F}, V_i\big(f_j\big)=F, \Theta\big(\varepsilon\big(f_j\big)\big)\neq 0} \frac{\Theta\big(W\big(f_j\big)\big)}{\Theta\big(\varepsilon\big(f_j\big)\big)}$$

$$14 \ nbFacts \leftarrow |\{f_j \in \mathcal{F} \,|\, \big(V_i, f_j\big) \in \mathcal{S}, \Theta\big(\varepsilon\big(f_j\big)\big) \neq 0\}|$$

$$15 \ \Theta\big(\varepsilon\big(V_i\big)\big) \leftarrow \frac{posFacts + negFacts}{nbFacts}$$

16 end for

17 end while

21 return Θ

In most scenarios, views only make positive statements, typically giving, for some query, the answer they have the most confidence in, but not giving the list of all possible false answers (which can be of unbounded size). Nevertheless, they focus on the situation where there are both positive and negative statements and use functional dependency information, if available, to infer possibly omitted negative facts. Considering the functional dependencies of the form "there is one and only one true answer to a question", they define a set of queries Q and each fact is associated with a reference query $ref\left(f_j \in Q\right)$. Then for each query $q \in Q$, they impose the following functional dependency constraints:

$$
\begin{cases}
\exists f_j \in F,\ \mathrm{ref}\left(f_j\right) = q \wedge W\left(f_j\right) = T \\
\forall f \in F - \left\{f_j\right\},\ \mathrm{ref}(f) = q \Rightarrow W\left(f_j\right) = F
\end{cases}
$$

These constraints express that each query has exactly one answer. Using the above constraint, they transform a problem with functional dependencies into a related problem with positive and negative statements. Specifically, given a set of views $V = \left\{V_1 \ldots V_m\right\}$, with no negative statements, and a set of queries Q verifying the above constraints, they modify the set of views into $V' = \left\{V_1', \ldots, V_m'\right\}$, by the following approach

$$
\begin{cases}
\forall f_j \in F,\ V_i\left(f_j\right) = T \Rightarrow V_i'\left(f_j\right) = T \\
\forall f_j \in F,\ \begin{pmatrix} V_i\left(f_j\right)\ \text{undefined} \wedge \exists f \in F, \\ \left(\mathrm{ref}(f) = \mathrm{ref}\left(f_j\right) \wedge V_i'(f) = T\right) \end{pmatrix} \Rightarrow \\
V_i'\left(f_j\right) = F
\end{cases}
$$

In other words, positive statements are kept, and negative statements are added for every unstated fact that refers to a query for which a positive statement has been made. This modified set of views is then applied to the aforementioned algorithms. When a view contradicts a functional dependency using more than one positive statement for the same query, all its positive statements are kept, even if they are inconsistent in such a case.

As reported in the work, experiments on both synthetic dataset and real-world datasets show that when using the above fixpoint algorithms, improvements can be obtain over the baselines, i.e., the basic VOTING algorithm and the TRUTH-FINDER of Yin et al., (2007).

Approaches Involved Copying Detection

As is assumed in the above approaches, data sources and facts are all probabilistically independent, but this is not always the case as copying between data sources is common in practice, especially on the web. Dong, Berti-Equille & Srivastava (2009a) consider how to find true values from conflicting information when there are a large number of data sources, among which some may copy from others. They present an approach that considers dependence between data sources in truth discovery. Intuitively, for a particular object, there are often multiple distinct false values but usually only one true value. Sharing the same true value does not necessarily imply sources being independent; however, sharing the same false value is typically a rare event when the sources are fully independent. Thus, if two data sources share a lot of false values, they are more likely to be dependent. They develop Bayes models to compute the probability of two data sources being dependent and take the result into consideration in truth discovery. Like all the above approaches, this work (Dong et al., 2009a) focuses on static information and considers a snapshot of data from different data sources.

Note that detection of dependence between data sources is based on knowledge of true values, whereas correctly deciding true values requires knowledge of source dependence. They are inter-dependence. So, they solve the problem by iteratively deciding source dependence and discovering truth from conflicting information.

Sharing the basic idea as (Yin et al., 2007), they present a different model for computing source accuracy and extend it to incorporate the notion of source dependence. To make models tractable, they only consider direct copying in copying detection and truth discovery and also cyclic copying is thought to be impossible.

Five computational models (depicted in Figure 3) are proposed in the work, and the core model Depen is based on the following three conditions:

Same source accuracy: For each object, all independent data sources have the same probability of providing a true value.

Uniform false-value distribution: For each object, there are multiple false values in the underlying domain and an independent source has the same probability of providing each of them.

Categorical value: For each object, values that do not match exactly are considered as completely different.

The Accu model is derived from the Depen model by relaxing the Same-source-accuracy condition. The other three models, i.e., AccuPR, Sim and NonUni, are derived from Accu.

Independent sources are assumed to be good under the following condition. For each $O \in \mathcal{O}$, let $\varepsilon(O)$ be the error rate of a source on O and $n(O)$ be the number of false values on O in the underlying domain. Then if

$$1 - \varepsilon(O) > \varepsilon(O) / n(O)$$

$$\text{(i.e., } \varepsilon(O) < n(O) / (n(O) + 1) \text{),}$$

independent sources in $\mathcal{V}$ are good. Involving discovering dependence between data sources, the Depen model copes with the truth discovery problem based on the VOTING approach under the assumption that all the data sources in $\mathcal{V}$ are good.

The computation of probability of dependence between sources in the Depen model requires several parameters: n ($n > 1$), the number of false values in the underlying domain for each object; c ($0 < c \le 1$), the probability that a value provided by a copier is copied; and ε ($0 \le \varepsilon < n / (n+1)$), the error rate. In the Depen model, for two data sources S_1 and S_2, they consider three sets of objects: $\bar{O}_t$, the set of objects on which the two sources provide the same true value, $\bar{O}_f$, the set of objects on which they provide the same false value, and $\bar{O}_d$, the set of objects on which they provide different values ($\bar{O}_t \cup \bar{O}_f \cup \bar{O}_d \subseteq \mathcal{O}$). The observation of $\bar{O}_t$, $\bar{O}_f$, $\bar{O}_d$ are denoted by Φ and k_t, k_f and k_d denotes their sizes respectively.

Figure 3. Computational models (Dong, Berti-Equille & Srivastava 2009a)

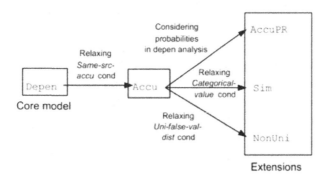

First, under the assumption that V_1 and V_2 are independent, denoted as $V_1 \perp V_2$, the probability that V_1 and V_2 provide the same true value for object O is

$$Pr\left(O \in \bar{O}_t | V_1 \perp V_2\right) = \left(1-\varepsilon\right)^2.$$

Under the Uniform-false-value-distribution condition, the probability that a data source provides a particular false value for object O is ε / n. Thus, the probability that V_1 and V_2 provide the same false value for O is

$$Pr\left(O \in \bar{O}_f | V_1 \perp V_2\right) = n \bullet \left(\frac{\varepsilon}{n}\right)^2 = \frac{\varepsilon^2}{n}.$$

Then the probability that V_1 and V_2 provide different values on an object O, is

$$Pr\left(O \in \bar{O}_d | V_1 \perp V_2\right) = 1 - \left(1-\varepsilon\right)^2 - \frac{\varepsilon^2}{n} = P_d$$

Assume that all the values of data sources are provided independently. The conditional probability of observation ϕ is

$$Pr\left(\phi | V_1 \perp V_2\right) = \frac{\left(1-\varepsilon\right)^{2k_t} \varepsilon^{2k_f} P_d^{k_d}}{n^{k_f}}$$

When V_1 and V_2 are dependent, denoted as $V_1 \sim V_2$, there are two cases where V_1 and V_2 provide the same value for an object. First, with probability c, one copies the value from the other and so the value is true with probability $1-\varepsilon$ and false with probability ε. Second, with probability $1-c$, the two sources provide the value independently and so its probability of being true or false is the same as in the case when V_1 and V_2 are independent. So, the probability is

$$Pr\left(O \in \bar{O}_t | V_1 \sim V_2\right) = \left(1-\varepsilon\right) \bullet c + \left(1-\varepsilon\right)^2 \bullet \left(1-c\right),$$

$$Pr\left(O \in \bar{O}_f | V_1 \sim V_2\right) = \varepsilon \bullet c + \frac{\varepsilon^2}{n} \bullet \left(1-c\right),$$

$$Pr\left(O \in \bar{O}_d | V_1 \sim V_2\right) = P_d \bullet \left(1-c\right).$$

The probability $Pr\left(\phi | V_1 \sim V_2\right)$ can be computed accordingly. By the Bayes Rule, the probability of $V_1 \sim V_2$ is given as

$$Pr\left(V_1 \sim V_2 | \phi\right)$$

$$= \frac{Pr\left(\phi | V_1 \sim V_2\right) Pr\left(V_1 \sim V_2\right)}{\begin{array}{c} Pr\left(\phi | V_1 \sim V_2\right) Pr\left(V_1 \sim V_2\right) + \\ Pr\left(\phi | V_1 \perp V_2\right) Pr\left(V_1 \perp V_2\right) \end{array}}$$

$$= \left(1 + \left(\frac{1-a}{a}\right)\left(\frac{1-\varepsilon}{1-\varepsilon+c\varepsilon}\right)^{k_t}\left(\frac{\varepsilon}{cn+\varepsilon-c\varepsilon}\right)^{k_f}\left(\frac{1}{1-c}\right)^{k_d}\right)^{-1}$$

Here $a = Pr\left(V_1 \sim V_2\right)$ ($0 < a < 1$) is the a-priori probability that two data sources are dependent. However, this equation does not indicate direction of dependence.

To perform the VOTING approach with involvement of data dependence, vote count of each value has to be computed. However, without knowing of the deterministic dependence relationship between sources, it is non-trivial to compute the vote count of a value. The straightforward but quite expensive approach is to enumerate all possible dependence cases of data sources. (Dong, Berti-Equille & Srivastava, 2009) propose to estimate a vote count by considering the data sources one by one.

For each source V, $\overline{Pre(V)}$ denotes the set of sources that have already been considered and

$\overline{Post}(V)$ denotes the set of sources that have not been considered yet. The probability that the value provided by V is independent of any source in $\overline{Pre}(V)$ is taken as the vote count of V. The vote count computed in this way is not precise because if V depends only on sources in $\overline{Post}(V)$ but some of those sources depend on sources in $\overline{Pre}(V)$, the estimation still (incorrectly) counts V's vote. To solve this problem, (Dong, Berti-Equille and Srivastava) take a greedy algorithm and consider data sources in such an order: in the first round, it selects a data source that is associated with a dependence of the highest probability; in later rounds, it selects a data source that has the maximal dependence on one of the previously selected sources each time.

Once an order of the data sources is decided, the probability that V provides a fact f independently of any data source in $\overline{Pre}(V)$, denoted by $I(V)$, is

$$I(V) = \prod_{V_0 \in Pre(V)} \left(1 - cP(V \sim V_0)\right)$$

The total vote count of f is $\sum_{V \in \overline{V}_O(f)} I(V)$, where $\overline{V}_O(f)$ is the set of data sources that provide f on O.

When knowing the vote count of each value, the true value can be discovered by voting. Algorithm VOTE in Algorithm 5 describes how to discover true values. VOTE iteratively computes the probability of dependence between each pair of data sources and the vote count of each value, and then for each object it takes the value with the maximal vote count as the true value. Notice that, in Line 12 of Algorithm 5, if there are several values winning the same number of votes, choose the previously selected one if possible or randomly choose one otherwise. This process repeats until the voting results converge. As reported in Dong et al., (2009a) when there are a finite number of objects in O, Algorithm VOTE converges.

The parameters in the model can be set initially according to a-priori knowledge of the data or by guessing a default value. During the voting process, in each iteration, α, ε and c can be refined based on the computed dependence probabilities and the discovered truth, and the new parameters will be used in the next iteration. As is reported in the work, different initial parameters settings lead to similar voting results.

Algorithm 5: The VOTE Algorithm (Dong, Berti-Equille and Srivastava 2009a)

Input: V, O
  Output: The true value for each object in O

1 for each $V_i \in V$ do $\overline{D}\overline{D}_0$
2 $\overline{D} = \varnothing$ //decided true values
3 $\overline{D}_0 = null$ //true values decided in the last round
4 while ($\overline{D} \neq \overline{D}_0$)
5 $\overline{D}_0 = \overline{D}$;
6 $\overline{D} = \varnothing$;
7 for each $V_1, V_2 \in V$ && $V_1 \neq V_2$
8 compute $Pr(V_1 \sim V_2)$;
9 end for
10 for each $O \in O$
11 compute vote count of each value of O;
12 select the value with the maximal vote count
    and add to $\overline{D}$;
13 end for
14 end while
15 return;

Unlike the Depen model only concerning about sources dependence to discover truth, the Accu model also considers accuracy (trustworthiness) of data sources when computing vote count. The Accu model computes a probabilistic distribution of various values in the underlying domain for a particular object.

For two data sources V_1 and V_2, $V_1 \rightarrow V_2$ denotes that V_1 is dependent on V_2. The accuracy of source V is denoted by $A(V)$, while the error rate of V is $\varepsilon(V) = 1 - A(V)$. When V_1 and V_2 are independent, we have

$$Pr\left(O \in \bar{O}_t | V_2 \perp V_1\right) = \left(1 - \varepsilon(V_1)\right)\left(1 - \varepsilon(V_2)\right) = P_t,$$

$$Pr\left(O \in \bar{O}_f | V_2 \perp V_1\right) = \frac{\varepsilon(V_1)\varepsilon(V_2)}{n} = P_f,$$

$$Pr\left(O \in \bar{O}_d | V_2 \perp V_1\right) = 1 - P_t - P_f.$$

While when V_2 copies from V_1 (similar for V_1 copying from V_2), the probabilities are

$$Pr\left(O \in \bar{O}_t | V_2 \rightarrow V_1\right) = \left(1 - \varepsilon(V_1)\right)\bullet c + P_t \bullet (1 - c),$$

$$Pr\left(O \in \bar{O}_f | V_2 \rightarrow V_1\right) = \varepsilon(V_1)\bullet c + P_f \bullet (1 - c),$$

$$Pr\left(O \in \bar{O}_d | V_2 \rightarrow V_1\right) = \left(1 - P_t - P_f\right)\bullet (1 - c).$$

Then similar to the Depen model, the probabilities of $V_1 \perp V_2$, $V_1 \rightarrow V_2$ and $V_2 \rightarrow V_1$ can be computed through the Bayes Rule.

Dong, Berti-Equille & Srivastava compute the accuracy of sources as the average probability of its facts being true:

$$A(V) = \frac{\sum_{f \in \bar{V}(V)} P(f)}{m}$$

Here $\bar{V}(V)$ is the values provided by V and m is the size of $\bar{V}(V)$. For each $f \in \bar{V}(V)$, $P(f)$ denotes the probability of f being true.

Consider an object $O \in \mathcal{O}$. Let $D(O)$ be the domain of O, including one true value and n false values. Let $\bar{V}_O$ be the sources that provide information on O. For each $f \in D(O)$, $\bar{V}_O(f) \subseteq \bar{V}_O$ is the set of sources that vote for f ($\bar{V}_O(f)$ can be empty). $\psi(O)$ denotes the observation of which value each $V \in \bar{V}_O$ votes for. To compute $P(f)$ for $f \in D(O)$, the probability of $\psi(O)$ conditioned on f being true needs to be calculated firstly. This probability should be that of sources in $\bar{V}_O(f)$ each providing the true value and other sources each providing a particular false value.

$$Pr\left(\psi(O) | f true\right) = \prod_{V \in \bar{V}_O(f)} A(V) \bullet \prod_{V \in \bar{V}_O - \bar{V}_O(f)} \frac{1 - A(V)}{n}$$

Among the values in $D(O)$, there is one and only one true value. Assume the a-priori belief of each value being true is the same β. Then $Pr\left(\psi(O)\right)$ is computed as

$$Pr\left(\psi(O)\right) = \sum_{f \in D(O)} \left(\beta \bullet \prod_{V \in \bar{V}_O(f)} A(V) \bullet \prod_{V \in \bar{V}_O - \bar{V}_O(f)} \frac{1 - A(V)}{n} \right)$$

By the Bayes Rule, $P(f)$ is

$$P(f) = Pr(f \text{ true} | \psi(O)) = \frac{\prod_{V \in \bar{V}_O(f)} \frac{nA(V)}{1 - A(V)}}{\sum_{f_0 \in D(O)} \prod_{V \in \bar{V}_O(f_0)} \frac{nA(V)}{1 - A(V)}}$$

To simplify the computation, Dong, Berti-Equille & Srivastava define the confidence of f, $C(f)$ as:

$$C(v) = \sum_{V \in \bar{V}_O(f)} \ln \frac{nA(V)}{1 - A(V)}$$

and the accuracy score of a data source V as

$$A'(V) = \ln\frac{nA(V)}{1-A(V)}$$

So we have

$$C(f) = \sum_{V\in\overline{V}_0(f)} A'(V)$$

Then the confidence of a value can be computed by summing up the accuracy scores of its providers. Finally, $P(f) = \dfrac{e^{C(f)}}{\omega}$, where $\omega = \sum_{f_0\in D(O)} e^{C(f_0)}$. Accordingly, a value with a higher confidence has a higher probability to be true; thus, values' confidence is used to discover truth.

Finally, if a source V copies a value f from other sources, V should be ignored when computing the confidence of f. So we have

$$C(f) = \sum_{V\in\overline{V}_0(f)} A'(V)I(V)$$

Here $I(V)$ is the probability that V provides f independently of any other data sources. The appropriate method used in the Depen model to estimate a vote count involves the computation of $I(V)$.

Based on the above Accu model, Dong, Berti-Equille & Srivastava give another algorithm, ACCUVOTE as shown in Algorithm 6, which is extended from VOTE to incorporate analysis of accuracy. ACCUVOTE conducts the analysis of both accuracy and dependence in each round. Specifically, ACCUVOTE starts by setting the probability of each value as one minus the overall error rate, iteratively (1) computes accuracy and dependence based on the confidence of values

computed in the previous round, and (2) updates confidence of values accordingly, and stops when the accuracy of the sources becomes stable. As is reported in (Dong, Berti-Equille and Srivastava, 2009), experiments show that when the number of objects is much more than the number of sources, the algorithm typically converges soon; nevertheless, the precise condition for convergence remains an open problem.

Algorithm 6: The ACCUVOTE Algorithm (Dong, Berti-Equille & Srivastava 2009a)

Input: $\mathcal{V}, \mathcal{O}$
  Output: the true value for each object in $\mathcal{O}$

1 set the accuracy of each sources as $1-\epsilon$;
2 while (accuracy of sources changes && no oscillation of decided true values)
3 for each $V_1, V_2 \in \mathcal{V}$ && $V_1 \neq V_2$ //compute dependence of each pair of sources
4 compute $\Pr(V_1 \sim V_2)$;
5 end for
6 sort sources according to the dependencies;
7 compute confidence of each value for each object;
8 compute accuracy of each sources;
9 end while;
10 for each $O \in \mathcal{O}$
11 among all values of O, select the one with the highest confidence as the truth;
12 end for;
13 return

As is stated before, Dong, Berti-Equille & Srivastava) also exploit several extensions of the Accu model by relaxing the Categorical-value condition and the Uniform-false-value-distribution condition, and by considering probabilities of a value being true in dependence discovery.

The Sim model is extended from Accu by incorporating the similarity model in Yin et al., 2007. The NonUni model considers false values that are not uniformly distributed. This model leads to the revised version of the probabilities $Pr(O \in \bar{O}_f \,|\, V_1 \perp V_2)$, and accordingly the revised version of $Pr(\psi(O)\,|\,\text{f true})$. While the AccuPR model incorporates the probability of a value being true in dependence discovery and captures the intuition that a frequent-occurring false value is not a strong indicator of dependence: a frequent false value tends to have a high probability of being true and thus lowers the probability of dependence between its providers.

As reported in Dong et al., (2009a), experiments on real-world and synthetic data show the following features of the above models.

In presence of source dependence, the models significantly improve truth-discovery results by considering dependence between sources; in absence of dependence, the models do not generate false dependence that can change the voting results, thus obtaining similar results as not considering dependence.

Though the algorithms do not tend to capture every variant of the real world, they are robust with respect to different settings of parameters, violations of assumptions, and indirect copying, and they apply well even if the real data do not conform to the models.

The models can effectively prevent falsification in most cases.

As a by-product, the source accuracy the models compute is similar to the percentage of true values over all values provided by the source.

A Semi-Supervised Learning Approach

As is shown above, most of existing approaches deal with the truth discovery problem using unsupervised learning methods. Yin & Tan (2011) proposed to use semi-supervised graph learning method with the help of ground truth data to cope with truth discovery problem, in 2011. As is reported in the work, this ground truth data, even

in very small amount, can greatly help to identify trustworthy data sources. Yin and Tan also derive the optimal solution to this semi-supervised truth discovery problem and provide an iterative algorithm that converges to it.

The input to the semi-supervised truth discovery problem is the same as the above traditional truth discovery problem, except that there is a subset of facts which are labeled as correct (i.e., ground truth facts). The goal is to assign a confidence score to each unlabeled fact, so that true facts have higher scores. A confidence score for a fact is defined to be a real value between -1 and 1. A score close to 1 indicates that a fact is believed to be true; while a score close to -1 indicates the reverse and a score close to 0 indicates that it is not known that the fact is true or false.

The proposed approach is based on two basic principles. First, as the principle utilized in all the above approaches, facts provided by the same data source should have similar confidence scores. The confidence scores of facts are estimated through the trustworthiness score of the data sources providing them. Second, value of implication between facts that is close to 1 indicates the facts should have similar confidence score, while negative value indicates that the two facts should have opposite confidence scores and they cannot be both true.

Formally, the semi-supervised truth discovery problem is defined as follows.

There are n facts $F = \{f_1, \ldots, f_n\}$, each provided by one or more of the m data sources $D = \{d_1, \ldots, d_n\}$. A subset of facts $F_l = \{f_1, \ldots, f_l\}$ is ground truth and thus labeled as true, while the remaining facts $F_u = \{f_{l+1}, \ldots, f_n\}$ are unlabeled. Each fact f is on an object $O(f)$. The implication between facts is denoted by $imp(f_1, f_2)$ ($-1 \le imp(f_1, f_2) \le 1$). Each data source can only provide one fact for each subject, although a fact can be a set-value, such as the authors of a book.

Yin and Tan model this problem as a graph optimization problem. The facts are modeled by a graph, with a node for each fact and an edge between each pair of related facts. An edge weight, w_{ij}, indicates relationship of two connected facts f_i and f_j. If f_i and f_j are provided by the same data source, then w_{ij} is set to a positive value $\alpha (0 < \alpha < 1)$. If f_i and f_j are on the same object (not in the same data source), then $w_{ij} = imp(f_1, f_2)$. Otherwise, w_{ij} is set to zero.

Consider an assignment of confidence scores to facts $c = \{c_1, \ldots, c_n\}$, where $c_i \in [-1, 1]$ is the score of f_i. The optimization aims to minimize the weighted sum of differences between the confidence scores of related facts. The loss function based on studies on semi-supervised graph learning (Zhou et al., 2004; Zhu et al., 2002; Zhu et al., 2003) can be utilized:

$$E'(c) = \frac{1}{2} \sum_{i,j} w_{ij} \left(c_i - c_j\right)^2,$$

where w_{ij} should be non-negative for all edges. But this option does not consider conflicting relationships between facts, which causes much information to be lost. Furthermore, $E'(c)$ can be easily minimized by assigning the score of 1 to each fact. Another option is to allow w_{ij} being negative. If $w_{ij} < 0$, then $E'(c)$ is minimized when c_i and c_j are different form each other. But under this situation, $E'(c)$ is not a convex function and may have many local minimums. Thus it is extremely difficult to optimize, especially for large-scale problems.

Finally, Yin and Tan choose a loss function from Goldberg et al., (2007), which can handle both positive and negative implications between facts:

$$E(c) = \frac{1}{2} \sum_{i,j} |w_{ij}| \left(c_i - s_{ij} c_j\right)^2,$$

where $s_{ij} = -1$ if w_{ij} is negative and $s_{ij} = 1$ otherwise.

In order to minimize $E(c)$, f_i and f_j should have similar confidence scores when $w_{ij} > 0$ (i.e., implication between f_i and f_j should be positive). When $w_{ij} < 0$ (i.e., implication between f_i and f_j should be negative), f_i and f_j should have opposite scores or scores both close to zero. The scores of labeled facts are fixed at 1 and cannot be changed. By minimizing $E(c)$, we get an assignment of scores that are not alone consistent with the relationships among facts, but also consistent with the scores given to the labeled facts.

An example graph of facts is shown in Figure 4. It contains seven facts $f_1, \ldots, f_7$ provided by three data sources D_1, D_2, D_3. f_1 is a ground truth fact. Because f_7 is mutual exclusive from f_1, $imp(f_1, f_7)$ should be close to -1. Thus f_7 will have a low confidence score, which also leads to a low score for f_6. f_2 and f_3 have high scores because they are provided by the same data source as f_1. f_5 is consistent with f_3 and thus has high score as well. f_4 also has high score because of its connections to f_2 and f_5.

In the work, Yin and Tan provide an analytical solution to minimize $E(c)$ and discuss when such a solution exists.

$E(c)$ is convex in c because each $\left(c_i - s_{ij} c_j\right)^2$ is convex. Therefore, to minimize $E(c)$, we only need to find c^* such that

$$\left. \frac{\partial E}{\partial c} \right|_{c = c^*} = 0,$$

Figure 4. An example graph of facts (Yin & Tan 2011)

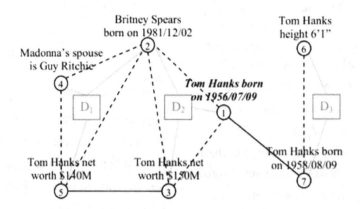

Under the constraint that $c_1,\ldots,c_l$ are fixed to their initial values. c can be split into the labeled set $c_l = (c_1,\ldots,c_l)$ and the unlabeled set $c_u = (c_{l+1},\ldots,c_n)$. With simple derivations, the above equation is equivalent to

$$\forall i \in \{l+1,\ldots,n\}, \sum_j |w_{ij}| c_i - \sum_j |w_{ij}| c_j = 0.$$

We define the weight matrix $W = [w_{ij}]$, diagonal matrix D such that $D_{ii} = \sum_j |w_{ij}|$, and matrix $P = D^{-1}W$. We split the weight matrix W into four blocks as $W = \begin{bmatrix} W_{ll} & W_{lu} \\ W_{ul} & W_{uu} \end{bmatrix}$, where W_{xx} is an $x \times y$ matrix. D and P are splitted similarly. Thus we can rewrite the above equation as

$$(D_{uu} - W_{uu})c_u - W_{ul}c_l = 0.$$

Therefore, we can solve

$$c_u = (D_{uu} - W_{uu})^{-1} W_{ul}c_l = (1 - P_{uu})^{-1} P_{ul}c_l,$$

if $(1 - P_{uu})$ is invertible.

However, $(1 - P_{uu})$ may be non-invertible. If an unlabeled fact f_k ($k \in (l,n]$) is not related to any labeled facts either directly or indirectly, we have $w_{ik} = w_{ki} = 0$ for any $i \neq k$, then the kth row and the kth column of the matrix $(1 - P_{uu})$ are 0, resulting in a non-invertible $(1 - P_{uu})$. The confidence score of f_k will remain undefined. In such cases $E(c)$ has multiple solutions, any confidence score f_k yields the same $E(c)$.

Yin and Tan solve this problem by introducing a "neutral fact" to the set of labeled facts. It has a confidence score of 0 and is connected to every unlabeled fact. Suppose f_1 is the neutral fact and has score $c_1 = 0$. The weight of the edge between f_1 and an unlabeled fact f_i must be above zero, i.e., $w_{1i} = w_{i1} > 0$. w_{1i} (w_{i1}) can be defined in many ways, as is shown in the work, the first definition is to use a constant weight:

$$w_{1i} = w_{i1} = \tau, i = l+1,\ldots,n,$$

where $\tau > 0$. The second definition is to assign a weight proportional to the total weight of edges from each node:

$$w_{1i} = w_{i1} = \mu \bullet \sum_{j>1} |w_{ij}|, \quad i = l+1, \ldots, n,$$

where μ is a small constant. The first definition is suitable for problems in which the distribution of edges is fairly uniform, i.e., the degrees of the nodes do not differ too much. The second definition is suitable for problems where different nodes have very different degrees, such as web-scale problems where some nodes have millions of edges while many others have only a few edges. With these considerations, $(1 - P_{uu})$ is positive-definite and is thus invertible. $E(c)$ has the unique solution $c_u = (1 - P_{uu})^{-1} P_{ul} c_l$.

Despite the above analytical solution, it is very expensive or impractical to compute. In a real-world truth discovery problem, the number of facts is usually large (tens of thousands), it is very expensive or impossible to compute the inverse of a matrix of such size. Yin and Tan solve this problem by an iterative procedure to compute c_u efficiently.

The goal of the iterative procedure is to compute $c_u = (1 - P_{uu})^{-1} P_{ul} c_l$ without involving matrix inversion or other expensive operations. The initial confidence score vector is set to $c^0 = (c_1, \ldots, c_l, 0, \ldots, 0)$, where c_i as the labeled data for $i = 1, \ldots, l$ while $c_i = 0$ for $i = l+1, \ldots, n$. Then the following steps are repeated until c converges.

Step 1: $c^t = Pc^{t-1}$

Step 2: Restore the confidence scores for the labeled facts, i.e., set $c^t_i = c_i$ for $i = 1, \ldots, l$.

It can be shown that the above steps are equivalent to computing $c^t_u = P_{uu} c^{t-1}_u + P_{ul} c_l$. Also, Yin and Tan have proved this procedure converges.

The iterative procedure presented above converges to the optimal solution and avoids comput-

ing matrix inverse. However, in reality, there are often millions times millions edges in the graph, which makes it impossible to materialize and store the matrices W and P. Yin and Tan give a way to decompose these matrices so that computation can be done in an affordable way.

Since in each iteration we need to compute $c^t = Pc^{t-1} = D^{-1} W c^{t-1}$, both D and W should be decomposed for efficient computation. A data source cannot provide multiple facts on the same object, i.e., if $d(f_i) \cap d(f_j) \neq \varnothing$, then $O(f_i) \neq O(f_j)$. W can be decomposed into two sparse matrices without overlapping entries: $W = W_s + W_d$, where $[W_s]_{ij} = \text{imp}(f_i, f_j)$ if $O(f_i) = O(f_j)$

and

$$[W_d]_{ij} = \alpha \bullet |d(f_i) \cap d(f_j)|$$

if $d(f_i) \cap d(f_j) \neq \varnothing$.

Also, D is decomposed as $D = D_s + D_d$, where $[D_s]_{ii} = \sum_j |[W_s]_{ij}|$ and $[D_d]_{ii} = \sum_j |[W_d]_{ij}|$.

W_s is usually a sparse matrix because the number of unique values for each subject is usually small. W_s can be stored as a sparse matrix and D_s can be computed from it. While W_d may contain billions or trillions of non-zero entries because some data sources may provide millions of facts. W_d thus needs to be decomposed further. Let T be a $n \times m$ matrix and

$$V_{ik} = \begin{cases} 1, & \text{if } d_k \in d(f_i) \\ 0, & \text{otherwise} \end{cases}.$$

It can be shown that

$$|d(f_i) \cap d(f_j)| = \sum_{k=1}^{m} V_{ik} V_{jk},$$

and thus $W_d = \alpha V V^T$.

Therefore,

$$Wc^{t-1} = W_s c^{t-1} + \alpha VV^T c^{t-1},$$

which can be easily computed because W_s is of manageable size, V is part of the input, and $VV^T c^{t-1}$ can be computed by two operations of multiplying a vector by a matrix.

D can be computed efficiently. D_s can be computed from W_s, and D_d can be computed as:

$$[D_d]_{ii} = \alpha \sum_j \sum_{k=1}^m V_{ik} V_{jk} = \alpha \sum_{k=1}^m V_{ik} \sum_j V_{jk}.$$

Let $|d_k|$ be the number of facts provided d_k. Obviously $|d_k| = \sum_j V_{jk}$, and thus

$$[D_d]_{ii} = \alpha \sum_{k=1}^m V_{ik} |d_k|.$$

In this way D_s and D_d can be pre-computed, and we can easily compute $c^t = D^{-1} W c^{t-1}$. Since the only operation involved in each iteration is multiplying a vector by a sparse matrix, we can easily implement this algorithm with MapReduce and run it in a distributed framework. Suppose there are n facts and m data sources and l be the total number of cases of a data source providing a fact, i.e., there are l non-zero entries in matrix V. Suppose for each fact f, on average there are q facts on the same objects as f. Then, the time complexity of this algorithm is $O((nq+l)t)$.

Note that, as is mentioned before, the neutral fact is important to the algorithm as it guarantees the existence of a unique solution and it is also important to the convergence of the iterative algorithm. As reported in the work, the neutral fact is also equivalent to introducing a small decay to the confidence scores of facts in each iteration.

As is reported in the work, experiments show the method achieves higher accuracy than existing approaches and can be applied on very large data sets.

SUMMARY

The truth discovery problem is ubiquitous in today's information life. It is often important to decide on the true facts because the false decision made on false facts can cause serious consequences. In this survey, we have reviewed different approaches to process the problem of truth discovery. We can see that the main approaches are to evaluate the interrelations between the trustworthiness of the data sources and the confidence of the facts provided by these data sources on different preconditions and assumptions. As the next step of study for this problem, mining more useful supporting relations between different facts may improve the quality of truth discovery significantly.

REFERENCES

Dong, X. L., Berti-Equille, L., & Srivastava, D. (2009a). Integrating conflicting data: The role of source dependence. *Proceedings of the VLDB Endowment*, 2(1), 550–561.

Galland, A., Abiteboul, S., Marian, A., & Senellart, P. (2010). Corroborating information from disagreeing views. In Proceedings of the Third ACM International Conference on Web Search and Data Mining (pp. 131-140). ACM.

Goldberg, A. B., Zhu, X., & Wright, S. (2007). Dissimilarity in graph-based semi-supervised classification. In Proceedings of Eleventh International Conference on Artificial Intelligence and Statistics (AISTATS) (Vol. 2, p. 46). AISTATS.

Yin, X., Han, J., & Yu, P. S. (2008). Truth discovery with multiple conflicting information providers on the web. *IEEE Transactions on Knowledge and Data Engineering*, 20(6), 796–808. doi:10.1109/TKDE.2007.190745

Yin, X., & Tan, W. (2011). Semi-supervised truth discovery. In Proceedings of the 20th International Conference on World Wide Web (pp. 217-226). ACM.

Zhou, D., Bousquet, O., Lal, T. N., Weston, J., & Schölkopf, B. (2004). Learning with local and global consistency. *Advances in Neural Information Processing Systems*, 16(753760), 284.

Zhu, X., & Ghahramani, Z. (2002). Learning from labeled and unlabeled data with label propagation (Technical Report CMU-CALD-02-107). Pittsburgh, PA: Carnegie Mellon University.

Zhu, X., Ghahramani, Z., & Lafferty, J. (2003). Semi-supervised learning using Gaussian fields and harmonic functions. In Proceedings of Machine Learning-International Workshop then Conference (Vol. 20, p. 912). Academic Press.

ADDITIONAL READING

Borodin, A., Roberts, G. O., Rosenthal, J. S., & Tsaparas, P. (2005). Link analysis ranking: algorithms, theory, and experiments. *ACM Transactions on Internet Technology*, 5(1), 231–297. doi:10.1145/1052934.1052942

Dong, X. L., Berti-Equille, L., Hu, Y., & Srivastava, D. (2010). Global detection of complex copying relationships between sources. *Proceedings of the VLDB Endowment*, 3(1-2), 1358–1369.

Dong, X. L., Berti-Equille, L., & Srivastava, D. (2009b). Truth discovery and copying detection in a dynamic world. *Proceedings of the VLDB Endowment*, 2(1), 562–573.

Kleinberg, J. M. (1999). Authoritative sources in a hyperlinked environment. [JACM]. *Journal of the ACM*, 46(5), 604–632. doi:10.1145/324133.324140

Page, L., Brin, S., Motwani, R., & Winograd, T. (1999). The PageRank citation ranking: bringing order to the web.

Wang, D., Kaplan, L., Le, H., & Abdelzaher, T. (2012, April). On truth discovery in social sensing: a maximum likelihood estimation approach. In Proceedings of the 11th international conference on Information Processing in Sensor Networks (pp. 233-244). ACM.

KEY TERMS AND DEFINITIONS

Facts: Information describing certain aspects of real-world entities that is claimed as true, whether or not it is right.

Fact Confidence: The confidence of a fact is the probability that this fact is true, to the best of our knowledge.

Fact Implication: The implication between two facts is each one's influence on the other one's confidence.

Source Dependency: If data source A copies facts from B, we say that A is dependent on B.

Truth Discovery: Given a set of views and a set of facts each provided by one or more data sources, how do we predict the confidence of each fact (i.e., likelihood of being true) and the trustworthiness of each data source.

Views: Data sources that contain a set of facts.

View Trustworthiness: The trustworthiness of a view is the expected confidence of the facts provided by this view.

Chapter 13
Query Processing Based on Entity Resolution

ABSTRACT

Dirty data exist in many systems. Efficient and effective management of dirty data is in demand. Since data cleaning may result in useful data lost and new dirty data, this research attempts to manage dirty data without cleaning and retrieve query result according to the quality requirement of users. Since entity is the unit for understanding objects in the world and many dirty data are led by different descriptions of the same real-world entity, this chapter defines the entity data model to manage dirty data and then it proposes EntityManager, a dirty data management system with entity as the basic unit, keeping conflicts in data as uncertain attributes. Even though the query language is SQL, the query in the system has different semantics on dirty data. To process queries efficiently, this research proposes novel index, data operator implementation, and query optimization algorithms for the system.

INTRODUCTION

Data quality has been addressed in different areas, such as statistics, management science, and computer science(Batini & Scannapieca, 2006). Dirty data is the main reason to cause data quality. Many surveys reveal that dirty data exist in most database systems. For example, a survey (Raman, DeHoratius & Ton, 2001) reports that over 65% of the inventory records at retailer Gamma were inaccurate at the store-SKU level. The consequences of dirty data may be severe. Having uncertain, duplicate or inconsistent dirty data leads to ineffective marketing, operational inefficiencies, inferior customer relationship

management, and poor business decisions. For example, it is reported (English, 1997) that dirty data in retail databases alone costs US consumers $2.5 billion a year. Therefore, several techniques have been developed to process dirty data to reduce the harm of dirty data.

Existing work on processing dirty data can be divided into two broad categories. The first category is data cleaning (Rahm & Do, 2000), which is to detect and remove errors and inconsistencies from data to improve data quality. However, data cleaning cannot clean the dirty data exhaustively and excessive. It may lead to the loss of information. Besides this, existing data cleaning techniques are generally time-consuming. Especially when the massive data is updated frequently, frequent data cleaning operation will greatly affect the ef-

DOI: 10.4018/978-1-4666-5198-2.ch013

ficiency of the system. Therefore, some researchers propose algorithms in the other category, to perform queries on dirty data directly and obtain query results with clean degree from the dirty data(Andritsos, Fuxman & Miller, 2006; Fuxman & Miller, 2005; Fuxman, Fazli & Miller, 2005).

Several models for dirty data management without data cleaning have been proposed (Boulos et al., 2005; Hassanzadeh & Miller, 2009; Widom, 2004). But most of these models only consider the uncertainty in values of the attributes and the quality degree of the data, without the consideration of the entities in real world and their relationships. In this paper, we focus on entity-based relational database model in which one tuple represents an entity. This model can better reflect the real world entities and their relationships.

In applications, the different representations of the same real-word entities often lead to inconsistent data, uncertain data or duplicate data, especially when multiple data sources need to be integrated (Dong, Halevy & Yu, 2009; Lenzerini, 2002). In the entity-based relational database, for the duplicate data referring to the same real-world entity, we combine these data, and for inconsistent data (or uncertain data), we endow each of them a value (we call it as quality degree) which reflects its quality. Example 1 shows this process.

Example 1: Consider a fragment of the dirty data shown in Table 1. In this table, we can easily identify that tuples 1, 3 and 6 refer to the same entity in the real world even though their

representations are different. By preforming entity resolution and combining these three tuples, we can get one entity tuple. In this process, we don't remove any data, because we are not completely sure which value is the correct (or real) one. By this table, we can only assume the value of the attribute "Name" is more likely to be "Wal-Mart", but we can't deny the value "Mal-Mart" completely. So, in entity-based relational database, we reserve all possible values of attributes, which implies that the value of one attribute in a tuple may be uncertain, and it may contain multiple values. We endow possible each attribute value with a quality degree in accordance with their proportion, as shown in Table 2. In tuples 1, 3 and 6, the value "Wal-Mart" appeases twice, so the quality degree is $2/3 \approx 0.67$. Similarly, other quality degrees can be given. Then we get an entity tuple as shown in Table 2.

As Example 1 shows, the entity-based relational database ingeniously processes the dirty data by entity resolution (Benjelloun et al., 2009; Y. Li, Wang, & Gao, 2011) and quality degree. Hence, an uncertain attribute value can be represented by a form: $((v_1,p_1),(v_2,p_2),...(v_m,p_m))$ where v_i is the possible value and p_i is the corresponding quality degree. Compared with the possible world model in the probabilistic database, the entity-based relational database model considers a tuple as an entity. Therefore, it does not generate all the

Table 1. A dirty data fragment

ID	Name	City	Zipcode	Phn	Reprsnt
1	Wal-Mart	Beijing	90015	80103389	Sham
2	Carrefour	Harbin	20016	80374832	Morgan
3	Wal-Mart	BJ	90015	010-80103389	Sham
4	Walmart	Harbin	20040	70937485	Sham
5	Carrefour	Beijing	90015	83950321	Morgan
6	Mal-Mart	Beijing	90015	80103389	Sham

Table 2. An Entity Tuple

ID	Name	City	Zipcode	Phn	Reprsnt
1	(Wal-Mart, 0.67), (Mal-Mart, 0.33)	(Beijing, 0.67), (BJ, 0.33)	(90015, 1.0)	(80103389, 0.67), (010-80103389, 0.33)	(Sham, 1.0)

possible world instances in query processing, which significantly increases the query processing efficiency.

With data model different from traditional relational model, the query in our system has different semantics compared to traditional relational database. With the consideration of multiple values of an attribute in the relation, the constraints in the query should take the uncertainty in attributes and constraint into consideration in two aspects. On one hand, the comparison between the value of attributes should consider the uncertainty in the values of attributes. On the other hand, since the values in attributes and constraints may contain error, the comparison between the attributes and the values in the constraints are approximate comparison instead of accurate comparison in traditional relational database.

As the queries have different semantics, the definitions of some data operators are redefined in our system. The projection operator is the same, but the selection and join operators are different. For example, the selection operator is a similarity search instead of accurate selection.

With different semantics in the query language, we develop novel techniques for efficiently query processing based on entity data model including similarity-based Operators, indices and query optimization

The remaining parts of this chapter are organized as follows. Firstly, we provides the data model in our system. Next, the architecture for entity-based database are discussed. Then details about the query processing methods are presented. We describe query optimization methods follow on. Finally, the reference is proposed.

ENTITY-BASED DATA MODEL

Definition of the Data Model

We firstly define the Uncertain Attribute Value in *Definition 1*. An uncertain attribute value not only contains possible values, but also contains the corresponding quality degrees. Then we give the definition of Entity in *Definition 2*. Entity is the basic unit of storage in the entity-based relational database system, containing a set of uncertain attribute values.

Definition 1 (Uncertain Attribute Value): An uncertain attribute value is a set of pair A= {(v,p)|v is possible value of the attribute and p is the quality degree of the value v}.

For an uncertain attribute value, it is clear the sum of quality degrees of all possible values is 1.

Definition 2 (Entity): An entity is a pair E= (K,A), where A is a set of uncertain attribute values and K is a set of keys that is to identify the entity uniformly (e.g., entity-ID).

Table 2 can help to understand these two definitions. Since we introduce the quality degree dimension in the definition of *Uncertain Attribute Value*, we need to define a new conception to reflect whether a tuple satisfies a query, and we call this conception *Similarity*.

Definition 3 (Similarity): For an uncertain values V in attribute *a* (we consider only numeric data type in this paper) and an atom constraint

C in form of $a@v$ where is a predicate symbol (e.g. $>$, $<$ ...) and v is a constraint, the similarity between them is defined as follows:

$$Sim\left(V@C\right) = \sum_{(v_i,p_i)\in V} sim\left(v_i@v\right)p_i \qquad (1)$$

$$sim\left(v_i@v\right) = \begin{cases} 1 & \text{where } v_i@v \\ 0 & \text{otherwise} \end{cases} \qquad (2)$$

For a selection query with a constraint $a<v$ (for the convenience, we use this form $a<v$ to represent a selection query in this paper), we consider that one tuple satisfies query with a similarity S, which can be calculated by Equation (1) and (2). We use an example to illustrate it.

Example 2: Consider a tuple t with value ((20, 0.1), (25, 0.4), (27, 0.4), (36, 0.1)) in attribute a, for two given queries, Q1 $a<22$ and Q2 $a<28$, the similarity between this tuple and query Q1 is 0.1 (0.1=1*0.1+0*0.4+0*0.4+0*0.1), and the similarity between this tuple and query Q2 is 0.9 (0.9=1*0.1+1*0.4+1*0.4+0*0.1).

With the support of the conceptions, some query operators are defined.

Operators of the Data Model

Selection Operator

As Example 2 shows, each query result satisfies the query with a similarity, since results with a low similarity are generally less interesting than higher similarity answers, we consider those results with a similarity less than a threshold τ (this parameter can be provided by user or the system sets a default value) as unsatisfied for a query. Therefore, the results of queries should be those answers that have a similarity exceeding a thresh-

old τ. So a query given by a $<_\tau$ x can be defined as an operator as follows:

$$Sim\left(a < x\right) > \tau \Leftrightarrow \sum_{(v_i,p_i)\in V} sim\left(v_i < x\right)p_i > \tau \qquad (3)$$

For example, in Example 2, if the threshold is fixed as 0.5, the tuple does not satisfy query Q1 but satisfies query Q2.

Entity Similarity Join Operator

Similarity join between two sets of tuples returns pairs of tuples satisfy that similarity values between the pairs are above a given similarity threshold. Currently, there are many methods to measure the similarity, such as edit distance, Hamming distance, Jacquard similarity, and cosine similarity. We consider the similarity based on edit distance connection. For a given two strings s and t, the edit distance of s and t $ed(s, t)$ is the number of a minimum editing operations (insert, delete, and replace) changing from s to t.

Considering that the attribute values are uncertain in the entity database, which may contain more than one value. We define entity similarity as follows.

Definition 4(Entity Similarity Join): Given two uncertain attribute value set R, S, and edit distance threshold τ, the entity similarity join picks all attribute value pairs satisfying as follows:

1. $r \in R \quad s \in S$
2. $\{(r,s) \mid r \in R \quad s \in S \quad v_{ri} \in r$
    $v_{sj} \in s \quad s.t. ed\left(v_{ri}, v_{sj}\right)k\}$

that is, there at least exists one possible value in r and s such that $ed(v_{ri}, v_{sj}) \leq k$ where v_{ri} represents the ith value of uncertain attribute value r.

Example 3: Table 3 presents entity attribute value set of R and S. and the edit distance threshold k is set as 3. The similarity join result is {(r1, s1),(r2, s2)}.This is because ed(Wal-Mart, Wal-mart)=1 $\leq$ 3 ed(John Strauss, John Strauss)= 0 $\leq$ 3.

Table 4 presents the join result.

Due to all possible values has a corresponding cleanliness in the entity database, the results of similarity join will also have a cleanliness that represents the quality of the result (reflecting the value of the results), as shown in Table 4. In Practical applications, we are only interested in a relatively high cleanliness results and lower cleanliness results will be ignored. So we consider another similarity join whose result reaches a certain cleanliness requirements (not less than a certain threshold), which is defined as follows:

Definition 5(Threshold Entity Similarity Join)
Given entity tables R, T,entity join attribute S, cleanliness threshold θ and edit distance threshold τ, the threshold entity similarity join operator on S of R and T returns the pairs (r_i, t_j) satisfying:

$$\{(r,s) \mid \sum_{ed(v_{ri}, v_{sj}) \leq k} p_{ri} \,^* p_{sj} \geq \theta\},$$

where p_{ri} is the cleanliness value of the i*th* possible value in attribute value r.

For example, if cleanliness threshold set as 0.3,then the result of threshold entity similarity join between *R* and *S* in *Table 3* contains no longer $\{(r_1, s_1)\}$. Because for (r_2, s_2), we have

$$\sum_{ed(v_{ri}, v_{sj}) \leq k} p_{ri} \,^* p_{sj} = 0.2 * 0.6 + 0.2 * 0.4 = 0.2 < 0.3,$$

that is, this result does not satisfy the requirement of cleanliness threshold.

THE ARCHITECTURE FOR ENTITY-BASED DATABASES

The framework of query processing in Entity-based Databases is the same as that of traditional relational databases (Garcia-Molina, Ullman, & Widom, 2000). With different semantics in the query language, we develop following three new techniques for efficiently query processing on the uncertain databases organized according to entities.

1. **Similarity-Based Operators:** With the definition of selection and join operators different from traditional relational database, we develop similarity search algorithm(Tong & Wang, 2012; X. W. Tong, Hongzhi; Li, Jianzhong; Gao, Hong, 2012) and similarity join algorithm(Liu, 2011) around the entity.
2. **Indices:** To process similarity selection and join efficiently, we designed novel index structures. The operator in our system is different from traditional similarity join in that the strings have weights. To handle the special operators in our system, the index considers not only more efficient string similarity search on string attributes(X. Tong & Wang, 2012), but also the similarity search of the combination of numerous and

Table 4. similarity join result of R and S

ID	R	S	Cleanliness
1	(Wal-Mart, 0.67), (Mal-Mart, 0.33)	(Wal-mart, 1.0)	1.0
2	(John Smith, 0.8), (John Strauss, 0.2)	(John Strauss, 0.6), (Johann Strauss, 0.4)	0.2

Table 3. entity table R, S

	R			S	
r_1	(Wal-Mart, 0.67), (Mal-Mart, 0.33)		s_1	(Wal-mart, 1.0)	
r_2	(John Smith, 0.8), (John Strauss, 0.2)		s_2	(John Strauss, 0.6), (Johann Strauss, 0.4)	

string attributes (X. W. Tong, Hongzhi; Li, Jianzhong; Gao, Hong, 2012), which can be used for the similarity search on weighted strings.

3. **Query Optimization:** With new operators in our system, for the query optimization, even though the query plan selection algorithms (Garcia-Molina et al., 2000) in classical relational databases could be applied in our system, the new estimation techniques for the operators should be developed. Thus we design novel result estimation algorithms for the selection and join operators in (Y. Zhang, Yang, & Wang, 2012) and (Y. Y. Zhang, Long; Wang, Hongzhi, 2012), respectively. Additionally, since the selectivity of join on multiple dirty relations is difficult to estimate, we propose a random algorithm for selectivity estimation and join order selection algorithm based the selectivity(Liu, 2012).

QUERY PROCESSING IN ENTITY-BASED DATABASES

Similarity Search in Entity-Based Databases

Similarity string handling in the application of computer systems plays an important role and is widely used in the database, information retrieval and other areas. However, similarity string matching also brings technical challenges. Firstly, it is not trivial to measure the difference between two strings. Secondly, even though many string measured functions have been proposed, it is costly to calculate these measured functions.

Based on the above discussion, for efficient string similarity search, a natural way is to build the appropriate indexing structure for the strings. Currently, the most extensive index structure for similarity string matching is inverted table structure that will split the string into grams, and measure the string by edit distance metric (Arasu, Ganti, & Kaushik, 2006; Behm, Ji, Li, & Lu, 2009; Goemans & Williamson, 1995; Hadjieleftheriou, Chandel, Koudas, & Srivastava, 2008; Hadjieleftheriou, Koudas, & Srivastava, 2009; Xiao, Wang, & Lin, 2008; Xiao, Wang, Lin, Yu, & Wang, 2011; Yang, Wang, & Li, 2008). Even though gram-based method can process similarity string matching efficiently in many cases, it has many weaknesses. First, it cannot effectively deal with the data update. Second, it has to introduce many collection operations when we use the inverted table to do the query, which increases the complexity of the query.

There are still a lot of non-inverted list indexing structures supporting similarity string search. For example, (Z. Zhang, Hadjieleftheriou, Ooi, & Srivastava, 2010) proposed edit distance tree structure that could hash each string into a number, and insert it into a B+ tree structure, which can support the data update well, but this structure emphasis on the ordering of the string too much and cannot pay full attention to the similarity of strings, therefore a large number of similar strings cannot be in the same leaf node, and the result is that the filter effect is not obvious, getting many alternative leaf nodes.

In summary, existing methods have drawbacks. We attempt to address these problems and design an index structure for efficient similarity string matching. Inspired by hash index and B+ tree, if similar strings are mapped into the same entry in the index, during the search, they can be accessed by once probing. Thus, the design of our index is to cluster the string set based on the similarity and build index with each cluster as an item. So similar strings can be accessed in batch in the index.

We choose a tree structure as the skeleton of our index, since such structure supports the data updating. Each node in the index corresponds to a set of similar strings. To represent the nodes in the index, for each node, we extract some grams from the strings in the corresponding string set, which are called feature grams. With feature grams, when some new strings are added to the set, they are added to the nodes with similar strings and distinguished from strings in other nodes. With this consideration, it is crucial to select the feature grams. To choose the feature grams, we use a cluster method to cluster the strings together and extract the feature grams from the center of each cluster. Our index is able to support threshold-based search, top-k search.

The rest of this part is organized as follows. Firstly, we discuss the necessary background and give some formal problem definitions. Then we present the basic principles of the Fgram-Tree. Finally, we describe details of the index building process and algorithm complexity.

Preliminaries

In this part we present some preliminary knowledge regarding string processing as well as the basic problem definition.

In the literature of similarity string matching, edit distance is commonly used to measure the similarity of two strings. We use edit distance to measure string similarity in our query process operations.

Definition 6 (Edit Distance): The edit distance between two strings s_i and s_j is the minimum number of single character edit operations (insertion, deletion, and substitution) that are needed to transform s_i to s_j. We denote the edit distance between as $ed(s_i, s_j)$.

Figure 1 shows a simple database table including 5 distinct strings and its general index structure. $ed(s_0, s_1)$ is 1, since s_0 is transformed to s_1 .with a substitute operation from single character 'y' to 'l'. Next, we give the formal definitions of string similarity search with respect to edit distance.

Figure 1. An example of string dataset and its general index structure(X. Tong & Wang, 2012)

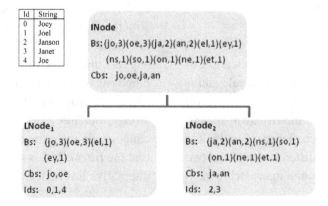

Definition 7 (Threshold-based Search): Given a query string q, a string set D and threshold θ. find all strings in D with edit distance no larger than θ..

In Figure 1, a threshold-based search query q ="Joe" with $\theta = 1$ .will return strings s_0, s_1 and s_4, .whose edit distances to q are no larger than 1.

Definition 8 (Top-k Search): Given a query string q and a string set D, find k strings in D with edit distance no larger than any other strings in D.

In Figure 1, a top-k search query $q=$ "Janet" with $k = 2$ will return strings s_2 and s_3, which .are more similar to q than any other strings in D.

When we do the similarity search, the algorithm of counting edit distance between two strings runs in $O\left(|s|^2\right)$ time for the length of strings: $|s|$, based on a standard dynamic programming method. As a result, when we deal with large amount of strings, we use various filtering techniques to prune the number of strings before counting edit distance. We split a string into grams.

Definition 9 (Ngram Split): Ngram split of a string is a set, that is composed by all the substrings with length N.

For example, the 2-gram split for "Joey" is {Jo, oe, ey}.

Some filters use the fact that if $ed\left(s_1, s_2\right) \leq \theta$, then the lengths $|s_1|$ and $|s_2|$ should differ by at most θ, and the number of common n-grams of them should be at least Num_c:

$$Num_c = Max\left\{|s_1|, |s_2|\right\} + 1 - \left(\theta + 1\right) * n \qquad (1)$$

Formula (1) is easy to understand. One single character edit operation could involve n grams at most, so θ operations involve $\theta * n$ grams at

most and a string contains $|s| - n + 1$ grams. As a result, the subtraction between two numbers is the least common n-grams.

Fgram-Tree

This part introduces the index structure and discusses query process methods including two kinds of similarity search queries.

Index Structure: We propose Fgram-Tree, a novel type of string indexing structure in a tree structure with each node representing a set of similar strings. Fgram-Tree pays more attention to the treatment of similar strings and supports threshold-based search, top-k search. We propose the formal definition of Fgram-Tree.

Definition 10 (Fgram-Tree) A Fgram-Tree is a tree structure where each leaf node is represented as a triple (bs, cbs, ids) and each intermediate node is a tuple (bs, cbs), where bs is a set of ngram splits of strings contained by all lower nodes and occurrences of each gram, cbs is the center of bs to represent bs, and Ids is the set of the strings attached to the node.

We use an example to illustrate our index. General index structure is shown in Figure 1. Similar strings s_0, s_1, s_4 are stored in LNode$_1$, and strings s_2, s_3 are stored in LNode$_2$. To reduce the storage overhead and the computing complexity, we store *bs* and *cbs* as bitmaps. Corresponding to each gram there are one bit in *bs* and a frequency of that gram. To facilitate the presentation, we do not use the bitmap form but the collection way in Figure 1, and we will discuss the problem by the collection way in the rest of the paper.

Query Process: In this part, we will discuss the algorithms for threshold-based search and top-k search based on our index.

Before the introduction of query process supported by Fgram-Tree, we give two filter conditions which are used in the query process and related to the similarity of strings. The basic idea of query process is that they are used to prune excess nodes impossible to contain similar strings with the query.

Condition 1: According to Formula (1), if the number of elements in intersection between the query string q and bs of node c is smaller than Num_c, node c must not contain a string similar with the query. Obviously, if the number of common n-grams bs sharing with q is smaller than Num_c, any string belonging to node c must not share such many grams with q, either.

Condition 2: If there is no intersection between a query q and cbs of node c, c must not contain a string meeting the query. We use center-based clustering method to construct our index and cbs is just the center for each cluster, thus it must intersect with q otherwise q does not belong to that cluster.

Threshold-Based Search: Firstly, we discuss threshold-based search. We use these two conditions to prune nodes to obtain the leaf nodes as few as possible. And then every string s in the obtained node set is verified to check whether s satisfies the constraint in the query. We give pseudo code of threshold-based search in Algorithm 1.

Algorithm 1 Threshold-basedSearch: (string q, tree node N, threshold θ)

1. **if** N is the leaf node **then**
2. **for** each $s \in N$ **do**
3. **if** Verify(q, s, θ) **then**
4. Add s in search result
5. **else**
6. **for** each child $c \in N$ **do**
7. **if** CommonGramBs(q, c, θ) **&&** CommonGramCbs(q,c) **then**
8. Threshold-basedSearch(q,c,θ)

Algorithm 1 traverses the nodes meeting Condition 1 and Condition 2 in the index recursively (Line 6-8) and verifies the strings in the visited the leaves (Line 1-4) by the verification algorithm only in $O(\theta|s|)$ mentioned in (Sakoe & Chiba, 1978). The strings satisfying the constraint are added to the final results. The function Common-GramBs() and CommonGramCbs() correspond to Condition 1 and Condition 2 respectively.

Top- K Search: Next, we discuss top-k search method. To take advantage of the feature of our index that similar strings are located in the same node in our index, we could firstly locate the leaf node where the most similar string with query q is by setting threshold 0 and choose k most similar strings in that node as the initialization result. Then we visit other nodes in the same way and update the result if a string with smaller threshold than the largest one in the result is found. Thus, we only need to access the index once. The top-k search algorithm is as follows:

Algorithm 2 Top-k Search: (string q, tree node N, threshold θ, result heap H)

1. **if** N is the leaf node **then**
2. **for** each $s \in N$ **do**
3. Geteditdistance(q, s)
4. Insert s into H
5. **if** $|H|>k$ **then** pop top entry
6. **else**
7. **for** each child $c \in N$ **do**
8. **if** CommonGramBs(q, c, θ) **&&** CommonGramCbs(q, c) **then**
9. Top-kSearch(q,c,θ,H)

In Algorithm2, we locate the nodes which contain the most similar string with q with the same pruning conditions as Algorithm 1(Line 7-9). We use a max-heap to keep the current top-k similar strings and directly calculate the edit distance in Geteditdistance()(Line 1-5). When a leaf node meets the conditions, for the strings in that leaf, we calculate their edit distances with q and insert them into the heap. If the number of elements in max-heap is more than k, we pop the strings with the largest distance.

Construction of Index Structure

According to above discussion, in order to filter more nodes in the same level, strings in the same node should be similar while those in different nodes should be not similar. Therefore, we design a center-based clustering method with each tree node equivalent to a cluster. *Cbs* in the index structure is just the center of our cluster. We design a center-based algorithm for the construction of such index in thispart. At first, we introduce the framework of our clustering method. Since center initialization, node selection and center update are basic operations for the clustering, we discuss them next respectively. At the end of this part, we analyze the time complexity of the index construction.

Overall Method: We show of overall framework of our method in this part by using a recursive approach to make a hierarchical clustering. In each level, firstly we initialize a suitable center *cbs* for each cluster. Secondly, we iteratively choose a center for every string and update the centers until the centers do not change. We show the overall index construction in Algorithm 3.

Algorithm 3 RecurMakeNode: (tree node N, int $r,$,int k)

1. **if**(the size of strings in $N > r$) **then**
2. InitNode(N)
3. **while**(true)
4. **for** each string s of N **do**
5. child node c=NodeChoice(s,N)
6. **for** each child node c of N **do**
7. SetCenter()
8. **if** each child c' *cbs* in N does not change **then**
9. **break**
10. **else return**
11. **for** each child node c of N **do**
12. **RecurMakeNode** (c,r,k)

The input of *Algorithm 3* is a tree node N which contains all the strings waiting to be clustered, the number k of clusters and the size r of strings in a child node. In order to take full advantage of the memory page size, k and r are by m emory limit. The output is the index based on tree with root N. And if the size of strings in a child node c is greater than r, the algorithm splits c (Line 2-9). Otherwise, it visits other nodes recursively. In Line 2, the center is initialized with InitNode(). Line 3-9 is the iterative process. The condition of ending iteration is that both the grams and their frequencies of all children nodes' cbs do not change (Line8-9). Line 4-5 chooses the suitable child node for s using NodeChoice(). Line 6-7 updates cbs of every child node using the method SetCenter().

Next, we will discuss the details about Init-Node(), NodeChoice() and SetCenter() respectively.

Center Initialization: In this part, we propose the method to initialize the center to accelerate the iteration rather than randomly generate centers.

Center-based clustering method is to select a center on behalf of the characteristics of each cluster. Clearly, two strings are similar if they have many common grams. Then we can extract some grams from every strings in the cluster to form a gram collection as the center, which share grams with each string. Moreover, we should extract the grams that similar strings share, because these grams could make similar strings located in the same cluster.

Based on above discussion, we pick some shared grams from *bs* as our center. And according to the idea of vote, the frequency of these shared grams should be higher than that of other grams. Thus, we choose some grams of high frequency to initialize our cluster center *cbs*. We use the trie structure(C. Li, Wang, & Yang, 2007)to initialize the center by picking some high frequencies grams from the trie in InitNode().

We develop an efficient three-step algorithm in Algorithm 4 to achieve the goal. Assume there are k centers and initialize for cbs_i ($i=1,2...k$).

In the first step, we construct a trie and select k grams in the leaf node belonging to different strings with the highest frequency and add them into $initgram_i$ ($i=1,2...k$) respectively (line 6-7).

In the second step, to each $initgram$, we find all of grams in the leaf node starting with n common characters with the gram in $initgram$, espacially that n is the length of grams in cbs and add these grams to $initgram$. (line 8-10)

In the last step, to each $initgram$, every gram in $initgram$ is split into standard grams. And we add them to the node center cbs. (line 11-12)

Algorithm 4 InitNode: (tree node N)

1. center cbs_i of N's every child ($i=1,2...k$)
2. $initgram_i \leftarrow (i=1,2...k)$
3. Heap $H \leftarrow \varphi$
4. TrieNode root $\leftarrow$ MakeTrie()
5. traverse the trie, $H \leftarrow k$ grams whose frequency is highest
6. **for** each $initgram_i$ **do**
7   $initgram_i \leftarrow H[i]$
8. **for** each substring s of $H[i]$ with length n **do**
9. **if**(a $gram$ begins with s in trie) **then**
10. $initgram_i \leftarrow gram$
11. **for** each $gram$ of $initgram_i$ **do**
12. $cbs_i \leftarrow$ the standard grams of $gram$

The main computation cost of Algorithm 4 is the construction of the trie with $O(N)$, since when the trie is constructed the cost of collecting high frequency grams(Line 7-12) is mainly trie traversal with time complexity $O(N)$.

Node Choice: In this part, we discuss the determination method of the clusters the strings belonging to in the iteration.

The goal is that strings in the same node should be similar but not similar to strings in other nodes. It means that strings in the same node should share more grams while less grams with those in different nodes. Thus, the smaller the intersection size of any centers is, the less common grams are in different nodes. Specifically, if we insert a string s into one node, the intersection size may become large. As a result, when we make node choice for a string, we should minimize the incremental intersection size after it is inserted.

To illustrate this problem clearly, we discuss the change of the intersection between two centers. Two $cbs_{1,2}$ divide the gram set into four subsets r_1, r_2, r_3, r_4. $cbs_1 = r_1 \bigcup r_3$, $cbs_2 = r_2 \bigcup r_3$. r_3 is the set of shared grams between cbs_1 and cbs_2, while r_1 and r_2 present their unique grams collections. r_4 is the set of all other grams not belonging to $cbs_{1,2}$. Obviously, $|r_3|$ is the intersection size and our goal is minimizing it after choosing a node for ngram split gs of a string. We give the choosing method as follows.

If $gs \bigcap r_1 = gs_1, gs \bigcap r_2 = gs_2$, we choose cbs_i where $|gs_i| = Max(|gs_1|, |gs_2|)$.

For the classification, we have two possible ways. The first is that gs is assigned to cbs_1. Such that $|r_3| = |r_3| + |gs_2|$. The second is that gs is assigned to cbs_2. Such that $|r_3| = |r_3| + |gs_1|$. Thus if $|gs_1| > |gs_2|$, we choose cbs_1 and otherwise we choose cbs_2. Therefore, we choose the center which has the most common grams with gs during the filtering of common grams with other centers. For the convenience of discussion, we define $|gs_i|$ as single covered degree *sc-degree*.

Based on the above discussion, we compute *sc-degree* for every center and select the center whose *sc-degree* is the largest. In the first step, we maintain the intersection between any two cbs represented by bitmap in a two-dimensional array to support the operation filtering of common grams with other centers, therefore it runs in $O(k)$

time where k is the number of clusters. In the second step, we select the center with the largest *sc-degree*. Obviously, the complexity of NodeChoice() is $O\left(k^2\right)$.

While querying a string q, CommonGramCbs() in Algorithm @.1, @.2 is used to judge whether there is a intersection between the ngram split gs of q and cbs. Because of our node choice method, gs must have a intersection with cbs which greatly enhanced filter function of the index.

Center Update: In this part, we introduce the update method of center cbs during the index construction.

In each iteration, if a gram is chosen as the center, it must be contained in the ngram splits of two strings. Therefore, we should choose the grams from those with frequencies no less than two. If we apply such update method, the number of grams in the center will be very large which may cause a new problem that many grams would lead to excessive iterations. Grams in each center must be constituted by each ngram split of the string waiting for clustering. According to the node choice method mentioned, to a string s, due to the center containing the overlapping part with ngram split of *s*, *s* will be chosen by this center. Then we can say that this overlap controls string *s*. Assuming that the number of elements in each overlapping set has taken to the minimum, then it is obvious that the center size will be minimal.

Next, we formally explain this process by drafting some definitions and get the conclusion in Theorem 1 that a large number of grams would not increase the iteration times.

Definition 11 (Control Effect): To a ngram split gs of s, if common(cbs_i, cover) $\geq$ common(cbs_j, cover)(j=1,2...k, j ≠ i) where Common(A,B) is sc-degree between set A and B and cover is the subset of gs, then cover determines which center s belongs to and every gram in cover has control effect to gs.

Definition 11 illustrates a control effect existing in a string s that means we may only compare a part of ngram split of s with the center to select the appropriate cluster rather than to compare the whole ngram split collection. Every center should be composed by covers and when each |cover| takes the min value, the center size will be minimal. Then, we define min cover set as well as the min center.

Definition 12 (Min Cover Set): Mcs is a min cover set, if its arbitrary subsets are not cover sets.

Definition 13 (Min Center): Min center Mcenter= $\left\{mcs_1, mcs_2 ... mcs_{|S|}\right\}$, mcs_i is the min cover set of s_i, $s_i \in S$, where S presents all of strings in one node.

Definition 13 shows the composition of the minimal center. Then we use above definitions to prove a theorem that implies larger center size would not increase the iteration times.

Theorem 1: When Mcenter converges, any center Lcenter with larger size satisfying $Lcenter \supseteq Mcenter$ must also converge.

Proof: Suppose that all the strings in one node is S, to each ngram split of string s in S, we divide it into two sets min cover set (*mcs*) and remaining set (*rs*). According to Definition 6, *mcs* could control any subset *sub* of *rs*, as a result, when *Mcenter* converges, every mcs_i (i=1,2...|S|) converges, then sub_i must converge. Obviously,

$$Mcenter = \left\{mcs_1, mcs_2 ... mcs_{|S|}\right\}$$

and the center

$$Lcenter = \left\{mcs_1 \bigcup sub_1, mcs_2 \bigcup sub_2 ... mcs_{|S|} \bigcup sub_{|S|}\right\},$$

therefore *Lcenter* converges.

Theorem 1 shows that due to the control effect, when Mcenter converges, Lcenter must also converge. In another word, their iteration times are the same. And because the size of Mcenter is smaller than Lcenter, the iteration times would not change with the increasing of center size.

We use SetCenter() to update the center in Algorithm 3. And because our method is based on operations of bitmap, the complexity of SetCenter() is $O(1)$ as well as judging convergence.

Complexity Analysis: In this part, we analyze the time complexity of index construction.

Algorithm 3 visits each node recursively. In every recursion, it contains two phases, initialization and iteration. The complexity of the initialization phase is the establishment of the trie with $O(N)$, where N is the number of strings. In iteration phase, because updating center and judging convergence run in constant time, the main consuming is choosing node with cost $O(k^2)$, where k is the number of clusters. Iteration phase has 2 levels of iterations with m and N times respectively, so the cost of the second phase is $O(mk^2N)$ where m is the iteration times when the center converges. As a result, in every recursion Algorithm 3 runs in $O(mk^2N)$ and in the whole recursive process Algorithm 3 runs in $O(mk^2NlogN)$. Because m would not increase with the bit size and m is far smaller than N in reality as well as k is a constant by memory limit, then the time complexity of Algorithm 3 is $O(NlogN)$.

Threshold Similarity Join in Entity-Based Databases

Existing similarity join algorithm can not be efficient to solve threshold entity similarity join. String-based similarity join only returns string pairs satisfying the similarity threshold, but threshold entity similarity join need to return entity pairs. Adopting the similarity join method based on string, we must first compute the string pairs satisfying similarity threshold, then aggregate strings according to the entity they are in, in addition, compute the entity similarity. Since each value of the entity attribute has cleanliness, the great string similarity value would not means great quality of entity pairs, which results in a large number of redundant computing. When entity relational table is large, the efficiency of this method is low. Therefore, String-based similarity join algorithm is not applicable to solve the problems of the threshold entity similarity join problem. In addition, set-based similarity join only considers the exact matching of the internal elements of the set. But threshold entity similarity join considers fuzzy matching, and also the quality of the elements in entity attribute.

For the problem discussed above, we proposed ES-JOIN algorithm (Liu, 2011),next we specify describe this algorithm. We firstly describe ES-JOIN algorithm framework structure. Then give description of specific ES-JOIN algorithm. Finally, we optimize ES-JOIN algorithm.

ES-JOIN Algorithm Framework Structure

In this part, we describe the basic idea and framework of the ES-JOIN algorithm through the link of entity databases and relational databases.

First, we try to solve entity similarity join using the method based on string similarity join. An entity attribute values can be represented by the following quadruple form in a relational database: *eid*, *cid*, value,pro. Considering entity attribute value $s = \{(p_1,\sigma_1),(p_2,\sigma_2)...(p_m,\sigma_m)\}$, we can put it into m rows, and each row represents a possible choice of S. Where m rows share an eid which uniquely identify an entity. The cid column sequentially values 1,2...m, indexing m selection values of S. The value column value stores m strings for the m selections, and pro represents string weight. The greater the weight, the higher quality of the S value. Entity attribute Name in *Table 5* specifically expressed in a relational database, as shown in Table 7:

Using string-based similarity join method, we should first split the entity join attributes into two tables R and T formed as shown in *Table 7*. Then adopt dynamic programming method to calculate edit distance between any two strings in R and T. If the edit distance is less than a given threshold value, we return them as the first step result. Then merge the first step results according to eid and return the final result.

Obviously, the cost of this method is very high. It needs to compute the edit distance between all possible values of the join attribute. While the time complexity of dynamic programming algorithm computing edit distance between two strings is $O(n^2)$, and space complexity is $O(n)$. Our goal is to design a good filter measures to reduce the string pairs and entity pairs that does not match as much as possible.

Existing research shows that using filter measures based on q-gram inverted index can prune large sting pairs that do not match, thereby reducing the number of calculations of the edit distance, and improving the efficiency of the implementation of the algorithm.

Based on the above description, we adopt the traditional filter-and-verify framework for ES-JOIN algorithm in this chapter

The specific process is shown in Figure 2:

Depicted in Figure 2, ES-join algorithm first merges the bilayer index to obtain initial candidate set, then filter the candidate set, finally compute similarity for generated candidate set to return the final result. This process is different from the string similarity join process: firstly, the bilayer

prefix index does not take string as the basic unit of the index, but the entity. Therefore, we do not need to merge string pairs in verify process. In addition, the ES-JOIN method can filter out the string pairs which similarity is high but the quality is very low in the filter stage, saving a lot of redundant computation.

Based on the framework of the ES-JOIN algorithm, *Algorithm 5* describes a specific implementation process.

Algorithm 5: ES-JOIN algorithm

Input: Entity table R,S, bilayer prefix index entity T_r, T_s on join attribute A, the edit distance threshold value τ, the similarity threshold θ

Output: Entity pair set *Result* meeting the join condition

1. $Result = \varnothing$
2.   The initial candidate
se*Cans*=Generate_candstruct(T_r,T_s)
3.   Candidate set *Canf*=Generate_cand(*Cans*)
4.   Result=verify(*Canf*)

Return Result: ES-JOIN algorithm adopts the bilayer prefix index structure to generate the candidate set. In the first step, Generate_candstruct merges bilayer prefix index and generates possible similar entity candidate pairs. In Step (2), Generate_cand use quality degree filtering candidate sets generated in the first step to generate the final candidate set. The finally step through iterative algorithm to verify the similar entity pairs, and ultimately return entity similarity join result.

Table 5. Custom information table

Id	Name	City
1	{Catherine,0.4;Kate,0.1;Kitty,0.5}	{NewYork,0.8;NY,0.2}
2	{Alexander,0.7;Ada,0.3}	{LasVegas,0.8;LV,0.2}
3	{Charles,0.8;Chunk,0.2}	{Chicago,0.8;CHI,0.2}

Figure 2. The framework of ES-JOIN algorithm (Liu, 2011)

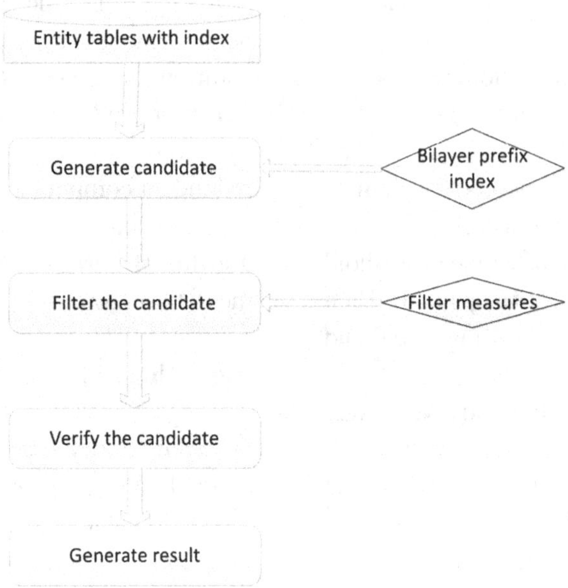

Table 7. The representation of entity in relational database

eid	cid	Name	Pro
1	1	Catherine	0.4
1	2	Kate	0.1
1	3	Kitty	0.5

ES-JOIN Algorithm and Analysis

In this part, we first introduce the bilayer prefix index structure, followed by describing how to merge the bilayer prefix index to generate candidate set, next using novel filter measures further filter the candidate set. Then verify the candidate sets, and return the final result. Finally, theoretically analysis the ES-JOIN algorithm.

Bilayer Prefix Index Structure

The similarity between entities can be converted to similarity between strings in entity. However, the existing prefix index based on string similarity join only return string pairs which satisfy the similarity condition, but does not reflect the entity similarity which string lies in. To solve this problem, we define a novel bilayer prefix index framework to produce similar candidate strings with entity information.

Bilayer prefix index is based on prefix index adopted in string similarity join. In string similarity join process, prefix index is an inverted index structure. The construction method is as follows: First, generate q-gram for all candidate strings. Secondly, sort all of the q-gram by IDF, i.e., the lower frequency q-gram is ranked in the front side of the sequence. Its intuitive idea is that the inverted list of a low frequency q-gram is relatively small, so the candidate set generated after prefix filtering is correspondingly small (Arasu et al., 2006). Again, sort the collection of q-grams of each string according to the order of the global q-gram.

Finally, the prefix index creates the inverted table for q-gram appearing in all string prefix length.

Different from string gram collection, multi-value characteristic of the entity attribute value determines the string q-gram generated in entity attribute is no longer a tuple of the form (l, g). We use the four-tuple (eid, cid, l, g) represents a q-gram. Specifically, eid represents entity number, all q-grams of one entity attribute value share a unique entity number. cid represents q-gram generated by the string which order is cid. i.e., the q-gram set of one string in entity attribute value shares a unique cid. Also, *l* represents the position information of the q-gram, g is the value of the q-gram.

Unlike existing prefix index based on string, bilayer prefix index takes the value of q-gram as index entries. The inverted table stores the entity number where .q-gram lies in. The second layer take eid as index entry, storing the 2-tuple structure (cid, Pro), where the value in the 2-tuple has the same meaning with corresponding q-gram. Using bilayer index, entity similar information can be reflected in the emerging index.

Example 4: In the entity Table 8 set $\tau = 1, q = 3$. The total sequence of the 3-gram in the value attribute is (bce, bcd abc). Therefore, bilayer prefix index is as Figure 3.

Candidate Set Generation

The candidate set is generated through two-step, the first step merges bilayer prefix index, and the second step filters off entities which does not meet the similarity threshold by filtering measures to obtain the similar entity pair candidate set.

Algorithm of Merging Bilayer Prefix Index and Analysis

Entity-based similarity join candidate set generation needs the merge the index of the two entity table .

Before merging process, we introduce a novel structure: entity candidate structure.

Definition 14 (Entity Candidate Structure Can_e): The similar characteristic of entity pair is denoted as:

$$(eid_1, eid_2) \rightarrow \{(eid_1.cid, eid_2.cid) \mid (C_{eid_1.cid} \cap C_{eid_2.cid}) \neq \varnothing\}$$

where (eid_1, eid_2) is an entity id pair, representing all entities which meet prefix filtering condition. C is the collection of q-gram of string prefix. *Cans* is entity candidate structure set. $Can_e.eid$ is denoted as $(eid_1, eid_2) . Can_e.cid$ is $(eid_1.cid, eid_2.cid)$ list satisfying $(C_{eid_1.cid} \cap C_{eid_2.cid}) \neq \varnothing$, $|Can_e.cid|$ is the length of the list and the weight of $(eid_1.cid, eid_2.cid)$ is equal to the product of the two string weight.

In the process of merging bilayer prefix index, we need first merge entities with the same q-gram. Then merge strings with the same prefix in merged entities to get entity candidate structure. After merging process, the entity candidate set directly takes entity as a basic unit, which save a lot of repetitive computations in string similarity filtration and verify stage.

Example 5: Suppose implementing similarity join operation on attribute Name of Table 5 and Table 6, set that $\tau = 2, \theta = 0.1$, entity candidate structure Can_e is shown in Figure 4:

Algorithm 6 describes the details of generating initial entity pair candidate structure.

Table 8. Entity table

eid	value
1	{abc,0.9;abcd,0.1}
2	{abce,0.5;bcd,0.5}

Figure 3. bilayer prefix index (Liu, 2011)

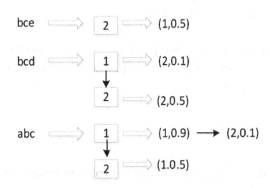

Algorithm 6: Generate_candstruct:

Input: Entity table R,S, bilayer prefix index T_r, T_s
Output: Entity pair candidate structure *Cans*.

1. $Cans = \varnothing$
2. Merge the inverted list with the same q-gram in T_r and T_s, consisting of entity pair candidate structure Can_e
3. For each Can_e
   a. If $Can_e.eid \in Cans.eid$,then insert $Can_e.cid$ into $Can_e.cid$ list of *Cans* by descending weight.
   b. If $Can_e.eid \notin Cans.eid$,then Can_e into *Cans*.
4. Return *Cans*

In the process of generating entity candidate structures, first we initialize *Cans* as empty. (the first step). Then merge bilayer prefix index on the join attribute. Based on each q-gram has a unique global sequence, we can take hash method by hashing inverted table with common q-gram into structure of Can_e to complete the second step. Then judge entity pairs in the generated Can_e whether has appeared in Cans. If so, merged the two Can_e structures (third step). In the merger process, do duplicate removal for cid pairs and insert cid pairs into *Cans* by descending weight. The purpose of step 3 is aggregating Can_e generated in the second

step by the same cid pairs (sum of the cid pairs is equal), and making each entity pairs appears only once in *Cans* after merging to simplify the next step of the filtering operation . In addition, ordering cid pairs is also in order to reduce the time complexity in the next filtration step by not traversing the entire cid pair list.

Algorithm time complexity analysis: Set $P(s) \bullet P(r)$ as prefix set of entity join attribute value, and $l_s(e)$ as the size of inverted index whose q-gram is e. Suppose the average number of entity attribute value as c. In order to get entity candidate structure set, Generate_candstruct needs to traverse the inverted table satisfying $qgram \in P(s) \cap P(s)$,which cost is equal to $\sum_{e \in P(s) \cap P(r)} (l_s(e) + l_r(e))$. Set the average length of the inverted table as l, the common q-gram number as n,and the size of the result which algorithm finally returns as C_Q . Then the average complexity of sorting in the third step is $O(c \log c \cdot C_Q)$. And the overall complexity of the algorithm is the two adding up, that is. $O(n \cdot l) + O(c \log c \cdot C_Q)$

Figure 4. Entity candidate structure Cane (Liu, 2011)

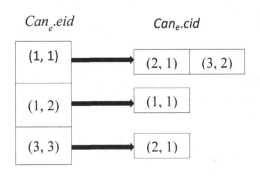

Algorithms of Filtering to Generate Candidate Set and Analysis

If all the merged eid pairs were inserted into candidate set, the candidate set will be very large. And the cost of computing edit distance between strings will seriously affects the performance of the algorithm. Therefore, we use filtering measures to filter merged index, further reducing the number of the candidate set.

By observing that larger weight strings contribute more to similarity between entities. If the match between larger weight strings can be determined as soon as possible, we can filter out more candidates, making the final candidate set as much as possible small.

Based on the above observations, we give two filters.

Property 1: Given attribute value

$$s = \{(p_1,\sigma_1),(p_2,\sigma_2)...(p_m,\sigma_m)\},$$

$$r = \{(q_1,\delta_1),(q_2,\delta_2)...(q_n,\delta_n)\}$$

similarity threshold θ, s,r ranking by descending weight. Suppose (cid_1,cid_2) was the first pairs in the entity candidate structure set,if

$$p_{cid_1} \cdot p_{cid_2} < \frac{\theta}{|Cane.cid|}, \text{ then}$$

$$d(Can_e.eid) < \theta$$

Proof: If s, r are similar, then

$$\sum\nolimits_{d(s_i,r_j)\le\tau} p_i \cdot q_j \cdot sim(s_i,r_j) \ge \theta.$$

Because

$$0 \le sim(s_i,r_j) \le 1,$$

so $\sum\nolimits_{d(s_i,r_j)\le\tau} p_i \cdot q_j \ge \theta$.

The number of string pairs which meet $d(s_i,r_j) \le \tau$ is $|Can_e.cid|$. According to the pigeonhole principle,if

$$\sum\nolimits_{d(s_i,r_j)\le\tau} p_i \cdot q_j \ge \theta,$$

then

$$p_i \cdot p_j < \frac{\theta}{|Cane.cid|}.$$

Again,

$$p_{cid_1} \cdot p_{cid_2} \ge p_i \cdot p_j,$$

so, if

$$p_{cid_1} \cdot p_{cid_2} < \frac{\theta}{|Cane.cid|}$$

then

$$\sum\nolimits_{d(s_i,r_j)\le\tau} p_i \cdot q_j < \theta,$$

that is $\sum\nolimits_{d(s_i,r_j)\le\tau} p_i \cdot p_j \cdot sim(s_i,r_j) < \theta$

Property 2: Let the cid pairs of entity candidate structure linked list be

$$(cid_{11},cid_{21}),(cid_{12},cid_{22})...(cid_{1m},cid_{2m}),$$

m denotes the length of linked list,suppose

$$k = \min\{j \mid \sum\nolimits_{i=1}^{j} p_i \cdot q_i \ge \theta\},$$

if $k > m$,then $d(Can_e.eid) < \theta$

Proof: If s, r are similar, then

$$\sum\nolimits_{d(s_i,r_j)\le\tau} p_i \cdot q_j \cdot sim(s_i,r_j) \ge \theta.$$

Because $0 \le sim(s_i,r_j) \le 1$ so

$$\sum\nolimits_{d(s_i,r_j)\le\tau} p_i \cdot q_j \cdot sim(s_i,r_j) \le \sum p_i \cdot q_j$$

If $k > m$, then

$$\sum\nolimits_{i=1}^{m} p_{cid1i} \cdot p_{cid2i} < \theta, \text{ i.e, } \sum p_i \cdot q_j < \theta \text{ so}$$

$$\sum\nolimits_{d(s_i,r_j)\le\tau} p_i \cdot p_j \cdot sim(s_i,r_j) \le \theta .$$

Property 1 simply determines whether the first cid pairs of the entity candidate structure list meets the similarity threshold. Properties 2 filter again the candidates which meet Property 1, further reducing the size of candidate set.

Example 6: Do similarity join on attribute "Name" in Table 5 and table 6. Suppose $\tau = 2, \theta = 0.5$. In example 4, the weight of cid pair (2,1) in entity pair(1,1) is 0.08 and the length of linked list is 2, while 0.08 is less than 0.5/2. Property 1 prunes entity pair (1,1). However, the weight of the first cid pair (1,2) in entity pair (1,2) is 0.32,, which is larger than 0.5/2, so (1,2) meet Property 1, while the addition of the weight of (1,2) and the weight of (2,1) is 0.44, which is less than 0.5. According to Property 2, entity pair (1,2) should be deleted from the candidate set.

From Property 1, in the entity candidate structure set, if the weight of the first cid pair is not large enough, the entity pairs must not meet similarity threshold, which can be directly filtered out.. Property 2 synthesizes the probability of entity pairs, further filtering the candidate which meet Property 1 but not meet similarity threshold. Algorithm 7 specifies the details to generate candidate using Property 1 and Property 2.

Algorithm 7: Generate_cand:

Input: Entity table R,S, entity candidate structure *Cans*

Output: Entity candidate structure *Canf*.

1. $Canf = \varnothing$
2. For $Can_e \in Cans$, retrieve cid linked list of $Can_e.eid$
   a. using Property 1 and Property 2 to filter
   b. if $Can_e.eid$ meet both of the filter condition, then insert $Can_e.eid$ into *Cans*

Return *Canf*

Generate_cand algorithm first let candidate set be empty, then retrieve each entity candidate structure, for each Cane, filtering by Property 1 and Property 2. Finally return the last candidate set.

Time complexity analysis: Generate_cand algorithm retrieve the entity candidate structure, its time complexity C_Q, i.e., $O(C_Q)$.

Verify Candidate Set Algorithm and Analysis

To generate entity candidate structure set, we need to compute the similarity value for each pair. Then compare with similarity threshold θ. If the similarity value larger than θ, then the two entities are similar, i.e., they can be joined together. Retriving all entity candidate structure set, the join result can be returned. Algorithm 8 describe the details of verify algorithm.

Algorithm 8 verify

1. $Result = \varnothing$
2. For $Can_e \in Cans$ retrieve the cid pair linked list of $Can_e.eid$
   a. Compute the edit distance of every cid pairs in linked list, then obtain their similarity value and add up to the eid pair similarity value.
   b. It the similarity of *eid* pair larger than θ, then inserted $Can_e.eid$ to Result set.

Return Result

Algorithm 8 iterative computes the similarity of entity candidate set. According to Generate_cand algorithm, the cid pair linked list contains all possible meeting eidt distance threshold string pairs. Verify algorithm compute the similarity of entity pair, finally return the correct join entity pair set.

Time complexity analysis: denote the average length of cid pair linked list of $Can_e.eid$ as $len(eid)$, the number of candidate as n, the average cost of computing similarity of every string pairs as cost, then the time complexity of verify algorithm is $O\big(cost \cdot len(eid)\big)$.

ES-JOIN Algorithm Analysis

The correctness of ES-JOIN algorithm: the candidate set generated by the Generate_candstruct and Generate_cand algorithm contains all possible join entity pairs. In verify algorithm, the cid pair linked list of $Can_e.eid$ contains all possible meeting edit distance threshold string pairs. Clearly, all entity pairs which meet the similarity threshold will be returned. S, the ES-JOIN algorithm is correct.

Time complexity analysis:the time complexity of ES-JOIN algorithm is the sum of the complexity time of the 2nd,3rd,4th step. The 2nd step merge prefix index, which time complexity is $O(n \cdot l) + O(c \log c \cdot C_Q)$. The 3rd step generate candidate by filtering process, which time complexity is $O(C_Q)$. And the time complexity of verify algorithm in the 4th step is $O\big(cost \cdot len(eid)\big)$. Therefore, the total time complexity of ES-JOIN algorithm is

$$O(n \cdot l) + O(c \log c \cdot C_Q) + O(C_Q) + O(cost \cdot len(eid)).$$

Specifically, l denotes the average length of inverted list, n denotes the number of common q-gram, C_Q denotes the size of merging bilayer prefix index, $len(eid)$ denotes the average length of cid pair linked listin candidate set $Can_e.eid$.

The Optimization of ES-JOIN Algorithm

This part discusses the strategy to further optimize the ES-JOIN algorithm.

Given entity attribute value set

$$s = \{(p_1, \sigma_1), (p_2, \sigma_2)...(p_m, \sigma_m)\},$$

$$r = \{(q_1, \delta_1), (q_2, \delta_2)...(q_n, \delta_n)\},$$

let r, s are sorted by weight descending. According to Property 1, after combined the bilayer prefix index, if the weight product of the first cid pairs is not big enough, the two entities are certainly not similar. That is, in the filtering process, string pairs bears little resemblance make fewer contribution to generate candidates (only used in Property. 2). Based on this, it should as much as possible, and as early as possible filter out those relatively large weight cid pairs in the process of generating candidate, further reducing the size of the candidate set, improving the execution efficiency of our algorithm.

Property 3: Given string σ_1, σ_2 edit distance threshold τ, if $d(\sigma_1, \sigma_2) \leq \tau$, then the first $q\tau + k$ prefix q-gram at least have K common q-gram .K is determined by using FixPrefixScheme framework (Wang, Li, & Feng, 2012), which Prunes similar entities using fixed-length prefix mechanism.

To filter relatively large cid pairs as much as possible, we can modify the length of the prefix. However, the increase of the length of prefix makes the size of the bilayer prefix index large, also keeps the merging bilayer prefix index algorithm Generate_candstruct cost up. In order to balance these two factors, the optimization algorithm only increases the prefix length of the largest weight entity string. The concrete practices are as follows: for the maximum weight entity string, increase its prefix length, and mark the cid which contains the increased prefix in the inverted index q-gram. In the process of merging bilayer prefix index, if there was a cid is marked, there should only merge the marked cid pairs. Then count the reduplicate cid pairs, if the number is less than the number of common q-gram should meet, the algorithm deletes the cid pairs from the eid linked list. This practice reduces the number of C_Q.

OPT_ES-JOIN algorithm has the same process as the ES-JOIN algorithm. While Generate_candstruct and Generate_cand algorithms change. In the process of merging bilayer prefix index, OPT_Generate_candstruct algorithm only merges the index items in inverted table which either is not marked or both are marked (in the step 2), and count the repeated cid pairs which both of cid in cid pairs are marked. According to Property 3, only if the cid pairs count is not less than k, the corresponding cid string pairs meet the edit distance threshold. Therefore, in OPT_Generate_cand algorithm, we first check counting array, then delete the cid pairs which do not meet the count condition before filter process. If the relatively large weight cid has been removed, then it will be easier to filter the entity pairs which do not meet similarity threshold. The OPT_Generate_cand algorithm is represented in Algorithm 9

Algorithm 9 OPT_Generate_cand algorithm:

1. $\mathrm{Re}\,sult = \varnothing$
2. For $Can_e \in Cans$ retrieve the cid pair linked list of $Can_e.eid$
    a. compute the edit distance of every cid pairs in linked list, then obtain their similarity value and add up to the eid pair similarity value.
    b. It the similarity of *eid* pair larger than θ ,then inserted $Can_e.eid$ to Result set.

Return Result

Example 7: Suppose $\tau = 1, q = 2$, entity attribute value {Microsoft,1.0}, {Macrofilt,1.0}, which prefix are {Mi,ic,cr} and {Ma,ac,cr}. After merging prefix index, this entity pairs is added to the entity candidate sets. Futhermore, the entity pairs meet Property 1and Property 2. Using the optimization algorithm, let k=2, according to Property 3, the number of common prefix must greater than 3. Obviously when the prefix length increase by 2, the common prefix number is 2, this entity cid pairs are filtered out.

Moreover,in the process of merging bilayer prefix index, we can adopt existing filter method such as suffix filtering to further reduce the candidate size.

QUERY OPTIMIZATION IN ENTITY-BASED DATABASES

This part we give one method of range query estimation, two methods of estimating threshold similarity join size and one strategy of multi-similarity join order selection in entity database .

Range Query Estimation

In this part, we describe our estimation methods in details. First,we give a preliminary query estimation method, which can well estimate unbounded range query (e.g., $a >_\tau x$ or $a <_\tau x$) result size. But for general range queries (e.g., $x_1 < a < x_2$), it often leads to underestimation. Then, a more accurate range query estimation method is proposed and it can well solve the underestimation problem which the former method encounters.

Preliminary Range Query Estimation Method

Existing query estimation methods are not suitable for range queries on entity-based relational database management system for reason that with the quality degree, the existing methods often lead to the overestimation. To solve this problem, we consider an unbounded range query Q by $a <_\tau x$ firstly, where a is an uncertain attribute value and τ is the similarity threshold. This query returns all tuples satisfying $Sim(a < x) > \tau$, which means that a satisfies the following relationship:

$$\sum_{(v_i, p_i) \in V} sim(v_i < x) p_i > \tau \qquad (2)$$

If all possible values of an uncertain value are sorted in database system, the relationship (3) is equivalent to calculate the cumulative distribution function $F_a(x)$, where $F_a(x) = \sum_{v_i < x} p_i$ and return the values satisfying $F_a(x) > \tau$.

Figure 5(a) shows an example of the cumulative distribution functions (CDF) of several tuples on attribute A, whose corresponding values are shown in Table 9. In the figure, each stacked line represents one tuple. The x-axis and y-axis respectively represent the attribute value and the similarity. The meaning of every stacked line is like the cumulative distribution function of every uncertain value. For example, the point P on the stacked line represents that the value of attribute A of tuple 3 is smaller than 35 with similarity 0.6. Therefore, with such a figure containing all tuples,

for a given query Q ($a <_\tau x_0$), the total number of tuples which satisfy query Q can be estimated directly. It is the number of stacked lines crossing the line segment l given by $x = x_0, \tau < y \leq 1$. This is an obvious conclusion and Theorem 2 shows the proof. The algorithm of query estimation is based on this conclusion.

Theorem 2: The number of tuples which satisfy query ($a <_\tau x_0$) is equal to the number of stacked lines crossing the line segment l given by $x = x_0$, $\tau < y \leq 1$.

Proof: One tuple corresponds a stacked line in the figure. The beginning point of each stacked line is (v_{min}, 0), and the end point is (v_{max}, 1). With the characteristic of the cumulative distribution functions, all stacked lines are monotonically increasing. Hence, all stacked lines go through an arbitrary line segment l given by $x = x_0, 0 \leq y \leq 1$, where $v_{min} \leq x_0 \leq v_{max}$. For the tuples which satisfy query ($a <_\tau x_0$), the intersection points of their stacked lines and the line segment l ($x = x_0, 0 \leq y \leq 1$) must be above the line $y = \tau$. Therefore, we can get the conclusion that the number of tuples which satisfy query ($a <_\tau x_0$) is equal to the number of stacked lines crossing the line segment l given by $x = x_0, \tau < y \leq 1$.

Histogram Structure

Based on the above discussion, we define a basic two-dimensional histogram. The range of input values is partitioned into $n * m$ buckets where n

Table 9. A Data Fragment

ID	A	B	......
1	((10, 0.1), (35, 0.3), (65, 0.5), (80, 0.1))	......	......
2	((20, 0.3), (50, 0.5), (80, 0.2))	......	......
3	((15, 0.6), (60, 0.2), (70, 0.2))	......	......

and m are the lengths of each dimension. A histogram bucket $H(i,j)$ covers the area given by

$$\left(i * \delta_x,\ j * \delta_s,\ (i+1) * \delta_x,\ (j+1) * \delta_s\right),$$

where δ_x and δ_s are the widths of histogram bket along x and y axis. Each bucket has a value, which stores the height of this bucket that records the number of tuples whose stacked lines intersect this bucket.

Obviously, the errors of the estimations using this histogram are associated to the number of the stacked line inflection points in buckets and do not exceed them. For example, as Figure 5(b) shows, H_i is a bucket of the histogram. Without the consideration of the y dimension, the stacked line l is a part of the CDF of one uncertain attribute value, and the dotted line τ represents the similarity threshold. Given two queries $Q1 : a <_\tau x_1$ and $Q2 : a <_\tau x_2$, where x_1, x_2 are located in the bucket H_i, and $x_1 \langle x_0,\ x_2 \rangle x_0$, the estimations using this bucket may lead to overestimation for query $Q1$ and underestimation for query $Q2$. On the contrary, if there is no inflection points in bucket H_i, the estimation for query $Q1$ (or $Q2$) (i.e., the number of stacked lines through bucket H_i above the dotted line τ) equals to the number of stacked lines crossing the line segment given by $x = x_1, \tau < y \leq 1$ (or $x = x_2, \tau < y \leq 1$ for $Q2$), which means the estimation is accurate according to Theorem 1. Hence in order to make the estimation more accurate, we need to ensure that the number of the inflection points in each bucket H_i is small enough.

In our approach, the histogram is firstly partitioned into p equal-width buckets, and we set the number of the inflection points in each bucket should not exceed ε ($\varepsilon = M / p$, where M is the total number of inflection points, which equals the number of all possible attribute values). When a bucket contains more than ε inflection points, this bucket is partitioned into q equal-width

buckets (generally, $q \ll p$, and q can be considered as a constant) and we set each new bucket containing ε / q inflection points. In the next process, for the buckets which do not meet the requisition, they are partitioned until that all buckets contain less than ε inflection points.

We now present the histogram construction algorithm. To facilitate the description of algorithm, we firstly summarize the main notations that will be used in our paper in Table 6. With these notations, *Algorithm 10* illustrates the detailed steps of histogram construction. Note that, we assume all possible values of an uncertain value are increasing in the database system, as shown in Table 9. For each uncertain value, it is supposed that all possible values are $v_0, v_1 \ldots v_{m-1}$ and the corresponding quality degrees are $p_0, p_1 \ldots p_{m-1}$, the interval $[v_{min}, v_{max}]$ can be divided into $m+1$ intervals: $[v_{min}, v_0),\ [v_0, v_1) \ldots [v_{m-1}, v_{max}]$. In each interval, we need to record value a in correct histogram buckets. For example, in $[v_{min}, v_0)$, value a should be recorded in buckets $H\left([v_{min}, v_0), 0\right)$, which represents $Sim(a < x)$ is 0, where $x \in [v_{min}, v_0)$. Similarly, value a should also be recorded in buckets:

$$H\left([v_0, v_1), p_0\right), H\left([v_1, v_2), p_0 + p_1\right) \ldots H\left([v_{m-1}, v_{max}], 1\right)$$

Meanwhile, the number of inflection points is stored in each bucket, and when the size of some bucket exceeds ε, it is partitioned into q equal-width buckets and the histogram is adjusted. *Algorithm 10* is the pseudo-code of this process, where symbol P_i represents the number of inflection points in bucket H_i.

Algorithm 10:

1.　　Initialize $H \leftarrow \varnothing$
2.　　**for** each uncertain value a **do**

3.   **for** each possible value v_k of an uncertain value **do**

4.   **for** all buckets meeting $v_{k-1} < l_i < v_k$ **do**

5. $H\left(i, F_a\left(l_i\right) / \delta_s\right)$++

6.   **end for**

7. P_i++

8.   **if** $P_i > \varepsilon$ **then**

9.   **partition** and **adjust** this bucket

10.   **end for**

11.   **for** all buckets meeting $r_i > max\left(v_k\right)$ **do**

12. $H\left(i, 1 / \delta_s\right)$++

13.   **end for**

14.   **end for**

Theorem 3: The time complexity of Algorithm 10 is $O\left(p\left(N + s\right)\right)$ and the space complexity is $O\left(ps\right)$.

Proof: This algorithm scans each tuple once and records each tuple in m appropriate histogram buckets, where m is the length of the histogram in x dimension. In the worst case, partition occurs per $\varepsilon\left(q-1\right) / q$ tuples, and partition times does not exceed $pq / \left(q-1\right)$ (i.e., $M / \left(\varepsilon\left(q-1\right) / q\right)$). Each partition adds $q-1$ buckets and adjusts s buckets along y axis, so

$$m < \left(q-1\right) pq / \left(q-1\right) + p = p\left(q+1\right).$$

Thus the time complexity is

$$O\left(p\left(q+1\right)N\right) + O\left(qspq / \left(q-1\right)\right)$$

and the space complexity is $O\left(p\left(q+1\right)s\right)$. Thus the time complexity is $O\left(p\left(N+s\right)\right)$ and the space complexity is $O\left(ps\right)$, because q can be considered as a constant.

Query Estimation Method

With the histogram structure, we can easily estimate query result size. Given a query $a <_\tau x_0$, query result size is estimated as the sum of the heights of the buckets where x_0 is located in and meet the similarity threshold. *Algorithm 10* shows this algorithm in details.

However, this algorithm is only applicable for the unbounded range queries in form of $a <_\tau x_0$. For anther unbounded range queries in the form of $a >_\tau x_0$, we need to perform an equivalent transformation to make *Algorithm 2* suitable for such form.

$$a >_\tau x_0 \Leftrightarrow Sim \left(a > x_0\right) > \tau \Leftrightarrow Sim \left(a < x_0\right) < 1 - \tau. \quad (3)$$

Such that *Algorithm 11* can also be used to estimate queries in the form as $a >_\tau x_0,$, with a modification of the loop range in *line 4*. For the queries in form of $a <_\tau x_0$ the result sets are the tuples satisfying $Sim \left(a < x_0\right) > \tau$, hence the loop

Figure 5. Example for showing the histogram structure(Y. Zhang et al., 2012)

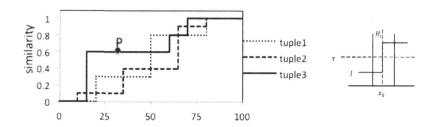

Table 10. Main notations

Notation	Meaning
τ	Similarity threshold
p, q	Initial granularity of partition and granularity of repartition
ε	Threshold of the number of inflection points in one bucket
l_i, r_i	Left boundary and right boundary of bucket H_i along x axis
δ_s, s	Width of buckets along y axis, where $s = 1 / \delta_s$
a_i	Uncertain values of attribute A ($0 \leq i < N$)
v_i, p_i	Possible values and quality degrees of an uncertain attribute value a
v_{min}, v_{max}	Minimum and maximum among all possible values of an attribute A
$sim\left(x_1, x_2\right)$	Similarity of $x_1 < a < x_2$ where a is an uncertain value
C	The number of tuples satisfying query Q

range is $\left[\tau / \delta_s, 1 / \delta_s\right]$, where δ_s is the width of buckets along y axis. On the contrary, for the queries in form of $a >_\tau x_0$, the result sets are the tuples satisfying $Sim\ (a < x_0) < 1 - \tau$ with the transformation (3). Therefore, the loop range should be modified to $\left[0, \left(1 - \tau\right) / \delta_s\right]$. Theorem 4 proves this estimation method is unbiased when p tends to infinity.

Algorithm 11

1.   **if** $x_0 < v_{min}$ **then return** 0
2.   **if** $x_0 > v_{max}$ **then return** N
3.   **let** $C = 0$ **and** find H_i meeting $l_i < x_0 \leq r_i$
4.   **for** j **from** τ / δ_s **to** $1 / \delta_s$ **do**
5. $C = C + H\left(i, j\right)$
6.   **end for**
7 **return** C

Theorem 4: The estimation method in Algorithm 11 is unbiased when p tends to infinity.

Proof: To facilitate the proof, we assume that $q = 2$, for other cases, the proof process is similar. As proved in Theorem 3, partition times does not exceed $2p$ (i.e., $pq / \left(q - 1\right)$), and each partition adds 1 (i.e., $q - 1$) buckets. Given a query $a <_\tau x_0$, we make the following assumptions. First, x_0 falls each bucket with equal probability. Second, n times partitions occur. Last, m buckets contain more than ε inflection points where $m \leq n$. With these assumptions, the total number of buckets along x axis is $p + n$. We have known the estimation error does not exceed the number of inflection points in bucket which x_0 is located in. Hence the expectation of estimation error is:

$$E\left(e\right) < \frac{p + n - m}{p + n}\varepsilon + \frac{m}{p + n}E'\left(e\right) = \frac{p + n - m}{p + n}\varepsilon + \frac{m}{p + n}\left(\varepsilon + \frac{M - m\varepsilon}{m}\right) = \varepsilon + \frac{M - m\varepsilon}{p + n} < \varepsilon + \frac{M}{p} = 2\frac{M}{p}.$$

Therefore, when p tends to infinity, the expectation of estimation error tends to 0, and this approach is unbiased.

We have discussed the unbounded range queries. Consider the general range query $x_1 < a < x_2$ and that is $Sim\left(x_1 < a < x_2\right) > \tau$. The unbounded range queries can be considered as a special case of the general range query. To estimate the general range query result size, with the application of the techniques in this part, a naïve method is proposed. Firstly, the numbers of tuples that satisfy query Q1 ($a <_\tau x_1$) and query Q2 ($a <_\tau x_2$) are estimated by *Algorithm 11*, and they are denoted by $C1$ and $C2$ respectively. We can use $C2 - C1$ to estimate the number of tuples that satisfy query Q ($x_1 < a < x_2$). Clearly, if we do not consider the threshold, this method is correct. However, it often leads to underestimation with the consideration of the effect of the similarity threshold on query result sizes. We show this point with an example as follows.

Example 8: Consider a tuple t, whose value is ((20, 0.25), (40, 0.2), (60, 0.3), (80, 0.25)) in attribute A, and give a query Q (30<a<50) with τ =0.2. Obviously, this tuple satisfies query Q. But, if we use the naïve method mentioned above, this tuple satisfies query $Q1$ ($a <_{0.2} 30$) and query $Q2$ ($a <_{0.2} 50$), and this means both the result set of query $Q1$ and the result set of query $Q2$ contain this tuple. Thus if $C2 - C1$ is used to estimate the result size of query Q, this tuple will be lost. The underestimation is led by repeatedly happening of such cases. However, for another query Q' (30<a<70) with τ =0.5,

this tuple will not be lost using the naïve method. Compared with query Q, query Q' has a wider query range and a different similarity threshold. It is because of these two characteristics that make this tuple not lost in query Q' result set.

As Example 8 shows, this naïve method may lead to underestimation. It is related to the width of query range and the threshold. With the shortcoming of this naïve method, we propose more accurate query range estimation method in next part.

Accurate Range Query Estimation

In this part, we present an accurate range query estimation algorithm, and it can solve the underestimation problem discussed in the above part. In order to adapt to general range queries, we add another dimension to the histogram. The meanings of two original dimensions do not change (the x axis and y axis respectively represent the end point of the query and the similarity), and the new additional dimension (z axis) represents the beginning of the query. Therefore, given a general range query Q ($x_1 < a < x_2$), we can estimate the size of query result set by counting the number of stacked lines crossing the line segment l given by $x = x_2$, $\tau < y \leq 1$ and $z = x_1$ similar to Figure 5(a). That is equivalent to executing a query Q' ($a <_\tau x_2$) on the plane, where $z = x_1$.

We call such new histogram as improved histogram. In this histogram, every plane on z axis is a basic histogram, corresponding to the constraint $z \leq x < v_{max}$ (clearly, it is not necessary to

Table 6. The user credit card transaction information

ID	Name	City	Date	money
1	{Kate,0.8;Kitty,0.2}	Beijing	2012-3-15	2000
2	{Katherin,1.0}	London	2012-3-15	5000
3	{chunk,0.4;chales,0.6}	London	2012-3-15	3000

store the whole range). The width of a bucket on z axis is controlled by an input parameter δ_z (in general, δ_z can be equal to $\left(v_{max} - v_{min}\right) / p$). The detailed algorithms for constructing this improved histogram and estimating the result size of a general range query are respectively presented in *Algorithm 12* and *Algorithm 13*. Compared with *Algorithm 10*, *Algorithm 12* only adds another layer of loops on z axis, but this improved histogram structure can give more accurate estimation than the basic histogram. *Theorem 5* gives the time and space complexity of the construction algorithm, and *Theorem 6* proves this estimation algorithm using this improved histogram is also unbiased when p tends to infinity.

Theorem 5: The time complexity of Algorithm 12 is $O\left(p^2\left(N + s\right)\right)$ and the space complexity is $O\left(p^2 s\right)$ with the assumption: $\delta_z = \left(v_{max} - v_{min}\right) / p$).

Proof: Compared with *Algorithm 10*, this algorithm only adds another dimension, and the length of this dimension is p. Therefore, similarly the analysis of the complexity of *Algorithm 10*, the time complexity of *Algorithm 12* is $O\left(p^2\left(N + s\right)\right)$ and the space complexity is $O\left(p^2 s\right)$.

Theorem 6: The estimation method in Algorithm 13 is unbiased when p tends to infinity.

Proof: Compared with the basic histogram discussed above, this improved histogram with more detailed information can get a more accurate estimation for general queries. Therefore, with the conclusion of Theorem 4, the estimation method using this improved histogram is also unbiased when p tends to infinity.

Algorithm 12:

1. Initialize $H \leftarrow \varnothing$

2. **for** each uncertain value a **do**
3. **for** each possible value v_n of an uncertain value **do**
4. **for** k **from** 0 to $(v_k - v_{min}) / \delta_z$ **do**
5. **for** all buckets meeting $v_{n-1} < l_i < v_n$ **do**
6. $H\left(k, i, sim\left(k^*\delta_z, l_i\right) / \delta_s\right)$++
7. **end for**
8. $P_{k,i}$++
9. **if** $P_{k,i} > \varepsilon$ **then**
10. **partition** and **adjust** this bucket
11. **end for**
12. **end for**
13. **for** k **from** 0 to $(v_k - v_{min}) / \delta_z$ **do**
14. **for** all buckets meeting $r_i > max\left(v_k\right)$ **do**
15. $H\left(k, i, sim\left(k^*\delta_z, l_i\right) / \delta_s\right)$++
16. **end for**
17. **end for**
18. **end for**

Algorithm 13:

1. **if** $x_1 < v_{min}$ **then let** $x_1 = v_{min}$
2. **if** $x_2 > v_{max}$ **then let** $x_2 = v_{max}$
3. **let** $C = 0; k = (x_1 - v_{min}) / \delta_z$ **and** find $H_{k,i}$ meeting $l_i < x_2 \leq r_i$
4. **for** j **from** τ / δ_s to $1 / \delta_s$ **do**
5. $C = C + H\left(k, i, j\right)$
6. **end for**
7. **return** C

Threshold Similarity Join Size Estimation

The Framework of Estimation Algorithm

This part focus on estimating the result size of threshold entity similarity join operator. We propose a sampling based algorithm that uses Locality Sensitive Hashing (LSH) to cluster similar objects. Compared with the traditional random sampling method, experimental results show that our method gives more accurate estimations.

Firstly, we will give out the frame of the estimation algorithm. The characteristic of threshold entity similarity join is that the result size will be close to (e.g., is the size of the join set). And when the similar threshold value is small, the join result size is relatively small.

The current existing methods on estimating the join result size are mainly based on sampling. Part of these methods could be applied on the estimation of the threshold similarity join discussed in this passage. However, there exists a significant defect in this state: they only applied to the situation where the threshold is relatively small and the join result size is relatively large. When we come to a larger threshold and a relatively small join result size, the estimation effect couldn't be guaranteed.

For the defects in the generally sampling method,(H. Lee, Ng, & Shim, 2011) proposed a sampling method based on the Locality Sensitive Hashing (LSH) to estimate the result size of the similarity self-join. (H. Lee et al., 2011) mainly solved the similarity join problems on vector(or set). The main idea is to hash similar vectors(or set) to the same bucket by applying Locality Sensitive Hashing method, and then sample in two cases. One is to sample from the same bucket to estimate the result size and the other is to sample from different buckets. By combining these two cases we could get a relatively accurate estimation value. In this method, even if the similarity threshold value is relatively large and the probability that sampling from the same bucket suit to the threshold is relatively large, the effect of the estimation result could be guaranteed because the objects in the same bucket are relatively similar.

Although this method could improve the estimation accuracy of the sampling method when the similar threshold is relatively high, this method only apply to the situation where the attribute is a single vector(or set). So this method doesn't apply to the threshold similarity join in entity relationship database discussed in this passage and mainly reflects in three aspects. First in the entity relationship database, each attribute could have multiple values; we need to take account of the effects of multiple possible values in the clustering process. Second in the entity relationship data model, we add the cleanness of data. The same possible values with different cleanness would result in different join result. Third (H. Lee et al., 2011) forces on similarity self-join and the sampling method would result in repeating sampling.

With consideration that the clustering sampling method could avoid the defects of general sampling method when the similarity is relatively large, the estimation algorithm in this passage based on this basic frame. To solve its shortcomings, we firstly purpose the Locality Sensitive Hashing algorithm based on the cleanness. This algorithm not only considers the multiple possible values of each attribute but also the influence of the cleanness corresponding to different values. In Example 9 we show the advantages of this algorithm. And to avoid repeating sampling, we use no-repeating sampling method in this algorithm.

Example 9: Consider two uncertain attribute values t1: {(Robert, 0.9), (Bob, 0.1)}and t2: {(Robert, 0.1), (Bob, 0.9)}. Suppose we use the method in(H. Lee et al., 2011) to consider all values, then t1 and t2 would be count 2 times. However, the algorithm in this passage would synthesize multiple values and count t1 and t2 only once. Secondly, method in (H. Lee et al., 2011)could reflect the influence of different cleanness value, so it could distinguish t1 and t2. In fact, given out t3: {(Robert,1)} with edit distance 2 and cleanness threshold 0.3, only (t1,t3) subject to the join condition and (t2,t3) doesn't. So t1 and t2 only have the same value but represent the different attribute value. The algorithm in this passage could distinguish t1 and t2 in the clustering process.

Algorithm 14 give out the basic frame of algorithm to estimate the result size of the threshold similarity join.

Algorithm 14: Join Estimation
Process 1: Data Preprocessing

Input: Uncertain attribute set R and S
Output: The cluster result set of R and S
// P,C refers to the similar pairs set and the cluster set
/*return all the similar pairs in R*/

1. PR ← LSH_Quality(R)←
2. PS ← LSH_Quality(S)
/*return the cluster result set in R*/
3. CR ←Clustering(PR)
4. CS ←Clustering(PS)

Process 2: Sampling Estimation

Input: The cluster result of uncertain attribute set R and S, similar threshold A, cleanness threshold ,
Output: The estimation value N on the size of the threshold similarity joins result
// SR, SS refers to the sampling set

1. SR ← Sampling(CR)
2. SS ←Sampling(CS)
3. N =0
4. for i from 1 to | SR |
/* each sampling set in SR */
5. for j from 1 to | SS |
/* each sampling set in SS */
6. n=0
7. for each pair(r, s)r∈SRi,s∈SSj
8. if $\sum_{sim(v_{r_i},v_{s_j})\geq\tau} p_{r_i} * p_{s_j} \geq \theta$ then
9. n++
10. end for
11. N += | CRi |*| CSj |*n/(| SRi |*| SSj |)
12. end for

13. end for
14. return N

The frame can be divided into two parts. Firstly pre-process the dataset to cluster similar attribute values, then samples from the cluster set to estimate the join result size.

The function sampling() applies random sampling for each cluster set to get sample sets and then make threshold similarity join on this sample set to estimate the join result size. That is suppose the join result size of the i-th cluster *CRi* with its sample set *Sri* and the j-th cluster *CSj* with its sample set S_{Sj} is n, then the estimation value of the join result size of *CRi* and *CSj* is | *CRi* |*| *CSj* |*n/(| *SRi* |*| *SSj* |). We estimate each join result size and add up to the estimation value of the total join result size.

For function Clustering(), we propose Locality Sensitive Hashing algorithm based on the cleanness, we will discuss it in details in the next part.

Locality Sensitive Hashing Clustering Algorithm Based on the Cleanness

The Locality Sensitive Hashing clustering algorithm is the core of the estimation method in this passage. We use this method to calculate all of the similar pairs and cluster on these similar pair results. Firstly we take an overview on the Locality Sensitive Hashing algorithm and then discuss how to apply this algorithm in entity relationship database with consideration of the influence of cleanness. Finally we describe the clustering algorithm.

Locality Sensitive Hashing Algorithm: Locality Sensitive Hashing algorithm was purposed firstly by Indyk and Motwani in(Indyk & Motwani, 1998) to solve the K-NN (K Nearest Neighbor) problem in high-dimension space. The main idea of this algorithm is to choose a cluster of Locality Sensitive Hashing functions based on given high-dimension vector set. Suppose that the less the angle of two vectors is, the closer their corresponding hash values are. So we could determine whether vectors are similar based on their hash values.(Charikar, 2002) discussed the Locality Sensitive Hashing functions in details and give out the following definitions.

Definition 14 (Locality Sensitive Hashing Functions): Given a cluster of hash functions H, if every two vector u, v∈Rm, h∈H we have

$$P(h_r(u) = h_r(v)) = sim(u,v) \qquad (3)$$

We could call them a cluster of Locality Sensitive Hashing functions, where sim(u,v) is the similarity measure functions.

Given m-dimension vector set, (Charikar, 2002) gives out a method to choose sensitive hashing functions: Randomly choose a m-dimension vector r, define sensitive hashing function as

$$h_r(u) = \begin{cases} 1 & if \ r \cdot u \geq 0 \\ 0 & if \ r \cdot u < 0 \end{cases}$$

Then given two vectors v and u, we have

$$P(h_r(u) = h_r(v)) = 1 - \frac{\theta(u,v)}{\pi} \qquad (4)$$

If the similarity measure function is cosine similarity, then the less their inner angle is, the larger the cosine value and the closer the two vectors are. Goemans and Williamson proved Equation (3) in(Goemans & Williamson, 1995).

To improve the accuracy of the hash functions, in practical applications, we generally choose multiple random vectors and use hash functions to get 0/1 value, this transfers a high-dimension vector to a 0/1 string. Suppose we choose d (d<<m) random vectors then each m-dimension vector is transferred into a d-length 0/1 string. According to (Ravichandran, Pantel, & Hovy, 2005) we have

$$P(h_r(u) = h_r(v)) = 1 - \frac{hamming\_distance(u,v)}{d} \qquad (5)$$

Where hamming_distance(u,v) indicates the hamming distance of u and v. The hamming distance of two 0/1 strings equals to the number of different values on the same position. For example the distance of 1011101 and 1101111 is 3. Based on Equation (3) and (5) we get

$$sim(u,v) = 1 - \frac{hamming\_distance(u,v)}{d} \qquad (6)$$

Thus, based on *Equation (6)*, we could transfer the problem that determine whether two vectors are similar to computing the hamming distance of the two corresponding 0/1 strings. If hamming distance is less than the threshold l, the two vectors are similar, or vice versa. The method to compute the hamming distance of two 0/1 strings is fast and effective. Thus we could quickly compute all of the similar pairs by applying Locality Sensitive Hashing algorithm.

In next part, we will discuss how to apply Locality Sensitive Hashing algorithm to compute all of the uncertain attribute similar pairs with consideration of multiple possible values and its corresponding cleanness.

Hashing Functions Based on Cleanness

The Locality Sensitive Hashing algorithm focuses on high-dimension vector. So we need to transfer each uncertain attribute value to a vector and consider the influence of different cleanness values. In this part, we discuss how to transfer each uncertain attribute value to a vector under the influence of different cleanness values and give out the Locality Sensitive Hashing algorithm based on this.

Vectorization on Uncertain Attribute Value

We apply edit distance to measure the similarity ot two strings. Existing similarity join methods based on edit distance are all done by q-gram. Q-gram is the consecutive sub-string of length q in string and q-gram set is the set of all q-grams in the string. Obviously the smaller of the edit distance between two strings, the more common q-grams between two strings. For example, given two strings s_1 and s_2, if $ed(s_1,s_2)<=k$, then the minimum number of the common q-grams between s_1 and s_2 is:

$$max\left(\left|s_1\right|,\left|s_2\right|\right)+1-\left(k+1\right)q \qquad (7)$$

Based on above analysis, each possible value in entity-relationship database owns its corresponding q-gram set and each uncertain attribute value owns its corresponding q-gram set (the union of the q-gram set of all possible values). We give out an example in *Table 11*. Note that in these sets we allow repeated elements such as two "ob".

From *Equation (7)*, for two similar strings s1 and s2 ($ed(s1,s2)<=k$), the minimum common q-gram number is $max(|s1|,|s2|)+1-(k+1)q$. We denote it as $L(s1,s2)$. With consideration of the features of the threshold entity similarity join (definition 3) in entity-relationship data model: the more similar tuple (r,s) is, the more their corresponding possible value similar pairs (ri,sj) are. So we have

Property 5: If the number of the corresponding possible value similar pairs is m, then the number of the common q-grams in the corresponding q-gram set is mL(ri,sj). So the more similar tuple (r,s) is, the more common q-grams in the corresponding q-gram set are and the more similar of the corresponding high-dimension vector is.

Based on Property 5, if we count all the q-grams of each uncertain attribute, then each attribute value could transfer to a high-dimension vector. Where each dimension corresponds to a different q-gram and the number of the dimensions equals to kinds of all the different q-grams in the uncertain attribute set. We call this process as vectorization of uncertain attribute values. Note that in the practical vectorization process, the cost to count all the q-grams may be large, so the dimension of the vector may be less than the kinds of different q-grams. In Figure 6 we propose the process of vectorization, in the example uncertain attribute values {(Robert,0.6),(Bob,0.4)}, the result of vectorization is <3,0,2,2,0>.

Hovever, the above process don't consider the influence of cleanness. For example with two uncertain attribute values {(Robert, 0.9), (Bob, 0.1)} and {(Robert, 0.1), (Bob, 0.9)}, the result of the above method is <3,0,2,2,0> without difference. To handle this condition, we could get another property.

Property 6: If the cleanness of tuple (r,s) is p and $p=\sum_{ed(v_{ri},v_{sj})\leq k}p_{ri}*p_{sj}$, then the pri and psj increase with p. So the larger the cleanness of tuple (r,s) is, the larger the cleanness of the corresponding common q-gram value is.

Table 11. 2-gram set of the uncertain attribute

Attribute	2-Gram Set
Robert	S_1:{Ro, ob, be, er, rt}
Bob	S_2:{Bo, ob }
{(Robert, 0.6), (Bob, 0.4)}	$S=S_1\cup S_2$:{ Ro, ob, be, er, rt, Bo, ob}

Based on Property 6, we improve the efficiency of the vectorization process by adding the influence of cleanness, which makes the resulted vector could represent the corresponding attribute value much more accuracy. In vectorization process, we only need multiple each g-gram with its cleanness value and then count. This could reflect the different cleanness value in the vectorization process. As showing in Figure 7, the vectorization result of {(Robert, 0.9), (Bob, 0.1)} is <1.9, 0, 1, 1.8, 0>, and the vectorization result of (Robert, 0.1), (Bob, 0.9)} is <1.1, 0, 1, 0.2, 0>. We find this vectorization method could reflect uncertain attribute value much more accuracy.

Detailed Algorithm

By Locality Sensitive Hashing algorithm, we could do vectorization on all uncertain attribute value. Based on this, we give out the detailed algorithm to compute all the similar pairs. Algorithm 15 describes this process.

Function *vertorize(s)* is used to do vectorization on *s* and returns a m-dimension vector. This process counts for the number of different q-gram

in the q-gram set. Suppose that the length of the strings in attribute value scopes in fixed range, then the function could finish in constant time, the time complexity is $O(1)$. Function hamming_ *distance(u_i,u_j)* computes the hamming distance of u_i and u_j. Due to each uncertain attribute value is transferred into a d-length 0/1 string and d<<m, the time complexity of this function is $O(1)$. Thus the time complexity of algorithm 15 is $O(1)$.

Algorithm 15: LSH Quality

Input: Uncertain attribute set S and hamming distance threshold l
Output: Uncertain attribute set S and all the similar pairs PS

1. randomly choose d m-dimension vectors { r1, ..., rd}
2. for each s∈S do
   /*vectorize on s to v */
3. v ← vectorize (s)
4. for each ri∈{ r1, ..., rd}
   //LSH function
5. ui ← $h_{r_i}(u)$

Figure 6. Vectorization of uncertain attribute (Y. Zhang et al., 2012)

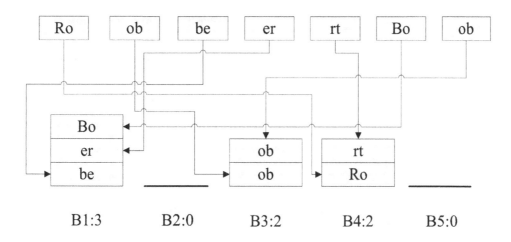

//transfer vector v to 0/1 string

6.   end for
7.   end for
8.   for each pair(ui, uj) do
9.   if hamming_distance(ui, uj) < 1 then
10.   PS ← (ui, uj)
11. end for
12. return PS

Clustering Algorithm

From Algorithm 15, we could get the set of all similar pairs. In this part we propose the clustering algorithm t to cluster similar uncertain attribute values. Thus we could sampling on each cluster set and estimate the result size of threshold similarity join.

Due to we have already get all the similar pairs, we regard each uncertain attribute value as a vertex and each similar pair as an edge between two vertices. After such transformation, we convert uncertain attribute set to a graph which reflects the similar relationship of all the uncertain attribute value. Thus the problem of clustering similar attribute values could be converted to the problem of graph clustering or community detection.

Recently many works have been done on graph clustering and community detection. In this study, we use the widely used CNM algorithm in community detection application r. This algorithm is based on integrity to divide clusters. Integrity is used to measure the effects of a division. Generally a good division is thought to have more edges in clusters but less edges between clusters. In CNM algorithm we define integrity as

$$Q = \sum_i (e_{ii} - a_i^2)$$

Inside this equation, e_{ij} refers to the ratio of edges connecting cluster i and cluster j, a_j refers to the ratio of edges in cluster i.

The main idea of this algorithm is to start with many clusters and merge clusters repeatedly to only one cluster in the direction of largest decrease of integrity. After this process we get a dividable cluster tree structure. Different method to divide this structure is corresponding to different cluster methods. While the method to get the largest integrity is the best division way. (Clauset, Newman, & Moore, 2004) discussed this algorithm in details.

By applying CNM algorithms to get cluster results, we could apply the sampling method discussed above to sample and estimate the result size of the threshold entity similarity join.

Compressed Histogram Based Entity Similarity Join Size Estimation

Using the weighted min-hash, we can get the min-hash signature of a property, which makes

Figure 7. Vectorization of uncertain attribute based on cleanness (Y. Zhang et al., 2012)

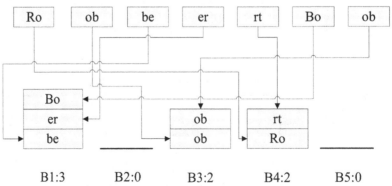

the property with the same dimensions and easy to use histogram to perform estimation, and then create its histogram, and finally use the improved discrete cosine transform to compress histogram information, which makes even for high dimensional data to ensure low error rate and low storage cost. We can use the compressed information directly to the cost estimation. In addition, this method can support dynamic data updates very well, which eliminate the need to periodically rebuild the histogram.

Min-Hash Signature

In order to conduct similarity join estimation using the property value statistics, but also to solve the problem of the attributes of model not only its value uncertain but also the number of its value not sure, we can use the min-hash methods to unify the property to a determined dimension, also it is convenience to create histogram. But it can only deal with the determined value, we requires new methods to solve uncertain attribute value. Therefore, we build the minimum hash signature of each attribute which is based on the weighted minimum hash method, the method can not only keep the attribute similarity, but also give full consideration of the impact of uncertain value cleanliness. Minimum hash signature method will be given below.

Build Min-Hash Signature

Min-Hash is a technology which quickly determines whether two sets similar, it is now widely used in applications related to the similarity. The main idea of the method is: h is assumed to be hash functions which will map set A and B to disjoint the numbers. For the set S, we use $h_{min}(S)$ to present the element whose value is the minimum of $h(x)$, where x belongs to the set S. Thus, only when the value obtaining $h_{min}(A \cup B)$ located in the $A \cap B$, we have $h_{min}(A) = h_{min}(B)$. Therefore, $Pr[h_{min}(A) = h_{min}(B)] = J_{AB}$. Thus we could use the hash functions whose numbers is k to construct a

set of signature, and we could use the similarity of the set of signatures to represent approximate similarity of the sets.

Definition 15. (Min-Wise Independent): Consider a set of random permutations $\Pi = \{\pi_1, ..., \pi_M\}$ on a universe $\Phi\{1,...,U\}$ and a set $r \subset \Phi$, let $min(\pi_i(r))$ denote $min(\{\pi_i(x)|x \in r\})$. With respect to two set r and s, Π is called min-wise independent, if $Pr(min(\pi_i(r)) = min(\pi_i(s))) = J_s(r,s)(J_s(r,s) = |r \cap s|/|r \cup s|)$.

Definition 16. (Min-Hash Signature): For a set r, we use $sig r = [min(\pi 1(r)), ..., min(\pi M(r))]$ to denote the signature of r.

The simplest min-hash is to use $M h_{min}(S)$ values which corresponding to the M fully independent hash functions to represent the min-hash signature of the set S, where M is a fixed integer parameter. Using this simple version to determine $J_s(A,B)$, supposed the number of the hash functions which $h_{min}(A) = h_{min}(B)$ is y, we use of y/M as the estimation of the signature.

Using the Min-Hash signatures, Js is estimated with

$$\hat{J}s(r,s) = \frac{|\{i \mid \min h_i(r) = \min h_i(s), 1 \le i \le M\}|}{M} . (8)$$

This estimation is the mean value of M different 0-1 random variables, where for each random variable, when $h_{min}(A) = h_{min}(B)$ the value is 1, otherwise is 0, thus y/M is unbiased estimation of $J_s(A,B)$, and also the average is an unbiased estimate. Let sig(r) denotes the signature of r, we use one example to show the use of the signature.

Example 10: Table 12 shows an example DB and corresponding signatures, sig(DB). The signature size M = 4 and the universe of hash functions is(Batini & Scannapieca, 2006; Eckerson, 2002; Garcia-Molina et al., 2000; Hassanzadeh & Miller, 2009; Raman et al., 2001). Hash functions are not shown.

Suppose that α = 0.5 is given. Using Equation (8), we can estimate Js(ri,rj) for ri,rj∈DB with their signatures. For instance, Ĵs(r1,r2)=0.5 since sig(r1) and sig(r2) match at two positions (i.e., the first and the second) out of 4 positions. The true similarity, Js(r1,r2)= $\frac{|\{10,19,52\}|}{|\{7,10,19,43,52,67\}|}$ =0.5. Considering all 5 sets in DB, there are 6 pairs {(r1, r2),(r1, r3), (r2, r3), (r1, r4), (r3, r4), (r2, r4)} that have at least two matching positions out of 4 positions in their signatures and thus Ĵs >= 0.5. Using the Min-Hash signatures, similarity estimation can be done by estimating the number of pairs (r, s), such that sig(r) and sig(s) overlap at least at $\lceil \alpha M \rceil$ positions.

Algorithm Design

We first use one example to show the compact of quality degree of attribute to the join result, and then give the algorithm of min-hash computation which consider the quality degree of attribute.

Example 11: Denote the attribute values of two relation are A1 ((10,0.1),(11,0.8), (12,0.05),(13,0.05)) and A2((11,0.7),(12,0.1),(14,0.1)), and supposed we use three hash function. The signature of A1 is (10,12,13) and the signature of A2 is (11,12,14), so J_s(A1,B2)=0.2, which is very low. But the quality degree similarity

larger than 0.2. So, we cannot simply consider the uncertain value of the entity-relationship data model.

The above transform simply consider the uncertain attribute value, in order to use the quality degree of uncertain value, the hash function can be deformed. We use the quality degree of the attribute value as weights, and together with the hash value of the uncertain values as parameters, to calculate again and we can re-obtain the set of values, and we select the hash value having the minimum uncertainty values as the final result of the hash function. The pseudo code of the algorithm is shown in *Algorithm 16*.

Algorithm 16: Algorithm of the min-hash signature of attribute.

Input: Attribute of a relation and a set of hash functions (the number is *K*)

Output: The min-hash signature of the attribute
// *R* represents a relation who need to compute min-hash signatures for its attribute

1.   for *i*=1 to |*R*|
2.   for *j*=1 to *K*
3.   create array *C* and *D*
4.   for *m*=1 to |*Ri*| //*Ri* represents the *i*th tuple's attribute
5.   *C*[*m*]=*Hj*(*Ri*[*m*]) //*Hj* represents the *j*th hash

Table 12. A sample and its signature

DB		sig(DB)	
r1	{7,10,19,52,67}	r1	{4,3,5,2}
r2	{10,19,43,52}	r2	{4,3,3,5}
r3	{10,13,43,52,67,85}	r3	{4,3,2,2}
r4	{10,38,43,49,80,94}	r4	{3,3,3,2}
r5	{3,25,29,47,50,66,73,75}	r5	{1,1,1,3}

is 0.8*0.7+ 0.05*0.1=0.565, which much   function

6. $D[m]=\beta*Hj(Ri[m])/pr(Ri[m])$
7. find minimum value of $D[min]$
8. put $C[min]$ as min $H_i(Ri)$
9. return C

Algorithm Analysis

Because the histograms need not to be established online, so the algorithm is an offline algorithm. When the hash values of the uncertain attribute values calculated, we do not immediately select the smallest hash value as the hash value, but to combine with the quality degree of the attribute. For example, the hash value could be multiplied by a coefficient and then divided by the quality degree of uncertain attribute values, so that we can make the high quality degree attribute value's hash value relative decrease, and relative increase a low quality degree hash value, it will make the high quality degree value with greater probability, and make the hash signature more representative. According to the sources of uncertain attribute values (such as data integration, etc.), some uncertain values of an attribute usually with high quality degree and others relatively low. Therefore, the min-hash signature can be a good choice of these representative uncertain values. The time complexity of the algorithm is O($K*|R|*$max($|Ri|$)), for the space complexity due to the uncertain value of the property has been normalized to the same size as the min-hash signature, it needs space O($K*|R|$).

The Histogram Information Compressed Using DCT

We can use the statistics of the attributes to conduct the join estimation, it is not only fast, but also is not affected by the data distribution. However, in order to obtain higher accuracy, the size of the histogram buckets need to divided very small. But, the number of histogram buckets is exponential growth with the growth of the dimension. In order to estimate join result using small size histogram

buckets in high-dimensional, we need to compress the histogram data, the compression methods are discrete Fourier transform, Haar transform, Karhunen Loeve transform (KLT), DCT and so on. But except DCT, other methods cannot solve the contradictions of energy compression and the amount of the calculation. DCT not only has better energy compaction characteristics, but also has a valid fast calculation algorithm. In addition, we can use the DCT characters of maintain the energy to conduct join estimation directly using the compression information. Therefore, we propose to use the DCT to compress histogram information, and use compressed information to conduct join estimation. In the realization of the fast calculation, we can not only obtain a low storage overhead, but also can ensure a low error rate. DCT cannot be used directly for multidimensional histogram data compression, it first needs to be expanded to multi-dimensional(J.-H. Lee, Kim, & Chung, 1999). Below we give a detailed description.

Discrete Cosine Transform

For a series of data $F=(f(0),f(1),...,f(N-1))$, DCT coefficients, $G=(g(0),g(1),...,g(N-1))$, are defined as follows:

$$k_u = \begin{cases} 1/\sqrt{2} \\ 1 \end{cases} \quad g(u) = \sqrt{\frac{2}{N}}k_u\sum_{n=0}^{N-1} f(n)\cos(\frac{(2n+1)u\pi}{2N})$$

for $u=0$, $u=0,...,N-1$ for $u\neq0$ $F=(f(0),f(1),...,f(N-1))$ is recovered by the inverse DCT defined as follows:

$$f(u) = \sqrt{\frac{2}{N}}\sum_{n=0}^{N-1} k_u g(n)\cos(\frac{(2n+1)u\pi}{2N}) \quad n=0,...,N-1.$$

1-dimensional DCT was extended to 2-dimensional DCT as follows: let [F]2 be an M×N matrix representing the 2-dimensional data and

[G]2 be the 2-dimensional DCT coefficients of [F]2. Then the element (u,v) of [G]2 is given by

$$g(u,v) = \sqrt{\frac{2}{M}} k_u \sum_{m=0}^{M-1} \left\{ \sqrt{\frac{2}{N}} k_v \sum_{n=0}^{N-1} f(m,n) \cos(\frac{(2n+1)v\pi}{2N}) \right\} \cos(\frac{(2m+1)u\pi}{2M}),$$

Its inverse is as follows:

$$f(m,n) = \sqrt{\frac{2}{M}} \sum_{u=0}^{M-1} k_u \left\{ \sqrt{\frac{2}{N}} \sum_{v=0}^{N-1} k_v g(u,v) \cos(\frac{(2n+1)v\pi}{2N}) \right\} \cos(\frac{(2m+1)u\pi}{2M})$$

$u=0,...,M-1$, $v=0,...,N-1$.

Now we generalize the above to the k-dimensional DCT recursively as follows:

Let $[F]_k$ be $N_1 \times N_2 \times {...} \times N_k$ k-dimensional data. Let $u(t)=(u_1,...,u_t) \subseteq (u_1,...,u_k)$ and $n(t)=(n_1,...,n_t)$ $\subseteq (n_1,...,n_k)$ for $1 \leq i \leq k$ and $u_i=0,...,N_i-1, n_i=0,...,N_i-1$. Let $G]_k$ be DCT coefficients of $[F]_k$. The formula is defined as follows:

$$G(u(1)) = \sqrt{\frac{2}{N_1}} k_{u_1} \sum_{n_1=0}^{N_1-1} f(n_1,...,n_k) \cos(\frac{(2n_1+1)u_1\pi}{2N_1})$$

$$G(u(t)) = \sqrt{\frac{2}{N_t}} k_{u_t} \sum_{n_t=0}^{N_t-1} G(u(t-1)) \cos(\frac{(2n_t+1)u_t\pi}{2N_t})$$

$$G(u(t)) = \sqrt{\frac{2}{N_t}} k_{u_t} \sum_{n_t=0}^{N_t-1} G(u(t-1)) \cos(\frac{(2n_t+1)u_t\pi}{2N_t})$$

$$F(n(1)) = \sqrt{\frac{2}{N_1}} \sum_{u_1=0}^{N_1-1} k_{u_1} g(u_1,...,u_k) \cos(\frac{(2n_1+1)u_1\pi}{2N_1})$$

$$F(n(t)) = \sqrt{\frac{2}{N_t}} \sum_{u_t=0}^{N_t-1} k_{u_t} F(n(t-1)) \cos(\frac{(2n_t+1)u_t\pi}{2N_t})$$

Then, k-dimensional DCT coefficients is given by $g(u_1,...,u_k)=G(u(k))$, and the inverse DCT transform is given by $f(u1,...,u_k)=F(u(k))$.

Properties of DCT

DCT has many desirable properties as follows: DCT is a linear transform; DCT is separable; DCT preserves the energy un the transform domain; DCT has the property of energy compaction and so on.

We found another property of DCT, which the paper referred to as DCT overall domain nature. We can see that DCT is the whole domain analysis which can be seen from the calculation of the DCT, so the big difference of the data could produce great influence on the results of the DCT transform. Take the 2-dimensional data as an example, if the maximum value and the minimum value of the data is a very big, then the DCT cannot play a effect compression, for example:

$$\begin{pmatrix} 100 & 10 & 9 \\ 8 & 100 & 5 \\ 1 & 2 & 3 \end{pmatrix} \xrightarrow{DCT} \begin{pmatrix} 79.3 & 37.5 & -23.1 \\ 46.1 & 46.5 & 25.6 \\ -23.8 & 24.0 & 77.2 \end{pmatrix},$$

but

$$\begin{pmatrix} 9 & 10 & 9 \\ 8 & 10 & 9 \\ 8 & 10 & 9 \end{pmatrix} \xrightarrow{DCT} \begin{pmatrix} 27.3 & -0.8 & -1.9 \\ 0.4 & 0.5 & 0.2 \\ 0.2 & 0.3 & 0.2 \end{pmatrix}.$$

Based on the above properties, if there is big difference between data values, the DCT cannot be used directly. Therefore, the data need to be processed firstly, which the large values of the data regions and small value region need to be separated, and then use the DCT compression separately.

Join Size Estimation Using DCT Compress Histogram Data

Using DCT compress histogram data to conduct join estimation also need to consider several aspects.

1. **The Partition of Histogram Data:** In view of the nature of the whole domain of the DCT which we found, it is that the greater difference of the data, the worse compression. In order to make DCT compression more effective, histogram data need to be divided between the big values and small values. As our article is focus on the min-hash signature's histogram data compression, through the analysis of the real data, we found that only several uncertainty attribute values with relatively large quality degree, so using the improved hash function, the probability of the value having a larger quality degree to be choose as the minimum hash value is high. Therefore, the value of the bucket of the histogram spindle direction should be relatively large, while others are more uniform (the so-called spindle i.e. meet the axis of the coordinate values are equal, for two-dimensional i.e. x = y, and the three-dimensional, i.e. x = y = z). So, the buckets of the spindle direction and other buckets compressed separately, the buckets of the spindle direction can also not be compressed but directly stored. In addition, the method can also be that to find the big data area and the small data area of histogram data, and then compression separately. Below is an example which to show the benefits of doing so.

Example 12: The result of directly conduct DCT on the 2-dimensional data is showed as follows:

$$\begin{pmatrix} 98 & 10 & 9 \\ 8 & 95 & 9 \\ 8 & 10 & 90 \end{pmatrix} \xrightarrow{DCT} \begin{pmatrix} 112.3 & 2.4 & -1.9 \\ 3.6 & 85.5 & 2.6 \\ 0.2 & 2.6 & 85.2 \end{pmatrix}$$

The result of the spindle large value data and the small value of the area are separated compressed is showed as follows:

$$\begin{pmatrix} 10 & 9 \\ 8 & 9 \\ 8 & 10 \end{pmatrix} \xrightarrow{DCT} \begin{pmatrix} 22.0 & -0.8 \\ 0.5 & 1.5 \\ 0.9 & 0.3 \end{pmatrix},$$

$$\begin{pmatrix} 98 & 95 & 90 \end{pmatrix} \xrightarrow{DCT} \begin{pmatrix} 163.4 & 5.7 & -0.8 \end{pmatrix},$$

if only select the large coefficients value of low frequency, the compression effect is significantly improved after compression separately.

2. **Geometrical Zonal Sampling:** After the histogram's DCT, the low frequency coefficients having larger values and the high frequency coefficients have small values, we can perform the estimation of meet a certain accuracy using only the larger coefficients, and this is the key to achieve data compression. How to choose the larger DCT coefficients, there are several main methods of geometrical zonal sampling(Rao, 1989), the methods can be extended to multidimensional, where only select a specific area of the DCT coefficients, and other regions is set to 0. Existing geometrical zonal sampling techniques include triangle, reciprocal, spherical, rectangular. Take the two-dimensional data for example, the results are shown in Figure 8:

Because we cannot determine which kind of sampling method is more suitable for the method proposed in this paper, so we will explain how to select the sampling method to make the proposed method become more effective through experiments.

3. **Dynamic Data Update:** In the case of data insert and delete frequently, it is important for updated data reflect to the statistic timely. Because DCT has the nature of the linear transformation, DCT-based compression histogram could spend small overhead to

reflect data updates rapidly. The following description of the process: when new data is inserted, the DCT coefficients calculated firstly, and then added to the saved DCT coefficients. In order to reflect the deletion data, we can subtract the DCT coefficients of the delete data from the DCT coefficient saved. In this way, you can reflect to the statistic data updates quickly, reducing the estimated error rate.

4. **Join Size Estimation:** In order to estimate the join size of two relations, we can use DCT compressed histogram data calculate directly. We first give an example to explain, and then correctness proof is given in the algorithm analysis.

Example 13: The direct join and DCT data join of two histograms:

$$
\begin{pmatrix} 9 & 10 & 9 \\ 8 & 7 & 9 \\ 8 & 10 & 8 \end{pmatrix} * \begin{pmatrix} 7 & 6 & 8 \\ 8 & 7 & 9 \\ 7 & 8 & 6 \end{pmatrix} = 573, \quad DCT \begin{pmatrix} 9 & 10 & 9 \\ 8 & 7 & 9 \\ 8 & 10 & 8 \end{pmatrix} * DCT \begin{pmatrix} 7 & 6 & 8 \\ 8 & 7 & 9 \\ 7 & 8 & 6 \end{pmatrix} =
$$

$$
\begin{pmatrix} 26, -0.408, -0.707 \\ 0.816, 0, 0.577 \\ 1.414, 0.577, -2 \end{pmatrix} * \begin{pmatrix} 22, -0.408, 0.707 \\ 0, -1, 1.732 \\ -1.414, 0.577, -1 \end{pmatrix} = 573.
$$

It is show that the DCT compressed histogram data can be used directly for join size estimation, and the estimation algorithm is given as following.

Algorithm 17: The algorithm of compressed histogram data using DCT.

Input: Multi-dimensional histogram of a relation F (it is supposed 3-dimensional)

Output: The histogram data G and H of multidimensional histogram F after the DCTb compression

1. for $i1=1$ to $N1$
2. for $i2=1$ to $N2$
3. for $i3=1$ to $N3$
4. if ($i1=i2\&\&i2=i3$)
5. save F[$i1,i2,i3$] in H[i1]
6. else
7. G[$i1,i2,i3$]=DCT(F[$i1,i2,i3$])
8. return G, H

Algorithm 18: The algorithm of join size estimation using compressed histogram data.

Input: The compressed histogram data of two relations

Output: The join size estimation of two relations

// Supposed compressed histogram data is a 3-dimensional data, and the histogram buckets division size are same.

// the histograms of two relations are $G1$ and $G2$, f is the sampling function

1. count $=0$
2. for i1 to min(N1,N2,N3)
3. count=count+H1[i1]*H2[i1]
4. for i1=1 to N1
5. for $i2=1$ to N2

Figure 8. Geometrical zonal sampling in 2-dimensional case (ZHANG Yan, 2012)

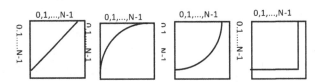

6.   for *i3*=1 to *N3*
7.   if f(*i1,i2,i3*)<=b
8.   count=count+*G1*[*i1,i2,i3*]*G2[*i1,i2,i3*]
9.   return count

We assume that two relations corresponding to the same histogram divided, on the basis of different situations, this algorithm can be simple extension. The Algorithm 17does not calculate spindle bucket data in the calculation of DCT coefficients, but directly store that; in the calculation of the rest of the DCT coefficients, it is going to get rid of the spindle data. The Algorithm 18 used to estimate the two relations' similar join results' size. Its first calculates the cumulative of the spindle bucket data's product, and then use sampling to calculate the cumulative of other DCT coefficients' product.

Algorithm Analysis

We first give the correctness of the algorithm:

Theorem 7: The energy maintenance of DCT. Denote *F*1 and *F*2 as two histogram data, the accumulation of corresponding elements' product is equal to the accumulation of its corresponding elements' products which belong to the corresponding *G*1 and *G*2 after DCT transformation, i.e.

$$\sum_{r \, and \, s \, are \, elements \, of \, same \, location \, of F1 and F2} r * s = \sum_{r' \, and \, s' \, are \, elements \, of \, same \, location \, of G1 and G2} r'* s'.$$

Proof: We start talking about the one-dimensional case, and then expanded to the multidimensional case. Denoted one-dimensional $\vec{F}$ =(f(0),...,f(N-1))^T, denoted the data after DCT as $\vec{G}$ =(g(0),...,g(N-1))^T, where

$$g(u) = \sqrt{\frac{2}{N}} k \sum f(n) \cos(\frac{(2n+1)u\pi}{2N})$$

$$k_u = \begin{cases} 1/\sqrt{2} \\ 1 \end{cases}$$

for *u*=0, *u*=0,...,*N*-1for *u*≠0 Denoted:

$$C_{N \times N} = \begin{pmatrix} 1/\sqrt{2}, & 1/\sqrt{2} & ,..., & 1/\sqrt{2} \\ \cos\frac{\pi}{2N}, & \cos\frac{3\pi}{2N} & ,..., \cos\frac{(2N-1)\pi}{2N} \\ \cos\frac{2\pi}{2N}, & \cos\frac{6\pi}{2N} & ,..., \cos\frac{(2N-1)2\pi}{2N} \\ & ... & ... \\ \cos\frac{(N-1)\pi}{2N}, & \cos\frac{3(N-1)\pi}{2N}, & ..., \cos\frac{(2N-1)(N-1)\pi}{2N} \end{pmatrix}$$

We get $\vec{G} = C_{N \times N} \vec{F}$. Let $\vec{F_1}$ and $\vec{F_2}$ be two histogram data, we can get the accumulation of the corresponding elements' products as $\vec{F_1}^T * \vec{F_2}$, and $\vec{G_1}^T * \vec{G_2} = \vec{F_1}^T * C_{N \times N}^T * C_{N \times N} * \vec{F_2}$. We can prove $C_{N \times N}^T * C_{N \times N} = I_D$ (unit matrix), so we can got $\vec{F_1}^T * \vec{F_2} = \vec{G_1}^T * \vec{G_2}$. For multidimensional case, as the same reason we got $\vec{F_1}^T * \vec{F_2} = \vec{G_1}^T * \vec{G_2}$. The theorem is a variant of the DCT maintain data energy QED.

Algorithm 17 belongs to data preprocessing and it is an offline algorithm, and the space needed is the space which could save the entire histogram data, and the algorithm can use DCT fast algorithm for information compression. The algorithm18 stores the data after the DCT compression and its storage space associated with the sampling threshold b. Because it is only need the compressed data, the greater of b, the greater the required storage space, the better accuracy of estimation result. In practical applications, it is possible to store the DCT coefficients within the sampling area in the certain order, so the time complexity of the algorithm is O(max(|G'_1|,|G'_2|)), where G'_1, G'_2 are respectively store data after sampling G'_1, G'_2.

Multi-Similarity Join Order Selection in Entity Database

The Size of the Entity Similarity Join Result Estimation

This part uses sampling method to estimate the size of entity similarity join result. The estimation process is to be divided into two steps: the first step is taking of samples and the second step is estimating the size of entity similarity join result based samples. And then we give an optimized algorithm.

MCMC Sampling Method Based on Entity

In practical applications, the distribution of data is unknown in many cases. So the sampling method must be independent of the specific distribution of data. In addition, the join operator occupies a very large sample space. For example, the join space of two 5K size tables up to 25000K. For this problem, the most common way is hash or aggregate data into different classes, then sample from these classes(H. Lee et al., 2011). However, due to the multi-value characteristic of entity, it does not guarantee that similar entities are gathered in same classes. So, these methods are no longer applicable to entity similarity join. Fortunately, the MCMC method(Hochba, 1997) is applicable to do sampling from the discrete distribution of the unknown, and very large sample space for parameter estimation. Therefore, we proposes entity-based MCMC methods to estimate the size of the entity similarity join result.

The entity-based MCMC method solves the sampling problem as follows. First it defines a traverse Markov chain as the sample space, the state set of the Markov chain is entity pair set satisfying the condition: $MinED \leq \tau$. That is,

$$\Omega(\tau) = \{(r_i, t_j) : r_i \in R \wedge t_j \in T \wedge d(r_i.A, t_j.A) \leq \tau\}.$$

Its stationary distribution is our required sampling distribution, that is, $|\Omega(\tau)| / |\Omega|$, where Ω is the Cartesian product of two tables. Suppose that sequence $X_0, X_1, ..., X_n$ is a section of the chain, $\mathfrak{M}_{join}$ can convergence to the stationary distribution from any one state. So after enough r steps, the distribution of the state will be close to the stationary distribution. Taking X_r as a starting point, remove the previous r value, $X_r, X_{r+1}, X_{r+2}...$ will eventually be as almost uniform sample from the stationary distribution.

The above sampling process can be divided into two parts: the construction of the Markov chain and the choice of sampling method.

The Construction of $\mathfrak{M}_{join}$ and its Properties

The initial state of $\mathfrak{M}_{join}$ can be any of the entity pair satisfying $MinED \leq \tau$. When calculating the current state, we randomly select an entity pair from Ω. If this entity pair was in $\Omega(\tau)$, then we take it as the current state. Otherwise, we copy previous state as the current state. Concrete construction method is described in Algorithm 19.

Algorithm 19: The construction of $\mathfrak{M}_{join}$ based on entity

1. X_0 is any entity pair of $\Omega(\tau)$
2. Compute X_{i+1}
    a. Uniform random select an entity pair (r_i, t_j) from $R \times S$
    b. If (r_i, t_j) is in $\Omega(\tau)$, $X_{i+1} = (r_i, t_j)$
    c. Else $X_{i+1} = X_i$.

The entity-based Markov chain constructed by Algorithm 19 has the following properties:

Property 7: $\mathfrak{M}_{join}$ has a unique stationary distribution.

Proof: Taking into account that all states in the state space $\Omega(\tau)$ belongs to a connected class, that is, any two states are reachable to each other. So $\mathfrak{M}_{join}$ is irreducible. In addition, this chain is aperiodic and limited, so it is traversed. Due to its limited, irreducibility and ergodicity, this chain $\mathfrak{M}_{join}$ has a unique stationary distribution and the stationary distribution $\pi_x = |\Omega(\tau)| / |\Omega|$ is evenly distributed.

By Property 7, when the number of running steps unlimited increases, $\mathfrak{M}_{join}$ converges to the uniform distribution $\pi_x = |\Omega(\tau)| / |\Omega|$. If the chain could run forever, then the final state will be a uniformly distributed state. Actually the chain only runs finite steps. Therefore, we use the method of Markov chain coupling to get an approximately uniform distribution. Sampling from the sample space obeying approximately uniform distribution, we will get an approximation uniform sample. Definition 16 gives definition of approximately uniform sample.

Definition 16: Let ω be the output of a sampling algorithm for a finite space Ω. For any subset S of Ω, if $|Pr(\omega \in S) - \dfrac{|S|}{|\Omega|}| \le \varepsilon$, then algorithm generates an $\varepsilon-$uniform sample of Ω

Obviously, the closer $\mathfrak{M}_{join}$ to the stationary distribution, the more uniform samples from sampling algorithm. Property 7 describes the convergence speed of $\mathfrak{M}_{join}$ to the nearly uniform distribution.

Property 8: Let $x = |\Omega| / |\Omega(\tau)| \bullet 0 < \varepsilon < 1$, through $x \ln(x / \varepsilon)$ steps, the sample drawn from $\mathfrak{M}_{join}$ is a $\varepsilon-$uniform sample.

Proof: We use the coupling lemma(Mitzenmacher & Upfal, 2005) to calculate the speed of $\mathfrak{M}_{join}$ convergence. First it needs to select a suitable coupling. Let R, S be the join entity tables. The Cartesian product Ω of two tables is numbered in sequence from 1 to $|\Omega|$. Given a copy of the chain in the different states, every time uniformly and randomly selects a location j. According to Algorithm 19, given the initial state, only if each of the entity pairs randomly selected by the algorithm is not in the state space, X_{t+1} is different from Y_{t+1}. In contrast, as long as the entity pair is in the state space, the two copies will inevitably become coupled. We simply define the number of times that must be selected entities before entity pair being in state space. Let $x = |\Omega| / |\Omega(\tau)|$, after the Markov chain running $x \ln x + cx$ steps, the probability of entity pairs which never be chosen to the state space $\Omega(\tau)$ is at most

$$(1 - \frac{1}{x})^{x \ln x + cx} \le e^{-(\ln x + c|)} = \frac{e^{-c}}{x}.$$

So the probability of entity pairs in the state space never be chosen is at most e^{-c}. Therefore, after going through $x \ln x + x \ln(1 / \varepsilon) = x \ln(x / \varepsilon)$ steps, the probability of chain not coupled at most ε. By coupling Lemma, after $x \ln(x / \varepsilon)$ steps, the sample extracted from $\mathfrak{M}_{join}$ is a uniform sample.

MCMC Sampling Algorithm Based on the Entity

This part determines the sampling sample space, discusses the specific sampling plan. Suppose R, S are two entities join tables, a simple sampling program estimating the join result size is as follows. Firstly we need to construct a Markov chain, taking Ω (Cartesian product of the two entities table) as state space. Then we randomly selected one entity pair from the Markov chain. If the extracted entity pair satisfied similar join conditions, then return $|\Omega|$, otherwise return 0. Theoretically, as long as experiments running a sufficient number of times, the average of estimated value can be close to exact solution by any degree accuracy. However, In fact this method can not get the expected result. We illustrate it using the following example. Suppose doing entity similarity join on entity attribute *A* in entity table *R, S,* suppoose entity *MinED* is 3. There are very few entity pairs satisfying the similarity condition, which account for only 0.001. So that even after a reasonable number of times of sampling, we obtain the desired results may also be 0. This indicates that, if the samples satisfy the conditions in the total sample space does not have enough dense, the estimated error of the result would be too large.

The Reasonable sampling plan should satisfy two conditions: (1) The sample space must contain all the sample which satisfy similarity condition. (2) The proportion of sample satisfying similarity condition in sample space should be sufficiently dense. By simple statistics of data in entity database, we observed that, if given a sample space $MinED \leq k$, in most cases, the sample which minimum edit distance has a few difference from k in the sample space $MinED \leq k$ is dense. For example, the sample $MinED \leq k-1$ in the sample space $MinED \leq k$ takes a large proportion. Without loss of generality, we assume that the proportion is in $[\theta_1, 1]$., θ_1 typically greater than 1/5. Based on the above observation, the estimation size of entity similarity join result can be obtained through indirect estimating the proportion of the sample Min $ED \leq k-1$ in the sample space Min $ED \leq k$. The specific idea is as follows:

Let $\Omega(i)$ be entity pairs which minimum edit distance satisfy that $MinED \leq i$, minimum edit distance threshold be τ, the maximum length of the join strings be len. Then the size of result which satisfy the join condition can be expressed as:

$$| \Omega(\tau) | = \frac{| \Omega(\tau) |}{| \Omega(\tau + 1) |} \times \frac{| \Omega(\tau + 1) |}{| \Omega(\tau + 2) |} \times ... \\ \times \frac{| \Omega(len - 1) |}{| \Omega(len) |} \times | \Omega(len) |$$

(9)

Since the edit distance of two strings is not greater than the length of the string, so $| \Omega(len) | = | \Omega |$. Then we can estimate the size of $\hat{r}_i = \frac{| \Omega(i) |}{| \Omega(i + 1) |}$ to obtain the final result.

Based on this idea, the sampling program is as follows:

Construct the Markov chain $\mathfrak{M}(i)$ whose state space is $\Omega(i)$ (entity pairs set which satisfy $MinED \leq i$)

Take samples from $\mathfrak{M}(i)$, calculate the proportion of the sample satisfying . $MinED \leq i-1$

The results of this sampling program is estimation value of $r_i = \frac{| \Omega(i) |}{| \Omega(i + 1) |}$

After determining the sampling plan, the specific algorithm estimating r_i. Analysis of the estimated error is given in following part.

The Size Estimation of Entity Similarity Join Result

In order to estimate the size of the entity similarity join result, r_i need to be estimated. We carry out random sampling program as follows: firstly take a sample from Markov chain $\mathfrak{M}(i)$ whose state space is $\Omega(\tau + i)$, then calculate whether the sample is in $\Omega(\tau + i-1)$. If so, the count is incremented. This process is repeated N times, and finally back to average value of count as the estimated value. Specific estimation algorithm is shown in Algorithm 20 And $\hat{r}_i$ estimated by the Algorithm 20 is an $(\varepsilon / 2m, \delta / m)$ approximation of r_i. We prove it in the following.

Algorithm 20: Estimate r_i

Input: Entity table R, S, minimum edit distance τ

Output: An estimation value of r_i X=0

1. Repeat

$$N = (648 / 5)m^2\varepsilon^{-2} \ln(2m / \delta) / \theta_1$$

times independent trials:

    a.   Sampling a
        $(\varepsilon\theta_1 / 6m) - uniform\ sample\ from\ \mathfrak{M}(i)$

    b.   If this sample was in $\Omega(\tau + i - 1)$, let X=X+1

2. Return $\hat{r}_i \leftarrow X / N$

The value of $|\Omega(\tau)|$ can be obtained by $\hat{r}_i$. Let m=len-τ. The estimation value of two entity tables join result size is $|\Omega| \prod_{i=1}^{m} \hat{r}_i$. According to Formula 9, $|\Omega|$ is known. After running m times Algorithm 20, the final result will be calculated by multiplying $\hat{r}_i$, we can get estimation value of $|\Omega(\tau)|$. Specific details are presented in Algorithm 21.

Algorithm 21: Estimate $|\Omega(\tau)|$: Mjoinsize

Input: Entity table R, S, minimum edit distance τ

Output: An approximation of $|\Omega(\tau)|$

1. $size \leftarrow |\Omega|$;
2. $For\ i \leftarrow m\ to\ i \leftarrow 1$
3. Construct a Markov chain whose sample space is $\Omega(\tau + i)$
4. Estimate the value of $r_i, \hat{r}_i$
5. $size = size \times r_i$
6. Return size.

The implementation process of Algorithm 21 indicates that the estimation algorithm is adaptive, that is, the larger the value of r_i, the faster the convergence rate of Markov chain. For example, in estimating r_m process, the Markov chain convergences in constant c step, and the total number of sampling is small.

With estimated results, next we need to define the estimated error. The value of entity Join result size is $|\Omega| \prod_{i=1}^{m} \hat{r}_i$ estimated by the algorithm, and the real value is $|\Omega| \prod_{i=1}^{m} r_i$ In order to calculate the estimated error, we have defined $R = \prod_{i=1}^{len} \hat{r}_i$. Particularly, in order to get an (ε, δ) approximate, we hope Pr($|$ R-1$| \le \varepsilon$) $\le 1 - \delta$

Theorem 8: $R = \prod_{i=1}^{len} \hat{r}_i$, $\Pr(| R - 1 | \le \varepsilon) \ge 1 - \delta$

In order to prove Theorem 1, we propose two lemma

Lemma 1: Suppose $m \ge 1$, $0 < \varepsilon \le 1$, the program of estimating r_i produce a $(\varepsilon / 2m, \delta / m)$ approximation of r_i.

In the proof of Lemma 1, we use the following theorem(Mitzenmacher & Upfal, 2005):

Theorem 9: Let $X_1, X_2, ..., X_n$ be independent and identically distributed indicator random variables, with $\mu = E[X_i]$. If

$$m \ge \left((3\ln(2 / \delta)) / \varepsilon^2\mu\right),$$

then

$$\Pr\left(\left|\frac{1}{m}\sum_{i=1}^{m} X_i - \mu\right| \ge \varepsilon\mu\right) \le \delta.$$

That is, m samples provide an $(\varepsilon \cdot \delta)$-approximation for μ.

The proof of Theorem 8: We first show that r_i is not too small, ensuring that samples satisfying join conditions in the sample space is sufficiently dense. Obviously,

$$\Omega(i) \in \Omega(i+1), r_i = \frac{|\Omega(i)|}{|\Omega(i+1)|} \geq \theta_1 \text{ (10)}$$

Now consider our N samples, and let $X_k = 1$ if the kth sample is in $\Omega(i)$ and 0 otherwise. Because our samples are generated by an $(\varepsilon \theta_1 / m)$-uniform sampler, each X_k must satisfy:

$$|\Pr(X_k = 1) - \frac{|\Omega(i)|}{|\Omega(i+1)|}| \leq \frac{\varepsilon \theta_1}{6m}$$

Since the X_k are indicator random variables, it follows that:

$$|E(X_k = 1) - \frac{|\Omega(i)|}{|\Omega(i+1)|}| \leq \frac{\varepsilon \theta_1}{6m}$$

and further, by linearity of expectations,

$$|E\left[\frac{\sum_{k=1}^{N} X_k}{N}\right] - \frac{|\Omega(i)|}{|\Omega(i+1)|}| \leq \frac{\varepsilon \theta_1}{6m}$$

We therefore have

$$|E\left[\hat{r_i}\right] - r_i| = |E\left[\frac{\sum_{k=1}^{N} X_k}{N}\right] - \frac{|\Omega(i)|}{|\Omega(i+1)|}| \leq \frac{\varepsilon \theta_1}{6m} \text{ (11)}$$

By combining (10) and (11), we have

$$E\left[\hat{r_i}\right] \geq r_i - \frac{\varepsilon \theta_1}{6m} \geq \theta_1 - \frac{\varepsilon \theta_1}{6m} \geq \frac{5\theta_1}{6}$$

By Theorem 9, if the number of samples N satisfies

$$N \geq \frac{3\ln(2m/\delta)}{(\varepsilon/6m)^2(5\theta_1/6)} = \frac{648}{5\theta_1}m^2\varepsilon^{-2}\ln\frac{2m}{\delta},$$

Then

$$\Pr(|\hat{r_i} - E\left[\hat{r_i}\right]| \geq \frac{\varepsilon}{6m}E\left[\hat{r_i}\right]) \leq \frac{\delta}{m}$$

Equivalently, with probability $1 - \frac{\delta}{m}$,

$$1 - \frac{\varepsilon}{6m} \leq \frac{r_i}{E\left[\hat{r_i}\right]} \leq 1 + \frac{\varepsilon}{6m} \quad (12)$$

As $|E\left[\hat{r_i}\right] - r_i| \leq \frac{\varepsilon \theta}{6m}$, we have:

$$1 - \frac{\varepsilon \theta_1}{6mr_i} \leq \frac{E\left[\hat{r_i}\right]}{r_i} \leq 1 + \frac{\varepsilon \theta_1}{6mr_i}$$

Using that $r_i \geq \theta_1$ then yields

$$1 - \frac{\varepsilon}{6m} \leq \frac{E\left[\hat{r_i}\right]}{r_i} \leq 1 + \frac{\varepsilon}{6m} \quad (13)$$

By combining (12) and (13)

$$1 - \frac{\varepsilon}{2m} \leq (1 - \frac{\varepsilon}{6m})(1 - \frac{\varepsilon}{6m}) \leq \frac{\hat{r_i}}{r_i} \leq (1 + \frac{\varepsilon}{6m})(1 + \frac{\varepsilon}{6m}) \leq 1 + \frac{\varepsilon}{2m}$$

That is, $\hat{r_i}$ is an $(\varepsilon/2m, \delta/m)$-approximation of r_i.

Lemma 2: Suppose that for all $i, \tau \leq i \leq len$, $\hat{r_i}$ is an $(\varepsilon / 2m, \delta / m)$-approximation for r_i. Then $Pr(|R - 1| \leq \varepsilon) \geq 1 - \delta$

Proof: For each $\tau \leq i \leq len$, we have

$$Pr(|\hat{r_i} - r_i| \leq \frac{\varepsilon}{2m} r_i) \geq 1 - \frac{\delta}{m}$$

Equivalently, $Pr(|\hat{r_i} - r_i| > \frac{\varepsilon}{2m} r_i) < \frac{\delta}{m}$

By the union bound, the probability that $|\hat{r_i} - r_i| > \bullet \varepsilon / 2m \bullet r_i$ for any i is at most δ. Therefore, $|\hat{r_i} - r_i| \leq \bullet \varepsilon / 2m \bullet r_i$ for all i with probability at least $1 - \delta$.

Equivalently, $1 - \frac{\varepsilon}{2m} \leq \frac{\hat{r_i}}{r_i} \leq 1 + \frac{\varepsilon}{2m}$ holds for all i with probability at least $1 - \delta$. When these bounds hold for all i, we can combine them to obtain

$$1 - \varepsilon \leq (1 - \frac{\varepsilon}{2m})^m \leq \prod_{i=1}^{m} \frac{\hat{r_i}}{r_i} \leq (1 + \frac{\varepsilon}{2m})^m \leq 1 + \varepsilon$$

giving the lemma.

The proof of Theorem 8: By lemma 1 and Lemma 2, we have $Pr(|R - 1| \leq \varepsilon) \geq 1 - \delta$

Optimization of the Algorithm Mjoinsize

We give an algorithm Mjoinsize to estimate $|\Omega(\tau)|$. Although the algorithm can guarantee the accuracy of the results, but the efficiency is very low. This is because we must construct Markov chain of $\Omega(i)$ sample space every time when Algorithm 20 estimates r_i every time. Furthermore, the sample extract from the Cartesian product, Markov chain convergence speed is very slow when i is very small.

In order to avoid constructing the Markov chain of $\Omega(i)$ sample space when i is very small, We give a novel estimator $\hat{r_i} = \frac{|\Omega(i)|}{|\Omega(i+l)|}$, where

$1 \leq l \leq len - i$. Compared with the original estimate $\hat{r_i} = \frac{|\Omega(i)|}{|\Omega(i+1)|}$, the convergence speed of Markov chain of $\Omega(i+l)$ sample space is faster than the Markov chain of $\Omega(i+1)$ sample space. And the estimation number of r_i will reduce at the same time. But the proportion of sample $MinED \leq k$ θ_i will smaller than θ_i in the sample space $MinED \leq k + l$. So the sampling number of Algorithm 20 will be increased. In order to balance the sampling number of Algorithm 20, the convergence speed of Algorithm 20, and the algorithm execution times, we need to select the appropriate value of l to make the least total sampling number.

When l was selected, the size of the similarity join result we need to estimate is

$$|\Omega(\tau)| = \frac{|\Omega(\tau)|}{|\Omega(\tau+l)|} \times \frac{|\Omega(\tau+l)|}{|\Omega(\tau+2l)|} \times \cdots \times \frac{|\Omega(\tau+ml)|}{|\Omega(len)|} \times |\Omega(len)|,$$

where

$$len - (\tau + ml) \leq l.$$

That is, $m = \left\lceil \frac{len - \tau}{l} \right\rceil$. If $r_i = \frac{|\Omega(\tau)|}{|\Omega(\tau+il)|}$, the way of estimating new r_i is similar to algorithm 2, the sampling number N, the Markov chain, and the sample counting conditions are changed.

The specific calculation process is as shown in Algorithm 22.

Algorithm 22: OPT_Mjoinsize:

Input: A entity relation table R, S, an edit distance threshold i

Output: The approximation of r_i

1.   X=0.

2. Repeat $N = 648m^2\varepsilon^{-2}\ln(2m/\delta)/\theta_l$ times independent tests

   a. Produce a $(\varepsilon\theta_1/m)$-uniform sample from $\mathfrak{M}(\tau+il)$;

   b. If this sample was in $\Omega(\tau+(i-1)l)$, X=X+1

3. return $\hat{r_i} \leftarrow X/N$

The Choice of L

Let N_{total} be the sampling number of estimating $\Omega(\tau)$, N_i be the sampling number of estimating r_i, $\theta_i = \theta^i$, we get the Equation (8) from Algorithm 22.

$$N_{total} = \prod_{i=1}^{m} r_m \qquad (13)$$

By algorithm 22, N_i is a function of l, $l = \left\lceil \dfrac{len-\tau}{m} \right\rceil$, so we can get l from optimizing m. And the optimized m can make the smallest N_{total}.

Theorem 3: The sampling number of estimating r_i N_i, is at least

$$x_i\ln x_i + cx_i + 2\times648m^2\varepsilon^{-2}\ln(2m/\delta)/5\theta_1^{\left\lceil\frac{len-\tau}{m}\right\rceil} \quad (14)$$

Proof: We known that the sampling number of estimating r_i from $\mathfrak{M}(i)$ is

$$N = 648m^2\varepsilon^{-2}\ln(2m/\delta)/5\theta_1^{\left\lceil\frac{len-\tau}{m}\right\rceil}.$$

In order to estimate r_i, we must sample at least N times after $\mathfrak{M}(i)$ nearly being steady in $x_i\ln x_i + cx_i$ steps. Therefore, the number of sample time constructing $\mathfrak{M}(i)$ is at least $x_i\ln x_i + cx_i + N$. And the number of sample time estimating r_i is at least

$$x_i\ln x_i + cx_i + 2\times648m^2\varepsilon^{-2}\ln(2m/\delta)/5\theta_1^{\left\lceil\frac{len-\tau}{m}\right\rceil}.$$

By Formula 9, $x_i = |\Omega|/|\Omega(\tau+il)|$ is a fixed value. Suppose that $k_i = 2\times648\varepsilon^{-2}/5$, then

$$N_i = x_i\ln x_i + cx_i + k_i\varepsilon^{-2}\ln(2m/\delta)/\theta_1^{\left\lceil\frac{len-\tau}{m}\right\rceil} \quad (15)$$

We optimize the value of m by derivation method.

$$\frac{dN_i}{dm} = \frac{\left(k_i m^2\varepsilon^{-2}\ln(2m/\delta)\right)'\theta_1^{\left\lceil\frac{len-\tau}{m}\right\rceil} - \left(k_i m^2\varepsilon^{-2}\ln(2m/\delta)\right)\left(\theta_1^{\left\lceil\frac{len-\tau}{m}\right\rceil}\right)'}{\left(\theta_1^{\left\lceil\frac{len-\tau}{m}\right\rceil}\right)^2}$$

$$= \frac{k_i\varepsilon^{-2}\left((2m+(len-\tau)\ln\theta_1)\ln(2m/\delta)+1\right)}{\left(\theta_1^{\left\lceil\frac{len-\tau}{m}\right\rceil}\right)}$$

$$\frac{dN_{total}}{dm} = \sum_{i=1}^{m}\frac{dN_i}{dm} = \qquad (16)$$
$$\sum_{i=1}^{m}\frac{k_i\varepsilon^{-2}\left((2m+(len-\tau)\ln\theta_1)\ln(2m/\delta)+1\right)}{\left(\theta_1^{\left\lceil\frac{len-\tau}{m}\right\rceil}\right)} =$$
$$\frac{k_i\varepsilon^{-2}\left((2m+(len-\tau)\ln\theta_1)\ln(2m/\delta)+1\right)}{\left(\theta_1^{\left\lceil\frac{len-\tau}{m}\right\rceil}\right)}\sum_{i=1}^{m}k_i\varepsilon^{-2}\cdot\frac{dN_{total}}{dm} = 0$$

Suppose that $\alpha=(len-\tau)\ln\theta_1$, we can simply Equation(16) as $\cdot 2m+\alpha)\ln(2m/\delta)+1=0$

Because of $\alpha\cdot\delta$ is known we can use plotting method to get the value of m.

In order to estimate the size of join result more effective, the Markov chain can be offline created. So we can get the estimation of r_i directly from the Markov chain created with offline. When data is update in the database, we use the following method to update the Markov chain: There are three operations in database update, increase, delete, and modify. The modified operation can be seen as first delete then added. Therefore, we only consider two cases: increase and deletion.

Without loss of generality, assuming that there are two join tables R and S, and a updating operation inserting r to R, we determine whether update the Markov chain with the probability of $|S|/(|R|+|S|)$. If so, we select a tuple from S randomly with the probability of $1/|S|$. Suppose that s is the selected tuple, we compute the minimum edit distance of r and s, then insert (r, s) is into $\mathfrak{M}(i)$ satisfying $i \geq MinED(r, s)$. For $\mathfrak{M}(i)$ satisfying the $i < MinED(r, s)$., the current state is the copy of the previous state.

To update the Markov chain with delete operation, we add a new list (tag) in the entity table. Tag is consists of a string, in which each character says it is drawn in which Markov chain. tag=0 says that it is not drawn. When deleting a tuple from R, we see tag firstly, finding out the Markov chain with the tag, then find the state of deleted entitles in the Markov chain and delete it.

Entity-Based Similarity Multi-Join Order Selection

Entity similarity multi-join cost relates to the size of intermediate results generated in the join process and whether the join table has index. According to the two factors, we establish the corresponding cost model. Then based on the cost we use the traditional multi-join optimization algorithm [15] to determine the multi-join order. The optimization algorithm uses the estimation method shown in the above part to estimate the entity similarity join result. This part focuses on introducing the cost model.

The most important in the model is the size of intermediate result. We use a example to illustrate it. Assuming that there are three table join R(a,b) ⋈S(b,c) ⋈T(d,a), and each the three table size is 1000. Any of the two table join result sizes shown in Table 13.

The result of three table join is fixed, so the efficiency of first join R and T is greater than the other cases. Therefore, the intermediate result size has an important influence on the efficiency of the actual join.

However, it can not reflect the actual cost of join all-right if we only consider the intermediate result size. If the two needed join tables have index in the join attribute, we can avoid scanning disk in the actual join process, and do join operator directly according to the index. This greatly reduces the number of I/O operation.

Because of these two considerations, we regard multi-join intermediate result size and whether has index as the total cost to optimize the join order. Cost model can be expressed as a function of two kinds of cost type.

$$
\begin{aligned}
\cos t\left(R,S:a\right) = {} & \alpha(Index\left(R:a\right)+Index\left(S:a\right) \\
& +\left(1-\alpha\right)(\cos t(R) + \cos t(S) + \quad (17) \\
& mresult(R) + mresult(S))
\end{aligned}
$$

where R and S can be regard as temporary table in the process of join, or original table. $\cos t\left(R,S:a\right)$ is the join cost of R and S on attribute a. Index(R) is the I/O cost, which has sense only if R is original table. We suppose that the temporary table exists in memory, and it does not need I/O operation. And $bool[R:a]$ shows that whether R has index on attribute a, 0 is no, otherwise is 1.

$$
Index(R:a) = \begin{cases} |R| & bool[R:a] = 0; \\ 0 & bool[R:a] = 1; \end{cases}
$$

And cost(R) is the cost of generating R, $mresult(R)$ is the size of generated temporary table in the process of connecting. Evidently, if R is original table, cost(R)=0, $mresult(R) = 0$. In addition, α is the weight of index structure in the total cost.

In the situation of R(a, b)⋈S(b, c)⋈U(c, d)⋈T(d, a), we can use the following formula to estimate the size.

$$\frac{|R(a,b)\infty S(b,c)|}{|R|} \times \frac{|U(c,d)\infty T(d,a)|}{|T|} \times |R(a,b)\infty T(d,a)|$$

Based on the cost model (12), we can use the existing multi-join sequence selection algorithm to optimize the order of multi-join. When the number of entity join tables is fewer (not more than five), dynamic programming selecting the join sequence method(Garcia-Molina et al., 2000) can return the optimal order of join by filling in the cost table, recording the minimum cost. However, when the number of entity join tables is large, dynamic programming will result in the calculation cost link exponential to the number of the join table. However, we can use a heuristic search strategy (Garcia-Molina et al., 2000), such as greedy algorithm to get a better join sequence. Specific algorithm is same as the traditional order selection algorithm, and not described here in details.

CONCLUSION

Since entity is the unit for understanding objects in the world and many dirty data are led by different descriptions of the same real-world entity, this chapter defines the entity data model to manage dirty data to keep conflicts in data as uncertain attributes. And then proposes EntityManager, a dirty data management system based on entity With entity data model different from traditional relational model, the query in our system has different semantics compared to traditional relational database. Novel techniques are developed for efficiently query processing including similarity-based Operators, indices and query optimization.

REFERENCES

Andritsos, P., Fuxman, A., & Miller, R. J. (2006). *Clean answers over dirty databases: A probabilistic approach.* Paper presented at the Data Engineering, 2006. New York, NY.

Arasu, A., Ganti, V., & Kaushik, R. (2006). *Efficient exact set-similarity joins.* Paper presented at the 32nd International Conference on Very Large Data Bases. New York, NY.

Batini, C., & Scannapieca, M. (2006). *Data quality.* Berlin: Springer.

Behm, A., Ji, S., Li, C., & Lu, J. (2009). *Space-constrained gram-based indexing for efficient approximate string search.* Paper presented at the Data Engineering, 2009. New York, NY.

Benjelloun, O., Garcia-Molina, H., Menestrina, D., Su, Q., Whang, S. E., & Widom, J. (2009). Swoosh: A generic approach to entity resolution. *The VLDB Journal—The International Journal on Very Large Data Bases, 18*(1), 255-276.

Boulos, J., Dalvi, N., Mandhani, B., Mathur, S., Re, C., & Suciu, D. (2005). *MYSTIQ: A system for finding more answers by using probabilities.* Paper presented at the 2005 ACM SIGMOD International Conference on Management of Data. New York, NY.

Charikar, M. S. (2002). *Similarity estimation techniques from rounding algorithms.* Paper presented at the Thiry-Fourth Annual ACM Symposium on Theory of Computing. New York, NY.

Table 13. The intermediate result size of three table join

	{R,S}	{R,T}	{S,T}
size	5000	2000	1000000

Clauset, A., Newman, M. E. J., & Moore, C. (2004). Finding community structure in very large networks. *Physical Review E: Statistical, Nonlinear, and Soft Matter Physics, 70*(6), 066111. doi:10.1103/PhysRevE.70.066111

Dong, X. L., Halevy, A., & Yu, C. (2009). Data integration with uncertainty. *The VLDB Journal, 18*(2), 469–500. doi:10.1007/s00778-008-0119-9

Eckerson, W. W. (2002). Data quality and the bottom line: Achieving business success through a commitment to high quality data. The Data Warehousing Institute, 1-36.

English, L. (1997). Plain English on data quality. *DM Review, 7,* 14–16.

Fuxman, A., Fazli, E., & Miller, R. J. (2005). *Conquer: Efficient management of inconsistent databases.* Paper presented at the 2005 ACM SIGMOD International Conference on Management of Data. New York, NY.

Fuxman, A. D., & Miller, R. J. (2005). First-order query rewriting for inconsistent databases. [Berlin: Springer.]. *Proceedings of Database Theory-ICDT, 2005,* 337–351.

Garcia-Molina, H., Ullman, J. D., & Widom, J. (2000). *Database system implementation* (Vol. 654). Englewood Cliffs, NJ: Prentice Hall.

Goemans, M. X., & Williamson, D. P. (1995). Improved approximation algorithms for maximum cut and satisfiability problems using semidefinite programming. *Journal of the ACM, 42*(6), 1115–1145. doi:10.1145/227683.227684

Hadjieleftheriou, M., Chandel, A., Koudas, N., & Srivastava, D. (2008). *Fast indexes and algorithms for set similarity selection queries.* Paper presented at the Data Engineering, 2008. New York, NY.

Hadjieleftheriou, M., Koudas, N., & Srivastava, D. (2009). *Incremental maintenance of length normalized indexes for approximate string matching.* Paper presented at the 35th SIGMOD International Conference on Management of Data. New York, NY.

Hassanzadeh, O., & Miller, R. J. (2009). Creating probabilistic databases from duplicated data. *The VLDB Journal—The International Journal on Very Large Data Bases, 18*(5), 1141-1166.

Hochba, D. S. (1997). Approximation algorithms for NP-hard problems. *ACM SIGACT News, 28*(2), 40–52. doi:10.1145/261342.571216

Indyk, P., & Motwani, R. (1998). *Approximate nearest neighbors: Towards removing the curse of dimensionality.* Paper presented at the Thirtieth Annual ACM Symposium on Theory of Computing. New York, NY.

Lee, H., Ng, R. T., & Shim, K. (2011). Similarity join size estimation using locality sensitive hashing. *Proceedings of the VLDB Endowment, 4*(6), 338–349.

Lee, J.-H., Kim, D.-H., & Chung, C.-W. (1999). *Multi-dimensional selectivity estimation using compressed histogram information.* Paper presented at the ACM SIGMOD Record. New York, NY.

Lenzerini, M. (2002). *Data integration: A theoretical perspective.* Paper presented at the Twenty-First ACM SIGMOD-SIGACT-SIGART Symposium on Principles of Database Systems. New York, NY.

Li, C., Wang, B., & Yang, X. (2007). *VGRAM: Improving performance of approximate queries on string collections using variable-length grams.* Paper presented at the 33rd International Conference on Very Large Data Bases. New York, NY.

Li, Y., Wang, H., & Gao, H. (2011). Efficient entity resolution based on sequence rules. In *Proceedings of Advanced Research on Computer Science and Information Engineering* (pp. 381–388). Berlin: Springer. doi:10.1007/978-3-642-21402-8_61

Liu, X., Wang, H., Li, J., & Gao, H. (2011). *Es-join: Similarity join algorithm based on entity research report*. Harbin Institute of Technology.

Liu, X., Wang, H., Li, J., & Gao, H. (2012). Multi-similarity join order selection in entity database. *Frontiers of Computer Science and Technology, 6*.

Mitzenmacher, M., & Upfal, E. (2005). *Probability and computing: Randomized algorithms and probabilistic analysis*. Cambridge, UK: Cambridge University Press. doi:10.1017/CBO9780511813603

Rahm, E., & Do, H. H. (2000). Data cleaning: Problems and current approaches. *A Quarterly Bulletin of the Computer Society of the IEEE Technical Committee on Data Engineering, 23*(4), 3–13.

Raman, A., DeHoratius, N., & Ton, Z. (2001). Execution: The missing link in retail operations. *California Management Review, 43*(3), 136–151. doi:10.2307/41166093

Rao, K. R. (1989). Discrete cosine transform-algorithms, advantage and applications.

Ravichandran, D., Pantel, P., & Hovy, E. (2005). *Randomized algorithms and nlp: Using locality sensitive hash function for high speed noun clustering*. Paper presented at the 43rd Annual Meeting on Association for Computational Linguistics. New York, NY.

Sakoe, H., & Chiba, S. (1978). Dynamic programming algorithm optimization for spoken word recognition. *IEEE Transactions on Acoustics, Speech, and Signal Processing, 26*(1), 43–49. doi:10.1109/TASSP.1978.1163055

Tong, X., & Wang, H. (2012). Fgram-tree: An index structure based on feature grams for string approximate search. In *Web-age information management* (pp. 241–253). Berlin: Springer. doi:10.1007/978-3-642-32281-5_24

Tong, X., Wang, H., Li, J., & Gao, H. (2012). *A top-k query algorithm for weighted string based on the tree structure index*. Paper presented at the In National Database Conference of China. Beijing, China.

Wang, J., Li, G., & Feng, J. (2012). *Can we beat the prefix filtering? An adaptive framework for similarity join and search*. Paper presented at the 2012 International Conference on Management of Data. New York, NY.

Widom, J. (2004). *Trio: A system for integrated management of data, accuracy, and lineage*. Technical Report.

Xiao, C., Wang, W., & Lin, X. (2008). Ed-join: An efficient algorithm for similarity joins with edit distance constraints. *Proceedings of the VLDB Endowment, 1*(1), 933–944.

Xiao, C., Wang, W., Lin, X., Yu, J. X., & Wang, G. (2011). Efficient similarity joins for near-duplicate detection. *ACM Transactions on Database Systems, 36*(3), 15. doi:10.1145/2000824.2000825

Yang, X., Wang, B., & Li, C. (2008). *Cost-based variable-length-gram selection for string collections to support approximate queries efficiently*. Paper presented at the 2008 ACM SIGMOD International Conference on Management of Data. New York, NY.

Zhang, Y., Yang, L., & Wang, H. (2012). Range query estimation for dirty data management system. In *Web-age information management* (pp. 152–164). Berlin: Springer. doi:10.1007/978-3-642-32281-5_15

Zhang, Y., Yang, L., & Wang, H. (2012). Similarity join size estimation with threshold for dirty data. *Journal of Computers, 35*(10).

Zhang, Y., Yang, Z.-S., Wang, H.-Z., Gao, H., & Li, J.-Z. (2012). Compressed histogram based similarity join size estimation for dirty database. *Mini-Micro Systems, 10.*

Zhang, Z., Hadjieleftheriou, M., Ooi, B. C., & Srivastava, D. (2010). *Bed-tree: An all-purpose index structure for string similarity search based on edit distance.* Paper presented at the 2010 International Conference on Management of Data. New York, NY.

ADDITIONAL READING

Andritsos, P., Fuxman, A., & Miller, R. J. (2006). Clean answers over dirty databases: A probabilistic approach. Paper presented at the Data Engineering, 2006. ICDE'06. Proceedings of the 22nd International Conference on.

Arasu, A., Ganti, V., & Kaushik, R. (2006). Efficient exact set-similarity joins. Paper presented at the Proceedings of the 32nd international conference on Very large data bases.

Batini, C., & Scannapieca, M. (2006). *Data quality.* Springer.

Behm, A., Ji, S., Li, C., & Lu, J. (2009). Space-constrained gram-based indexing for efficient approximate string search. Paper presented at the Data Engineering, 2009. ICDE'09. IEEE 25th International Conference on.

Benjelloun, Omar, Garcia-Molina, Hector, Menestrina, David, Su, Qi, Whang, Steven Euijong, & Widom, Jennifer. (2009). Swoosh: a generic approach to entity resolution. The VLDB Journal—The International Journal on Very Large Data Bases, 18(1), 255-276.

Boulos, J., Dalvi, N., Mandhani, B., Mathur, S., Re, C., & Suciu, D. (2005). MYSTIQ: a system for finding more answers by using probabilities. Paper presented at the Proceedings of the 2005 ACM SIGMOD international conference on Management of data.

Charikar, M. S. (2002). Similarity estimation techniques from rounding algorithms. Paper presented at the Proceedings of the thiry-fourth annual ACM symposium on Theory of computing.

Dong, X. L., Halevy, A., & Yu, C. (2009). Data integration with uncertainty. *The VLDB Journal, 18*(2), 469–500. doi:10.1007/s00778-008-0119-9

Eckerson, W. W. (2002). Data quality and the bottom line: Achieving business success through a commitment to high quality data. The Data Warehousing Institute, 1-36.

English, L. (1997). Plain English on data quality. *DM REVIEW, 7,* 14–16.

Fuxman, A., Fazli, E., & Miller, R. J. (2005). Conquer: Efficient management of inconsistent databases. Paper presented at the Proceedings of the 2005 ACM SIGMOD international conference on Management of data.

Fuxman, A., & Miller, R. J. (2003). Towards inconsistency management in data integration systems. In IIWeb (pp. 143-148).

Fuxman, A. D., & Miller, R. J. (2005). *First-order query rewriting for inconsistent databases Database Theory-ICDT 2005* (pp. 337–351). Springer.

Garcia-Molina. (2000). *Hector, & Ullman, Jeffrey D.* New Jersey: Jennifer Widom Database System Implementation Prentice Hall.

Garcia-Molina, H., Ullman, J. D., & Widom, J. (2000). *Database system implementation* (Vol. 654). Prentice Hall Englewood Cliffs.

Goemans, M. X., & Williamson, D. P. (1995). Improved approximation algorithms for maximum cut and satisfiability problems using semidefinite programming. [JACM]. *Journal of the ACM, 42*(6), 1115–1145. doi:10.1145/227683.227684

Hadjieleftheriou, M., Chandel, A., Koudas, N., & Srivastava, D. (2008). Fast indexes and algorithms for set similarity selection queries. Paper presented at the Data Engineering, 2008. ICDE 2008. IEEE 24th International Conference on.

Hadjieleftheriou, M., Koudas, N., & Srivastava, D. (2009). Incremental maintenance of length normalized indexes for approximate string matching. Paper presented at the Proceedings of the 35th SIGMOD international conference on Management of data.

Hassanzadeh, Oktie, & Miller, Renée J. (2009). Creating probabilistic databases from duplicated data. The VLDB Journal—The International Journal on Very Large Data Bases, 18(5), 1141-1166.

Hochba, D. S. (1997). Approximation algorithms for NP-hard problems. *ACM SIGACT News, 28*(2), 40–52. doi:10.1145/261342.571216

Indyk, P., & Motwani, R. (1998). Approximate nearest neighbors: towards removing the curse of dimensionality. Paper presented at the Proceedings of the thirtieth annual ACM symposium on Theory of computing.

Lee, H., Ng, R. T., & Shim, K. (2011). Similarity join size estimation using locality sensitive hashing. *Proceedings of the VLDB Endowment, 4*(6), 338–349.

Lee, J.-H., Kim, D.-H., & Chung, C.-W. (1999). Multi-dimensional selectivity estimation using compressed histogram information. Paper presented at the ACM SIGMOD Record.

Lenzerini, M. (2002). Data integration: A theoretical perspective. Paper presented at the Proceedings of the twenty-first ACM SIGMOD-SIGACT-SIGART symposium on Principles of database systems.

Li, C., Wang, B., & Yang, X. (2007). VGRAM: Improving performance of approximate queries on string collections using variable-length grams. Paper presented at the Proceedings of the 33rd international conference on Very large data bases.

Li, Y., Wang, H., & Gao, H. (2011). *Efficient Entity Resolution Based on Sequence Rules Advanced Research on Computer Science and Information Engineering* (pp. 381–388). Springer. doi:10.1007/978-3-642-21402-8_61

Liu, xueli, Wang, Hongzhi, Li, Jianzhong, Gao, Hong. (2011). Es-join: Similarity join algorithm based on entity Research Report Harbin Institute of Technology.

Liu, xueli, Wang, Hongzhi, Li, Jianzhong, Gao, Hong. (2012). Multi-similarity join order selection in entity database. Frontiers of Computer Science and Technology, 6.

Mayfield, C., Neville, J., & Prabhakar, S. (2010, June). ERACER: a database approach for statistical inference and data cleaning. In Proceedings of the 2010 international conference on Management of data (pp. 75-86). ACM.

Mitzenmacher, M., & Upfal, E. (2005). *Probability and computing: Randomized algorithms and probabilistic analysis.* Cambridge University Press. doi:10.1017/CBO9780511813603

Rahm, E., & Do, H. H. (2000). Data cleaning: Problems and current approaches. *A Quarterly Bulletin of the Computer Society of the IEEE Technical Committee on Data Engineering, 23*(4), 3–13.

Raman, A., DeHoratius, N., & Ton, Z. (2001). Execution: The missing link in retail operations. *California Management Review, 43*(3), 136–151. doi:10.2307/41166093

Rao, Kamisetty Ramamohan. (1989). Discrete Cosine Transform-Algorithms, Advantage and Applications.

Ravichandran, D., Pantel, P., & Hovy, E. (2005). Randomized algorithms and nlp: using locality sensitive hash function for high speed noun clustering. Paper presented at the Proceedings of the 43rd Annual Meeting on Association for Computational Linguistics.

Sakoe, H., & Chiba, S. (1978). Dynamic programming algorithm optimization for spoken word recognition. Acoustics, Speech and Signal Processing. *IEEE Transactions on, 26*(1), 43–49.

Tong, X., & Wang, H. (2012). *Fgram-Tree: An Index Structure Based on Feature Grams for String Approximate Search Web-Age Information Management* (pp. 241–253). Springer. doi:10.1007/978-3-642-32281-5_24

Tong, X., Wang, H., Li, J., & Gao, H. (2012). A top-k query algorithm for weighted string based on the tree structure index. Paper presented at the In National Database Conference of China.

Wang, H., Li, J., Wang, J., & Gao, H. (2011). *Dirty data management in cloud database Grid and Cloud Database Management* (pp. 133–150). Springer. doi:10.1007/978-3-642-20045-8_7

Wang, J., Li, G., & Feng, J. (2012). Can we beat the prefix filtering?: an adaptive framework for similarity join and search. Paper presented at the Proceedings of the 2012 international conference on Management of Data.

Widom, Jennifer. (2004). Trio: A system for integrated management of data, accuracy, and lineage. Technical Report.

Xiao, C., Wang, W., & Lin, X. (2008). Ed-join: an efficient algorithm for similarity joins with edit distance constraints. *Proceedings of the VLDB Endowment, 1*(1), 933–944.

Xiao, C., Wang, W., Lin, X., Yu, J. X., & Wang, G. (2011). Efficient similarity joins for near-duplicate detection. [TODS]. *ACM Transactions on Database Systems, 36*(3), 15. doi:10.1145/2000824.2000825

Yang, X., Wang, B., & Li, C. (2008). Cost-based variable-length-gram selection for string collections to support approximate queries efficiently. Paper presented at the Proceedings of the 2008 ACM SIGMOD international conference on Management of data.

Zhang, Y., Yang, L., & Wang, H. (2012). Range query estimation for dirty data management system Web-Age [Springer.]. *Information & Management*, 152–164.

Zhang, Y., Yang, L., & Wang, H. (2012). Similarity join size estimation with threshold for dirty data. *Journal of Computers, 35*(10).

Zhang, Z., Hadjieleftheriou, M., Ooi, B. C., & Srivastava, D. (2010). Bed-tree: an all-purpose index structure for string similarity search based on edit distance. Paper presented at the Proceedings of the 2010 international conference on Management of data.

KEY TERMS AND DEFINITIONS

Database Structure: Entity database has the same structure with traditional relation database.

Data Quality: There are some materials to improve data quality which includes data cleaning and models for dirty data management without data cleaning. While the data cleaning can not clean the dirty data thoroughly, it also may delete useful information. And models for dirty data such as probabilistic model has limitation to express dirty data. That's why we introduce entity data model.

Join Order Selection: Join operator is an important factor to influnce the performance of query evaluation. When the number of join tables is larger than two, the join order directly affect the effectiveness of join algorithm. There are only works about solving the join order selection problem in traditional relation database. Understating the basic idea of join order selection strategy in relation database, you can get a deep sight of the method of entity join order selection.

Query Size Estimation: Query size estimation is an routine process in query optimization, which includes selection size estimation and join size estimation. The technique doing size estimation almost adopts random sampling or clustering. The existing work helps us understanding the details of this technique and providing theoretical basis and specific operation in entity database system.

Similarity Search/Join Based on Entity: There has been lots of work dong similarity search/join problem based on string and set. They provides basic framework and some proven techniques to do similarity search/join based on entity.

Section 4
Applications for Entity Resolution

Chapter 14
Duplicate Record Detection for Data Integration

ABSTRACT

In information integration systems, duplicate records bring problems in data processing and analysis. To represent the similarity between two records from different data sources with different schema, the optimal bipartite graph matching is adopted on the attributes of them, and the similarity is measured as the weight of such matching. Based on similarity estimation, the basic idea in this chapter is to estimate the range of the records similarity and to determine whether they are duplicate records according to the estimation. When data integration is performed on XML data, there are many problems because of the flexibility of XML. One of the current implementations is to use Data Exchange to carry out the above operations. This chapter proposes the concept of quality assurance mechanisms besides the data integrity and reliability.

INTRODUCTION

Information integration systems have been widely used. When integrating data from heterogeneous and autonomous data sources, multiple records representing the same entity are often obtained. Such records are called duplicate records. In an information integration system, duplicate records not only cause data redundancy, resulting in the waste of network bandwidth and storage space, but also provide users too many useless duplicate results. In order to increase the efficient and usability of information integration systems, it is necessary to eliminate duplicate records. Duplicate record detection, which is to partition the record set into clusters each representing the same entity, is the first step of duplicate record elimination..

Because of its widely applications, many techniques have been presented to deal with duplicate records detection. (Elmagarmid et al. 2007) is a survey of the early work of duplicate records detection. Some recent work (Bilenko et al.2003, Chandel et al. 2007, Chaudhuri et al. 2003, Cohen et al. 2000) adopt similarity functions of textual similarity, such as edit distance or cosine similarity. Those methods consider that the records corresponding to the same entity are textually similar, and are indeed useful for catching most kinds of typographic errors. The major drawback of textual similarity is that it may be misleading in the conditions of heterogeneous expressions (e.g. J. Smith is short for both John Smith and Jane Smith). Some methods based on segmentation (Borkar et al. 2001, Sarawagi et al.

DOI: 10.4018/978-1-4666-5198-2.ch014

2004, Viola et al. 2005) are proposed. Segmentation is to partition a string into its constituent components. Segmentation-based methods can solve the problem of heterogeneous expressions in some degree. There are also some other similarity descriptions are proposed. (Cohen et al. 2004) uses a similarity function to address this problem in this setting. Transformation-based and grammar-based methods are proposed in (Arasu.et al. 2008) and (Arasu et al. 2009), respectively. However all these methods does not consider the problem that the records may have various schema or attribute order and not practical for duplicate detection on records from heterogeneous data sources.

To represent the similarity of records with heterogeneous schemas, optimal bipartite graph matching is adopted (naïve Optimal Bipartite Matching Based, OBMAB) (Mohan et al. 2009). The pair of records is modeled as a bipartite graph with each node as an attribute, each edge as connecting a pair of attributes one from each record. The weights of edges are the similarity between corresponding pair of attributes. With such model, the similarity of two records is defined as the weight of optimal matching in corresponding bipartite graph. Such definition can describe the similarity of any records with different schema. As the comparing records are not necessarily having the same attribute number and order, the method is more suitable for the detection of the duplicate records from heterogeneous data sources effectively. However, each record needs to compare with a large number of records before it is assigned to the appropriate cluster. The method is not suitable for large data set. Moreover, a record will not be classified into a cluster even if only one record and the current record do not meet the requirements of similarity. This makes the method sensitive and results in low recall, which is the ratio of the detected duplicate records to all the duplicate records. Take the following case as an example.

Example 1: Records in $\{R_1$(John Smith, 18), R_2(John Smith, 18, England), R_3(John Smith, England, 18)$\}$ all refer to the student named John Smith. While processing R_4 (John Smith, England), with OBMAB, the similarity of R_1 and R_4 is 0.5. However, if the condition that R_4 belongs to the cluster is larger than 0.5, R_4 will not be classified to the cluster, although R_4 has a high similarities with R_2 and R_3. If we reduce the constraint to 0.4, the records as (Jane Smith, 18) can be classified into this cluster.

To make OBMAB practical, we proposed Similarity Estimating Duplicate Record Detection (SEDRD). For a record R and a cluster C, the upper and lower bounds of the similarity between R and any record in C can be estimated in $O(1)$ time. These bound are used to determine whether R should belong to C. As the result, during the processing of R, the computation of the similarity between R and the records in C is avoided and the processing is accelerated. Another benefit of our method is that the restriction of each cluster is relaxed and the recall is improved.

The optimal-matching-based methods for duplicate record detection are studied in this chapter. With the ability of measure the similarity of records with heterogeneous schemas, such methods are suitable for duplicate detection on records from heterogeneous data sources. An estimation method of the range of optimal-matching-based similarity is presented based on the properties of edit distance as the base of efficient duplicate record detection method. With the estimated ranges of optimal-matching-based similarity, an optimized method for record detection is presented to improve the naïve method in both efficiency and effectiveness. Extensive experiments are performed to show that our method outperforms existing methods in both efficiency and effectiveness.

Independently developed producers for example Amazon, eBay etc. bring about non-standard data in their respective databases. Consequently, when integrating data from different sources, the lack of a standard data schema is a severe problem. Subsequently Schema-Mapping targeting at the uniformity of data schema is a primary operation. To guarantee the quality of generated data is the main part in data exchange and information integration. We have a very good understanding of mappings between relational schemas (see, e.g., recent SIGMOD and PODS keynotes on the subject (Bernstein et al. 2007, Kolaitis, et al.2005)); several advanced prototypes for specifying and managing mappings have been developed and incorporated into commercial systems (Miller et al. 2001, Popa et al. 2002). There are techniques for using such mappings in data integration and exchange, and tools for handling mappings themselves, for example, for defining various operations on them (Kolaitis et al.2005, Bernstein et al.2006, Chiticariu et al. 2006, Fagin et al.2005, Madhavan et al. 2003, Nash et al. 2007). But much less is known about mappings between XML schemas.

However, more and more of today's data are represented in non-relational form. In particular, XML is increasingly popular, especially for data published on the Web and data exchanged between organizations. (Weis et al. 2005) XML data has become the standard of information conversion and integration on the Internet because of the usability of XML. Nevertheless, it's difficult for computer to automatically operate and analyze heterogeneous XML information, so information cannot be extracted and collected effectually. For that reason, Schema-Mapping is required to integrate originally heterogeneous XML information into same Schema. Since XML data is semi-structured, traditional Schema-Mapping operation on the heterogeneous XML data cannot guarantee the quality of generated data. Our work in this chapter is committed to achieving Schema-Mapping with Quality Assurance for XML Data Exchange.

The problem we faced has some properties: Heterogeneous Representation (HR) and Inconsistency Hidden (IH) in the semi-structure. 1. HR means that different sources for example Amazon, eBay etc. have different schemas to describe their data. As a semistructured data description language, XML allows the same data is organized various forms through attributes and elements. 2. IH means that inconsistent data appear in the generated result after the Schema-Mapping operation.

For example, two people, Jack Baker and Jason Brown, are obvious two persons. In the circumstances of writing the full name, they can be distinguished automatically by computer. As a matter of fact, data are not invariably standard as our example. In some case, they both are written as J. B. and to computer, J. B. is one person. Otherwise, Jack Baker is written as Jack B. and computer cannot identify that both names refer to the same person. The former phenomenon is called Homonymy-Name-Problem (HNP), and the latter phenomenon is called Synonym-Name-Problem (SNP).

In general, there are some traditional methods to solve the information integration problem. (Feng et al. 2009, Lu et al. 2003, Zhou et al. 2008, Liu et al. 2007) carry out a technique about Schema-Mapping between relational database and XML data. In fact, data integration or data Exchange is an operation of high CPU and Memory cost in database. The predecessor's contribution cannot be simply used in the XML database. Even if the technology of predecessor is applied to implement a system, the system cannot guarantee the quality of data.

In this chapter, we are determined to address HNP and SNP to improve data quality. Since entity in the XML data is not correctly identified, HNP and SNP emerge. This will cause that we cannot get complete and accurate information about one entity on the whole. Solving HNP raises the rate of precise (accurate) and solving SNP raises the rate of recall (complete). So we introduce entity identification into Schema-Mapping and bring on

Schema-Mapping based on entity. In this chapter, we first summarize the predecessor's works about Schema-Mapping and find the ignored on their methods. Subsequently, we put forward a method with data quality assurance which addresses HNP and SNP based on entity. Afterward a strategy comes up to automatically locate the node with sensitive quality. Ultimately, we prove our algorithm is practicable, feasible and valid through experiment. The major content of this paper is from (Li, Wang, Li & Gao 2010) and (Bian, Wang & Gao 2011). The entity resolutions of relational database (Chapter 5 and Chapter 6) and XML data (Chapter 7) could be applied as the preprocessing phrase in the techniques in this Chapter.

The rest of this chapter is organized as follows: Section 2 introduces some background knowledge. Section 3 presents the duplicate record detection method which based on similarity estimation. a motivating example is presented about XML schema mapping. Section 4 describes the model and criterion and gives the detailed methods. Experimental results and analysis are reported in Section 5. Section 6 concludes the whole chapter.

PROBLEM DEFINITION

In this section, we define the problem of detecting duplicate records and introduce the naïve duplicate records detection method based on optimal bipartite graph matching.

Duplicate Records Detection

With the consideration of transitivity of duplication relationship between records, duplicate record detection is defined as follows.

Definition 1 (Detection of duplicate records on data set *R*): Given a original record set R = {$R_1, R_2, ..., R_m$}, detection of duplicate records on is defined as follows.

A required similarity ε is given. Divide R into several disjoint subsets $S_1, S_2, ..., S_n$, each S_i meet the following 3 properties.

1. For ∀ *S*i, any two records in Si have a similarity which is not lower than ε;
2. For ∀ S_i, S_j (i≠j), we have $S_i \cap S_j = \varnothing$;
3. For ∀ S_i, S_j (i≠j), $S_i \cup S_j$ does not meet 1).

The Naïve Duplicate Records Detection Method

The naïve OBMAB method involves three key technologies.

The Similarity of Attributes: The attributes' similarity is defined based on edit distance (Ristad, E. S. et al. 1998) as it can be applied to a variety of attributes. The edit distance of A_1 and A_2 is dis(A_1,A_2), and the lengths are len(A_1), len(A_2). The similarity of A_1 and A_2 is defined as follows, where m represents the maximal value of len(A_1) and len(A_2).

$$Sim(A_1, A_2) = \frac{dis(A_1, A_2)}{m} \qquad (1)$$

The Similarity of Records: Taking the difference of attributes' positions, the loss of some attributes into consideration, the similarity of records is defined based on a bipartite graph as follows.

R_1 and R_2 are two records. A complete bipartite graph B=($V_1 \cup V_2$, E, W) is built. Each node u in V_1 and v in V_2 represents R_1's attribute A_{1i} and R_2's attribute A_{2j}, respectively. E=$V_1 \times V_2$, the weight function W: E→(0,1) is defined as W(u,v)=Sim(A_{1i},A_{2j}), while Sim($A_{1i,} A_{2j}$) is the attribute similarity. M=(V',E') is the optimal match of B. Sim(R_1, R_2) denotes similarity of R_1 and R_2.

$$Sim(A_1, A_2) = \frac{\sum_{e \in E'} W(e)}{\max(m, n)} \qquad (2)$$

m and n represents the number of attributes of R1 and R2, respectively.

Kuhn-Manures algorithm (Kuhn et al. 1955, Munkres et al. 1957) (KM algorithm) is a good choice to find the optimal match, so it can be used to compute the similarity of records (Mohan et al. 2009).

Detection of Duplicate Records: The main idea is for each $R_k R$, search in the stack to find which cluster R_k belongs to. If R_k does not belong to any existing cluster, build a new cluster for R_k.

The method uses a stack S to store the records (signature record) which represents the existing clusters. Each signature record has a bucket to store the records belonging to the cluster. Before a record R_k is classified to a cluster, it should compare with the signature records (denoted by R_s) in S, from the top to the bottom. If the similarity of R_k and R_s is no less than required similarity ε, then R_k is compared with the records in the bucket of R_s. And if all the similarities are no less than ε, R_k enter the bucket of R_s. At the end, each R_s in the stack and the records in R_s's bucket are classified into a cluster. All the clusters form a division satisfying Definition 1. Figure1 shows the method's framework.

The method has two problems. The one is that it needs to compare a large number of records pairwise. The other is that a strict duplicate records judgment condition results in a low rate of recall. An optimized method is to be proposed in section 3.

Schema-Mapping

Let us consider a scenario that a company which has a large number of chapter information organized as Schema S carries out data integration that need to update data Schema. We can abstract a simple problem as Figure 2 from Schema-Mapping. For the reason that we mainly focus on XML data which can be represented as node labeled trees (Mohan, L. et al. 2009), the following example will be shown in the form of tree structure. The meaning of label in our example is described in Table 1.

In the source, RS shows three different chapter which can be distinguished by title of chapter or chapter's authors. RT shows the author information from original data (after data integration based value). However in the target data, except for the same name (L.Y.), the author of t_1 and the author of t_2 could not be identified one person, and this is HNP. On the contrary, t_2's author L.Y. and t_3's author Y.L. are seen as two people even though there is a co-author (SunZhen), and this

Figure 1. Framework of the naïve method

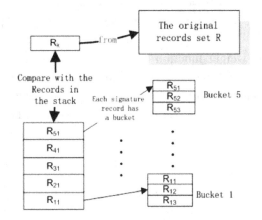

Figure 2. Xml data tree and XML schema tree

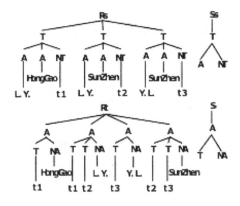

is SNP. Not only co-author is the description of author, but also tree structure and lable value are the descriptions.

DUPLICATE RECORD DETECTION BASED ON SIMILARITY ESTIMATION

In this section, we present an efficient duplicate record detection method based on similarity estimation. At first, the basic idea of our method is presented. Then, we introduce the method's theoretical basis and underlying assumption . Thirdly, we present the efficient duplicate record detection based on similarity estimation . At last, detailed discussions are given.

The Main Idea and Framework

In order to facilitate the following discussion, the symbols to be referred are listed.

The framework of our algorithm is shown as follows.

Step 1: Initialize the stack S, ε, **u_con** and **l_con.**
Step 2: Get a record R_k from R,
Step 3: Search in S to find an R_s whose similarity is no less than ε with R_k.
Step 4: IF R_s can not be found, THEN move to step 5.

ELSE estimate R_k.ub_sim and R_k.lb_sim.
IF R_k.ub_sim$\geq$u_con and R_k.lb_sim$\geq$l_con,

THEN R_k enters R_s's bucket and move R_s to the top of the stack.
ELSE move to step 3 to find a new R_s.

Step 5: Push R_k into the stack.
Step 6: IF all the records have been processed, THEN end the algorithm.

ELSE move to step 2.

The basic idea of the acceleration of the comparison is to estimate the upper and lower bounds of the similarities of R_k and records in each cluster (denoted as R_k.ub_sim and R_k.lb_sim) very efficiently and determine the cluster R_k belonging to with the bounds instead of the real similarities. Given an upper and lower bound (u_con and l_con, called required bounds and considered as the required upper and lower bounds of every bucket). For each R_k, instead of computing the similarities of R_k and all the records in the bucket, an upper and lower bound of the similarities R_k.ub_sim and R_k.lb_sim are estimated. If R_k.ub_sim and R_k.lb_sim is no less than u_con and l_con, respectively, then R_k enter the bucket.

The Method's Theoretical Basis and Underlying Assumption

In this section we present two properties as the basis of the similarity estimation method. The estimating method in this chapter is based on the following property.

Table 1. The notations used in example

Number	Lable	Description
1	R_s	Root of source data tree
2	R_T	Root of target data tree
3	S_s	Root of source schema tree
4	S_T	Root of target schema tree
5	T	One piece of paper, means Title
6	A	One author, means Author
7	NT	Title of paper, means Name of Title
8	NA	Author name, Name of Author

Table 2. Symbols and meaning

Symbol	Meaning	Symbol	Meaning
Sim(Ri,Rj)	The similarity of Ri and Rj.	Match(A)	The attributes belonging to the records in Rs.bucket and matching attribute A.
Sim(Ri,Rj).lb	The lower bound of Sim(Ri,Rj).	Akl	The attributes which belong to Rk, and matches attribute Asi.
Sim(Ri,Rj).ub	The upper bound of Sim(Ri,Rj).	Akl.ub_dis	The upper bound of the edit distance between Akl and the attributes in Match(Akl)
Rs	The signature record in the stack being processing now	Akl.lb_dis	The lower bound of the edit distance between Akl and the attributes in Match(Akl).
Rs.bucket	The bucket corresponding to Rs	Sim(Akl,Match(Akl)).lb	The lower bound of the similarity between Akl and the attributes in Match(Akl).
Rb	The records in Rs.bucket	Sim(Akl,Match(Akl)).ub	The upper bound of the similarity between Akl and the attributes in Match(Akl).
Rk	The record being processing now	Akl.max_len	max{Asi.max_len,len(Akl)}
Rk.lb_sim	The lower bound of the similarities between Rk and **Error! Reference source not found.**Rb	Akl.min_len	min{Asi.min_len,len(Akl)}
		Asi	The ith attribute of Rs
		Asi.ub_dis	Asi's upper bound of edit distance
Rk.ub_sim	The upper bound of the similarities between Rk and **Error! Reference source not found.**Rb	Asi.max_len	The maximal string length of Match(Asi)
		Asi.min_len	The minimal string length of Match(Asi)

Proporty 1: A_1, A_2 and A_3 are three strings. $dis(A_i,A_j)$ is the edit distance of A_i and A_j, let $dis(A_1,A_2)=d_1$, $dis(A_2,A_3)=d_2$, $dis(A_1,A_3)=d_3$. d_1, d_2, d_3 satisfy the inequality:

$$d_1 - d_3 \leq d_2 \leq d_1 + d_2 \tag{3}$$

Assumption 1 is another useful property for similarity estimation.

Assumption 1: $R_1(A_{11}, A_{12}, A_{13})$, $R_2(A_{21}, A_{22}, A_{23})$, $R_3(A_{31}, A_{32}, A_{33})$ are three records. The matching attributes of R_1 and R_2 are (A_{11}, A_{21}), (A_{12},A_{22}), (A_{13},A_{23}), the matching attributes of R_2 and R_3 are (A_{21},A_{31}), (A_{22},A_{32}), (A_{23},A_{33}). Then, the matching attributes of R_1 and R_3 are (A_{11},A_{31}) (A_{12},A_{32}) (A_{13},A_{33}).

Even though Assumption 1 cannot be proven theoretically, it coincides with the intuition that if the attribute A and B refer to the same information, and the attribute B and C refer to the same information, then A and C also refer to the same information.

The Method of Similarity Estimation

In this section, we will introduce a simple estimation method first. With it as a component, we introduce the method suitable for large data set.

The Simple Estimation Method: In this subsection, the simple method to estimate the bounds of *Sim(A, C)* with *Sim(A, B)* and *Sim(B, C)*, where all of A, B and C can be attributes or records.

First, consider the case with 3 attributes. A_1, A_2 and A_3 matches with each other. $dis(A_i,A_j)$ represents the edit distance of A_i and A_j. $dis(A_1,A_2)=d_1$, $dis(A_1,A_3)=d_3$. According to

Property 1, $dis(A_2,A_3) \in (d_1-d_3, d_1+d_3)$. According to Equation (1), $Sim(A_2,A_3) \in (1-(d_1+d_3)/m, -(d_1-d_3)/m)$.

For the introduction of the record estimation method, Perfectly Matched Records Pair (PMRP) is defined.

Definition 2 (Perfectly Matched Records Pair, PMRP): R_1 and R_2 are two records. If for R_1's attributes set A_1 and R_2's attributes set A_2, there is a one-to-one mapping $T: A_1 A_2$, $T(A_{1i})=A_{2j}$ iff the jth attribute of R_2 (denoted by A_{2j}) matches with the ith attribute of R_1 (denoted by A_{1i}), then (R_1, R_2) is a Perfectly Matched Records Pair. (R_1, R_2) being PMRP means that for any R_1's attribute A_{1i}, there is an R_2's attribute A_{2j} matching A_{1i}, and for any R_2's attribute A_{2j}, there is an A_{1i} matching A_{2j}.

For any matching attribute pair (A_{2j}, A_{3k}) with A_{2j} and A_{3k} as attributes in R_2 and R_3, respectively, based on Assumption 1 and the fact that (R_1, R_2) and (R_1,R_3) are both PMRPs, there is a attribute A_{1i} in R_1 satisfies (A_{1i}, A_{2j}) and (A_{1i}, A_{3k}). The upper and lower bound of $Sim(A_{2j}, A_{3k})$ can be estimated from $Sim(A_{1i}, A_{2j})$ and $Sim(A_{1i}, A_{3k})$ in the method discussed above.

With the range of similarity of any matching attribute pair of R_2 and R_3 estimated, $Sim(R_2, R_3)$ is estimated. In the bipartite graph B built on (R_2, R_3), each $W(e)$ $(e=(A_{2j}, A_{3k})\in E')$ is $Sim(A_{2j}, A_{3k})$. The bounds and exact value of $W(e)$ are denoted by $W(e).ub$, $W(e).lb$ and $W(e).val$, respectively. By substituting $W(e).ub$ and $W(e).lb$ into formula, $Sim(R_2, R_3).ub$ and $Sim(R_2, R_3).lb$ can be estimated.

$$Sim(R_2, R_3) \in \left[\frac{\sum_{e\in E'} W(e).lb}{\max\{m,n\}}, \frac{\sum_{e\in E'} W(e).ub}{\max\{m,n\}} \right] \quad (4)$$

The method works well in the records set containing only PMRPs. But in the original records set, records are heterogeneous. To deal with this problem, some preparations are required to make sure that each records pair (R_i, R_j) satisfy the PMRP.

Similarity Estimating Preparations: For the cluster C, a record R_s is in the stack. During the determination of whether a record R_k belongs to the cluster C, R_k should be compared with R_s first. If $Sim(R_s, R_k) \geq \varepsilon$, as the preparation, a record R_k^* forming PMRP with R_s is generated from R_k using Rule 1. The similarity bound $Sim(R_k^*, R_s).ub$ and $Sim(R_k^*, R_s).lb$ are estimated. If the similarity bound satisfy the required bound, then R_k^* enter the bucket of R_s.

Rule 1: For each attribute A_{si} of R_s,

1. If there is an A_{kl} in R_k matching A_{si}, then A_{kl} is the jth attribute of R_k^*.
2. Otherwise the ith attributes of R_k^* is an empty attribute to match A_{si}.

The attributes of R_k matching no attribute of A_{si} are ignored. It is easy to see that (R_k^*, R_s) is PMRP. In R_s.bucket, the records are generated using Rule 1 for computation convenience. They all have same attributes number. In order to access original records, each R_k^* has been linked to corresponding R_k. To facilitate our method, we use symbol R_k instead of R_k^* in the following descriptions.

Since (R_k, R_s) is PMRP and for each R_b in R_s.bucket, (R_b, R_s) is PMRP, (R_k, Rb) is also PMRP. For each attribute A_{kl} of R_k, since the attribute of R_s matching A_{kl} is A_{si}, $Match(A_{kl})=Match(A_{si})$, where $Match(A_{si})=\{A_{sij}| A_{sij}$ is an attribute of $RT\in$ Rs.bucket and Asij matches Asi}. Therefore, when estimating the similarity bounds of Rk, It needs to estimate the similarity bounds of each attribute Akl and the attributes in Match(Akl) (Sim(Akl,Match(Akl)).ub and Sim(Akl,Match(Akl)).lb) first.

Estimating the Similarity Bounds of Attributes: The estimation is based on the following Theorem.

Theorem 1: For any attribute Asi of Rs it is supposed that the attribute in Rk matching Asi is Akl. Then,

$$Sim(A_{kl}, Match(A_{si})).ub = 1 - (dis(A_{kl}, A_{si}) - A_{si}.ub\_dis) / A_{kl}.\max\_len \quad (5)$$

$$Sim(A_{kl}, Match(A_{si})).lb = 1 - (dis(A_{kl}, A_{si}) + A_{si}.ub\_dis) / A_{kl}.\min\_len \quad (6)$$

where $A_{si}.ub\_dis = max(dis(A_{si}, A_{sij})), \forall A_{sij} Match(A_{si}) = Match(A_{kl}) A_{kl}.max\_len$ and $Akl.min\_len$ be the maximum and the minimum string length of Akl and all the attributes in $Match(Akl)$.

Proof. As discussed in the last section, $Match(A_{si}) = Match(A_{kl})$. According to Property 1 and Equation (3), $\forall sij Match(A_{si})$, $dis(A_{kp}, A_{sij})$ $(dis(A_{kp}, A_{si}) - dis(A_{si}, A_{sij}), dis(A_{kp}, A_{si}) + dis(A_{si}, As_{ij}))$.

$A_{si}.ub\_dis = max\{dis(A_{si}, A_{sij})\}$, then, $dis(A_{kp}, A_{sij})$ $(A_{kl}.lb\_dis, A_{kl}.ub\_dis)$, where

$$A_{kl}.ub\_dis = dis(A_{kl}, A_{si}) + A_{si}.ub\_dis \quad (7)$$

$$A_{kl}.lb\_dis = dis(A_{kl}, A_{si}) - A_{si}.ub\_dis \quad (8)$$

According to Equation (1), it implies that for $\forall A_{sij} Match(A_{si}) = Match(A_{kl})$, $Sim(A_{kp}, A_{sij})$ $(1 - A_{kl}.ub\_dis/A_{kl}.min\_len, 1 - A_{kl}.lb\_dis/A_{kl}.max\_len)$. That is,

$$Sim(A_{kl}, A_{sij}).ub = 1 - A_{kl}.lb\_dis / A_{kl}.\max\_len = 1 - (dis(A_{kl}, A_{si}) - A_{si}.ub\_dis) / A_{kl}.\max\_len \quad (9)$$

$$Sim(A_{kl}, A_{sij}).lb = 1 - A_{kl}.lb\_dis / A_{kl}.\min\_len = 1 - (dis(A_{kl}, A_{si}) + A_{si}.ub\_dis) / A_{kl}.\min\_len \quad (10)$$

For $\forall A_{sij} Match(A_{si})$, $Sim(A_{kp}, Match(A_{si})).ub = Sim(A_{kp}, A_{sij}).ub$, and $Sim(A_{kp}, Match(A_{si})).lb = Sim(A_{kp}, A_{sij}).lb$. In order to compute the bound, for each attribute A_{si} of a record R_s in the stack, three values, the maximal length of the strings in

Match(A_{si}) (denoted by $A_{si}.max\_len$), the minimal length of the strings in Match(A_{si}) (denoted by $A_{si}.min\_len$) and $A_{si}.ub\_dis$ are maintained. The steps of computation are illustrated with an example.

Example 2: Suppose the attribute A_{kl}= "John_Simth", A_{si}= "J.Smith", Match(A_{kl}) =Match(A_{si}) ={J_Smith, John.Smith}. For A_{si}, $A_{si}.max\_len=10$, $A_{si}.min\_len=7$ and $A_{si}.ub\_dis=3$. It can be computed that $dis(A_{kl}, A_{si})=4$, $A_{kl}.min\_len=10$, $A_{kl}.max\_len=10$. Based on these values,

$$Sim(A_{kl}, Match(A_{si})).ub = 1 - (dis(A_{kl}, A_{si}) - A_{si}.ub\_dis) / A_{kl}.\max\_len = 1 - (4 - 3) / 10 = 0.9$$

$$Sim(A_{kl}, Match(A_{si})).lb = 1 - (dis(A_{kl}, A_{si}) + A_{si}.ub\_dis) / A_{kl}.\min\_len = 1 - (4 + 3) / 10 = 0.3$$

That is, $\forall Asij \in Match(Asi)$, the similarity of Akl and $Asij$ belongs to $[0.3, 0.9]$.

Note that the upper bound may greater than 1, and the lower bound may less than 0. When these happen, the upper bound is set to 1, and the lower bound is set to 0.

Estimating the Similarity Bounds of Records: Intuitively, for each attribute A_{kl} of R_k, substituting $W(e)$ for $Sim(A_{kp}, Match(A_{kl})).ub$ and $Sim(A_{kp}, Match(A_{kl})).lb$ in Equation (2), an upper bound and a lower bound of the similarity of R_k and the records in R_s.bucket is obtained,

$$R_k.ub\_sim = \frac{\sum_{l=1}^{n} Sim(A_{kl}, Match(A_{kl})).ub}{n} \quad (11)$$

$$R_k.lb\_sim = \frac{\sum_{l=1}^{n} Sim(A_{kl}, Match(A_{kl})).lb}{n} \quad (12)$$

where n is the number of attributes in a record.

Detailed Discussion

The Parameters: It is very important to choose the parameters ε, u_con, l_con when detecting duplication. The chosen of parameters depends on the requirement of precision, efficiency and recall. Parameters with high value will result in high precision but low efficiency and recall. Some techniques of machine learning (Alpaydin et al. 2004) can be used to choose them. Also, experiences are helpful when choosing them.

Other discussion: SEDRD can compensate the two shortcomings of the naïve method introduced in section 2. Firstly, SEDRD reduces the cost of operations. The method estimates the bounds of the algorithm in $O(1)$ time. A record only needs to compare with the signature records in stack rather than all the records in the buckets. Second, SEDRD improves the recall. When the required bounds are relaxed, it is not as strict as in the naïve method for a record to enter a bucket. The recall is improved.

The worst case of our methods exists in the case without duplicate records in the original record set R. In such case, each record in R belongs to a cluster by itself and our method has to spend $O(|R|^2)$ time to search the whole stack for each record in R. However, in general cases, the operation cost is much less, because a record only needs to compare with the signature records in the

stack. Especially, for another extreme case with all the records in R belonging to the same cluster, the time complexity of the naïve method is $O(|R|^2)$ while that of our method is $O(|R|)$, because there is always only one record in the stack.

SCHEMA MAPPING

Model and Criterion

In this section, we introduce a new model based on entity to solve Schema-Mapping, and propose a criterion to validate that our solution is able to achieve high precision and recall. The model is illustrated as Figure 3 which shows fundamental processes in Schema-Mapping.

We use precision and recall as metrics to evaluation. In order to calculate precision and recall, we generate artificial data. Considering the truth of research team, first of all team data are generated, and every team contains dozens of authors. Then paper data are generated, and every paper is written by several authors from one team. Every person-name might appear in one or more teams, and the aim is to produce HNP. When using person-name in paper, the string of person-name might be mixed into noise information, and the aim is to produce SNP. To evaluate precision, we compare output set with "Gold-Answer" from

Figure 3. Data exchange with schema schema-mapping

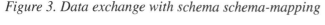
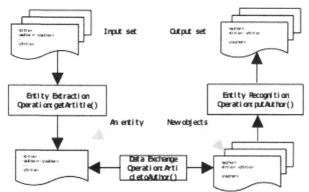

process of generation. Let O means the set of object-pairs which describe one entity in both output set and Gold-Answer. Let P means the set of object-pairs which describe one entity in output set and different entities in Gold-Answer. Let Q means the set of object-pairs which describe different entities in output set and one entity in Gold-Answer. Then the precision Pre is $\frac{|o|}{|o|+|P|}$ while there recall Rec is $\frac{|o|}{|o|+|Q|}$. For instance, the output set is R_T in Figure 2, and Gold-Answer is shown in Figure 4. O={<t2,t3>}, P={<t1,t2>} and Q={<t2,t3>}. Pre=0.5 and Rec=0.5.

Data Exchange with Schema-Mapping

In this section, the processes of our model are detailed introduced. The Input set is broken down by the Entity Extraction process into separate entity. One or more objects are come into being from every entity by the Data Exchange process. And the Output set is organized by new entities generated from the Entity Recognition process.

Entity Extraction

The Entity Extraction component is used to extract entities from Input set, and this process ensures that the entity agrees with the source schema. Considering example in Figure 2, R_S is Input set,

Figure 4. Gold-answer

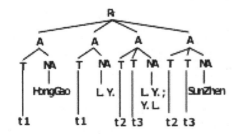

and every T, son of R_S, is extracted as one entity. The detailed procedures are shown in Operation 1.

Operation 1: getArticle()

1. 1.for each document do
2. get every article element;
3. do ArticletoAuthor();
4. 4.end for;

Operation 2: ArticletoAuthor()

1. 1.for each article element
2. get every author element;
3. restructure author element;
4. get the structure information of every author;
5. do putAuthor();
6. end for;

Data Exchange

The Data Exchange component is used to exchange the old data into new data. And this process acting on old entity retains structure information for produced entities. The detailed operation is various because of different source and target schemas. For our example, the procedures are shown in Operation 2.

In our example, structure information is Co-Author, and this is stored in list authors.

Entity Recognition

The Entity Recognition component is used to distinguish new entity and locate it. And this process aims at solving SNP and HNP through entity recognition. The basic plan is shown in Figure 5. At entrance, edit-distance between strings (Ristad et al. 1998) and string transformations (Arasu et al. 2009) are commendable to find out the hidden objects which are the potential same entity. At exit, the structure information is exploited to eliminate the objects which describe different entity. The procedure is shown in Operation 3.

In the circumstances of data integration and schema mapping, the entity recognition method based on tree edit distance (Lu et al. 2001) cannot work well. The approach which only considers the simple but significant structure information will obtain a high precise result within reasonable time. In the example, CoAuthor is chosen as structure information.

In operation 3, the entity_set stores all entities and their structure information, dynamic managed in the process of handling object one by one. Similarly the list stores all entities that are candidates of the object, author element. In real application, we have millions of objects that do not necessarily fit in the memory and need to be stored on disk. In putAuthor(), content of entity is stored in entity_set, which can be put in disk. This problem can be solved through adding a mapping structure between entity_set in memory and disk.

- Broad-Entrance

Broad-entrance is realized by the sentence:list=entity.find(author.name);

Method find() is defined at entity, and its input is a string of author name while its output is the list of similar entities. The method introduced in (Ristad et al. 1998) and (Arasu et al. 2009) certainly work well in real application. In this chapter, our approach below swift obtains list of authors.

Figure 5. Basic plan

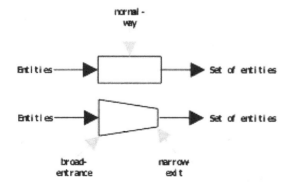

In the process of Broad-Entrance, the purpose is to guarantee all entities which are referred by name value are returned. Obviously the string of name is simple but the information hidden carries main ability of distinguish. So the value of name becomes the foundation of Broad-Entrance. Approach in (Broder et al. 1997), originally proposed in (Manber et al. 1994), takes as signature all values having a hash value that is divisible by a constant m. When the value of object matches several entities, those entities are returned. This can work well based on clean data where different values mean different entity. Actually there is not clean data in specific applications. One way to deal with this is to replace each string by a set of chunks - e.g. words, q-grams(Shannon et al. 1948) or v-grams(Li et al. 2007) occurring in it, and then to compare these sets of chunks. A method for converting strings into sets of chunks is called a chunking strategy. A very simple way for comparing string value based on chunks is to form for each string the set of chunks occurring in any of its values, and then compare these sets. Such an approach has been suggested in (Dasu et al. 2002). Technically this can be done exactly as before the only difference is that we are now comparing sets of chunks instead of strings containing the original values. While this gives us a rough estimate on whether two strings have something in common, it is not very accurate since information held by structure is not taken into account (Köhler et al.2010).

By means of chunks, the original value is broken into more short strings. Then the chunks are hashed into different numerical values. The minimum value is chosen as the signature of the set of chunks and the entity. The signature of object obtained as the same method matches entities, then the candidate entities is discovered by filter.

- Narrow-Exit

Narrow-exit is realized by the sentence: e.match(author);

Coauthor is the description of the detected object which means variable author in instance, and stores all coauthors organized as one set. Through comparing the description with existing entities one by one, the truth that the object belongs to a certain entity is discovered. By utilizing Jaccard Measure (Hamers et al. 1989), compare method determines the relation between the object and the entity.

Our approach to schema mapping based on entity is separated into above three operations. To derive the complexity of our method, assume that each of N articles has exactly A authors, and each of M authors has B coauthors. Then the time to process our input set RS is $O(N \times A \times (M + c \times (A-1) \times B)) = O(N \times A \times M)$. Here c means the number of similar authors. Due to $M >> (A-1) \times B$, the runtime is mainly decided by the scale of article and author.

Mechanism of Automatically Positioning with Quality Problem

The model proposed in above section solves the quality problem with given position. In fact, the schema and data are all the information we can get, and the position with quality problem cannot be discovered immediately. The way exploiting programmer's experience can help to manually distinguish the position with quality problem. But it's not a general method. In consequence, the mechanism of automatical positioning with quality problem is proposed in this section.

To realize the auto-mechanism, DTD document, the description of XML data, is detailed analyzed. There are some discoveries:

1. Attribute never needs to be treated as one entity. When the XML data is organized as an XML tree, the attribute can be seen as attribute node.
2. It is probability that the number of certain type node under its father node is only 1 or 0.

A naïve idea is that father node absorbs the single child node as attribute, and a tree which retains main nodes is reorganized. This trick can cut down many weak branches in order to minish the structure of main entity. Based on this idea, the method of weak branch converged is proposed.

- **An Example of Weak Branch Converged:** The example in motivation is too simple; factually data have more complex structure. Schema S in Figure 6 is article description with more detailed information. Known from common sense, article has one publisher and one conference; author has one age and one gender. Through weak branch converged, S is reformed into S'.

Schema S which has 8 nodes without the root contains 2 main nodes: article and author. The pruning effects of strategy causes the space reduction which makes the processes of data exchange and entity recognition work.

- **The Strategy of Weak Branch Converged:** As the target, a reduced structure is the form which makes the Data Exchange easy-handle. And the strategy is used to transform the complex data schema into a simple schema. Some definitions are given as below:
  ○ **Central-Node:** Is a relation between two or more nodes which satisfy many-to-many relationship. In Figure 5, article and author are central-node by common sense.
  ○ **User-Node:** User might care some specific nodes.
  ○ **Kernel-Node:** The nodes satisfied central-node ship or designated by user.

The reduction process is that Kernel-nodes absorb non-Kernel-nodes. And target structure is made up of Kernel-nodes.

- **An Implement of Weak Branch Converged:** A common-sense fitted assumption: if A and B have non-kernel-node relationship, they can be detected in local information. This is suitable in mostly circumstances, because information is gathered locally in the process of schema exchange between schema S and schema T. Therefrom three rules for recognition is given as below: 1. If A is B's father in both schema and A:B=1:1, node A absorbs node B and inherits all son nodes under B. 2. If A is B's father in one schema, A:B=1:1 and B is A's father in the other, B:A=1:1, A absorbs node B and inherits all son nodes under B in both schema under the circumstances (e.g. A has no brother node in latter schema). 3. A is B's father and A:B=1:1 in one schema. B is A's father, B:A=1:more, and the type of A is the only type of B's son nodes. Under this circumstances node A absorbs B.

Apply the above rules iteratively until all father-son pairs dissatisfy adsorbility. We use convergence ratio (CR for short) to judge the effect of reduction. CR=U/O, where U means node number of schema T and O means node number of schema S.

EXPERIMENT EVALUATIONS

Duplicate Record Detection

Experiments were run on AMD Sempron 3000+ with 512M memory. We do the experiment both on real and virtual data set. For real data set, the records comes from the website of ACM and DBLP are used to test the efficiency and effectiveness. For the virtual data set, we use the data generator and noises tool to get duplicate records. The differences between two duplicate records are: 1) attributes' positions difference, 2) the loss of some attributes, and 3) typographic errors. Data generator is used to generate some benchmark records randomly, and for each benchmark record, some modify operations are used to modify the benchmarks to get duplicate records.

When generating duplicate records, there are two main parameters: the number of the benchmark records (denoted by NR), and the number of duplicate records for each benchmark record (denoted by ND). In order to ensure the accuracy of the experiments, we need to fix NR first. NR is set to be 100. That is, we generate a record set which contains 100 benchmark records, and then modify (no more than 50%) the records to generate ND duplicates. ND is changed to control the size of R. Since the modification of the benchmark records is no more than 50%, we set $\varepsilon=0.6$, which is a little higher than the lowest similarity.

Figure 6. Weak branch converged

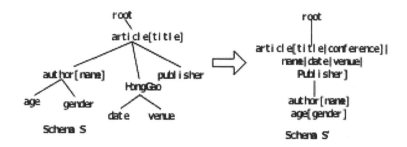

Original data sets with different size are used to test efficiency, adn ε=0.5, u_con=0.6, l_con=0.5. The result is shown in Figure 7. We put the size of R on X-axis and time cost on Y-axis. To test the effectiveness, we use a data set with 50 records, and set ε=0.7, u_con=0.8, l_con=0.3. Our algorithm gets 45 clusters. That is quite similar with the divide result of human beings, which is 48 clusters.

Schema Mapping

Here we present experiment to evaluate our method work well.We ran all of the experiments on an Intel dual core 2.4 Ghz Windows machine with 1G RAM. Our code was implemented by Code::Blocks 8.02.

- **Precision and Recall:**

The result on real data is shown in Table 3.

From the results, we can draw some conclusions: 1. Different sources have different situations, and the results of our method are all very perfect. 2. The less objects described the same entity, the better result.

For precision measure, it has nothing with the number of groups and the number of every group's papers, and decreases with the number of every group's authors. For recall measure, there is no explicit relationship between recall and number of groups. It increases with the number of every group's papers and decreases with the number of every group's authors.

- Convergence Ratio

The result on real data is shown in Table 4.

It is very common that schema can be converged. And from real data, the converged operation brings about a striking effect (see the small ratio).

CONCLUSION

Provide discussion of the overall coverage of the chapter and concluding remarks. The duplicate detection method based on optimal bipartite graph matching can deal with record set with attributes' position differences, the loss of some attributes, and typographic errors to a certain extent. The

Figure 7. The efficiency results

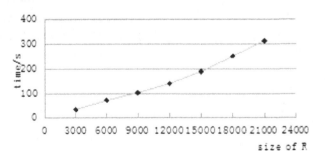

Table 3. Results of different resources

Data Source	Number of Entities	Number of Objects	Pre	Rec	
DBLP	14	50	97.2	96.5	
Book-Order	28	45	98.5	100	
CD	17	20	100	100	
Course	26	28	100	100	

Table 4. Results of weak branch converged

Source	Type	Original Node Number	Result Node Number	Ratio
paper	DTD	8	2	0.25
Book-Order	Schema	12	4	0.33
CD	Schema	7	1	0.14
Hardware	DTD	7	2	0.29

naïve method for such similarity has two short-comings. First, it costs too much time. Second, the strict classification requirements make a low recall. In this chapter, we present an efficient and effective duplicate records detecting method. With the estimation of similarities, such method can efficiently divide the original records set. That not only reduces the times of comparisons, but also improves the recall. Theoretical analysis and experimental results show that the method proposed in this chapter is correct and effective.

Our future work includes more accurate estimation of bounds and indices structure for the acceleration of the search in stack.

We have introduced the model and method to solve the data transformation problem with quality assurance. The new model settles HNP and SNP, and the method is based on entity. Meanwhile, a strategy is given to find nodes with sensitive quality. Finally, we prove our technique through experiment.

REFERENCES

Alpaydin, E. (2004). *Introduction to machine learning*. Cambridge, MA: MIT Press.

Arasu, A., Chaudhuri, S., & Kaushik, R. (2008). Transformation-based framework for record matching. In *Proceedings of Data Engineering* (pp. 40–49). IEEE.

Arasu, A., Chaudhuri, S., & Kaushik, R. (2009). Learning string transformations from examples. *Proceedings of the VLDB Endowment, 2*(1), 514–525.

Arasu, A., & Kaushik, R. (2009). A grammar-based entity representation framework for data cleaning. In *Proceedings of the 2009 ACM SIGMOD International Conference on Management of Data* (pp. 233-244). ACM.

Bernstein, P. (2006). *Implementing mapping composition*. VLDB.

Bernstein, P. (2007). Model management 2.0:manipulating richer mappings. In *Proceedings of SIGMOD 2007*. ACM.

Bian, X., Wang, H., & Gao, H. (2011). Schema mapping with quality assurance for data integration. [APWeb.]. *Proceedings of APWeb, 2011*, 472–483.

Bilenko, M., & Mooney, R. J. (2003). Adaptive duplicate detection using learnable string similarity measures. In *Proceedings of the Ninth ACM SIGKDD International Conference on Knowledge Discovery and Data Mining* (pp. 39-48). ACM.

Borkar, V., Deshmukh, K., & Sarawagi, S. (2001, May). Automatic segmentation of text into structured records. *SIGMOD Record, 30*(2), 175–186. doi:10.1145/376284.375682

Broder, A. Z. (1997). On the resemblance and containment of documents. In *Proceedings of Compression and Complexity of Sequences* (pp. 21–29). IEEE.

Chandel, A., Hassanzadeh, O., Koudas, N., Sadoghi, M., & Srivastava, D. (2007). Benchmarking declarative approximate selection predicates. In *Proceedings of the 2007 ACM SIGMOD International Conference on Management of Data* (pp. 353-364). ACM.

Chaudhuri, S., Ganjam, K., Ganti, V., & Motwani, R. (2003). Robust and efficient fuzzy match for online data cleaning. In *Proceedings of the 2003 ACM SIGMOD International Conference on Management of Data* (pp. 313-324). ACM.

Chiticariu, L., & Tan, W. C. (2006). Debugging schema mappings with routes. In *Proceedings of the 32nd International Conference on Very Large Data Bases* (pp. 79-90). VLDB Endowment.

Cohen, W. W. (2000). Data integration using similarity joins and a word-based information representation language. *ACM Transactions on Information Systems*, *18*(3), 288–321. doi:10.1145/352595.352598

Cohen, W. W., & Sarawagi, S. (2004). Exploiting dictionaries in named entity extraction: Combining semi-markov extraction processes and data integration methods. In *Proceedings of the Tenth ACM SIGKDD International Conference on Knowledge Discovery and Data Mining* (pp. 89-98). ACM.

Dasu, T., Johnson, T., Muthukrishnan, S., & Shkapenyuk, V. (2002). Mining database structure, or, how to build a data quality browser. In *Proceedings of the 2002 ACM SIGMOD International Conference on Management of Data* (pp. 240-251). ACM.

Elmagarmid, A. K., Ipeirotis, P. G., & Verykios, V. S. (2007). Duplicate record detection: A survey. *IEEE Transactions on Knowledge and Data Engineering*, *19*(1), 1–16. doi:10.1109/TKDE.2007.250581

Fagin, R., Kolaitis, P. G., Popa, L., & Tan, W. C. (2005). Composing schema mappings: Second-order dependencies to the rescue. *ACM Transactions on Database Systems*, *30*(4), 994–105. doi:10.1145/1114244.1114249

Feng, Y. E., & Jingsheng, X. (2009). Mapping XML DTD to relational schema. In *Proceedings of Database Technology and Applications* (pp. 557–560). IEEE.

Hamers, L., Hemeryck, Y., Herweyers, G., Janssen, M., Keters, H., Rousseau, R., & Vanhoutte, A. (1989). Similarity measures in scientometric research: The Jaccard index versus Salton's cosine formula. *Information Processing & Management*, *25*(3), 315–318. doi:10.1016/0306-4573(89)90048-4

Köhler, H., Zhou, X., Sadiq, S., Shu, Y., & Taylor, K. (2010). Sampling dirty data for matching attributes. In *Proceedings of the 2010 International Conference on Management of Data* (pp. 63-74). ACM.

Kolaitis, P. G. (2005). Schema mappings, data exchange, and metadata management. In *Proceedings of the Twenty-Fourth ACM SIGMOD-SIGACT-SIGART Symposium on Principles of Database Systems* (pp. 61-75). ACM.

Kuhn, H. W. (1955). The Hungarian method for the assignment problem. *Naval Research Logistics Quarterly*, *2*(1-2), 83–97. doi:10.1002/nav.3800020109

Li, C., Wang, B., & Yang, X. (2007). VGRAM: Improving performance of approximate queries on string collections using variable-length grams. In *Proceedings of the 33rd International Conference on Very Large Data Bases* (pp. 303-314). VLDB Endowment.

Li, M., Wang, H., Li, H., & Gao, H. (2010). Efficient duplicate record detection based on similarity estimation. [WAIM.]. *Proceedings of WAIM*, *2010*, 595–607.

Liu, Y., Wang, T., Yang, D., & Tang, S. (2007). Propagating functional dependencies from relational schema to XML schema using path mapping rules. In *Proceedings of International Conference on Internet Computing,* (pp. 294–299). Academic Press.

Lu, C. L., Su, Z.-Y., & Tang, C. Y. (2001). A new measure of edit distance between labeled trees. In COCOON 2001 (LNCS), (vol. 2108, pp. 338–348). Berlin: Springer.

Lu, S., Sun, Y., Atay, M., & Fotouhi, F. (2003). A new inlining algorithm for mapping XML DTDs to relational schemas. In *Conceptual modeling for novel application domains* (pp. 366–377). Berlin: Springer. doi:10.1007/978-3-540-39597-3_36

Madhavan, J., & Halevy, A. Y. (2003). Composing mappings among data sources. In *Proceedings of the 29th International Conference on Very Large Data Bases* (vol. 29, pp. 572-583). VLDB Endowment.

Manber, U. (1994). Finding similar files in a large file system. In *Proceedings of the USENIX Winter 1994 Technical Conference* (Vol. 1). USENIX.

Milano, D., Scannapieco, M., & Catarci, T. (2006). Structure aware xml object identification. In *Proceedings of VLDB Workshop on Clean Databases* (CleanDB). Seoul, Korea: VLDB.

Miller, R. J., Hernandez, M. A., Haas, L. M., Yan, L. L., Ho, C. T. H., Fagin, R., & Popa, L. (2001). The Clio project: Managing heterogeneity. *SIGMOD Record*, *30*(1), 78–83. doi:10.1145/373626.373713

Mohan, L., Hongzhi, W., Jianzhong, L., & Hong, G. (2009). Duplicate record detection method based on optimal bipartite graph matching. *Journal of Computer Research and Development*, *46*, 339–345.

Munkres, J. (1957). Algorithms for the assignment and transportation problems. *Journal of the Society for Industrial and Applied Mathematics*, *5*(1), 32–38. doi:10.1137/0105003

Nash, A., Bernstein, P. A., & Melnik, S. (2007). Composition of mappings given by embedded dependencies. *ACM Transactions on Database Systems*, *32*(1), 4. doi:10.1145/1206049.1206053

Popa, L., Velegrakis, Y., Hernández, M. A., Miller, R. J., & Fagin, R. (2002). Translating web data. In *Proceedings of the 28th International Conference on Very Large Data Bases* (pp. 598-609). VLDB Endowment.

Ristad, E. S., & Yianilos, P. N. (1998). Learning string-edit distance. *IEEE Transactions on Pattern Analysis and Machine Intelligence*, *20*(5), 522–532. doi:10.1109/34.682181

Ristad, E. S., & Yianilos, P. N. (1998). Learning string-edit distance. *IEEE Transactions on Pattern Analysis and Machine Intelligence*, *20*(5), 522–532. doi:10.1109/34.682181

Sarawagi, S., & Cohen, W. W. (2004). Semi-markov conditional random fields for information extraction. *Advances in Neural Information Processing Systems*, *17*, 1185–1192.

Shannon, C. E., & Weaver, W. (1948). *A mathematical theory of communication.*

Viola, P., & Narasimhan, M. (2005). Learning to extract information from semi-structured text using a discriminative context free grammar. In *Proceedings of the 28th Annual International ACM SIGIR Conference on Research and Development in Information Retrieval* (pp. 330-337). ACM.

Weis, M., & Naumann, F. (2005). DogmatiX tracks down duplicates in XML. In *Proceedings of the 2005 ACM SIGMOD International Conference on Management of Data* (pp. 431-442). ACM.

Zhou, R., Liu, C., & Li, J. (2008). Holistic constraint-preserving transformation from relational schema into XML schema. In *Database systems for advanced applications* (pp. 4–18). Berlin: Springer. doi:10.1007/978-3-540-78568-2_4

ADDITIONAL READING

Bilenko, M., & Mooney, R. J. (2002). *Learning to combine trained distance metrics for duplicate detection in databases. Technical Report AI 02-296, Artificial Intelligence Lab*. University of Texas at Austin.

Chaudhuri, S., Ganjam, K., Ganti, V., & Motwani, R. (2003, June). Robust and efficient fuzzy match for online data cleaning. In *Proceedings of the 2003 ACM SIGMOD international conference on Management of data* (pp. 313-324). ACM.

Cohen, W. W. (2000). Data integration using similarity joins and a word-based information representation language. [TOIS]. *ACM Transactions on Information Systems*, *18*(3), 288–321. doi:10.1145/352595.352598

Cohen, W. W., Kautz, H., & McAllester, D. (2000, August). Hardening soft information sources. In *Proceedings of the sixth ACM SIGKDD international conference on Knowledge discovery and data mining* (pp. 255-259). ACM.

Cohen, W. W., & Richman, J. (2002, July). Learning to match and cluster large high-dimensional data sets for data integration. In *Proceedings of the eighth ACM SIGKDD international conference on Knowledge discovery and data mining* (pp. 475-480). ACM.

Cohen, W. W., & Sarawagi, S. (2004, August). Exploiting dictionaries in named entity extraction: combining semi-markov extraction processes and data integration methods. In *Proceedings of the tenth ACM SIGKDD international conference on Knowledge discovery and data mining* (pp. 89-98). ACM.

Cook, D. J., & Holder, L. B. (1994). Substructure discovery using minimum description length and background knowledge. *arXiv preprint cs/9402102*.

Durbin, R., Eddy, S. R., Krogh, A., & Mitchison, G. (1998). *Biological sequence analysis: probabilistic models of proteins and nucleic acids*. Cambridge university press. doi:10.1017/CBO9780511790492

KEY TERMS AND DEFINITIONS

Central-Node: Is a relation between two or more nodes which satisfy many-to-many relationship. article and author are central-node by common sense.

Kernel-Node: The nodes satisfied central-node ship or designated by user.

Perfectly Matched Records Pair (PMRP): R_1 and R_2 are two records. If for R_1's attributes set A_1 and R_2's attributes set A_2, there is a one-to-one mapping T: $A_1 A_2$, $T(A_{1i}) = A_{2j}$ iff the jth attribute of

R_2 (denoted by A_{2j}) matches with the ith attribute of R_1 (denoted by A_{1i}), then (R_1, R_2) is a Perfectly Matched Records Pair. (R_1, R_2) being PMRP means that for any R_1's attribute A_{1i}, there is an R_2's attribute A_{2j} matching A_{1i}, and for any R_2's attribute A_{2j}, there is an A_{1i} matching A_{2j}.

The Similarity of Attributes: The attributes' similarity is defined based on edit distance (2) as it can be applied to a variety of attributes.

The Similarity of Records: R_1 and R_2 are two records. A complete bipartite graph B=$(V_1 \cup V_2,$ $E, W)$ is built. Each node u in V_1 and v in V_2 represents R_1's attribute A_{1i} and R_2's attribute A_{2j}, respectively. $E=V_1 \times V_2$, the weight function W: $E \rightarrow (0,1)$ is defined as $W(u,v)=\text{Sim}(A_{1i}, A_{2j})$.

User-Node: User might care some specific nodes.

Chapter 15
Entity Resolution in Bibliography Information Management

ABSTRACT

Entity resolution, that is to build corresponding relationships between objects and entities in dirty data, plays an important role in data cleaning. In bibliography information management system, the confusion between authors and their names often results in dirty data. That is, different authors may share the identical name, and different names may correspond to the identical author. Therefore, the major task of entity resolution is to distinguish entities sharing the same name and recognize different names referring to the same entity. However, current research focuses on only one aspect and cannot solve the problem completely. To address this problem, in this chapter, EIF, a framework of entity resolution with the consideration of the both kinds of confusions, is proposed. With effective clustering techniques, approximate string matching algorithms, and a flexible mechanism of knowledge integration, EIF can be widely used to solve many different kinds of entity resolution problems. In this chapter, as an application of EIF, the authors solve the author resolution problem. The effectiveness of this framework is verified by extensive experiments.

INTRODUCTION

In bibliography information management, entities are often queried by their names. For example, researchers are often queried by their names on dblp. Unfortunately, dirty data often lead to incomplete or duplicated results for such queries. From different aspects, there are two major problems. On the one hand, a name may have different spellings and one entity can be represented by multiple names. For example, the name of a researcher "Wei Wang" can be both written as "Wei Wang" and "W. Wei". Another example of this confusion is movie names. Such as the movie called "Hong lou ment" can also be represented as "A Dream in Red Mansions". On the other hand, one name can represent multiple entities. For example, when querying an author named "Wei Wang" in dblp, the database system will output seven different authors all named "Wei Wang". In this chapter, the former problem is called name variant for brief and the latter is called name sharing.

DOI: 10.4018/978-1-4666-5198-2.ch015

Entity resolution techniques are to deal with these problems. This is a basic operation in data cleaning and query processing with quality assurance. Given a set of objects with name and other properties, the goal of this operation is to split the set into clusters, such that each cluster corresponds to one real-world entity.

Some techniques for entity resolution have been proposed. Some of them have been introduced in Chapter 3 and Chapter 9. However, each of these techniques focuses on one of the two problems. The techniques for the first problem are often called "duplicate detection" (Newcombe, Kennedy & Axford 1959). These techniques usually find duplicate records by measuring the similarity of individual fields (e.g. objects with similar names). Different approaches are used to compare the similarity. These techniques are based on the assumption that duplicate records should have equal or similar values. With the second problem existing simultaneity, records with the same name referring to different entity cannot be distinguished. As far as we know, the only technique for the second problem is presented in (Yin, Han & Yu 2007). It identifies entities using linkage information and clustering method. From the experiment in (Yin, Han & Yu 2007), it takes a long time for object distinction; therefore it is not suitable for entity resolution on large datasets. Besides, this method distinguishes objects by assuming that the objects have identical names. If this method is used to solve entity resolution problem, in which the assumption is unsatisfied, the results might be inaccurate. In summary, when these two aspects of problems both exist, current techniques cannot distinguish objects effectively.

For entity resolution in general cases, new techniques with the ability of dealing with both these problems are in demand. For effective entity resolution, this chapter proposes EIF, an entity resolution framework. With effective clustering techniques, approximate string matching algorithms and a flexible mechanism of knowledge

integration, EIF can deal with both the two aspects of the problems. Given a set of objects, EIF split them into clusters, such that each cluster corresponds to one entity. In this chapter, as an application of EIF, we process an author resolution algorithm for identifying authors from the database with dirty data. For the simplicity of discussion, in this chapter, we only focus on relational data. The techniques in this chapter can also be applied to semi-structured data or data in OO-DBMS by representing each object as a tuple of attributes. The content of this chapter is from Li, Wang, Gao & Li (2010).

The contributions of this chapter can be summarized as following:

1. EIF, a general entity resolution framework by using name and other attributes of objects, is presented in this chapter. Both approximate string matching and clustering techniques can be effectively embedded into EIF, domain knowledge integration mechanism as well. This framework can deal with both name variant and name sharing problems. As we know, it is the first strategy with the consideration of both problems.
2. As an application of EIF, an author resolution algorithm is proposed by using the information of author name and co-authors to solve author resolution problem. It shows that by adding proper domain information, EIF is suitable to process problems in practice.
3. The effectiveness of this framework is verified by extensive experiments. The experimental results show that the author resolution algorithm based on EIF outperforms the existing author resolution approaches both in precision and recall.

The rest of this chapter is organized as follows. The entity resolution framework EIF is introduced in Section 2. In Section 3, we demonstrate how to apply EIF on author resolution. Related work is introduced in Section 4. In Section 5, the effectiveness of the algorithm based on EIF is evaluated by experiments. Section 6 concludes the whole chapter.

THE ENTITY RESOLUTION FRAMEWORK: EIF

In this section, we propose an entity resolution framework EIF. EIF consists of two parts. The first is a classifier based on object name to put the objects whose names might refer to the same name in one class, vice versa. The second part is to partition objects in each class and combine these partitions to generate a global partition. This global partition is the final result. In the final result, objects in the same cluster correspond to one entity, vice versa.

The Introduction to the Framework

The input of EIF is a set of objects, denoted by N. N can be represented as a graph $G = (V, E)$ with $\forall v \in V$ corresponding to an element in N. The initialization of E is null. Firstly, EIF classifies the objects by their names. If the names of two objects are similar, they are classified in one class. Note that one object can be classified into multiple classes. Secondly, EIF generates edges in G. sim(u, v) is defined to be the similarity function of objects u and v according to the domain knowledge. It can be computed from name and other attributes of u and v. Edge (u, v) is added if the value of $sim(u, v) \geq \Delta$ (the determine of threshold Δ will be discussed later). Thirdly, induced subgraph of each class is generated and is partitioned into clusters by domain knowledge. Finally, the global partition is obtained from local partitions generated; the objects belonging to each cluster in the final partition refer to the same entity. The flow of EIF is shown in Algorithm 1.

Algorithm 1 the EIF

Input: A set of objects N with each object consisting of a name and some other attributes.

Ouput: A partition of N, $R = \{G_1, G_2, ..., G_t\}, G_1 \cup G_2 \cup ... \cup G_t = N, G_i \cap G_j = \emptyset, 1 \leq i < j \leq t$. Objects in the same cluster refer to the same entity.

1. **Initialization:** $G_N = (V, E), V = N, E = \emptyset$.
2. Classify N into $N_1, N_2, ..., N_k$ by comparing the names of objects, satisfying $N = N_1 \cup N_2 \cup ... \cup N_k, \forall a, b \in N_i$, the names of a and b are similar; $\forall a \in N_i, b \in N_j (i \neq j)$, the names of a and b are not similar.
3. Define the similarity function sim and the threshold Δ by using the domain knowledge or machine learning approaches. Given u, $v \in N_i, 1 \leq i \leq k$, the larger sim(u, v) is, the more similar u and v are. $\forall u, v \in V$, if $sim(u, v) \geq \Delta$, insert edge (u, v) to G_N.
4. The subgraph of G_N induced by node set N_i is denoted by $G_N[N_i]$. That is $G_N[N_i] = G_N - \overline{N_i}$, where $\overline{N_i} = V(G_N) - N_i, (1 \leq i \leq k)$. A partition of each induced subgraph $G_N[N_i]$, denoted by $R_i (1 \leq i \leq k)$, is obtained by domain knowledge. $\forall a \in G_N[N_i]$, the class object a belongs to in the partition R_i is denoted by $R_i(a)$.
5. The global partition $R = \{G_1, G_2, ..., G_t\}$ is combined from the partitions of all the induced subgraphs: $R_1, R_2, .., R_k$, satisfying $\forall a, b \in V$, if $\exists R_i, R_i(a) \neq R_i(b)$ (a and b are not in the same cluster in the partition R_i), then $R(a) \neq R(b)$; otherwise, $R(a) = R(b)$.
6. Return R.

Both sim and Δ can be obtained by domain knowledge. For example, if at least two names occur simultaneously in two publications as authors, by the domain knowledge, we know that these authors with the identical name in these two publications are very likely to refer to the same author. Therefore, the similarity function can be defined as the size of intersection of co-author sets, and Δ can be set to 2.

Induced Subgraph Partition Method

Step 4 is to partition the objects in induced subgraph. Effective clustering approaches are applied to perform such partition, domain knowledge as well. In this chapter, an iteration method is used. In iteration, nodes u and v satisfying one of these two conditions are found: 1)$N(u) \subseteq S(v)$ or $N(v) \subseteq S(u)$; 2)$|N(u) \cap N(v)| \geq \lambda \times |N(u) \cup N(v)|$, where for any node v, we denote the set of neighbours of v (including v) in G_N as $N(v)$ and the initial node set of v as $S(v)$.

For each edge $e = (u, v) \in E$ in the induced subgraph $G_N[N_i]$, if e satisfies one of the above conditions, u and v are considered to refer to one entity in N_i and should be partitioned into the same cluster. Once u and v are considered to refer to one entity, (u, v) is contracted and u, v are merged to one node u', where the original node set of u' is denoted as $S(u')$, $S(u') = S(u) \cup S(v)$ and $N(u')$ is denoted as the union of neighbours of u and v, $N(u') = N(u) \cup N(v)$.

The iteration terminates when no more nodes can be merged. The result is the partition of N_i. Each node $u \in N_i$ represents an entity in N_i and $S(u)$ represents the set of objects referring to this entity. The algorithm of this method is shown in algorithm 2.

Algorithm 2 Author Resolution with Similar Names Algorithm

Input: $G_N[N_i] = (V', E')(V'=N_i \subseteq V, E' \subseteq E)$
Output: G_N' (each node in G_N' corresponds to the objects referring to the same entity)

1. $G_N' = G_N[N_i]$;
2. **for each** $v \in V$ **do**
3. $S(v) = \{v\}$;
4. **for each** $e = (u, v) \in E$ **do**
5. **if** $|N(u) \cap N(v)| / |N(u) \cup N(v)| > \lambda$ **then**
6. replace u and v with u';
7. $N(u') = N(u) \cup N(v)$;
8. $S(u') = S(u) \cup S(v)$;
9. UpDate = true;
10. **if** UpDate = true **then**
11. goto 2;
12. **return** G_N'

Since the time complexity of step 1-3 of EIF depends on domain knowledge, we only focus on step 4-5. According to our analysis, in the worst case, the time complexity of step 4 is $O(|V'||E'|)$ and the time complexity of step 5 is $O(|V'|)$.

Example: In this subsection, we demonstrate the flow of EIF with Example 1.

Example 1: There are six publications each with a list of authors, and each publication has an author named "Wei Wang" or "Wang Wei". By domain knowledge, it is known that these two names might refer to an identical name. For simplicity, the task of entity resolution in this example is to distinguish the authors named "Wei Wang" or "Wang Wei". The information is shown in Table 1. In EIF, the entity resolution consists of the following steps.

- **Step 1:** Generate the corresponding graph G_N of N. Each node in G_N corresponds an author (for simplicity, objects A-F with name "Wang Wei" or "Wei Wang" are considered). (Figure 1(a))
- **Step 2:** Classify the objects by comparing their names. Since we only distinguish the objects with similar names "Wei Wang" or "Wang Wei", all nodes in G_N belongs to the same class N_1. (Figure 1(b))
- **Step 3:** Suppose the similarity function is defined as the size of intersection (including the author himself) of co-author set and the threshold Δ is set to be 2. Therefore, for any two objects u and v, if the intersection of their co-author sets is in size of at least 2, an edge (u, v) is inserted into G_N. (Figure 1(c))

Table 1. Objects in publications

Obj_ID	Pub_ID	Object Name	Co-Auhtos	Obj_ID	Pub_ID	Object Name	Co-Auhtos
A	1	Wei Wang	Dylan	D	4	Wang Wei	Bob, Mike
B	2	Wei Wang	Bob	E	5	Wang Wei	Dylan
C	3	Wei Wang	Dylan, Mike	F	6	Wang Wei	Bob

- **Step 4:** Partition the objects in the induced subgraph with $\lambda = 1/2$. Since $N(A) \cap N(C) = \{A, C, E\}, N(A) \cup N(C) = \{A, C, D, E\}$, so $|N(A) \cap N(C)| = 3$, $|N(A) \cup N(C)| = 4$, and $|N(A) \cap N(C)| / |N(A) \cup N(C)| = 3/4 \geq \lambda = 0.5$. The condition 2) is satisfied, A and C are considered to refer to one entity. A and C are merged into A'. $N(A') = N(A) \cup N(C)$, and $S(A') = S(A) \cup S(C) = \{A, C\}$. In the same way, A' and E are merged into A'' with $N(A'') = N(A') \cup N(E) = \{A, C, D, E\}$ and $S(A'') = S(A') \cup S(E) = \{A, C, E\}$. For A'' and D, since $N(D) = \{C, B, D, F\} \not\subset S(A'')$ and $N(A'') = \{A, C, D, E\} \not\subset S(D)$, condition 1) is not satisfied. Moreover, $N(A'') \cap N(D) = \{C, D\}$, $N(A'') \cup N(D) = \{A, B, C, D, E, F\}$, so $|N(A'') \cap N(D)| / |N(A'') \cup N(D)| = 1/3 < \lambda$. Condition 2) is not satisfied either. Therefore, A'' and D are not merged. Step 4 of EIF is iterated until no more edge can

be contracted. Finally, the partition of N_1 is obtained, which is $\{\{A, C, E\}, \{B, D, F\}\}$. (Figure 1(d-e))

- **Step 5-6:** In Step 5, since there is only one class N_1, the final result is the partition of N_1, denoted as R_1. Return R_1 in Step 6(The algorithm ends).

THE AUTHOR RESOLUTION ALGORITHM BASED ON EIF (AI-EIF)

Both problems of name variant and sharing exist in author resolution of publications. Different authors may share identical or similar names; an author name may also have different spellings in different publications, such as abbreviation, different orders of family name and given name and so on. Therefore, EIF can be applied to the author resolution problem. In this section, we will discuss how to apply EIF to design author

Figure 1. The flow of EIF applied in author resolution (Li, L., Wang, H., Gao, H. & Li, J. 2010)

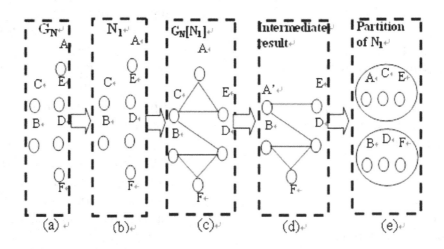

resolution algorithm. Example 1 has shown the major processing of the application of EIF in author resolution. In this section, methods based on domain knowledge of publications will be discussed in detail.

Classification of Objects on Names

According to the EIF, the author resolution algorithm should classify the objects by names in step 2 of Algorithm 1. Objects with similar names should be classified in the same class. Our task is to define the similarity judgement rules between names.

Since author names are in type of string with special formats, rule-based strategies can be used in this step. The matching rules of name in (Michael 2003) are used as the rules in this chapter. These rules enumerate diversities of name spellings.

With these matching rules, we define conditions of classification. An intuitive idea of classification is to make the nodes in the same class match each other, which can be proved to be an NP-Hard problem. Due to limitations on space, we eliminate the proof.

In order to efficiently solve this problem, we propose a heuristic rule-based strategy. The heuristic rules are as follows:

1. If names a and b are matching, then Class(a) = Class(b),
2. If Class(a) = Class(b), and Class(b) = Class(c), then Class(a) = Class(c),

where for name a, we denote the class a belongs as Class(a). According to the heuristic rules, we propose the rule-based strategy. This strategy includes the following steps:

1. Find all matching pairs of name sets by rules in (Michael 2003). Each matching pair is considered as a class,
2. Merge two classes if their intersection is not empty,

3. Repeat step 2) until no more classes can be merged.
4. All classes are output.

When the classes of names are generated, a classification of objects is obtained. However, such classification cannot distinguish objects effectively because of name sharing. As a further step, we propose a partition algorithm in the next section to solve the problem of name sharing.

Partition of Objects based on Clustering

After authors are classified by names, we implement the 3-5 steps in EIF by entity resolution with similar names algorithm.

The first step of this algorithm is to add edges. Each edge $e = (u, v)$ in G_N represents u and v might be the same real-world entity. The rules of whether (u, v) should be added into G_N is determined by domain knowledge and the values of attributes of u, v. The domain knowledge for author resolution is as follows.

1. The more similar the research areas are, the more possible the objects with the similar names refer to the same entity.
2. The larger the intersection set of co-authors is, the more possible the objects with the similar names refer to the same entity.

These rules can be described as similar functions. Before the functions are defined, some basic functions are introduced. Consider two objects aut1 and aut2, aut1 is in publication p1 and aut2 is in publication p2. aut1 and aut2 have similar names. It means that after classification, aut1 and aut2 are in the same class. Denote the set of citations of publication p as C(p), the set of author names of p as A(p). The domain similarity function and co-authors similarity function are defined as follows:

1. Domain similarity of objects aut1 and aut2: $f((aut1),(aut2)) = |C(p1) \cap C(p2)|$;
2. Co-authors similarity of objects aut1 and aut2: $g((aut1),(aut2)) = |A(p1) \cap A(p2)|$

Combining above two similarities, the similarity function **sim** is defined as:

$$sim((aut1),(aut2)) = a*f((aut1),(aut2)) + b*g((aut1),(aut2)) \ (0 \leq a \leq b \leq 1, \ a+b=1),$$

where parameters a, b can be determined by domain knowledge or machine learning approaches.

According to the similarity function **sim** and the threshold Δ, edges are added into G_N in the following rule:

$$\forall u, v \in V, \text{ if } sim(u, v) \geq \Delta, \text{add edge } (u, v) \text{ into } E$$

Step 3 in EIF for author resolution repeats to added edges into E in above rule and terminates until no more edge can be added.

EXPERIMENTS

In order to verify the effectiveness and efficiency of EIF, we perform the extensive experiments. The experimental results and analysis are shown in this section.

Experimental Settings

1. **Experimental Environment:** We ran experiments on a PC with Pentium Processor 3.20 GHz CPU, 512 RAM. The operation system is Microsoft Window XP. We implemented the algorithms using VC++ 6.0 and SGI's stl library. We have implemented the author resolution algorithm based on EIF, called AI-EIF. We evaluate our framework on both real dataset and synthetic data set and show the effectiveness and efficiency of our algorithm.

2. **Data Sets:** In order to test the algorithm in this chapter, three datasets are used. The first is the dataset used in (Yin, Han & Yu 2007) for comparisons. The second is the DBLP(http://dblp.uni-trier.de/) to test the effectiveness and efficiency of our algorithm on real data. In order to test the impact of parameters on our algorithm, synthetic data is used as well. We designed a data generator for generating publication with authors. The parameters include the number of authors per publications(#aut/per pub), the number of publications(#pub) and the ratio of the number of names to the number of authors(#name/#aut). For each author as an entity, its name is chosen randomly from the name set. To simulate real life situations, the authors forms a scale-free network(Barabasi, A. L., Bonabeau, E., 2003) which models the co-author network among them. For each publication, its authors are a group of randomly selected co-authors in this network.

3. **Measures:** In order to test the effectiveness of AI-EIF, we compare the entity resolution results of EIF with manually resolution results. Manually resolution is to manually divide the objects into groups according to author's home pages, affiliations and research areas shown on the papers or web pages. According to the definitions in (Yin, Han & Yu 2007), we define the manually partition is C, and the experimental results of AI-EIF is C*. Let TP (true positive) be the number of pairs of objects that are in the same cluster in both C and C*. Let FP (false positive) be the number of pairs of objects in the same cluster in C* but not in C, and FN (false negative) be the number of pairs of references in the same cluster in C but not in C*. Therefore the precision and recall are defined as follows: precision = TP / (TP + FP), recall = TP / (TP + FN).

4. **Parameters Setting:** Since only co-author information is used in the experiments, a =

0, b = 1. For the algorithm, we set Δ = 2 and λ = 0.05. The default setting of our data generator is that: #name/#aut = 0.9, #pub = 1000, #aut/per pub = 4.

Experimental Results on Real Data

We test both efficiency and effectiveness of the algorithm on DBLP. We extract information of all 1119K publications for author resolution. The processing time of AI-EIF on DBLP is 1.64 hours.

In order to test the effectiveness of AI-EIF, we randomly pick 8 names from all 2074K author names in DBLP and identify them manually. Each of the 8 names corresponds to multiple authors. The basic information of them is shown in Table 2, including the number of authors (#aut) and number of references (#ref). Table 2 also shows the precisions and recalls of each name by AI-EIF. From the result, the precisions are always 100%. It means that AI-EIF always divide objects referring to different authors into different clusters. The average of recall is greater than 90%. It means that in most of time, objects referring to the same entity are in the same cluster.

From the experimental results, it is observed that the recall is affected by the connection between any two authors in the set of authors who cooperated with the author u, denoted as Co(u). For any two authors in Co(u), if they cooperated, the connection between them is tight, otherwise it is loose. Take the author named Michael Siegel in Weizmann Institute of Science(WIS) as an example, in all his publications, there are 8 publications he

cooperated with some people in WIS, and there are 3 other publications he cooperated with some people in Institut für Informatik and Praktische Mathematik(IIPM). Since the co-operator set in WIS never cooperate with the co-operator set in IIPM, the connection between these two co-operator set is loose. Therefore, in our algorithm, the objects referring to the author Michael Siegel in WIS are partitioned into 2 clusters.

Comparison Experiments

As far as we know, DISTINCT(Yin, Han & Yu 2007) is the best author resolution algorithm. Therefore, we compare AI-EIF with DISTINCT. Since DISTINCT only tests its quality for distinguishing references, we compare precision and recall results of AI-EIF with DISTINCT. We test our algorithm using the same test data as (Yin, Han & Yu 2007). We test AI-EIF on real names in DBLP that correspond to multiple authors. 8 such names are shown in Table 3, together with the number of authors and number of references.

The experimental comparisons of precisions and recalls are also shown in Table 3 respectively. From Table 3, it can be seen that AI-EIF outperforms DISTINCT both in precision and average recall.

Changing Parameters

According to our analysis, the effectiveness and efficiency of AI-EIF are influenced by the parameters: λ, #aut/per pub, #name/#aut and #pub.

Table 2. Names corresponding to multiple authors and accuracy of AI-EIF

Name	# aut	# ref	precision	recall	Name	# aut	# ref	precision	recall
Michael Siegel	5	45	1.0	0.804	Hui Xu	13	34	1.0	1.0
Qian Chen	9	39	1.0	0.949	Hai Huang	15	44	1.0	0.780
Dong Liu	12	36	1.0	0.870	Zhi Li	11	32	1.0	1.0
Lin Li	11	30	1.0	0.933	Jian Zhou	12	38	1.0	0.895
Average			1.0	0.904					

Table 3. Names corresponding to multiple authors and comparison results

Name	# aut	# ref	Precision DISTINCT	Precision EIF	Recall DISTINCT	Recall EIF
Hui Fang	3	9	1.0	1.0	1.0	1.0
Ajay Gupta	4	16	1.0	1.0	1.0	0.882
Rakesh Kumar	2	38	1.0	1.0	1.0	1.0
Michael Wagner	5	24	1.0	1.0	0.395	0.620
Bing Liu	6	11	1.0	1.0	0.825	1.0
Jim Smith	3	19	0.888	1.0	0.926	0.810
Wei Wang	14	177	0.855	1.0	0.814	0.933
Bin Yu	5	42	1.0	1.0	0.658	0.595
Average			0.94	1.0	0.802	0.871

The experimental results are shown in Figure 2 to Figure 7.

We test the impact of λ on real data. For the convenience of observation, only the experimental results of publications of Wei Wang in UNC(entity 0) and Wei Wang in Fudan(entity 1) are shown. The experiment results are shown in Figure 2. From Figure 2, it is observed that the recall decreases with the increase of λ. It is because the bigger λ is, the stronger the similarity matching condition of objects is. Therefore, more and more objects referring to the same real-world entity are partitioned into different clusters. This leads to the decrease of recall. Another observa-

tion is that in most cases the precision is not affected by λ, while in a few cases, when λ is too small (e.g. λ=0.01 in our experiments), the precisions are no longer 100%. In another word, the larger λ is, the stronger the matching condition is and the higher the precision is, vice versa.

The conclusion drawn from the experiments of changing λ is that the smaller λ is, the lower the recall is and the higher the precision is; vice versa.

In Figure 3 we test the efficiency by changing #pub from 500 to 5000, #aut = 500. From Figure 3, it can be seen that the run time is approximately linear to the number of publications. It is because according to the analysis in Section II-D, the run time is approximately linear to the

Figure 2. λ VS recall

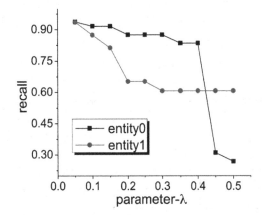

Figure 3. Exe.time VS #pub

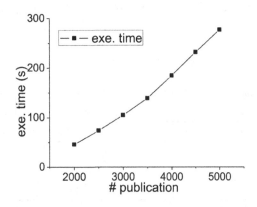

Figure 4. Precision VS #name/#aut

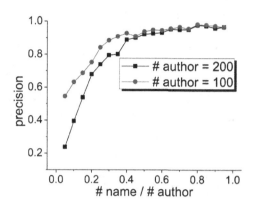

number of objects, which is linear to the number of publications.

In Figure 4 and Figure 5 we test the impact of the ratio of name number and entity number on effectiveness by changing #name/#aut from 0.05 to 0.95. From Figure 4, it can be seen that the bigger the ratio of the number of names to the number of authors is, the higher the precision is. That is because, the bigger the ratio is, the smaller the probability of different authors having same name is, the less objects referring to different authors are divided into same cluster, the higher precision is. From Figure 5, recalls are insensitive to the ratio of number of names to the number of authors. That is because, FN is insen-

sitive to the probability of different authors having same name.

We test the impact of the number of authors per publication on effectiveness by changing #aut/per pub from 2 to 11. The precision is insensitive to the number of authors in each publication. It shows that the precision of our algorithm is assured. Figure 6 shows the impact of #aut/per pub on recall. Recall increases more and more slowly with the #aut/per pub. The recall increasing with #aut/per pub is because the more number of co-authors in each publication are, the more co-authors are connected by this publication, the higher the connections between co-authors are. Since the connections between co-operators of this author are higher, the recall gets larger. This result is coincident with the analysis of the experimental results of the changing of λ. The reason for the incremental speed getting slower with #aut/per pub is that marginal impact of the number of authors per publication on the recall decreases.

In Figure 7 we test the efficiency by changing #aut/per pub from 2 to 14. From Figure 7, it can be seen the run time increases more and more slowly with #aut/per pub. The increasing of run time with #aut/per pub is because the more co-authors in each publication, the more information is to be processed. The increment speed of run time becomes slower is because even though the

Figure 5. Recall VS #name/#aut

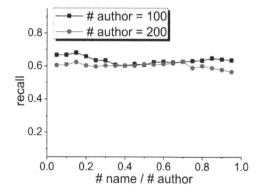

Figure 6. Recall VS #aut/per pub

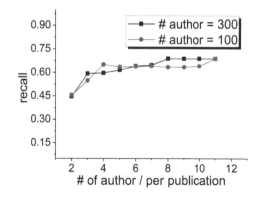

Figure 7. Exe.time VS # aut/per pub

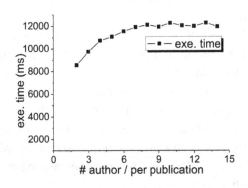

number of co-authors gets larger, the probability of two objects referring to the same author will not get larger in the same scale. It means that the number of objects to process will not increase in the same scale.

CONCLUSION

In this chapter, we study the entity resolution problem, and propose a general framework of entity resolution, EIF. Both clustering techniques and domain knowledge are effectively integrated in EIF, which can process the data with both problems of name variant and name sharing. Both effectiveness and efficiency are verified.

REFERENCES

Barabasi, A. L., & Bonabeau, E. (2003). Scale-free networks. *Scientific American, 288*, 50–59. doi:10.1038/scientificamerican0503-60 PMID:12701331

Li, L., Wang, H., Gao, H., & Li, J. (2010). EIF: A framework of effective entity identification. [WAIM.]. *Proceedings of WAIM, 2010*, 717–728.

Michael, L. (2003). Computer science digital libraries - A personal view. *JBIDI, 21*.

Newcombe, H., Kennedy, J., & Axford, S. (1959). Automatic linkage of vital records. *Science, 130*, 954–959. doi:10.1126/science.130.3381.954 PMID:14426783

Yin, X., Han, J., & Yu, P. S. (2007). *Object distinction: Distinguishing objects with identical names*. ICDE. doi:10.1109/ICDE.2007.368983

ADDITIONAL READING

Arasu, A., Chaudhuri, S., & Kaushik, R. (2008). *Transformation-based framework for record matching*. ICDE.

Arasu, A., Chaudhuri, S., & Kaushik, R. (2009). *Learning string transformations from examples*. VLDB.

Arasu, A., Kaushik, R. (2009). A grammar-based entity representation framework for data cleaning. SIGMOD, 233-244.

Arasu, C. R., & Suciu, D. (2009). *Large-scale deduplication with constraints using Dedupalog*. ICDE.

Barabasi, A. L., & Bonabeau, E. (2003). Scale-Free Networks. *Scientific American, 288*, 50–59. doi:10.1038/scientificamerican0503-60 PMID:12701331

Chaudhuri, S., Chen, B. C., Ganti, V., & Kaushik, R. (2007). *Example-driven design of efficient record matching queries*. VLDB.

Chen, Z., Kalashnikov, D. V., Mehrotra, S. (2009). Exploiting context analysis for combining multiple entity resolution systems. SIGMOD, 207-218.

Culotta, A., & McCallum, A. (2005). Joint deduplication of multiple record types in relational data. CIKM, 257–258.

Dong, X., Halevy, A., & Madhavan, J. (2005). Reference reconciliation in complex information spaces. SIGMOD, 85–96.

Koudas, N., Sarawagi, S., Srivastava, D. (2006). Record linkage: similarity measures and algorithms. SIGMOD, 802-803.

Koudas, N., Saha, A., & Srivastava, D. et al. (2009). *Metric functional dependencies*. ICDE.

Michael L. (2003). Computer Science Digital Libraries - a personal view. JBIDI, 21.

Milch, B., Marthi, B., Sontag, D., Russell, S., & Ong, D. L. (2005). BLOG: Probabilistic models with unknown objects. In IJCAI-05, pp.1352–1359.

Newcombe, H., Kennedy, J., & Axford, S. (1959). Automatic Linkage of Vital Records. In Science, vol. 130(pp. 954-959).

Singla, P., & Domingos, P. (2005). *Object resolution with attribute-mediated dependences*. PKDD.

Whang, S. E., Menestrina, D., Koutrika, G., Theobald, M., Molina, H. G. (2009). Entity resolution with iterative blocking. SIGMOD, 219-232.

Yin, X., Han, J., & Yu, P. S. (2007). *Object Distinction: Distinguishing Objects with Identical Names*. ICDE. doi:10.1109/ICDE.2007.368983

KEY TERMS AND DEFINITIONS

Entity Resolution: Given an data object set U, entity resolution is to partition U into groups $R_U=\{R_1,...,R_k\}$ such that objects which are determined to refer to the same real-world entity are in the same group while objects which are determined to refer to different entities are in different groups and R_U also satisfies that, i) $R_1 \cup ... \cup R_k = U$; ii) $\forall R_i$, $R_j \in R_U$, $R_i \cap R_j = \varnothing$.

Induced Subgraph: Let G=(V,E) be a graph and V'⊆V is a subset of vertices of G. The subgraph of G induced by V' is the subgraph G'=(V',E') of G such that, for all u,v∈V', (u,v)∈ E iff (u,v)∈ E'.

Name Sharing: The problem that a name is shared by multiple entities is called name sharing.

Name Variant: The problem that a real-world entity has multiple names is called name variant. Name variant can be caused by abbreviations, different orders and misspellings.

Precision: Let C be the correct entity resolution result, C* be the experimental result of entity resolution. Let TP (true positive) be the number of pairs of objects that are in the same cluster in both C and C*. Let FP (false positive) be the number of pairs of objects in the same cluster in C* but not in C, and FN (false negative) be the number of pairs of references in the same cluster in C but not in C*. The precision denoted by pre is defined as pre= TP / (TP + FP).

Recall: Let C be the correct entity resolution result, C* be the experimental result of entity resolution. The recall denoted by rec is defined as rec = TP / (TP + FN), where TP (true positive) is the number of pairs of objects that are in the same cluster in both C and C* and FN (false negative) is the number of pairs of references in the same cluster in C but not in C*.

Similarity Function: Taken a data object pair (o_i, o_j) as input, similarity function $sim(o_i, o_j)$ returns a non-negative number such that the more similar o_i and o_j are, the larger the value of $sim(o_i, o_j)$ is.

Chapter 16
Product Entity Resolution in E-Commerce

ABSTRACT

With the rapid development of e-commerce, there is a huge amount of commodity data on the Internet. Users are always spending a lot of time looking for the exact product. Therefore, finding products representing the same entity is an effective way to improve the efficiency of purchasing. Due to frequently missing or wrong values and subjective difference in description, traditional method of entity resolution may not have a good result on e-commerce data. Therefore, a set of algorithms are proposed in data cleaning, attribute and value tagging, and entity resolution, which are specialized for e-commerce data. In addition, user's actions are collected to improve the classification result. The chapter evaluates the effectiveness of the proposed algorithms with real-life datasets from e-commerce sites.

INTRODUCTION

With the rapid development of the Internet, more and more users choose to purchase products on the network. However, with the advent of C2C online shop, the amount and the variety of product increase rapidly. The same product may have a different description in different sellers, which a lot of products exist lack of information, error information and other issues. For example, there are 6 million sellers and almost 0.8 billion products in taobao.com, in which most of the products are input manually. This makes the product information very subjective differences in description and users may take a long time to find the exact product that they want.

Therefore, the entity classification on e-commerce data has high value. Entity resolution technology is relatively mature, but they are mostly for the structured data or relational data, as in Chapter 5 and Chapter 6, they cannot get the desired results on e-commerce data. Compared to the traditional entity identification technology, entity classification on e-commerce data faces greater challenges:

1. Incomplete description of product. E-commerce data generally include the product name, price, shipping costs, seller and the description information of product. Product name contains very little amount of information and the description also lack of

DOI: 10.4018/978-1-4666-5198-2.ch016

detailed information. Consider "Camera", for example, the title contains general camera model, brand information, and this information exists in the natural text, computer hardly know which attribute each word represents. Most of information in description for business promotional information, the lack of a camera pixel, lens type.

2. Product description inconsistent. Different sellers have a different description of the same product. For example, for a camera Powershot A4000 IS, some sellers describe it as Powershot A4000 IS while some describe it as A4000.

3. Product description miscellaneous. The description is mixed with information of other products, such as " Similar products that are hot recommended like (Canon) PowerShot A3300 Camera 1600 Megapixel 3 inch LCD promotional price 918.00 Nikon COOLPIX S3300 1600 Megapixel 2.7 inch display new spot promotional price 808.00", which is in fact, it is a sentence from the description of the product "Sony W630". So, these descriptions of promotional merchandise will cause a lot of interference in entity classification.

We use an example to illustrate these problems. As shown Figure 1, the model of the first product should be PowerShot A3300 IS, half of the content of the title is advertising message. The second product is also likely to cause confusion, users cannot determine the product model "G1X" or "PowerShot G1 X" or "PowerShot G1X". The third product, it is not a same class with the first two product. Description in Figure 2, contains more than a package of product information, such as "SanDisk 32G SD," "MINI tripod."

As we can see in this example, there is significantly difference between e-commerce data and structured relational data. Existing entity resolution algorithms for structured data have achieved more satisfactory results. Algorithm described in Whang, Menestrina, Koutrika, Theobald, & Garcia-Molina (2009, June) has reached more than 90% in accuracy with 2,000,000 dataset. However, they will not be able to solve the three basic problems of e-commerce data previously described, so most of these algorithms cannot directly applied on e-commerce data. For these problems, we designed and implemented an online real-time processing of massive e-commerce data query system. The system has the following characteristics:

1. The product data is real-time, the search results are consistent with the e-commerce

Figure 1. Some different produce information of Canon camera

Figure 2. The description information returned from the results in Figure 1

```
The Canon G1X full set of standard (new original genuine
support counter detection)
The SanDisk 32GSD/C10 Speed ??mainstream memory card (Genius 5-
year warranty)
Senior product wins backup battery (Genius
five-year warranty)
Canon G1X special holster (tailor-made ??high-end utility)
MINI tripod
Spree [High Speed ??Card Reader + Professional HD cable +
Digital Wipes + LCD Film + lens cleaning pen]+LCDSending 150
yuan worth of gold free after-sales three years (testing fee /
maintenance fee / return postage is free), the pro! Allows you
to buy the rest assured that with the happy after-sales peace
of mind.
```

system. Product data integration of multiple shopping site, is a one-stop search system.

2. Search results in accordance with the entity to distinguish, users can quickly find what they want

3. The user can manually adjust the products category, the system can learn to optimize entity classification algorithm. The behavior of click an item will also be fed back to the system to improve the result. With the system being used by more and more users, the classification results will be more and more accurate.

The contribution of this chapter, can be summarized as the following:

1. This chapter presents an integrated e-commerce site and returns the search results in different entities of real-time commodity search system. The system is the first real-time processing of e-commerce entity resolution system.

2. We established a Filter ad rule base for e-commerce product data, integrated the attributes and attribute values of products with high weight, constitute a more detailed product information library, this information will be useful in other areas.

3. We make use of users' behavior in product entity classification system to optimize the results.

This system has been demoed as Wang, Zhang, Li & Gao (2013). Some techniques introduced in Chapter 3 and Chapter 4 can be applied for entity resolution for e-commerce data.

The organizational structure of this chapter is as follows: Section 2 is some related work about entity classification. In section 3, we describe the overall architecture and four important part of the system. In section 4, we use real-life dataset from taobao.com to evaluate the effectiveness of this system. Finally we draw the conclusion in section 5.

RELATED WORK

Entity resolution on e-commerce data is a more cutting-edge research area, the current study mainly stays in the direction of data mining (Raghavan 2005). E-commerce collaborative filtering research has existed for quite a long time, many e-commerce sites already use the technology, and the more serious problem they face is the ever-growing amount of product data quality issues. Köpcke, Thor, Thomas, & Rahm

(2012, March) proposed a special entity resolution algorithm for e-commerce data, but the main idea of this algorithm is to extract characteristic words to represent the product (it is called product code in that paper), they are lack of comparison for detailed properties of products. And without the consideration of the impact of dirty data on the system, the result is not good enough.

As a long-standing problem of data cleansing, there are a large number of references which proposed their own algorithms. As shown in Yu (2002), the correct rate of data cleaning system has reached 90%, but most of these algorithms is aimed at structured data and they are not suitable for e-commerce data, Gomory, Hoch, Lee, Podlaseck & Schonberg (1999) pointed out the importance of data cleaning in e-commerce system, but did not propose a specific method of cleaning.

Part of speech tagging is quite mature in the field of natural language processing, and many other models, such as HMM, maximum entropy, conditional random field, SVM have achieved better results in dealing with the problem of speech tagging. However, due to the special nature of the e-commerce data, and real-time requirements of the system, they cannot be directly applied to the part of speech tagging. Kannan, Givoni, Agrawal & Fuxman (2011, August) gives an unstructured product data structured approach, but the method of property values n-gram (n=4) method to obtain a huge amount of merchandise word, cannot meet the real-time requirements. The method relies on off-the-shelf product attribute library and cannot cope with the rapid changes in the e-commerce data.

SYSTEM DESIGN

The main idea of this system is to return results of the integration of multiple data sources, classification of query results according to their description, and to provide users with a friendly interface, users can view results classified by entities and quickly find what they really want. User can participate in the entity classification to optimize the system and click on the search results or adjust their class. These operations can achieve the purpose of optimizing search results, then making the result become increasingly accurate with more and more users to use this system.

System Architecture

The system architecture shown in Figure 3, it gets real-time raw product data through the shopping site API, advertisements. Useless information in raw data will be removed through a data cleaning module (Module 1) segmentation. The cleaned data will input into POS module (Module 2) to identify the product attributes and attribute values (we name it attributes tuple) and set the initial weights of attributes tuples. The results (attribute, value, weight) are stored in the local database. Entity Resolution module (Module 3) takes all attributes tuple as input to classify the original results by entity classification, users' behavior of clicking or adjusting the product will be input into feedback module(Module 4) to modify the weight of involved attributes tuples.

The following will introduce the four main modules of the system and its main algorithm. Modules are not completely independent.

Data Cleaning

The data quality of e-commerce product data is a serious problem, we can find all kinds of problems just consider the product title. For an example with name "Mainland licensed +invoices original charger Samsung ST77 Panoramic digital camera reduction 65", it is a product title, we can easily find many useless punctuations and some advertising which has nothing to do with the product. If we keep these information, there will be adversely affected in entity resolution module.

In order to take an effective entity resolution, system tokenizes product title and description

Figure 3. System architecture

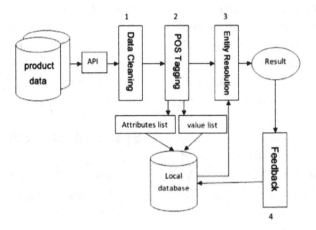

while cleaning. As there is generally no standard grammatical structure in title and description, and most e-commerce terms are not included in current thesaurus. Using existing algorithms cannot get the desired results, and efficiency cannot meet the requirements of real-time query. Therefore, the system does not use existing algorithms. We combine data cleansing and segmentation, and use regular expression to extract useful information from title and description, which excluded the advertising words and other useless information. This method reduces the time of dealing with such long description information, and makes the system to achieve real-time query request.

Based on different data quality issues, e-commerce data cleaning consists of three parts:

1.   Remove the ad.

We use the rule-based approach to find ad words and remove them. It is an offline processing step. We design the rule-based ad-cleaning method and create an ad words rule base to do the cleaning work.

All the rules in the rule base are in the form of regular expression. According to the different categories of ad, we divided the rule base into three categories, 1) Feature based rule, such as

"Package one", "Package two", "Package three", most words behind these phrases are useless information. 2) Combination of specific words. 3) Rules of the relationship between products, such as "received in 10 minutes". Such word appears only in the virtual products, while "free shipping", "genuine licensed" may appear in a variety of products with different categories. But in different categories, the similarity is very small except ad words. The first two kinds of rules are added manually, category 3 is got by the machine statistical learning methods.

2.   Clean the title.

After removing ad information, there still exists some data quality problems, such as special punctuation, not normal split and merge of products useful information, information duplication and contradictions. Take product "Frozen price 10x Optical zoom Nikon Digital Camera S8100VS9100 S8000S8200" as an example, after removing ad information, we get "10x Optical zoom Nikon Digital Camera S8100VS9100 S8000S8200", the symbol "\/" should be replaced with a space, S8000S8200 is not normal merger phenomenon, and it's conflict with the previous described information.

In this chapter, we use regular expression to exclude special punctuation marks and the problems of not normal split and merge of products information. We record the relative position of the word in the title to make the involved attributes tuples get different weights, thereby reducing the interference of the contradictions among product information. Algorithm is designed as follows.

Algorithm 1 Parser

Input: All products title

Ouput: Inverted index of all products according to the split words and each word has a weight

1. all_words = ∅
2. **for all** item∈item_list **do**
3. Match all Chinese, English, numbers, '.', '-' And so such special characters, get word_list, and record the word location at the same time
4. **for all** w∈word_list **do**

If the length of Chinese word w is greater than 6, replace it with 2-gram segmentation

5. **end for**
6. all_words = all_words ∪ word_list
7. **end for**
8. //calculate the weight
9. **for all** w∈all_words **do**

the weight of w is equal to the number of products that contain word w divided by wi, while wi is the most popular word

10. **end for**
11. **return** all_words

Algorithm Parser takes the title of all products as input and uses regular expressions to extract useful information. If a Chinese word is longer than 6, it is spit with 2-gram. Finally we get the word list all_words, it contains the position of each word in product title and the weight is calculated based on the frequency the word appears.

Table 1 is the result of comparison between ICTCLAS algorithm and Parser algorithm, we use 40 items from "camera" category. The right one has removed advertisements and other useless information. Seen better results of the right one, and it has a higher algorithm efficiency.

3. Clean the description (referred as desc)

Table 1. Top 10 words before and after data cleaning (title)

Results by Ictclas		Our Results	
Words:	**Weight:**	**Words:**	**Weight:**
Camera	1.0	Canon	1.0
Digital	0.833	Digital Camera	0.684
Canon	0.75	Sony	0.421
Genuine	0.638	Canon Digital Camera	0.368
Licensed	0.527	w630	0.315
[	0.5	Fuji	0.315
]	0.5	canon	0.263
Bag	0.416	Megapixel	0.263
HS	0.361	ixus 115 hs	0.263
IXUS	0.333	Camera	0.263

As is more special in product description, desc has a large amount of information, useless information. However, attributes and attribute values will generally appear in pairs in desc, which is not possible in title, so desc is more useful when finding attributes tuples. Thus, we designed a specialized cleaning algorithm for desc.

Most of the information contained in title is attribute values. Therefore, according to the results obtained, we can build a small vocabulary. There has been some rough classification in some e-commerce sites and pre-set some of the optional attributes and attribute values. We add this useful information into our vocabulary, and designed specific extraction rules for algorithm 1. We use modified Parser to do desc information extraction and keep words that have a small distance with the words in title, such as less than 5. This method can exclude most of the information that cannot be paired in module 3, Thereby reducing the time overhead of the system in the subsequent module.

The algorithm is shown as follows.

Algorithm 2 ParserForDesc

Input: All desc information and original classification list involved in the e-commerce website

Output: Inverted index of all products according to the split words and each word has a weight

1. build the vocabulary
2. design the extraction rules for desc and add them to Parser
3. **for all** item∈item_list **do**
4. desc_words = Parser(item.desc) //use the modified algorithm Paresr to extract desc, keep words that have a distance less than 5 with the words in title.
5. **end for**
6. update words' weight
7. **return** desc_words

The weight of the resulting word is calculated according to the following equation:

Assuming a total of K products, i represents the i-th items, w.wt represents the weight of word w

The number of word w appears in item i

The total number of words in item i's desc

$$w.wt = \max_{i=1}^{K} \left(\frac{\text{The number of word w appears in item i}}{\text{The total number of words in item i's desc}} \right)$$

Seen by the comparison of the results in Table 2, algorithm ParserForDesc got a better result than ICTCLAS. It kept most of useful words and their original structure.

Part of Speech

In data cleaning step, we removed most of the dirty data and after that we get a list of products indexed by their words. The purpose of this module is to tag the words obtained from previous module, and give them a weight according to their importance in entity resolution step. Specifically, we use the words in the title to match all attribute tuples pre-set by e-commerce sites and find out all attribute tuples in desc information and save them into local database for subsequent queries.

Table 2. Top 10 words before and after data cleaning (desc)

Results by Ictclas		Our Results	
Words:	Weight:	Words:	Weight:
Product surface	0.333	Nikon	0.875
:	0.333	Canon	0.857
Pictures	0.333	Sony	0.769
+	0.161	Casio	0.666
\	0.134	Brand	0.578
,	0.096	Fuji	0.567
Special offer	0.05	Pixels	0.333
dollars	0.048	ixus 220 hs	0.3
buying	0.048	ixus 125 hs	0.288
Price	0.048	ixus 310 hs	0.278
Promotions	0.045	600Mega	0.230

The part of speech in this chapter is different with that in natural language processing. The purpose of this module is to mark a word obtained from the previous module as an attribute or an attribute value. There is no standardized syntax structure in product information. If we use existing machine learning method to do POS tagging, we will meet two problems: One problem is the larger input of this module, results in reduced efficiency; the other problem is that machine is difficult to learn useful mark rules in non-standard information. Since the system's purpose is to classify products from e-commerce sites in real time, high-efficiency is required, so we designed a POS tagging algorithm for real-time processing of product information.

For product titles, the information do not contain attribute tuples, but only attribute value. These values are very useful information, such as brand names, product type. E-Commerce sites have given most of these attributes. They have main list of values. Combining with the position of the word in the title, we can get attribute tuples easily with the list.

Since the length of title is limited, we cannot get enough information from title. desc information is helpful in entity resolution if we find out the attribute tuples in it. In desc, although there is a lot of useless information, it has a normal syntax structure, attributes and attribute values appearing in pairs, such as "battery capacity: 1300mAh", "1300mAh battery capacity". So we can tag them according to their frequency and the distance between the attribute and its value.

Specifically, for an attribute w and its value v, we assume these two words appeared in N products at the same time, then we can get their average distance according to the following formula:

$$\overline{D} = (\sum_{j=0}^{N} D_j) / N$$

Wherein D_j is the distance of the words w and v in the j-th product. According to the habits of sellers in describe a product, attribute and values are appearing in pairs and with a small distance, so the smaller of the results from formula(1), the higher probability of the two words w and v to be an attribute tuple. Hence we get such a formula:

$$P = 1 / \overline{D}$$

We select attribute tuples in accordance with the threshold value, but by the formula (2), we can only judge whether w, v is an attribute tuple, cannot ascertain which is attribute and which is attribute value. Under normal circumstances, one attribute has multiple values, so the frequency of attributes will be higher than its values. Assuming the word w appeared in Nw products, word v appeared in Nv products, so we can use the following formula to distinguish the attribute and attribute value:

$$W(w,v) = N \div \left(\max\left(N_w, N_v\right) * \overline{D} \right) + w.wt + v.wt$$

where w.wt and v.wt are their weights obtained from module 2 and W(w,v) is finally determined attribute tuples' right weight.

The feasibility of the algorithm can be seen from Table 3, with most correct paired with a higher weight. Although the result of some mismatches, such as "Nikon - coolpix s3300", is not presented in attribute tuple relationship, this relationship is only as a basis of the product classification, not all product attributes are presented to users. Hence these data is still useful to the system.

Entity Resolution

After the processing of all above modules, the system has got relatively regular product data to do efficient entity resolution. In order to make

Table 3. Top 10 attribute tuples find in desc information

Attribute	Value	Weight
Nikon	coolpix s3300	0.5
Model	powershot sx150 is	0.5
Model	dsc-w630	0.5
Dust-proof	Antifreeze	0.333
Effective Pixels	400Mega	0.25
Lens Type	Telescopic	0.235
Anti-shake	Optics Anti-shake	0.152
Effective Pixels	ex-zs5	0.142
Waterproof	Antifreeze	0.125
Sony	1500Mega	0.111

this module more efficient, we organized attribute tuples into the following form:

In this chapter, entity resolution is based on similarity. As shown from Figure 4. Attributes separate all products into a sub-block. Since a product may have more than one attribute, but two products can only take a value at one attribute, similarity of the products in the sub-block can be added, and can only take a maximum if they are in different blocks.

Specifically, the similarity between any two products can be obtained by the following formula:

Suppose there are M sub-blocks, blockj is the j-th block, wi∈blockj means word w_i is an value in blockj, $w_i \in A \cap B$ means that w_i appears in both A and B's desc, attr$_j$[w$_i$]. w$_t$ is the weight of attribute tuple (attrj, w$_i$).

$$sim\left(A, B\right) = \sum_{j=1}^{M} \left(\max_{wi}^{wi \in blockj \wedge wi \in A \cap B} \left(attr_j \left[w_i \right].wt \right) \right)$$

By the above formula we can get the similarity between any two products, which form a similarity matrix. The similarity matrix can be treated as an undirected graph with one vertex representing one product and an edge weight being the similarity between the two products. If the similarity is zero, then there is no edge between that two vertices. For any pair of products A, B, if sim (A, B) is greater than the threshold, then the A, B will in the same category. Considering the transmission of similarity, i.e. A and B, B and C, their similarity is greater than the threshold, the A and B are similar too. So we can use breadth-first search strategy to traverse all of the vertices and the condition of accessing to the new vertex is that the similarity is greater than threshold. If one search cannot access any more vertex, then that search is finished, all vertices constituting a classification are accessed, and they are deleted from graph the a new vertex is chosen randomly to start a new search, until the graph is empty. The specific algorithm is as follows.

Algorithm 3 EntityResolution

Input: Graph G(V,E)
    Output: Classifications

1. Initialization classification results set = ∅
2. Set threshold k
3. Arbitrarily select a vertex to do a breadth-first search, the search conditions is that the value of the edge is greater than k
4. If there is no edge greater than k, finish this search, add all visited vertices to a new

Figure 4. Relationship between products

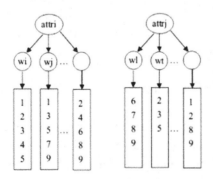

category, and delete these vertices and edges from the graph.

5. Return to step 3 until finished traversing all vertices

Get the top-3 attribute values as the category name, so that user can determine whether they want to view the products under the classification according to the attribute values listed.

Space complexity of the algorithm: The algorithm needs to save a similarity matrix with size |V + E| and a vertex status list with size |V| as the list stored product category information. The total space complexity is $O(2|V|+|E|)$.

The time complexity of the algorithm: The undirected graph was stored in an adjacency matrix and the loop detection matrix with | V | vertices, so the time complexity is $O(|V|^2)$.

Figure 5 is a result of classification for top-40 products from "camera" category. Category name is top-3 attribute values, we can see the system has reached the distinguish affect, users can quickly navigate to the products they want.

Feedback

Users' behaviors play a significant role in guiding the entity resolution. Generally, in a query result, user continuously click products have a higher similarity; user view the number of products in a classification to a certain extent on the accuracy of

Figure 5. Partial results of this system

the classification. Therefore, we use user feedback to improve the quality of the results.

Since e-commerce data changes quickly, we do not save product data in a local database, we just store attribute tuples. Hence we cannot change product's category permanently. The algorithm in this module is different with those widely used collaborative filtering algorithms. The main idea of our algorithm is to make use of users' behaviors to correct the weight of attribute tuples in the local database, so that we can get a more precise result in next classification.

System is mainly based on two user behavior data to modify the weight:

1. The list of user clicked products
2. The list of user modified classification.

For the first kind data, the habits of users when searching a product, they click product from the same class, and the majority of these product they clicked do have obvious common features. Therefore, we improve the weights of common attribute tuples under the list. Specifically, it is assumed that the public words for the list is W1, for any word w∈W1, the word w associated attribute tuple's weight is old_wt and its weight is updated to new_wt where

$$new\_wt = \sqrt{old\_wt}$$

So as calculated by formula(3), the weight will continue to close to 1.

For the second kind of data, the user adjusts product i from class cat_a to class cat_b. It means that the similarity between product i and producs in cat_a is lower the that with products in cat_b. Assume that the common words list between product i and cat_a is W2, and W3 for cat_b, so we reduce the weight of attribute tuples that W2 involved and increasing the weight that W3 involved. Finally, it means that we reduced the

probability of product i that has been assigned to cat_a, and increased the probability to cat_b, and use the following formula to update the weight:

$$new\_wt = old\_wt * e^{-1}$$

So calculated by formula (4), the weight of attribute tuples that involved in W22 will keep close to 0. For W3, we use the same formula (3) to modify its weight.

EXPERIMENT

The purpose of this chapter is to achieve an efficient and accurate online product classification. In order to test the effectiveness of the system, we use real product data from taobao.com for experiment. Based on the characteristics of real-time search, users cannot view to many products in one query, for example, taobao only return 40 products for one query in the first page. So we use 40-200 different sizes of datasets to test the system's recall rate, accuracy, efficiency, and the accuracy of data cleaning module and POS tagging module. To exclude the interference of the network access time, we crawled products from taobao's API, but did not do any pre-processing. The results are consistent with real-time access.

Effectiveness of Data Cleaning Module and POS Tagging Module

We combine the result of data cleaning module and POS tagging module, and calculated its accuracy, the results are as shown below:

As can be seen from Figure 6 (a), data cleaning module had almost cleaned 70% of dirty data. We found that, the 30% dirty data remain was ad information and our next work is to improve the rule base, so as to improve the accuracy of the data cleaning module.

The accuracy of POS tagging module is about 50%, mainly because there are too many other products description interferences. And the calculation of accuracy only considers whether correctly identified the attribute tuples, but does not consider the weight of that tuples. Such as tuple (Nicon, coolpix s3300, 0.5) is a false match, but it is still a useful tuple for entity resolution.

Comparisons

The algorithm used for comparison is from a taobao-based real-time product retrieval system which has already been online used. The system uses only the title information, and split title with white space, and uses 2-gram to split words that are longer than 5. The word weight calculation method is consistent with us, but they do not consider products' desc information and product brand, model, etc. attribute information and its weight, and no removal of the impact of ad. They finally use Jaccard similarity to classify all products.

Performance Test

We use products under "camera" category to do 5 tests The dataset size is 40, 80, 120, 160, 200.

We can see from Figure 6 (b) and (c), racall rate and accuracy tend to decrease with the increase of dataset size. However, consider that users cannot view too many products in one search. In the case with smaller data sets, recall rate and accuracy can be accepted. In Figure 6 (c), the accuracy of the proposed algorithm is relatively more stable than the comparison algorithm, so we can conclude that a classification based on detailed information is more reliable than that just rely on word frequency. When dataset size increases, word frequency cannot distinguish products effectively. Figure 6 (d) shows the comparison algorithm's time consumption is lower than the proposed algorithm, in real system, we can use cache method. When a user is watching products in the first page, we process the second page data at background, reducing the

Figure 6. Experimental results

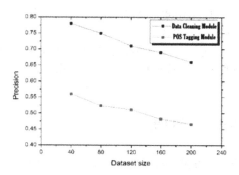

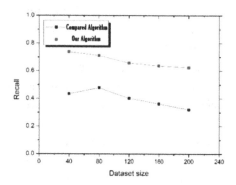

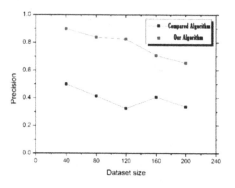

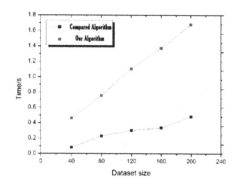

efficiency impact on system, while we can get relatively high recall rete and accuracy.

In this chapter, we consider the actual demand of a system, so we use a certain amount of time to exchange for a higher recall rate and accuracy, thereby increasing the system's utility.

CONCLUSION

In this chapter, we designed an entity classification system for e-commerce products including data cleaning, POS tagging, entity resolution and feedback module, detail described a strategy for entity classification of unstructured data. We use rule-based ad extraction, product attributes extraction based on the context, similarity-based entity classification, as well as to optimize the results based on users' behavior. Finally, we use real product data and verified the effectiveness of this system. The future work is to use more types of products to verify its effectiveness, and design a cloud-based identification method for huge amounts of data.

REFERENCES

Gomory, S., Hoch, R., Lee, J., Podlaseck, M., & Schonberg, E. (1999). *E-commerce intelligence: Measuring, analyzing, and reporting on merchandising effectiveness of online stores.* IBM Watson Research Center.

Kannan, A., Givoni, I. E., Agrawal, R., & Fuxman, A. (2011). Matching unstructured product offers to structured product specifications. In Proceedings of the 17th ACM SIGKDD International Conference on Knowledge Discovery and Data Mining (pp. 404-412). ACM.

Köpcke, H., Thor, A., Thomas, S., & Rahm, E. (2012). Tailoring entity resolution for matching product offers. In Proceedings of the 15th International Conference on Extending Database Technology (pp. 545-550). ACM.

Raghavan, N. S. (2005). Data mining in e-commerce: A survey. *Sadhana*, *30*(2-3), 275–289. doi:10.1007/BF02706248

Wang, H., Zhang, X., Li, J., & Gao, H. (2013). ProductSeeker: Entity-based product retrieval for e-commerce. In Proceedings of SIGIR 2013, (pp. 1085-1086). ACM.

Whang, S. E., Menestrina, D., Koutrika, G., Theobald, M., & Garcia-Molina, H. (2009). Entity resolution with iterative blocking. In Proceedings of the 35th SIGMOD International Conference on Management of Data (pp. 219-232). ACM.

Yu, C. (2002). Data cleaning method. *Journal of Computer Applications*, *22*(12), 128–130.

ADDITIONAL READING

Agrawal, R., & Ieong, S. (2012, August). Aggregating web offers to determine product prices. In Proceedings of the 18th ACM SIGKDD international conference on Knowledge discovery and data mining (pp. 435-443). ACM.

ALPAR, F. Z. (2010). Matchmaking Framework for B2B E-Marketplaces. *Informatica Economica*, *14*(4), 164–170.

Barbosa, G. P., & Silva, F. Q. (2001). An electronic marketplace architecture based on technology of intelligent agents and knowledge. In *E-Commerce Agents* (pp. 39–60). Springer Berlin Heidelberg. doi:10.1007/3-540-45370-9_4

Bazzanella, B., Palpanas, T., & Stoermer, H. (2009, August). Towards a general entity representation model. In Information Reuse & Integration, 2009. IRI'09. IEEE International Conference on (pp. 431-432). IEEE.

Gopalakrishnan, V., Iyengar, S. P., Madaan, A., Rastogi, R., & Sengamedu, S. (2012, October). Matching product titles using web-based enrichment. InProceedings of the 21st ACM international conference on Information and knowledge management (pp. 605-614). ACM.

Kim, Y. G., Lee, T., Chun, J., & Lee, S. G. (2006). Modified naïve bayes classifier for e-catalog classification. In *Data Engineering Issues in E-Commerce and Services* (pp. 246–257). Springer Berlin Heidelberg. doi:10.1007/11780397_20

Kolomvatsos, K., & Hadjiefthymiades, S. (2013). An extended Q-gram algorithm for calculating the relevance factor of products in electronic marketplaces. *Electronic Commerce Research and Applications*. doi:10.1016/j.elerap.2012.12.005

Kopcke, H., Thor, A., & Rahm, E. (2010). Learning-based approaches for matching web data entities. *Internet Computing, IEEE, 14*(4), 23–31. doi:10.1109/MIC.2010.58

Köpcke, H., Thor, A., & Rahm, E. (2010). Evaluation of entity resolution approaches on real-world match problems. *Proceedings of the VLDB Endowment, 3*(1-2), 484–493.

Miklós, Z., Bonvin, N., Bouquet, P., Catasta, M., Cordioli, D., Fankhauser, P.,..., & Stoermer, H. (2010, January). From web data to entities and back. InAdvanced Information Systems Engineering (pp. 302-316). Springer Berlin Heidelberg.

Nguyen, H., Fuxman, A., Paparizos, S., Freire, J., & Agrawal, R. (2011). Synthesizing products for online catalogs. *Proceedings of the VLDB Endowment, 4*(7), 409–418.

Thor, A. (2010). Toward an adaptive string similarity measure for matching product offers. GI Jahrestagung (1), 702-710.

KEY TERMS AND DEFINITIONS

Entity Resolution: Identify the data objects referring to the same real-world entity from a data object set.

E-Commerce: A type of industry where buying and selling of product or service is conducted over electronic systems such as the Internet and other computer networks.

Data Cleaning: The process of detecting and correcting (or removing) corrupt or inaccurate records from a record set, table, or database.

Data Mining: The computational process of discovering patterns in large data sets involving methods at the intersection of artificial intelligence, machine learning, statistics, and database systems. The overall goal of the data mining process is to extract information from a data set and transform it into an understandable structure for further use.

Semi-Structured Data: A form of structured data that does not conform with the formal structure of data models associated with relational databases or other forms of data tables, but nonetheless contains tags or other markers to separate semantic elements and enforce hierarchies of records and fields within the data.

Chapter 17
Entity Resolution in Healthcare

ABSTRACT

Abbreviations are common in biomedical documents, and many are ambiguous in the sense that they have several potential expansions. Identifying the correct expansion is necessary for language understanding and important for applications such as document retrieval. Identifying the correct expansion can be viewed as a Word Sense Disambiguation (WSD) problem. Previous approaches to resolving this problem have made use of various sources of information including linguistic features of the context in which the ambiguous term is used and domain-specific resources, such as UMLS. This chapter compares a range of knowledge sources, which have been previously used, and introduce a novel one: MeSH terms. The best performance is obtained using linguistic features in combination with MeSH terms.

INTRODUCTION

When we talk about an entity, it may refer to a person, a department, a team, corporation, cooperative, partnership, or other group with whom it is possible to conduct business. In the formal definition, an entity is something that exists by itself, although it need not be of material existence. In particular, abstractions and legal fictions are usually regarded as entities. In general, there is also no presumption that an entity is animate. Entity resolution is the process of finding non-identical duplicates in a relation and merging the duplicates into a single tuple (record). Record linkage is the process of finding related entries in one of more related relations in a database and creating links among them. Entity resolution and record linkage are important steps in data cleaning, which is removal of inaccuracies in databases and, as such, is part of populating a data warehouse. Generally,

data warehouses are important repositories for organization reporting on historical data. Where this information is derived from entities in the organization's concern, it is important for the underlying data to be as accurate as possible. Additionally, because duplicate entries are not allowed in databases, entity resolution can be useful in establishing when a tuple about to be entered will be a copy of one already present. Hence, it is very useful in maintaining of the integrity of a traditional database by providing accurate and consistent data. Moreover, entity resolution, also known as data matching or record linkage, is the task of identifying and matching records from several databases that refer to the same entities. Entity resolution is an important information quality process required before accurate analyses of entity-related data are possible. In the real life, we usually come across that something refers to the same real-world entity but in different representa-

DOI: 10.4018/978-1-4666-5198-2.ch017

tions. Also, this situation will happen frequently. For example, both CA and California refer to the same state of the United States but within different characters and length. Particularly, what we should do when come across this situation is to remove the situation of duplicate records that have same meaning but different characters in our databases.

Health information exchange (HIE) is the mobilization of healthcare information electronically across organization within a region, community or hospital system. Health information exchange systems facilitate the efforts of physicians and clinicians to meet high standards of patient care through electronic participation in a patient's continuity of care with multiple providers. The health information exchange implementation challenge will be create a standardized interoperable model that is patient centric, trusted, longitudinal, scalable, sustainable, and reliable. However, many health organizations are increasingly faced with the challenge of having large databases containing references to patients, physicians, drugs, and other entities that need to be matched in real-time with a stream of query records also containing entity references. Often, different people from different places may provide the same information with different forms in all kinds of data types. How to determine which one will be the useful and whether they are the same is meaningful for HIE to construct their systems. Hence, Entity resolution is a core process in health information exchange systems that have been evolving to address this problem. Most existing entity resolution methods focus on automated entity resolutions which are not perfect and face a precision-recall trade-off. By contrast, hand-cleaning methods even with visualization support can be slow and inefficient in finding duplicates but tend to be high precision, because there is a human-in-the-loop marking the final resolution decision. However, inspecting a large data set and hunting for duplicates can be like looking for the proverbial needle in a haystack. Therefore, while these approaches may have high precision, they tend to have low recall.

The number of documents discussing biomedical science is growing at an ever increasing rate, making it difficult to keep track of recent developments. Automated methods for cataloging, searching and navigating these documents would be of great benefit to researchers working in this area, as well as having potential benefits to medicine and other branches of science. Lexical ambiguity, the linguistic phenomenon where a term has more than one potential meaning, makes the automatic processing of text difficult. For example, "cold" has several possible meanings in the Unified Medical Language System Metathesaurus including "common cold", "cold sensation" and "Chronic Obstructive Airway Disease". The ability to accurately identify the meanings of terms is an important step in automatic text processing. It is necessary for applications such as information extraction and text mining which are important in the biomedical domain for tasks such as automated knowledge discovery. The NLM Indexing Initiative attempted to automatically index biomedical journals with concepts from the UMLS Metathesaurus and concluded that lexical ambiguity was the biggest challenge in the automation of the index process. Liu, Lussier & Friedman (2001) reported that an information extraction system originally designed to process radiology reports had problems with ambiguity when it was applied to more general biomedical texts. During the development of an automated knowledge discovery system Weeber found that it was necessary to resolve the ambiguity in the abbreviation MG in order to replicate a well-known literature-based discovery concerning the role of magnesium deficiency in migraine headaches (Weeber, Mork & Aronson 2001).

Word Sense Disambiguation (WSD for brief) is the process of resolving lexical ambiguities. WSD has been actively researched since the 1950s and is regarded as an important part of the process of understanding natural language texts. Schuemie provide an overview of WSD in the biomedical domain. Previous researchers have used a variety of approaches for WSD of biomedical text. Some of them have taken techniques proven to be effective for WSD of general text and applied them to ambiguities in the biomedical domain, while others have created systems using domain-specific biomedical resources. The techniques introduced in Chapter 3, Chapter 4, Chapter 5, and Chapter 9 could also be applied for WSD for different data format. However, there has been no direct comparison of which information sources are the most useful or whether combing a variety sources, a strategy which has been shown to be successful for WSD in the general domain, also improves results in the biomedical domain.

In this chapter, we will introduce how to process entity resolution in health information exchange, particularly, based on word sense disambiguation. We also introduce an effective and efficient method with the balance between the rate of precision and the rate of recall, though there are so many methods that have been proposed with high accuracy. We compare the effectiveness of a variety of knowledge sources of WSD in the biomedical domain. These include features which have been commonly used for WSD of general text as well as information derived from domain-specific resources. One of these features is MeSH terms, which we find to be particularly effectively when combined with generic features.

BACKGROUND

The office of the national coordinator for health information technology defines health information exchange as the electronic movement of health-related information among organizations according to nationally recognized standards definition further detailed by the Arkansas office of health information technology, which defines health information exchange as the system that provides the ability to electronically connect and exchange information between individuals and places, which includes the technology that allows real-time information to be shared in a secure and confidential manner, so that treatment can be rendered when and where it is needed.

Achieving statewide health information exchange structure requires tackling an array of barriers. One of important and of significant concern, there are a mass of uncertain and imprecise references to the entities in healthcare IT systems, such as physicians, hospitals, testing laboratories, doctor's offices, clinics and payers. The absence of unique identifiers for the underlying entities frequently results in databases that contain multiple references to the same entity. This can lead not only to data redundancy and inconsistency but also to inaccuracies in information visualization, query processing, and knowledge extraction. Entity resolution, which is the process of determining whether two references to real-world objects are referring to the same object or different objects, is a critical solution to identity references of Master Patient Index and Provider Index and Control the information quality in the health information exchange system.

Various researchers have explored the problem of disambiguating global abbreviations in biomedical documents. Gaudan et al. (2005) distinguishes two types of abbreviations, global and local. Global abbreviations are those found in documents without the expansion explicitly stated, while local abbreviations are defined in the same document in which the abbreviation occurs. Our work is concerned with the problem of disambiguating global abbreviations. Gaudan et al. (2005) point out that global abbreviations are often ambiguous.

Various researchers have explored the problem of disambiguating global abbreviations in biomedical documents. Liu et al. (2001, 2002) used several domain-specific knowledge sources to identify terms which are semantically related to each possible expansion but which has only one sense themselves. Instances of these terms were identified in a corpus of biomedical journal abstracts and used as training data. Their learning algorithm uses a variety of features including all words in the abstract and collocations of the ambiguous abbreviation. They report an accuracy of 97% on a small set of abbreviations. Liu et al. (2004) present a fully supervised approach. They compared a variety of supervised machine learning algorithms and found that the best performance over a set of 15 ambiguous abbreviations, 98.6%, was obtained using Naïve Bayes. Gaudan et al. (2005) uses a Support Vector Machine trained on a bag-of-words model and report an accuracy of 98.5%. Yu et al. (2006) experimented with two supervised learning algorithms, Naive Bayes and Support Vector Machines. They extracted a corpus containing examples of 60 abbreviations from a set of biomedical journal articles which was split so that abstracts in which the abbreviations were defined were used as training data and those in which no definition is found as test data. Abbreviations in the test portion were manually disambiguated. They report 79% coverage and 80% precision using a Naive Bayes classifier. Pakhomov (2002) applied a maximum entropy model to identify the meanings of ambiguous abbreviations in 10,000 rheumatology notes with around 89% accuracy. Joshi et al. (2006) disambiguated abbreviations in clinical notes using three supervised learning algorithms (Naive Bayes, decision trees and Support Vector Machines). They used a range of features and found that the best performance was obtained when these were combined. Unfortunately direct comparison of these methods is made difficult by the fact that various researchers have evaluated their approaches on different data sets.

A variety of approaches have also been proposed for the problem of disambiguating local abbreviations in biomedical documents. This task is equivalent to identify the abbreviation's expansion in the document. The problem is relatively straight-forward for abbreviations which are created by selecting the first character from each word in the expansion, such as "angiotensin converting enzyme (ACE)", but is more difficult

when this convention is not followed, for example "acetylchlinesterase (ACE)", "antisocial personality (ASP)" and "catalase (CAT)". Okazaki et al. (2008) recently proposed an approach to this problem based on discriminative alignment that has been shown to perform well. However, the most common solutions are based on heuristic approaches. The most likely one is identified by searching for the shortest candidate which contains all the characters in the abbreviation in the correct order.

ABBREVIATION DISAMBIGUATION SYSTEMS

The abbreviation disambiguation system is based on a state-of-the-art WSD system that has been adapted to the biomedical domain by augmenting it with additional knowledge sources. The system on which our approach is based (Agirre and Mart´ınez, 2004) participated in the Senseval-3 challenge (Mihalcea et al., 2004) with a performance close to the best system for the lexical sample tasks in two languages while the version adapted to the biomedical domain has achieved the best recorded results (Stevenson et al., 2008) on a standard test set consisting of ambiguous terms (Weeber et al., 2001).

This system is based on a supervised learning approach with features derived from text around the ambiguous word that are domain independent. We refer to these as generalfeatures. This feature set has been adapted for the disambiguation of biomed-ical text by adding further linguistic features and two different types of domain-specific features: CUIs (as used by McInnes et al. 2007) and Medical Subject Heading (MeSH) terms. This set of features is more diverse than have been explored by previous approaches to abbreviation disambiguation.

This part sources from Stevenson, Mark, et al (2009).

The NLM-WSD Data Set

WSD has been actively researched since the 1950s and is regarded as an important part of the process of understanding natural language texts.

Research on WSD for general text in the last decade has been driven by the SemEval evaluation frame-works which provide a set of standard evaluation materials for a variety of semantic evaluation tasks. At this point there is no specific collection for the biomedical domain in SemEval, but a test collection for WSD in biomedicine was developed by Weeber et al. (2001), and has been used as a benchmark by many independent groups. The UMLS Metathesaurus was used to provide a set of possible meanings for terms in biomedical text. 50 ambiguous terms which occur frequently in MEDLINE were chosen for inclusion in the test set. 100 instances of each term were selected from citations added to the MEDLINE database in 1998 and manually disambiguated by 11 annotators. Twelve terms were flagged as "problematic" due to substantial disagreement between the annotators. There are an average of 2.64 possible meanings per ambiguous term and the most ambiguous term, "cold" has five possible meanings. In addition to the meanings defined in UMLS, annotators had the option of assigning a special tag ("none") when none of the UMLS meanings seemed appropriate. Various researchers have chosen to evaluate their systems against subsets of this data set. Liu et al. (2004) excluded the 12 terms identified as problematic by Weeber et al. (2001) in addition to 16 for which the majority (most frequent) sense accounted for more than 90% of the instances, leaving 22 terms against which their system was evaluated. Leroy and Rindflesch (2005) used a set of 15 terms for which the majority sense accounted for less than 65% of the instances. Joshi et al. (2005) evaluated against the set union of those two sets, providing 28 ambiguous terms. McInnes et al. (2007) used

the set intersection of the two sets (dubbed the "common subset") which contained 9 terms.

The 50 terms which form the NLM-WSD data set represent a range of challenges for WSD systems. The Most Frequent Sense (MFS) heuristic has become a standard baseline in WSD (McCarthy et al., 2004) and is simply the accuracy which would be obtained by assigning the most common meaning of a term to all of its instances in a corpus. Despite its simplicity, the MFS heuristic is a hard baseline to beat, particularly for unsupervised systems, because it uses hand-tagged data to determine which sense is the most frequent. Analysis of the NLM-WSD data set showed that the MFS over all 50 ambiguous terms is 78%. The different subsets have lower MFS, indicating that the terms they contain are more difficult to disambiguate. The 22 terms used by (Liu et al., 2004) have a MFS of 69.9% while the set used by (Leroy and Rindflesch, 2005) has an MFS of 55.3%. The union and intersection of these sets have MFS of 66.9% and 54.9% respectively.

The Thesaurus

The feature set contains a number of parameters (e.g. thresholds for unigram and CUI frequencies). These parameters were set to the same values that were used when the system was applied to general biomedical terms (Stevenson et al., 2008) since these were found to perform well. We also use the entire abstract as the context of the ambiguous term for relevant features rather than just the sentence containing the term. Effects of altering these variables are consistent with previous results (Liu et al., 2004; Joshi et al., 2005; McInnes et al., 2007) and are not reported here.

Linquistic Features

The system uses a wide range of domain-independent features that are commonly employed for WSD.

- **Local Collocations:** A total of 41 features which extensively describe the context of the ambiguous word and fall into two main types: (1) bigrams and trigrams containing the ambiguous word constructed from lemmas, word forms or PoS tags (assigned using maximum-entropy-based part of speech tagger) and (2) preceding/following lemma/word-form of the content words (adjective, adverb, noun and verb) in the same sentence with the ambiguous abbreviation. For example, consider the sentence below with the target abbreviation BSA.

Lean BSA was obtained from height and lean body weight ...

The features would include the following: left-content-word-lemma "lean BSA", right-function-word-lemma "BSA be", left-POS "JJ NNP", right-POS "NNP VBD", left-content-word-form "Lean BSA", right-function-word-form "BSA was", etc.

- **Syntactic Dependencies:** These features model longer-distance dependencies of the ambiguous words than can be represented by the local collocations. Five relations are extracted: object, subject, noun-modifier, preposition and sibling. These are identified using heuristic patterns and regular expressions applied to PoS tag sequences around the ambiguous word. In the above example, "heparin" is noun-modifier feature of "adjustment".

- **Salient Bigrams:** Salient bigrams within the abstract with high log-likelihood scores computed from the NLM-WSD corpus, as described by Pedersen. In the experiments, bigrams that occur more than once and have a log-likelihood higher than 6.635 are included as features.

- **Unigrams:** Lemmas of all content words (nouns, verbs, adjectives, adverbs) in the target word's sentence and, as a separate feature, lemmas of all content words within a $\pm$ 4-word window around the target word, excluding those in a list of corpus-specific stop words (e.g. "ABSTRACT", "CONCLUSION"). In addition, the lemmas of any unigrams which appear at least twice in the entire corpus and are found in the abstract are also included as features.

However, we found that removing these features including syntactic dependencies led to a small increase in performance. The likely reason for this is that these features are noisy since the dependencies are difficult to identify accurately. In addition the heuristics used were not developed to be applied on biomedical documents.

Concept Unique Identifiers (CUIs)

The different senses of a word are often obtained from a sense inventory such as a dictionary or other resource. The Unified Medical Language System (UMLS) is one such sense inventory for the biomedical and clinical domain. In the UMLS, senses (or concepts) associated with words and terms are enumerated via Concept Unique Identifiers (CUIs).

The UMLS is more than just a dictionary of different word senses but also a framework encoded with different semantic and syntactic structures. Some such information includes related concepts, semantic types and semantic relations. A semantic type is a broad subject categorization assigned to a CUI. A semantic relation is the relationship between two semantic types.

MetaMap maps terms in biomedical text to senses (i.e. concepts) in the UMLS by identifying the CUIs of the content words in the text. MetaMap can be thought of as an all-words disambiguation system, and assigns a CUI (sense) to every word or term that it can in a running text using rules and patterns. The approach is based on supervised learning, where we collect some number of manually disambiguated examples of a given word, and learn a model from that data that only assigns senses to that target word. Thus, MetaMap is a broad coverage tool while our approach is more fine-grained and specific to a few words.

We follow the approach presented by McInnes et al. (2007) to generate features based on UMLS Concept Unique Identifiers (CUIs). The MetaMap program (Aronson, 2001) identifies all words and terms in a text which could be mapped onto a UMLS CUI. MetaMap does not disambiguate the senses of the concepts, instead it enumerates likely candidate concepts. For example, MetaMap will segment the phrase "Lean BSA was obtained from height and lean body weight ..." into four chunks: "Lean BSA", "obtained", "from height" and "lean body weight". The first chunk will be mapped onto three CUIs: "C1261466: BSA (Body surface area)", "C1511233: BSA (NCI Board of Scientific Advisors)" and "C0036774: BSA (Serum Albumin, Bovine)". The chunk "lean body weight" is mapped onto two concepts: "C0005910: Body Weight" and "C1305866: Body Weight (Weighing patient)".

CUIs occurring more than twice in an abstract are included as features. CUIs have been used for various disambiguation tasks in the biomedical domain, including disambiguation of ambiguous general terms (McInnes et al., 2007) and gene symbol disambiguation (Xu et al., 2007), but not, to our knowledge, for abbreviation disambiguation.

Medical Subject Headings (MeSH)

The Medical Subject Headings (MeSH) is the National Library of Medicine's controlled vocabulary thesaurus. MeSH was introduced in 1963. Created and updated by the United States National Library of Medicine (NLM), it is used by the MEDLINE/PubMed article database and by NLM's catalog of book holdings. It consists of sets of terms naming descriptors in a hierarchical structure that permits searching at various levels of specificity. The yearly printed version was discontinued in 2007 and MeSH is now available online only. It can be

browsed and downloaded free of charge through PubMed. By the way, MeSH has been translated into numerous languages.

MeSH is the National Library of Medicine's controlled vocabulary thesaurus. It consists of sets of terms naming descriptors in a hierarchical structure that permits searching at various levels of specificity. MeSH descriptors are arranged in both an alphabetic and a hierarchical structure. At the most general level of the hierarchical structure is very broad headings such as "Anatomy" or "Mental Disorders." More specific headings are found at more narrow levels of the twelve-level hierarchy, such as "Ankle" and "Conduct Disorder". Until now, there are 26,853 descriptors in 2013 MeSH, as well as over 213,000 entry terms that assist in finding the most appropriate MeSH Heading. For example, "Vitamin C" is an entry term to "Ascorbic Acid". In addition to these headings, there are more than 214,000 headings called Supplementary Concept Records (formerly Supplementary Chemical Records) within a separate thesaurus.

The descriptors or subject headings are arranged in a hierarchy. A given descriptor may appear at several locations in the hierarchical tree. The tree locations carry systematic labels known as tree numbers, and consequently one descriptor can carry several tree numbers. For example, the descriptor "Digestive System Neoplasms" has the tree numbers C06.301 and C04.588.274; C stands for Diseases, C06 for Digestive System Diseases and C06.301 for Digestive System Neoplasms; C04 for Neoplasms, C04.588 for Neoplasms By Site, and C04.588.274 also for Digestive System Neoplasms. The tree numbers of a given descriptor are subject to change as MeSH is updated. Every descriptor also carries a unique alphanumerical ID that will not change.

Most subject headings come with a short description or definition. See the MeSH description for diabetes type 2 as an example. The explanatory text is written by the MeSH team based on their standard sources if not otherwise stated. References are mostly encyclopaedias and standard textbooks of the subject areas. References for specific statements in the descriptions are not given, instead readers are referred to the bibliography.

In addition to the descriptor hierarchy, MeSH contains a small number of standard qualifiers (also known as subheadings), which can be added to descriptors to narrow down the topic. For example, "Measles" is a descriptor and "epidemiology" is a qualifier; "Measles/epidemiology" describes the subheading of epidemiological articles about Measles. The "epidemiology" qualifier can be added to all other disease descriptors. Not all descriptor/qualifier combinations are allowed since some of them may be meaningless. In all there are 83 different qualifiers.

In addition to the descriptors, MeSH also contains some 139,000 Supplementary Concept Records. These do not belong to the controlled vocabulary as such; instead they enlarge the thesaurus and contain links to the closest fitting descriptor to be used in a MEDLINE search. Many of these records describe chemical substances.

The MeSH thesaurus is used by NLM for indexing articles from 5,400 of the world's leading biomedical journals for the MEDLINE®/PubMED® database. It is also used for the NLM-produced database that includes cataloging of books, documents, and audiovisuals acquired by the Library. Each bibliographic reference is associated with a set of MeSH terms that describe the content of the item. Similarly, search queries use MeSH vocabulary to find items on a desired topic.

The Medical Subject Headings Section staff continually revises and updates the MeSH vocabulary. Staff subject specialists are responsible for areas of the health sciences in which they have knowledge and expertise. In addition to receiving suggestions from indexers and others, the staff collect new terms as they appear in the scientific literature or in emerging areas of research; define these terms within the context of existing vocabulary; and recommend their addition to MeSH. Professionals in various disciplines are also consulted regarding broad organizational changes and close coordination is maintained with various specialized vocabularies.

Learning Algorithms

We compared three machine leaning algorithms which have previously been shown to be effective for WSD tasks.

- **The Vector Space Model (VSM):** A memory-based learning algorithm which was used by Agirre and Martínez (2004). Each occurrence of an ambiguous word is represented as a binary vector in which each position indicates the occurrence/absence of a feature. A single centroid vector is generated for each sense during training. These centroids are compared with the vectors that represent new examples using the cosine metric to compute similarity. The sense assigned to a new example is that of the closest centroid.
- **The Naive Bayes (NB):** Classifier is based on a probabilistic model which assumes conditional independence of features given the target classification. It calculates the posterior probability that an instance belongs to a particular class given the prior probabilities of the class and the conditional probability of each feature given the target class.
- **Support Vector Machines (SVM):** Have been widely used in classification tasks. SVMs map feature vectors onto a high dimensional space and construct a classifier by searching for the hyper-plane that gives the greatest separation between the classes.

We used our own implementation of the Vector Space Model and Weka implementations (Witten and Frank, 2005) of the other two algorithms.

EVALUATION CORPUS

The most common method for generating corpora to train and test WSD systems is to manually annotate instances of ambiguous terms found in text with the appropriate meaning. However, this process is both time-consuming and difficult (Artstein and Poesio, 2008). An alternative to manual tagging is to find a way of automatically creating sense tagged corpora. For the translation of ambiguous English words Ng et al. (2003) made use of the fact that the various senses are often translated differently. For example when "bank" is used in the 'financial institution' sense it is translated to French as "banque" and "bord" when it is used to mean 'edge of river'. However, a disadvantage of this approach is that it relies on the existence of parallel text which may not be available. In the biomedical domain Liu et al. (2001, 2002) created a corpus using unambiguous related terms although they found that it was not always possible to identify suitable related terms.

Corpus Creation

Liu et al. (2001) also made use of the fact that when abbreviations are introduced they are often accompanied by their expansion, for example "BSA (bovine serum albumin)". This phenomenon was exploited to automatically generate a corpus of abbreviations and associated definitions by replacing the abbreviation and expansion with the abbreviation alone. For example, the sentence "The adsorption behavior of bovine serum albumin (BSA) on a Sepharose based hydrophobic interaction support has been studied." becomes "The adsorption behavior of BSA on a Sepharose based hydrophobic interaction support has been studied."

We used this approach to create a corpus of sense tagged abbreviations in biomedical documents using a set of 21 three letter abbreviations used in previous research on abbreviation disambiguation (Liu et al., 2001; Liu et al., 2002; Liu et al., 2004). Possible expansions for the majority of

these abbreviations were listed in these papers. For the few remaining ones possible expansions were taken from the Medstract database (Pustejovsky et al., 2002).

The retrieved documents are then processed to remove the expansions of each abbreviation. The Schwartz and Hearst (2003) algorithm for identifying abbreviations and the relevant expansion is then run over each of the retrieved abstracts to identify the correct expansion. The expansion is removed from the document and stored separately, effectively creating a sense tagged corpus. For convenience the abstracts are converted into a format similar to the one used for the NLM-WSD corpus (Weeber et al., 2001).

The resulting corpus consists of 55,655 documents. It can be seen that there is a wide variation between the number of abstracts retrieved for each abbreviation. CSF occurs in 14,871 abstracts and ASP in just 71. There is also a wide variation between the frequency of the most common expansion with over 99% of the occurrences of "CSF" representing one expansion ("cerebrospinal fluid") while for "ASP" two of the five possible expansions ("antisocial personality" and "aspartate") each account for almost 34% of the documents. In addition, several abbreviations have expansions which occur only rarely. For example, two of the expansions of "APC" ("atrial pressure complexes" and "aphidicholin") each have only a single document and account for just 0.03% of the instances of that abbreviation.

Corpus Reduction

Given the diversity of the abbreviations which were downloaded from Medline, both in terms of number of documents and distribution of senses, sub-sets of this corpus that are more suitable for WSD experiments were created. Corpora containing 100, 200 and 300 randomly selected examples of each abbreviation were generated and these are referred to as Corpus.100, Corpus.200 and Corpus.300 respectively.

Some of the 21 abbreviations were not suitable for inclusion in these corpora. Abbreviations were not included in the relevant corpus if an insufficient number of examples were retrieved from Medline. For example, only 71 abstracts containing "ASP" were retrieved and it is not included in any of the three corpora. Similarly, "ANA" and "FDP" are not included in Corpus.200 or Corpus.300 and "DIP" not included in Corpus.300. In addition, rare senses, those which represent less than 1% of the occurrences of an abbreviation in all retrieved abstracts, were discarded. Finally, two abbreviations ("ACE" and "CSF") have only one sense that is not "Rare" and these were also excluded from the reduced corpora.

Consequently, Corpus.100 contains 18 abbreviations ("ACE", "ASP" and "CSF" are excluded), Corpus.200 contains 16 ("ANA" and "FDP" are also excluded) and Corpus.300 contains 14 ("DIP" and "PVC" also excluded). Where an abbreviation is included in more than one corpus, all the examples in the smaller corpus are included in the larger one(s). For example, the 100 examples of "APC" in Corpus.100 are also included in Corpus.200 and Corpus.300.

The best performance is obtained using a combination of the linguistic and MeSH features, a pattern observed across all test sets and machine learning algorithms. Although the increase in performance gained from using both the linguistic and MeSH features compared to only the linguistic features is modest it is statistically significant, as is the difference between using both linguistic and MeSH features compared with using the MeSH features alone (Wilcoxon Signed Ranks Test, p <0.01).

Combining MeSH terms with other features generally improves performance, suggesting that the information contained in MeSH terms is distinct from the other knowledge sources. However, the inclusion of CUIs as features does not always improve performance and, in several cases, causes it to fall. This is consistent with McInnes et al. (2007) who concluded that CUIs were a useful information source for disambiguation of biomedical

text but that they were not as robust as a linguistic knowledge source (unigrams) which they had used for a previous system. The most likely reason for this is that our approach relies on automatically assigned CUIs, provided by MetaMap, while the MeSH terms are assigned manually. We do not have access to a reliable assignment of CUIs to text; if we had WSD would not be necessary. On the other hand, reliably assigned MeSH terms are readily available in Medline. The CUIs assigned by MetaMap are noisy while the MeSH terms are more reliable and prove to be a more useful knowledge source for WSD.

The Vector Space Model learning algorithm performs significantly better than both Support Vector Machine and Naive Bayes (Wilcoxon Signed Ranks Test, p <0.01). This pattern is observed regardless of which set of features are used, and it is consistent of the results in Senseval data from (Agirre and Mart´ınez, 2004).

Performance using MeSH terms as the only feature is better than using CUIs alone when the Naive Bayes and Support Vector Machine Learning algorithms are used. However, this is reversed for the Vector Space Model. The most likely reason is that the MeSH terms are far more sparse than CUIs which hinders this algorithm's performance.

Per-Word Analysis

The performance of Leroy and Rindflesch's system is always lower than the best result for each word. The systems reported by Joshi et al. (2005) and McInnes et al. (2007) are better than, or the same as, all other systems for 14 and 12 words respectively. The system reported here achieves results equal to or better than previously reported systems for 33 terms.

There are seven terms for which the performance of our approach is actually lower than the MFS baseline. (In fact, the baseline outperforms all systems for four of these terms.) The performance of our system is within 1% of the baseline for five of these terms. The remaining pair, "blood pressure" and "failure", are included in the set of problematic words identified by (Weeber et al., 2001). Examination of the possible senses shows that they include pairs with similar meanings. For example, the two senses which account for 98% of the instances of "blood pressure", which refer to the blood pressure within an organism and the result obtained from measuring this quantity, are very closely related semantically.

Linguistic Features

The WSD algorithm uses a wider range of linguistic features than previous approaches. The results show a comparison of each of the three types of linguistic features described in the Features section. Each type of feature is used alone and as part of a pair. Performance of each type of feature used alone is above the relevant MFS baseline, indicating that all three provide useful information for disambiguation. Unigrams are the most effective, followed by salient bigrams with local collocations the least effective. A possible reason for this may lie in the fact that local collocations comprise an extensive feature set, some of which may be redundant or noisy. For all words the pairing of local collocations with unigrams is the most effective with performance only 0.1% less accurate than combining all three types of linguistic features. However, combining salient bigrams with unigrams generates the best results over each of the four subsets and actually outperforms the combination of all three feature types for two of them.

CONCLUSION

The experiment shows that each of the three types of information (linguistic, CUIs and MeSH) can be used to create a classifier which achieves a reasonable level of disambiguation, since performance exceeds the relevant baseline score. This suggests that each of these can contribute to the disambiguation of ambiguous terms in biomedical text. In addition, disambiguation is improved by combining information sources. This is consistent with results over general text. For example, Stevenson and Wilks and Harley and Glennon showed that WSD could benefit from use of several different types of information from a dictionary. More recently Specia et al. showed that a combination of information sources could improve disambiguation of Portuguese verbs.

Combining MeSH terms with other features generally improves performance, suggesting that this provides the classifier with information not available from the others. An important difference between MeSH terms and the other features (linguistic and CUIs) is that they are assigned to the entire abstract rather than just individual terms and, as such, provide information about the topic of the abstract which would be hard to derive from more local features. This can be seen in the example usage of "adjustment" in the Features section above. The abstract in which this term is used discusses the treatment of coronary angioplasty using heparin, an anticoagulant. This abstract does not include the term "anticoagulant" but is assigned the MeSH term "D27.505.954.502.119: Anticoagulants". It would be difficult to determine that this abstract discusses anticoagulants using only the kinds of linguistic features used by many WSD systems. However, MeSH terms provide a way of identifying this information. These findings in this study are consistent with results from WSD of general text.

Unlike MeSH terms, the inclusion of CUIs as features does not always improve performance and, in several cases, causes it to fall. This is consistent with McInnes et al who concluded that CUIs were a useful information source for disambiguation of biomedical text but that they were not as robust as one type of linguistic information (unigrams) which they had used for a previous system. However, in some ways this result is surprising since CUIs are derived from UMLS, a resource which contains all the information in the MeSH hierarchy (the MeSH hierarchy is a subset of UMLS). The most likely reason for this is that our CUI assignment, provided by MetaMap, is automatic.

MetaMap does not attempt to disambiguate terms which map onto more than one UMLS concept so this CUI assignment is noisy.

This chapter has compared a variety of information sources for word sense disambiguation of ambiguous biomedical terms. The most accurate results can be achieved using a combination of linguistic restores commonly used for word sense disambiguation of general text. According to the situation that may happen in the real world, involving of health information exchange systems, we import the entity resolution technique to resolve them.

The several methods that have been proposed in the above could be demonstrated effective and efficient on the area of health information. Certainly, the main methods involve the specific data sets as training sets, and it is acknowledged that specific data could improve the accuracy of model and could also improve the rate of recall in some way. As we can know from the above, the decline of word sense disambiguation could solve the problem of duplicate records in databases and help us to remove duplicate records. In further study, a data-adaptive method to process entity resolution in health information exchange will be deeply studied.

REFERENCES

Agirre, E., & Martinez, D. (2004). The Basque Country University system: English and Basque tasks. In *Proceedings of the 3rd ACL Workshop on the Evaluation of Systems for the Semantic Analysis of Text (SENSEVAL)* (pp. 44-48). ACL.

Aronson, A. R. (2001). Effective mapping of biomedical text to the UMLS metathesaurus: The MetaMap program. In *Proceedings of the AMIA Symposium*. American Medical Informatics Association.

Artstein, R., & Poesio, M. (2008). Intercoder agreement for computational linguistics. *Computational Linguistics, 34*(4), 555–596. doi:10.1162/coli.07-034-R2

Gaudan, S., Kirsch, H., & Rebholz-Schuhmann, D. (2005). Resolving abbreviations to their senses in Medline. *Bioinformatics (Oxford, England), 21*(18), 3658–3664. doi:10.1093/bioinformatics/bti586 PMID:16037121

Joshi, R., Reingold, A. L., Menzies, D., & Pai, M. (2006). Tuberculosis among health-care workers in low-and middle-income countries: A systematic review. *PLoS Medicine, 3*(12), e494.

Leroy, G., & Rindflesch, T. C. (2005). Effects of information and machine learning algorithms on word sense disambiguation with small datasets. *International Journal of Medical Informatics.*

Liu, H., Lussier, Y. A., & Friedman, C. (2001). Disambiguating ambiguous biomedical terms in biomedical narrative text: An unsupervised method. *Journal of Biomedical Informatics, 34*(4), 249–261. doi:10.1006/jbin.2001.1023 PMID:11977807

Liu, H., Teller, V., & Friedman, C. (2004). A multi-aspect comparison study of supervised word sense disambiguation. *Journal of the American Medical Informatics Association, 11*(4), 320–331. doi:10.1197/jamia.M1533 PMID:15064284

McInnes, B. T. (n.d.). National library of medicine participation program report. *National Library of Medicine.*

Mihalcea, R., Chklovski, T., & Kilgarriff, A. (2004). The senseval-3 English lexical sample task. In *Proceedings of Senseval-3: Third International Workshop on the Evaluation of Systems for the Semantic Analysis of Text* (pp. 25-28). Academic Press.

Nakov, P. I., Schwartz, A. S., & Hearst, M. (2004). Citances: Citation sentences for semantic analysis of bioscience text. In *Proceedings of the SIGIR'04 Workshop on Search and Discovery in Bioinformatics* (pp. 81-88). ACM.

Okazaki, N., Ananiadou, S., & Tsujii, J. I. (2008). A discriminative alignment model for abbreviation recognition. In *Proceedings of the 22nd International Conference on Computational Linguistics* (vol. 1, pp. 657-664). Association for Computational Linguistics.

Pustejovsky, J., Castano, J., Saurí, R., Rumshinsky, A., Zhang, J., & Luo, W. (2002). Medstract: Creating large-scale information servers for biomedical libraries. In *Proceedings of the ACL-02 Workshop on Natural Language Processing in the Biomedical Domain* (vol. 3, pp. 85-92). Association for Computational Linguistics.

Stevenson, M., Guo, Y., Gaizauskas, R., & Martinez, D. (2008). Disambiguation of biomedical text using diverse sources of information. *BMC Bioinformatics*, 9(Suppl 11), S7. doi:10.1186/1471-2105-9-S11-S7 PMID:19025693

Weeber, M., Mork, J. G., & Aronson, A. R. (2001). Developing a test collection for biomedical word sense disambiguation. In *Proceedings of the AMIA Symposium*. American Medical Informatics Association.

Xu, H., Fan, J. W., Hripcsak, G., Mendonça, E. A., Markatou, M., & Friedman, C. (2007). Gene symbol disambiguation using knowledge-based profiles. *Bioinformatics (Oxford, England), 23*(8), 1015–1022. doi:10.1093/bioinformatics/btm056 PMID:17314123

Yu, Z., Tsuruoka, Y., & Tsujii, J. I. (2003). Automatic resolution of ambiguous abbreviations in biomedical texts using support vector machines and one sense per discourse hypothesis. In Proceedings of the SIGIR (Vol. 3, pp. 57-62). ACM.

ADDITIONAL READING

Bhattacharya, I., & Getoor, L. (2004, August). Deduplication and group detection using links. In KDD workshop on link analysis and group detection.

Bilenko, M., & Mooney, R. J. (2003, August). Adaptive duplicate detection using learnable string similarity measures. In Proceedings of the ninth ACM SIGKDD international conference on Knowledge discovery and data mining (pp. 39-48). ACM.

Christen, P., & Churches, T. (2005, April). A probabilistic deduplication, record linkage and geocoding system. In Proceedings of the Australian Research Council Health Data Mining Workshop, Canberra, Australia.

Cohen, W. W., & Richman, J. (2002, July). Learning to match and cluster large high-dimensional data sets for data integration. In Proceedings of the eighth ACM SIGKDD international conference on Knowledge discovery and data mining (pp. 475-480). ACM.

Jaro, M. A. (1978). *Unimatch: A record linkage system: Users manual.* Bureau of the Census.

Joshi, M., Pakhomov, S., Pedersen, T., & Chute, C. 2006. A comparative study of supervised learning as applied to acronym expansion in clinical reports. In Proceedings of the Annual Symposium of the American Medi-cal Informatics Association, pages 399–403, Washing-ton, DC.

Joshi, M., Pedersen, T., & Maclin, R. 2005. A Compara-tive Study of Support Vector Machines Applied to the Word Sense Disambiguation Problem for the Medical Domain. In Proceedings of the Second Indian Confer-ence on Artificial Intelligence (IICAI-05), pages 3449–3468, Pune, India.

Lanktree, C., & Briere, J. (1991, January). *Early data on the Trauma Symptom Checklist for Children (TSC-C)*. Paper presented at the meeting of the American Professional Society on the Abuse of Children, San Diego, CA.

Leroy, G., & Rindflesch, T. (2005). Effects of Information and Machine Learning algorithms on Word Sense Disambiguation with small datasets. *International Journal of Medical Informatics*, *74*(7-8), 573–585. doi:10.1016/j.ijmedinf.2005.03.013 PMID:15897005

Liu, H., Johnson, S., & Friedman, C. (2002). Automatic Resolution of Ambiguous Terms Based on Machine Learning and Conceptual Relations in the UMLS. *Journal of the American Medical Informatics Association*, *9*(6), 621–636. doi:10.1197/jamia.M1101 PMID:12386113

Liu, H., Lussier, Y., & Friedman, C. (2001). Disambiguating ambiguous biomedical terms in biomedical narrative text: An unsupervised method. *Journal of Biomedical Informatics*, *34*, 249–261. doi:10.1006/jbin.2001.1023 PMID:11977807

Liu, H., Teller, V., & Friedman, C. (2004). A Multiaspect Comparison Study of Supervised Word Sense Disam-biguation. *Journal of the American Medical Informatics Association*, *11*(4), 320–331. doi:10.1197/jamia.M1533 PMID:15064284

Ristad, E. S., & Yianilos, P. N. (1998). Learning string-edit distance. Pattern Analysis and Machine Intelligence. *IEEE Transactions on*, *20*(5), 522–532.

Smith, T. F., & Waterman, M. S. (1981). Identification of Common Molecular Subsequences. *Journal of Molecular Biology*, *147*, 195–197. doi:10.1016/0022-2836(81)90087-5 PMID:7265238

Ullmann, J. R. (1977). A binary n-gram technique for automatic correction of substitution, deletion, insertion and reversal errors in words. *The Computer Journal*, *20*(2), 141–147. doi:10.1093/comjnl/20.2.141

Waterman, M. S., Smith, T. F., & Beyer, W. A. (1976). Some biological sequence metrics. *Advances in Mathematics*, *20*(3), 367–387. doi:10.1016/0001-8708(76)90202-4

Weeber, M., Mork, J., & Aronson, A. 2001. Developing a Test Collection for Biomedical Word Sense Disambiguation. InProceedings of AMAI Symposium, pages 746–50, Washington, DC.

Witten, I., & Frank, E. (2005). *Data Mining: Practical machine learning tools and techniques*. San Francisco: Morgan Kaufmann.

KEY TERMS AND DEFINITIONS

Computational Linguistics: An interdisciplinary field dealing with the statistical or rule-based modeling of natural language from a computational perspective.

Entity Resolution: Identify entity that in real world or some domains.

Learning Algorithm: A method based on machine learning and data mining.

Statistical Classification: A problem of identifying to which of a set of categories a new observation belongs, on the basis of a training set of data containing observations whose category membership is known.

Supervised Learning: A kind of machine learning task of inferring a function from labeled training data.

Unsupervised Learning: The problem of trying to find hidden structure in unlabeled data.

Word Sense Disambiguation: Governs the process of identifying which sense of a word is used in a sentence, when the word has multiple meanings.

Compilation of References

Adamic, L. A., & Adar, E. (2003). Friends and neighbors on the web. *Social Networks, 25*(3), 211–230. doi:10.1016/S0378-8733(03)00009-1

Agirre, E., & Martinez, D. (2004). The Basque Country University system: English and Basque tasks. In *Proceedings of the 3rd ACL Workshop on the Evaluation of Systems for the Semantic Analysis of Text (SENSEVAL)* (pp. 44-48). ACL.

Al-Kamha, R., & Embley, D. W. (2004). Grouping search-engine returned citations for person-name queries. In Proceedings of the 6th Annual ACM International Workshop on Web Information and Data Management (pp. 96-103). ACM.

Alpaydin, E. (2004). *Introduction to machine learning.* Cambridge, MA: MIT Press.

Andritsos, P., Fuxman, A., & Miller, R. J. (2006). *Clean answers over dirty databases: A probabilistic approach.* Paper presented at the Data Engineering, 2006. New York, NY.

Antonellis, I., GarciaMolina, H., & Chang, C. (2008). Simrank++: Query rewriting through link analysis of the click graph. In *Proceedings of PVLDB 2008.* PVLDB.

Arasu, A., & Kaushik, R. (2009). A grammar-based entity representation framework for data cleaning. In *Proceedings of the 2009 ACM SIGMOD International Conference on Management of Data* (pp. 233-244). ACM.

Arasu, A., Ganti, V., & Kaushik, R. (2006). *Efficient exact set-similarity joins.* Paper presented at the 32nd International Conference on Very Large Data Bases. New York, NY.

Arasu, A., Chaudhuri, S., & Kaushik, R. (2008). Transformation-based framework for record matching. In *Proceedings of Data Engineering* (pp. 40–49). IEEE.

Arasu, A., Chaudhuri, S., & Kaushik, R. (2009). Learning string transformations from examples. *Proceedings of the VLDB Endowment, 2*(1), 514–525.

Arasu, A., Ré, C., & Suciu, D. (2009). Large-scale deduplication with constraints using dedupalog. In *Proceedings of Data Engineering* (pp. 952–963). IEEE.

Aronson, A. R. (2001). Effective mapping of biomedical text to the UMLS metathesaurus: The MetaMap program. In *Proceedings of the AMIA Symposium.* American Medical Informatics Association.

Artstein, R., & Poesio, M. (2008). Intercoder agreement for computational linguistics. *Computational Linguistics, 34*(4), 555–596. doi:10.1162/coli.07-034-R2

Aslam, J. A., Pelekhov, E., & Rus, D. (2004). The star clustering algorithm for static and dynamic information organization. *J. Graph Algorithms Appl., 8*, 95–129. doi:10.7155/jgaa.00084

Bagga, A., & Baldwin, B. (1998). Algorithms for scoring coreference chains. In Proceedings of the First International Conference on Language Resources and Evaluation Workshop on Linguistics Conference (Vol. 1, pp. 563-6). Academic Press.

Bagga, A., & Baldwin, B. (1998). Entity-based cross-document coreferencing using the vector space model. In *Proceedings of the 17th International Conference on Computational Linguistics* (vol. 1, pp. 79-85). Association for Computational Linguistics.

Bansal, N., Blum, A., & Chawla, S. (2002). Correlation clustering. In *Proceedings of FOCS.* FOCS.

Bansal, N., Blum, A., & Chawla, S. (2004). Corrlation clustering. *Machine Learning, 56*(1-3), 89–113. doi:10.1023/B:MACH.0000033116.57574.95

Barabasi, A. L., & Bonabeau, E. (2003). Scale-free networks. *Scientific American*, *288*, 50–59. doi:10.1038/scientificamerican0503-60 PMID:12701331

Barabási, A., & Albert, R. (1999). Emergence of scaling in random networks. *Science*, *286*(5439), 509–512. doi:10.1126/science.286.5439.509

Barabási, A., & Albert, R. (1999). Mirror, mirror on the web: A study of host pairs with replicated content. *Computer Networks*, *31*, 1579–1590. doi:10.1016/S1389-1286(99)00021-3

Barbay, J., & Kenyon, C. (2002). *Adaptive intersection and t-threshold problems*.

Batini, C., & Scannapieca, M. (2006). *Data quality*. Berlin: Springer.

Bayardo, R. J., Ma, Y., & Srikant, R. (2007). Scaling up all pairs similarity search. In *Proceedings of WWW*, (pp. 131-140). IEEE.

Behm, A., Ji, S., Li, C., & Lu, J. (2009). *Space-constrained gram-based indexing for efficient approximate string search*. Paper presented at the Data Engineering, 2009. New York, NY.

Benjelloun, O., Garcia-Molina, H., Menestrina, D., Su, Q., Whang, S. E., & Widom, J. (2009). Swoosh: A generic approach to entity resolution. The VLDB Journal—The International Journal on Very Large Data Bases, *18*(1), 255-276.

Berkhin, P. (2006). A survey of clustering data mining techniques. In *Grouping multidimensional data* (pp. 25–71). Berlin: Springer. doi:10.1007/3-540-28349-8_2

Bernstein, P. (2007). Model management 2.0: manipulating richer mappings. In *Proceedings of SIGMOD 2007*. ACM.

Bernstein, P. (2006). *Implementing mapping composition*. VLDB.

Bertini, M., Del Bimbo, A., & Nunziati, W. (2006). Video clip matching using mpeg-7 descriptors and edit distance. In Image and video retrieval (pp. 133-142). Berlin: Springer.

Bhattacharya, I., & Getoor, L. (2005). Relational clustering for multi-type entity resolution. In *Proceedings of the 4th International Workshop on Multi-Relational Mining* (pp. 3-12). ACM.

Bhattacharya, I., & Getoor, L. (2007). Collective entity resolution in relational data. *ACM Transactions on Knowledge Discovery from Data*, *1*(1), 5. doi:10.1145/1217299.1217304

Bian, X., Wang, H., & Gao, H. (2011). Schema mapping with quality assurance for data integration.[APWeb.]. *Proceedings of APWeb*, *2011*, 472–483.

Bilenko, M., & Mooney, R. J. (2003). Adaptive duplicate detection using learnable string similarity measures. In Proceedings of the Ninth ACM SIGKDD International Conference on Knowledge Discovery and Data Mining (pp. 39-48). ACM.

Bille, P. (2005). A survey on tree edit distance and related problems. *Theoretical Computer Science*, *337*(1), 217–239. doi:10.1016/j.tcs.2004.12.030

Borkar, V., Deshmukh, K., & Sarawagi, S. (2001, May). Automatic segmentation of text into structured records. *SIGMOD Record*, *30*(2), 175–186. doi:10.1145/376284.375682

Boulos, J., Dalvi, N., Mandhani, B., Mathur, S., Re, C., & Suciu, D. (2005). *MYSTIQ: A system for finding more answers by using probabilities*. Paper presented at the 2005 ACM SIGMOD International Conference on Management of Data. New York, NY.

Brian, H. A. Y. E. S., Brunschwiler, T., Dill, H., Christ, H., Falsafi, B., Fischer, M., & Zollinger, M. (2008). Cloud computing. *Communications of the ACM*, *51*(7), 9–11. doi:10.1145/1364782.1364786

Brizan & Tansel. (2006). A survey of entity resolution and record linkage methodologies. *Communications of the IIMA*, *6*(3).

Broder, A. Z. (1997). On the resemblance and containment of documents. In *Proceedings of Compression and Complexity of Sequences* (pp. 21–29). IEEE.

Cai, J., & Strube, M. (2010). Evaluation metrics for end-to-end coreference resolution systems. In Proceedings of the 11th Annual Meeting of the Special Interest Group on Discourse and Dialogue (pp. 28-36). Association for Computational Linguistics.

Carvalho, J. C., & da Silva, A. S. (2003). Finding similar identities among objects from multiple web sources. In *Proceedings of the 5th ACM International Workshop on Web Information and Data Management* (pp. 90-93). ACM.

Chandel, A., Hassanzadeh, O., Koudas, N., Sadoghi, M., & Srivastava, D. (2007). Benchmarking declarative approximate selection predicates. In *Proceedings of the 2007 ACM SIGMOD International Conference on Management of Data* (pp. 353-364). ACM.

Charikar, M. S. (2002). *Similarity estimation techniques from rounding algorithms*. Paper presented at the Thiry-Fourth Annual ACM Symposium on Theory of Computing. New York, NY.

Charikar, M., Guruswami, V., & Wirth, V. (2005). Clustering with qualitative information. *Journal of Computer and System Sciences*, *71*(3), 360–383. doi:10.1016/j.jcss.2004.10.012

Chaudhuri, S., Ganjam, K., Ganti, V., & Motwani, R. (2003). Robust and efficient fuzzy match for online data cleaning. In *Proceedings of the 2003 ACM SIGMOD International Conference on Management of Data* (pp. 313-324). ACM.

Chaudhuri, S., Ganti, V., & Kaushik, R. (2006). A primitive operator for similarity joins in data cleaning. *ICDE, 5*.

Chaudhuri, S., Sarma, A. D., Ganti, V., & Kaushik, R. (2007). Leveraging aggregate constraints for deduplication. In *Proceedings of SIGMOD*. ACM.

Chiticariu, L., & Tan, W. C. (2006). Debugging schema mappings with routes. In *Proceedings of the 32nd International Conference on Very Large Data Bases* (pp. 79-90). VLDB Endowment.

Cho, J., Shivakumar, N., & Garcia-Molina, H. (2000). Finding replicated web collections. *SIGMOD Record*, *29*(2), 355–366. doi:10.1145/335191.335429

Clauset, A., Newman, M. E. J., & Moore, C. (2004). Finding community structure in very large networks. *Physical Review E: Statistical, Nonlinear, and Soft Matter Physics*, *70*(6), 066111. doi:10.1103/PhysRevE.70.066111

Cohen, W. W., & Sarawagi, S. (2004). Exploiting dictionaries in named entity extraction: Combining semi-markov extraction processes and data integration methods. In *Proceedings of the Tenth ACM SIGKDD International Conference on Knowledge Discovery and Data Mining* (pp. 89-98). ACM.

Cohen, W. W., Ravikumar, P., & Fienberg, S. E. (2003). A comparison of string distance metrics for name-matching tasks. In *Proceedings of the IJCAI-2003 Workshop on Information Integration on the Web (IIWeb-03)* (Vol. 47). IJCAI.

Cohen, W. W. (1998). Integration of heterogeneous databases without common domains using queries based on textual similarity. *SIGMOD Record*, *27*(2), 201–212. doi:10.1145/276305.276323

Cohen, W. W. (2000). Data integration using similarity joins and a word-based information representation language. *ACM Transactions on Information Systems*, *18*(3), 288–321. doi:10.1145/352595.352598

Cormen, T. H., Leiserson, C. E., & Rivest, R. L. (1990). *Introduction to algorithms*. Cambridge, MA: McGraw Hill and MIT Press.

Cover, T. M., & Thomas, J. A. (2012). *Elements of information theory*. New York: Wiley-Interscience.

Dasu, T., Johnson, T., Muthukrishnan, S., & Shkapenyuk, V. (2002). Mining database structure, or, how to build a data quality browser. In *Proceedings of the 2002 ACM SIGMOD International Conference on Management of Data* (pp. 240-251). ACM.

Dean, J., & Ghemawat, S. (2008). MapReduce: Simplified data processing on large clusters. *Communications of the ACM*, *51*(1), 107–113. doi:10.1145/1327452.1327492

Demaine, E. D., Emanuel, C., Fiat, A., & Immorlica, A. (2006). Correlation clustering in general weighted graphs. *Theoretical Computer Science*, *361*(2), 172–187. doi:10.1016/j.tcs.2006.05.008

Dittrich, J.-P., & Seeger, B. (2001). *GESS: A scalable similarity-join algorithm for mining large data sets in high dimensional spaces.*

Dong, X., Halevy, A., & Madhavan, J. (2005). Reference reconciliation in complex information spaces. In *Proceedings of the 2005 ACM SIGMOD International Conference on Management of Data* (pp. 85-96). ACM.

Dongen, S. V. (2000). *Graph clustering by flow simulation.* (PhD thesis). University of Utrecht, Utrecht, The Netherlands.

Dong, X. L., Berti-Equille, L., & Srivastava, D. (2009a). Integrating conflicting data: The role of source dependence. *Proceedings of the VLDB Endowment, 2*(1), 550–561.

Dong, X. L., Halevy, A., & Yu, C. (2009). Data integration with uncertainty. *The VLDB Journal, 18*(2), 469–500. doi:10.1007/s00778-008-0119-9

Eckerson, W. W. (2002). Data quality and the bottom line: Achieving business success through a commitment to high quality data. The Data Warehousing Institute, 1-36.

Elmagarmid, A. K., Ipeirotis, P. G., & Verykios, V. S. (2007). Duplicate record detection: A survey. *IEEE Transactions on Knowledge and Data Engineering, 19*(1), 1–16. doi:10.1109/TKDE.2007.250581

English, L. (1997). Plain English on data quality. *DM Review, 7*, 14–16.

Fagin, R., Kolaitis, P. G., Popa, L., & Tan, W. C. (2005). Composing schema mappings: Second-order dependencies to the rescue. *ACM Transactions on Database Systems, 30*(4), 994–105. doi:10.1145/1114244.1114249

Fan, W., Jia, X., Li, J., & Ma, S. (2009). *Reasoning about record matching rules.* Paper presented at VLDB. Lyon, France.

Fan, X., Wang, J., Pu, X., Zhou, L., & Lv, B. (2011). On graph-based name disambiguation. *Journal of Data Quality.*

Fan, W., Geerts, F., & Wijsen, J. (2012). Determining the currency of data. *ACM Transactions on Database Systems, 37*(4), 25. doi:10.1145/2389241.2389244

Fan, W., Li, J., Ma, S., Tang, N., Wu, Y., & Wu, Y. (2010). Graph pattern matching: from intractable to polynomial time. *Proceedings of the VLDB Endowment, 3*(1-2), 264–275.

Fan, W., Li, J., Ma, S., Wang, H., & Wu, Y. (2010). Graph homomorphism revisited for graph matching. *Proceedings of the VLDB Endowment, 3*(1-2), 1161–1172.

Fan, X., Wang, J., Pu, X., Zhou, L., & Lv, B. (2011). On graph-based name disambiguation. *J. Data and Information Quality, 2*(2), 10.

Fellegi, I. P., & Sunter, A. B. (1969). A theory for record linkage. *Journal of the American Statistical Association, 64*(328), 1183–1210. doi:10.1080/01621459.1969.10501049

Feng, Y. E., & Jingsheng, X. (2009). Mapping XML DTD to relational schema. In *Proceedings of Database Technology and Applications* (pp. 557–560). IEEE.

Flake, G. W., Tarjan, R. E., & Tsioutsiouliklis, K. (2004). Graph clustering and minimum cut trees. *Internet Mathematics, 1*(4), 385–408. doi:10.1080/15427951.2004.10129093

Fogaras, D., & Rácz, B. (2005). Scaling link-based similarity search. In *Proceedings of the 14th International Conference on World Wide Web.* IEEE.

Frey, B. J., & Dueck, D. (2007). Clustering by passing messages between data points. *Science, 315*, 972. doi:10.1126/science.1136800

Fuxman, A., Fazli, E., & Miller, R. J. (2005). *Conquer: Efficient management of inconsistent databases.* Paper presented at the 2005 ACM SIGMOD International Conference on Management of Data. New York, NY.

Fuxman, A. D., & Miller, R. J. (2005). First-order query rewriting for inconsistent databases.[Berlin: Springer.]. *Proceedings of Database Theory-ICDT, 2005*, 337–351.

Galland, A., Abiteboul, S., Marian, A., & Senellart, P. (2010). Corroborating information from disagreeing views. In Proceedings of the Third ACM International Conference on Web Search and Data Mining (pp. 131-140). ACM.

Garcia-Molina, H., Ullman, J. D., & Widom, J. (2000). *Database system implementation* (Vol. 654). Englewood Cliffs, NJ: Prentice Hall.

Gaudan, S., Kirsch, H., & Rebholz-Schuhmann, D. (2005). Resolving abbreviations to their senses in Medline. *Bioinformatics (Oxford, England), 21*(18), 3658–3664. doi:10.1093/bioinformatics/bti586 PMID:16037121

Getoor, L., & Machanavajjhala, A. (2012). Entity resolution: theory, practice & open challenges. *Proceedings of the VLDB Endowment, 5*(12), 2018–2019.

Goemans, M. X., & Williamson, D. P. (1995). Improved approximation algorithms for maximum cut and satisfiability problems using semidefinite programming. *Journal of the ACM, 42*(6), 1115–1145. doi:10.1145/227683.227684

Goldberg, A. B., Zhu, X., & Wright, S. (2007). Dissimilarity in graph-based semi-supervised classification. In Proceedings of Eleventh International Conference on Artificial Intelligence and Statistics (AISTATS) (Vol. 2, p. 46). AISTATS.

Gomory, S., Hoch, R., Lee, J., Podlaseck, M., & Schonberg, E. (1999). *E-commerce intelligence: Measuring, analyzing, and reporting on merchandising effectiveness of online stores*. IBM Watson Research Center.

Guha, S., Jagadish, H. V., Koudas, N., Srivastava, D., & Yu, T. (2002). Approximate XML joins. In *Proceedings of the 2002 ACM SIGMOD International Conference on Management of Data* (pp. 287-298). ACM.

Hadjieleftheriou, M., Chandel, A., Koudas, N., & Srivastava, D. (2008). *Fast indexes and algorithms for set similarity selection queries*. Paper presented at the Data Engineering, 2008. New York, NY.

Hadjieleftheriou, M., Koudas, N., & Srivastava, D. (2009). *Incremental maintenance of length normalized indexes for approximate string matching*. Paper presented at the 35th SIGMOD International Conference on Management of Data. New York, NY.

Hamdoun, O., Moutarde, F., Stanciulescu, B., & Steux, B. (2008). Person re-identification in multi-camera system by signature based on interest point descriptors collected on short video sequences. In *Proceedings of Distributed Smart Cameras* (pp. 1–6). IEEE.

Hamers, L., Hemeryck, Y., Herweyers, G., Janssen, M., Keters, H., Rousseau, R., & Vanhoutte, A. (1989). Similarity measures in scientometric research: The Jaccard index versus Salton's cosine formula. *Information Processing & Management, 25*(3), 315–318. doi:10.1016/0306-4573(89)90048-4

Han, J., & Kamber, M. (2000). *Data mining: Concepts and techniques*. San Francisco: Morgan Kaufmann.

Hassanzadeh, O., & Miller, R. J. (2009). Creating probabilistic databases from duplicated data. *The VLDB Journal—The International Journal on Very Large Data Bases, 18*(5), 1141-1166.

Hassanzadeh, O., Chiang, F., Miller, R., & Lee, H. C. (2009). Framework for evaluating clustering algorithms in duplicate detection. *PVLDB, 2*(1), 1282–1293.

Hassanzadeh, O., & Miller, R. J. (2009). Creating probabilistic databases from duplicated data. *The VLDB Journal, 18*(5), 1141–1166. doi:10.1007/s00778-009-0161-2

Haveliwala, T. H., Gionis, A., & Indyk, P. (2000). Scalable techniques for clustering the web. *WebDB*, 129-134

Hernández, M. A., & Stolfo, S. J. (1995). The merge/purge problem for large databases. *SIGMOD Record, 24*(2), 127–138. doi:10.1145/568271.223807

Hochba, D. S. (1997). Approximation algorithms for NP-hard problems. *ACM SIGACT News, 28*(2), 40–52. doi:10.1145/261342.571216

Hopcroft, J. E. (2008). *Introduction to automata theory, languages, and computation* (3rd ed.). New Delhi: Pearson Education India.

Indyk, P., & Motwani, R. (1998). *Approximate nearest neighbors: Towards removing the curse of dimensionality*. Paper presented at the Thirtieth Annual ACM Symposium on Theory of Computing. New York, NY.

Jaro, M. A. (1989). Advances in record-linkage methodology as applied to matching the 1985 census of Tampa, Florida. *Journal of the American Statistical Association, 84*(406), 414–420. doi:10.1080/01621459.1989.10478785

Jeh, G., & Widom, J. (2002). SimRank: A measure of structural-context similarity. In *Proceedings of KDD*. KDD.

Joshi, S., Agrawal, N., Krishnapuram, R., & Negi, S. (2003). A bag of paths model for measuring structural similarity in web documents. In *Proceedings of the ninth ACM SIGKDD International Conference on Knowledge Discovery and Data Mining* (pp. 577-582). ACM.

Joshi, R., Reingold, A. L., Menzies, D., & Pai, M. (2006). Tuberculosis among health-care workers in low-and middle-income countries: A systematic review. *PLoS Medicine*, *3*(12), e494.

Junker, M., Hoch, R., & Dengel, A. (1999). On the evaluation of document analysis components by recall, precision, and accuracy. In *Proceedings of Document Analysis and Recognition* (pp. 713–716). IEEE.

Kade, A. M., & Heuser, C. A. (2008). Matching XML documents in highly dynamic applications. In *Proceedings of the Eighth ACM Symposium on Document Engineering* (pp. 191-198). ACM.

Kannan, A., Givoni, I. E., Agrawal, R., & Fuxman, A. (2011). Matching unstructured product offers to structured product specifications. In Proceedings of the 17th ACM SIGKDD International Conference on Knowledge Discovery and Data Mining (pp. 404-412). ACM.

Knuth, D. E. (1973). Sorting and searching. *The Art of Computer Programming, 3*.

Köhler, H., Zhou, X., Sadiq, S., Shu, Y., & Taylor, K. (2010). Sampling dirty data for matching attributes. In *Proceedings of the 2010 International Conference on Management of Data* (pp. 63-74). ACM.

Kolaitis, P. G. (2005). Schema mappings, data exchange, and metadata management. In *Proceedings of the Twenty-Fourth ACM SIGMOD-SIGACT-SIGART Symposium on Principles of Database Systems* (pp. 61-75). ACM.

Kolb, L., Kopcke, H., Thor, A., & Rahm, E. (2011). Learning-based entity resolution with MapReduce. In Proceedings of the Third International Workshop on Cloud Data Management (pp. 1-6). ACM.

Köpcke, H., Thor, A., Thomas, S., & Rahm, E. (2012). Tailoring entity resolution for matching product offers. In *Proceedings of the 15th International Conference on Extending Database Technology* (pp. 545-550). ACM.

Kopcke, H., Thor, A., & Rahm, E. (2010). Evaluation of entity resolution approaches on real-world match problems. *Proceedings of the VLDB Endowment, 3*(1-2), 484–493.

Kopcke, H., Thor, A., & Rahm, E. (2010). Learning-based approaches for matching web data entities. *IEEE Internet Computing, 14*(4), 23–31. doi:10.1109/MIC.2010.58

Koudas, N., Sarawagi, S., & Srivastava, D. (2006). Record linkage: Similarity measures and algorithms. In *Proceedings of SIGMOD*. ACM.

Koudas, N., & Sevcik, K. (1998). High dimensional similarity joins: Algorithms and performance evaluation. In *Proceedings of Data Engineering*. IEEE.

Kuhn, H. W. (1955). The Hungarian method for the assignment problem. *Naval Research Logistics Quarterly, 2*(1-2), 83–97. doi:10.1002/nav.3800020109

Laender, H., Gongalves, M. A., Cota, R. G., Ferreira, A. A., Santos, R. L., & Silva, A. J. (2008). Keeping a digital library clean: new solutions to old problems. In Proceedings of the Eighth ACM Symposium on Document Engineering (pp. 257-262). ACM.

Lee, J.-H., Kim, D.-H., & Chung, C.-W. (1999). *Multidimensional selectivity estimation using compressed histogram information.* Paper presented at the ACM SIGMOD Record. New York, NY.

Lee, H., Ng, R. T., & Shim, K. (2011). Similarity join size estimation using locality sensitive hashing. *Proceedings of the VLDB Endowment, 4*(6), 338–349.

Leitão, L., Calado, P., & Weis, M. (2007). Structure-based inference of xml similarity for fuzzy duplicate detection. In *Proceedings of the Sixteenth ACM Conference on Conference on Information and Knowledge Management* (pp. 293-302). ACM.

Lenzerini, M. (2002). *Data integration: A theoretical perspective.* Paper presented at the Twenty-First ACM SIGMOD-SIGACT-SIGART Symposium on Principles of Database Systems. New York, NY.

Leroy, G., & Rindflesch, T. C. (2005). Effects of information and machine learning algorithms on word sense disambiguation with small datasets. *International Journal of Medical Informatics*.

Levenshtein, V. I. (1966). Binary codes capable of correcting deletions, insertions and reversals. *Soviet Physics, Doklady, 10,* 707.

Li, C. Bin Wang, & Yang, X. (2007). VGRAM: Improving performance of approximate queries on string collections using variable-length grams. In *Proceedings of the 33rd International Conference on Very Large Data Bases.* VLDB Endowment.

Li, C., Lu, J., & Lu, Y. (2008). *Efficient merging and filtering algorithms for approximate string searches.*

Li, C., Wang, B., & Yang, X. (2007). *VGRAM: Improving performance of approximate queries on string collections using variable-length grams.* Paper presented at the 33rd International Conference on Very Large Data Bases. New York, NY.

Li, L., Wang, H., Gao, H., & Li, J. (2010). EIF: A framework of effective entity identification. In *Proceedings of WAIM 2010.* WAIM.

Liben-Nowell, D., & Kleinberg, J. (2007). The link-prediction problem for social networks. *Journal of the American Society for Information Science and Technology, 58*(7), 1019–1031. doi:10.1002/asi.20591

Li, L., Li, J., Wang, H., & Gao, H. (2011). Context-based entity description rule for entity resolution.[CIKM.]. *Proceedings of CIKM, 2011,* 1725–1730.

Li, L., Wang, H., Gao, H., & Li, J. (2010). EIF: A framework of effective entity identification.[WAIM.]. *Proceedings of WAIM, 2010,* 717–728.

Li, M., Wang, H., Li, H., & Gao, H. (2010). Efficient duplicate record detection based on similarity estimation. [WAIM.]. *Proceedings of WAIM, 2010,* 595–607.

Lin, B., Shah, R., Frederking, R., & Gershman, A. (2010). Cone: Metrics for automatic evaluation of named entity co-reference resolution. In Proceedings of the 2010 Named Entities Workshop (pp. 136-144). Association for Computational Linguistics.

Lin, Z., Lyu, M. R., & King, I. (2009). MatchSim: A novel neighbor-based similarity measure with maximum neighborhood matching. In *Proceedings of the 18th ACM Conference on Information and Knowledge Management.* ACM.

Liu, X., Wang, H., Li, J., & Gao, H. (2012). Multi-similarity join order selection in entity database. *Frontiers of Computer Science and Technology, 6.*

Liu, Y., Wang, T., Yang, D., & Tang, S. (2007). Propagating functional dependencies from relational schema to XML schema using path mapping rules. In *Proceedings of International Conference on Internet Computing,* (pp. 294–299). Academic Press.

Liu, H., Lussier, Y. A., & Friedman, C. (2001). Disambiguating ambiguous biomedical terms in biomedical narrative text: An unsupervised method. *Journal of Biomedical Informatics, 34*(4), 249–261. doi:10.1006/jbin.2001.1023 PMID:11977807

Liu, H., Teller, V., & Friedman, C. (2004). A multi-aspect comparison study of supervised word sense disambiguation. *Journal of the American Medical Informatics Association, 11*(4), 320–331. doi:10.1197/jamia.M1533 PMID:15064284

Liu, X., Wang, H., Li, J., & Gao, H. (2011). *Es-join: Similarity join algorithm based on entity research report.* Harbin Institute of Technology.

Li, Y., Wang, H., & Gao, H. (2011). Efficient entity resolution based on sequence rules. In *Proceedings of Advanced Research on Computer Science and Information Engineering* (pp. 381–388). Berlin: Springer. doi:10.1007/978-3-642-21402-8_61

Lu, C. L., Su, Z.-Y., & Tang, C. Y. (2001). A new measure of edit distance between labeled trees. In COCOON 2001 (LNCS), (vol. 2108, pp. 338–348). Berlin: Springer.

Lu, S., Sun, Y., Atay, M., & Fotouhi, F. (2003). A new inlining algorithm for mapping XML DTDs to relational schemas. In *Conceptual modeling for novel application domains* (pp. 366–377). Berlin: Springer. doi:10.1007/978-3-540-39597-3_36

Madhavan, J., & Halevy, A. Y. (2003). Composing mappings among data sources. In *Proceedings of the 29th International Conference on Very Large Data Bases* (vol. 29, pp. 572-583). VLDB Endowment.

Maidasani, H., Namata, G., Huang, B., & Getoor, L. (2012). Entity resolution evaluation measures.

Manber, U. (1994). Finding similar files in a large file system. In *Proceedings of the USENIX Winter 1994 Technical Conference* (Vol. 1). USENIX.

Manning, C. D., Raghavan, P., & Schütze, H. (2008). *Introduction to information retrieval* (Vol. 1). Cambridge, UK: Cambridge University Press. doi:10.1017/CBO9780511809071

McCallum, A., Nigam, K., & Ungar, L. H. (2000). Efficient clustering of high-dimensional data sets with application to reference matching. In Proceedings of the Sixth ACM SIGKDD International Conference on Knowledge Discovery and Data Mining (pp. 169-178). ACM.

McInnes, B. T. (n.d.). National library of medicine participation program report. *National Library of Medicine.*

Meila, M. (2007). Comparing clusterings—An information based distance. *Journal of Multivariate Analysis, 98*(5), 873–895. doi:10.1016/j.jmva.2006.11.013

Menestrina, D., Whang, S. E., & Garcia-Molina, H. (2009). Evaluating entity resolution results (extended version).

Menestrina, D., Whang, S. E., & Garcia-Molina, H. (2010). Evaluating entity resolution results. *Proceedings of the VLDB Endowment, 3*(1-2), 208–219.

Michael, L. (2003). Computer science digital libraries - A personal view. *JBIDI, 21.*

Mihalcea, R., Chklovski, T., & Kilgarriff, A. (2004). The senseval-3 English lexical sample task. In *Proceedings of Senseval-3: Third International Workshop on the Evaluation of Systems for the Semantic Analysis of Text* (pp. 25-28). Academic Press.

Milano, D., Scannapieco, M., & Catarci, T. (2006). Structure aware xml object identification. In *Proceedings of VLDB Workshop on Clean Databases* (CleanDB). Seoul, Korea: VLDB.

Miller, R. J., Hernandez, M. A., Haas, L. M., Yan, L. L., Ho, C. T. H., Fagin, R., & Popa, L. (2001). The Clio project: Managing heterogeneity. *SIGMOD Record, 30*(1), 78–83. doi:10.1145/373626.373713

Mitzenmacher, M., & Upfal, E. (2005). *Probability and computing: Randomized algorithms and probabilistic analysis.* Cambridge, UK: Cambridge University Press. doi:10.1017/CBO9780511813603

Mohan, L., Hongzhi, W., Jianzhong, L., & Hong, G. (2009). Duplicate record detection method based on optimal bipartite graph matching. *Journal of Computer Research and Development, 46,* 339–345.

Monge, A. E., & Elkan, C. (1996). The field matching problem: Algorithms and applications. In *Proceedings of the Second International Conference on Knowledge Discovery and Data Mining* (pp. 267-270). Academic Press.

Monge, A., & Elkan, C. (1997). An efficient domain-independent algorithm for detecting approximately duplicate database records. In *Proceedings of the SIGMOD Workshop on Research Issues on Data Mining and Knowledge Discovery (DMKD).* Tuscon, AZ: ACM.

Munkres, J. (1957). Algorithms for the assignment and transportation problems. *Journal of the Society for Industrial and Applied Mathematics, 5*(1), 32–38. doi:10.1137/0105003

Nakov, P. I., Schwartz, A. S., & Hearst, M. (2004). Citances: Citation sentences for semantic analysis of bioscience text. In *Proceedings of the SIGIR'04 Workshop on Search and Discovery in Bioinformatics* (pp. 81-88). ACM.

Nash, A., Bernstein, P. A., & Melnik, S. (2007). Composition of mappings given by embedded dependencies. *ACM Transactions on Database Systems, 32*(1), 4. doi:10.1145/1206049.1206053

Newcombe, H., Kennedy, J., & Axford, S. (1959). Automatic linkage of vital records. *Science, 130,* 954–959. doi:10.1126/science.130.3381.954 PMID:14426783

Okazaki, N., Ananiadou, S., & Tsujii, J. I. (2008). A discriminative alignment model for abbreviation recognition. In *Proceedings of the 22nd International Conference on Computational Linguistics* (vol. 1, pp. 657-664). Association for Computational Linguistics.

Orenstein, J. (1991). An algorithm for computing the overlay of k-dimensional spaces. In O. Günther, Oliver, & H.-J. Schek (Eds.), Lecture Notes in Computer Science: Advances in Spatial Databases (Vol. 525, pp. 381–400). Berlin: Springer. http://dx.doi.org/ doi:10.1007/3-540-54414-3_48

Popa, L., Velegrakis, Y., Hernández, M. A., Miller, R. J., & Fagin, R. (2002). Translating web data. In *Proceedings of the 28th International Conference on Very Large Data Bases* (pp. 598-609). VLDB Endowment.

Puhlmann, S., Weis, M., & Naumann, F. (2006). XML duplicate detection using sorted neighborhoods.[Berlin: Springer.]. *Proceedings of Advances in Database Technology-EDBT, 2006*, 773–791.

Pustejovsky, J., Castano, J., Saurí, R., Rumshinsky, A., Zhang, J., & Luo, W. (2002). Medstract: Creating large-scale information servers for biomedical libraries. In *Proceedings of the ACL-02 Workshop on Natural Language Processing in the Biomedical Domain* (vol. 3, pp. 85-92). Association for Computational Linguistics.

Raghavan, N. S. (2005). Data mining in e-commerce: A survey. *Sadhana, 30*(2-3), 275–289. doi:10.1007/BF02706248

Raghunathan, K., Lee, H., Rangarajan, S., Chambers, N., Surdeanu, M., Jurafsky, D., & Manning, C. (2010). A multi-pass sieve for coreference resolution. In Proceedings of the 2010 Conference on Empirical Methods in Natural Language Processing (pp. 492-501). Association for Computational Linguistics.

Rahm, E., & Do, H. H. (2000). Data cleaning: Problems and current approaches. *A Quarterly Bulletin of the Computer Society of the IEEE Technical Committee on Data Engineering, 23*(4), 3–13.

Raman, A., DeHoratius, N., & Ton, Z. (2001). Execution: The missing link in retail operations. *California Management Review, 43*(3), 136–151. doi:10.2307/41166093

Rao, K. R. (1989). Discrete cosine transform-algorithms, advantage and applications.

Rastogi, V., Dalvi, N., & Garofalakis, M. (2011). Large-scale collective entity matching. *Proceedings of the VLDB Endowment, 4*(4), 208–218.

Ravichandran, D., Pantel, P., & Hovy, E. (2005). *Randomized algorithms and nlp: Using locality sensitive hash function for high speed noun clustering.* Paper presented at the 43rd Annual Meeting on Association for Computational Linguistics. New York, NY.

Recasens, M., & Hovy, E. (2010). Coreference resolution across corpora: Languages, coding schemes, and preprocessing information. In Proceedings of the 48th Annual Meeting of the Association for Computational Linguistics (pp. 1423-1432). Association for Computational Linguistics.

Ristad, E. S., & Yianilos, P. N. (1998). Learning string-edit distance. *IEEE Transactions on Pattern Analysis and Machine Intelligence, 20*(5), 522–532. doi:10.1109/34.682181

Russell Index, R. C. (1992). *U.S. patent 1,435,663.* Retrieved from http://patft.uspto.gov/netahtml/srchnum.htm

Russell Index, R. C. (1998). *U.S. patent 1,261,167.* Retrieved from http://patft.uspto.gov/netahtml/srchnum.htm

Sakoe, H., & Chiba, S. (1978). Dynamic programming algorithm optimization for spoken word recognition. *IEEE Transactions on Acoustics, Speech, and Signal Processing, 26*(1), 43–49. doi:10.1109/TASSP.1978.1163055

Sarawagi, S., & Bhamidipaty, A. (2002). Interactive deduplication using active learning. In *Proceedings of the Eighth ACM SIGKDD International Conference on Knowledge Discovery and Data Mining* (pp. 269-278). ACM.

Sarawagi, S., & Kirpal, A. (2004). *Efficient set joins on similarity predicates.*

Sarawagi, S., & Cohen, W. W. (2004). Semi-markov conditional random fields for information extraction. *Advances in Neural Information Processing Systems, 17*, 1185–1192.

Shannon, E., & Weaver, W. (1948). A mathematical theory of communication.

Singh, S., Subramanya, A., Pereira, F., & McCallum, A. (2011). Large-scale cross-document coreference using distributed inference and hierarchical models. In Proceedings of the 49th Annual Meeting of the Association for Computational Linguistics: Human Language Technologies (vol. 1, pp. 793-803). Association for Computational Linguistics.

Singla, P., & Domingos, P. (2005). Object identification with attribute-mediated dependences. In *Proceedings of PKDD*. PKDD.

Smith, T. F., & Waterman, M. S. (1981). Identification of common molecular subsequences. *Journal of Molecular Biology, 147*(1), 195–197. doi:10.1016/0022-2836(81)90087-5 PMID:7265238

Stevenson, M., Guo, Y., Gaizauskas, R., & Martinez, D. (2008). Disambiguation of biomedical text using diverse sources of information. *BMC Bioinformatics, 9*(Suppl 11), S7. doi:10.1186/1471-2105-9-S11-S7 PMID:19025693

Stoyanov, V., Cardie, C., Gilbert, N., Riloff, E., Buttler, D., & Hysom, D. (2010). Reconcile: A coreference resolution research platform.

Strehl, A., Ghosh, J., & Mooney, R. (2000, July). Impact of similarity measures on web-page clustering. In *Proceedings of Workshop on Artificial Intelligence for Web Search* (AAAI 2000) (pp. 58-64). AAAI.

Swamy, C. (2004). Correlation clustering: Maximizing agreements via semidefinite programming. In *Proceedings of the Annual ACM-SIAM Symposium on Discrete Algorithms* (SODA), (pp. 526–527). New Orleans, LA: ACM.

Tai, K. C. (1979). The tree-to-tree correction problem. *Journal of the ACM, 26*(3), 422–433. doi:10.1145/322139.322143

Tan, P. N. (2007). *Introduction to data mining.* New Delhi: Pearson Education India.

Tejada, S., Knoblock, C. A., & Minton, S. (2002). Learning domain-independent string transformation weights for high accuracy object identification. In *Proceedings of the Eighth ACM SIGKDD International Conference on Knowledge Discovery and Data Mining* (pp. 350-359). ACM.

Tejada, S., Knoblock, C. A., & Minton, S. (2001). Learning object identification rules for information integration. *Information Systems, 26*(8), 607–633. doi:10.1016/S0306-4379(01)00042-4

Tian, Y., & Patel, J. M. (2008). Tale: A tool for approximate large graph matching. In Proceedings of Data Engineering, (pp. 963-972). IEEE.

Tong, X., Wang, H., Li, J., & Gao, H. (2012). *A top-k query algorithm for weighted string based on the tree structure index.* Paper presented at the In National Database Conference of China. Beijing, China.

Tong, X., & Wang, H. (2012). Fgram-tree: An index structure based on feature grams for string approximate search. In *Web-age information management* (pp. 241–253). Berlin: Springer. doi:10.1007/978-3-642-32281-5_24

Vernica, R., Carey, M. J., & Li, C. (2010). Efficient parallel set-similarity joins using MapReduce. In *Proceedings of the 2010 International Conference on Management of Data* (pp. 495-506). ACM.

Verykios, V. S., Moustakides, G. V., & Elfeky, M. G. (2003). A Bayesian decision model for cost optimal record matching. *The VLDB Journal, 12*(1), 28–40. doi:10.1007/s00778-002-0072-y

Vilain, M., Burger, J., Aberdeen, J., Connolly, D., & Hirschman, L. (1995). A model-theoretic coreference scoring scheme. In Proceedings of the 6th Conference on Message Understanding (pp. 45-52). Association for Computational Linguistics.

Viola, P., & Narasimhan, M. (2005). Learning to extract information from semi-structured text using a discriminative context free grammar. In *Proceedings of the 28th Annual International ACM SIGIR Conference on Research and Development in Information Retrieval* (pp. 330-337). ACM.

Viyanon, W., & Madria, S. K. (2009). A system for detecting xml similarity in content and structure using relational database. In *Proceedings of the 18th ACM Conference on Information and Knowledge Management* (pp. 1197-1206). ACM.

Viyanon, W., Madria, S. K., & Bhowmick, S. S. (2008). XML data integration based on content and structure similarity using keys. In *On the move to meaningful internet systems: OTM 2008* (pp. 484–493). Berlin: Springer. doi:10.1007/978-3-540-88871-0_35

Wang & Fan. (2011). Object identification on complex data: A survey. *Chinese Journal of Computers, 34*(10).

Wang, H., Zhang, X., Li, J., & Gao, H. (2013). Product-Seeker: Entity-based product retrieval for e-commerce. In Proceedings of SIGIR 2013, (pp. 1085-1086). ACM.

Wang, J., Li, G., & Feng, J. (2012). *Can we beat the prefix filtering? An adaptive framework for similarity join and search.* Paper presented at the 2012 International Conference on Management of Data. New York, NY.

Wang, X., Smalter, A., Huan, J., & Lushington, G. H. (2009). G-hash: Towards fast kernel-based similarity search in large graph databases. In *Proceedings of the 12th International Conference on Extending Database Technology: Advances in Database Technology* (pp. 472-480). ACM.

Wang, H. Z., & Fan, W. F. (2011). Object identification on complex data: A survey. *Jisuanji Xuebao, 34*(10), 1843–1852.

Wang, H., Li, J., Wang, J., & Gao, H. (2011). Dirty data management in cloud database. In *Grid and cloud database management* (pp. 133–150). Berlin: Springer. doi:10.1007/978-3-642-20045-8_7

Wang, J., Li, G., Yu, J. X., & Feng, J. (2011). Entity matching: How similar is similar. *Proceedings of the VLDB Endowment, 4*(10).

Wang, X., Huan, J., Smalter, A., & Lushington, G. H. (2010). Application of kernel functions for accurate similarity search in large chemical databases. *BMC Bioinformatics, 11*(Suppl 3), S8. doi:10.1186/1471-2105-11-S3-S8 PMID:20438655

Watts, D. J., & Strogatz, S. H. (1998). Collective dynamics of 'small-world' networks. *Nature, 393*(6684), 440–442. doi:10.1038/30918

Weeber, M., Mork, J. G., & Aronson, A. R. (2001). Developing a test collection for biomedical word sense disambiguation. In *Proceedings of the AMIA Symposium*. American Medical Informatics Association.

Weis, M. (2005, August). Fuzzy duplicate detection on XML data. In *Proceedings of VLDB 2005 PhD Workshop*. VLDB.

Weis, M., & Naumann, F. (2004). Detecting duplicate objects in XML documents. In *Proceedings of the 2004 International Workshop on Information Quality in Information Systems* (pp. 10-19). ACM.

Weis, M., & Naumann, F. (2005). DogmatiX tracks down duplicates in XML. In *Proceedings of the 2005 ACM SIGMOD International Conference on Management of Data* (pp. 431-442). ACM.

Weis, M., & Naumann, F. (2006). Detecting duplicates in complex xml data. In *Proceedings of Data Engineering* (pp. 109–109). IEEE.

Whang, E., Benjelloun, O., & Garcia-Molina, H. (2009). Generic entity resolution with negative rules. The VLDB Journal—The International Journal on Very Large Data Bases, 18(6), 1261-1277.

Whang, S. E., Menestrina, D., & Koutrika, G. (2009). *Entity resolution with iterative blocking.* Paper presented at SIGMOD. Providence, RI.

Whang, S. E., Menestrina, D., Koutrika, G., Theobald, M., & Garcia-Molina, H. (2009). Entity resolution with iterative blocking. In Proceedings of the 35th SIGMOD International Conference on Management of Data (pp. 219-232). ACM.

Widom, J. (2004). *Trio: A system for integrated management of data, accuracy, and lineage.* Technical Report.

Winkler, W. E. (1990). String comparator metrics and enhanced decision rules in the Fellegi-Sunter model of record linkage.

Wu, W., Li, H., Wang, H., & Zhu, K. Q. (2012). Probase: A probabilistic taxonomy for text understanding. In *Proceedings of the 2012 International Conference on Management of Data* (pp. 481-492). ACM.

Xiao, C., Wang, W., Lin, X., & Shang, H. (2009). Top-k set similarity joins. In *Proceedings of ICDE*, (pp. 916-927). ICDE.

Xiao, C., Wang, W., Lin, X., & Yu, J. X. (2008). Efficient similarity joins for near duplicate detection. In *Proceedings of WWW*, (pp. 131-140). IEEE.

Xiao, C., Wang, W., & Lin, X. (2008). Ed-join: An efficient algorithm for similarity joins with edit distance constraints. *Proceedings of the VLDB Endowment, 1*(1), 933–944.

Xiao, C., Wang, W., Lin, X., Yu, J. X., & Wang, G. (2011). Efficient similarity joins for near-duplicate detection. *ACM Transactions on Database Systems, 36*(3), 15. doi:10.1145/2000824.2000825

Xu, H., Fan, J. W., Hripcsak, G., Mendonça, E. A., Markatou, M., & Friedman, C. (2007). Gene symbol disambiguation using knowledge-based profiles. *Bioinformatics (Oxford, England), 23*(8), 1015–1022. doi:10.1093/bioinformatics/btm056 PMID:17314123

Xu, R., & Wunsch, D. (2005). Survey of clustering algorithms. *IEEE Transactions on Neural Networks*, *16*(3), 645–678. doi:10.1109/TNN.2005.845141 PMID:15940994

Yan, X., Yu, P. S., & Han, J. (2005). Substructure similarity search in graph databases. In *Proceedings of the 2005 ACM SIGMOD International Conference on Management of Data* (pp. 766-777). ACM.

Yang, X., Wang, B., & Li, C. (2008). *Cost-based variable-length-gram selection for string collections to support approximate queries efficiently*. Paper presented at the 2008 ACM SIGMOD International Conference on Management of Data. New York, NY.

Yin, X., & Tan, W. (2011). Semi-supervised truth discovery. In Proceedings of the 20th International Conference on World Wide Web (pp. 217-226). ACM.

Yin, X., Han, J., & Yu, P. S. (2007). *Object distinction: Distinguishing objects with identical names*. ICDE. doi:10.1109/ICDE.2007.368983

Yin, X., Han, J., & Yu, P. S. (2008). Truth discovery with multiple conflicting information providers on the web. *IEEE Transactions on Knowledge and Data Engineering*, *20*(6), 796–808. doi:10.1109/TKDE.2007.190745

Yu, Z., Tsuruoka, Y., & Tsujii, J. I. (2003). Automatic resolution of ambiguous abbreviations in biomedical texts using support vector machines and one sense per discourse hypothesis. In Proceedings of the SIGIR (Vol. 3, pp. 57-62). ACM.

Yu, C. (2002). Data cleaning method. *Journal of Computer Applications*, *22*(12), 128–130.

Zhang, L., Vaisenberg, R., Mehrotra, S., & Kalashnikov, D. V. (2011). Video entity resolution: Applying ER techniques for smart video surveillance. In Proceedings of Pervasive Computing and Communications Workshops (PERCOM Workshops), (pp. 26-31). IEEE.

Zhang, Y., Yang, Z.-S., Wang, H.-Z., Gao, H., & Li, J.-Z. (2012). Compressed histogram based similarity join size estimation for dirty database. *Mini-Micro Systems, 10.*

Zhang, Z., Hadjieleftheriou, M., Ooi, B. C., & Srivastava, D. (2010). *Bed-tree: An all-purpose index structure for string similarity search based on edit distance*. Paper presented at the 2010 International Conference on Management of Data. New York, NY.

Zhang, Y., Yang, L., & Wang, H. (2012). Range query estimation for dirty data management system. In *Web-age information management* (pp. 152–164). Berlin: Springer. doi:10.1007/978-3-642-32281-5_15

Zhang, Y., Yang, L., & Wang, H. (2012). Similarity join size estimation with threshold for dirty data. *Journal of Computers*, *35*(10).

Zhou, D., Bousquet, O., Lal, T. N., Weston, J., & Schölkopf, B. (2004). Learning with local and global consistency. *Advances in Neural Information Processing Systems*, *16*(753760), 284.

Zhou, R., Liu, C., & Li, J. (2008). Holistic constraint-preserving transformation from relational schema into XML schema. In *Database systems for advanced applications* (pp. 4–18). Berlin: Springer. doi:10.1007/978-3-540-78568-2_4

Zhu, X., & Ghahramani, Z. (2002). Learning from labeled and unlabeled data with label propagation (Technical Report CMU-CALD-02-107). Pittsburgh, PA: Carnegie Mellon University.

Zhu, X., Ghahramani, Z., & Lafferty, J. (2003). Semi-supervised learning using Gaussian fields and harmonic functions. In Proceedings of Machine Learning-International Workshop then Conference (Vol. 20, p. 912). Academic Press.

About the Author

Hongzhi Wang, Ph.D., is an associate professor in the Massive Data Computing Center at Department of Computer Science and Technology, Harbin Institute of Technology, Harbin, China. He received his BSc, MSc, and PhD degree in computer science from Harbin Institute of Technology in 2001, 2003, and 2008, respectively. His research interest is data and information management in general, particularly in areas of big data management, data quality, XML, and graph data management. He has published more than 100 papers in conferences and journals. He was also awarded as a Microsoft Fellow, an IBM PhD Fellowship, and a Chinese Excellent Database Engineer. His doctoral dissertation was selected as the outstanding doctoral dissertation by the China Computer Federation.

Index

T

U

V

W